Locke: A Biography

This is the first comprehensive biography in half a century of John Locke — "a man of versatile mind, fitted for whatever you shall undertake", as one of his many good friends very aptly described him. Against an exciting historical background of the English Civil War, religious intolerance and bigotry, anti-government struggles and plots, and the Glorious Revolution of 1688, Roger Woolhouse interweaves the events of Locke's rather varied life with detailed expositions of his developing ideas in medicine, theory of knowledge, philosophy of science, political philosophy, philosophy of religion, and economics. Chronologically systematic in its coverage, this volume offers an account and explanation of Locke's ideas and their reception, while entering at large into the details of his private life of intimate friendships and warm companionship, and of the increasingly visible public life into which, despite himself, he was drawn — Oxford tutor, associate of Shaftesbury, dutiful civil servant. Based on broad research and many years' study of Locke's philosophy, this will be the authoritative biography for years to come of this truly versatile man whose long-standing desire was for quiet residence in his Oxford college engaged in the study and practice of medicine and natural philosophy, yet who, after years in political exile, finally became an overworked but influential public servant who is now seen as one of the most significant early modern philosophers.

Roger Woolhouse is Emeritus Professor of Philosophy at the University of York. He is the author of many journal articles and books on early modern philosophy, including *The Empiricists, Descartes, Spinoza, Leibniz,* and, with R. Francks, *Leibniz's "New System"*.

Locke
A Biography

ROGER WOOLHOUSE
University of York

CAMBRIDGE
UNIVERSITY PRESS

_192_
_w_
npl

CAMBRIDGE UNIVERSITY PRESS
Cambridge, New York, Melbourne, Madrid, Cape Town, Singapore, São Paulo

Cambridge University Press
32 Avenue of the Americas, New York, NY 10013-2473, USA

www.cambridge.org
Information on this title: www.cambridge.org/9780521817868

First published 2007

Printed in the United States of America

A catalogue record for this publication is available from the British Library.

Library of Congress Cataloguing in Publication data

Woolhouse, R. S.
John Locke : a biography / Roger Woolhouse.
p. cm.
Includes bibliographical references and index.
ISBN-13: 978-0-521-81786-8 (hardback)
ISBN-10: 0-521-81786-2 (hardback)
1. Locke, John, 1632–1704. I. Title.

B1296.W66 2006
192–dc22
[B]

2006027992
ISBN 978-0-521-81786-8 hardback

To Shirley
sine qua non

"I believe you and your parts such that you may well be said to be *homo versatilis ingenii,* and fitted for whatever you shall undertake".

John Strachey to John Locke, 18 November 1663

Contents

Illustrations follow page xviii.

Preface

John Locke (1632–1704) has been the subject of various biographies, short memoirs, and biographical sketches. Some are by people who knew him: Pierre Coste (Coste 1705), Jean Le Clerc (Le Clerc 1705), Damaris Cudworth Masham (D. Masham 1704), and the third Earl of Shaftesbury (Shaftesbury 1705). Others were written at varying degrees of distance from him: Lord King's *Life and Letters* (King 1884) is a rather random miscellany of transcripts of some original manuscripts; as H. R. F. Bourne, Locke's first systematic biographer, commented, King "seems to have made no effort at all to string them [the available original materials] together in any order or to combine with them such information as he could procure from other sources". Though King had available to him a huge amount of material which had come down to him from Locke's cousin Peter King, to whom he left his manuscripts, this was unfortunately not available to Bourne; otherwise his two-volumed *Life of John Locke* (1876), which he rightly claims to be "orderly and comprehensive", would be even better than it is. In more recent times Maurice Cranston was not subject to these restrictions, and for his equally systematic *John Locke: A Biography* (1957) he had available the original materials (and more) belonging to Lord King. They (or most of them) had eventually been bought in 1948 from Lord Lovelace, one of King's descendants, by the Bodleian Library, University of Oxford.

The raw material (whether in the Bodleian or elsewhere) which exists for Locke's biography is remarkably extensive. Besides the letters and other documents which went out of Locke's hands, the escritoire he willed to Peter King contained an amazing variety of manuscripts.

Alongside drafts of his serious writings there is material of a surprising kind, surprising not only that it ever existed, but also that Locke kept it (kept, rather than failed to throw away or lose) to the end of his days. Often with cross-references from one place to another, he recorded (with notes and quotations) his extensive reading on many topics, he collected recipes (both medical and culinary), and he noted his daily movements and purchases; he listed his belongings, his books, and the state of his various business affairs and investments. It may be something to smile at, but it is no joke to say that when he died he left behind him his laundry lists.*

For general biographical purposes, perhaps the most important parts of this material are the letters sent or drafted by Locke and received by him. Cranston used these to very good effect, and his work with them must have been very onerous, since many of them existed only in manuscript. Since then, due to the absolutely invaluable and monumental labours of E. S. de Beer, these letters (more than 3600 of them) are readily and conveniently accessible in transcribed, translated, and edited form in *The Correspondence of John Locke* (dB). (Though I have followed de Beer's enumeration of them I have not, for reasons of copyright, always quoted from his presentation of these letters.) These eight (so far) volumes are part of the definitive Clarendon Edition of Locke's works, which unfortunately does not yet contain what is another of the more important elements of primary biographical material, the journals which Locke kept from 1675, and of which only some parts have been transcribed and published (Aaron and Gibb, Dewhurst 1963a, Leyden, Lough).

There were two different calendars in use in Locke's time: the new-style Gregorian calendar in much of Europe, and, running ten days behind this, the old-style Julian in England. With the occasional double date (e.g. 11/21 June), I have used the former when Locke was out of England. Sometimes the year was taken to begin in April (as the British financial year now does), so that dates between January and April were sometimes written with two years, e.g. "17 February 1692/93" (and, very occasionally, "17 February 1692" has to be understood as a date in the calendar year 1693). I have normalised all dates to the relevant calendar year. (Incidentally, there is no question but that for Locke, by contrast with the twentieth-century politicians who ushered in the new millennium at the end of 1999, the eighteenth century began in 1701, not 1700.)

The money of account in Locke's time was pounds (£), shillings (s: twenty to the pound) and pence (d: twelve pennies to the shilling). Over his life a pound was worth almost one hundred times more than now.

Throughout this book, where appropriate, "he" is to be understood as "he/she", "mankind" as "humankind", and so on. In quoting from seventeenth- and eighteenth-century texts I have often modernised some spelling and punctuation.

The book contains two sets of notes. Those indicated with a numerical superscript are purely bibliographical; those indicated with an asterisk are discursive and further the exposition.

I am very grateful to the late Terry Moore of Cambridge University Press for his initial invitation to write this book. For their help and encouragement in the writing of it I want to thank Bruno Balducci, Janique Balducci, John Bradley, Laura Dosanjh, Bob Gutteridge, Gloria Gutteridge, Roland Hall, Shirley Hawksworth, Roma Hutchinson, Patrick Murphy, Bill Sheils, Clair Souter, Clive Souter, Tim Stanton, Jan van der Werff, Susan van der Werff, and an anonymous reader for the Press. The inter-library loan department of the University of York has as always been very helpful. Finally, I want particularly to thank the Leverhulme Foundation for the financial support of an Emeritus Fellowship (2002–2004), which enabled library visits and the purchase of microfilms.

I am grateful for permission to quote from copyright and other material as follows: to Blackwell's Publishing (from Dewhurst 1963b); to Brynmill Press (from Watson); to Calgary University Press (from Bennett and Remnant); to Cambridge University Press (from the Farr and Roberts transcription of Locke 1690d, Laslett's introduction to Locke 1689d, Lough, Abrams, and Sommerville); to the Maurice Cranston estate (from Cranston); to Elsevier (from Dewhurst 1954b); to Johns Hopkins University Press (from Dewhurst 1960a); to *Journal of Church and State* (from Biddle); to the Newberry Library, Chicago (from E. Masham); to Oxford University Press (from Dewhurst 1962b, Haley, Kelly, Leyden, Nuovo, Ogg 1955, Tyacke 1997a, and Wainwright); to Prometheus Books (from Romanell's transcription of Locke 1666b); and to Springer (from Montuori).

I am further grateful to Oxford University Press for permission to quote from E. S. de Beer's *The Correspondence of John Locke* (letters L3, L4, L5, L6, L8, L17, L18, L22, L27, L29, L30, L43, L48, L54, L59, L65, L66, L68, L69, L70, L71, L72, L74, L77, L79, L80, L81, L82, L83,

L84, L86, L87, L88, L89, L91, L93, L94, L95, L97, L101, L111, L112, L113, L119, L129, L133, L154, L157, L163, L176, L178, L184, L185, L191, L205, L208, L209, L217, L219, L220, L222, L225, L232, L251, L279, L304, L306, L313, L314, L323, L326, L329, L358, L366, L359, L372, L386, L390A, L396, L397, L407, L410, L415, L421, L428, L431, L432, L473, L509, L511, L528, L546, L584, L645, L660, L666, L673, L677, L684, L688, L693, L690, L699, L704, L706, L748, L779, L784, L787, L794, L796, L797, L803, L805, L815, L823, L824, L825, L827, L830, L837, L839, L851, L857, L861, L865, L873, L874, L876, L879, L896, L905, L939, L968, L974, L978, L982, L1003, L1040, L1042, L1044, L1085, L1099, L1100, L1107, L1110, L1117, L1120, L1122, L1127, L1131, L1146, L1147, L1152, L1165, L1200, L1213, L1322, L1323, L1325, L1330, L1333, L1342, L1344, L1353, L1375, L1429, L1450, L1488, L1510, L1542, L1544, L1548, L1549, L1551, L1559, L1562, L1564, L1567, L1572, L1575, L1590, L1606, L1627, L1635, L1678, L1679, L1750, L1760, L1788, L1790, L1804, L1821, L1826, L1853, L1856, L1860, L1862, L1869, L1901, L1920, L1939, L1944, L1961, L1971, L1974, L1980, L1987, L1990, L2002, L2003, L2036, L2092, L2094, L2160, L2179, L2209, L2218, L2228, L2229, L2230, L2232, L2233, L2239, L2278, L2281, L2312, L2314, L2315, L2318, L2323, L2340, L2352, L2359, L2378, L2395, L2413, L2460, L2493, L2498, L2512, L2525, L2535, L2536, L2597, L2610, L2615, L2634, L2643, L2652, L2656, L2693, L2734, L2776, L2800, L2825, L2843, L2866, L2880, L2883, L2896, L2945, L2979, L3014, L3074, L3108, L3142, L3144, L3147, L3153, L3164, L3186, L3197, L3201, L3209, L3219, L3248, L3269, L3284, L3309, L3310, L3311, L3326, L3364, L3367, L3369, L3373, L3376, L3394, L3412, L3415, L3418, L3419, L3461, L3467, L3469, L3471, L3475, L3485, L3500, L3506, L3513, L3522, L3524, L3539, L3541, L3553, L3555, L3556, L3558, L3566, L3572, L3573A, L3582, L3591, L3600, L3627, L3631, L3640, L3641, L3647).

Other quotations from Locke's correspondence are from Abrams (L75); Bonno (L2236); Bourne (L200, L240, L237, L238, L249, L259, L269, L270, L295, L328, L352, L374, L426, L475, L1121, L1773, L2124, L2301, L2327, L2426, L2603, L3275); Boyle 1772: *Works*, vols. 5, 6: L175, L197, L228, L335, L397, L478, L1422; Brewster, vol. 2 (L1517); Campbell (L3631); Christie, vol. 2 (L235, L255, L322, L620); Cranston (L751, L752); Dewhurst 1960b (L1785, L2219, L2224, L2227, L2956), 1962b (L1096, L1292, L2055), 1963b (L1290, L1299, L3299); Forster 1830 (L991, L993, L998, L1356, L2640; Forster 1847 (L2424, L2956, L3198); Historical Manuscripts Commission, Fifth Report, App. (L1776); King 1884 (L110, L176, L177, L180, L182, L186, L187, L204, L219,

L260, L297, L417, L532, L795, L828, L982, L1116, L1309, L1332, L1357, L1405, L1499, L1519, L1619, L1659, L1663, L1664, L1843, L1846, L1964, L1977, L2091, L2100, L2131, L2172, L2181, L2186, L2288, L2306, L2384, L2468, L2518, L2851, L2855, L3107, L3272, L3275, L3287, L3375, L3511, L3551, L3573, L3468); Locke 1823: vols. 9, 10 (L1515, L1530, L1538, L1544, L1563, L1579, L1592, L1593, L1609, L1620, L1643, L1652, L1655, L1661, L1665, L1685, L1693, L1744, L1857, L1887, L1921, L1965, L1966, L2059, L2100, L2115, L2129, L2131, L2189, L2202, L2240, L2243, L2254, L2288, L2310, L2340, L2376, L2395, L2407, L2414, L2490, L2514, L2846, L3234, L3278, L3293, L3301, L3306, L3328, L3361, L3465, L3470, L3498, L3504, L3504, L3537, L3542, L3544, L3548, L3556, L3565, L3570, L3608, L3613, L3624, L3636); Lough (L310); Newton (L1513); Ollion (L467, L475, L492, L508, L556, L565, L587, L626, L633, L656, L790, L1172, L2412); Rand 1927 (L264, L782, L705, L709, L770, L771, L773, L774, L777, L791, L799, L801, L807, L817, L822, L829, L844, L845, L886, L929, L943, L989, L999, L1000, L1020, L1026, L1038, L1045, L1047, L1050, L1057, L1077, L1102, L1113, L1128, L1167, L1220, L1326, L1423, L1431, L1433, L1439, L1440, L1442, L1455, L1471, L1476, L1483, L1501, L1502, L1538, L1544, L1565, L1571, L1576, L1586, L1625, L1644, L1799, L1836, L1872, L1903, L1908, L1972, L1985, L1988, L1992, L2001, L2018, L2067, L2071, L2090, L2113, L2139, L2243, L2356, L2376, L2398, L2408, L2414, L2420, L2447, L2575, L2576, L2585, L2812, L2695, L2719, L2747, L2763, L2768, L2787, L2812, L2817, L2859, L3058, L3138, L3223, L3400, L3465); Tanner 1929 (L405); *The Monthly Repository of Theology and General Literature*, vol. 13 (1818) (L1107, L1120, L1147, L1572, L1901, L2209); Trotter, vol. 1 (L3234).

Others (with grateful acknowledgement) are from manuscripts in the Bodleian Library, University of Oxford: MS Locke c.19, fols. 116 (L307), 120 (L309), 141 (L389), 10v (L614), 147r (L618), 150r (L624), 112 (L653), 100r (L748), 111r (L1028), 40 (L1129), 101–102r (L1166), 107r (L1192), 159r (L1545), 161 (L1563), 96 (L1890), 185 (L2363), 178r (L2451); MS Locke c.22, fols. 173 (L51), 177 (L85), 175 (L105), 3 (L106), 5 (L115), 7 (L118), 15 (L155), 40 (L590), 42v (L645), 50v (L775), 55v (L889), 58v (L932), 61 (L957), 64v (L985), 69rv (L1019), 71r, 72r (L1225), 82r, 82v (L1248), 85v (L1256), 86v–87r (L1266), 88v (L1277), 90r–91r) (L1301), 92r, 93rv (L1307), 94rv, 95rv (L1312), 81r (L1329), 115v–116r) (L1378), 99rv (L1403), 102rv (L1420), 104 (L1424), 121r (L1589), 125r (L1655), 20r (L1929), 144v (L2975), 152r (L3195), 159r (L3324), 161r (L3358), 166r (L3477), 168r (L3511); MS Locke b.8, no. 168 (L772); MS Locke f.6, pp. 34–35, 20 (L687, L696). Yet others (with grateful acknowledgement) are from manuscripts in the British Library: Add MS 6194, pp. 248–9 (L417); Add MS 22910, fol. 507 (L2808); Sloane MS 4036, fols. 185 (L1785), 290r (L2219), 294 (L2227).

Acknowledgements are due to the Bodleian Library, University of Oxford, the British Library, the National Archives, and the Newberry Library, Chicago, for quotations (identified, via the References and Bibliographical Notes) from manuscripts in their collections.

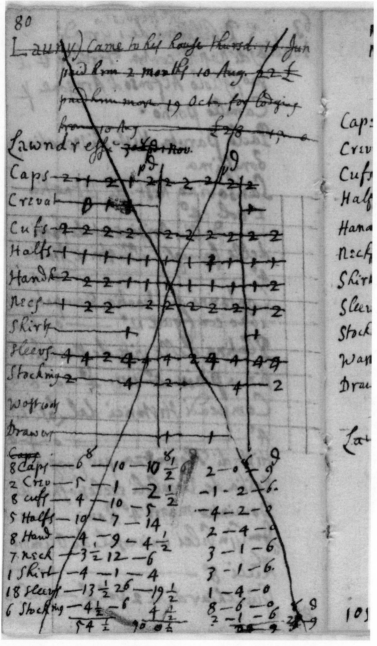

Rent record and laundry lists (1677); see pp. 138, xxviii. (Reproduced by permission of the Bodleian Library, University of Oxford, from MS Locke f.15, p. 80.)

Locke's last portrait (1704), for Anthony Collins, by Godfrey Kneller; see pp. xv, 456. (Reproduced by permission of Virginia Museum of Fine Arts, Richmond. Bequest of Dr Bernard Samuels in memory of his mother Kathleen Boone Samuels.)

Locke's birthplace, *circa* 1885; see p. 6. (Reproduced by permission of PFD on behalf of the Estate of Maurice Cranston.)

Example of Locke's shorthand (trans. at Leyden: 257); see p. 57.
(Reproduced by permission of the Bodleian Library, University of
Oxford, from MS Locke f.1, p. 404.)

An Essay concerning

The Understanding, Knowledge,

Opinion

~~Belief~~ & Assent

1 § Since it is the Understanding that sets man above ~~all other~~ sensible beings & gives him all that dominion wch he hath over them it is certainly a subject even for its nobleness worth ones labour to enquire into, & wch perhaps hath been less seriously considerd then ye worth of the thing & ys nearness it hath too us seems to require. The understanding like the eye whilst it makes us see & perceive all other things, takes noe notice of it selfe, & it requires art & pains to set it at a distance from it selfe & make it its owne object. But what ever be the difficultys that lye in ys way of this enquiry whatever it be yt keeps us soe much in the dark to our selves, sure I am that all the light we can let in upon our owne minds all ye acquaintance we can make with our owne understandings will not only be very pleasant, but bring us great

First page of draft B of *De Intellectu*; see p. 106. (Reproduced by permission of the Bodleian Library, University of Oxford, from MS Locke f.26, p. 3.)

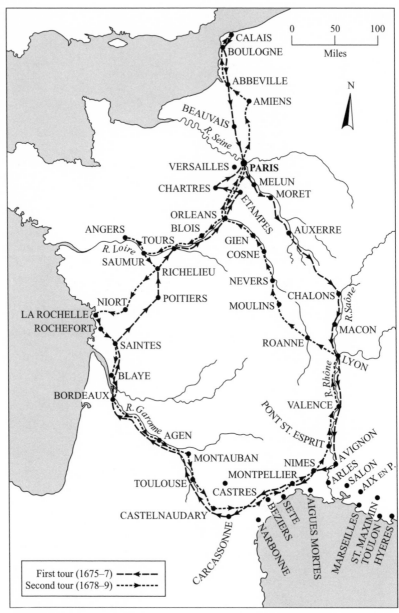

Locke's Tours of France 1675–1679. (Reproduced by permission of Cambridge University Press from John Lough, *Locke's Travels in France* (1675–1679), 1953.)

Locke's Netherlands.

50

Mar: 26 letter — : — : 4
27 for Hartland's horse — : 1 : 6
letter — : — : 2
Inck: for bottels — : 4 : —
29 ale & bottels — : 9 : —
1 tt of Sugar — : 1 : 4
clarret glass — : — : 6
Apples — : 1 : —
2 tt of Candels — : — : 10
30: for buckles rings & stable — : — : 9
& y͏e sadle
31: for y͏e horse at Wicomb — : 3 : —
3 bottels of sider — : 3 : —
Apples — : — : 3
Cont — : 2 : 6
Apr: 2 carrying Sr I. Neil's trone — : — : 8
Candels — : — : 5
Tobacco & pipe — : — : 5
9: letter — : — : 2
16: carriage of a litle box — : — : 6
Candels — : — : 5
mending y͏e Portmantel — : 2 : 6
2 letters — : — : 4
17 Gunpowder — : — : 4
18 for mending y͏e sadle & fast-
ning y͏e horse shoos at reding — : 1 : 4
for a strap & sowing y͏e bridle at Worc: — : — : 4

Example of Locke's accounts; see p. 237. (Reproduced by permission of the Bodleian Library, University of Oxford, from MS Locke f.15, p. 50.)

COPY FOR WRITING DESIGNED BY LOCKE.

Copy for writing designed by Locke; see p. 254. (Reproduced by courtesy of the University of Liverpool Library, from Thomas I. M. Forster, *Original Letters of Locke, etc.* 1830.)

The earliest known portrait of Locke (c. 1672–76), by John Greenhill. (Reproduced by permission of the National Portrait Gallery.)

Page from Locke's weather register at Oates; see p. 307. (Reproduced by permission of the Bodleian Library, University of Oxford, from MS Locke d.9, p. 486.)

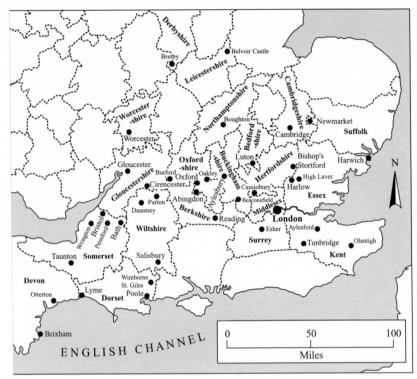

Locke's England.

Introduction

"A man of versatile mind"[1]

In his later years John Locke had "forgot the year of his birth" (though "he believed that he had set it down somewhere"*). Not knowing exactly where he had been born, his friends took some months after his death to locate the record of his baptism in the register of All Saints' Church, Wrington, Somerset. They were then able to complete the Latin obituary he had composed for himself, and to have it engraved on the marble tablet which was set, adjacent to his tomb, into the south-facing wall of All Saints' Church, High Laver, a small Essex village one hundred and twenty miles to the east of his birthplace.

Siste Viator, Hic juxta situs est JOHANNES LOCKE .... Stay, traveller: near this place lies JOHN LOCKE. If you ask what sort of man he was, the answer is that he was contented with his modest lot. Bred a scholar, he used his studies to devote himself to truth alone. This you may learn from his writings which will show you anything else that is to be said about him more faithfully than the doubtful eulogies of an epitaph. His virtues, if he had any, were too slight for him to offer them to his own credit or as an example to you. Let his vices be buried with him. Of good life, you have an example, should you desire it, in the gospel; of vice, would there were none for you; of mortality, surely (and you may profit by it) you have one here and everywhere. That he was born on the 29th of August in the year of our Lord 1632, and that he died on the 28th of October in the year of our Lord 1704, this tablet, which itself will quickly perish, is a record.[2]

The tablet (now inside the church) has not perished yet. As for his writings, it is striking that these were published only towards the end

1

of his seventy-two-year life. Had he not survived a winter sea-journey back from Holland after five years of political exile which ended with William of Orange's "Glorious Revolution" of 1689, his life and work would probably have had little more record than that tablet itself. For that first year back in England, when he was approaching sixty, saw the publication of the three works on which his fame rests, and which, over three hundred years later, are still on the curriculum at universities the world over: *An Essay concerning Human Understanding*, *Two Treatises of Government*, and *A Letter concerning Toleration*. Without them he would not soon have been recognised by Voltaire as, along with Newton, among the "greatest philosophers, as well as the ablest writers of their age"; without them there would have been no grateful plaque near his tomb remembering that "his philosophy guided the founders of the United States of America".[3]

A student required to read the *Essay*, with its tendency to repetition and perhaps prefaced with an engraving of one of the Kneller portraits of a gaunt, rather forbidding, ageing man, would easily come to what is perhaps the popular view of Locke as stern, distant, perhaps boring: George Eliot conjured up her Mr Casaubon by making him "remarkably like the portrait of Locke".* There can be no doubt that he was a deeply serious man, trustworthy and reliable, with a keen sense of duty and loyalty, but any view of him as the embodiment of a heavy gravity is mistaken, at least according to the obituarial eulogies of friends. Far from "assuming . . . airs of gravity" Locke disapproved of them, and looked on them as "an infallible mark of impertinence"; he would indeed sometimes make fun of them, and "divert himself with imitating that studied gravity, in order to turn it the better to ridicule; and upon this occasion he always remembered this maxim of La Rochefoucault, which he admired above all others, that gravity is a mystery of the body, invented to conceal the defects of the mind". Nevertheless, the view of Locke as having a stern distance did have some contemporary currency:

Many who knew him only by his writings, or by the reputation he had gained of being one of the greatest philosophers of the age, having imagined to themselves beforehand that he was one of those scholars that, being always full of themselves and their sublime speculations, are incapable of familiarising themselves with the common sort of mankind, or of entering into their little concerns or discoursing of the ordinary affairs of life, were perfectly amazed to find him nothing but affability, good humour, humanity, pleasantness.[4]

It was not, however, that affability and pleasantness were ever-present. Though no one was

less magisterial, or dogmatical than he; or less offended with any man's dissenting from him in opinion: there are yet an impertinent sort of disputants who though you have answered their arguments over, and over again, will still return to them, and still repeat the same things, after having been ever so often beaten out of them. With these Mr Locke would be apt sometimes to speak a little warmly; for which yet he would oftener blame himself than anybody else saw cause for him to to do.[5]

Locke was a man who liked company and conversation, and who, in his turn, was valued for his amusing and affable company. He had, it was said, "all the good qualities, that could render his friendship pleasant and agreeable". Pierre Coste's picture of him is entirely believable: "when an occasion naturally offered, he gave himself up with pleasure to the charms of a free and facetious conversation. He remembered a great many agreeable stories, which he always brought in properly; and generally made them yet more delightful, by his natural and agreeable way of telling them". Yet, Coste also makes plain, this affability was not always completely spontaneous, and was some-times something Locke exercised, almost dutifully, in the service of a higher seriousness. What Locke "chiefly loved", Coste said, was "truths that were useful, and with such fed his mind, and was generally very well pleased to make them the subject of his discourse"; but he believed that the very pursuit of "serious and important occupations" required, as a beneficial contrast, that we spend some part of our life in "mere amusements, and it was at least partly for this reason that he would give himself over to free and easy conversation".[6] We might also suppose that, amusing and agreeable as he might genuinely have been on such occasions, he would not for a moment have abandoned his cautious inclination, apparent throughout his life, towards reserve, control, and even secrecy.

Both Pierre Coste and Damaris Masham remarked something we have seen already in Locke's habit of recording and note-taking, that he "above all things, loved order" and was an "exact keeper of accounts". This was surely a polite way of saying that he was "anally retentive", strong-willed, obsessively anxious for control; and, given these characteristics, it is noteworthy that his life did not take the shape he seems for a long time ideally to have wanted — that of "a retired single life" of residence in his Oxford college, combining an interest in experimental iatrochemistry (chemistry as applied to medicine) and other areas of natural philosophy with practice as a physician: "Dr Locke", as his contemporaries in fact often referred to him. Chronic ill-health and a strong sense of duty were impediments to this, as of course were external events at whose mercy he continually felt himself to be.

"Troubles and business", he said, "will in spite of the gentler fluxes of our inclinations carry us which way they please." By the time he was in his forties he was "accustomed to have fortune...dispose of me contrary to my design and expectation"; and he spoke of being under the influence of some unknown "witchcraft" and of being ridden by goblins who make use of us "to trot up and down for their pleasure and not our own". But at least as important as external events was that, despite an awesome capacity for hard work and focused concentration, there was, overall, a certain lack of single-mindedness – a breadth of interest and ability, which, though it certainly did not waste his talents, got in the way of any narrow expression of them. "I believe you and your parts such", a friend once told him, "that you may well be said to be *homo versatilis ingenii* [a man of versatile mind], and fitted for whatever you shall undertake."[7]

Upbringing and Education (1632–1658)

John Locke's great-grandfather, Sir William Locke, was said to be "the greatest English merchant under Henry the Eighth". His activities as a mercer dealing in silk and velvet were continued by his son Nicholas, who moved from Buckland Newton, Dorset, to Pensford, in Somerset, where he built up a flourishing business, collecting in, and shipping on, the woollen cloth woven in cottages throughout the west of England. Nicholas had a number of children, two girls, Frances and Anne, and four sons: John, the eldest son, born in 1606, did not follow his father into the cloth trade, but turned instead to the law; Peter (1607–86), initially a tanner, later earned a living as a landowner; Edward (1610–63); and Thomas (1612–64), who became a rich brewer in Bristol. All these children were said to have been "persons of very exemplary lives".[2]

John was twenty-three in July 1630, when he married Agnes Keene, ten years his senior and said to have been "a most beautiful woman". Her family was local to Wrington where, about ten miles from Pensford, various members owned land and houses. Her elder brother took both her father's name, Edmund, and his trade of tanner; another brother, John, was an attorney.[3]

John and Agnes Locke had been married just over a year when, on 29 August 1632, their first child, John, was born; their second, Peter, died in infancy; and their third, Thomas, was born in August 1637. Throughout their marriage John and Agnes lived at Belluton, in a house given to them by Nicholas Locke. Their son John was not born here, however, but in Wrington, in what had been Agnes's grand-parents' home but which was then lived in by her brother.[4] The house,* which existed into Victorian times, was immediately adjacent to the north side of the church where John was baptised on the day of his birth.

At first, John Locke senior was clerk to Justices of the Peace, who included Alexander Popham, a considerable landowner and Member of Parliament for Bath at various times; later he practised as an attorney and had responsibility for the county drainage sewers. The manage-ment of land and tenements that he was left by his father also occupied him. Details of these occupations and preoccupations over a quarter century are recorded in his notebook in which there are records of local assize cases and their juries, forms of court oath, receipts for rents, and lists of liabilities for taxes.[5]

Little is known of the influence of Agnes on her son John. Later he would say that she had been "a very pious woman and an affectionate mother". In letters to his father he mentioned her only to the extent of asking him to "remember my humble duty to my mother". More is known of the father's influence (perhaps an indication that it was stronger). "I have often heard . . . that he was a man of parts", it would be reported years later:

Mr Locke never mentioned him but with great respect and affection. . . . His father used a conduct towards him when young, that he often spoke of with great approbation. It was this being severe to him by keeping him in much awe, and at a distance while he was a boy; but relaxing still by degrees of that severity as he grew up to be a man, till (he being capable of it) he lived perfectly with him as a friend. . . . He has told me that his father, after he was a man, solemnly asked his pardon for having struck him once in passion as a boy; his fault not being equal to that correction.[6]

In retrospect Locke approved of this upbringing, as is witnessed not only by that report, but also by some remarks he made in a book on child rearing he published towards the end of his life. Here he said that many fathers make the double mistake of indulging their children when they are little and then being more severe and reserved in later years. This tends to produce "an ill understanding between father and son", whereas if the son's later friendship is to be had, an early strict discipline and severity should gradually be relaxed as the father admits the maturing boy "into a nearer familiarity".[7] We do not know how Locke felt as a child, but the relationship certainly flourished in the long term: the report that they came to live "perfectly together as friends" is supported by the cordiality and devotion of his letters to his father.

As a child, Locke must have been exposed to his father's non-professional interests, and something of what they were can again be found in his father's notebook. Recorded there are various medical prescriptions, "against the plague", "for consumption and cough", "for a sprain on a horse"; there are details of bell-ringing changes, and a list of "The seven wonders of the world". At a higher level of intel-lectuality, there are notes on "History, Ethic, and Dialectic", and Latin entries concerning divine providence and predestination. We know too that Locke senior borrowed from a local vicar such books as Procopius' *History of the Wars of the Emperor Justinian*, Anthony Cade's *A Justification of the Church of England* (1630), Richard Overton's *Man's Mortality* (1643), and a book of poems. But what the father tried to teach the son, both formally and informally, or what his early hopes for him were, is unknown. At some point he seems to have had ambitions for him as "a scholar".[8]

Locke's childhood home at Belluton was on the northern ridge of the Chew valley, five or six miles south of the great trading port of Bristol, overlooking the small market town of Pensford and looking across to the Mendip Hills. The local rural economy was largely based on wool: sheep farming, wool spinning, and cloth weaving. But there was also lead and coal mining in the Mendips, and Pensford itself was located in a coal field (part of which would form an element in Locke's later business interests).

The house at Belluton no longer exists, but an inventory taken at the time of Locke senior's death gives some impression of it, with a list of the contents of nine rooms – parlour, hall, kitchen, study, buttery, outward chamber, inner chamber, hall chamber, and stable. For example,

Parlour. Two table-boards, six cushions, two carpets, two sideboards, six chairs, two cast-iron dogs and one back; *Kitchen.* Three pairs of tongs, one fire shovel, one iron fork, three pairs of hangels, two dripping pans, two frying pans, two pairs of pothooks, three spits, one pair of cast dogs, one pair of grills with a bar, one beef fork, one chopping knife, one gridiron, one jack, one smoothing iron, two brand irons, one cleaver, one sideboard; *Inner chamber.* One standing bedstead, with cord matt vallence and curtains, one flock bed, two feather bolsters, two pillows, one pair of blankets, two white coverlets, one green rug, one press, one round table, one desk, one coffer, one trunk.

The overall value of the contents amounted to about £80.[9]

About three miles southwest of Pensford was the manor house of Sutton Court, where, a couple of years younger than he, one of Locke's childhood (and lasting) friends, John Strachey, lived. The two boys must have explored the various nearby antiquities (which years later Locke would describe to John Aubrey): at Stanton Drew, more or less midway between their two homes, was a complex Stone Age megalithic site, part of which was the standing stone of Hautville's Quoit; two miles away from Belluton, to the northwest, were the remains of Maes Knoll, a Celtic Iron Age camp.[10]

In 1642, within days of Locke's tenth birthday, civil war broke out between the Parliamentary army and that of the King, Charles I. Recalling this eighteen years later he would write, "I no sooner perceived myself in the world but I found myself in a storm, which has lasted almost hitherto".[11]

A number of disagreements and discontents (economic, political, religious) led up to the war. One of these concerned Charles's attempt at personal rule without the aid (the hindrance, as he saw it) of Parliament, which had not been called between 1629 and 1640. Apart from anything else, a clear and direct problem for the King in this was his need for money, for he was expected to "live of his own" in normal circumstances, and except in an emergency could not impose taxation without the agreement of Parliament. In 1634 Charles decided that the prevalence of piracy on English ships and shores, and the weakness of the navy, constituted just such an emergency, and he revived an old tax of Ship Money, extending it to the inland counties. As a clerk to the local Justices, Locke's father was involved with the imposition of this hugely unpopular tax, and his notebook contains details of shipping belonging to Somerset ports, and of amounts due from various individuals.

Charles's leanings towards personal rule were associated with his religious views, and these too brought him into conflict with his subjects, many of whom had puritan views. He had a firm belief in the divine right of kings and in the congruence of the English state and the Anglican Church. William Laud, his Archbishop of Canterbury since 1633, though an unswerving Protestant, was in no way in sympathy with puritan thinking, according to which the Calvinist-influenced reformation of an earlier century had not gone far enough in purifying and purging the church from its association with Catholic Rome. Unlike the puritans, he believed in an episcopalian hierarchy for the church and in the apostolic succession of bishops; he believed in a decent conformity to a traditional and ceremonial order of church service according to the Prayer Book; he believed in bowing at the name of Jesus, making the sign of the cross, wearing of surplices by the clergy, and in placing the altar behind rails. He believed too that once the religious observances of the morning service were performed, Sunday was a day for innocent enjoyment and recreation, for dancing, drinking, and the playing of games.

For the Calvinistic puritans, however, these beliefs and practices were too heavily redolent of Catholicism; and such activities outside of church were in clear breach of the injunction to keep the Sabbath holy, an injunction which required sermonising and serious study of the Bible, rather than a merely conforming observance of what to them were suspicious rituals.

There is little direct evidence as to how "puritanical" Locke's upbringing was, but it seems likely that his family were Calvinists, with leanings to Presbyterianism. His grandfather, Nicholas Locke, did as a Calvinist might, and willed money to the church in Pensford for a weekly Bible lecture. Locke's description of his mother as having been "a very pious woman" is some indication too, as perhaps is the ardent puritanism of the rector of Wrington, by whom his mother had him baptised. The religious tendency of people in the local area, and of Locke's relations, point this way too, as does Locke's father's service in the Parliamentary army.[12]

Matters which exercised puritans certainly exercised Locke's father, for his notebook shows a concern with questions such as "Whether bowing towards an altar is lawful?", "Whether the order of bishops is of divine institution?", "Whether bowing at the name of Jesus be a pious ceremony?", "Whether in the election of ministers the voice of the people is required?", and "Whether a minister may with a safe conscience administer the sacrament to one not kneeling?"[13]

Parliament had eventually been allowed to meet in 1640, and the next year issued a Grand Remonstrance which challenged the King's authority and fitness to rule. When armed resistance to the crown began to break out in 1642, Locke's father's employer, Alexander Popham, raised his own regiment of cavalry, becoming a colonel in the Parliamentary army. Earlier in the year Locke's father had publicly announced assent to Parliament's protest, and he soon became a captain in Popham's regiment. His notebook contains lists of local footsoldiers, pikemen and musketeers, and notes on the loading of muskets.[14]

Despite initial successes Parliamentary forces in the West Country were defeated at Devizes, and by the latter half of 1643 Somerset was in the King's control. It seems likely that both Popham and Locke's father left the army at this point (and so were not amongst the Parliamentary forces which eventually regained control).[15] Though their political cause finally prospered, both Popham and Locke senior suffered considerable material loss in the civil war. Popham's house was burnt by the Royalists, and as for Locke, it was later said (on the basis of his son's testimony) that as "a captain in the Parliamentary army ... [he was] by that means a private sufferer in those public calamities: which probably was the sole cause of his fortunes being impaired".[16]

On the other hand, the support that Locke senior had given to Popham over the years, both in peacetime and in war, was recognised in a way which hugely determined the future life of his son. As a member of Parliament, Popham was privileged to nominate boys for entry into Westminster School in London, and he successfully nominated the young John Locke. The boy's life would undoubtedly have taken a very different course had he not (probably in 1646, the year of his fourteenth birthday) left his home in rural Somerset and made the hundred or so mile journey to Westminster, one of the finest schools in the country.[17]

1646–1652: "A VERY SEVERE SCHOOL"[18]

At Westminster, Locke joined about two hundred and fifty other boys, some a few years younger. About forty were King's Scholars (the name being retained by the Royalist headmaster), who boarded in the school. Others were "oppidans", the sons of local residents, who lived at home; or "pensioners", who boarded in the house of a master or of a member of the Westminster Abbey Chapter. Locke himself was a "peregrine", one of the boys who, having to come to school from the country, lived with friends or relations or simply took suitable lodgings nearby, in his case with a Mrs Susan Bates.[19]

Towards the end of 1649 Locke started a careful account of his income and expenditure, something he would continue thoughout his life. His father had arranged for him to receive regular money via a London man, "cousin William Strickland", half-yearly sums varying from £6 to £14. With this he "paid my laundress for two quarters 12s", "paid to Mr Busby ... for a quarter £1", and paid out for "mending my clothes 4d", "for the woman who makes the beds", "paper 5d", "soling a pair of shoes 1s 5d", "2s 6d when I was sick of the flux", "turnip seed for my mother 8d" (enclosed in a letter home); toiletries such as "wafers and washballs", candles, and haircuts about four times a quarter, figure regularly. Items such as these are interspersed with books he bought: Lucan's *Pharsalia* in English and Latin, George Abbot's *A Brief Description of the Whole World* (1599), Thomas Godwin's *Roman Antiquities* (1614).[20]

The Head Master, Richard Busby, had been appointed in 1638 when the school was governed by the Chapter of the Abbey. But, even though he was a staunch Royalist, the Parliamentary Committee which had governed it since the end of the civil war had allowed him to stay. He was an energetic and dedicated teacher, devoted to bringing out the best in his boys; he composed his own Latin, Greek, Hebrew, and Arabic grammars for their use. No doubt it was a recognition of his abilities that allowed him to continue, for he seems not to have taken much trouble to hide his continuing Royalist sympathies; the reported view of John Owen, the Dean of Christ Church, Oxford, was that "it would never be well with the nation till this school was suppressed". In 1644 Busby was required, under pain of suspension from office, to subscribe to the Presbyterianism of the National Solemn League and Covenant, yet though the recorded explanation of his failure to do so (he was "sickly") is rather slim, no action was taken against him. None was taken in 1648 either, when, as the scaffold was being prepared in nearby Whitehall on "that black and eternally infamous day of the king's murder", Busby called the school together and (so Robert South, one of Locke's contemporaries and lifelong acquaintances, recorded) "publicly prayed" for King Charles just "an hour or two ... before his sacred head was struck off". But Busby was loyal to his school too and his position in it: after the Restoration, when he showed Charles II round the school, he risked appearing disrespectful and kept his hat on, lest his boys "think that there was anyone greater than himself within the walls of his School".[21]

During his years at Westminster, Locke was exposed to a curriculum that included Latin, Greek, Hebrew, and Arabic, with a smaller measure of geography, geometry, and arithmetic. These last were taught through the medium of Latin, which he learnt to pronounce as though it were English — a fact which later led to problems when conversing in Latin with foreigners.[22]

In 1650 Locke was thought suitable to enter the "challenge" competition for election to a King's Scholarship, a procedure which required a knowledge of Latin, and of grammar, and an ability in prose or verse composition. Whether or not his earlier expenditure of one shilling for "Pies against the election" helped, he was successful, being placed tenth on the list of twenty candidates.[23]

Something of Locke's life as a King's Scholar residing in the school can be learnt, from an account of the curriculum in the upper forms, which another pupil gave. The day began shortly after five with Latin prayers followed by ablutions. Between six and eight, pupils were first drilled in Latin and Greek grammar, and then were put to composing Latin verses on set themes, or to expounding Latin or Greek authors such as Cicero, Livy, Homer, and Xenophon, and to reciting from memory. Next there was an hour for some food and drink, and for taking stock — for "recollection of ourselves and preparation for future exercises". The period between nine and eleven began with selected boys reading out their Latin or Greek prose or verse compositions on themes which had been given them the previous evening — "some to be examined and punished, others to be commended and proposed to imitation". The rest of this two-hour period was given over to extempore translation of unseen passages into Latin or Greek, and to exposition by the master of something from a Latin or Greek author on which the pupils were to be tested that afternoon. There was no complete rest from academic work during the dinner hour from twelve to one, for (as at supper time too) the pupils practised reading Latin manuscripts, "to facilitate the reading of such hands".[24]

Dinner over, the afternoon was no less intense than the morning. For two hours the text which a master had expounded earlier "was to be exactly gone through by construing and other grammatical ways, examining all the rhetorical figures and translating it out of verse into prose, or out of prose into verse; out of Greek into Latin, or out of Latin into Greek"; the passage had then to be memorised for the next day. Between three and four "they had a little respite"; though only a little, for the break was partly for "fitting themselves for their next task". This was a miscellany of some study of rhetoric, and of further practice in unseen translation from Latin or Greek. Before leaving the school room for supper they were given a theme on which to construct some Latin or Greek prose or verse for the next day. After supper, at any rate in the light summer evenings, there was instruction in geography, and pupils of the upper forms were "practised to describe, and find out cities and countries in the maps".

On Saturdays the pace slowed considerably, for the record shows no more than practising Greek and Latin declamations. On Sundays, however, besides prayers and services in the Abbey, the boys, at any rate those of the upper forms, were set to memorising the catechism in Greek or to practice in construing the Greek Gospel. In the afternoon they composed verses on the morning sermon or gospel readings, and listened to expositions of classical authors.

The dense concentration of classical languages and literature pervaded the disciplinary system too, a system which initially was the responsibility of the boys themselves, some of whom were appointed monitors. Their every order and (on Friday mornings) their list of complaints were strictly in Latin; and punishment was by way of linguistic exercises or "scholastic tasks, as repeating whole orations out of Tully, Isocrates, Demosthenes, or speeches out of Virgil, Thucydides, Xenophon, Euripides, etc." But punishment was in the hands, literally, of the masters too: Dryden reported that "Master Busby used to whip a boy so long, till he made him a confirmed blockhead". Years later Locke would describe Westminster as a "very severe school", and in composing some directions for education of children he was decisively against the "discipline of the rod": use of this "instrument of government" did not turn children towards their books and away from pleasure, rather it simply reinforced sensual motivation by pleasure and aversion. Locke's most viciously unpleasant critic would say of him (fairly or unfairly we do not know) that "surely the fear of the school-master's rod (which with some trembling he mentions ... [more than once]) was betimes begot in his mind by his early deserving it".[25]

There were other elements in Westminster education about which, in later life, Locke had critical things to say. He was particularly against the study of rhetoric, which he thought was of little use in learning to speak "handsomely". He was similarly against the composition of themes and verses in Latin. It is good, he later thought, that boys should learn to speak well on a variety of topics, but the medium of Latin and choice of topics such as "Omnia vincit amor" (Love conquers all), things of which they "want knowledge", are hardly good means to this end: it is "a sort of Egyptian tyranny, to bid them make bricks who have not yet any of the materials".[26]

In May 1651 Locke was joined at the school by his young brother, who had been brought from Somerset by their mother. Thomas joined as a peregrine, just when, as a King's Scholar, John had ceased to be one. His finances were in John's hands, who carefully recorded items such as "a satchel for my brother 1s" and a "pair of gloves for my brother".[27]

Success in the "minor" election for King's Scholarships meant more than free board and lodging within the precincts of the school. It also brought entitlement to compete in the "major" election for a further scholarship to one of the university colleges with which Westminster had a special relationship, Christ Church Oxford and Trinity College Cambridge, each of which took a minimum of three Westminster boys each year. In May 1652 the nineteen-year-old Locke became a candidate.

The elections aimed to test the candidates' confidence and mental agility rather than their knowledge, and a main feature was the delivery in the school, on the second Monday in the Easter term, of an oration composed in Latin, Greek, or Hebrew. Candidates could express a preference for one university or the other, which they did by composing an address to the relevant elector. Locke prepared to address himself to the Dean of Christ Church: "having now served for some years under the standards of grammar, and having mastered the *Iliad* of Homer, [I] am seeking to reach that Ithaca of yours, the University. . . . Let your favouring voice . . . set me, after my wretched buffeting . . . in a place of perfect peace and tranquillity, the University."[28]

Before the election, Locke told his father that the Latin oration he had prepared was not to be delivered (perhaps Busby had advised against it for some reason), but that the Hebrew one he had since composed was. He wanted him to say nothing about this, "for there has been something already spoken abroad more than has been for my good". Whatever it was that was being spread around, Locke's warning to his father highlights the fact that the election process involved a considerable amount of personal lobbying and petitioning, and of partiality on the part of the electors. Locke's father took part in this himself, writing a letter to General Charles Fleetwood, a former Parliamentary commander and now a governor of Westminster. The letter was relayed via a Captain Smith who, the schoolboy Locke reported, "has promised me to do his utmost" and is "most ready and willing to lay out himself for the accomplishment [of my election]". Another letter was written to Busby, and further help seems to have been solicited from Colonel Popham through whose patronage Locke was at Westminster in the first place; for it was probably to Popham that he wrote, again in Latin, "Remember, I beseech you, by whose supporting voice and by whose introduction I was once placed within these walls, and let me be permitted on the ground of that old favour now also to hope for and earnestly to solicit your patronage".[29]

As the election approached Locke had high hopes. He told his father, "I doubt not much of the election with the help of some friends which I shall diligently labour for". Then, a week later, he wrote that he had "to my utmost done what lies in me for the preparation both of myself and friends for the election". His optimism was not complete, however, for he asked his father to advise him what to do if he failed, but it was well founded for it seems that he was amongst the Head Master's favourites, one of his so-called "white boys": Busby, he informed his father, had promised "to do what he can which I cannot doubt of having so many assurances of his love he has made choice of my oration before any of the rest to be perhaps spoken at the Election". Well might the hopeful boy say that "Mr Busby [was not] any way wanting", for besides having promised him that his Hebrew oration would be amongst those presented in public, Busby had even "spoken to the Electors in my behalf".[30]

We can only speculate about what Locke's father would have advised for him in the event of failure to win one of the scholarships which would take him to university: to follow him in becoming a country lawyer comes to mind. But advice was not needed, and that spring month he was chosen for one of the Christ Church scholarships (he was placed last in a list of six), which would take him to Oxford.[31]

1652–1656: "NO VERY HARD STUDENT"[32]

Having left school, Locke presumably spent the summer, and his twentieth birthday, at home in Somerset. Towards the end of the year he made the sixty-mile journey to Oxford, to take up his Studentship. For his first few days there he seems to have had his patron Alexander Popham for company. Excited by the prospect of the "more than ordinary advantages" and "learning" which Oxford had to offer, the chance to converse with "all the worthys and most admired persons of former ages", Locke wrote to Popham thanking him for "my first days enjoyment, wherein you were pleased to afford your company and happiness".[33]

Through his careful financial accounts, we can follow Locke on his arrival at Christ Church, taking possession of his belongings from the carrier, getting a college porter to take them to his rooms (whose furniture, linen, and hangings he had probably bought from the previous occupant at a discount of one third), having his bed put up. Once he was settled in, the following picture of a quarter's expenses was typical (except, perhaps, for the medicine and sickness):

Paid my tutor for a quarter pupillage £1; paid him more for books which he paid for £1.11.0; paid to my bedmaker for three quarters of a year 15s; paid my laundress for one quarter 5s; to the House [i.e. Christ Church] £2.7s; paid to Mr Waxland money formerly borrowed in full £1.8.10; for a pair of boots 16s; for physic £1.03.0; laid out in my journey into the country when you [his father?] were sick and another since 15s.[34]

Described in the college records as "generosi filius", son of a gentleman, Locke matriculated on 27 November, though Westminster Students were not formally admitted to their Studentship until December. Then, in the cathedral, he would have formally sworn to observe the statutes, ordinances, and decrees of the college; to obey the Dean and other officers; and to act to the credit of Christ Church.[35]

Christ Church was unlike other colleges in more than one way. It embodied both a cathedral and a college, both of which were governed by the Dean and Chapter, with the educational work of the college being supervised by the Dean, the Sub-Dean, and their annually elected officers. The government of other university colleges, for example, Trinity College Cambridge to which some of Locke's schoolfellows had been elected, was in the hands of the Master and Fellows. At Christ Church, the nearest equivalent to Fellows were those of its Students who were of Master of Arts status, the difference being that they were not members of their governing body.

Locke would have been admitted to Christ Church along with forty or so other undergraduates. While all of these might be loosely referred to as "students", unlike him they were not all holders of a Studentship. Christ Church had an establishment of one hundred of these, many of them being filled by Westminsters. So though Locke was a Student, other undergraduates were admitted as Noblemen, Noblemen Commoners, Commoners, and Servitors (who received a free education in return for various domestic duties).[36]

The statutory course of studies required by the university for the B.A. degree had last been laid down by Archbishop Laud in 1636, when he was Chancellor of the University. Laud's Statutes had been part of his response to his belief that the puritan threat to the authority of the monarch and the established Church (which eventually led to the civil war) had some basis in a failure of university discipline and order. According to them, attendance was required in the first year at the twice-weekly lectures of the university lecturers in grammar, and in rhetoric, and on Aristotle, Cicero, or Quintilian. From then on there were lectures in logic and moral philosophy, and attendance three days a week at disputations as an observer. In the third year there were lectures by the Professor of Greek on various classical authors (some of which Locke would already have studied at Westminster), including Homer, Demosthenes, Isocrates, and Euripedes. The undergraduate now had to partake in two disputations, as an opponent and as a respondent; successful completion of this qualified him as a "general sophister" and saw him awarded a book of Aristotle's logic; after further terms of logic, and two final disputation performances, he was in a position to petition for his B.A.[37]

Lectures, disputations, and tutorials were in Latin, and one aim of the statutes was that students should be able to converse easily in it: "The examination is not to be on philosophical subjects merely ... and a principal object of inquiry with the examiners shall be with what facility the several persons have of expressing their thoughts in Latin ... on matters of daily occurrence."[38]

This course prescribed by university statute may not always have been followed in practice. For one thing, the colleges made parallel educational provisions for the four-year curriculum: at Christ Church a good part of these consisted of lectures on Aristotle (*Prior Analytics*, in the first year; *Categories*, *Posterior Analytics*, and *Topics* in the second; *Ethics* and *Physics* in the third; his scientific works in the fourth). There were also the classes of the college lecturers in rhetoric and in Greek to attend, classes which consisted of examined lectures and compositions on set themes. In addition, the Christ Church undergraduate education included declamations in Latin and Greek and participation in disputations.

The tutorial system also meant that an undergraduate's education may not always have followed a statutory course. Each undergraduate was required to have a tutor from amongst the graduates in his college. Though they were appointed by the Dean, tutors were not college officers and were paid directly by their tutees. Locke's tutor was Thomas Cole, an ex-Westminster boy, about six years older, to whom

he paid £1 a quarter. Not responsible for any formal teaching, Cole
would have been expected to supervise, even on a daily basis, Locke's
life and activities; to oversee his moral development and to direct
his studies by prescribing reading and private study in areas outside
of the formal curriculum, in mathematics and natural philosophy for
example, or more recent philosophy such as that of Descartes or
Gassendi.[39]

Locke's retrospective judgement on his first few years of university
study was not flattering. "I have often heard him say", it was later
reported,

> that he had so small satisfaction there from his studies, as finding very little
> light brought thereby to his understanding, that he became discontented with
> his manner of life, and wished his father had rather designed him for anything
> else than what he was destined to: apprehending that his no greater progress
> in knowledge proceeded from his not being fitted, or capacitated to be
> a scholar.[40]

The stress on the academic exercises of declamations and presentations in Latin and Greek, and of the practice of formal disputations,
was one thing he disliked. Some years later he spoke against "captious
logical disputes, or set declamations . . . upon any question". The first
of these "teaches fallacy, wrangling, and opinionatry", while the second
"sets the thoughts upon wit, and false colours, and not upon truth".
They all "spoil the judgement, and put a man out of the way of
right and fair reasoning". He "never loved the trade of disputing in
public", a friend would say, "but was always wont to declaim against
it as being rather invented for wrangling or ostentation than to
discover truth".[41]

Locke was also against much of the curriculum's content. The
formalities of Aristotelian logic which drilled a student in "predicaments and predicables", and in the "mode and figure" of arguments,
was not a good foundation for right reasoning and judgement. "I have
seldom or never observed anyone to get the skill of reasoning well,
or speaking handsomely, by studying those rules which pretend to
teach it." He was similarly critical of the content of the lectures, and
would later "complain of the method he took in his studies at first . . .
and [say] that he lost a great deal of time, when he first applied himself
to study, because the only philosophy then known at Oxford was the
Peripatetic, perplexed with obscure terms and stuffed with useless
questions".[42]

Dislike of his undergraduate curriculum which "kept him from being any very hard student" turned Locke instead (it was reported) to seek out "the company of pleasant, and witty men, with whom he likewise took great delight in corresponding by letters. And in conversation, and these correspondences, he, according to his own account of himself, spent for some years much of his time." One of these was Samuel Tilly, the son of the vicar of Keynsham (four miles north of Locke's home at Pensford), and an Oxford student a couple of years senior. During a visit to Somerset towards the end of his undergraduate course Locke wrote to Tilly, back in Oxford, hoping for a letter in return:

I exceed you in that which men esteem the greatest happiness of their lives, that I have a better friend than you can hope for. I mean sir yourself from whose friendship besides common and familiar offices I can expect miracles such as these, that you should make me sensible of some delight whilst I am away from you, this you can do by ... writing.[43]

Another "pleasant and witty" man with whom Locke both conversed and corresponded during his undergraduate years was Thomas Grenfeild, an ex-Oxford man, fourteen years older and a local vicar in Somerset. Locke told him that "besides common helps he will stand in need not only of the lively genius and serenity of the spring but the warmth and vigour of summer that writes to you. You are not of the number of those with whom every scribbling ... will pass for an obligation."[44]

Locke had been at Oxford for nearly a year when, in June 1653, heads of colleges were instructed by the Parliamentary Visitors to purge themselves of any undergraduates who were not good puritans. Locke survived, but this could mean that the Dean, John Owen, had not followed the instruction strictly, rather than that education under the Royalist Busby had had no effect on Locke's religious sympathies.[45]

The following year Locke contributed to a volume of verses* written by a wide variety of members of the University, which the college published in honour of Oliver Cromwell who had recently signed a peace treaty with the Dutch. He wrote a short Latin piece, and a longer English one which began:

> If Greece with so much mirth did entertain
> Her *Argo*, coming laden home again,
> With what loud mirth and triumph shall we greet
> The wish'd approaches of our welcome fleet,

> When of that prize our ships do us possess
> Whereof their fleece was but an emblem —
> Peace.[46]

Little is known of Locke's movements during his undergraduate years. Twice in 1653 he visited his father (who on one occasion was ill), and in February 1654 he made the two-day coach journey to London. Perhaps it was on this later occasion that he made the visit to a family at Hampton Court which he referred to in some rather clumsy and unskilfully mannered letters of thanks:

The same greatness of those favours I received from everyone ... which exacts a more than ordinary return of thanks, the same also pleads an excuse for the delay of my acknowledgement. [The] small and common courtesies ... that you conferred on me overwhelm and fill the soul, and leave no room for any other thoughts than of their greatness, which rather amaze the mind, than compose it for a due return of thanks.

The "due return" included a book on heraldry, which his correspondent had wanted to read. Touchingly, the book contained a secret message Locke had written in some kind of invisible ink: "I must add one petition that ... you would take out a leaf of clean paper inserted at the beginning of this book and when you are alone warm it very hot by the fire."[47]

Later that year, in the autumn, Locke's mother was taken ill, and died, and presumably he was in Somerset for her funeral. He was certainly there the next year, in September. He graduated the following February, aged twenty-three, after eleven terms of the statutory twelve.[48]

1656–1658: "A MOST LEARNED AND INGENIOUS YOUNG MAN"[49]

In the summer after graduation, Locke was at home with his father. Perhaps he spent time with Grenfeild, he certainly did with Francis Atkins, another local friend and one with lively interests in the opposite sex. Atkins asked for his company on a journey he was about to make. Though he was going on some business, "it may be Cupid may be one of the actors in our comical journey: and to that purpose I have sent already ... to my mistress to meet me.... I cannot promise you she is handsome; but this, though I think she has the more scarlet in her cheek of the two, yet you shall be her judge." Atkins concluded his letter even more tantalisingly, "my service to your bedfellow, for so I think she is at this time".[50]

Whether or not he accompanied Atkins on the "comical journey", Locke left Pensford certainly before the end of October. Rather than going to Oxford he took the coach from Bath to London, a one-hundred-mile journey which was marked by having to sit opposite a "mountain of flesh that called herself a merchant's wife". "She was so gross", Locke told his father, "that she turned my stomach and made me sick the two first mornings and the third I was like to be buried, for had the coach (as it might) overturned and she fell upon me I should have been dead and buried at a time." With no clear evidence to the contrary in the record of Locke's life, someone might be tempted to infer that behind the humour of this report there was some deep-rooted fear of the female body as such; more clearly, though, it does illustrate that by this time his father was no longer "keeping him in much awe, and at a distance" and that he now "lived perfectly with him as a friend".[51]

Having taken lodgings near his old school at Westminster, Locke was prevented by wet weather from pursuing the "business" which had brought him to London, business for which, he told his father, it would be "very material" to get a letter from Alexander Popham. He passed some time in Westminster Hall, observing the Parliamentary examination of James Nayler, a Quaker called the Son of God by his followers, and who earlier in the year had entered Bristol in the manner of Christ entering Jerusalem. Locke's own "business" was probably that of seeking admission to one of the Inns of Court, for he was admitted to Gray's Inn that December.[52]

Locke did not stay in London to study law; instead he returned to Oxford, to work towards the M.A. The three-year curriculum involved more participation in disputations, and the delivery of six formal lectures. Attendance was also required at lectures on geometry and astronomy, Hebrew and Greek, and natural philosophy and metaphysics. Some of these requirements were met by arrangements made internally by Christ Church: the college provided for participation in disputations, for declamations, and for the delivery of six lectures on Aristotle; it also provided lectures by the Junior Censor in Natural Philosophy, and the Senior Censor in Moral Philosophy. Within this broad curriculum, M.A. students were no longer subject to close supervision and direction, and were expected to follow their own particular specialised academic interests.[53]

Locke graduated M.A. in June 1658, not long before his twenty-sixth birthday. By that time he had "acquired the reputation of learning".

He was, it was said, "looked upon as one of the most learned and ingenious young men in the college".[54] That report was made by James Tyrrell, an undergraduate, ten years Locke's junior, and a man who would feature (in varying degrees of friendship) in Locke's life to the end.

College Offices and Medical Studies (1659–1667)

In the spring, Locke, now approaching twenty-seven, was encouraged to think of marriage by his father who urged him to make a point of being in Pensford that July, a certain widow, "young, childless, handsome, with £200 per annum and £1000 in her purse may possibly occasion your stay here".[2] Presumably the matter was further discussed, but it came to nothing. Even if the widow's money was sufficient for her and a new husband, Oxford had far more to offer. Still with his Studentship, without any college responsibilities and not registered for any further degree, Locke was free to follow his own inclinations and interests.

Whether or not Locke saw the widow there, he did go to Pensford in the summer. His father was thinking of moving to nearby Stanton Drew, a plan in which Locke saw "many conveniences". Whatever these were, the move was not made: possibly because he was ill (perhaps a recurrence from the previous year). This, and the fact that he too was unwell, kept Locke in Somerset longer than he intended. On the whole he was "melancholy and discontented": since coming into the country, he wrote to a friend, "I have been either not well or not at rest".[3]

The cause of the discontent was that rural life was no exchange for the sophistication of Oxford, the "learning [and] civility" to which he had grown accustomed. "I am", Locke wrote back to Oxford, "in the midst of a company of mortals that know nothing but the price of corn and sheep [and] that can entertain discourse of nothing but fatting of beast and digging of ground." Remarks such as this show how far he felt his education had separated him from his original surroundings. They were common in the letters he wrote this year from "Zomerzetshire", as he called it in imitation of the local accent. He referred to "barbarism", and the "clownery of the country". "I am", he told his friends, disparagingly rather than approvingly, "in a country where art hath no share in our words and actions, you can meet with nothing here but what is the innocent product of nature", and referred to "bonny country girls that have not one jot of dissimulation in them". It was clear that the locals who had known him as a child saw what he had now become; though whether they took him as seriously as he did himself is not clear. He reported "being the prime statesman of the place, and the dictator of intelligence". "You would laugh", he said, presumably with humour but none too modestly for all that, "to see how attentive the gray-heads be to my reports . . . how they bless themselves at my relations, and go home and tell wonders and prophesies of next year's affairs."[4]

Something he was missing was his circle of friends in Oxford, two days away. Besides Samuel Tilly, there was William Uvedale and Gabriel Towerson, "the grave Mr Towerson" as Locke called him. The circle also included, in Uvedale's words, "the three ladies . . . or Godesses at B.H.". "B.H.". was Black Hall in St Giles', the home of John Evelegh, a clergyman; "the Godesses" included Anne, the second of his five daughters, and Elinor Parry (now about eighteen or nineteen), whose brother John was a fellow of Jesus College. When the friends (the "club" as Towerson called them) met at Black Hall, they engaged in the formalised social practices of the time such as the appointment by lot on 14 February of "valentines" for the coming year, and spent time in reading or discussing light-hearted romances such as Loveday's *Hymen's Praeludia*, Madeleine de Scudéry's *Le Grand Cyrus*, Francis Osborne's *Remedies of Love* and *Advice of a Father to his Son*, and William Davenant's *The Tragedy of Albovine, King of the Lombards*. Locke himself wrote one such romance, and sketched out a play, "Orozes, King of Albania".[5]

A good number of the letters (or their drafts) that passed between Locke and these friends have survived, and these, even more than those he wrote to Tilly and Grenfeild during his undergraduate years, show his delight in such correspondence. He had by now, if not before, been impressed by the letters of Jean-Louis Guez which had been published as models of style (if "I had his volume by me I had thence transcribed an answer" to you, he told one correspondent); and his letters to "the club" display how his own letters had advanced in the skilful elaboration of metaphors and conceits.[6]

The emotional depth of many of these letters (those to, as well as from, Locke) is difficult to judge. Though full of protestations of affection, and avowals of romantic inclination, their stylised and polite gallantry seems designed to keep serious emotion at arm's length, or at any rate to hide it under playfulness. Some of the letters between the males of the group tend towards gallantry too, certainly they are barely more free and open; nevertheless their talk about the godesses at Black Hall does betray real excitement and frisson.

Anne Evelegh was William Uvedale's valentine, but this did not mean the letters which passed between her and Locke (of whom she was perhaps somewhat in awe) could not be full of playful compliments. Locke's relationship with her seems to have been nothing more than friendly and companionable. Her letters to him in Pensford bemoan in the most flattering way the absence of his "sweet society and pleasing company"; they charmingly regret that Somerset outvies Oxford in owning "so exquisite and so virtuous a soul", "the completest man that ever the world brought forth". But they all make plain that these are the sentiments of everyone at Black Hall, including her parents, and not just, not especially, hers: fortune "frown[s] on us in depriving us all this while of your sweet company". Except for a reference to Uvedale's success in getting a fellowship at All Souls, and a brief reference to Locke's health, her letters to him, as his to her, contained nothing at all by way of reports of day-to-day doings, no news or comment. In a draft letter Locke spoke of his good fortune in having had from her "wrapped up in one sheet delicates enough to feast me a whole week"; but the letter to which he was replying contained nothing but elaborate compliment combined with perhaps genuine protestations of being unworthy of their friendship. For his part, Locke did no more than return the compliments: along with "my admiration of your extraordinary accomplishments . . . I might justly wonder at that prodigality wherewith you cast away those flowers of rhetoric upon me did I not consider that those rarities grow naturally and flourish continually in you".[7]

So Locke's friendship with Anne Evelegh, although genuine enough, appears to have had no particular depth to it. She wrote, she said, "to make you laugh: and to serve for a diversion in the country". On the other hand, his "real friendship" with Elinor Parry, some years his junior, was not, as he said, "tied always to the ceremonious rules and

compliment".[8] It certainly seems to have involved something more —
though it is not easy to work out exactly what her feelings were, for her
letters to Locke from this period have not survived, and we have merely
drafts of his to her.

In February she had been appointed his valentine; and he wrote her
a letter devoted to expressing his satisfaction: "Had your choice alone
bestowed on me what I now partly owe to chance I had wanted nothing
of perfect happiness. However as it is my condition is too glorious to
let me be insensible of it and I will be content with the enjoyment of
a blessing without examining how I came by it."[9] The conventions of
politeness and civility required no less than all of this, and there was
nothing to be read between the lines.

How things went between St Valentine's day in February and the
summer when Locke left Oxford for Pensford we do not know, but
what was probably his first letter to her from Somerset was perhaps
more than merely conventional. He complained that being away from
her was bad enough, but, to compound the evil, she had not written.
He spoke as though he saw this failure as almost cruelly intentional on
her part: not only had he been "forsaken", but worse, was "banished
and treated as an outlaw with whom there is held no commerce",
"forbidden all hopes of intelligence with those persons that made me
sensible of my life". "Having no longer converse with the living" he was
as good as dead. He begged her to write and to "redeem" him, "your
letter alone will enlarge me".[10]

Locke was in his "melancholy condition" for a week more, until
eventually a letter arrived. His spirits rose immediately, and now he was
regretful it would take two days or so for him to tell her this: "The
inhabitants of this world are clogged with dull earth which obeys not
the nimbler motion of their spirits, else . . . I had not made use of these
slow paced messengers to convey my thanks." Apparently rather
suggestively he continued: "Could my body remove with my thoughts
I believe you would have reason to complain of my too frequent visits,
and possibly some times at midnight you would find other company
at Black Hall besides sleep and pleasant dreams." Perhaps it was
just conventional modesty and indicated nothing that Locke thought
the "excellent epithets" in her letter were "misplace[d] upon me",
but the ending of his reply does seem to show that he felt himself to
be clumsily unworthy, still the country boy of his youth: "I am the
same rough thing still that I was when I left you and I fear I shall
grow worse in a country famous for rustics. Which however it may

endanger that small stock of civility I am owner of yet it shall never impair that esteem I have for you." Another close female friend of a later year would record that Locke's eventual easy, unconstrained manner was not "had naturally" but acquired "from the company he had kept".[11]

At the very beginning of September there was another letter from Elinor. It too was received with a perhaps slightly abject "gratitude". It immediately changed despondency into joy: "I wonder with what spell it is that you convert your ink into so efficacious a balsam, that when I thought myself in a condition destined to misery beyond remedy and beyond comfort behold two or three drops have revived me." Rightly or wrongly, Locke was able to find in the letter some-thing different from the friendship expressed by Anne Evelegh (from whom he had received a letter at the same time): "I admire the gallantry and composure of your expressions, but it is that vein of goodness that runs through it that I take myself to be concerned in, and it is this that makes me adore the graces of your letter that they are kind as well as handsome, and that you have made them smile upon me".[12]

Locke's next letter, perhaps two weeks later, adds to the impression that without her he felt empty and lifeless, as nothing without recognition from her. Compared with the delights of her company and conversation, all else lacked pleasure and satisfaction; and again he spoke of "my melancholy", "my misery". As though his continued existence somehow depended on her, he begged for "some room in your thoughts" and for "your remembrances".[13]

We learn from this letter that Elinor's brother had recently been in Somerset, and that Locke had had a meeting with him, probably in Bath. Elinor sent some silk flowers as a "memento", and Locke, though knowing her "remembrances are not to be bought", had nevertheless discussed with her brother (as "one that best knows you") "what things are fittest to suggest them". He had decided to send her some silver which had been coloured gold by the action of the heavily mineral spring water of Bath.

Elinor seems to have objected to Locke's having talked to her brother about her; and, from this point on, tensions began to appear in their relationship, even though for some weeks yet it consisted only of what Locke's father once called "paper visits". Perhaps she was becoming uneasy with the weight of Locke's emotions, for she seems to have told him to curb his pen. He was apologetic of course, and promised obedience to her "power" and "empire", even though possibly he could not see his fault:

If you are resolved to exercise your rigour I know not how to help it; this I know my pen hath not deserved to lose that liberty you desire to take from it unless you think none deserves to speak to you or of you but your own.... Whatever mistakes [my pen] may have run into it never adventured on the boldness to describe you and it has been always wise enough to know that you are not to be drawn but by yourself.... [W]hen you are resolved to appear to the world you must like the heavenly bodies dress yourself in your own beams and with your own light show yourself to our wonder: a mischief on my pen, I think you are in the right indeed and it ought to be imprisoned.[14]

Besides now appearing to be warning Locke to keep his distance, emotionally speaking, Elinor had also begun to tease. Perhaps she just could not cope with what she was beginning to experience as serious advances which made some demand on her (was she not ready for any involvement?), or perhaps, as coming from Locke, she simply did not find them welcome (did she find him too ponderous? too gauche? too bookish?). She seems teasingly to have suggested that his anxiety to get back to Oxford was focused on his new friend Towerson. He did not deny that Towerson's friendship was something he valued and he even asked Elinor to "persuade him into a belief of it". But he complained that "had you not preferred railery to truth", she would have acknowledged herself as the person that would really draw him back. Perhaps hinting that Elinor had mentioned Towerson because he was on *her* mind, he concluded reproachfully, "am I indeed so unfortunate as to have no other friend left in Oxford but Mr T.... Is it possible that a month's absence should ruin a friendship that I thought everlasting." He would know by her next letter, he said, "what judgement I shall make of my condition" but was sure that "jesting will not always last, and you will not in a frolic make yourself sport with tormenting me"; and indeed Elinor's reply was evidently not displeasing.[15]

For one thing, she appears to have asked Locke to perform some task or errand on her behalf, a task which he delightedly carried out since it "satisfied me something for not seeing you that I was about your business". For another, she appears to have reassured him with "professions of friendship". Though Locke gallantly said he would not "sully the glory of such a favour by owing it to any other cause than

merely your goodness", he seems to have wanted more and still felt the
need to make his own feelings plain:

I would not have my happiness alloyed with the mixture of any other
consideration, yet if I may be permitted to plead the high esteem I shall always
have for you.... I mention this now not that I think you unacquainted with the
temper of my heart, but because I herein give you the greatest assurances of
sincerity can be imagined since I am in a country where art hath no share in
our words and actions.[16]

Locke's next surviving draft replied to something less satisfying.
Though he had found in Elinor's last letter "the kind and the
comfortable", and an "assurance...of your friendship", he had also
found more "railery and challenges", and provocative things of
"stomach and daring". To what extent and in what way Elinor had
been reacting to things she had found, or had imagined she had found,
in a previous (now lost) letter from him is not clear. Unlikely as it may
seem in view of his rather abject and subservient attitude, Locke had
been accused of being "invincible and unconquerable". He put on a
brave face and did not neglect to laud her with compliment, but he was
obviously hurt by what he took to be some criticism. Perhaps a little
mystified, he could not forbear complaint. How could she "that can be
so obligingly perfectly good when you please as if you were made for
nothing else, ever be otherwise"? "A face that becomes smiles so well
should never put on frowns.... You should follow the bent of your own
temper and be perfectly generous and I should receive one letter from
you full of free and open kindness."[17]

It looks likely that, as Locke had hoped, Elinor replied to this "by
return of the carrier". She enclosed some ribbon as a token of
friendship and reconciliation, and by the middle of December
Locke was able to write, in great delight, "All's well, the quarrel is
ended...and I think it is very hard for us long to be enemies. But were
I stubborn you know how to mollify me, and had I set up my strongest
resolution to stand out you have found a way to take me in and bring
me to conditions." Was he acknowledging here the kind of fault that
might have led to Elinor's earlier complaint of his being "invincible and
unconquerable"? Or was he confessing that, even though she had given
him good cause to "stand out", his resolution would inevitably have
failed? Perhaps the latter, for though gratefully acknowledging the end
of the quarrel, he could not bring himself to accept that things were
well enough to be left alone. He felt compelled to question the present

of the ribbon and just what it signified: "When I consider all the circumstances I am ready to conclude ... that either you have very little love who are forced to buy it, or that you think any good enough for me since you send me that which is so slight and fading and lies open to everyone's purchases." Had she, he asked, "sent your heart with this"? "Pray tell me too whether yours be true love or no. . . . If it be, certainly it is the coldest that ever was, for I dare say if one were covered all over with this sort of love it would scarce make one warm, and one might nevertheless freeze and starve to death."[18]

Locke had said in his previous letter that if only Elinor would reply to his worries he would not trouble her again before his return to Oxford, but he could not rest: "Pardon me that contrary to my promise I beg the trouble of another letter, but it very much concerns me to be well assured in this point, before I resolve to remove hence where every chimney offers the comfort of a warm sun to a place where it seems fire heats not and flames have no warmth."

JANUARY–DECEMBER 1659: "STUDY IN EARNEST"[19]

After his M.A. Locke began "to study in earnest ... apply[ing] himself principally to physic". For some time he had been interested in medicine: perhaps even prior to going to Oxford in 1652 he had collected some remedies for common troubles such as ague, measles, sore throat, toothache, and rheum. The recipes were distinctly homely: for toothache "take your own water and rock alum and boil together and lay it to your teeth with a fine cloth", for some hurt to the eye "take some of the water that grows in bladders on elm trees and apply it"; there is even one from "A.L.", perhaps his mother Agnes.[20]

At the beginning of 1658, shortly before his M.A., a letter from John Strachey characterised Locke as a doctor, and in that same year Locke's notebook began to show a more substantial and sophisticated concern with medicine and associated scientific matters. There is a note on observing the circulation of blood in a frog by stripping it of its skin and holding it up against the sun. There are also notes from various medical authors, from the ancient to, mainly, the recent: Hippocrates, Pierre Borel, Ralph Bathhurst, Francis Glisson, and Lambert Velthuysen.[21]

During the months in Pensford in the latter half of 1659 Locke began a fresh medical notebook. Again there are recipes and cures which he must have collected from local people, but most of the book is taken up with notes on the reading he was doing, particularly the works of the Galenist chemist Daniel Sennert.[22]

The seriousness of Locke's interest in medicine in the late 1650s is shown by a list of around two thousand medical authors, and the titles of twenty-five medical books. His medical reading* was certainly quite intense between the completion of his M.A. and 1661 when he took on some responsibilities in Christ Church; and, to take a larger period, in the years between 1658 and early 1667 well over a half of his reading was in the area of medicine and natural science.[23]

Yet medicine was not Locke's only intellectual interest during the summer months of 1659 in Pensford. In September, Henry Stubbe (another Westminster Student at Christ Church, and Locke's senior by two years) sent him a book he had recently published, *An Essay in Defence of the Good Old Cause; or a discourse concerning the rise and extent of the power of the civil magistrate in reference to spiritual affairs.* Stubbe shared the views of the college Dean, John Owen, an Independent, who, as an advocate of toleration, was against the idea of any religious imposition by the state: as there was no agreed and infallible reading of the Bible, people should be free to think and worship as they saw fit. Stubbe was not alone in following Owen for, so he had reported in 1656, all ex-Westminster scholars at Christ Church (which, if the report was correct, would include Locke) were "Dr Owen's creatures and had promised to defend liberty of conscience".[24]

After a week's "hasty perusal" of the book, Locke wrote to Stubbe what has been called "the earliest document in our possession containing a reasoned argument" by him. He had read the book "with infinite satisfaction". His only worry was Stubbe's extension of toleration to Catholics. Expressing a common view, Locke could not accept that this "can consist with the security of the Nation.... I cannot see how they can at the same time obey two different authorities carrying on contrary interests". The danger to the state inherent in a subject's owing an allegiance to Rome was heightened by the nature of that outside authority. Rome's authority was "backed with an opinion of infallibility and holiness ... not limited by any contract and therefore not accountable to anybody". Locke implicitly recognised that it might be different if the Pope claimed purely spiritual jurisdiction, but even then there could be difficulties: "you know how easy it is", he put it to Stubbe, "under pretence of spiritual jurisdiction to take in all secular affairs since in a commonwealth wholly Christian it is no small difficulty to set limits to each and to define exactly where one begins and the other ends". A second problem implicit in the nature of Catholics' allegiance to Rome was that it meant their home state could have no reason to trust them. Indeed Catholics, or so it was generally held, were not obliged to "keep faith with heretics [= Protestants]". What guarantee can be had "of their fidelity and obedience from all their oaths and protestations, when that other sovereignty they pay homage to is acknowleged by them to be owner of a power that can acquit them of all perfidy and perjury"?[25]

Leaving aside this scruple about toleration of Catholics, which would remain with him throughout his life, Locke doubted that, whatever the strength of the theoretical case for religious toleration, it was possible in practice that people of different beliefs would "quietly unite...under the same government...and hand in hand march to the same end of peace and mutual society though they take a different way to heaven".[26]

JANUARY–OCTOBER 1660: "I SHALL NOT WILLINGLY BE DRAWN FROM HENCE"[27]

In November, Locke had been visited in Pensford by one of his friends from "the club", William Uvedale, who had travelled from his family home in Hampshire. His later letter of thanks told Locke that both he (Uvedale) and Gabriel Towerson had been made fellows of All Souls College, and mentioned he had heard that Locke was not to be expected back in Oxford "until after winter"; in fact Locke was there by early January.[28]

Even though it had then supported him through six years of formal university study, the Studentship to which Locke had been elected had not come to an end with his M.A.: the average tenure of the Studentships was around fifteen years, though given certain provisos and circumstances they could be held for life. The intention was to ensure a supply of educated parochial clergy, so as soon as a Student entered holy orders and took up a living away from Oxford, or as soon as he married, his tenure came to an end. But having entered holy orders it was still possible to remain a Student (perhaps with the intention of studying for a higher degree in divinity) so long as any living taken was poorly remunerated or not more than thirty miles from Oxford.[29]

There was some inexorability in the progress from Student to clergyman. Initially elected as *discipuli*, of which there were forty,

Students gradually gained seniority through length of residence, and not long after graduation migrated into the group of forty *philosophi*, some of whom might take orders. By the beginning of 1659, not many months after taking his M.A., Locke had been about the twenty-sixth most senior in this group. He would have expected eventually to become one of the next group of twenty *theologi*, when he would have a relatively immediate obligation to take holy orders, or at least to be preparing to do so. However, despite their intention that Students should take orders, the rules made provision for certain exceptions. The Crown could grant a dispensation from taking orders; and, even apart from such royal intervention, there were four special Faculty Studentships (five after 1665). These, by contrast, could only be held by laymen, and were awarded by the college to graduate *philosophi* for the purpose of training as lawyers or physicians.[30]

Locke might, then, at the beginning of 1660, have been expected to register for a further degree, in theology (particularly for a Student, now twenty-second among the *philosophi*), or perhaps in law or medicine, but he did not do so.[31]

At least two possibilities seem to have been in the air as regards his hopes and intentions (neither of which involved going into the Church). Four years earlier, shortly after his B.A., he had been admitted to Gray's Inn in London; and, though he had then returned to Oxford, the idea of studying to become a lawyer seems still to have been a possibility, though not an attractive one, as appears from letters Locke wrote in March to William Carr, Popham's brother-in-law, who had recently started legal studies himself. He spoke of Carr's head being "stuffed like a tailor's pocket with fragments of parchment and scraps of old moth eaten leases", and said that this gave him "a quarrel to our profession and makes me slow to remove from a college to an Inn of Court": "I shall never expect to find so much satisfaction at Gray's Inn as I do at Christ Church."[32]

Medicine was another, and more attractive, possibility. Locke quite clearly had a serious interest in this, and as a means of livelihood it was something he had discussed with his father during their recent time together. The question had evidently arisen of entering into some sort of medical collaboration or practice with a local doctor, Dr Ayliffe Ivye; but he was no more enthusiastic about taking up life in Somerset than he had been about going to Gray's. "I find no disappointment at all in the delay of your treaty with Dr Ivye", he wrote to his father not long after his return to Oxford, "since I shall not willingly be drawn from hence."[33] In fact, whatever the expertise and knowledge of Dr Ivye as a physician, there could hardly have been a better place than Oxford for Locke to pursue his interest in medicine, even apart from his having his Studentship there.

After the B.A. and M.A., the statutory Oxford route to medical practice was to the B.M. (three years) and the D.M. (four years). The B.M. was sufficient for an official licence to practise (either from Oxford or from the Royal College of Physicians in London), but the D.M. was a requirement for fellowship of the Royal College. It was quite possible, however, to practise (perhaps in an apprentice or assistant capacity) on the basis of an M.A.; and some country physicians worked on their own without any formal qualifications, perhaps not even a B.A. The experience and practical skills acquired in this way, or by reading and study outside of a formal curriculum, might later lead to a B.M. or a licence.[34]

To what extent Locke had it in mind eventually to earn a living as a practising physician is not clear, but in any case a serious interest in medicine could find expression in Oxford in ways other and perhaps better than being registered for a degree and following a formal course of study. It was an extraordinarily thriving centre of scientific activity of many kinds, in particular those kinds which related to medicine, such as anatomy, chemistry, and physiology. One of the brightest and best and still rising stars was Robert Boyle, five years Locke's senior, who in 1655 had set up a laboratory there. He had begun with an interest in chemistry, often from the point of view of its application to medicine (or physic), his first publication being *An Invitation to a Free and Generous Communication of Secrets and Receipts in Physick*.[35]

Locke first met Boyle probably during the first months of 1660, perhaps through the mediation of Richard Lower, who had been two or three years his senior at Westminster and Christ Church: with active interests in anatomy, physiology, and chemistry, Lower was already a medical practitioner in association with his mentor Thomas Willis, who became Sedleian Professor of Natural Philosophy that year. It was quite evidently the convergence of Locke's and Boyle's interests in iatrochemistry that gave meaning to the new acquaintanceship for him, and he lost little time in letting Dr Ivye know about it. Ivye congratulated him on his introduction to Boyle, and even hoped to benefit from it himself: he hoped Locke would "let slip no occasion whereby you may better yourself, and so me, by your acquaintance with Mr Boyle. I long to have an account of my queries." Whether or not

Ivye benefited from Locke's new contact with Boyle, Locke himself certainly did, being given recommendations for reading and access to the books in Boyle's study.[36]

It was perhaps under the influence of Boyle, with his broad interests in natural philosophy, that for a couple of years into the 1660s, Locke's reading widened from medicine to encompass physics, in particular Descartes's physics. In later years he would tell a friend that the dissatisfaction he had had with his earlier curriculum was cured by Descartes. For a time, he told her, he had thought his problem with it "proceeded altogether from a defect in his understanding". It was not until he came to read some Descartes that he got "a relish of philosophical studies": he was "rejoiced in reading of these because though he very often differed in opinion from this writer, he yet found that what he said was very intelligible".[37]

It was not just the attractiveness of Oxford as a centre of research in medicine and related subjects which led Locke to tell his father that he would "not willingly be drawn from hence"; he saw his agreeable pattern of life in Oxford and Christ Church as providing the security of some kind of predictability and familiarity in a troubled and unsettled world. He would not want to leave "whilst things are in these uncertain hurries, nor think to enter upon a steady course of life whilst the whole nation is reeling".[38]

What Locke was referring to was the confused political situation which had followed the death of Oliver Cromwell in 1658, and the succession of his son Richard as Lord Protector. The previous year Richard Cromwell had been overturned by the army, and, as Locke observed to his father shortly after his return from Pensford, Parliament, whose relations with the army were unstable, had that very month invited General Monck in Scotland to come to its aid with his army. The national situation was a deep worry to him; "it appears to me", he told his father, "altogether lowering and cloudy and I fear a storm will follow. Divisions are as wide, factions are as violent and designs as pernicious as ever.... In this posture of affairs I know not what to think, what to say. I would be quiet and I would be safe, but if I cannot enjoy them together the last certainly must be had at any rate."

Locke was so moved by the uncertainties of the political situation, which gave some indication of leading to another civil war, that he even envisaged himself taking up arms, though on which side he did not know: "In this time when there is no other security against men's passions and revenge but what strength and steel yields I have a long time thought the safest condition to be in arms could I be but resolved...for whom to imploy them." Let me know, he asked his father, "which way your arms are like to point".[39]

This letter, so open about Locke's emotions regarding national affairs, is untypical. With few exceptions, the (surviving) letters which he had written so far contained no record of his feelings during the years of the civil wars and of Cromwell's rule, following the beheading of Charles I.

This reserve seems to have softened after the end of Cromwell's "reign" in September 1658, though it is noticeable that (with one exception) the change only pervaded Locke's letters to his father. A draft of a letter to Elinor Parry (written during the very disturbed period after the fall of Richard Cromwell in May 1659, and before the rise of General Monck in February 1660) does mention the political situation. But there is no anxiety or worry in the passing reference, which is made only for use as a conceit in paying court to Elinor. Her virtue, he said, gave her a "title to empire", and "possibly it is the only thing wherein all the dissenting factions now in England would agree, viz. that you ought not only to be general but sovereign".[40]

It is not until the period following Cromwell's death, then, that we begin to learn, almost exclusively in his letters to his father, something of Locke's feelings about national events. We perhaps also begin to learn why we had heard nothing of them earlier. One reason may have been that, out of caution (perhaps sensible, perhaps neurotic), Locke simply did not set down on paper (or asked to have it destroyed) anything that might commit him politically in an unpredictable situation. So, a long and open passage in a letter to his father in 1659 ends by apologising that what he had been saying was both "what you are well acquainted with already", and also risky: "a comment on these times is as dangerous as to you useless, and therefore fit for nothing but the fire".[41]

Another possible reason why he was unrevealing of his feelings is that he hid them from himself. With some degree of intent, Locke seems to have averted his eyes during the years of political turmoil and tried to cultivate an other-worldliness. In June 1659, shortly before his extended visit to Pensford, he had written that the "health and quiet" he was pleased to have learnt his father was then enjoying was "a blessing this tumbling world is very sparing of"; but then he went on,

[handwritten margin note: Did L. often ask correspondents to burn his letters?]

"though I cannot remember any days of my life wherein I have enjoyed more". His rather paradoxical explanation was that

all these tossings have served but to rock me into a pleasant slumber, whilst others dream ... of nothing but fire, sword, and ruin. . . . I have taught my hopes to overlook my fears and suppress those troubles. . . . That which I look to is the hand that governs all things, that manages our chaos and will bring out of it what will be best for us.[42]

So if his letters generally did not express anxieties and opinions about the political situation, it was perhaps because of an adopted stance of keeping quiet, of averting himself from national affairs, and of turning his thoughts to other things. There was, though, one other person besides his father whom he seems to have entrusted with his deeper feelings. This was Thomas Westrowe, whom he knew at Christ Church, and with whom he evidently had a free and informal friendship. In October 1659 Locke wrote to him in rather pessimistic, despairing terms about how people's lives and actions had been guided. What "rules us all under the title of reason" is nothing more than our fanciful imagination, he said.

Where is that great Diana of the world, Reason; everyone thinks he alone embraces this Juno, whilst others grasp nothing but clouds ... and there is not a man but thinks he alone hath this light within and all besides stumble in the dark. It is our passions, that brutish part, that dispose of our thoughts and actions, we are all centaurs and it is the beast that carries us.[43]

The following month he again wrote to Westrowe, troubled by the confused situation following Richard Cromwell's fall: "Oh for a pilot that would steer the tossed ship of this state." His response had been to harden himself ("methinks I find myself ... half iron already") and to "turn a churlish insensible outside to the world".[44]

Yet on a personal level Locke was forced to see that withdrawal from the world was "not a sure remedy against its troubles". Five months later, when he had news that his father was ill with what seems to have been a recurring complaint, Locke recognised that "I had begun to arm myself against the evils of the world, but I find myself wounded in a place unguarded, and it will be but in vain to endeavour to harden oneself, whilst nature, virtue and gratitude will keep some places continually sensible".[45]

The troubled political situation which had so disturbed Locke for the past year reached some kind of resolution in May with the restoration of Charles II. At first he seems to have had some concern that this was not going to provide the peace and security he craved, for in early August, during the Restoration visitation to the university, he warned an acquaintance "not to expect that I alone should preserve my reason clear in a place where everyone has his clouded and disturbed by no ordinary fear". Oxford now, he said, "is not a place for serene thoughts...[and] you will not blame me if my hands shake in a storm".[46]

OCTOBER–DECEMBER 1660: "WHETHER THE CIVIL MAGISTRATE MAY LAWFULLY IMPOSE"[47]

In October and into November, Locke was in Pensford. Quite possibly he saw Dr Ivye and discussed medical matters with him, for they had been keeping up a correspondence, but much of his time must have been spent in writing to Gabriel Towerson about what was called the "law of nature". Their letters continued discussions they had been having for some time; indeed their concern with the topic had become something of a joke. Writing to Locke, William Uvedale said, "I do not intend to trouble you with any discourse of the Law of Nature, or (what is more proper for me) a dispute about the motion of the diaphragm [i.e. about laughter]", and Towerson himself seems to have been tiring of it: "The papers that have past between us", he wrote at the beginning of November, are now "so voluminous that I conceive it more difficult to inform ourselves of the state of the controversy between us." He intended, he said, "to put a period to this controversy, if I find you inclinable thereto".[48]

Two important books on the subject had been published during the year. One of these, *De Officiis secundum Naturae Jus*, was by Robert Sharrock, and, particularly since he was part of Robert Boyle's circle, it is very possible that Locke had read it; the other, which he evidently did read, was Samuel Pufendorf's *Elementa Jurisprudentia Universalis*.[49]

By "natural law" was meant a God-given morality. But is there really such law? How do we know there is? How can we discover its content? By early November it seems Towerson and Locke were agreed that there *is* a law of nature, but that further discussion was needed about how we know this. Could, for example, "the being of the law of nature...be evinced from the force of conscience in those men who have no other divine law [such as the revelation of the Scriptures] to square their actions by"? Towerson, though not Locke, believed that it could.[50]

Besides thinking about natural law, Locke was also thinking about the question of religous toleration, which had been raised by Stubbe's book the previous year. He had suggested to Stubbe that in all likelihood toleration could not work in practice, and this belief pervaded the lengthy piece he was writing on Stubbe's topic of "the power of the civil magistrate in reference to civil affairs".

In fact it was not Stubbe who inspired him to address this question, but rather Edward Bagshaw, the author of "The Great Question concerning things indifferent in religious worship", a short pamphlet that had been published in September. Locke may have seen this prior to its publication, for it may have circulated around Christ Church, of which Bagshaw too was a Student. But if not, he took no more than about eight weeks to compose his systematic rejection of it, and by early December had completed what has become known as his "First Tract on Government". It was headed, in scholastic style as though for an academic disputation, "Question. Whether the civil magistrate may lawfully impose and determine the use of indifferent things in reference to religious worship".

Behind this question lay the assumption that if it were not that God, who has authority over us, wishes us to act in certain ways we would have unrestricted liberty, and everything would be morally "indifferent". But not everything is morally neutral for God has set laws for us, and some things are morally obligatory or commendable, and some are forbidden. These laws, these expressions of God's will, are made known to us in two ways: either by "the discoveries of reason, usually called the law of nature", or by "the revelations of his word" in the Scriptures.[51]

One part of God's will is that we should live in societies, and our liberty is further restricted by laws promulgated by the "magistrate", the sovereign or government: some things which are morally indifferent, indifferent with respect to God's law, may be subject to civil imposition. At issue between Locke and Bagshaw was whether the magistrate had any right to legislate as to ways of religious worship about which God had not ruled and so left "indifferent". Can he, for example, rule on whether we should bow at the name of Jesus, wear a surplice in preaching, kneel at the sacrament, or on where the communion table should be placed, on whether there should be a set liturgy?

Heated disagreement about ways of worship (bowing, crossing, kneeling) had of course been a pre-civil war issue between the Anglican

Church and nonconforming puritans who wished to worship in their own way; and, even with the disestablishment of Anglicanism, disagreement continued during the years of the interregnum between the puritans and the newer sects, such as the Quakers. There is no doubt that Locke's view, in disagreement with Bagshaw, that determinations about such things can be imposed by the magistrate, was fuelled by the anxiety and fearfulness which the events of the civil war and the interregnum, "which have so wearied and wasted this poor nation", had produced in him. These encouraged him to think that the "good and peace" of the people would benefit from imposition of the practices of the re-established Church of England by the newly-restored King.[52]

Bagshaw thought that, as the Bible made plain, a government had no right to enforce ways of worship. Locke disagreed; but he did not think there are no restrictions on, or criteria governing, the impositions a sovereign may make. He has been "entrusted with the care of society", and his law-making must be guided by this trust.[53]

It was not, Locke said, that he had no love of liberty. But he was obviously imbued by a gloomy distrust of human nature, clearly fearful of the consequences of religious freedom; he thought that the experience of the interregnum years showed that were such freedom generally allowed, "it would prove only a liberty for contention, censure and persecution and turn us loose to the tyranny of a religious rage". It would soon be found, he thought, "that the practice of indifferent things not approved by dissenting parties, would then be judged as anti-Christian and unlawful [i.e. against the Bible] as their injunction is now [i.e. by Bagshaw]". He was suspicious that religious liberty would be taken advantage of: "Grant the people once free and unlimited in the exercise of their religion and where will they stop.... Will it not be religion to destroy all that are not of their profession?" We need, said Locke, only to look back on recent years to see that religious freedom "was the first inlet to all those confusions...and destructive opinions that overspread this nation".[54]

Locke's foreboding about how religious liberty might be used, and the "respect and veneration" he said he had for authority, contrasted with a worry of Bagshaw's about how a power of imposition might be used: "For do we but once grant that the magistrate has a power to impose, and then we lie at his mercy how far he will go." Locke thought this worry unrealistic, for it would always be in the magistrate's interest "to use no more rigour than the temper of the people and the necessity of the age shall call for, knowing that too great checks as well as too loose a rein may make this untamed beast to cast his rider".[55]

But even if Locke were right that the civil imposition of religiously indifferent things would be for the "good and peace" of the people, it still did not follow it would be legitimate and not, as Bagshaw thought, against God's will. Locke had a single and short argument showing that it *is* legitimate, and that (within the moral limits set by God's law) the magistrate is free to pass any law which, in his view, conduces to the civic good.

According to Locke, a sovereign's authority to restrict liberty is legitimate only as derived from God's "natural original power and disposure of the liberty of man". It is only from the authority of God himself, either directly or indirectly, that the "laws do fundamentally derive their obligation". Locke did not decide whether rulers have authority directly by divine right, or indirectly, with their legislative power being "derived from, or conveyed... by, the consent of the people". But in either case, he argued, they are free to pass any law, so long as in their view it conduces to the good of society. If the sovereign has been "immediately commissioned by God", then, clearly, the only bounds to his laws can be ones set by God. If, on the other hand, his authority and power comes indirectly from God via popular consent, then he has, Locke argued, been entrusted with "as full a power" over their actions as they themselves have; that is to say, any respect in which God's law has not restricted human liberty is one the magistrate, to whom that liberty has been entrusted, has a right to legislate over.[56]

Of course it would be different if God willed there be some free and indifferent things which we are not at liberty to give up to the magistrate. Locke did not think it could be shown that this is God's will, but since it was part of Bagshaw's case that it could, and that legislation with respect to religious worship was explicitly ruled out in the Bible, a large part of his tract was devoted to specific texts which Bagshaw cited in his support.

The relation of individual conscience to the magistrate's impositions was one important point which arose. We are enjoined, Bagshaw pointed out, to "do unto others as you would have others do to you", but "who is there would have his conscience imposed upon"?[57] Does Locke's view (that a magistrate may legitimately pass any law which is not inconsistent with laws God has already promulgated and which he thinks is for the good of society) mean that he may legitimately pass laws which go against some people's conscience, i.e. which they think are inconsistent with God's laws?

Locke plainly thought it would not be workable in practice for a magistrate's hands to be tied in this way. For one thing, Bagshaw's position that people's consciences should not be imposed upon in spiritual as opposed to civil matters is unstable: "a decency of habit according to the fashion of the place" might seem to be a civil matter, but wearing a hat in church was made a matter of conscience by the Quakers: "there is no action so indifferent which a scrupulous conscience will not fetch in with some consequence from Scripture and make of spiritual concernment". Consciences may differ, moroeover, as on the very question at issue, "some being as conscientiously earnest for conformity as others for liberty".[58]

There is some suggestion in what Locke said that scruples about imposed ways of worship are really of no importance, for such impositions pertain only to outward actions and not to inner beliefs, the "substantial parts of religion": all God looks for in worship is the "sacrifice of a broken and contrite heart", which is something which "may be willingly and acceptably given to God in any place or posture". Whatever impositions the magistrate makes, inner "faith and repentance" are not under his jurisdiction, for he has "no commission to examine the hearts, but to take care of the actions of his subjects". In any case it is impossible that he could have: beliefs "cannot be wrought into the hearts of men" by any power but God's.[59]

Even so, Locke did not want to deny that "conscience is tenderly to be dealt with, and not to be imposed on". But his interpretation of conscience and its scruples enabled him to hold that no tying of the magistrate's hands is involved. Legislating in a way unacceptable to conscience is not imposing upon it, he said; claiming that such legislation is enjoined by God's law and so is something which conscience should require, is. Imposing on conscience is "the pressing of...laws...as of divine original...and in themselves obliging the conscience, when indeed they are no other but the ordinances of men".[60]

While it was supposed there were many things pertaining to religious practice which God had left indifferent, uniformity in such practice was not, it seemed to many people including Locke, one of them: "let all things be done decently and in order", St Paul had said. For Locke this did not mean that the magistrate necessarily had to impose a decent uniformity, but it did mean that it could not be wrong for him to do so if he judged it would conduce to the peace. Exactly what order this uniformity should take was still indifferent, of course, and it was up to the magistrate to decide, and to decide, Locke envisaged, according to the general taste of each community. God has left it "to the discretion of those who are entrusted with the care of the society to determine what shall be order and decency.... Our rudeness [is] others' civility... and should the eastern and turbanned nations embrace Christianity it would be as uncomely to them to be bare in the public worship of God as to us to be covered."[61]

DECEMBER 1660–DECEMBER 1662: "QUIET AND SETTLEMENT"[62]

His father was probably already unwell when Locke returned to Oxford in November; he certainly was by the end of the year: "I cannot be safe so long as I hear of your weakness, and that increase of your malady upon you", Locke wrote to him shortly before Christmas. He again hoped it was just an old, recurring complaint which their doctor, Dr Edmund Meara, had "more than once put a stop to".[63] A few days later, however, he was at his father's bedside.

Meara was "of the opinion that Captain Locke has the regions of the liver and mesentery so much out of order that there are little hopes of repairing them". All he could recommend was strengthening nourishment: "jellies of hartshorn and ivery... with agrimony, liverwort, harts tongue, maidenhair, raisins, red rose buds, anise seeds, and veal or pullet".[64] At the end of the first week of January things were worse, and, apparently not completely satisfied with Meara's diagnosis and prognosis, Locke sought a second opinion, from Dr Ivye.

"The painful increase of my father's weakness", Locke told Ivye, "with the addition of a feverish distemper... has by my persuasions made him not only willing but desirous to see you.... Your own eyes and inquiry may possibly give you better discoveries of his disease and condition than my descriptions could." Whatever Ivye thought or did, Locke's father died a month later.[65]

He had made his will in mid-December as his illness increased, and had written to his elder son in a despondent mood, saddened at how little he had to pass on to him and Thomas. Locke would be reported as saying years later that the civil war was "probably the sole cause of his fortunes being impaired"; exactly in what way this was supposed to have happened was left unexplained, but perhaps there is a connection with something he said in a letter to his father early in 1658.

He referred to some "business" in progress, business which seems to have related to some promises made regarding services the elder Locke had performed, and which, if it miscarried, might leave the family with merely some few acres of land to sell. Perhaps referring to Alexander Popham, under whom his father had served in the civil war, Locke "hotly" told his father that he could not "see your services so rewarded, repeated promises so slighted and juggling in a great man without being moved".[66]

In the event the elder son, John, was left some specially designated belongings (some bedding, two pieces of arras, a watch, an antimonial cup, a brewing furnace) and a house and grounds, leased from Popham. He was not, however, to come into full possession of this last for four years, during which all rents and profits were to go towards "the payment of my debts". Even after this period some part of the rent was to go to the younger son, Thomas, who was also left various tenements and lands and the rest of his father's goods and chattels.[67]

Though he had no formal responsibilities under the will — Thomas was named as executor, with their uncle Peter as an "overseer trustee and assistant" — Locke stayed on in Pensford, seeing to his father's affairs. He made an inventory of his father's goods, both at Belluton and at his uncle Edward's; together with credits and the leasehold property (worth £400) his total valuation was just over £500.[68]

In March, still in Pensford, Locke had some correspondence with Gabriel Towerson. Towerson was keen for him to publish the tract against Bagshaw, which Locke had sent him in early December. He had heard that Bagshaw's book was "so well liked" that it was probably going to be reprinted: "you may perhaps do God and the church a piece of seasonable service if you would be pleased to print your answer to it". Towerson repeated his urging the following month, when he had recently heard Bagshaw preach: he "insisted on his old theme, and though he prayed for Archbishops and Bishops yet he took away their power and made it a mark of AntiChrist to impose ceremonies.... This I thought good to inform you of ... that you might know there may be some necessity that your papers should see the light."[69]

Towerson seems to have had some effect for at some point (certainly later than the opening of Parliament in early May) Locke composed a "Preface to the Reader" of the tract, clearly with publication in mind. He had evidently decided by now, and with considerable relief, that nothing but good was going to come of the return of the King. Reflecting on past years he wrote that "I no sooner perceived myself in the world but I found myself in a storm, which hath lasted almost hitherto, and therefore cannot but entertain the approaches of a calm with the greatest joy and satisfaction". His earlier uncertainties and worries melted away. The restoration of the monarchy "has brought with it that quiet and settlement which our own giddy folly had put beyond the reach, not only of our contrivance, but hopes", he said. "I would [hope] men would be persuaded to be so kind to their religion, their country and themselves as not to hazard again the substantial blessings of peace of settlement."[70]

Prepared as he was for publication, Locke nevertheless showed some aversion to it, and the "Preface" spoke of the tract as "being forced into the public" by the "importunity" of his friends. No doubt one general reason for this aversion to entering into what was a polemical exchange was what Locke in a later year would refer to as "my unmeddling temper, which always sought quiet and inspired me with no other desires, no other aims than to pass silently through this world with the company of a few good friends and books". But, natural as that reticence might have been, it had been reinforced by the political disturbances through which he had lived. Repeating what he had said to Tilly five years earlier, that it was *writing* "that has set almost all the world in an uproar and at varience", Locke's "Preface" gave as a reason against publishing the tract that he had always been "an enemy to the scribbling of this age and often accused the pens of Englishmen of as much guilt as their swords". Less blood would have have been spilled, he said, "had men been more sparing of their ink"; the recent "furies, war, cruelty, rapine, confusion...have been conjured up in private studies".[71]

In the event, the tract was not published, but there must have been some further, more immediate and circumstantial reason. Locke had been still interested in his manuscript in early November, when he sent a copy to Tilly, apparently asking him for some judgement about its public worth, and allowing him to consult others. It was, however, not until the following March that Tilly returned the papers; his judgement (and that of his consultants) was that they contained "nothing dissonant from truth, much that may tend to public satisfaction". Tilly remarked that Bagshaw's arguments against imposition of religious practices were shortly to be answered in the way Zeno's arguments against the possibility of motion had been – "by doing what he pretended could not be done". Presumably what he had in mind was the bill for Uniformity which had been going through Parliament (and which would receive the royal assent the following May): this imposed a revised prayer book, a requirement to adopt the liturgy of the now re-established Church of England, and required Presbyterian ministers to acknowledge episcopal authority or face dispossession of their livings. It is likely that (against the background of his general reluctance) it was the lack of need for them that led Locke to decide against publication of his arguments for religious imposition. Despite his early upbringing, the reintroduction of episcopal Anglicanism would probably not have been unwelcome to him; certainly it would not have been to his friends, such as John Parry, Samuel Tilly, and Gabriel Towerson, who all inclined in that direction.[72]

Towerson was not the only person in Oxford with whom Locke corresponded in the first months of the year while he was occupied in Pensford with his father's affairs. A draft of a letter written in early January shows he was still thinking of Elinor Parry, as a source of life and authentification: "all those few minutes of time they [my thoughts] can get from a sadder employment are spent with you.... This indeed may seem but a thin and airy refreshment, compared with those real enjoyments your presence affords, which are so rich and lasting that their very memory is not without some satisfaction."[73]

Elinor seems to have promised that when he returned to Oxford he would have a friend's sympathy in his bereavement, but when he arrived back in April he found her gone to London. We do not know how strongly he reproved her for not telling him that she was going, but the burden of her response seems to have been as on previous occasions, that he must not presume too much: "I expect a kindness and behold a quarrel", he wrote to her in reply:

I am chid because I am not inspired with the gift of prophesy and neither the heavens nor you afforded me means to perceive your motion at fifty mile distant and it is ill nature in me which in any other would be reason to look for anything in the same place it was left in. This I must confess is a cunning, I will not say how kind a way, of acquitting yourself by casting guilt on another and I must be content to be faulty because you were silent.

She seems, moreover, to have made no attempt to divert him from, or to sympathise with, the "pressure of sadness" about his father; rather she seems to have put him at arm's length and refused, or was emotionally unable, to join with him in any way. "You tell me you intended me something of mirth", Locke complained, "but withhold it from me only because I am sad, and I must not expect from you any diversions or remedies of my melancholy till it be first gone." This, he said, is "as commendable a charity as . . . not administer[ing] physic till the disease be removed".[74]

He was clearly wounded by Elinor's distancing of him, and perhaps began to have his doubts: "I know not why you should put my friendship always upon such hard exercise"; "I cannot promise you that my confidence shall always be able to bear up against such contrary appearances". Yet it was still in him to think the best of her: "I will believe as long as I can that your thoughts are better than your letter"; "I yet kiss [your hand] while it is striking me and I cannot but wish all happiness to that person which detains me from a designed comfort in my greatest need of it and at a time when if friendship had been silent pity would have pleaded for more tenderness".[75]

When Locke returned to Oxford in April, to find Elinor visiting London, it was as more than just a Student of Christ Church. He was now one of ten college officers, having been elected the previous Christmas Eve as lecturer in Greek for the year. This post, for which he received payment of £2.13s.4d, and to which he was re-elected at the end of the year, was one step up in seniority from the four college lectureships in dialectic or logic, posts usually held by senior B.A.s but ones for which he had earlier been passed over.[76]

Soon afterwards his college responsibilities increased still further, for by May he had also become a tutor, an appointment which he held until 1667, and which, though made by the Dean, was not an official college post. He had only a couple of pupils at first, but in some years that number increased to ten and over; on average he earned about £30–35 a year from the work.[77]

The books he recommended his pupils to buy were on logic (by Robert Sanderson, Martin Smiglecius, Samuel Smith, and Zabarella) and metaphysics (Flavel, Scriblerius, and Burgersdicius); classical texts in Greek (Lucian) or Latin (Cicero, Justin, Juvenal, Lucan, Ovid, and Seutonius); the more recent Thomas Godwin's *Roman Antiquities*, Hugo Grotius's *De Veritate*, and Richard Allestree's very recent *The Whole Duty of Man*, a popular devotional work of orthodox Anglicanism, and one which Locke would recommend to the end of his life as "a methodical system" of morality. Many of the academic exercises (translations, verses, and essays) that his pupils and other undergraduates did for him have survived as mountings in two bound volumes of botanical specimens which he began to collect in 1661, accumulating nearly one thousand specimens over the next five or six years.[78]

Rather more than his own tutor had been, he was responsible for the finances of his pupils (some of whom were rather younger than he had been); and of course he kept a careful record of what he paid out for them: matriculation fees and caution money, payment for their rooms, for their laundress and bedmaker. Letters from parents show how he had to concern himself with his pupils' domestic details, such as ordering their furniture and overseeing the choice of a new summer suit. With a fussiness which he himself (certainly in later years) was well able to match, Locke was instructed by the family servant of one pupil, who had recently changed rooms, that the curtains and other handings were to be

taken down...brushed and well folded up and laid aside in some spare corner with some careless cloth thrown over them till it be certain whether Sir Charles shall keep his lodgings he now is in for if he should be put to remove again then probably those hangings may be again of use to him. [Care must be taken]...that no rats get into them which is very usual when they lay by.[79]

Being accountable in this way meant that Locke had to face complaints from parents about the expense of it all:

We have perused your accounts and notes of receipts and disbursements, and do believe have assessed them right.... Only I do not understand why barbers, laundresses and woman to make beds and sweep chambers or such like should be paid for no service or work done by the quarter, when either one come up in the middle of a quarter or are absent a third part or half a quarter together.

Naturally, parents' concerns were not always financial: "be pleased to keep him to his study and that he avoid ill company", he was told; "put so much employment on him as may keep him out of idleness and unnecessary wandering about the town".[80]

Locke was conscientious in his pastoral duties, and his pupils seem to have liked him for it. The one that changed rooms did change them again: the thirteen-year-old Sir Charles Berkeley shortly moved again, not this time elsewhere in Christ Church, but to Cambridge, from where he frequently wrote to his former tutor asking him to visit (with the promise that he would see old friends from Westminster).[81]

A very long letter of advice Locke wrote to a leaving pupil shows how seriously he took his duties (as also, perhaps, himself):

Though you have put off your gown...you are not yet got beyond my affection and concernment.... You [must] now begin to think yourself a man, and necessary that you take the courage of one. I mean not such a courage as may name you one of those daring gallants...but a courage that may defend and secure your virtue and religion. For, in the world you are now launching into, you will find, perhaps, more onsets made upon your innocence than you can imagine; and there are more dangerous thieves than those that lay wait for your purse, who will endeavour to rob you of that virtue.... I could wish you that happiness as never to fall into such company,... but you may withold your heart where you cannot deny your company, and you may allow those your civility who possibly will not deserve your affection.... I do not in this advise you... to avoid company or not enjoy it. One may certainly with innocence use all the enjoyments of life, and I have always been of opinion that a virtuous life is best disposed to be the most pleasant, for certainly, amidst the trouble and vanities of this world, there are but two things that bring a real satisfaction with them, that is, virtue and knowledge. What progress you have made in the latter, you will do well not to lose. Your spare hours from devotion, business, or recreation (for that, too, I can allow where employment... gives a title to it) will be well bestowed in reviewing or improving your university notions, and if... I could afford your studies any direction or assistance, I should be glad and you need only let me but know it.

He concluded with some advice which can be seen from time to time in his own behaviour: "To be thought [both] prudent and liberal, provident and good-natured, are things worth your endeavour to obtain, which perhaps you will better do by avoiding the occasions of expenses than by a frugal limiting them when occasion has made them necessary."[82]

In the course of 1661 (and perhaps into 1662), and possibly as a lecture or as a contribution to some debate within the college, Locke wrote a short Latin essay headed, again in scholastic style, "Is it necessary that an Infallible Interpreter of Holy Scripture be granted in the Church? No". In attacking the Roman Church's claim that the Pope is "the sole infallible interpreter" of the Bible, the essay in effect showed that Locke's assertion, in his tract against Bagshaw, of the magistrate's right to make religious impositions does not inevitably lead to Rome, and this may indeed have been its aim.[83]

Why would God, Locke asked, have left us in need of an infallible interpreter? Does he "address men in such a way that he cannot be understood without an interpreter?" In any case, such an interpreter will not be able "to contribute anything to the solution of problems of faith or to the establishment of peace among Christians" unless he could infallibly demonstrate his infallibility.[84]

Locke went on to point out the lack of homogeneity in the contents of Scripture; there are historical facts, rules of conduct, and articles of faith, and not all of these categories require an infallible interpreter.

Some questions which can be raised (what exactly was the forbidden fruit? where was the Garden of Eden?) are not worth settling, and "can safely be ignored". In fact "they hardly seem to concern the Scripture, which is the standard of faith and conduct". Some other matters (such as "the trinity of persons in the divine nature", "the union of divine and human nature in the person of the mediator", and "the infinity and eternity of God"), though they are "profound mysteries... which utterly transcend the human intellect", were intended by God only to be believed and not to be understood: "the way in which they are true cannot be expressed in discourse nor grasped by the mind", and human interpretation of them is impossible. So far as rules of conduct, such as the duties of justice, chastity, charity, and benevolence, are concerned, it is "most necessary to salvation" that we are clear about them. But no infallible interpreter is in place here either, for these things are "so clear and unambiguous that virtually nobody can doubt them".[85]

In one case, however, Locke did concede the need for what might be called, in a certain sense, an "infallible" interpreter. There are things which the Bible has left indeterminate, and so which are by their nature indifferent. For example, according to St Paul "all things [should] be done decently and in order": for this precept to be applied, some interpretation is required. In itself this did not preclude interpretation by each individual, unless decency and order were thought to require uniformity; but in the light of what Locke had argued the previous year about religious impositions, it is no surprise that he did not think in these terms, but assigned the task to the "fathers and leaders" of the established Church. In these matters, he said, they "can be called" infallible, adding that their "infallibility is directive not definitive". It is not definitive for they may not necessarily be right in what they say, but this does not detract from their "directive" infallibility, the fact that, whatever they decide, their decisions are to be followed by anyone who "applies himself to both obedience and the peace of the church".[86]

On Christmas Eve 1662 Christ Church appointed Locke as lecturer in Rhetoric for the following year, a post for which he received £5, and which involved giving a course of lectures. It was perhaps in this connection that he readdressed the question he had first considered two years earlier, "Whether the civil magistrate may incorporate indifferent things into the ceremonies of divine worship and impose them on the people". The resulting "slight sketch", which has become

known as the "Second Tract on Government", was half the length of
the first; it merely "touched lightly on" the arguments against his
unchanged view that the magistrate does indeed have that power.
Written in Latin and heavy with rhetorical flourishes, it has the
appearance of being a formal contribution to an academic debate, to
a "mock battle" or "private fencing-match", as he put it.[87]

Though the anxiety and the gloomy view of human nature which
were so evident in the first tract were not now entirely absent, some of
the earlier emotional energy had gone. The Restoration had brought,
with the return of an established Anglicanism and an imposed
religious uniformity, a "new posture of affairs and . . . [a] well-composed
order of society". The chaos of argument and "heady ferment of
passions" about the right of the magistrate to impose some uniformity
of religious practice had receded, because, in Locke's view, it should
now have been clear that "civil obedience, even in the indifferent
things of divine worship" is a Christian duty. Bearing in mind the
"tossing and vain threats of the waves from which they [had] just
escaped" and the restoration of peace and calm, Locke "hoped that
nobody [now] will be so obstinate and stiff-necked as to attempt further
civil changes or to disparage the magistrate's power in respect of
indifferent things".[88] Locke was now, whatever his earliest religious
affiliation had been exactly, clearly committed to the Church of
England in its re-established form. Whether or not he might have
initially hoped for a more comprehensive settlement as perhaps had
been envisaged by the King, he seemed happy with the arrangements
Parliament had come to.

But, less emotional though they might have become, there had been
no radical shift in Locke's views over the past two years; the central
points he made are the same, though sometimes put more clearly and
effectively: God's laws are made known to us by reason and by
revelation; so long as he has in mind the public good, the sovereign can
legislate over any matter which God has left undetermined; the fact that
a given civil law is against our conscience is not a reason for disobeying
it; though the "essence and soul of religion" consists in the "inner
worship of the heart", God requires worship to be public and open,
and has left it to the state to decide on the form and order of that
public worship.[89]

Locke's account of "liberty of conscience" remained essentially
unchanged too, though he now explained the matter at greater length
and in more formal terms. The obedience we owe to the magistrate's

impositions, even when we think them unjust, is no imposition on or infringement of the liberty of our conscience, which requires only an "assent of the will"; our consciences would be imposed upon only if the magistrate claimed that the content of some law was something required by God, for this would be an infringement of our "liberty of judgement". The liberty of the conscience is, he now put it, not a "liberty of will", but rather a "liberty of judgement". It is not obvious, however, that this is an entirely satisfactory view: given that "the law of conscience" is "that fundamental judgement... concerning any possible truth of a moral proposition about things to be done in life", and so has to do not simply with judgements but with judgements about what is to be done, it still might be felt that we go against our consciences when, even if the magistrate does not claim it is required by God, we do something which we think is wrong.[90]

JANUARY 1663—NOVEMBER 1665: "NO LAW WITHOUT A LAW-MAKER"[91]

Along with everything else, Locke had been maintaining his interests in natural philosophy. During 1661 and 1662 he had attended medical lectures given by Thomas Willis; pervading these was a theory of disease and illness which, though partly mechanistic, made much use of the idea derived from Jan Baptista van Helmont that basic to the world were organic processes such as fermentations. Locke took notes on a wide variety of topics ranging from arthritis to epilepsy and hysteria. Now, in 1663, he enrolled on a course given by Peter Stahl, a German chemist whom Boyle had brought over to provide expert assistance in the laboratory, and as a knowledgeable resource. Lower had already attended such a course, and it was perhaps on his recommendation that Locke joined the "club" that Stahl organised between 23 April and 30 May, at a price of £3 per head. Anthony Wood was one of the ten or so in the group, and Locke apparently struck him as "a man of turbulent spirit, clamorous and never contented": while the others "wrote and took notes from the mouth of their master... the said J. Locke scorned to do it; so that every man besides, of the club were writing, he would be prating and troublesome". Wood did not say whether he found Locke any more pleasant on the two occasions during the course they were together in a small group at a ninepenny supper; but he was in any case wrong to say that Locke "scorned" to take notes on the chemical experiments and medical recipes which

Stahl discussed, demonstrated, and got his students to carry out and prepare, for they still exist.[92]

At the time Locke was still among the *philosophi*, and was not yet committed to entering the clergy. The question of doing so did arise, however. It looks as though towards the end of the year he received an offer of an ecclesiastical living. The document which the Dean of the college signed in October, to the effect that Locke was of good character and orthodox in religion, could have been called for by such an offer. The following month, moreover, Locke asked Thomas Strachey about accepting a living. Perhaps it was one within thirty miles of Oxford, for the question seems to have been whether he should accept it as a means of keeping his Studentship. Strachey thought Locke was cut out for something better than a country parsonage; he urged him not to worry about his Studentship, not to worry that "you shall never meet with the like again". Such timidity offered only a bleak prospect, Strachey said; if it came to it Locke should bravely "put to sea": "Neptune is not so merciless as most men fancy".[93]

Locke rejected the offer, though he hardly "put to sea" and, presumably because it was still possible to do so, decided to leave things as they were. He took on a more senior college post (with an emolument of £7 10s) of Censor in Moral Philosophy, to which he was elected at the end of the year for the following twelve months.[94]

This new post required him to deliver a course of lectures, and it would seem that his chosen subject was what he had discussed with Gabriel Towerson in 1660, and on which he had continued working, "The law of nature". At any rate, that subject is treated in some Latin essays which were begun during that earlier discussion and completed during Locke's year as Censor.[95]

In his two tracts on government Locke had made use of the idea of God-given natural law, but had left undiscussed many things about it. In what have come to be called his "Essays on the Law of Nature", Locke addressed some basic questions: "Is there really a rule of morals, or law of nature given to us?", "Are we bound by it?", "How do we know it?", and "What is its basis?"

One thing which indicated to Locke that there were objective moral laws was the fact of human conscience. In their earlier discussions Locke and Towerson had agreed that there *is* a law of nature, and had begun to ask how it related to conscience. In the "Essays", Locke now expressed the view that the very fact that people's consciences make judgements about what is morally right (even though those judgements may disagree or may not be correct) presupposes the existence of such laws.

Throughout these essays is the conception of law which was embodied in the earlier tracts, according to which law presupposes a law-giver, who is superior to the things to which the law applies, and of whose will the law is an expression. This conception is obviously applicable to civil laws, and Locke construed moral laws similarly except that the authority whose will they are, was conceived to be our creator. However, whereas all civil laws are "positive", announced directly, not all moral laws are. They may be "positive" and announced or "revealed" by our creator, or they may be discoverable by some natural means, other than directly from their promulgator. It is in this latter case that Locke spoke of moral laws as "natural laws". Of course, even though this is what Locke meant by "law of nature", it does not necessarily follow that there actually is any such thing. It was part of his aim in the "Essays" to show that there is.

"God shows Himself to us as present everywhere", Locke began, "as much in the fixed course of nature now as by the frequent evidence of miracles in time past." So the existence of God will not be denied, so long as we recognise "the necessity for some rational account of our life, or that there is a thing that deserves to be called virtue or vice". Stemming from God's will, Locke continued, are laws by which "the heaven revolves in unbroken rotation", and as there is nothing which does not similarly "admit of valid and fixed laws of operation", no one will suppose that we alone are exempt from laws.[96]

God's laws are appropriate to the kind of thing to which they apply. "Since man has been made such as he is, equipped with reason and his other faculties and destined for this mode of life, there necessarily result from his inborn constitution some definite duties for him." We are "bound to love and worship God and also to fulfil other things appropriate to the rational nature, i.e. to observe the law of nature".[97]

Our rational nature not only determines our governing laws, but also means we have the capacity to search for and discover them: "the decree of a divine will [is] discernible by the light of nature [reason]... indicating what is and what is not in conformity with rational nature".

What exactly is the "light of nature", and is it really by its means that we know the law of nature? Locke did not rule out the possibility of our being informed of moral law by revelation; but this would be learning it directly, as positive and not as natural law. Divine inspiration or heavenly illumination are not "natural" means of knowledge, and it is whether we can learn God's will naturally that Locke was investigating.

Besides "the light of nature", by which Locke meant our faculties of understanding, reason, and sense-perception, there are other natural means which might be suggested as the source of knowledge of natural law.

One of these was "inscription". Some people hold, he said, that the "law of nature is inborn in us and . . . implanted by nature". Amongst the reasons Locke gave for rejecting this was the fact of moral disagreement. If moral precepts were stamped on our minds, why is "one rule of nature and right reason . . . proclaimed here, another there"?[98]

Locke's keen awareness of moral differences was derived not only from observation of his own society but also from his fascinated reading of the accounts of travellers and merchants in the Americas and the East, an interest which would remain with him all his life. Many of these accounts seemed to show there was no natural innate morality, even amongst uncorrupted "primitive peoples". No one, Locke argued, "who consults the histories both of the old and the new world, or the itineraries of travellers . . . will believe that the law of nature is best known and observed among these primitive and untutored tribes, since among most of them there appears not the slightest trace or track of piety, merciful feeling, fidelity, chastity, and the rest of the virtues".[99]

"Tradition" was another possible natural source of moral precepts. Perhaps they are "transmitted to us by parents, teachers, and all those who busily fashion the manners of young people and fill the still tender souls with the love and knowledge of virtue". Locke did not doubt that many precepts are learnt in this way, but in the end tradition is hardly satisfactory as a source of moral knowledge, he said. It carries the risk that people's rules of what is right and good are simply the customs and the common opinion of their society. They may, that is, be guided "by belief and approval" and not by what is genuinely God's will as embodied in the law of nature; indeed this must be so in at least some cases since there is "so much variety among conflicting traditions".[100]

Tradition cannot anyway, Locke pointed out, be the original source of knowledge of our duties since it must itself have a source in "an original author" who discovered the law of nature in some other way.[101] Given the keen awareness that Locke exhibited about the variability of traditions, not merely within a state (as with different religious sects) but also between different nations, it is perhaps surprising that he should think of traditions having, somewhat artificially, a single "author" rather than having grown up communally.

A third possible source for our knowledge of natural law which Locke considered was general consent. Perhaps customs, actions, and opinions manifest a kind of "natural consent... to which men are led by a certain natural instinct", showing both that there is natural law and what it is. This idea too was dismissed on the basis of the moral variability so evident to "anyone who consults the history of the world".[102]

Locke concluded that the natural means by which we *do* acquire our knowledge of natural law indeed is "the light of nature", our natural faculties of understanding, reason, and sense-perception. Prior to explaining how the two faculties of reason and sense-perception working together can lead us to the law of nature, Locke reviewed his conception of law: If we are to understand that we are bound by some law, we must know "there is a law maker, i.e. some superior power to which [we are] rightly subject". We must also know "that there is some will on the part of that superior power with respect to the things to be done by us, that is to say, that the law-maker... wishes that we do this but leave off that".[103]

What Locke said here points to a further argument he might have brought against the idea that the source of our knowledge of natural law is "inscription". Even if there were, inscribed on our souls, the precept that we should keep promises, we still would not know that this inscription was the work of a superior law-maker who wants us to keep promises, and who would punish us if we do not. However, in going on to show how reason and sense-perception can lead us to knowledge of the law of nature, he tried at the same time to show how those essential prerequisites can also be established.

Our senses reveal to us a regular and beautiful world, one which, we realise, could not have come about by chance. So we "infer that there must be a powerful and wise creator". Because this divine creator is wise he must have created the world with a purpose, and there must be things he wants us to do, and which, since he has authority over us as dependent creatures, we have an obligation to do: "in so far as we are subject to another we are so far under an obligation". What we are commanded to do can partly be gathered from the apparent "end in view for all things" – namely, that they are intended by God "for no other end than His own glory". They can be further gathered from reflection on our own constitution, faculties, and experiences, all of which seem to dispose us not only to "praise, honour and glory... so great and so beneficent a creator", but also, in order the better to fulfil our needs, to live in society with each other.[104] What have been imposed on us, then, are duties to God, to our neighbours, and to ourselves.

Locke did, then, go some way to attempt to establish the prerequisites to there being a law of nature: the existence of a superior God on whom we are dependent and whose will, which we are obliged to follow, we can discover. But he certainly did not go all the way, for he said at one point that not only God, but also the immortality of our souls, "must be necessarily presupposed if natural law is to exist", the reason being that just as "there is no law without a law-maker", so "law is to no purpose without punishment".[105] It cannot be said, however, that he even tried here to show that there is divine punishment in store for us in some afterlife if we do not obey God's laws.

At the end of the year, when Locke retired as Censor of Moral Philosophy, he delivered, in accordance with tradition, a valedictory speech, a mock funeral oration to "bury" the censor. He chose for this academic exercise (performed in Latin) to consider the question, "Can anyone by nature be happy in this life?" In a semi-humorous fashion, he gave the answer "No". Death, he proclaimed, is a deliverance from the futility of life: "However much happiness nature may promise, what she in fact offers is little and trifling, as can be seen well enough from the complaints of the whole of mankind." Even philosophy cannot make men happy; it "holds out her many riches, but they are all mere words.... Those pointed and shrewd discourses concerning the highest good do not heal human misfortune any more than fist and sword cure wounds."[106]

Some of one of Locke's drafts of this oration is in a form of shorthand* (based on a system invented by Jeremiah Rich), which Locke had, it seems, just begun to use and which he would use for many years to come, in journals and notebooks, sometimes for the odd word or sentence, sometimes at greater length. Years later he said that the art of shorthand is worth learning, both "for despatch in what men write for their own memory" and also for "concealment of what they would not have lie open to every eye". Examples of both these uses occur in his papers. It was clearly for concealment that he used it to record where he had left his will, that a certain person was a liar, and his observation in a French inn that a certain Catholic priest was sharing his bed with a woman.[107]

Locke now (January 1665) had no official college post, though he continued as a tutor. More importantly, he also continued with his scientific inquiries. He had had an interest for some time in the nature of blood, and recently, towards the end of the previous year, had made some notes about the purpose of our respiration of air in relation to the blood.[108]

Various aspects of respiration had been studied for some years in Oxford. Experiments carried out by Boyle and Robert Hooke in 1659, in which air was pumped out from a glass globe or "receiver" into which various objects and materials could be introduced, had shown that air was essential both for fire and for life. Fire was quickly extinguished in the rarefied air of an evacuated receiver, and birds swooned and soon died unless they were revived by the readmission of air. But why did we need to breathe air in and out in order to live?

One function commonly attributed to respiration was to rid the blood of waste products, "excrementitious steams", as Boyle put it, which we breathed out. Locke aligned himself with this: "One use of respiration seems to be for the carrying away those vaparous excrement[s] of the blood which are usually called fuliginos, which finding a fit receptacle in the pores of the air drawn into the lungs insinuate themselves and so are cast out in expiration." He noted that air could become filled with such "steams" and so be unfit for respiration, pointing out that this would explain why people faint in enclosed spaces.[109]

Boyle's experiments had suggested that cleansing could not be the only purpose of respiration. Stifling by an over-concentration of exhaled waste products would certainly explain why a bird in a closed receiver would eventually die even without any evacuation of air; but it would not explain why birds died more quickly in a partially evacuated receiver, for with more room for them the exhaled waste products should be less stifling. Boyle therefore tended towards thinking that the air brought something to the body, as well as taking something away, but he was undecided what it might be.[110]

Locke also followed some of the programme of experiments and investigations concerning the blood, and the part it played in respiration, which Lower, Boyle, and others had embarked on the previous year. In particular he recorded some of Lower's observations on the differing colours of blood taken from veins and arteries, and speculated that the florid colour of arterial blood might be due to its mixture with air, perhaps because of some "nitrous salt" in it.[111]

At the end of the previous year, when he wrote his short note on respiration, Locke had been confident that there was something more to respiration than the cleansing of the blood, and he had at least the beginnings of a view what it was. Noting that air is required to ferment and volatilize vegetable substances, and for combustion (which itself seemed akin to a process of volatilization), he theorised that "another use of respiration seems to be, to mix some particles of air with the blood and so to volatilize it".[112] He seemed, though, to have had no thoughts about how air might volatilize the blood, or what the purpose of its doing it might be.

Now, when he thought further about fermentation and volatility, and the part that air played in it, he tended towards the idea that air contained a light and insubstantial nitrous salt which contributed to combustion and fermentation and, by a volatilization of the blood which fitted it in some way for a kind of "nourishment" for the body, was an essential element in respiration. Some such idea, that air contained some active nitrous salt, akin to saltpeter (potassium or sodium nitrate, which in fact are potent oxidizing agents), went back to Paracelsus in the previous century, and the suggestion that, when inspired, it served as food to the blood had been advocated in Ralph Bathurst's lectures in Oxford, when Locke was an undergraduate.[113]

In a comment on Lower's observations about the differences between arterial and venous blood Locke wrote: "Probably it is the nitrous salt in the air that gives it [arterial blood] this tincture and volatilizes it, and the volatile part in circulation being either transmuted into nourishment of the part, the remaining blood in the veins is less spirituous... and therefore is returned by the veins to the lungs and heat to be new volatized." This could be tested, he suggested, by distilling venous and arterial blood to see whether they yielded different quantities of salt; possibly it was some such test he carried out the following June, when, after distilling some human blood for over twelve hours, "there came white fumes but I saw no salt stuck to the receiver".[114]

NOVEMBER 1665–FEBRUARY 1666: "TOOK COACH FOR GERMANY"[115]

The first cases of bubonic fever in what became the "Great Plague" had begun to appear in early 1665, and by the spring those who could had left London. This included the King, who eventually set up court in Oxford in September, where, shortly afterwards, he held a short session of Parliament, seeking a vote of money for the war with Holland which he had declared in March. Some of what he obtained was allotted to diplomatic efforts, one of which was aimed at securing at least the neutrality of the Elector of Brandenburg, some of whose territory was adjacent to Holland. In pursuance of this a mission under Sir Walter Vane was sent to Cleves, in the lower Rhineland, to where the Elector had recently moved.

In what must have been an exciting first excursion out of his narrow world of academic Oxford and rustic Somerset and into one of foreign travel and international affairs, Locke, now aged thirty-three, went with Vane, as his secretary. "Monday 13 November 65 we took coach in Oxford for Germany", he recorded in a memorandum book, as also that Sir Walter had given him £10 the day before. How exactly the appointment came about is not clear. Locke could easily have met the King himself since the court had been set up at Christ Church, and there was a potential intermediary, literally a friend at court, in William Godolphin, secretary to Lord Arlington, a man of considerable influence with the King, and he, as is clear from Locke's letters to him from Cleves, had a direct interest in the mission. Locke had known him at Westminster and then at Christ Church, just as he had also known, again from schooldays, another of Arlington's secretaries, Joseph Williamson; and he too evidently had a connection with the mission.[116]

Part of Locke's responsibility during his three months in Cleves was to write out Vane's official letters about the progress of negotiations with the Elector. Less officially, he also kept his eyes and ears open in order to inform Godolphin, not simply about the progress of the mission as he saw it, but also about all the other political events and personalities associated with the Elector and the war. His reports show considerable nervous diffidence about having been thrown into a world of which he had had no experience, and of uncertainty about the extent of his success in his "watching brief". Telling Godolphin what he could about the Elector's finances, his counsellors, and about the comings and goings of envoys from various parties with an interest or involvement in the war, he said:

how our affairs stand in the Court and what progress is made you will better understand by Sir Walter's dispatches, in which, whatever shall be found,

I desire I may be considered only as a transcriber tied to a copy even to the very spelling and sometimes so straightened in time that haste makes my hand worse than it would be. If my intelligence be not so considerable as you may expect you will pardon it to my want of experience and language not of will and endeavour.

Having promised to try to learn more, he again wrote apologetically about his performance as an informant, hinting that besides his inexperience and lack of language, their dispatches were being intercepted. Particularly with an insecure mail, Locke may also have been inhibited by thinking that he should not show (perhaps merely to the various foreign envoys busy in Cleves, but perhaps also to Sir William Vane himself) more curiosity than his official brief would have warranted. It is certain that he would have felt freer had he been senior enough to be privy to the official diplomatic code: again apologising for his inexperience, he wrote to Godolphin, "the mistakes of these conjectures you will excuse in one not versed in affairs of this nature, and has not all the conveniencies of informing himself, which yet I should not think convenient to write thus, could I have obtained the use of the cypher".[117]

Besides receiving no letters from Godolphin, Locke had none from his friends either, and wondered whether his were reaching them. Deprived of news from England, he began to feel lonely and isolated. He comforted himself in what he found to be "a barren place, and the dull frozen part of the year" by "writing long letters with little in them" to John Strachey, letters which he often did not dispatch (perhaps intending to hand them over personally in England). So while he wrote to Godolphin exclusively about the diplomatic mission and the comings and goings of foreign envoys, he wrote to Strachey about his own doings during "off duty" periods, and about life as it was lived in Cleves. What he chose for comment must be evidence of what interested him on his first time out of England; but he obviously had an eye too on what he thought might interest Strachey or, more accurately, amuse him — for his very successful attempts at wit and humour are the most noticeable things about the letters he wrote for him. The wit, as in a letter which described an official dinner the Elector gave for the English mission, cannot be described as kindly; it tended to be chauvinistically disparaging and, perhaps rather naïvely, superior.[118]

Locke developed the theme that the Elector's dinner was not entirely to his liking: "I had no great pleasure in a feast where, amidst a great deal of meat and company, I had little to eat, and less to say. The advantage was, the lusty Germans fed so heartily themselves, that they regarded not much my idleness." The food was not good: the meats were "all so disguised, that I should have guessed... they had a mind to pose than to feed us. But the cook made their metamorphosis like Ovid's, where the change is usually into the worse." What do you think, he asked Strachey, of "hen and cabbage" and "powdered beef covered over with preserved quinces"? (Yet "one thing there is that I like very well", he brought himself to say, "is that they have good salads all the year, and use them frequently".)[119]

Locke also recorded for Strachey's amusement his attendance at a number of church services. In the Lutheran church he "found them all merrily singing with their hats on; so that by the posture they were in, and the fashion of the building, not altogether unlike a theatre, I was ready to fear that I had mistook the place"; the delivery of the sermon "was not very pleasant" and if the preacher's "matter were no better than his delivery, those that slept had no great loss, and might have snored as harmoniously". At a Christmas Day service at the Catholic church the choir "had strong voices, but so ill-tuned, so ill-managed, that it was their misfortune, as well as ours, that they could be heard... everyone had his own tune". At another Catholic service he came in for "a good sprinkle of holy water"; "now I may defy the devil", he said. Then, in a Calvinist church, he saw a christening, at which there was a good number of "godfathers and godmothers, of which they allow a greater number than we do, and so wisely get more spoons".[120]

Locke's raconteurial abilities and inclinations are further illustrated by his account of buying some gloves:

You must not expect anything remarkable from me all the following week, for I have spent it in getting a pair of gloves.... Three days were spent in finding out a glover, for... their shops are so contrived, as if they were designed to conceal, not expose their wares; and though you may think it strange, yet, methinks, it is very well done, and it is a becoming modesty to conceal that which they have reason enough to be ashamed of.... The two next days were spent in drawing them on, the right hand glove (or as they call them here, handshoe), Thursday, and the left hand, Friday, and I'll promise you this was two good days work, and little enough to bring them to fit my hands and to consent to be fellows, which, after all, they are so far from, that when they are on, I am always afraid my hands should go to cuffs, one with another, they so disagree: Saturday we concluded on the price.

A week for a pair of gloves was not out of the way:

A pair of shoes cannot be got under half a year. I lately saw the cow killed, out of whose hide I hope to have my next pair. The first thing after they are married here is to bespeak the child's coat, and truly the bridegroom must be a bungler that gets not a child before the mantle be made; for it is far easier here to have a man made than a suit.[121]

But the jocularity of Locke's reports to Strachey masked a more serious impression made on him by witnessing the variety of sects and denominations, which were allowed freely to worship in Cleves. In one letter he at first likened Catholics and their priests to a model of the Christmas nativity he saw near the high altar: "A little without the stable was a flock of sheep, cut out of cards; and these, as they then stood without their shepherds...methought represented these poor innocent people, who, whilst their shepherds pretend so much to follow Christ, and pay their devotion to him, are left unregarded in the barren wilderness." But then, in a moment of real openness, he said:

but to be serious with you, the Catholic religion is a different thing from what we believe it in England. I have other thoughts of it than when I was in a place that is filled with prejudices, and things are known only by hearsay. I have not met with any so good-natured people or so civil, as the Catholic priests, and I have received many courtesies from them, which I shall always gratefully acknowledge.[122]

In his tracts on government Locke had not believed that people of different religious persuasions could easily and peaceably live together, and be freely left to their own modes of worship: "Grant the people once free...in the exercise of their religion and where will they stop...will it not be religion to destroy all that are not of their profession." But what he saw in Cleves made him think again, and not just about Catholics. He wrote to Boyle that there was no more uniformity in the religion of the people of Cleves than there was in their irregular streets, and that (using a phrase he was fond of) "they quietly permit one another to choose their way to heaven":

This distance in their churches gets not into their houses...for I cannot observe any quarrels or animosities amongst them upon the account of religion. This good correspondence is owing partly to the power of the magistrate, and partly to the prudence and good nature of the people, who...entertain different opinions, without any secret hatred or rancour.[123]

When he began this letter Locke was regretful he had nothing of real and lasting interest to report to Boyle concerning natural philosophy. But in the end he was able to add a postscript retailing a first-hand account he had just had from an envoy in another mission of a copper mine in Hungary where iron appeared to be changed into copper by dripping water. Unfortunately, this scientific exchange was cut short by the political events which had made it possible – "I had not time", Locke concluded, "to enquire after more particulars, being hastily called away".

Keenly aware of what he had left behind in Oxford, Locke complained to Boyle that "their physicians go the old road, I am told, and also easily guess at by their apothecary's shops, which are unacquainted with chemical remedies". He had "not yet heard of any person here eminently learned", but his best chance seemed to be "one Dr Scardius [Schard], who, I am told, is not altogether a stranger to chemistry. I intend to visit him as soon as I can get a handsome opportunity." When Locke got to meet Schard he found him even more interesting and informative than he had expected. Schard encouraged him in chemical experimenting, and they later corresponded about various chemical preparations.[124]

In early February, Locke wrote to Strachey that though the Elector was professing neutrality, "I will whisper in your ear that I think he leans to the Dutch and we have but little hopes of him". What Locke did not whisper was that the English government was not prepared to pay the price the Elector wanted for his neutrality. The mission left Cleves and Locke was back in London some days later.[125]

Why exactly did Locke go to Germany with Sir Walter Vane? No doubt the short-term adventure of a first journey abroad appealed to him, and perhaps some desire for social advancement, a sense of duty, or wanting to oblige, were involved too (though these last cannot have been the whole story, for before long he would refuse further, similar offers).

What certainly seems to have played a part is that there were some aspects of his life at Oxford of which he was weary and from which he wanted to be away. His letter to Boyle makes clear that his interests in chemistry and medicine had not waned, but he seems, after his years of college duties, to have become jaded with traditional academic life. This emerges from one of the letters to Strachey, as does the interesting fact that he appears to have had some anxiety that his life was not entirely under his own control, and that somehow he was doomed to academia:

The old opinion, that every man had his particular genius that ruled and directed his course of life, has made me sometimes laugh to think what a pleasant thing it would be if we could see little sprites bestride men ... [which] ride them about, and spur them on in that way which they ignorantly think they choose themselves. ... To what purpose this from Cleves? I will tell you: if there be any such thing ... certainly mine is an academic goblin. When I left Oxford, I thought for a while to take leave of all University affairs, and should have least expected to have found anything of that nature here at Cleves of any part of the world. But do what I can, I am still kept in that tract.

Locke then told of no less than three tedious scholarly encounters to which "my invisible master ... having mounted me rode me out". The first was a "divinity disputation" which he was made to suffer by a

young sucking divine, that thought himself no small champion; who, as if he had been some knight-errant, bound by oath to bid battle to all comers, first accosted me in courteous voice; but the customary salute being over, I found myself assaulted most furiously, and heavy loads of arguments fell upon me ... the end of all [being] some rubbish of divinity as useless and incoherent as the ruins the Greeks left behind.

Being "too far from my own dunghill", as he described Oxford, "to be quarreling", Locke was uncertain why he had been picked out.

The second encounter to which Locke's academic sprite rode him was with a "learned bard in a threadbare coat, and a hat, that though in its younger days it had been black, yet it was grown grey with the labour of its master's brains. ... His two shoes had but one heel, which made his own foot go as uneven as those of his verses." The next day Locke was again ridden out by "my University goblin", this time "to a foddering of chopped bay or logic":

poor *materia prima* was canvessed cruelly, stripped of all the gay dress of her forms, and shown naked to us, though I must confess I had not eyes good enough to see her; however, the dispute was good sport, and would have made a horse laugh, and truly I was like to have broke my bridle. The young monks (which one would not guess by their looks) are subtile people, and dispute as eagerly for *materia prima*, as if they were to make their dinner on it. ... I being a brute, that was rode there for another's pleasure, profited little by all their reasonings, and was glad when they had done, that I might get home again to my ordinary provender, and leave them their sublime speculations.[126]

Locke's performance in Cleves had been sufficiently impressive for him to receive, again perhaps at the direct instigation of Godolphin,

another offer in the diplomatic service. He cannot have been back
in England for much over a day before he told Strachey, "I am
now offered a fair opportunity of going into Spain with the
Ambassador*.... If I go, I shall not have above ten days' stay in
England." He had obviously liked his two months in Cleves well
enough to make the immediately required decision a difficult one.
"I am pulled both ways by divers considerations, and do yet waver",
he said. "I intend tomorrow for Oxford, and shall there take my
resolution." One thing he must have taken into consideration was the
length of time he thought he would have been away (in fact it would
have been two years). Perhaps his "academic goblin" was
not immediately in evidence when he got back to Oxford, and after
no more than five days there Locke reported that

> those fair offers I had to go to Spain have not prevailed with me: whether fate
> or fondness kept me at home I know not; whether I have let slip the minute that
> they say everyone has once in his life to make himself, I cannot tell: this I am
> sure, I never trouble myself for the loss of that which I never had.

(Later in the year he had a chance to reconsider when the opportunity
arose of going as secretary with the envoy to Sweden.)[127]

FEBRUARY–JULY 1666: NATURAL PHILOSOPHY: PRACTICAL AND THEORETICAL

Having decided against staying out in the wider world, Locke resumed
his life in Oxford. He had hoped to go to Somerset to stay with
Strachey and to see to his property there, as soon as he returned from
Cleves. But during his first weeks back in Oxford some "troubles and
business" were preventing him from making the journey.[128]

Seeing Elinor Parry can hardly have counted either as "trouble" or
as "business"; now calling herself "Scribelia" and Locke "Atticus", she
had told him when he was away that she was keeping "her valour to
disenchant you after your adventures". Perhaps his "academic goblin"
was riding him again, and the "trouble" related to his work as a college
tutor which continued for some months; but likely the "business" was
his own, and generated by his scientific interests. He started doing
chemical experiments and making medicines with two interested
people, Lister Blount and David Thomas, and over the next months,
sometimes with guidance from Schard in Cleves, made a large number
of preparations.*[129] Locke's association with Blount seems not to

have extended beyond this period, but David Thomas (about two years his junior) would be a lifelong and close friend.

By April he was able to get away to Somerset and into the second week of the month had been there for some days, staying at Sutton Court with Strachey, entertaining him with tales of Cleves. He needed to see to the property he had inherited from his father (to which he had added a leasehold cottage, bought from his sister-in-law following his brother's death in 1663). It was his first visit since the previous April, the month he had come into full possession of the property (which after careful survey he valued at £872).[*130]

Towards the end of the month Locke returned to Oxford. An outbreak of the plague in Somerset led him to go sooner than he intended, but he had had enough time to make some observations he had promised Boyle. Boyle had provided him with a barometer to measure the pressure in the Mendips lead mines. Unfortunately, as he told Boyle, he was "able to do so little in the attempts I have made to serve you". Access to the mine was not a matter of being lowered down a vertical shaft; rather, the miners climbed down, through cracks and faults in the rock. Yet the difficulty this made for carrying the barometer down was not all, and Locke gave a vivid picture of the immiscibility of the interests of the unsophisticated miners ("who could give me very little account of anything, but what profit made them seek after") and those of an educated experimental philosopher: "the sight of my engine, and my desire of going down into some of their gruffs [mines], gave them terrible apprehensions; and I could not persuade them but that I had some design". The more Locke and Strachey said to allay their doubts served only to make "them disbelieve all we told them; and do what we could, they would think us craftier fellows than we were.... The women too were alarmed, and think us still either projectors or conjurors."[131]

But Locke was able to do some experiments one morning on a hill at Stowey, near Sutton Court.[132] He found that at the top the barometer's mercury had fallen about three-eighths of an inch, and that in general, "both going up and going down, I observed, that proportionably as I was higher or lower on the hill, the mercury fell or rose". He suspected that, besides the instrument readings, Boyle would have liked to know "the perpendicular height of the place I made the experiment in", but he was not able to provide this.

Locke carried on making barometrical observations, for on 24 June he began making daily (sometimes twice, thrice, or more) records of the weather, using, besides his barometer, a thermoscope and hygrometer, and making an estimate of the wind speed. With some interruptions this habit, which he believed would be to the "great advantage of mankind", would persist throughout his life; one of his thoughts, which he shared with Boyle and others, was that there might be some connection between disease epidemics and the weather.[133]

Some of the information that Locke gathered on his excursion in the Mendips about the need for a constant flow of fresh air into the mines was used in *Respirationis Usus*, a manuscript which he worked on in May and November. Written in Latin, this uncompleted draft carries the marks of a formal disputation, and perhaps Locke's intention was to capitalise on the thinking and reading he had done in recent years to produce something for submission towards a medical qualification.

By this time Locke had come to some view about what it might be that was brought to the body by the air in respiration, and he expounded it against the background of the generally accepted idea that a natural heat of the heart was essential to life. As he put it, "Nature's aim seems to have been to foster that universal heat or fire of our life. For we live as long as we burn, and are nourished by the same fire." Now according to the Galenists, with whom Locke began as the formal target of his piece, "the first purpose of respiration [is] the cooling of the heart", to prevent it from overheating. As against this, others held that the air feeds rather than cools the vital flame in the heart. Boyle's air-pump experiments supported or at least were consonant with this, for they showed that air was necessary both for animal life and for combustion. At one finely balanced point Locke said, "it is so far hidden among the mysteries of nature whether our continual breathing fosters or checks our native fires", yet, he added, "if you weigh up everything more carefully you can scarcely believe that timid nature would have made these bellows of our lungs of such sort that they were liable to extinguish the flame".[134]

Clearly, the vital heat of the heart needed fuel, and this, said Locke, is supplied to it by the blood, in the form of a "continual generation and flux of fine spirits". These are produced by "various ferments" and "digestions" in the stomach and the intestines, which all "work together to produce something which can be burned so that the vital flame may have its fuel".[135]

Yet this is not sufficient, Locke argued, and in order for there to be "a continuous and constant provision of animal spirits" by the blood to the heart to serve it as combustible fuel, the products of digestion which are carried in the blood need to made combustible, need to be "changed into a subtle and volatile material". This change, Locke suggested, is brought about by something in air, so that one purpose of respiration is to ensure that the products of digestion are combustible.[136]

Alluding to Boyle's experiments, Locke pointed to the close connection between air and combustion, and to how without air it is impossible, with however violent a fire, to burn "substances normally volatile and responsive to heat". There is, he said, some substance in the air which is necessary for combustion and volatilization, and in respiration this substance is carried to the body in order to volatilize the blood. So "air serves rather to foster the heart's heat than to cool it". This could be proved experimentally: people die in mines without fresh air; this happens not because of excessive burning in the heart (for they can die in mines which are very cold), rather they die because "the heart for lack of fuel gradually dies down". Flames die out too, but no one says this is because of excessive heat.[137]

Locke had, at least tentatively, already reached this conclusion in his short note "Respiratio" two years earlier, and then had shortly come to think that the crucial element of the air was, as he says here, some "volatile salt", a "highly volatile interior spirit" or "acid".[138] But he had not explained there that the purpose of such volatilization is to make the products of digestion suitable as fuel for the heart.

Locke's idea that digestion and volatilization of the blood involved "ferments" was perhaps derived from Thomas Willis, whose lectures he had attended a few years earlier. Willis had speculated in his *De Fermentatione* (1656) that underlying such things as digestion, putrefaction, effervesence, and the "working" of yeast, lay "fermentation", a mixing of particles of different kinds – spiritous, sulphurous, saline, aqueous, and earthy.[139]

3

Exeter House, London (1666–1675): "One Accident in My Life"[1]

JULY 1666–MAY 1667: "FALLING INTO A GREAT MAN'S FAMILY"[2]

According to Anthony Wood's contemporary biographical sketch, "rather than tak[ing] orders and be[coming] a minister according to the church of England, [Locke] entered on the physic line, ran a course of chemistry and got some little practice in Oxon". This "little practice" was with David Thomas, for besides working with him in the preparation of iatrochemicals, Locke assisted Thomas when he began to take on patients, having in April received a licence to do so. One was an infant boy who suffered from rickets; he died, and Thomas and Locke took the opportunity of doing a thorough post-mortem examination of his liver, heart, lungs, and other organs ("the head we had not time to open"). Locke made lengthy notes on their observations, observations which led him to raise a number of queries about a possible connection between rickets and diseases of the lungs. Learning of Locke's activities with Thomas, which we may suppose he now intended to continue as his life's work, Strachey teasingly addressed him as "Mr Doctor".[3]

In early July when Thomas was in London buying chemicals and other materials, he asked Locke to get "twelve bottles of water for my Lord Ashley, to drink in Oxford...if you can possibly do it, you will very much oblige him and me".[4] This chance event proved to be a turning point in Locke's life.

"My Lord Ashley" was Anthony Ashley Cooper, Baron Ashley of Wimborne St Giles, near Salisbury in Dorset. Now in his forties, he had been subject for twenty years to almost daily attacks of violent pain in his side. He also suffered from jaundice, with its accompanying ill-effects of weakness and loss of appetite, and in the earlier months of this year his health had been particularly poor. He found acidic mineral waters to be something of a tonic, and Locke's commission from Thomas was for spring water from Astrop, a village seventeen miles from Oxford.[5]

Astrop was not developed as a spa, the therapeutic value of its water having been recognised only two years earlier (in fact by Richard Lower), and it would certainly have been more pleasant for Ashley to take the water in Oxford. In any case, his fourteen-year-old son and heir, also Anthony Ashley Cooper, was an undergraduate at Trinity College and he probably wanted to spend some time in Oxford with him.[6] But Ashley was faced with having to make the further journey to Astrop, for, when they met, Locke had to tell him that, certainly through no fault of Thomas's and despite his own best efforts, the dozen bottles of water were not there ready in Oxford.

Ashley was a man of great charm, affable, cultivated, and confident, and took the thwarting of his plans well. We are told by someone who must have had the report from Locke that Ashley "in his wonted manner, received him very civilly; accepting his excuse with great easiness: and when Mr Locke would have taken his leave of him, would needs have him stay to sup with him". Locke too had something to do with his friendly reception, for Ashley was "much pleased ... with his conversation": this presumably began with formalities relating to Thomas, and to Ashley's son's education and his tutors at Trinity College, but eventually it ran as far as poetry. Another later report, this time by Ashley's grandson, tells how Locke, "at that time a student in physic ... though he had never practised physic, yet appeared to my grandfather to be such a genius that he valued him above all his other physicians".[7]

Locke was no less attracted to Ashley, as he told friends in later life. "But if my Lord was pleased with the company of Mr Locke, Mr Locke was yet more so with that of my Lord Ashley: and he has often said, that it perfectly charmed him." Indeed, so pleased were the two with each other that Locke accepted Ashley's invitation to drink the waters at Astrop with him. "My Lord did understand you intended to bear him company", Ashley's servant wrote from Astrop in early August. "He has now commanded me to let you know he has a bed...for you and if you can dispense with your own occasions, desire you would come over tomorrow to us...pray forget not to bring the verses upon the wits." Locke went to Astrop, but exactly when is not clear.*[8]

On 4 September, at 1 p.m., Locke recorded that while it had been "Fair" four hours earlier, there was now "Dim reddish sun-shine"; "this unusual colour of the air", he wrote, "which, without a cloud appearing, made the sun beams of a strange red dim light, was very remarkable". News had not yet reached Oxford of the great fire that had broken out in London two days earlier, but, as he later added, "the smoke of London then burning, which, driven this way by an easterly wind, caused this odd phenomenon". A few days later a member of Ashley's household suggested that, since the fire (which burned till 5 September) "will certainly occasion great business for physicians", he should come to London. Whether or not this thought figured in Locke's mind, or whether he was just responding to Ashley's invitation to visit him "as soon as he could", Locke left Oxford in early October for Exeter House, Shaftesbury's home in the Strand, between the City of London and Westminster.[9]

The so-called "Great Fire of London" and its aftermath would have been one topic of conversation between Locke and Ashley, but another must have been Locke's plans and ambitions, and it was presumably at Ashley's request that in early November Lord Clarendon, the Chancellor of Oxford University, agreed to recommend to the Vice-Chancellor that Locke be allowed to proceed towards the degree of Doctor of Medicine without qualifying first for the Bachelor's degree:

I am very well assured that Mr John Locke...has employed his time in the study of physic to so good purpose that he is in all respects qualified for the degree of Doctor in that faculty...; but not having taken the degree of bachelor in physic, he has desired that he may be dispensed with to accumulate to that degree, which appears to me a very modest and reasonable request he professing himself ready to perform the exercises for both degrees. I therefore give my consent that a dispensation to that purpose be proposed for him.[10]

We can only guess what Locke might have said to Ashley about this, but presumably he was intending to work as a physician; he is unlikely to have wanted an M.D. merely in formal recognition of his informally acquired knowledge. More pressing, though, was the matter of his Studentship. Since the beginning of the previous year he had been in the ranks of the *theologi*, and pressure would have been increasing on him to take holy orders (probably by the end of the year if he were not to lose his Studentship).[11] Getting a faculty Studentship, in medicine, would have been an ideal solution (except that it too required celibacy and would not consist with the "pleasant hopes" he shortly claimed to be harbouring regarding Elinor); and being an M.D. would have fitted him for this.

It does not seem, however, that Clarendon's recommendation was ever submitted to the university and it looks as though Locke decided against "performing the exercises" for the M.B. and M.D. In any case, less than two weeks after Clarendon wrote his letter, Locke tried something else to relieve the pressure on him to go into the Church, this time by way of an approach to the college. Again Ashley must have used his influence on behalf of his new friend, and the King himself (who perhaps remembered Locke's service in Cleves with the diplomatic mission) ordered him dispensed from the need to take holy orders. In mid-November the Secretary of State wrote, on behalf of the King, to the Dean of Christ Church:

Whereas we are informed that John Locke... is of such standing as by the custom of that college he is obliged to enter into holy orders or otherwise to leave his student's place there, at his humble request that he may still have further time to prosecute his studies without that obligation, we are graciously pleased to grant him our royal dispensation, and do accordingly hereby require you to suffer him... to hold and enjoy his said student's place in Christ Church, together with all the rights, profits, and emoluments thereunto belonging without taking holy orders.[12]

In late November, Locke returned to Oxford (with an invitation to be again at Exeter House at Christmas, or indeed at "any time"). Perhaps Ashley was already pressing Locke to make Exeter House his home (he certainly was by the following Easter), and Locke needed time to reach a decision, or to sort out his affairs. Otherwise, we may suppose, he went back to Oxford simply "to prosecute his studies" further (as the King's dispensation had put it). Thomas was certainly anxious to have him back for the last reason. He had expected him sooner, and needed his help with their chemical experiments and preparations.[13]

The dispensation meant that one source of heart-searching was absent when, soon after getting back to Oxford, Locke was offered the chance of an ecclesiastical appointment in Ireland. But since the offer was from Elinor Parry's brother, who, with his sisters, had recently removed to Dublin where he was now Dean of Christ Church, there must have been other corners of his heart to search. "What your resolutions are as to a calling", Parry wrote,

> and whether England be the place you only intend to fix in I know not; but in case you think fit to venture your fortunes with us here, and take orders, I...doubt not but in a little time to get you to be Chaplain to my Lord Duke and the first Dignity that falls, especially in my own Cathedral... I do really believe to procure for you so that in a little time I am confirmed I shall see you very handsomely provided for...without being a constant preacher.[14]

As Parry urged, Locke was speedy in his reply, pointing out that he "must needs be very quick or inconsiderate, that can on a sudden resolve to transplant himself from [his] country, affairs, and study, upon a probability". He did of course say that quite apart from its intrinsic attractiveness, Dublin was a desirable place "because of the conversations of those I love and company of my friends", but, perhaps a little tartly, he went on to suggest that he would need to *earn* the advancements Parry confidently expected for him, and "my want of fitness may possibly disappoint". Suppose, he said, "I should put myself into orders, and, by the meanness of my abilities, grow unworthy such expectations, (for you do not think that divines are now made, as formerly, by inspiration and on a sudden, nor learning caused by laying on of hands)".[15]

What also clearly weighed with him was not only that he might have to give up and "lose all my further study" in medicine, but that the commitment to holy orders would be for life; he would be putting himself "into a calling that will not leave me...a profession from whence there [is no]...return". In 1663, as we have seen, Locke refused a preferment, and apparently there had been other such offers, for "the same considerations", he told Parry, "have made me a long time reject very advantageous offers of several very considerable friends in England".

In this case, however, there was a further consideration – Parry's sister Elinor. What understanding there had been between her and Locke when she removed to Dublin – which cannot have been more than a very few months after he returned from Cleves – has to be gleaned from the draft of the letter he wrote her at the same time as he replied to her brother. Besides repeating to her what he had said to him, Locke showed very considerable regret that this way in which they could have been together was not really possible:

I with discontent reflect upon my misfortune that makes me uncapable of [accepting the proposals]. O my best are all my pleasant hopes returned to the same place they were.... I long to be with you and only desire to come handsomely so that we may enjoy one another and ourselves. But I find I am a little unfortunate and by several ways am led to the prospect but shut off from the possession of my happiness.

Locke also chided Elinor for not writing:* "You have let me know so little of the state of your affairs.... I wish heartily you had not been so silent: you cannot think that since you went I have ... laid no designs or made me no concernment; and can you believe twenty four [hours] time enough to consider, dispose, and alter all?"[16]

Elinor was passionate and emotionally beckoning in her response to Locke's decision. (Because her feelings for him were now more mature and settled? Or because the reinforcing of their geographical separation obviated any need to keep him at arm's length?) "She bids me tell you", Elinor wrote of herself,

she repines at this separation and as her kindness would persuade her to patience and hope for the sight of you, yet her despair is greater, and more firmly fixed it is not grounded on any hindrances this side as she knows: she is as heartily real in her affection as ever neither does she now practice that nicety of disowning it ... if you are the yet passionate Atticus and the real one you ever was you will hide nothing from her, she must share in your concerns as she has share in your heart and you must tell her all things.... My best shall I never see you: shall I always lament your absence without any hopes.[17]

A couple of months later she worried that she had not recently had a letter from him: "Are you changed and do you now think indifferently of the affection you have framed in my soul.... I must tell you I have breathed your name often ... and as often called you. But in vain.... When you come in my thoughts I groan to death."[18]

Having determined, as Locke said to John Parry, not "to lose all my further study", he continued with it, and towards the end of the year he composed a short essay on diseases, *Morbus*. His opening suggestion, that there may be "another and more rational theory of diseases" than those of the Galenists and the Paracelsians, is supported by the claim that in general some things are "produced by seminal principles" and others "by bare mistion [mixture] of the parts", perhaps helped along by heat and cold.[19]

By "seminal principles or ferments" Locke meant "some small and subtle parcels of matter which are apt to transmute far greater portions of matter into a new nature", though "how these small and insensible ferments, this potent Archeus works I confess I cannot satisfactorily comprehend, though the effects are evident".[20] Locke was aligning himself here with an account of nature which derived from Paracelsus and, more immediately, from van Helmont, an account which took as its model for events and processes in the world organic processes such as fermentations and decompositions, or the growth of a seed or plant, and which supposed that such processes were guided by an active spiritual principle, an archeus.

Locke's belief at this time, as he went on to argue, was that we cannot even begin to understand things like the growth of different plants from apparently identical seeds planted in the same soil, or the development of a chicken from the liquid in an egg, in any other way than by the operation of such seminal principles and ferments. In particular, they cannot be explained as Boyle, following Descartes, hoped to explain them, in terms of some mechanism, modelled (as in Descartes's case) on the example of sieves which allow through different amounts of liquid or strain out differently sized particles.[21] Surely, Locke said, the different growths of cuttings of mint and of marjoram in the same water cannot be "effected by barely straining it [the water] through the different pores of those plants, but must be wrought in some more powerful way.... I believe all the straining in the world would scarce make the parts of water produce the smell of either of those plants."

Having aligned himself with the Paracelsian approach to nature in general, Locke suggested that some diseases "spring from these ferments", and he instanced the production of scabs in contagions such as the "itch", and the corrosiveness of some "eating ulcers". But to an extent he also aligned himself with Galenic theory according to which diseases were produced by an imbalance of the four humours of the body; though he did not accept that different bodily constitutions produced diseases, they still might be differently susceptible to them (just as different seeds thrive better in different soils): "sanguine complexions", he said, "are observed more easily to admit the seminal principles of the plague".[22]

Yet, as he had indicated at the outset, Locke did not think that everything was to be understood in terms of "seminal principles" and "ferments". Some things involved no more than the "mixing of parts" of two different substances, often to produce a third quite different from either, such as the production of a third chemical from the mixture of "acid and volatile salts". The difference between the results of seminal principles and those of "mixing of parts" is that without any alteration in themselves, seminal principles, "small and insensible" though they are, alter what they act on; whereas "mixing" involves similar quantities of both substances, each of which is altered in the "mixing". It is easy, Locke said, to see the difference, as to "way of production and method of curing", between the "ebullition of the blood" caused by too much drinking of wine, and that produced by "the biting of some venemous beast". It might be thought that Locke's proposal of "mixture of parts" as the explanation of some processes and events partly aligned him with Descartes's and Boyle's mechanical picture of the world, but it is just as easy to think that the alignment is with van Helmont's non-mechanical recognition of inorganic chemical reactions which produce a compound irreversibly different from the chemicals which were "mixed".[23]

Locke was continuing with his chemical studies too, in collaboration with Thomas. In the first months of the new year he was at work (following some instructions from Boyle) on the distillation of oil of vitriol and spirit of wine, and on the first day of April he completed and wrote up an experiment he had begun on lead ore the previous June.[24]

But he had by now decided to accept Ashley's patronage at Exeter House, and that same day he wrote out an account of the laboratory expenses ("Mr Thomas £22 5s 5d, Mr Blunt £5 15s 11d, JL £4 13s 5d), and shortly afterwards went to Somerset, "for some little stay" he told Boyle when he wrote asking whether there were any investigations he could make for him in the Mendips. He was there with Strachey at Sutton Court until the end of April. Perhaps he then went straight to London; at any rate he was at Exeter House by the end of May (when he recorded receiving some clothes and linen that he had sent earlier from Oxford). He was now, as a friend would later report, "with my Lord Ashley as a man at home; and lived in that family much esteemed not only by my lord, but by all the friends of the family".[25]

JUNE–DECEMBER 1667: "WITH MY LORD ASHLEY AS
A MAN AT HOME"[26]

Lord Ashley, into whose household Locke entered at the age of almost
thirty-five, was ten years his senior and a highly skilled and experienced
politician and administrator. His life and experience had been quite
unlike Locke's: a baronet from the age of ten, he had had some formal
education in his teens at Exeter College, Oxford, and at Lincoln's Inn
in London. He was married at eighteen and a Member of Parliament
for Tewkesbury at nineteen. In the civil war he was first neutral, then
joined the Royalists, and then, less than a year later, changed sides,
fighting with troops he had himself raised. During the Commonwealth
period he served on local committees in the southwest, later in various
parliaments, and then as a member of Cromwell's executive government, the Council of State. He eventually left Cromwell's service
and gradually moved into opposition to him. As a member of the
Convention Parliament of 1660 he was chosen as one of twelve to go
to Holland to acknowledge Charles II as King. Ashley had had a lot
to offer the new government, in which he was made a Privy Councillor.
In 1661, newly ennobled, he became Chancellor of the Exchequer,
a position in which he had worked hard, and still held when he met
Locke.[27]

Though Locke surely did not decide lightly, it probably would
not have needed much to persuade him to make the move from
Oxford. The Black Hall "club" had long since disbanded: Tilly,
Towerson, and Uvedale had left Oxford (the first two having taken
orders); Anne Evelegh had married and gone to Ireland; and, most
particularly, Elinor Parry was gone too. His medical acquaintances
and colleagues were dispersing also: Boyle and Lower to London,
Thomas to Salisbury. At Exeter House he could expect to meet,
besides the "great men of those times", a wide variety of people
connected with the administration of the country and the world
of learning.[28] Besides, he could return to Oxford, temporarily or
permanently, whenever he wanted: relieved of the obligation to
prepare for holy orders, he was perfectly secure in the tenure of his
valuable Studentship.

In moving to London, Locke might have thought that he had at last
thrown off the "academic goblin" which had mounted him in Oxford
and which had accompanied him to Cleves. He might have thought
too that he could now "rule and direct his course of life" himself.

In fact, however, living with Ashley would gradually produce fresh "little sprites" to bestride him.[29]

Locke did not go to Exeter House as a paid employee, but under Ashley's patronage, and it was evidently understood that he would be there for long enough to have made it worthwhile to sub-let his Christ Church rooms (for about £10 per annum). It was presumably understood too that he was to have responsibility for the education of Ashley's son, and that his developing knowledge and expertise as a physician would be called on. Some notes he made on cases between 1667 and 1670 show that he certainly advised members of the Ashley household on medical matters large and small, but he was not, straightforwardly, "the family physician"; by 1673 the various medicines prescribed for Exeter House were mostly not at his order. His main aim, however, would have been to continue his study of medicine and associated matters, and to extend his experience as a physician. If he had not, during the first six months at Exeter House, yet set about "attempting any farther experiments in Chemistry" of the kind he had been engaged in with Thomas, it was not, he told Boyle, that his fingers did not "still itch to be at it", but because there was no room for it, and because he was likely before long "once more [to] cross the seas".[30] Was he, perhaps, going to take Ashley's son abroad?

A few years later a lady of Locke's acquaintance would flatter him regarding the "excellent faculty which you possess in perfection, of talking ingeniously upon every subject, and inventing new ones... whenever the dullness of your friends sets your charity, or your good nature on work to relieve them". His attractiveness as a good companion to both sexes, of all ages, and of all sorts and conditions, and his facility as a conversationalist also featured in the posthumous memoirs written by his friends. One of these hinted that his habit of easy, unconstrained informality was not natural, but acquired "from the company he had kept", while another was more explicit that his ability to make his "conversation so agreeable to all sorts of people", his "obliging and benevolent manners", his "easy and polite expression", were developed during the years he spent with Ashley, when he "had the advantage of becoming acquainted with all the polite, witty, and agreeable part of the court".[31]

To some degree this characteristic was surely there before Locke met Ashley — it was, after all, an element in the initial formation of their friendship — but the move to Exeter House must have been the beginning of the transformation of an awkwardly studious and quiet reserved man who, even at thirty five, was still perhaps rather gauche, into an assured and confident gentleman, with that civility which (so it was reported) he "thought not only the great ornament of life...that gave lustre and gloss to all our actions", but also "a Christian duty that deserved to be more inculcated as such, than it generally was".[32]

Exeter House certainly introduced him to a wider world than Oxford, and to new acquaintances. It was perhaps at Ashley's table that he first met Samuel Pepys, when the Navy Board clerk was dining there in September. He soon became a welcome visitor at nearby Northumberland House, the London home of the Earls of Northumberland. He knew some members of the household from as long ago as his schooldays (the Reverend Thomas Blomer, the family chaplain; Dr John Mapletoft, first a family tutor and then its physician), and forged new friendships with others, such as Margaret Beavis, one of Lady Northumberland's attendants. They came to speak of themselves as "brother" and "sister", and spent "agreeable hours" together, reading and conversing "in the pretty arbour at the end of the fine garden" at Northumberland House. It was perhaps she who introduced him into the home of Thomas Grigg, a prebendary of St Paul's. The happiness of the hours he spent there, he told her, was second only to the time he spent with her. Grigg and Locke were likely distantly related (via Locke's uncle Peter's wife); while his wife, Anna, was very possibly Margaret Beavis's sister.[33]

Locke also soon met, and began an association with, Dr Thomas Sydenham, whose medical practice encompassed Exeter House. Sydenham had a particular interest in infectious fevers, such as were common at the time; his *Methodus Curandi Febres*, published the previous year, listed the cases he had attended since he began his work in London, and had treated by his chosen method of "cooling", instead of with the standardly prescribed "heating medicines". Perhaps Locke had already read this when he met Sydenham, but in any case he was soon interested enough in what Sydenham was doing and thinking to be accompanying him regularly on his visits to patients. By April of the next year Sydenham, in writing to Boyle, spoke of "my friend Mr Locke...who has troubled...himself in visiting with me very many of my varioulous [suffering from smallpox] patients especially".[34]

The first-hand experience Locke gained with Sydenham and what he learnt of Sydenham's methods and ideas completely transformed his thinking not only about medicine but about our knowledge of the natural world in general. Sydenham saw little point in inquiring into the nature of disease, or in producing some encompassing theory of the inner workings of the world in general or the human body in particular, and indeed was pessimistic about the chances of doing so. Diseases were to be approached, not in an a priori fashion, but by careful and systematic observation of the way they developed and of the effect of various treatments on them.

The following year, when the second edition of Sydenham's book appeared, it was prefaced with a poem in which Locke eulogised at least part of this approach. Sydenham, Locke wrote, opposed "both fever and the schools". He eschewed abstract medical theorising and discussion: "not for him, fires of occult corruption or those 'humours' that breed fevers.... What hope of health if fictitious fluid burns within?"; "not for him those squabbles whose heat exceeds the fevers". Describing Sydenham's whole approach some years later, Locke approvingly said: "general theories...are, for the most part, but a sort of waking dreams". Thus "the Galenists' four humours, or the chemists sal, sulphur, and mercury, or the late prevailing invention of acid and alkali, or whatever hereafter shall be substituted to these with new applause, will, upon examination, be found to be but so many learned empty sounds, with no precise determinate signification". People begin at the wrong end when they "lay the foundation in their own fancies, and then endeavour to suit the phenomena of diseases, and the cure of them, to those fancies". Instead of this "romance way of physic", doctors should set themselves first

nicely to observe the history [i.e. the course] of diseases in all their changes and circumstances...wherein...men...may be convinced of their error by unerring nature and matter of fact.... There is nothing left for a physician to do, but to observe well,...and thence make to himself rules of practice: and he that is this way most sagacious will, I imagine, make the best physician.[35]

The re-establishment of a strong Church of England at the Restoration was something to which Locke had looked forward. But it had not resulted in the peaceful religious uniformity he had wanted. Instead there had been the separation and persecution of many nonconformists who did not agree with the ceremonials of the re-established Anglicanism. The King himself had not been in favour of the Act of Uniformity, which in 1662 had formally established a firmly episcopal

Church with a clearly set-out and required liturgy, and which had seen to it that most official positions were held by Anglican communicants. He would have preferred a tolerant broadening of the Church and the suspension of penal laws against any remaining dissenters. All along, Ashley's position had been that of the King: both were opposed to the Conventicle Act of 1664 (which forbade nonconforming religious assemblies of over five, on pain of fines, imprisonment, and transportation), and the Five Mile Act of 1665 (which prohibited dissenting clergymen or schoolmasters from living within five miles of a city). Ashley certainly supported, and probably advised, Charles during discussions which began during Locke's first year in London, on the possibility of getting support for measures which would comprehend some dissenters within a widened Church, and tolerate any who still lay outside.[36]

It was against this background that, whether merely stimulated or actually requested by Ashley, Locke composed an "Essay concerning Toleration", the last part of which reads as though it was intended to be seen by the King. He set out to address the question of liberty of conscience, a question which "has for some years been so much bandied amongst us". On the one hand were those who "preach up absolute obedience" to imposed doctrines and ways of worship, and on the other were those who "claim universal liberty in matters of conscience". Locke's thought was that each side had claimed too much: while there are *some* things that have "a title to liberty", there are *others* where "imposition and obedience" are in place.[37]

It is often remarked that the "Essay" (perhaps under the influence of Ashley, perhaps because the restored Church had been too narrow and strict for Locke's own liking) differed from Locke's earlier tracts on government in being less authoritarian, more tolerant. Yet the differences are not all doctrinal; some are of stress and emphasis, and derive from a more optimistic assessment of human nature.

Whereas earlier Locke had been concerned to stress the extent of the magistrate's right to make religious impositions, he was now more concerned to stress its limits. As he now explained things, there are some "opinions and actions [which] in themselves concern not government and society at all", which are beyond the magistrate's reach, and which "have an absolute and universal right to toleration". He sharply distinguished these from "practical ... opinions, by which men ... regulate their actions with one another" and which (perfectly in accordance with the "Tracts") are to be tolerated only so long as "they do not tend to the disturbance of the state, or do not cause greater inconveniences than advantages to the community".[38]

The opinions which have an absolute right to toleration are "purely speculative" ones, for example, "belief in the Trinity, purgatory, transubstantiation...Christ's personal reign on earth" They "come not within the magistrate's cognisance" and are to be tolerated by him, because whatever my beliefs are on these matters they "cannot by any means either disturb the state or inconvenience my neighbour".[39]

Though the earlier "Tracts" did not explicitly pick out any such beliefs "as were above the reach of government", they were in fact implied by what Locke said there, since he recognised that the magistrate "has no commission to examine the hearts, but to take care of the actions of his subjects". Moreover the argument of the "Essay" that even were they within his cognisance, the magistrate could not possibly have power over our beliefs since we ourselves do not, just underlines and stresses a point he had already made in the "Tracts".[40]

As for the actions which are of no concern for the magistrate and which have "just claim to an unlimited toleration", these are ones which relate to the "manner of worshipping my God". Like my speculative opinions, these are things between God and me: "kneeling or sitting in the sacrament can in itself tend no more to the disturbance of the government or injury of my neighbour than sitting or standing at my own table".[41]

According to the earlier tracts, such things *would* have been within the province of the magistrate. Indeed, Locke's thought then had been that the magistrate had a duty to rule about them in order to provide a uniformity of order and decency in religious practice. This difference quite possibly reflected Locke's having come to a different view of his fellows, one which can be seen in the fact that the "Essay" was structured, as the earlier "Tracts" were not, by a distinction between actions which have no relation to other people and those which do. Locke's earlier thought had been that such a distinction was unstable. Some people, he thought, could take exception to almost anything others did and find it un-Christian and religiously unlawful. "Grant the people once free and unlimited in the exercise of their religion", he said, "and will it not be religion to destroy all that are not of their profession?" When he came to write the "Essay", however, his feelings seem to have changed, perhaps partly as a result of having observed in Cleves that a religiously mixed society could nevertheless be a peaceful one. He still had some caution, however, for even though the magistrate should have no concern with actions and beliefs which contain nothing which, if it be "done sincerely and out of conscience", can "make me either the worse subject to my prince or worse neighbour to my fellow-subject", he expressed just the sort of worry which had been so prominent in the "Tracts": "unless", he said, "it be that I will, out of pride or overweeningness of my own opinion and a secret conceit of my own infallibility, . . . force and compel others to be of my mind or censure and malign them if they be not".[42]

But along with this softening of attitude, Locke had also come to believe that conscientious scruples about ways of worship are of some importance. Whereas he had earlier thought that worship, "the sacrifice of a broken and contrite heart", was something which "may be willingly and acceptably given to God in any place or posture", he now thought that such things should be "wholly between God and me". Worship, which is that "homage which I pay to God", must be done "in a way I judge acceptable to him".[43]

Though Locke now insisted that ways of worship will "necessarily produce no action which disturbs the community", his new belief in their importance required some amendment to what could be said about conscience. He was no less adamant than he had been earlier that the magistrate cannot let people's conscientious objections carry any weight in his law-making. But he moved away from thinking that we should always obey whatever the magistrate required (an obedience which he originally thought involved no imposition on our conscience since we still retained our "liberty of judgement"). He now thought that a law to which we conscientiously object *is* an imposition on our conscience and that we *should* disobey it. At the same time, however, we are bound "quietly to submit to the penalty the law inflicts"; in this way we secure for ourselves both our "grand concernment in another world and disturb not the peace of this".[44]

The firm view to which Locke had come, that the proper concern of the magistrate is wholly secular, solely with "the quiet and comfortable living of men in society one with another" and in no way at all with "their concernments in another life", stood over and against a prominent strand of Anglican thought according to which the state had a duty to act in tandem with the Church to penalise dissenters and to bring them to recognise the correctness of the Church's ceremonials and doctrines. His view related to a conviction not only that one must find one's own way to heaven, but also that the magistrate, or the established Church, is in no privileged position to judge on such matters. They have "no more certain or more infallible knowledge of the way to attain [heaven] than I myself".[45]

In a second part of the "Essay", Locke considered the practical application of these general ideas, in particular to the then-present state of affairs in England. Sometimes talking of "us" and "we", he aligned himself with the established order, and, in occasionally addressing "you", seemed to be offering advice to the King.

One difficulty he noted for the application of the principles he had argued for was that people usually "take up their religion in gross", so that purely speculative opinions, which should be tolerated, may be held "all at once in a bundle" with some dangerous practical opinions which should not. A further practical matter which needed to be considered was that, as he assessed them, people tend to "grasp at dominion" when they see the chance of it. Groups of people, although initially come together for innocent reasons, such as those of religion, might eventually become so numerous as to "seem visibly to threaten the peace of the state".[46] Given sufficient numbers the Quakers, he thought, were just such a group.

"Papists", or Roman Catholics, were an example of those who combined harmless speculative beliefs with "dangerous opinions, which are absolutely destructive to all governments but the Pope's". They do not, Locke said, allow freedom of religion to those who dissent from theirs; they owe a blind obedience to the Pope who would allow them to "dispense with all their oaths, promises, and the obligations they have to their prince", especially if he is not a Catholic. Such opinions, as with any others that are potentially destructive of civil peace, have no right to toleration. Moreoever, in Locke's view, it was better if they do not have it: not only is tolerating "papism" likely to encourage it, but also restraining it will be productive of religious unity for it will "knit all the protestant party firmer to our assistance and defence". Various dissenting groups, perhaps suspicious of what they see as Catholic tendencies in orthodox Anglicanism, are more likely to "unite in a common friendship" with the established Church when they see that "we really separate from and set ourselves against the common enemy both to our church and all protestant professions".[47]

Locke did not claim that intolerance of Catholics would deal with all the animosities, both towards the state and the established Church, which were harboured by the "fanatics" amongst Protestant dissenters. But while not saying that they and their opinions, in so far as they were subversive, had any right to toleration, he thought that in fact they should be dealt with gently and with circumspection. Persecution and force will not work, and will merely make them band together as "secret malcontents", rather than "open dissenters" in disparate groups; but "courtesy, friendship, and soft usage" may get them to change their views. Then, even "if they do not part with their opinions [they] yet may [be] persuade[d]...to lay by their animosities, and become friends to the state, though they are not sons of the church".[48]

JANUARY–DECEMBER 1668: "TURNING HIS THOUGHTS
ANOTHER WAY"[49]

In May 1668, when Locke had been at Exeter House for about a year, a medical crisis* developed. The abdominal pain and jaundice which Ashley had suffered for years increased and was accompanied by vomiting. The purge which Francis Glisson, one of the King's physicians, recommended, only increased the pain and produced an ostrich-egg-sized tumour below the ribs. In June, under Locke's direction, this was cauterised and drained; and after six weeks of daily draining there was merely a watery discharge. Much to the delight of contemporary satirists, a silver tube was inserted to keep the aperture open and drained.[50]

During this year Locke was giving much thought to the theory of medicine too, and composed "Anatomie", a piece thoroughly imbued by the empirical, anti-theoretical methodology he had been coming to in his association with Sydenham, the methodology of careful observation according to which "what we know of the...constitution of health, and the operations of our own bodies, is only by the sensible effects".[51]

In "Anatomie", Locke expressed scepticism about our ability to come to know "the contrivances by which nature works" and stepped back from the positive ideas he had put forward earlier in his note on diseases. He was now quite agnostic about what those "contrivances" might be, allowing the Cartesian mechanical theory of strainers as much credence as that of Paracelsian ferments: "what ferments, strainings, mixtures and other changes" the juices of the body undergo, whether nature works by one or all of these ways, is likely always to be a question. He similarly turned his back on his earlier speculations about the purpose of respiration: controversies among "the learned", he now disparagingly said, are likely to produce more doubts than any clear solution as to whether respiration serves "to cool the blood, or give vent to its vapours, or to add a ferment to it, or to pound and mix its minute particles".[52]

Along with the theories of "the learned", anatomy (which would have included physiology) is also unlikely, he argued, to improve "the practise of physic" or to help establish "a true method" in it. It does have some particular uses (in surgical operations such as trepanning; in guiding the application of externally applied remedies; and in prognostications about wounds and diseases of the organs), but it is not of much general use to the physician in his treatment of diseases. On the face of it, it might seem that anatomy provides insight into the workings of the body, but one of Locke's points was that it does not: all it can do is expose "the gross and sensible parts of the body", it cannot show us how they work. Nature operates at a level below anything revealed to the observation of the anatomist, he said, even when that observation is assisted by the microscope. He repeatedly stressed that "after all our porings and mangling the parts of animals we know nothing but the gross parts, see not the tools and contrivances by which nature works".[53]

Furthermore, even if we could come to know nature's contrivances, we would still not, Locke argued, know how to cure various diseases. How would knowing that "the pores of the parenchyma of the liver or kidneys were either round or square and that the parts of urine and gall separated in these parts were in size and figure answerable to those pores" help us to to know "the cure either of the jaundice or stoppage of urine"?[54]

Locke also insisted, following Sydenham, that knowledge of cures, of the composition and dosage of suitable medicine, is not to be got from theorising, but from experience, from "a diligent observation of these diseases, of their beginning, progress, and ways of cure". A physician can do this without carefully inquiring "into the anatomy of the parts", just as well as a gardener, "by his art and observation", can cultivate fruit "without examining what kinds of juices, fibres, pores etc. are to be found in the roots, bark, or body of the tree".[55]

Ashley had been so impressed by Locke and his contribution during his medical crisis that he made some attempt to turn him *away* from medicine. According to Ashley's grandson, Locke became so esteemed by Ashley "that as great a man as he had experienced him in physic, he looked upon this but as his least part; he encouraged him to turn his thoughts another way; nor would he suffer him to practise at all in physic, except in his own family, and as a kindness to some particular friends". Instead he "put him upon" studying "whatsoever related to the business of a Minister of State, in which he was so successful, that my grandfather began soon to use him as a friend, and consult with him on all occasions of that kind".[56] From this point on, Locke's life began to take a new turn. It would, increasingly, be less determined by his own primary interests in medicine, and more by Ashley's own political concerns. It would eventually lead to exile and the disreputation of being known, not for his own sake, simply as "Dr Locke", but as "he that belonged to the Earl of Shaftesbury" (as Ashley became).

One completely new way in which Ashley, as Chancellor of the Exchequer, turned Locke's thoughts in the later months of the year was to economic theory, in particular to the question of interest rates, which had been discussed in Parliament under the stimulus of a recent book, *Brief Observations concerning Trade, and Interest of Money*. Against a background of falling land rents and sluggish trade, its author, Josiah Child, proposed a lowering of the official interest rate from 6 to 4 per cent. As the example of Holland shows, he argued, a low interest rate goes along with national prosperity. Child and other advocates of interest rate reduction argued that it would stimulate trade: with cheaper money more businesses would start up, and producers would invest more in their undertakings; there would, moreover, be an increase in the circulation of money and producers would get better prices for their goods.[57] They further argued that land would increase in value, and also that the Crown would be helped with repayment of its debts.

Locke composed a short piece against reduction, "Some of the Consequences that are like to follow upon lessening of interest to four per cent", dedicating it to Ashley in acknowledgement of his patronage. Prominent in what he wrote were so-called "mercantilist" ideas about a country's economy: a country is richer in proportion to its stock of precious metals such as silver (the main raw material for the national coinage) and gold; a circulation of money is required within the country to enable the production of goods and their sale, to "drive the wheels of trade", as Locke put it.[58] These two ideas are connected in that circulation of money (and hence production of goods) can be increased by an increase in the supply of money, and that supply in its turn is to be increased by the importation of precious metals for the coining of money, an importation which results from a surplus of domestic exports over foreign imports.

Locke argued that reducing the legal interest rate would, despite what its proponents thought, in fact slow the wheels of trade: economic activity, both domestically and in terms of export, would suffer. Within the country there would be less money circulating or "stirring in trade", since a lower rate would not compensate for the risk people take in lending it out.[59] The scarcity of money would, furthermore, lead to a fall in prices and hence to a reduction in the value of exports.

Later in the year Locke more than doubled the size of his paper. In a "Supplement" he considered what effect a reduction of the interest rate would have on the value of land and of annuities, and on the value of money in respect of its power to purchase commodities. He concluded that as interest rates go down, the value of land increases, annuities increase less so, and (at least to begin with) the purchasing power of money is unchanged.[60]

JANUARY 1669—DECEMBER 1670: "A LOVE OF ALL SORTS OF USEFUL KNOWLEDGE"[61]

In April, Locke received a letter from Elinor Parry. Unfortunately we do not have the letter to which it replied, and we know little of how much or what had passed between them during the two years since he had decided not to join her and her brother in Dublin. During the weeks after telling her of that decision (when he had protested "I long to be with you"), he seems to have been slow to write again; she worried that he had "changed", and begged him not to "think indifferently of the affection you have framed in my soul". But whatever he did feel then it seems clear that by now his feelings had undergone a change. The roles they first occupied had reversed. Elinor was now the supplicant, for it appears from this letter that Locke had reacted stiffly to an earlier one in which she seems to have made some demand which he was not inclined to meet. It appears too that he had advised her against placing too much weight on their relationship — though she evidently found it hard to believe he really meant this. "My dear Atticus", she wrote,

how hard is it for you to disguise your soul and heart to one that knows it so well as I do and how ill does such grave council become your pen as you would persuade me to follow.... As I know you love me still in spite of all my follies you have over-acted the indifferent part.... Take all the peace you can possible in the assurance that I love you tenderly...and that I am certain I shall see you yet unless you take a greater care to be rid of me than to keep me.

Whether Locke replied to this letter we do not know, but their relationship was about at an end. There is no reason to think that he made any effort to "keep her", and before long she married a Richard Hawkshaw in Dublin.[62]

Besides seeing an end to Locke's relationship with Elinor, this year also saw an even closer one with Ashley in respect of his business and personal affairs. Since his mid-twenties Ashley had involved himself in overseas colonies; he had been a joint owner of a sugar plantation in Barbados; and in 1663 was one of the eight Lords Proprietors to whom Charles II granted the northeastern American colony of Carolina. The powers and rights of the Proprietors were considerable: though their charter required elected assemblies, civil and government appointments were in their hands, as was the determination of the laws and the civil structure of the colony; further, the first seven years of importation into England of various goods (silks, wines, currants, oil, and olives) were to be free of customs duties. Development of the colony had at first been rather haphazard, and unguided by the Proprietors, until Ashley moved to persuade his colleagues into greater activity, activity for which he now got Locke to act in a secretarial capacity.

In April the Proprietors began fitting out three ships with 140 prospective settlers and the goods, arms, implements, and other paraphernalia necessary for the settling, planting, and general working of the colony. In July, before the ships left, they approved a formal "Fundamental Constitutions of Carolina" to govern the colony. This specified various government positions to be filled by the Proprietors themselves; it imposed certain divisions of the land (into counties, subdivided into various hereditary baronies and land for "the people"); set up a number of supreme courts; and determined the constitution of the Parliament, which was automatically to meet every two years. There were further articles which, while specifying that freemen must "acknowledge a God; and that God is publicly and solemnly to be worshipped", tolerantly allowed that any seven or more people who agree in religion may set up their own church (though it was hoped that "Jews...and other dissenters from the purity of the christian religion" would "by good usage and persuasion...be won over to embrace and unfeignedly receive the truth". (Catholics were simply not mentioned.)[63]

Locke's first editor included the "Constitutions" as one of his works: Locke himself, Desmaizeaux said, had "presented it, as a work of his, to one of his friends, who was pleased to communicate it to me". Locke did indeed, as we will see, speak in terms which could imply that the "Constitutions" were his; but his words are consistent with his having just played a part,* albeit an actively contributory one, in its composition. This, after all, is what was said by Sir Peter Colleton, one of the Proprietors who approved the "Constitutions" and who were in any case ultimately responsible for their promulgation as their own: writing to Locke in 1673 about the progress of the colony, he referred to "that excellent form of Government in the composure of which you had so great a hand". No doubt Locke's "hand" extended to his having many unofficial discussions on the matter with Ashley, who, as the most proactive of the Proprietors, must bear initial responsibility for shaping and drawing up the "Constitutions".[64]

In fact, even Desmaizeaux did not think that Locke agreed with all of the "Constitutions". A clause added in 1670 deemed that despite the lack of religious imposition, and the freedom for a group of like-minded people to set up their own church, the Anglican Church would become the state church; and this, according to Desmaizeaux, "was not drawn up by Mr Locke; but inserted by some of the chief of the proprietors, against his judgement; as Mr Locke himself informed one of his friends". But whatever his involvement in the composition of the "Constitutions", Locke did seem to have a close attachment to it. Over the years he gave copies to friends, and just months before his death he was still interested enough for it to be a topic of discussion.[65]

Locke acted as secretary of the Lords Proprietors until 1675, arranging and keeping minutes of their meetings, summarising and taking note of official letters sent between England and Carolina, exchanging letters himself with officials in the colonies. His interest in the colony extended to devoting some thought to constructing a decimal system of coinage and measurements for it.[66]

In the summer Locke became involved in Ashley's personal affairs too when he was given responsibility for arranging the marriage of Ashley's son, now seventeen, to Lady Dorothy Manners, daughter of the Earl of Rutland. According to Ashley's grandson, a child of this marriage, his father "was too young to choose a wife for himself, and my grandfather too much in business to choose one for him", so the whole matter "was thrown upon Mr Locke, who being already so good a judge of men, my grandfather doubted not of his equal judgement in women". Locke surely did not have a completely free hand in choosing the bride and agreeing the settlement, but he obviously played an important intermediary part. Recognising both this and earlier services, Ashley wrote to him at Belvoir Castle, the Rutlands' seat in Leicestershire where the wedding was to take place, "Sir, you have in the greatest concerns of my life been so successively and prudently kind to me that it renders me eternally, your affectionate and faithful friend".[67]

Together with Ashley's son and his new wife, Locke stayed on at Belvoir after the marriage at the end of September – perhaps because Ashley, who had returned to London, had not settled where his son and new daughter-in-law were to live. But by mid-October a train of coaches and carriages, under Locke's supervision and joined by Ashley for the final leg from Luton, was on its way south. Having been informed of his friend's return to London, Thomas wrote hoping that Locke would now be free to visit him in Salisbury. He too was shortly to be married, and teasingly suggested that perhaps Locke, now the expert, could give "advice concerning wedding clothes and the fashions".[68]

Thomas referred to his wife-to-be (Honor, sister of John Greenhill, the portrait painter) as "Parthenice", a name taken from Charles Sorel's *The Extravagent Shepherd: or, the History of the Shepherd Lysis*, from where Locke and his friends, following a recent whimsical French practice, took other names. Thomas himself became known as "Adrian", Locke as "Carmelin", and James Tyrrell as "Musidore".[69]

Locke's help was also sought in getting a supply of antimony. About a month later Thomas was wanting other chemicals too, and described the preparations he had been engaged upon. If only Locke were there to join him! "If you were here, or could spend this winter a fortnight or three weeks in Sarum we might, it may be, perform some good operations."[70]

Though Locke had not needed, had not been able, to be as active as Thomas in the actual preparation of medicines, he had been giving serious thought to the subject, and during this year had worked on a manuscript entitled *De Arte Medica*. The three thousand or so words he wrote were merely the introduction to a far larger project, which he got no further than barely outlining: to consider the "present state of...medicine...in reference to diseases and their cure", and the "steps whereby it grew to that height", and how it might "be brought nearer to perfection".[71] All that Locke said about this was completely in tune with the new ideas he had begun to have about medicine since coming to London and working with Sydenham, and which he had already expressed in "Anatomie".

His introductory remarks are striking for their stress on the importance of medicine as something which can make a practical difference: "Length of life, with freedom from infirmity and pain . . . is of so great concernment to mankind that there can scarce be found any greater undertaking than the profession to cure diseases." Moreover, in the curing of disease the developing of "rules of practice" is far more important than building up a body of theory which has little practical application.[72]

Locke was clear that "rules of practice" are to be "founded upon unbiassed observation" of "the operation of nature and the event of things"; and he extended these considerations about the importance of useful knowledge and the way to acquire it beyond medicine to natural philosophy in general. The point of "knowledge of natural bodies" in general, its "end and benefit", "can be no other than the advantages and conveniences of human life"; and the way to attain these is by practical experience and observation:

The beginning and improvement of useful arts, and the assistances of human life, have all sprung from industry and observation. True knowledge grew first in the world by experience and rational operations, and, had this method been continued, and all men's thoughts been employed to add their own trials to the observation of others no question physic, as well as many other arts, had been in a far better condition than now it is.[73]

Why medicine, as a practical discipline, is less advanced than it might have been is, Locke thought, because, not content "to observe the operation of nature", "the learned men of former ages" had been inquisitive about the deeper causes of those things. They had "employed a great part of their time and thoughts in searching out the hidden causes of distempers, [and] were curious in imagining the secret workmanship of nature and the several imperceptible tools wherewith she wrought". It was plainly Locke's view that though it is natural to us to do this ("it is very agreeable to the nature of man's understanding"), nevertheless there is an objectionable pride in it. The pride lies partly in that such knowledge would not actually be useful, but also, more radically, in that we are incapable of it:

proud man, not content with that knowledge he was capable of and was useful to him, would needs penetrate into the hidden causes of things. . . . Whereas his narrow, weak faculties could reach no further than the observation and memory of some few effects produced by visible and external causes, but in a way utterly out of the reach of his apprehension, it being perhaps no absurdity to think that this great and curious fabric of the world, the workmanship of the Almighty, cannot be perfectly comprehended by any understanding but his that made it.[74]

The upshot had been that people had gone in for pointless speculation, filling the world with books and disputes:

He that thinks he came to be skilled in diseases by studying the doctrine of the humours, that the notions of obstructions and putrefaction assist him in the cure of fevers, or that by the acquaintance he has with sulphur and mercury he was led into this useful discovery that what medicines and regimen as certainly kill in the latter end of some fevers as they cure in others, may as rationally believe that his cook owes his skill in roasting and boiling to his study of the elements, and that his speculations about fire and water have taught him that the same seething liquor that boils the egg hard makes the hen tender.

Locke's plain implication is that the model for the physician should be the artisan, such as a ploughman, tanner, smith, or baker, rather than "the scholar and philosopher". Speculations

however curious and refined or seeming profound and solid, if they teach not their followers to do something either better or in a short and easier way than otherwise they could, or else lead them to the discovery of some new and useful invention, deserve not the name of knowledge, or so much as the waste time of our idle hours to be thrown away upon such empty, idle philosophy.[75]

In making these points, it should be noted, Locke had in mind not only medicine particularly, but any study of the natural world.

Along with noting features of Locke's character such as his ability to make easy conversation with all sorts and conditions of people, two of the long obituaries written by his friends would make a point of remarking on his preference for and interest in the practical knowledge of the artisan. According to one of them, "it was his peculiar art in conversation, to lead people to talk of what they understood best. With a gardener he discoursed of gardening; with a jeweller of a diamond; with a chemist of chemistry." In this way Locke

had acquired a very good insight into all the arts, of which he daily learnt more and more. He used to say, too, that the knowledge of the arts contained more true philosophy, than all those fine learned hypotheses, which, having no relation to the nature of things, are fit for nothing at the bottom, but to make men lose their time in inventing, or comprehending them. A thousand times have I admired how, by the several questions he would put to artificers, he would find out the secret of their art, which they did not understand themselves, and oftentimes give them views entirely new, which sometimes they put in practice to their profit.

According to another report, he was

alike conversable with all sorts of people, and equally pleased and profitted all; which proceeded not purely from his singular humanity, and good breeding, that taught him to accommodate himself to everyone but also from his real persuasion that he could learn something which was useful, of everybody: together with a universal love of all sorts of useful knowledge: from whence, and his custom of suiting his discourse to the understanding, and proper skill of everyone he conversed with, he had acquired so much insight into all manner of arts, or trades, as was to everybody very surprising: for a stranger might well have thought that he had made each of these matters his study, or practice: and those whose professions these things were often owned they could learn a great deal from him concerning them; and did frequently beg his direction or advice therein.[76]

There is no reason to doubt the range and flexibility of Locke's mind which is recorded here, but one wonders whether the exchange of useful information really was quite as mutual as this.

In August of the next year (1670) Locke was called upon for his medical expertise. The young Dorothy Cooper was in danger of losing not only the baby she was carrying, but also her own life; in the event the pregnancy was to continue successfully to the end of its term. The same month Locke attended Thomas Grigg, who was suffering from some kind of fever; unfortunately, despite all that Locke could do, he died.[77]

It should be no surprise that in writing to Mapletoft the previous month Locke had referred to medicine as "our profession", nor indeed that not long after that he again tried to have this formally recognised, by getting the degree of Doctor of Medicine. In November, Ashley asked the Chancellor of Oxford University to include Locke amongst the recipients of a number of honorary degrees which were to be awarded to mark a visit by the Prince of Orange. However, learning that both the Dean of Christ Church (John Fell) and the Provost of Eton (Richard Allestree) were against the award, Locke asked Ashley to withdraw the nomination.[78]

Thanks to the King's earlier dispensation from taking holy orders, Locke was perfectly secure in the tenure of his Studentship at Christ Church, but in seeking the M.D. he may have had in mind that the degree could count in his favour in the award of a medical faculty Studentship. Such an award was certainly in his mind, for, having withdrawn the nomination, Ashley asked Fell to give the next vacant faculty place to Locke.[79]

In September, Margaret Beavis (who had recently married Thomas Blomer) reminded Locke that he had promised to travel to France the following spring with the Northumberland household. His reply alarmed her, for he seems to have said that doing so would save his life. "You may easily imagine", she wrote from the Northumberland's country seat, "what my concern is when you so plainly tell me that it is France must give you life." Coming from a man "not accustomed to represent things worse than they are", this could only "create such apprehensions in me as must of necessity be very uneasy and lasting". "My dear brother", she said, "my present impatience will be to hear that your cough is abated."[80]

This is the first we have heard of Locke, now thirty-eight, being seriously troubled by a cough, though it may not have been the first episode of what was to prove to be a chronic problem, in which the cough was joined by difficulty in breathing. He was suffering from what he believed was phthisis or consumption (which seems to have killed his brother), and though in fact his problem was more probably asthma and chronic bronchitis, the notorious London air was no better for those conditions. Some notes he transcribed from Sydenham illustrate his situation. People are prone to consumption in London because

we live here in a perpetual mist, the sun not being powerful enough to dissipate the clouds. And with this mist are mixed the fumes that arise from the several trades managed here, but especially the sulphur and fumes of sea coals* with which the air is repleted, and these being sucked into our lungs and insinuating into the blood itself give an occasion to a cough.

The notes go on to describe a pattern which Locke's life came exactly to fit: "We see that people, upon the winter's coming on, returning out of the country into London presently fall a coughing, and these coughs do easily vanish the first day's journey after they leave London."[81]

Fourteen years later, at a point when the future looked bleak and uncertain, Locke would say that it was at least partly because of his "consumptive disposition" that he never pursued medicine as a profession. It "forbade me a settled abode to look after others health and gave me work enough to take care of my own". A close friend of later years similarly recorded that it was partly because of his ill-health that he never engaged in medicine professionally, "not being well able to bear the fatigue those must undergo who would bring themselves into any considerable practice". Locke also complained that living at Ashley's, in some way as his aide and secretary, had diverted him from this, which had been his original plan: "if I had spent those years I lived with him in the public practice of physic, I believe I may say without boasting, that I might have made myself another manner of establishment, than I now have". Perhaps it was simply a different slant on the same basic facts that led his later friend to say that he had no need, being able to "live at his ease" without doing so.[82]

JANUARY–SEPTEMBER 1671: "WHAT I THINK ABOUT THE HUMAN UNDERSTANDING"[83]

In February, Locke attended Ashley's daughter-in-law in the successful birth of what Ashley had all along confidently expected to be a boy. The new and excited maternal grandmother was full of "friendly droles" when she wrote to thank Locke for his help in bringing to the "noble family so hopeful an heir, that early accosts ladies in bed and manages a weapon at three days old".[84]

Dorothy Cooper's pregnancy had not been without its dramas and she later spoke of the "cough [and] heaviness of heart" she had had during it. She had previously had a miscarriage, and this "heaviness of heart" is perhaps what Locke had in mind in some notes he later made on midwifery. The fear of miscarriage, he suggested, can of itself lead to abortion: "For the mind being kept in constant apprehension of miscarriage every least occasion turns that apprehension into real fright. . . . Hence we see that amongst the poor and labouring country women not one of ten miscarry in comparison of the aborting to be found amongst people of quality."[85]

When the child, a third Anthony Ashley Cooper, was three he came under the guardianship of his grandfather, and, no doubt partly influenced by Locke, would grow up to be a moral philosopher of some significance, as witnessed by the three volumes of his *Characteristics of Men, Manners, Opinions, Times* (1711). As he reported many years later, Locke, "my friend and foster-father", was given considerable responsibility for his upbringing: "In [my] education from the earliest infancy [he] governed according to his own principles." As the eldest son, he said, "I was . . . taken by my grandfather and bred under his immediate care, Mr Locke having the absolute direction of my education."[86]

During the summer Locke worked on a manuscript he headed "Sic Cogitavit de Intellectu humano Jo: Locke an 1671": "What I think about the human understanding, John Locke, 1671. The human understanding together with the certitude of knowledge and the firmness of assent." Though the date "10 July" makes an incidental appearance in it (a date at which he was perhaps at St Giles with Ashley), the manuscript had its roots in discussions Locke had had at Exeter House earlier in the year, with James Tyrrell, David Thomas, and other friends, perhaps including Nathaniel Hodges (familiarly known as "Lysis"), an old friend from Christ Church and now Ashley's chaplain. At one of these, so Tyrrell recalled some years later, the discussion had been "about the principles of morality and revealed religion", and we might suppose from this that Locke was still concerned with some of the questions he had discussed earlier in his "Essays on the Law of Nature".

Looking back on the occasion himself, Locke later wrote that the friends "found themselves quickly at a stand, by the difficulties that rose on every side". "After we had puzzled ourselves", he said, "without coming any nearer a resolution of those doubts which perplexed us, it came into my thoughts that we took a wrong course." Rather than concerning themselves specifically and narrowly with the nature of their knowledge of morality and religion, they should first consider the wider question of the nature of the human understanding as such, in order to see just what it was capable of. It occurred to Locke, then, that "before we set ourself upon inquiries of that [narrower] nature, it was necessary to examine our own abilities, and see what objects our understandings were, or were not fitted to deal with". His friends "all readily assented...and agreed, that this should be our first inquiry". They agreed too that Locke should lead the way, and so he "set down against our next meeting" some "hasty and undigested thoughts, on a subject I had never before considered".[87]

By July these first "hasty and undigested thoughts" had grown to about three thousand words. The manuscript opened with a firm and bold suggestion about human knowledge, a suggestion from which Locke never deviated, and one which is crucially important for his subsequent place in the history of philosophy: "I imagine that all knowledge is founded on and ultimately derives itself from sense, or something analogous to it." The mind "at first it is probable to me is rasa tabula", Locke wrote, and in much of what followed he was simply embroidering and developing this central core of what became known as "empiricism".[88]

The first step in this derivation of knowledge is that "our senses...give us the simple ideas or images of things and thus we come to have ideas of heat and light, hard, soft"."Analogous to" sense is "the other fountain of all our knowledge", which is "nothing but the experience of the operations of our own minds", from which we get the ideas of thinking, believing, desiring, and so on.[89]

Locke thought of our minds as being passive in their reception of these simple ideas: "the understanding can no more refuse to have those...than a mirror can refuse [the ideas that]...the objects set before it do therein produce". Similarly, and as with a mirror, the mind cannot "produce in itself" any simple ideas.[90]

Simple ideas passively acquired in this way are the elements of complex ideas, for example the ideas of gold, the sun, or a horse. These complexes may themselves be received in sensory experience, "united mixed or coexistent from things without", but, besides this, the mind itself can actively "unite, combine, enlarge, compare, etc. these simple ideas together and thereof make new complex ones".[91]

The necessarily passive reception of simple ideas and the active construction of complex ideas out of them, means that simple ideas, or rather the words which stand for them, "are not capable of any definition", whereas those for complex ideas are, for the definition of a word, Locke's thought was, is the enumeration of the ideas composing the idea it stands for. "All the words in the world and efforts at a definition will not give a blind man any idea of black or white...those simple ideas being to be conveyed to the mind no other way but by the senses themselves."[92]

Locke went on to distinguish complex or "collected" ideas into two. Most obviously there are complex ideas of material things, both natural substances such as iron or horses (or artificial things such as watches or pistols). What Locke said about the formation of these ideas of substances and about the inclusion in them of the idea of a "substratum" would eventually involve him in considerable controversy. "The senses...find that a certain number of...simple ideas go constantly together which therefore the understanding takes to belong to one thing", and because we "cannot apprehend how they should subsist alone", we suppose they "rest and are united in some fit and common subject which being as it were the support of those sensible qualities we call substance or matter [or "substratum"]".[93]

A second kind of complex idea are "relations", the ideas we form when we "compare and consider" either one thing with "reference to" another (such as when two men are considered as "father" and "son"), or one idea with another ("whiter"), or an action with a law or rule ("so are virtues or vices, justice, temperance").[94]

Since his inquiry into the human understanding had been initiated by questions about the "principles of morality and revealed religion", Locke focused particularly on the third kind of relational idea, the ones we have of "the rectitude of actions", to show how, in accordance with his claim about the origin of knowledge, these terminate in ideas derived from sense or reflection. "To murder is willingly and with design to kill a man", and all the ideas involved here, the ideas of "thinking of a thing and purposing of it beforehand, a man, of life or a power to move and perceive of itself and some other such sensible simple ideas, and of doing some action to that man to make that power to cease", can all be reduced to simple ideas derived from observation of the world or our own minds. We then find these ideas "comprehended in this one word murder" either "to agree or disagree with something that [we] conceive to be a law" and so call murder good or bad.[95]

Though our understanding is bounded by the ideas we have from sensation, those ideas are not knowledge as such. Though knowledge is "founded" on sense and "ultimately derives itself" from there, it requires us to "join" ideas together, or "separate" them "by way of affirmation or negation". For example, we "join" the ideas of whiteness and milk when, "affirming" the one of the other, we assert that milk is white.[96]

Locke continually stressed that there is a crucial difference between "the understanding of words" and "the knowledge of things". In our use of words for various complex ideas (particularly those of substances) we may talk misleadingly and at cross-purposes, even confusedly and unintelligibly. Different people may have different complex ideas, under the same name; for a child a certain colour alone may be sufficient to make something gold, while for someone who has "oftenest and with greatest care examined" gold, many more qualities are needed. The fact that our "definitions of...words are often very imperfect" is "the foundations of great errors and disputes"; but these disputes, Locke was concerned to stress, are verbal and not real. "They are errors and disputes rather about the signification of words than the natures of things."[97]

This distinction between our words and ideas on the one hand, and things on the other, figures in a point Locke frequently made about universal propositions about substantial beings – for example that milk is white. Whether or not we have knowledge of such propositions, and what kind of knowledge it is, differs according as the idea of whiteness is or is not contained in my idea of milk. In the first case "the proposition is always true but also only verbal"; in the second the proposition is real, but "not certainly true nor have I a certain knowledge of it".[98]

Though we should not take "verbal" propositions to be other than what they are, Locke did not dismiss them out of hand; indeed, much of his discussion was devoted to knowledge of propositions whose truth depends solely on the meanings of words and the relations of ideas. There are various such cases where "we may have a certain knowledge of the connection and consequence of words, to which having affixed constant and defined signification . . . we may with great certainty join them . . . in propositions as their definitions happen to make them fit to be so joined". Some are "universal affirmative identical propositions" which affirm one idea of itself (a swallow is a swallow); some are "universal negative propositions" which deny one idea of another (two is not equal to three); finally there are affirmations where one idea "comprehends" (rather than is identical with) another, such as that milk is white, where the idea of whiteness is "contained in the definition" of milk. "Books of metaphysics, school divinity, and some sort of natural philosophy" are filled with such propositions whose truth "depends on the very nature of the ideas we have" but where, unfortunately, people not only fail to use their words "constantly and steadily in the same signification" but also make the mistake of "thinking such propositions to be about the realities of things and not the bare signification of words".[99]

In contrast to these propositions, which "only prove suppositions made in my own mind", are those about the "reality of things existing without me". Here our affirmations are based not on our own ideas but "are grounded upon the repeated exercise of our senses about that object, which we call experience and observation". There are different kinds of these propositions which "I can no other way possibly know but by my senses".[100]

There are, to begin, "particular propositions" about individual substantial things, for example, that "the milk I drink now is white". As with propositions which depend solely on our ideas, we do have certain knowledge here too – or, rather, we do as long as "our senses conversant about those particulars do or have informed us" about the colour of the milk. Of course, if, on the basis of being so "informed" by my senses, I affirm that this milk is white, I am also affirming there really is something "without my mind" which "answers to" my ideas of milk and whiteness. Locke said of an affirmation of the existence of something that "the testimony of my eyes, which are the proper and sole judges of this thing" is relied on with great certainty. He can, he said, no more doubt of the existence of the paper he was writing on than of his own existence. This is not to say that the certainty from the "testimony of our senses" is complete, but that "it is as great as our frame can attain to [and] as our condition needs". Our senses "serve to our purposes well enough"; not even a sceptic requires "greater certainty to govern his actions by".[101]

When Locke turned from these propositions about particulars, to general "instructive" propositions about the world, he found that their grounding in experience and observation was insufficient to give us certain knowledge. Indeed, he concluded, "most of those propositions we think, argue, reason, discourse, nay act upon are not evident and certain, and we cannot have undoubted knowledge of their truth". Though we have often found certain ideas going together they may, for all we know "by the testimony of [our] senses", not always do so. "If I say I know this universal proposition to be true that all loadstones will draw iron it is certainly true when I include this power of drawing iron in the very idea of the thing I call a loadstone." On the other hand, "if I say that a stone of such colour, weight, hardness . . . which usually meet in a loadstone will certainly draw iron, of this I have no certain knowledge".[102]

Besides affirmations about substantial beings, Locke also considered relational affirmations, where one thing is compared with another. Geometrical and arithmetical propositions are one sort of example here, and Locke was at least inclined to suppose them to be like instructive affirmations about substantial beings in that we make them "by constant observation of our senses especially our eyes". The three angles of a triangle have been found to be equal to two right angles "in several triangles and by nobody found in any one triangle otherwise"; similarly, it is by "repeated observations" that we find that two is greater than one, for they "always retain the same proportion whenever we compare them together". But he did not apply to them his general dogma that universal propositions are either certain but verbal, or instructive though not certain, for though based on observation he said that "we may be allowed" to have a certain knowledge of them. Exactly why this is so, why they "pass into . . . universally acknowledged truth", is not completely clear. One element in his thought was that there is something particularly compelling in the visual *comparison* of a pair of objects with a single other, or in the observed measuring of the angles of a triangle and their *comparison* with two right angles; there is a kind of visual demonstration which is absent when we simply observe the attraction of iron by a loadstone. Another element was that we can be sure, for a reason he did not bring out, that our ideas of mathematical figures, the "connection of ideas within us", will, unlike our ideas of substantial beings, "always exactly agree" with "their existing so without us".[103]

Moral affirmations are another example of relating one thing (in this case, an action) to another (a rule). As in his "Essays on the Law of Nature", Locke said that moral standards are "the rules set to our actions by the declared will of another who has power to punish"; and in order to come to a knowledge of them, we must show that there is "a law giver with power and will to reward and punish" and show "how he has declared his will and law". It is, however, an indication of how Locke's inquiry had begun to take on a life of its own that he said no more about such matters, which are the very ones which preceded and gave rise to it. For the moment, he said, and until he can find a "fit place" to speak of such things, namely "god, the law of nature and revelation", he will say only that given such rules the agreement or disagreement of an action with them "is as easily and clearly known as any other relation".[104]

From the certainty of knowledge, Locke moved on to "the several degrees and grounds" of "probability and assent, or faith". Many propositions are not certain, and we lack "undoubted knowledge of their truth"; nevertheless, Locke noted, they are not all of a piece. Some "border so near upon certainty, that we make no doubt at all of their truth", while others move "from the very neighbourhood of certainty and evidence quite down to improbability and unlikeliness even to the confines of impossibility".[105]

We might have expected that Locke would have considered here those universal propositions about substantial beings of which he said earlier we can have no certain knowledge (for example, gold is fusible, where fusibility is not part of the idea of gold). He did speak of some of these as "highly probable" and implied that their probability depended on our having observed a large number of positive, and no negative, instances. But the detail he then went into does not fit such cases and relates rather to particular propositions, as that Caesar made a speech at the battle of Munda, of which, had we been there, we would have certain knowledge. "In knowledge we first receive the impressions or sensations of the thing, and the alteration in our understanding is made by the reality of what we know", but with probability and opinion, as when I did not see and hear Caesar, "that which makes me believe is some thing extraneous to the thing I believe". Among such extrinsic considerations are the "agreeableness to our own experience" (is it our experience that generals make speeches before battles?), and the "testimony of witnesses vouching their experience".[106]

Locke inquired whether our assent to a proposition is always in proportion to the evidence for it. Rather to his dismay he quickly concluded this often is not so, and propounded an ideal of leisured, free, and impartial inquiry. Not only does "a difference of degrees in men's understandings, apprehensions, and reasoning" mean that the available evidence is not always weighed properly, but also evidence is not always collected in the first place. Some people lack "convenience or opportunity", involved as they are in "labour and enslaved to the necessities of their mean condition"; others are subject, not to a material enslavement, but to one of their understandings, by censorship: "this is generally the case of all those who live within the reach of the inquisition that great office of ignorance...where the good Catholic is to swallow down opinions as silly people do empirics' pills without knowing what they are made of or how they will work". Finally, and rather disparagingly, Locke observed that wishing not to disturb their "opinions, lives or designs" some people will not look at the available evidence ("some men will not read a letter which is suspected to bring ill news"). Others will not give it its due weight, and "will believe that to be flesh which he sees to be bread", because he has come to accept he must believe what his church teaches.[107]

Of the ideas which occurred in the course of Locke's discussion there are two which, though he did not dwell on them, would become increasingly central in his thought. One is an idea which chimes well with what he had written in "Anatomie" and *De Arte Medica* about the importance of an observational and experiential, non-theoretical approach to the natural world: though there are limits to our understanding and to what we can know, we nevertheless can know what we need to know. Our faculties, our understanding and senses, are not suited "to the extent of beings and a perfect clear comprehensive knowledge of them", but they are what "our condition needs" and "serve to our purposes well enough".[108]

The other is an idea embodied in Locke's two examples of things which lie beyond our reach: the means by which material things act on us (so as to produce sensations), and those by which they act on each other (as when a loadstone attracts iron). In what he said here he now seemed inclined to accept, along with Boyle, the Cartesian picture of the world, which he had rejected in his earlier discussion of disease, namely, that the modus operandi may in some way be mechanical. For, he quite positively said, what he would increasingly come to think, that what our senses fail to reveal to us are the shape, size, and motions of various minute particles. If we could discover these we would know how, for example, cold freezes water "as we do the way how a joiner puts several pieces of wood together to make a box or table which by tenons, nails, and pins we well enough perceive how it hangs together"; and the "motions of an animal would be as intelligible to us as those of a watch". It may be, however, that, despite the rather enthusiastic detail, Locke was simply referring to one possible account of the matter, rather than committing himself to it, for he also referred (albeit in passing) to the possibility that a sensation of whiteness is produced, not mechanically by the action of particles, but by some "essence nature or formality" of whiteness.[109]

SEPTEMBER–DECEMBER 1671: "PROFITABLE TO THE LIFE OF MAN"[110]

In the early autumn Locke's chronic cough gave him reason to get out of London. He went first to Oxford; then, in early October, to Salisbury to see Thomas, and then, after a few days there, to see Strachey in Somerset. He was so much concerned about his health that he spoke of final "farewells" and of "the solitariness of the grave". He wrote from Salisbury to Mapletoft in London that while he was in Oxford "either my constantly being abroad in the air as much as the clouds would permit, or in good company at home, made me believe I mended apace, and my cough sensibly abated". But he feared that the Salisbury air "will not be so advantageous to me; for at best I have but made a stand, if not gone backwards". He also referred, rather anxiously, to his thinness:

I must conclude my carcass to be made of a very ill composition that will not grow into good plight in fresh air...and, whilst my mind is at perfect ease in so full an enjoyment of what I most desire, methinks my body should batten [grow fatter]. What will be the issue I know not; but if I should return that burly man you speak of, I shall put nothing into your embraces you will not have a just title to.[111]

Worried for his friend, Mapletoft had arranged some "winter quarters" for him, apparently with a doctor in Montpellier in the south of France. Thanking him, Locke ruefully wrote that he would "be no more fit for that excellent person's company than if I were really taken out of the grave and however you have dressed me up to him you will use your friend the doctor little better than he that joined the living and the dead together". Towards the end of October, now at Sutton Court, Locke again thanked Mapletoft for the "concernment you express for my health, and the kindness wherewith you press my journey into France". He would soon be back in London, "and then having made you judge of my state of health, desire your advice what you think best to be done...nothing will be able to make me leave those friends I have in England but the positive direction of some of those friends for my going".[112]

Before the year was out, Locke put aside the now rather untidy manuscript concerning the human understanding on which he had worked during the summer. Under a rather grander and more formal heading, "An Essay concerning the Understanding, Knowledge, Opinion and Assent", he made a fresh start*, though sometimes with passages copied directly from the earlier draft. For some reason, work on it came to rather an abrupt halt for he stopped in mid-sentence; he stopped in mid-discussion too, just at the point where, having dealt with ideas, he was about to move on to knowledge and opinion, his set topic.

In his first draft Locke had got down to business immediately, as though in some urgency to work things out for himself; he now began with a couple of elegant scene-setting paragraphs which read as though intended for other readers. The examination of how the understanding comes by its ideas and knowledge, and how far they extend, though it will "be very pleasant" in itself, was done not just for its own sake, nor was it explained in terms of Locke's initial interest in the foundations of morality. Developing an idea of which there was just a passing hint earlier, it now explicitly set out to contribute to an understanding of what it is to be human and of our place in the world, and of how, given that we are as we are, we should most usefully and sensibly conduct ourselves in matters of inquiry, particularly as concerns action. "The understanding", he began, is that which "sets man above the rest of sensible beings, and gives him all that dominion which he has over them"; and, he continued, his chief aim in inquiring into it was "to find out those measures whereby a rational creature, put in that state which man is in in this world, may and ought to govern his opinions and actions depending thereon".[113]

One immediate advantage, Locke said, in coming to see that there are limits to our understandings is that we will be "content to sit down in a quiet ignorance of those things which upon examination we shall find to lie beyond the reach of our capacity". We will escape the pride and vanity of "not being content with that knowledge [we are] capable of" and of wilfully trying to "penetrate into the hidden causes of things".[114]

One thing that must have led Locke to make something of a fresh start was realising that his account of our ideas and knowledge as ultimately derived from sensation and reflection, should be prefaced by discussing an opposing "received opinion", "that there are in the mind of man some innate principles . . . which it receives in its very first being, and brings into the world with it". While he had recognised at the end of the earlier draft that this doctrine of innateness might be used as an objection against him, he had now decided that it should be dealt with at the outset, and at some considerable length. What he said was developed even further at a later date, and we will consider it then (pp. 226 ff. below).[115]

In this second draft Locke dwelt at greater length than before on his core idea, that all the notions we shall ever have, "all those sublime thoughts which tower above the clouds, and reach as high as heaven itself", all "take their rise and footing" from experience. Indeed, this second draft consists basically of a filling out of some parts of the framework he had earlier provided. There is, for instance, discussion of different mental faculties (retention, discerning) which deal with our ideas; and the classification of these ideas is developed by the (tentative and unemphatic) addition to "substances" and "relations" of a third sort of complex idea, "modes": ideas such as "modesty" and "gratitude", which are like many relations in having to do with "ways of our considering" things, and unlike those of substances which we "gather . . . from things as they are in themselves". Then, with the aim of illustrating how our ideas "all terminate in and are concerned

about" ideas derived from sensation or reflection, he analysed three
(time, place, and causality) which "seem to be most remote" from these
sources. His discussion of the origin of various units of measurement
certainly goes to illustrate his point, but it also illustrates the way in
which his work on human understanding had begun sometimes to
involve a digressing, away from the overall thrust of his investigation,
into a detailed treatment of topics which had simply occurred to his
lively mind as he went along.[116]

Something which Locke himself called a "digression", but which,
certainly as his thinking later developed, would become of considerable
importance, was his discussion of words. He had already said much
about words and language in the first draft but he said more here, and
made some further points. Our words for simple ideas are "perspic-
uous, determinate, clear, and distinct", but this is not so for those for
complex ideas, ideas which (particularly in the case of substances) are
collections "often very perfunctorily and heedlessly taken up...one
man's complex idea seldom agreeing with another, and often differing
from his own that he had yesterday". Such ambiguous and ill-defined
words serve us "well enough with common affairs of life and
conversation", but they often lead to disputes which are merely
verbal "wrangling about sounds". Such disputes are quite barren, yet
they are, he said (no doubt remembering his formal studies as a
student), actually encouraged by "a great part of scholastic learning".
The "learned arts of disputing" have contributed to confusing the
meaning of words and making them "more undetermined and
doubtful than they were before in ordinary conversation". In contrast
to the "artificial ignorance and learned gibberish", as he saw it, of
scholastic philosophy, Locke continually opposed the "useful arts",
knowledge which is "profitable to the life of man" and for which we
owe more to artisans, to "the illiterate and contemned mechanic", than
to "the disputing and wrangling philosophers".[117]

So far as the imperfections, the ambiguities and indeterminacies,
of the names of substances go, Locke suggested that what was needed
was some collaborative effort (no doubt with the help of artisans) to
construct complete descriptions of things, by "searching out all their
qualities and properties" – though he recognised this was more easily
said than done: it would require "a laborious and exact scrutiny into
the nature of things"; besides which, "though there is a foundation in
nature for the dividing of things into sorts and tribes", we hardly ever

know "the precise bounds, where one ends and another begins". One thing he was adamant about, however, was that words are the "invention of man", and that what they stand for are collections of sensible ideas and not, as the scholastics supposed, for substantial forms and essences from which those ideas or qualities were supposed to flow. Talk of such "forms" was pointless and empty, he thought: how would anyone decide that some matter had within it the "form of gold" except by observing in it the qualities which we had collected together?[118]

One of the early and lasting actions performed by King Charles at the Restoration had been to give a Charter to the "Royal Society of London for the Improving of Natural Knowledge". The Society had grown out of various informal and semi-formal experimental philosophy groups in Oxford and London, and in November of 1668, his second year in London, Locke had been elected and admitted as a Fellow,* joining two hundred or so others, of varying degrees of importance, from major active scientists such as Boyle, Hooke, and Lower, to merely interested virtuosi such as John Aubrey. Attendance at meetings was not recorded, but the minutes for March 1670 note his taking part in a discussion on a dog's anatomy.[119]

Much of the thinking of many in the Royal Society about the nature and acquisition of natural knowledge had a consonance with what Locke had written in "Anatomie" and *De Arte Medica* about medical knowledge specifically, and with what he now said in "de Intellectu". Many of the ideas he expressed can be found in the writings of other members of the Royal Society such as Boyle and Hooke, and in its early official *History* (1667) by Thomas Sprat: the stress that knowledge of the natural world (whether of its diseases or of its plants and minerals) is at least to be begun by compiling what were called "natural histories", by "serious diligent observation" of the overt and manifest properties and behaviour of things, rather than by theorising about the unobservable workings of nature; the suggestion that the physician and any others who seek knowledge of the natural world should model themselves on practical artisans rather than on the "the scholar and philosopher" with his a priori speculative "gibberish"; the suggestion that the gentleman natural philosopher should be like the humble artisan, the "contemned mechanic", and aim to acquire knowledge which is useful and profitable to human life; and finally, the suggestion that all of this might best be done collaboratively, by people acting in concert to carry out a programme of investigation.[120]

JANUARY 1672–NOVEMBER 1675: "THAT TETHER WHICH CERTAINLY TIES US"[121]

Locke did not take up the "winter quarters" in Montpellier which Mapletoft had fixed up for him, and he seems to have been in London over the winter, and into the spring and summer. Whether or not involvement with Ashley's business prevented his going, he certainly continued to spend time on it, not only on such mundanities as making arrangements for meetings of the Lords Proprietors of Carolina, but on more weighty matters too.[122]

In March, carrying out a secret agreement he had with the French, the King declared war against the Dutch. Just prior to this, in a move which would have got him the support of nonconformist dissenters who for the past years had been subjected to persecution, he also issued a Declaration of Indulgence, which laid aside penal laws against all nonconformists, including Catholics, though the latter were still not allowed public worship.[123]

In order to solidify support for his policy of war even further, the King gave honours to various members of the government, including a peerage to Ashley who became Earl of Shaftesbury. Ashley's elevation occasioned him to have his portrait painted by John Greenhill, which in its turn led Locke to compose some verses praising Greenhill's skill:

> In your matchless pieces may be seen,
> strength, vigour, beauty, humour, life, and mien;
> which when we view, and sadly find that they,
> are than ourselves, less subject to decay;
> we think ourselves, the shadows that do fade,
> and should be lost, but for your timely aid.[124]

At the beginning of September the Lords Proprietors of Carolina, who two years earlier had been given the Bahamas by the King, made a grant of land on New Providence to a "Company of Adventurers", with a view that they would organise trade between there and England. Locke subscribed £100 towards the required £1600 (shortly afterwards taking over the interest which Mapletoft had bought). Some months later Sir Peter Colleton, the deputy-governor of Barbados, told Locke he thought the trade "will turn to account", but advised that, not being on the spot, he should not get involved in planting. About two and a half years later Locke sold much of his stock, at a 27 per cent profit.[125]

A further colonial enterprise, in which Locke became involved towards the end of the month, was by way of an investment of £400 in the Royal African Company, a reconstituted company whose trade partly consisted in the transport of slaves from the Gold Coast for sale in the West Indies and by whose new charter Locke was incorporated as a "Trader and Adventurer".*[126]

Shortly after the first meeting of the Bahaman adventurers in September, Locke was able to leave London for France with members of the Northumberland household. In inviting him, Lady Northumberland, no doubt advised by Mapletoft, seems to have been concerned for Locke's health. After a stay of two or three weeks in Paris, Locke returned to London whilst the others travelled on south for the winter.[127]

Short as his time away had been, it had done his lungs some good, and had elevated his spirits even more. The excited delight of a letter to Strachey in rural Somerset from "your quondam friend John, now fashionable Monsieur John" shows some uncertainty whether to scoff at French modishness or to be self-congratulatory at being a man of the world. You are, he told Strachey, about

to be beatified by the refined conversation of a man that... can tell you which side of his two-handed hat ought to be turned up, and which only supported with an audace. I fear you have the unpardonable ignorance not to know what an audace is; to oblige you then, know that what an untravelled Englishman would take to be a piece of ordinary loop lace made use of to support the overgrown brims of a flapping hat has by the virtuosos and accomplished gallants of Paris, when I was there, been decreed to be an audace.... You see what a blessing it is to visit foreign countries and improve in the knowledge of man and manners.

You could not, he said, have learnt this at Sutton Court, "but now I have ... enriched your understanding ... let it not make you proud, that belongs to us only that have taken pains and gone a great way for it". Later in the letter Locke ruefully remarked that if the French air had "given me but half so much health as it has vanity, I shall quickly be as strong as I am now conceited. I only wish this puffing up would make me in truth more bulky."[128]

These of course were immediate reactions to the surface of things, and before he was much older and with a deeper experience of the country, Locke would say that he was not much of a lover of French fashions.[129] Even this brief visit showed him things of which he disapproved, and with its acidic humour about foreign ways, particularly about religious practices, the letter is reminiscent of those he wrote Strachey from Cleves on his first visit abroad. In a reference to the religious houses he saw in Paris he said, "I saw there men that had forsaken the world and women that professed retirement and had poverty [who] have yet in the ornaments of their buildings and the hatchments of their trinkets all the mighty riches exquisite art could produce."

He would have liked to spend the whole winter away with the Northumberland entourage; his early return was out of duty. "You know", he wrote to Mapletoft, "that our journey as well as pilgrimage in this world have their settled bounds, and none of us can go beyond the extent of that tether, which certainly ties us." Clearly, at the other end of the tether was the newly enobled Earl of Shaftesbury, and Locke (who now had his own private colonial interests) was soon assisting him in his work with a new Council of Trade and Plantations which he had been instrumental in forming. Shaftesbury had been made the Council's President (an appointment which enabled him, from an official position, to see to his personal overseas business investments).[130]

Shortly afterwards, in November, Shaftesbury rose even further, when the King promoted him to the position of Lord Chancellor, making him the most powerful minister in the government. This in itself would have increased any work Locke was informally involved in with Shaftesbury, but in addition to that his patron had him appointed Secretary of Presentations – a post (with a salary of £300 a year) which involved the supervision of all ecclesiastical matters that came under the Lord Chancellor's remit, including the bestowal of various ecclesiastical benefices. As a result of Shaftesbury's patronage, Locke was now in a position to bestow some himself. He soon thought of trying to do something for Thomas Blomer and was involved the following year in the appointment of Hodges to prebends at Norwich and Gloucester cathedrals.[131]

"The confusion and disorder of new affairs" with Shaftesbury, to which Locke, as "a man not versed in the world", was now exposed meant that he was unable to keep up his interests in medicine and natural philosophy as much as he would have liked, as he wrote to Mapletoft (now in Aix): "Dr Sydenham and I mention you sometimes, for we do not now meet often, my business now allowing me but little leisure for visits; but I hope I shall in a short space bring it to better terms." The minutes of the Royal Society also show that his time for such interests was limited: at a meeting early in November he had reported making some experiments with the attractive powers of a sulphur ball and "promised that he would bring it to the society at the next meeting". But though he was there the following week he "excused himself, that he had forgot it, promising to bring it at the next". He seems not to have done this, and perhaps he was over-estimating what he had time for: that same month he allowed himself to be elected (for the second time) to the Society's council and was at the meeting in December when he was sworn in, but he never attended the council during his year of office. It was perhaps due to his involvement with Shaftesbury's "new affairs" both that a journey to New England was projected around this time and that it came to nothing.[132]

Conscious of his new importance as Lord Chancellor, Shaftesbury wanted somewhere grander than Exeter House for his London home. Locke sounded out the possibility of taking over Northumberland House, but in the end Shaftesbury decided on leasing more rooms in Exeter House and on making some alterations* there.[133]

When, after a break of nearly two years, Parliament reassembled in February 1673, Shaftesbury was required to present a justification of the government's recent policies. In what was one of the most famous speeches of his career he sought Parliamentary support for the Declaration of Indulgence and, particularly, for the war against Holland. Unknown to Shaftesbury, what lay behind these policies was the secret Treaty of Dover of 1670 into which Charles had entered, with the encouragement of some of his advisers and his brother James who, like himself, was leaning towards Catholicism. "Being convinced of the truth of the Roman Catholic Religion", as the Treaty read, Charles had agreed with Louis XIV that, with French financial support and when the state of the country seemed right, he would declare himself a Catholic and restore England as a Catholic country; and that France and England would then jointly declare war on the Dutch. All that was known to Shaftesbury and others who were not privy to Charles's full intention had been the agreement with France for war against the Dutch. Moreover, though the relief which Charles's Declaration of Indulgence offered to Protestant dissent was welcome to Shaftesbury, he did not know that its explicit mention of Catholic recusants was a small move towards the Catholicization which Charles had secretly agreed with Louis.[134]

As Lord Chancellor, Shaftesbury served as "the King's mouth" and had to "speak the King's sense", and, according to his grandson's later account, he did not wholly approve of the words he uttered: the speech as first written and as seen by Locke, became, as it passed through the King's council, "very different, and...was altered". He said that Shaftesbury's "concern and trouble" about this had been so strong that, despite his usual facility, he had to call on Locke to help him out when he delivered the speech, "to stand at his elbow, with the written copy, to prompt him in the case of failure in his repetition". No doubt when Shaftesbury later came to realise something of what had lain behind the King's policies he regretted his earlier support for them, but there is no unbiased reason to think that his speech did not represent his view at the time and that the alterations which were made to it were other than minor.[135]

In the event, the King was forced to abandon the Declaration: on the one side by bishops who supported penalties for dissent, and on the other by parliamentarians who objected to the King using his prerogative in this matter. Though against the *King's* suspending the penal laws, the Commons was in favour of toleration for Protestant dissent and tried to introduce a Bill to that effect. The prorogation of Parliament at the end of March interfered with this, but not with a Test Act which banned from public office any who would not take the sacrament in the Church of England and declare a disbelief in transubstantiation. This Act had arisen partly out of an increasing worry in the country about the growth of Popery; it certainly revealed that James, the heir to the throne, had by now converted to Catholicism, for it led him to step down as Lord High Admiral.[136]

In August or early September, after three months of "great rains, that produced greater floods than were known in the memory of man", Locke was able visit Strachey at Sutton Court. A visit to Somerset was hardly as ambitious as one to New England, but any journey at all out of London became yet more difficult when in the second half of the year Locke took on more work for Shaftesbury, this time in a more public role. The Secretary of the Council of Trade and Plantations, Benjamin Worsley, a dissenter, was another casualty of the Test Act; and in October, Locke was sworn in in his place, at an annual salary of £500, taking on further responsibility the next month as Treasurer (at £100 a year). Many of his letters in this and the following year are witness to his involvement with both the Council and the Lords Proprietors of Carolina, and also to his own interest in the Bahamas.[137]

Thanks to his association with Shaftesbury, Locke now held two official posts, but he was not to remain in them both for long. Like others, Shaftesbury had begun to suspect that something lay behind Charles's foreign policy and the French alliance; he had begun to see political dangers in James's Catholicism and openly to oppose him. For his part he was suspected by the King of planning to get Parliament to break the alliance and to end the war, and, pressed by James, the King decided to do without him. In November he dismissed him as Lord Chancellor together with all that went with that, including his appointment of Locke as Secretary for Presentations.[138]

But Shaftesbury's and Locke's work with the Council of Trade and Plantations continued (into the following year, when the Council ceased work and was eventually formally dissolved); and in November, Shaftesbury was responsible for setting up and chairing a sub-committee, one of whose tasks was to look into the desirability of setting the interest rate at 4 per cent. In the six years since he had composed his manuscript on the interest rate Locke had continued to think about economic matters, but it was no doubt as a result of Shafestbury's involvement with this committee that early in 1674 he took out the manuscript for some further work.[139] One of the more substantial of the amendments and additions he made related to international exchange rates. These depend, he argued, partly on the extent to which the ratio of national wealth in relation to domestic trade differs between two countries, and partly on the balance of trade between them.

With the Council of Trade about to be dissolved, Locke stood to lose a £600 annual income. "I am sorry you are like to fare so ill in your place", Shaftesbury told him; and it was with this at least partly in mind that he arranged for Locke to receive a £100 annuity, "for I would leave you free from care, and think of living long and at ease". This was not an outright gift, for Locke himself paid for the security of the annuity (the ninety-nine-year lease of a farm on Shaftesbury's Dorset estate), but it was sold him for the very favourable amount of £700.[140]

Towards the end of the year (1674) Locke was suffering some "distemper" which was not responding to treatment. Sydenham was not surprised: he thought Locke was simply overworked and run down, "broken with business", and "disquieted" due to his age (forty-two), his chronic ill-health, and the approach of winter. He advised him to take it easy, "cherish yourself as much as you possibly can": "bed very early at night at eight", and adopt a simple, plain, and easily digestible diet.[141]

Despite his now having become a secretary and adviser to Shaftesbury, Locke still had his interests in medicine and seems to have seen his long-term future as still lying there. In early February (1675) the university granted him grace to supplicate for the degree of Bachelor of Medicine, which was duly awarded. It then granted the new "Medicinae Baccalaureo" a licence to practise medicine, and, most importantly, Christ Church appointed him to the faculty Studentship which he had long wanted, the first vacancy since Shaftesbury had petitioned in 1670 that he be appointed to the next one. This was not entirely to the satisfaction of everyone in the college: "Locke has wriggled into Ireland's faculty place, and intends [in July] to proceed Doctor in Physic", Humphrey Prideaux reported.[142]

Perhaps Locke had sought the M.B. degree so as to be more formally fitted for appointment to a medical Studentship. But now that that appointment had been made there was no longer any material point in aiming for the Doctor of Medicine degree.* A faculty Studentship could be held for life, entirely free of any pressure to enter holy orders (in any case a requirement from which he had of course been dispensed in 1666), and if he wished to practise medicine he had the licence to do so.

For some time in the autumn Locke was with Shaftesbury at St Giles. They may well have discussed, if not begun to compose together, a lengthy propaganda pamphlet, *A Letter from a Person of Quality, to his Friend in the Country*. In an account of recent and not so recent political events, the *Letter* portrayed Thomas Danby (who had displaced Shaftesbury as the King's chief minister) as attempting to revive a High Church Cavalier party: it argued that there was a movement (in which the King himself was not necessarily directly implicated) to "declare the government absolute and arbitrary; and allow monarchy, as well as episcopacy, to be jure divino, and not to be bounded or limited by any human laws"; it argued that there was a "resolve to take away the power and opportunity of parliaments to alter any thing in church or state; only leave them as an instrument to raise money, and

to pass such laws as the court and church shall have a mind to";
it argued against the Act of Uniformity and defended the Declaration
of Indulgence. It was anonymously published and on sale at the
beginning of November, when it was immediately condemned by the
Lords, who ordered it to be burnt, and set up a committee to discover
who had had it printed.[143]

For some years the *Letter* was attributed to Locke, but when his first
editor included it in a posthumous collection of his works he said only
that Shaftesbury "desired Mr Locke to draw up this relation; which he
did under his lordship's inspection, and only committed to writing
what my lord Shaftesbury did in a manner dictate to him". It is in fact
uncertain who composed the pamphlet, but at the very least it was done
in some collaboration with and probably with the help of
Shaftesbury.[144]

Four days after the Lords ordered the *Letter* to be burnt, Locke left
for France. A quarter of a century later, Shaftesbury's grandson would
connect the two events. Remarking that Locke's chronic ill-health
"served as a very just excuse", he explained Locke's departure in terms
of the publication of the *Letter*:

When my grandfather quitted the Court and began to be in danger from it,
Mr Locke now shared with him in dangers as before in honours and
advantages. He entrusted him with his secretest negotiations, and made use of
his assistant pen in matters that nearly concerned the State, and were fit to be
made public to raise that spirit in the nation which was necessary against the
prevailing Popish Party. It was for something of this kind that got air, and out of
a great tenderness for Mr Locke, that my grandfather, in the year 1674 [*sic*
1675], sent him abroad to travel.[145]

The suggestion that Locke's departure was connected with the
reaction to the *Letter* cannot be right, for it was planned before the
Letter was published. The fact is that if Locke's health was an "excuse",
then it was indeed a "very just one". Even if Shaftesbury's having
"quitted the Court" gave Locke the opportunity, there is every reason
to think that he went for nothing more than his health: the extent to
which it was mentioned far exceeded any need there could have been
to use it as a cover. In November his uncle Peter, who had had the sad
news "of the return of your cough", prayed "the Lord give good
success in your intended voyage or journey into France in order to your
health". The "just excuse" continued to figure, not only in correspondence from those who were in the know, but also in Locke's immediate
movements in France. Not long after his arrival there, Shaftesbury's

steward, Thomas Stringer, wrote that "your friends here are mightily concerned for your welfare, and desire to see you return in perfect health"; moreover Locke's condition certainly explains the fact that Montpellier in the south of France was his specific destination. The climate of its area was generally recognised as being beneficial for pulmonary consumption, or phthisis, the wasting disease which Locke believed he had; an added attraction was the location in Montpellier of a renowned medical school.[146]

4

France (November 1675–May 1679)

Locke would be in France for three and half years. He had not intended this when he left, though he had thought he would be away long enough to make it necessary and worthwhile, in early November, to put a number of carefully listed articles (including his weather-recording instruments and, ironically, "a large map of France") into the keeping of the Christ Church chaplain; to inventory the furniture in his rooms (which, though free to him, he was able to sublet for £2 10s a quarter); and to inform the Dean of his intended absence (on the grounds of health, and during which he continued to receive a college stipend of about £80 a quarter).[1]

Once these matters were settled Locke returned to London. Here, on 12 November, the day he took a boat down river to Gravesend to embark for France, he made a list of the things (from "one scrutoir" and "a trunk with drawers" down to "three handkerchiefs") he was leaving at Exeter House.[2]

Having set sail on the evening tide, he reached Calais two days later. With him was George Walls, an Oxford friend about fourteen years his junior, who had been his pupil at Christ Church and who was now a clerical student there. Their journey had been a matter of some gossip in the college. Humphrey Prideaux, the college librarian, told a friend, "George Walls goes to London...in order to a journey into France. What is his business there I know not, unless it be to be Dr John Locke's chaplain, whom he accompanies thither." On the passage to France, Locke and Walls had "the happiness of my Lord

Ambassador's protection", for they had been invited to sail with the party of John Berkeley, incidentally one of the Lords Proprietors of Carolina, who was going to Paris as the English ambassador.[3]

During the eleven days' ride to Paris, Locke passed an unpleasant night at Poix, for the beds "seemed to be ordained for antidotes for sleep". The problem was not their hardness, which "is a quality I like", but rather their smell, which was tolerable only because "a large, convenient hole in the wall at my bed's head powered in plenty of fresh air". Things were far better at Tillart where, in one of the very few instances he ever recorded, Locke felt some susceptibility to a female face. There were "clean sheets of the country, and a pretty girl to lay them on". Do not wonder, he wrote back to England, "that a man of my constitution and gravity mention to you a handsome face amongst his remarks, for I imagine that a traveller, though he carries a cough with him, goes not yet out of his way when he takes notice of strange and extraordinary things".[4]

Of his short stay of ten days in Paris, Locke recorded not much more than that "the greatest part of the people had colds as they had in England when we left", and that he visited the then almost completed military hospital, Les Invalides, "a magnificent building" which moved him to make the pedestrian note, "length of front 320 of my paces".[5] From Paris he and Walls set out on what was to be for Locke the first of two circuitous tours:* down to Montpellier, where he stayed for fifteen months before returning north in 1677. (The second tour, again as far south as Montpellier, occupied the summer and autumn of 1678.)

In France, Locke recorded his daily experiences, observations, and thoughts in a series of journals written on plain pages bound with a printed almanac for the year. (The series would continue until the year of his death, though the initially sometimes quite lengthy entries would become sparser and shorter over the years. In Locke's systematic way these journals often have cross-references to other of his note-books, and his rather random daily jottings often formed the basis of a letter back to England, or were copied into other more focused places.

One of the journals contains an account of some very general heads under which Locke thought that notes should be made and arranged. He was thinking at the time of his extensive *reading*, but the account gives some insight into the interests underlying the huge amount of disparate material he recorded in France, partly from reading but largely from *observation*. There are four "principal parts or heads of things to be taken notice of": "the knowledge of things, their essence and nature, properties, causes and consequences of such species, which I call philosophica"; "history wherein it being both impossible in itself, and useless also to us to remember every particular I think the most useful to observe the opinions we find amongst mankind concerning god, religion, and morality and the rules they have made to themselves or practise has established in any of these matters... or things that are commanded, forbidden, or permitted by their municipal laws in order to civil society"; "what things we find amongst other people fit for our imitation, whether politic or private wisdom. Any arts conducing to the convenience of life"; and "any natural productions that may be transplanted into our countries or commodities which may be an advantageous commerce".[6]

There is much in the journals he kept in France that might be arranged under "Philosophica", the first of these four heads. Often, of course, this reflects Locke's interest in medicine and pharmaceutical recipes, but also there is information concerning the cabinet collections of natural history specimens and other curios shown him by various people, and there are daily records of the wind strength and direction, and of hygrometer readings. There are, too, the frequent comments he makes on flora and (though, curiously, hardly ever) fauna (the birds in one rare entry are caged).

Under "History" might be put the details of the circumstances and facts relating to religious belief and practice which he recorded: the number of Protestants in various areas of Catholic France, the condition of Jews, local ecclesiastical government and affairs, details of churches, monasteries and convents, and of life in them. Though the Edict of Nantes officially accorded French Protestants some protective toleration, this was hardly complete and was in any case gradually being eroded under Louis XIV, as Locke from time to time noted: a Protestant hospital confiscated; Protestants banned from civic office; churches demolished (one on the grounds that the Protestant psalm singing "disturbed the service" in the nearby Catholic church); Protestant ministers forbidden to teach classes of more than two. Naturally Locke was interested in whether such discouragements led Protestants to convert, and there was mixed evidence about this. At Nîmes he noted that not many of them "go over", and was told elsewhere that numbers remained pretty constant; on the other hand he was told that "the number of Protestants within these twenty or thirty last years are manifestly increased and do daily, notwithstanding their loss everyday of something, some privilege or other". Despite all of this, Locke had only one occasion to note that some Protestants had complained to officials about not having what security the Edict supposedly guaranteed them; in Montpellier, at least, it seems that on a personal level and aside from government persecution, and the behaviour of the Catholic clergy towards them, Protestants and "papist laity live together friendly enough in these parts".[7]

Locke's attitude towards Catholicism, particularly its clergy, is usually disparaging, as when he notes the use of images of God, the displays of saintly relics, and, particularly, the behaviour of the clergy (the "mistress in the town" and the "very fine boys" in the train of a cardinal being recorded in shorthand).[8]

Under the two heads of "History" and that of "politic wisdom" could go the mass of information Locke recorded about the various structures of local government he encountered in different places, the kinds and levels of taxes levied, the wages earned, and the cost of various goods. Perhaps this would be the place too for the frequent detail about regional systems of weights and measures, and of coinage. (Lengths are sometimes converted into "grys" and "philosophical feet", units in a system of decimal measurement* he was developing.)[9]

There is much in the journals relevant to "arts conducing to the conveniences of life" and "natural productions and commodities". The descriptions of the countryside, villages, and towns through which Locke passed typically embody notes (sometimes running to two or three thousand words) on the local, mainly rural, industry and economy: winemaking, olive oil production, rearing of silkworms and silk-making, sea-salt recovery, production of soap, wax, turpentine, and verdigris. There are frequent notes concerning the appearance of the agricultural workers, their methods, their tools and implements, the fertility or otherwise of the soil, and the crops; and there are records of methods of food preparation, in one case for a green salad with over twenty ingredients.[10]

As for the fourth head for note-taking, Locke continually had in mind "natural productions that may be transplanted into our countries"; the cultivation of olives, grapes, and other fruit such as plums and oranges, always caught his attention. This interest was both encouraged by and partly on behalf of Shaftesbury, who provided him with lists of trees, cuttings, and seeds he wanted. They were destined partly for Shaftesbury's own gardens in Dorset, but the plantations in Carolina were quite prominent in Locke's mind. Entries made at Bordeaux and in the Loire valley read, "Prunelles Q. How to cure them and take order to have three trees sent to England by first opportunity and the like for anything else that may be fit for Carolina, particularly their little fig of Provence", and, again, "Loire: Q. What fruits good there for Carolina or England particularly the plumbs of Tours, prunes de St Margaret."[11]

But some place would remain to be found for references to the various odd sights which caught Locke's eye and which he thought worth noting ("a flock of sheep following the shepherd apace in the highway"; "a company of women riding out of town, most on asses, some behind men on horses, some with their faces to the far side"); for the observations and measurements of antiquities and grand houses; and for the old wives' tales he records and (often) appears to give credence to ("Query. Whether as they say here linen washed in the old of the moon will be stiffer than what is washed in the new").[12]

Locke's journals also tell us of his various modes of travel through France. Often it was on horseback (daily distances up to ten leagues, or thirty English miles), sometimes in the company of a local carrier or "messager" (taking goods from one place to another on a given route), sometimes with a specially engaged "voiturin" who accompanied them as a guide, arranged for food and lodging along the way, and returned after a few days, with the horses, to his place of origin. Sometimes it was by public "diligences", coaches drawn by eight horses, travel by which (up to fifty miles a day) could involve being on the road by four in the morning, and journeying on for an hour or two after the evening meal. Sometimes it was by river boat (up to thirty miles or more a day), which might be privately engaged along with a waterman, or might be public (perhaps run in an organised way in conjunction with a coach). On one occasion, "fearing the heat", Locke and a companion hired a litter.[13]

Locke and Walls left Paris in mid-December; five days' travel by public coach took them to Chalon. (On the way he noted, and recorded in shorthand, that each night two of his fellow travellers, an "abbé and a woman lay in the same chamber".) At Chalon they transferred to a boat which, over two days, went down the Saône to Lyon. "The passage ... was very easy and convenient and the river very quiet", so much so that they spent some time playing cards ("doubles"), "at which I having won the French were willing to avoid paying".[14]

Some years later a friend said that Locke would only ever play cards "out of complaisance": "Although being often in company with those who used it, he could play very well, if he set about it. But he would never propose it, for he said it was but an amusement for those who wanted conversation." And in fact on this occasion on the Saône it was probably *he* that "wanted conversation", for lack of French; for only a few days later, while looking at a "closet", or cabinet of curiosities, his interest was thwarted by the collector "having not Latin nor I French". It is quite likely that he was already in the process of remedying the situation by reading in French a chapter of the New Testament each day, a method which he recommended as the best way to learn a language. Within three weeks he had taken further steps, for, he recorded early on in the new year, "This day I got a French master who was to teach Mr Walls and me one hour per diem five days in the week at four crowns per month". Even so, his Latin continued to be of use, for Monsieur Pasty's instructions and Locke's notes on the lessons were in Latin.[15]

In Lyon, Locke and Walls visited two Englishmen, one of whom, William Charleton, became a friend for life. He was a keen collector, particularly of coins and natural history specimens, and the results of his enthusiasm, which Locke encouraged, would eventually form a part of the British Museum. Together they examined an extensive collection of "pretty curiosities" got together by "an old, morose, half-mad gent". Locke thought some of the items "tricks rather than experiments", but did find two things that "were of use" — devices for perspectival drawing. He showed the same utilitarian seriousness in his attitude to the cathedral clock: what people "most looked at" in it were the movements of various mechanical models (a dove, an angel, the Virgin), but these were "of least moment, there being other things far more considerable in it", such as "the place of the sun, the dominical letter, epact, golden number, moveable feasts, etc".[16]

After a few days in Lyon, Locke, Walls, and now Charleton, rode southward down the Rhône valley to Avignon, which they reached on the last day of the year. The next day ("so warm that we dined without fire with the windows open") was spent looking round the town — churches, papal palace, and Jewish quarter ("the nastiest and most stinking [place] that ever I was yet in, and they all clad like beggers, though we were told some of them were rich"). On the second day of the new year they crossed the Rhône and rode southwest to Nîmes, where the remains of a Roman amphitheatre and aqueduct took up all of Locke's attention: he evidently spent a considerable time measuring them (sometimes using "my sword, which was near about a philosophical yard long") in great detail.[17]

JANUARY 1676—MARCH 1677: MONTPELLIER

Locke and his companions arrived at Montpellier late on 4 January. How long he expected or intended to stay is not clear. Towards the end of February, Exeter House seems to have been expecting him back "in a little time", and at the end of June, Anna Grigg reported that Stringer had told her he was "returning" (but she may have meant "to Paris", for Stringer was intending to meet Locke there).[18] In the event he stayed fifteen months in the south of France, until March of the following year.

Based in Montpellier, Locke spent time exploring the region. On a couple of occasions in March he went for some days to the west (Frontignan, Sète, Aigues-Mortes, Peccais); a large part of April was devoted to a more extensive tour of Provence to the east (Arles, Marseilles, Toulon, Hyères, Aix, Avignon, Tarascon); and, to shelter from the summer heat, he removed for two to three months at the end of June to a farm in the nearby village of Celleneuve. ("Began with my barber of Celleneuve" he recorded on 28 June.)

Locke's medical and pharmaceutical interests are a continual presence in his journals during this period, whether in records of discussions at Aix with Dr Claude Brouchier (to whom he was directed by Mapletoft), or in a recipe for haemorrhoids given him by Madame Michard, the farmer's wife in Celleneuve. Indeed, one attraction of Montpellier was the concentration of doctors to be found there. Many of these were connected with the university and medical school, though (apart from the "physic garden") Locke seems not to have got much from these institutionally: disputations he attended at the school struck him as containing "much French, hard Latin, little logic, and little reason", and "great violence of Latin and French, grimace and hand". In fact the doctors with whom Locke seems to have had most contact were two who, as Protestants, were not eligible for posts at the university: Pierre Magnol and Charles Barbeyrac (whose pupil Sydenham had been), from whom Locke took extensive case notes, and accounts of various operations and remedies.[19]

Locke was himself consulted about the health of two English travellers, Sir John and Lady Chicheley, and he had his own health to consider too. Shortly after his arrival in Montpellier he had written for advice to Mapletoft, who then consulted with Sydenham. Sydenham advised that the "main stress" of Locke's cure would be in the change involved by his eating the local diet, without which not much was to be expected from the Montpellier air. Unfortunately, during the first three or so months there his cough got worse, though by May he had reported back to England that he had recovered considerably; by the end of the year his health was still on the increase, even if not perfect. He was not, it appears, alone: at the beginning of November he recorded "as much coughing at church as ever I heard in London".[20]

Besides the Chicheleys, Locke met other English people in Montpellier. One, in particular, was Thomas Herbert, a young man of twenty who, as Earl of Pembroke (1683), would become an influential patron and friend; he grew into a man of some learning with an interest in ideas whose discussion he encouraged.[21]

The summer months that Locke spent at the farm at Celleneuve provided considerable time for study and thought. One thing he seems to have been engaged upon was a biblical concordance. Besides this, he was also thinking about a number of topics which had, or would come to have, a relation to the investigations he had started five years earlier into the nature of the understanding: the distinction between simple and complex ideas, extension and space, and faith and reason.[22]

This last topic would become increasingly important in Locke's thinking about our understanding and the limits to our knowledge. What concerned him was where the boundary between faith and reason lay. There are cases, he saw, where, due to lack or imperfection of our ideas, we cannot reach knowledge by the use of reason; for example, our limited ideas about the operations of God and of our minds do not allow us to decide questions of predestination and free will. In such cases, to which "reason, acting upon our natural ideas, cannot reach", we may have to rely on "faith and revelation". Having noted that we can have no faith in revelation any further than we know it is genuine, he pointed out that a supposed revelation cannot be genuine if it contradicts what we already know, for "God, the bountiful author of our being", would not "overturn all our principles and foundations of knowledge, [and] render all our faculties useless" in this way. But to say that faith and reason cannot be in opposition, is not to say that a genuine revelation, as from the Holy Scriptures, might not inform us concerning "matters above our reason", matters about which our reason simply cannot decide. Indeed, he concluded, it is here, in the distinction between matters of reason and matters above reason, where the boundary of faith and reason lies.[23]

Locke applied this conclusion, that reason can never be opposed to faith and genuine revelation, to the case of transubstantiation, a doctrine which is based on a certain interpretation of revealed truth. "All the principles of our knowledge, all the evidence of sense" do not permit us to believe that the consecrated Host is not bread but flesh:

It is a thing we exercise our senses and knowledge on and not our faith, and so clear that there is not room to doubt. For the reality and essence of bread being in respect of us nothing but a collection of several simple ideas, which make us know it, distinguish it from flesh, and call it bread, it is as impossible for a man, where he finds that complex idea to know it to be flesh or receive it to be such, as it is to believe himself a loaf.

Locke's thought here was not that it is contrary to reason that God might perform miracles; he was not saying that, as they are above reason, no faith is to be had in miracles. Indeed, unless we used the principles of our knowledge and understanding to rule out that the consecrated Host is not really bread, we would be ruling out that there could be any genuine miracles which are above reason. We would be ruling out that

God work a miracle to convince [us] of anything that indeed was a real transubstantiation and like the other of God's miracles, which always, by addressing themselves to the senses...confirmed some doctrines of faith, but never, beginning at the other end, made use of invisible miracles to destroy the testimony of our senses, overturn all our knowledge, and confound all measures of faith and reason.[24]

Faith and reason, then, are never opposed, Locke concluded. The province of faith and of biblical revelation begins where our sense and reason fail us "in the discovery of many truths necessary for us to know...[for] our salvation". That Christ died to save us is one such case, being something which "reason tracing its own ideas...would never arrive at".[25]

Locke also noted down some thoughts about atheism. He could not accept that an unbiased mind could, given all the available proofs, fail to find the existence of God more probable than not. But even if "the seeming probability lay on the atheist's side", the different consequences of the two opinions were very different, and anyone "who would pass for a rational creature...[and] has the least care or kindness for himself" should be clear which opinion to opt for. "Infinite misery...will certainly overtake the atheist" if he is wrong, whereas even if the believer is wrong and fails to achieve "everlasting happiness", the worst that can happen to him is "eternal insensibility".[26]

Locke's mind turned also to less weighty things, such as spelling reform. The words "to, too, two" have the same pronunciation but a different spelling, while in the words "gin, begin" the same characters are pronounced differently. Remarking that he had long thought "that things ought to be regulated by their ends", he noted that since "letters are but the lasting marks of sounds" it would be far better if we brought "our spelling nearer to our pronounciation". This would, he acknowledged, mean losing the etymologies of some words, "the marks of their pedigrees", but this might not be an entirely bad thing. It would put an end to arguments about the meanings of various words in ancient documents, and release us for the more useful search "into the inside and truth of things". The symbols in Locke's system of shorthand represent the sound rather than the spelling of a word, and it was suggested by Wolfgang von Leyden, to whom we owe our understanding of that system, that there is a connection between Locke's use of shorthand and his interest in phonetical spelling.[27]

A further thing to which Locke devoted his solitary hours at Celleneuve, at least partly as "a not unprofitable way of improving my French", was translating into English three essays from Pierre Nicole's *Essais de morale* (1671), "On the existence of God", "On the weakness of man", and "On the way of preserving peace". He later presented them to Lady Shaftesbury:

It was a bold thing for one that had but begun to learn French to attempt a translation out of it... [but] since one is allowed to bring vanity with one out of France, and with confidence to present as marks of respect at home any toys one has picked up abroad, I now have to make use of my privilege of a traveller, and to offer to your ladyship a new French production in a dress of my own making.[28]

Early in February, Locke composed in his journal a long note which again addressed the topic which had first concerned him in 1671 in his first writings on the human understanding, the "extent and measure" of knowledge. In doing so it developed and expanded on ideas the seeds of which were present earlier: ideas which had just begun to set what at first might have seemed to be a quite narrow and restricted project against the background of a larger religious and moral vision of mankind, a view of the meaning of our lives and our relation to God.

The note began with the firm thought that there are some things which we cannot know, some things into which our understandings and faculties cannot penetrate: "our minds are not made as large as truth nor suited to the whole extent of things". This, however, is no reason for despair; it ought not to "discourage our endeavours in the search of truth or make us think we are incapable of knowing anything because we cannot fully understand all things". There are things we can know, and these, thanks to God's goodness, are just those things we need to know. The faculties "we are sent out into the world furnished with" are perfectly sufficient and adequate so long as we confine our search "within those purposes and direct it to those ends which the constitution of our nature and the circumstances of our being point out to us".[29]

Our condition on earth necessitates food, drink, clothing, shelter, and medicine, and so "one large field for knowledge proper" is what is "for the use and advantage of men in this world". We should seek ways "to shorten or ease our labours ... or procure new and beneficial productions whereby ... things useful for the conveniencies of our life may be increased or better preserved". Our minds are suited to such investigations even though "perhaps the essence of things, ... their secret ways of working ... be as far from our capacity as it is beyond our use". On the other hand, there are many things about which we might speculate, but knowing them would be "of no solid advantage to us nor help to make our lives the happier".[30]

But besides the question of our earthly well-being there is "another and that the main concernment of mankind". If we make use of our faculties we can see "that there is a supreme ruler, and an universal law", and it is "possible and at least probable that there is another life wherein we shall give an account for our past actions in this to the great god of heaven". It is, then, important to us to know what that law is which we are "to live by here and shall be judged by hereafter". And here too, said Locke, we have been "furnished with principles of knowledge and faculties able to discover light enough to guide".[31]

In short, our "business" in this world is, first, to work towards a life of material health, ease, and pleasure, and, second, to hope for and work towards a comfortable life in another world when this one has ended. For these we need no other knowledge than "the history and observation of ... natural bodies", and of "our duties in the management of our own actions". We have no reason to complain if our understandings "leave us perfectly in the dark" about some things. In his wisdom and goodness God has enabled us to know what we need to know.[32]

In March 1677, after about fifteen months in Montpellier, Locke had a letter from Sir John Banks, a self-made businessman. Banks wanted his eighteen-year-old son Caleb to spend five or six months in France "to see and observe what so short a time may permit". He asked Locke to join the youth in Paris, as soon as he could, and to "have him under your friendship and conduct". Banks had thought carefully about this plan for his only son. Questions whether Locke was suitable and likely to be prevailed upon had been raised not only with Shaftesbury (who recommended these plans of "my intimate good friend" to Locke), but with various others, including Samuel Pepys.[33]

Though Locke had turned down a similar request the previous year, he agreed to this one. In fact Banks had left him with little choice or time for consideration, and was assuming Locke's agreement (partly because he had learnt from Stringer that Locke was intending soon to return to Paris anyway). Towards the end of the month, leaving Walls in Montpellier, Locke set out for Paris.[34]

He also left behind Denis Grenville, an English clergyman he had met towards the end of the previous year. Though Locke never showed any sign of wanting to shun or avoid him, Grenville seems to have been something of an unpredictable self-obsessive, excitable, self-dramatising, and importunate. He was certainly aware of a certain instability in himself; "to bespeak the truth", he told Locke, "I am made up in a manner of contradictions". His life was something of a mess: with a tendency to living beyond his means and an unhappy marriage to a woman who became manic-depressive, he faced antagonism from his father-in-law, the Bishop of Durham. When Locke met him he was travelling with his sister, in temporary flight from his unhappy life in England.[35]

Grenville regretted his "over-wisdom and cautiousness" in not immediately seeking Locke's friendship at their first meeting, for he had not had enough of Locke's company when he learnt that Locke was to leave Montpellier, and there is no sign of wisdom or caution in his dramatic "Blunt Demand" of Locke "to know whether your resolution to return be unalterable": "give me leave", he begged, "to make an assault on you ... to continue somewhat longer in these parts". He went on to speak of being "willing to purchase" Locke's friendship and conversation".[36]

In another letter, a few days later, Grenville told Locke that he wanted from him his thoughts on five matters: recreation, business, conversation, study, and devotion. His concern with these was not one of detached interest, for he went on to speak about his own worrying inability to work out a satisfactory modus vivendi in which he would neither harm himself with too much solitude, contemplation, and study, nor waste both his time and his spirit in hunting, shooting, and angling, or in cards and backgammon.[37]

In themselves Grenville's five topics were of serious interest to Locke, and perhaps it was just for this reason that, only three days later, he made a lengthy and (so far as we have it) objective reply about the first; certainly he was either not struck by Grenville's importunate manner or did not mind it. As for Grenville, he seems to have been beside himself with excitement at having engaged Locke's attention, and wrote again immediately: after "many earnest desires" God has at last "directed me to such a person as you seem to be, and with which ... I find nothing to jar", he told Locke. He proposed that they should try never to be more than a day's journey apart, that they should be together the coming winter, that every three months they should make a two- or three-week tour, and that they should visit Italy together.[38]

Locke thought well enough of the more than a thousand words on recreation which he composed for Grenville to retrieve them from him later and to copy them down in his journal; and rightly so, even though they show, from the very start, an attitude very distant from what now prevails. (Grenville was similarly concerned for his own papers and letters, asking Locke to save them from the usual fate of such such things, "that of the bum".) Recreation, Locke wrote, is "a thing ordained not for itself but for a certain end. That end is to be the rule and measure of it." Its point lies beyond its being pleasurable in itself and preferable to work, even though it certainly is "the doing of some easy or at least delightful thing". Its point is that by restoring "the mind or body tired with labour to its former strength" it fits them "for new labour".[39]

Apart from ruling out that recreation could be an end in itself, what Locke said here might today seem just good pragmatic sense. In order to get more work from a servant someone would be well advised not to overwork him, and it would be sensible for someone intent on getting more done to take some time off occasionally. But this is not how Locke was thinking exactly. To begin with, "recreation supposes labour and weariness, and therefore he that labours not has no title to it"; that is, someone not working not merely has no need for recreation, but no entitlement to it. Moreover, and crucially,

Locke thought of each of us as having "a calling", some work or employment which we have a duty to do since God has called us to it; and that brings with it a further duty to keep ourselves fit for our calling. In short, we should "design our diversions to put us in a condition to do our duty".

As to what these recreational diversions should be and how long we should spend on them, we should do no more and no less than what will make us fit to do more of that employment to which we think ourselves called. This will vary from person to person and from calling to calling. Different people have different bodily and mental constitutions, and are "called" to different work. There can, said Locke, be "no general rule set...concerning the time, manner, duration or sort of recreation that is to be used". The only rule is that people's recreation should be what "their experience tells them is suited to them, and proper to refresh the part tired". What that is may not always be obvious, and we may go wrong: "We must beware that custom and the fashion of the world, or some other interest does not make that pass with us for recreation which is indeed labour to us...; playing cards for example...is so far from fitting some men for their business and giving them refreshment, that it more discomposes them than their ordinary labour." Even if this idea of our having a calling, for which we have a duty to keep ourselves in condition, is alien to us today, some of Locke's practical suggestions may not be lost on us: it is best that our work and play are different, for "the properest recreation of studious, sedentary persons...is bodily exercise. To those of bustling employment sedentary recreations."[40]

Though Locke did not send them to Grenville he also, the day after he left Montpellier and during the following weeks, wrote down some ideas concerning another of Grenville's topics, "Study", a piece which has signs of being conceived as a chapter of a larger project. Since, as he noted, "the end of study is knowledge", it is no surprise that there were ideas here which he had recently recorded in his piece on "Knowledge", and which were becoming abiding themes in his thought: since there are limits to our knowledge, such as "the essences...of substantial beings" and "how nature in this great machine of the world produces the several phenomena", it would be "of great service to us to know how far our faculties can reach" so that we will not waste time and "pry too curiously" into things beyond us. But these limits are not such that we can know nothing; on the contrary, we can know what is useful and important to us: "that which seems to me to be suited to the end of man and lie level to his understanding is the improvement of natural experiments for the conveniences of this life and the way of ordering himself so as to attain happiness in the other".[41]

As for study itself, by which we attain knowledge, we should, our lives being short, and there being much to learn, "take the straightest and most direct way we can". This means avoiding the books of the scholastics, which, with their "maze of words and phrases", provide no "progress in the real knowledge of things"; it means being primarily interested in truth rather than in what opinions other people happen to have held; it means eschewing the study of history for its own sake rather than for what it can tell us about human life; and it means avoiding as our main aim "remote useless speculations" such as where the Garden of Eden was, or what kind of bodies we shall have at the resurrection.[42]

The body and mind must, Locke wrote, each be "in a temper fit for study". It is good to press on with study when the mind is "willing . . . and goes at ease", but we must not press too much or too often: "our bodies and our minds are neither of them capable of continual study". Moreover, we should bring to our studies "a mind covetous of truth", a mind wary of taking on received opinions without examination, wary of opinions which happen to suit our temporal advantage.[43]

There are, Locke thought, two areas of study which are "every man's business". "The first and chiefest" is that which concerns "our great business and interest", namely, how we may get to heaven. Second in importance to "happiness in the other world" is our happiness in this, which requires a study of prudence, the knowledge of the "conduct and management of ourselves in the several occurrences of our lives".[44] What should be studied beyond these two areas is a matter of what our own particular calling in life is.

Locke noted that his own studies had often been rather unsystematic: "I have changed often the subject I have been studying, read books by patches and as they have accidentally come in my way and observed no method or order in my studies." In response to this he had found it a help to draw up a map or scheme of a general area of interest, which would "serve like a regular chest-of-drawers to lodge those things orderly and in their proper places which came to hand confusedly and without any method at all". A good example of just such a "chest of drawers", together with contents, has come down to us in a theological notebook Locke began in 1694.[45]

"Converse with books", however, despite its reputation of being so, was not, Locke thought, "the principal part of study". By itself it got no further than "collecting the rough materials". Equally important were meditation by oneself and "discourse with a friend". In a later year he would stress the importance of the last even more: "Meditating by oneself", he said, "is like digging in the mine": whether what is brought up "contains any metal in it, is never so well tried as in conversation with a knowing judicious friend, who carries about him the true touch-stone, which is love of truth in a clear-thinking head".[46]

MARCH 1677–JULY 1678: PARIS

Rather than retrace his earlier direct journey through the Rhône-Saône valley, Locke at first went northwestward to Bordeaux. Whereas before he had used the southerly flow of the Saône and Rhône towards Montpellier, he was now able to take advantage of the westerly flow of the Garonne; and after four days on horseback he took a canal boat from Carcassonne to Toulouse, and then various boats down the river to Bordeaux, which he reached in early April.

These couple of weeks were not the most pleasant he had spent on a journey. Once it was "very hot all day", at other times it was "as cold as it could be without freezing". In his various overnight lodgings (one was "the most cut-throat house I was ever in"), he was more than once "ill treated" and had to suffer "an ill dinner". But such annoyances and inconveniences were nothing to the unpleasant time he had on the Garonne, when he became ill with a "feverish and an extraordinary pain in my head". During "a very cold and untoward passage by water...a great pole...fell upon my head in the boat", though Locke was not sure exactly what had caused his trouble. "But willing above all to secure my head as much as I could if that had received any harm I took a clyster in the afternoon and the next morning the pain in my head continuing with great violence, I bleeded, I believe between eleven and twelve ounces. It proved afterwards a tertian ague." This illness (whose course he reported to Sydenham) delayed him for six weeks, until well into May when he resumed his journey, though not recovered sufficiently to do justice to the sights: at Lusignan "are some of the walls remaining of the prettiest park I ever saw, which would deserve a description, were I in health and humour".[47]

Caleb Banks left England about the time Locke left Montpellier, and was already in Paris when his tutor-to-be arrived at the beginning of June. John Banks had already given favourable accounts of the boy: "a reasonable scholar", "the french tongue...perfect". Yet "good and governable" as he might also have been, Caleb made no mention of the fifty pounds his father had promised Locke in order to "equip" himself, presumably in a decent fashion in the capital after months in the provinces; and though Locke felt obliged to write at some length to Banks about this, he explained that he thought it best if Caleb were not reminded about it, lest it bias him at the start against his tutor. He took the opportunity of continuing at some length, in a rather pompous, pontificating way, about how he had always thought that those who have to do with young gentlemen "mistake their business quite, and put themselves out of a capacity of doing them that good they might" by not getting their friendship from the start. (He seems – as also in later letters to Banks – to have been striving to impress with the seriousness and reflectiveness with which he was approaching the care of his son.) Locke respectfully further suggested that all money from Banks, even if it were for Caleb personally, should come first to him (Locke), so as "to afford me opportunity...to discourse with him about the regulation of his expenses"; unfortunately, it took some time for the three to adjust themselves to each other on the matter.[48]

There was vagueness and indecision as to how long Caleb would be in France, and what they would do. Initially Banks did not intend the stay to be more than about five or six months, and left it to Locke to decide whether they should stay in Paris or travel. But soon after Locke's arrival in Paris (already two months since Caleb had left England), Banks, to Locke's politely hidden annoyance, became rather more directive; he suggested they should stay in Paris for "yet some time", and confessed to apprehension about Caleb's travelling in the heat of the summer months. Towards the end of July, however, he had agreed that, if Locke "judge it best", they should make a tour of the Loire in October and November; after all it seemed this is what Caleb had a fancy for. Then, a couple of weeks later, things were much less certain again: Banks reported that his wife could not "bear the thoughts of any such undertaking", and that he could not bear giving her "that occasion of disquiet". As a consequence he had tried to persuade his son that "Paris answers all", and asked Locke "to divert my son from the desire of going further".[49]

Locke was not prepared just to bow passively to this; perhaps he thought that, having been given tutorial responsibility, he had a positive duty to press the educational case against remaining in Paris. He treated Banks to some well-organised thoughts on this matter:

As to the improvements of travel, I think they are all comprehended in these four: knowledge, which is the proper ornament and perfection of the mind; exercise, which belongs to the body; language, and conversation. Of all these, exercise only is that which seems to persuade the spending his time in Paris.... They who imagine that the improvements of foreign conversation are to be sought by making acquaintance and friendships abroad seem to me wholly to mistake the matter.... The great benefit to be found by travel is by constant changing of company, and conversing every day with unknown strangers is to get a becoming confidence, and not to be abashed at new faces, to accustom oneself to treat everybody civilly, and to learn by experience that that which gets one credit and recommends one to others is not the fortune one is born to, but the riches of the mind, and the good qualities one possesses. And were it not for this one thing I know not why young gents should not be sent for breeding rather to the court of England than to the inns and eating houses of France.[50]

Over their first summer together in Paris relations between Locke and Caleb seem to have been strained. Apart from the initial uneasinesses about control of the purse-strings, it is not clear what their problems were, and whether it was Caleb or Locke that had been complaining back to the Bankses. At first the Bankses thought of bringing things to an end. In September, Pepys told Caleb's mother that "the more I think on it the more I concur with your...present thoughts of sending for Mr Banks..., for I am no wise satisfied that matters either are or are now likely to come into that posture which I could wish they were in between him and Mr Locke". But things seem to have got better, or perhaps the Bankses decided to let them ride, for they neither called Caleb back nor stood by their intention in June of Caleb's coming home at Christmas.[51] Locke and his charge remained in Paris for the rest of the year, and the question of a return to England did not recur until the following spring.

Banks again at first left it largely to Locke to decide what to do: "write me freely what you think best, in regard to my son's return or longer stay and how long". He had some worry about rumours of impending war between England and France, but thought that so long as the English ambassador felt safe in Paris he should feel the same about his son; so in April he agreed with his wife that Caleb should stay abroad for another two or three months. Halfway into this time, however, Caleb asked for a further extension, and reopened the question of journeying to the Loire. Eventually, in June, after Caleb had been in Paris for a whole year, this was agreed to, with two months being allowed for the tour.[52]

About this time Locke had a letter from Dr Thomas Coxe (who had been one of those who approved of Locke's taking charge of Caleb), which revealed something of the tensions which lay behind the indecisions, the changes of mind, and procrastinations to which Locke had been exposed by the Bankses (and which perhaps had infected his relations with Caleb). Lady Banks, he said, "has been passionately desireous for a long while that her son should return without any further delay". Sir John had been "content to gratify him in his desire of staying some longer time"; and Coxe himself had "thought it had been no way amiss to let him have passed two or three months in a slow and gradual making that which they call the little Tour* of France". But, said Coxe, Lady Banks would hear nothing of it. However, "it is now again in consideration whether this may not be done at this time". Coxe himself was still in favour of such a tour, even though the approaching hot summer made the timing less than ideal, and he did warn Locke of "the chief inconvenience" in the Loire, namely, "the multitude of young unexperienced youths of our own nation and Germans, that flock thither"; but, he said, for "your peace and ease I know you will endeavour to avoid" them.[53]

Locke's reply was equally revealing of the frustration and exasperation he had felt at the Bankses' ditherings. He had had more than a year of "letters from home setting but short limits to our stay", despite his urging the benefits to the "naturally bashful" Caleb of getting out of Paris. Now, having missed the expected chance of a spring return ("the proper time for my return into our English air", and also when he had "prepared all my friends and some business to expect me"), he found that the Bankses had eventually, and with an unsuitable season for travel approaching, "come to the execution of that which was the thing proposed" when he sent Caleb to France in the first place. Locke must have supposed these complaints would go no further than Coxe, for he was certainly conscious of and concerned for his own position and reputation (after all he had been recommended to Banks by his patron Shaftesbury):

the respect I have for Sir John and his family makes me consent to make my little affairs give way to the design he has for improving his son, and perhaps the relation, that the world will think I had to him, makes me more than a little cautious that no haste of mine should cut him short of any improvement that longer time abroad might afford him. For if the critical world can find anything to lay hold on at his return I know where the censure will light, let the fault be where it will.[54]

Despite these frustrations Locke's time during the year in Paris had not been wasted. At the very first he had been unable to get about, for the fever he had suffered on the way there had left him with weak legs, but within two days of arriving in Paris he had written to Boyle asking him to "recommend me to the acquaintance of any one of the virtuosi you shall think fit here".[55] Paris, with its Royal Academy and Observatory, was the intellectual capital of Europe, and presumably Boyle did not leave Locke to find his own entry into it, but we do not know what help and suggestions he offered.

We do know, though, that from the very start he got intellectual sustenance from Moïse Charas with whom he initially stayed. Charas, a master apothocary (later to become royal apothecary to Charles II), worked as a demonstrator in Chemistry at the Botanical Gardens, and had recently published a pharmacological work, *Pharmacopée royale galénique et chimique* (1676).[56]

In June, Locke moved from Charas's to the house of Gilles de Launay* where he stayed until mid-October. De Launay was a follower of the French anti-Cartesian philosopher Pierre Gassendi; Locke bought or was given some of his books but there is no record of any conversations they might have had.[57]

Around this time Locke's friend John Mapletoft was contemplating marriage, an event which would have involved his giving up the professorial chair of Physic at Gresham College, which he had occupied for two years. He promised that he would do what he could for Locke to succeed him. In the event, Mapletoft postponed marriage for two years, when, perhaps now too taken up in Shaftesbury's business, Locke seems no longer to have been interested in the post.[58]

By early October, Locke had met Henri Justell, a scholar and librarian, whose house was the focus for regular gatherings of intellectuals, local and visiting, Catholic and Protestant. At their first recorded meeting Justell told him about the Duke of Hanover's coach (in fact invented by the German philosopher, Leibniz, a visitor to Justell's), "which at night he turned into a tent, and which will serve also for a boat". Through Justell, Locke became acquainted, even friendly, with a variety of people whose interests he shared; possibly it was through him that he first met the Dutch physicist Christian Huygens. He performed experiments on the behaviour of water in a vacuum, and a surgical operation on a dog's leg done with a M. Hubin, from whom he also took down a mercury cure for skin diseases; he made observations at the Royal Observatory of the Moon, Jupiter, and Saturn, under the guidance of Giovanni Cassini, who a year or so earlier had detected the main divisions in the rings of Saturn.[59]

Locke also met François Bernier, with whom he shared more than one interest: besides having trained and practised as a doctor, Bernier had recently published an *Abrégé de la philosophie de Gassendi*. But it was Bernier's first-hand knowledge of the Orient, where he had spent a number of years and on which he had published a number of travel books, that seems to have excited Locke most, chiming as it did with the interest in foreign places and ways already observable in his "Essays on the Law of Nature". "Though I find pleasure and profit in hearing him [Bernier] disputing amongst the philosophers", Locke said, "I should...prefer him to tell us something about the manners and doings of Eastern peoples and the things he has observed in those parts." "We have long been overloaded", Locke thought, "with philosophy and disputations, whilst we have little or nothing in the way of trustworthy accounts of happenings amongst foreign nations."[60]

Another visitor at Justell's was Nicholas Toinard, with whom Locke quickly formed a rather intense friendship. Toinard, a Catholic about three years Locke's senior and a lifelong bachelor, had trained as a lawyer but was sufficiently wealthy to live a life indulging his rather varied intellectual and scholarly interests, which (as manifested in discussions and correspondence with Locke) ranged from new technology, natural philosophy, and medicine, through geographical exploration to biblical scholarship. Locke described him as "a very good mechanic, besides an admirable scholar".[61]

On what must have been his first visit to Toinard's own chambers Locke was exposed to his host's enthusiasm for guns: he was shown "several fashions", some of them of Toinard's own design, and given an account of breech loading and of bullet making. On the same occasion, Locke recorded, "Mr Toinard showed me his harmony of the Evangelists printed in a new manner which I think may be very useful". This brief note referred to what was one of Toinard's most abiding and focused interests, which was to harmonise the various parts of the New Testament as they were found in early Greek texts, so that a single integrated narrative could be constructed. In accordance with his "new manner" the four Gospel texts were placed in parallel columns, the various parts of their Greek narratives being aligned and related as appropriate. Each page was headed with the dates and places of the various events, and, in a fifth column, Toinard constructed a "definitive" Latin summary. When Toinard had his *Harmonia* of the Gospels privately printed a year or so later, Locke inscribed his copy as having been presented by Nicolas Toinard of Orléans:

the best of men, graced with virtues of the old school yet of great charm, with a most acute and shrewd intellect, with learning of every kind, deeply versed in Greek and Hebrew scholarship, and in chronology too, as is clear from this Harmony, built up by him on new foundations . . .; moreover a friend greatly to be cherished on many accounts: furnished and enriched me with this welcome and priceless gift.[62]

Included in Toinard's circle was John Brisbane, a man attached to the English embassy and who became secretary to the Admiralty in 1680 (Toinard and Locke referred to him as the Sea Captain). Brisbane was not the only person Locke knew with the embassy, for the wife of the English ambassador himself (Ralph Montague) had been Locke's friend and neighbour in London, Lady Northumberland. She had retained her title after her first husband had died about eight years earlier, and she was still accompanied by the Blomers.

One winter evening Locke was called upon to minister to Lady Northumberland. The immediate trouble was "a violent rhume in her teeth which puts her to a very great torment", and Margaret Blomer begged Locke to come and to bring with him "the best blistering plaster you can . . . she is not willing to try any more French experiments". The earlier "French experiments", which evidently had not got to the bottom of the trouble, had concerned the extraction of a tooth, which proved to be sound. The fits with which Locke was confronted were fearsome. During them "she gave many shrieks. At every shriek her mouth being drawn towards the right ear, and when the fit was over she told me that the pain shot itself all at once like a flash of fire all over that side of her cheek up to her ear, into her teeth." Locke seems to have been present at the bedside almost continously for the next two weeks, applying blistering plasters, purging, and soothing the gums with laudanum-based ointments. He described the case, which he recognised as having to do primarily with the nerves (in fact trigeminal neuralgia), rather than with the teeth themselves, in very lengthy detail both in his journal and to Mapletoft, from whom along with other London doctors such as Sydenham he took advice. For his attentions Locke was rewarded with "a pair of silver candle sticks and a silver standish with ink box and sand box and a silver bell".[63]

Lady Northumberland was not the only member of the English community that Locke treated. Besides prescribing for a maid at the ambassador's who was suffering from a fever, he treated Thomas Herbert, now in Paris on his way back to England, for sickness, vomiting, and a swollen testicle, a Mrs Sandys for dysentry and diarrhoea, and attended a Mr Robinson, one of Sydenham's patients.[64]

In March, Denis Grenville sent Locke some of his own thoughts on three of the topics (temporal business, study, conversation) that he had earlier asked about. Whereas Locke's thoughts on recreation had been quite objective, Grenville's focused on his personal difficulties. In each of the three cases he had problems which all, quite clearly, arose from chronic indecision and inability to stick to a course of action. Locke's reply, which he was not long in making, recognised that there was indeed a unity in Grenville's problems: "the great difficulty, uncertainty, and perplexity of thought you complain of in these particulars arises, in a great measure from this ground, that you think that a man is obliged strictly and precisely at all times to do that which is absolutely best". If, Locke said, "we were never to do but what is absolutely the best, all our lives would go away in deliberation, and we should never come to action". Grenville's general problem did indeed seem to be that he could "never come to action", which Locke saw more as an intellectual error than as a flaw of character or personality. He argued that though "our duty is sometimes so evident . . . that there is no latitude left", this is rarely so, and it cannot be that in every situation there is *the one* thing to be done, *the best* course of action. God would not have imposed on us, his weak and fallible creatures, the need always to come to such a judgement, about which we would always be running the risk of being mistaken.[65]

Locke added a further consideration which he said related to a "fancy", an "odd notion of mine", something "I have often thought", namely, that "our state here in this world is a state of mediocrity, which is not capable of extremes". He thought of this idea as something which "will be applicable in several cases", and it had already cropped up in the note he had written the previous year on study, where it captured the idea that our faculties in this world, unlike those of angels, have their limits. Its point here, however, was to give a further demonstration that it is wrong to think there is always *the best* thing to do, "we are not capable of continual rest nor continual exercise . . . not able to labour always with the body nor always with the mind".[66]

JULY–OCTOBER 1678: AN EXTENDED "LITTLE TOUR" OF FRANCE

At the beginning of July, Locke began careful preparations for Caleb's "little tour" to the Loire. Four boxes were packed with books, and a black trunk filled (according to his systematic listing) with things such as clothes, razors, knives and forks, along with pages of Toinard's "*Harmonia*" and two manuscripts of his own – the translation of Nicole's essays he had done in Celleneuve, and a manuscript entitled "Essay de Intellectu". The silver items given him by Lady Northumberland after her illness, having been carefully weighed, were put into the safekeeping of Brisbane. As for what he needed, he made a careful "note of linen taken with me", shirts, handkerchiefs, caps, cuffs, and woollen stockings.[67]

A few days later he and Caleb left Paris for the southwest, probably travelling in their own coach, as Coxe had advised. In two days they were at Orléans. This was Toinard's home town, and he had provided Locke with letters of introduction to friends and acquaintances. Toinard must have been quite a presence to Locke, for besides being entertained by his friends Locke was shown some of his technological inventions at work. Toinard had had the idea, for example, of closing bottles not with the usual corks or wooden stoppers, but with screw-threaded glass stops, and at the bottle factory Locke saw these in production. He was also shown, by the Abbé François Gendron, a small portable mill that Toinard had designed, which, according to the detailed description Locke recorded of it, would grind "corn enough in twenty-four hours for one hundred men".[68]

A good amount of time was spent in discussion of medical matters with another of Toinard's friends, Dr Godefroy. Locke had noticed that "the town abounds in lame and crook backed people", and was told by Godefroy that, in a curiously indirect way, their spinal deformation was due to the strength of the local wine: the wine and the quality of the air made young children cough and the coughing "puts out their backbones when they are yet tender". Gout was another common complaint in Orléans, and Godefroy again put this down to the local wine. He told Locke of a friend who "designed to make himself a friar because his gout made him unfit for anything".

In prudent preparation for the "austerities" of the religious life he began to drink less; but "having left off wine a little he found himself cured of the gout and so remains ever since".[69]

Locke and Caleb were in Orléans until the end of July, longer than they had originally intended. Your city is like you, Locke told Toinard, "it does not readily let go those whom it has once taken to itself". (By this time their correspondence already amounted to six typically rather lengthy letters — a measure of how much they had taken to each other.) But behind Locke's flattery was the mundane reality that Caleb had been laid low with dysentry. Predictably, when she heard of this, Caleb's mother was even "more desirous of his coming home".[70]

From Orléans they travelled by boat down the Loire, aiming for Blois, forty or so miles away. A contrary wind and a fellow passenger fearful of the waves forced a stop halfway, at Avery, where their timid new acquaintance, a Madame de Richmond, introduced them to a local "person of quality" in whose house, complete with a carp-filled moat, they "were well received and lodged". Though they set out again the next day, Locke had found time to compile a list of the half-dozen best pears in their host's garden.[71]

They had been recommended to stay at the "Galère" in Blois. Locke liked it "very well"; it was not "horrid dear" as an earlier inn had been, and meals were reasonably priced "if you bargain". They spent some time visiting local stately homes and gardens. Several pages of Locke's journal are devoted to a plan and detailed description of one of these, Chambord, a house belonging to the King. At another house, Beauregard, Locke's interests were caught less by the gallery ("where are the pictures of most of the considerable personages of these later ages, but not extremely well done") than by the technology in the courtyard where there were "several things very well contrived". These, which he recorded in much detail, related to a well whose water was drawn by a pair of ingeniously counterbalanced buckets.[72]

The day after these visits Locke wrote to Boyle asking whether there was any information he could seek out, or commission he could undertake for him, "in the part of France I am now rambling". Passing on information he had had in recent letters from Toinard, he told Boyle about the invention in Paris of a hygrometer which "besides marking the moistness of the air, will also be improved to wind up a pendulum; which, if it succeeds, will be a kind of perpetual motion". He also told him of another ingenious attempt, using a design of

Toinard's, to use the air as a source of energy: "a watchmaker ... is now at work upon a movement, that the air will wind up".[73]

After a week in Blois, Locke and Caleb continued their "rambling" down the Loire, to Tours. It was rather cold during their four days there, so much so that Locke "found it convenient to get on my flannel shirt" (one of those carefully itemised before the departure from Paris). Properly clothed, he and Caleb surveyed the town from the top of St Gatien tower, and visited a Capuchin convent and a Benedictine monastery. He was very interested in the town's unfortunately declining silk-weaving industry, on which he made lengthy notes about its various aspects, technical, social, and economic.[74]

From Tours they continued down river to Saumur, "a little town just under an high hill upon the edge of the Loire". Here Locke reflected on the financial aspects of the journey so far. The "Trois Mores" where they were now lodging was treating them "well" at four-fifths the price of the rather indifferent "St Marthe" at Tours; the boat from Blois to Tours, which at the time he had thought cost "but very little", now struck him, after further experience, as "a little too dear". And, as at all of their stops, he made notes on the local fruit in all its variety. He listed the plums ("Roche Corbon, red and large", "Ste. Katherine, large and yellow") and pears ("La Rousselette", "Le poire de Citron"), and described the method used to dry them. Peaches such as "La Belle Chevereuse" or "Le gros pay d'Italy" were also dried and, their stone being removed, "a little peach thrust into its place ... makes the other larger and better".[75]

After a week in Saumur, Locke and Caleb made for Angers, covering the last two or three miles on horseback. Locke considered that the locals "made use of our necessity" for they charged him 50 per cent over the odds for the horses.[76]

The notes Locke made on the Minims' church in Angers at first showed the objectivity of the genuinely curious – about the various kinds of masses that could be bought, about the cost of celebrating them to perpetuity, or of having the Host exposed. But anti-Catholic prejudice came to the fore in his remark that "if there be any benefit to be had from these things, it is it seems only for those who have ... money enough to pay for them". His reaction to the "abundance of relics" he saw at the cathedral of St Maurice makes one wonder why he went there if not to deride and have his prejudices reinforced. Nothing could be seen of the wood of the true Cross "but the gold and silver that covered it", and the milk of the Virgin, which was supposedly there along with some of her hair and a piece of her petticoat, was "out of sight". The porphyry water pot, purportedly one of those in which Jesus produced wine, was "hard of digestion" as being too costly for the wedding host at Cana and ornamented in a non-Jewish fashion.[77]

The practical, down-to-earth aspect of Locke's mind came out with regard to an organ he saw being made. What initially made it worth remark was that it had more stops than usual. But Locke was obviously far more taken with the keys which were made from horse bone which will "never grow yellow as ivory does"; and he recorded the recipe for whitening them.[78]

Along with all of this Locke was able during the days in Angers to give some thought to his investigations *"de intellectu"*, and he made some notes on ideas of "complex modes", one of the kinds of idea which in his earlier thinking had not been clearly distinguished from others; one example (boucaning, or cooking by smoking) was taken from a book he was reading about a journey made the previous century in Brazil by Jean de Léry.[79]

From Angers, Locke and Caleb made their way back to Saumur, where they stopped, again at the "Three Moors", for just one night. "Fearing the heat", which was becoming intense, they had "hired a litter for ourselves" carried by two men (and two horses for the servants Locke and Caleb had with them). Toinard's advice had been to get to La Rochelle via Thouars, Fontenay, and Marans, but Locke decided otherwise, and to go via Richelieu and Niort. For the next day's journey to Richelieu, via Chinon up the river Vienne, they took horses and another man for a guide. Chinon, though "a little, dirty, poor town", did at any rate produce walnut oil, the method for which Locke wrote down. By contrast, the château at Richelieu was "the most complete piece of building in France", the town itself being "built with the same exactness". They spent one night in Richelieu (at the "Puis d'or", "not very well") and left the next day, the last in August.[80]

Two days later they were at La Rochelle, where, Locke noted, "This is the first time I ever saw the [Atlantic] ocean".[81] They had for a companion a local doctor, M. Beaulot, who took them round the many pits where salt was recovered by evaporation of sea water, and with whom Locke discussed the locally endemic diseases.

Even before they got to La Rochelle, it had been agreed, at Caleb's enthusiastic urging, that it would not be the furthermost point of their journey and that they would go further south, via Bordeaux, to Toulouse. The Bankses had been anxiously reluctant about this, of course, and their friend Pepys, "being a daily witness of the uneasiness of my Lady's life under the apprehensions of her son's going still further from home", wrote to Locke suggesting that they should certainly start their return at Toulouse.[82]

Without covering the same ground twice, the obvious way back to Paris from Toulouse was to travel east into Languedoc, along the valley of the partly completed Canal du Midi to Montpellier (and then to travel north up the Rhône valley to Lyon). Locke looked forward to being in Montpellier again and wrote to Charleton expressing his "hopes to have the satisfaction...of seeing you and of throwing myself into the arms of a friend...where I think myself so safe and so happy".[83]

Locke and Caleb left La Rochelle in early September for Bordeaux. On the way, at Rochefort, on the strength of introductions from Toinard, they were dined by the governor, and conducted round the recently developed and important shipbuilding town, with its planned right-angled grid of wide streets (such that "one sees from one end of the town to the other").[84]

At Bordeaux, Caleb wrote to his mother expressing a wish to go to Italy; this was entirely with Locke's concurrence, for he was keen to visit Rome. Caleb asked Pepys to persuade his parents into it. Predictably, Sir John was torn. Like Pepys, he thought the plan a good one in itself; moreover he clearly wanted to satisfy his son and believed the journey would not involve putting off a return to London beyond the spring, the earliest time he could anyway have reasonably hoped for. (He recognised that, from Locke's point of view, getting to London for the approaching winter "would have been an inconvenient time to your own health after all your time spent abroad in respect thereto".) On the other hand, he told Locke, "finding my wife so much concerned if the post do not every week bring letters, I can then think of nothing but his [Caleb's] return". However, with Pepys's help, Lady Banks was persuaded and it was agreed they would go to Italy, on condition she heard from Caleb every week, and that he was home in the spring of the following year.[85]

The new plan coincided with the old as far as Lyon, where, instead of continuing north to Paris, they would turn east and cross the Alps. Accordingly, towards the end of September, they left Bordeaux for Toulouse, which they reached five days later. Here, while staying at "the Navarre", Locke wrote in his journal that "the happiness of man consists in pleasure, whether of body or mind":

that this is so I appeal not only to the experience of all mankind and the thoughts of every man's breast but to...the scripture which tells that at the right hand of God...are pleasures for ever more, and that which men are condemned for is not for seeking pleasure but for preferring the momentary pleasures of this life to those joys which shall have no end.

He also, in complete contrast, noted two or three curiosities he learnt from a M. Breteile: "rub your hand over with a pounded snail and then pour on it boiling wax and it will not scald".[86]

Locke and Caleb reached Montpellier in mid-October, when Locke re-established contact with, amongst others, William Charleton, Pierre Magnol, and Pierre Jolly. With Jolly he made careful observations of a total eclipse of the moon, an account of which he sent to Robert Hooke, now the secretary of the Royal Society.[87]

The day after the eclipse Locke and Caleb left Montpellier. The more than two weeks they had been there had not been enough for Locke to enjoy the company of his friends to the full; leaving so soon was "the most unacceptable thing [that] has happened to me all my journey", he told Charleton. But they needed to get across the Alps before the winter snows, and so they travelled quickly northwards to Lyon, which they reached in just less than a week.[88]

The prospect had not looked good, for, as Locke wrote to Charleton the next day, "the cold and hard winds we had in our faces almost all the way hither has the last week covered the tops of the hills [with snow] as I came along". And, sure enough, they had arrived in Lyon only to be thwarted, "the first of those that are come too late to pass the mountains this winter". Locke thought that "with good luck one might bustle through" the snow, but since there was no necessity for it ("I am not passing over the hills for a warm benefice to thaw me again...and M. Banks is not the Pope's nephew...get[ting] to Rome to make his fortune"), he decided to continue on to Paris. Some months later Locke said that had it not been for his responsibility for Caleb he would have pressed on; but, as it was, he was clearly very disappointed. "If all the world should go to Rome", he wrote resignedly to Mapletoft,

I think I should never, having been twice firmly bent upon it, the time set, the company agreed, and as many times defeated.... Were I not accustomed

to have Fortune to dispose of me contrary to my design and expectation,
I should be very angry to be thus turned out of my way when I imagined myself
almost at the suburbs of Rome, and made sure in a few days to mount the
Capitol and trace the footsteps of the Scipios and the Caesars.

It is not obvious when Locke had earlier intended a journey to Rome,
though during his lengthy stay in Montpellier two years earlier he had
made extensive jottings on travel in Italy and what to do and see in
Rome.[89]

Locke and Caleb left Lyon for Paris in mid-November, not
then knowing that "though the first falling of the snow had
made the passage mighty inconvenient and pretty dangerous,
yet... afterwards... fair weather had much mended it, and... people
went and came without any great difficulty". They reached Paris at
the end of the month.[90]

The day before they left Lyon, Locke had taken a young Swiss into his
service as a "laquais", a manservant or lackey, and, kitted out in a new
livery coat, he was now travelling up by boat, the cheapest service
between Lyon and Paris. In some way Sylvanus Brownower was
a replacement for John Wheelock, a servant Locke had had two years
previously (at a wage of usually £5 per annum); he, however, had been
taken on by the Shaftesburys when Locke left for France. Brownower
would be with Locke for nearly twenty years, perhaps because, as was
observed, Locke "was very kind to his servants and would take the
trouble to instruct them with a great deal of mildness, after what
manner he expected to be served by them". One of Wheelock's duties
had been to shave his master, and perhaps this also fell to Syl (as he
became known), but he became invaluable in more substantial ways:
as a highly trusted secretary, transcribing his manuscripts, acting as
an amanuensis, and (being a talented artist) producing drawings
when necessary, including portraits of his master.[91]

A little over a year earlier Mapletoft had written to Locke, obviously
in reply to something he had said, "I think you are much in the right
when you resolve not to buy a wife, and doubt not but most of the
married men in England will be on your side". But the idea of marrying
seems to have remained on Locke's mind, for he later mentioned it to
Stringer too, who was "at some dispute whether it is the improvement
you have made by your travels in strength and vigour, or the thoughts
of old age and infirmities... that puts you in mind of getting a wife".[92]
Locke had certainly reported an improvement in his health since

coming to France, but nothing we know of his life so far, apart from his relationship with Elinor Parry, indicates that any interest he might have had in a wife would be increased by or require strength and virility. It seems more likely that, at a couple of years short of fifty, it was "thoughts of old age and infirmity" that were weighing with him. If so, it seems probable that they were similarly at work in his taking on a new manservant.

For a year or so after this, marriage kept cropping up as a topic of extremely light-hearted discussion between Locke and his bachelor friends in Paris. At one point Locke would tell Toinard he had got for him "a beautiful young girl to be your wife", and though it appeared that someone in particular was in mind, the very idea was clearly something of a joke. "If she does not suit you after some trial", Locke said, "you can sell her...at so much a pound − just as I have seen them sell pigs at Montpellier": "I think [she] would bring you in five or six shillings a pound, for she is handsome, young, very tender, and in good condition for the market." By this time Locke seems to have reached the conclusion that marriage and death "are nearly the same thing", and we can only speculate as to why he was not inclined towards, or even inclined against, marriage.[93] It would certainly have interfered with the control that was possible to him in a bachelor life; he would have forfeited his Christ Church Studentship, and would have had to put his mind to regular medical practice, to earning money as opposed to receiving grateful gifts for services rendered. Added to this, however, and as just mentioned, he seems never to have had any interest in the kind of sexual life that marriage would have afforded. Perhaps he simply had no sexual drives at all, but it is easy to think of them as there, but repressed out of some distaste or, again, some fear of losing control. His friendship with Toinard, though apparently never physical, is sometimes suggestive of homosexuality.

NOVEMBER 1678–MAY 1679: PARIS

Locke now settled in for another winter in Paris, taking up the acquaintances and activities he had left behind earlier in the year, such as, for example, spending time at the observatory with the astronomers the Abbé Jean Picard and Olaf Rømer. Toinard was again a regular companion. The details of his project for harmonising the Scriptures must have figured large in their conversations, but they also discussed a report "for certain" of man-powered flight, a method to make sea water drinkable, the relative speed of carrier pigeons and horseback riders (sixteen times quicker), and a model Toinard had made of a breech-loading cannon. Their relationship was sufficiently close and informal as to allow Locke to speak for Toinard, and at rather short notice: "I promised you to Mr Brisban today at dinner. I will come to your place around midday in order to lead you to the rendezvous."[94]

Shortly after he arrived back in Paris, Locke received a letter from Denis Grenville which enclosed an account of some of his concerns regarding "Devotion". As before, these were entirely personal and of the kind Locke had heard before. He was continually indecisive as to the relative importance of "the nice and punctual performances" of the outward forms of devotion ("prefixed times", "such and such postures of body") as compared with an "inward and spiritual temper of soul"; he was continually indecisive too about the relative importance of devotion, converse, study, business, and recreation. Locke suggested that he really should decide once and for all, and get it firmly fixed in his mind, whether or not he accepted "that we are not obliged to do always that which is precisely best". It had, said Locke, usually been his way with himself, "to which, I think, I owe a great part of my quiet", firmly to establish his principles as he went along.[95]

In February, Locke filled a dozen pages in his journal with statements of various laws. These were not the laws of some real country about which he had been reading, for they were headed "Atlantis" and he concluded them with his own initials, indicating that they represented his own thoughts. They dealt with things such as marriage ("A marriage wherein the man is not fourteen nor the woman thirteen shall be ipso facto nul"), public service ("He that is seventy years old shall be at liberty to refuse any public employment or office whatsover"), taxation ("he or she that has ten children living shall be exempted and free from all public taxes and burdens"), and begging ("beggars shall ipso facto be taken and sent to the public work house and there remain the rest of their lives"; "If any one shall relieve a beggar without giving notice of his begging ... to the tithing man he shall be liable to pay double his tax"). (If we are inclined to remark on the harshness of these laws about begging, we should not ignore the gloss Locke adds to them: "But nothing herein shall be construed to hinder the charity of well disposed people to bestow their charity ... on poor people in their own houses ... that do not go about begging").[96]

These laws were far more detailed than the "Constitutions of Carolina" with which Locke had been involved ten years earlier. Yet they seem to have been intended, like them, for some New World colony: one of them (in fact headed "Carolina" rather than "Atlantis") concerned what should be done "in dealing with the indians" ("one should never pardon on any consideration the murder of any of our people...but in all other injuries received it may be convenient to forgive and be reconciled upon other considerations"). Detailed laws for some colony (whether actual or possible) were on Locke's mind presumably because of discussions he had been having with his friends in Paris, for they seem to have been very interested in what had been worked out for Carolina. In September 1667 Stringer had sent Locke a copy of the "Constitutions" (along with some flannel shirts), and Toinard told Locke some months later that he had been thinking about the laws of Carolina in relation to persecution. The discussions that must have taken place in Paris were continued by correspondence with Toinard and with Justel after Locke's eventual return to England.[97]

To an extent the discussions Locke had with Toinard about distant colonies were close to their hearts, because the two friends were taken with the idea of escaping from the sins of Europe (as they put it) to the French Indian Ocean colony of Bourbon (now Réunion) or to Carolina (of which Locke had years earlier been made a Landgrave and given some land). In the very first letter Toinard wrote Locke after their final parting in Paris, he talked (albeit incidentally) of preparing himself for the voyage to Carolina or Bourbon. Shortly afterwards, Locke said that for his part

if the wickedness of our Europeans will not leave even one so manly and so honest as you are at peace I am quite ready to go with you to the Isle of Bourbon...[or] to Carolina, where there is a very fine island which they have done me the honour to name after me.* There you can be emperor, for I can answer for it that everything which bears the name of Locke is certain to obey you.

Locke later said he would follow Toinard anywhere: "only find a healthy and tranquil country, where your conversation can be hoped for, and I will be ready to follow you to this earthly paradise which will be the fulfillment of all my desires".[98]

Perhaps this idea was largely fantasy; it certainly never came to anything (but then neither did any of their plans for seeing each other again in Paris or London). But for Toinard at least it was not entirely light-hearted: "think seriously", he wrote to Locke towards the end of 1681, "of removing to Carolina, of which you have up till now spoken in a playful way as between friends". (Two years earlier Toinard had said that he thought Locke was as serious about going to Carolina as he was about getting married.)[99]

The decision that Locke and Caleb would leave Paris in the spring remained firm. As regards his health, Locke was probably not too concerned about returning to England: towards the end of the year he had told Banks that he dared to think his "lungs are pretty well" and "will bear the sea coal smoke of London". But there was much discussion about the route to be taken, as much as there had been in the first place about what they would do in France. Caleb wanted to go via Flanders and Holland; but this would have involved waiting until May when the roads would be properly open, and Banks was also afraid they might encounter pillaging soldiers. Eventually, when Locke and Caleb left Paris at the beginning of May, they made, not for Holland, but for Calais on the French coast. They were accompanied by Olaf Rømer, who was making a visit to England, and of course by Locke's new manservant, Syl.[100]

Locke was not happy to leave Paris and his friends there, particularly Toinard, "assuredly the best". Before embarking on the *Charlotte* in Calais, he wrote, in the terms of tender affection which would continue in his letters to him, that his heart had been so heavy on the journey there that he could hardly find a post-horse which could gallop carrying such a great weight. The yacht sailed on 28 April/8 May. Lack of wind forced them to anchor in the Thames estuary for a time (during which Locke examined and made notes on Rømer's tinderbox, and discussed with him the speed of light which some years earlier Rømer had proved to be finite). Eventually, on 30 April, Locke landed at the Temple stairs, after nearly three and a half years in France.[101]

5

Thanet House and London
(May 1679–September 1683)

Let us pray no Papist Heir may England's sceptre sway.*

While Locke was in France, Shaftesbury moved his London household into the City, to Thanet House in Aldersgate Street, and it was there that Locke went on his return. On a larger scale, other things had happened while he was away. Even before he left for France there had been anxieties both about the King's style of government (his attempts, by prorogation and adjournments, to rule without Parliament) and his policies (toleration of Catholics, and his alliance with the absolutist Catholic Louis XIV in the Dutch war). Even without knowledge of the secret treaty between Charles and Louis, there were fears that the Protestant religion and Parliamentary government were under threat, both from inside and outside the country, and that England might become, like France, a Catholic country under an absolute ruler. The fear of the "popery" of a Catholic absolutism increased during Locke's years in France, and the summer before his return seemed to receive some very concrete justification when a certain Titus Oates had testified (falsely as it happens) to the existence of a Catholic-inspired plot to kill King Charles and to have him succeeded by his openly Catholic brother James, a man who had continually encouraged Charles in his attempts at arbitrary government. This revelation of a supposed "Popish Plot" was soon followed by the discovery that Louis had been financing Charles to enable him to rule without

Parliament and the money it might vote him. Shaftesbury used all of this to stir up anti-Catholic and anti-Jamesian feeling. His new popularity forced the King to bring him back into office, as Lord President of a new Privy Council (an event which took place days before Locke left France and which he described to Toinard as a "great change").[1]

It would later be reported by a friend that it was no accident that Locke had arrived back at this important juncture in his patron's affairs for, she said, "the Earl of Shaftesbury being made Lord President of the Council, Mr Locke (as it is said) was sent for home", while Bourne, a little differently, said that "in anticipation of that appointment, probably as soon as he saw his way to a return to power, he invited Locke to come back to England and to resume his former relations with him as adviser upon all affairs of public importance". Yet Locke's return to England at this particular time had had a clear and natural projection since the previous October when his plan to cross the Alps into Italy had been thwarted. There is no evidence that he was "caused . . . at Shaftesbury's request, to hurry home when he did".[2]

In April, after suggestions in the Commons that James knew of the "plot", the conclusion had been reached that at any rate his being a Catholic and his being next in line of succession had of itself encouraged Papist conspiracies against "the King and the Protestant religion". Besides his Catholicism, which by itself would have made his succession abhorrent to the many who jealously guarded their Protestantism, there was also his impatience with Parliamentary government. But even though he found James's open Catholicism a political embarassment, Charles was hot to defend his right to succeed, and, to forestall any suggestion of his being excluded from the succession, he offered (perhaps not sincerely) that constitutional limitations might be placed on the power of any Catholic monarch.[3]

Some (including Shaftesbury) objected to limitations that they might lead to the destruction of the monarchy as such, others that they would not work in practice; and Locke had been back in England for less than a week when the Commons debated an exclusion bill "to disable the Duke of York to inherit the crown of England".[4] The bill got through its two first readings, but before it reached a third, the King caused its failure by proroguing Parliament until mid-August.

The bill was not very specific about who would succeed if James were excluded, thus avoiding the risk of dividing those who supported it. It did say that the Crown should descend as though James were dead (i.e. to his children), and this implied that his Protestant daughter Mary, wife of the equally Protestant William of Orange, would be next in line. While some favoured this, it was clear that the whole problem would re-emerge if James's present wife had a son before Charles died. Another person with considerable support as a possible successor was Charles's son, the Duke of Monmouth; but he was illegitimate and, despite recurring claims and rumours, Charles denied that he had ever married the mother. Even as one of the main proponents of exclusion, and as someone who often found it convenient to ally with Monmouth, Shaftesbury's own views about the succession were never made clear.[5]

The "great agitation" and "trouble" Locke had found himself surrounded by since his arrival back in London must have been particularly intense at Thanet House, and shortly after the prorogation of Parliament and the failure of the exclusion bill he "retired to the country" for a couple of weeks. Even here there must have been much political discussion for he was at Bexwells in Essex, where Shaftesbury's steward Stringer had a house; but perhaps he went simply to escape London, for despite his optimism the previous winter Locke's health was not, it was later said, "so established but that after his return he was still less able than formerly, to continue long in London without retreating ... to recover the prejudice his health received from the smoke of that vast quantity of sea coal which is burnt in this great city".[6]

There is no record of what Locke did for Shaftesbury during his first months back in England, but he seems to have been kept busy, generally unable to "dispose of myself as I have wished" and "finding myself in places I had not chosen to be". His political sympathies were becoming more obvious: specifically mentioning Locke, Wood recorded that "After the breaking out of the popish plot several of our scholars were tried [i.e. put to the test] and at length were (1680) discovered to be whigs" – that is, amongst those (often nonconformists and dissenters) who saw Popery and non-Parliamentary government as the greatest threats to the country, in contrast with the loyalist high Anglican "tories" who, reminded of the situation prior to the civil war, saw popular opposition to the King as an even greater threat.[7]

Olaf Rømer stayed in London for about a month, though Locke was unable to see him as much as he would have liked for his lodgings were some way from Thanet House. He did, however, take him to visit

Boyle and arranged for him to meet Flamsteed, the Astronomer Royal. One particular interest which Locke and Rømer shared (along with others in Paris such as Picard) was the standardisation and comparison of units of length and other quantities such as weight.[8]

Earlier in the century the Italian physicist Galileo had shown that a pendulum's period of swing is proportional to its length, and, given this, the Royal Society had proposed as a standard unit of length a pendulum whose period of swing is one second – a length which in London, so Rømer informed Locke after making the observations (which Locke himself intended to do), turned out to be 39 inches. On the basis of the length of a "pendulum of seconds", Locke devised a system which he explained to Boyle later that year. He defined what he called a "philosophical or universal foot" as one-third of a pendulum of seconds (i.e. 13 inches, a length happily quite close to the English foot). This was then divided into ten "inches", the inch into ten "lines", and the line into ten "grys" – so that a grys was one-thousandth of a philosophical foot. (The "grys", though differently valued, had figured in the non-absolute system of decimal measurement Locke had devised some years earlier for Carolina.) This measure of a philosophical foot, he told Boyle, "whatever it be for other purposes, I thought the fittest for philosophical communications"; he encouraged his friends to use it, giving them folding boxwood rulers he had had made to embody it.[9]

Locke used these units when he sent Toinard the measurements of a "pigeon hole" cabinet he designed for the storage of rolled papers, such as letters and other manuscripts: a square of 3460 grys divided into 100 square holes of 765 grys in depth with walls of a thickness of 36 or 37 grys, so each pigeon hole was 300 by 300 by 765 grys deep. Toinard thought the idea was wonderful, as did everyone to whom he described "le cabinet de monsieur Locke".[10]

Presumably Rømer was equally impressed when he saw the cabinet during his visit, but he was in some doubt about the philosophical foot as an absolute measure, since he found that a pendulum of seconds in London was slightly longer than one in Paris. Such puzzling variations with latitude were first clearly indicated by the observations made by the French astronomer Jean Richer at the beginning of the decade. As it happens, while Rømer was in London, Toinard had a visit from Richer, who persisted in his claims about this variation, even when faced with Toinard's objection that Picard had found no difference between Copenhagen and Montpellier.[11] In fact there *is* a difference between these two places, more indeed than between London and Paris, for the earth is not perfectly spherical and gravitational force, together with the length of a pendulum of seconds, decreases towards the equator.

During this year the many friends Locke had left behind in Paris must have often been in his mind, not least because Toinard kept them there by his reports of toasts to Locke's health at their informal discussion groups and dinners. Besides constantly plying Locke with requests for a large variety of objects (books, book catalogues, crayons, knives and forks, seeds, marine charts, maps of London, fishing rods, hooks and lines), Toinard's letters were so crammed with questions, information, and ideas that Locke was forced to ask him to write on larger paper and with wider margins to give room for annotating and summarising their contents. Locke's less frequent replies tended not to open up fresh topics or even to develop those offered by Toinard, and if there is possibly something rather mechanically dutiful about them, this was surely more for reasons of time than of interest: in May he said that since his return there had simply been no time for the sort of conversation he enjoyed with Toinard.[12] There is no sign that he regretted the frequency and easy light-hearted closeness of Toinard's letters.

A regularly occurring topic in Toinard's letters (in this and later years) was his project for scriptural "harmonisation". He had been moving on from his "Evangelical Harmony" of the Gospels to a "Harmony Davidica" of the books of Kings, Chronicles, and the Psalms, and regularly sent Locke samples and versions of his work. Locke's interest in the whole project was markedly encouraging (he hoped Toinard would do the whole Bible) and more than politely enthusiastic. He reported on Toinard's work to others, all of whom, Boyle in particular, were keen to see it, he said. He offered his comments on the problem which often exercised Toinard as to the best way to present the complex results of his attempts at harmonisation. One of the more difficult aspects of the project, so Toinard found, and one which occupied Locke too, was the dating of the various biblical events.[13]

The activities of their friend Picard at the Paris observatory were another regular topic. He was engaged in determining the longitude of various places by means of the method proposed by Galileo of using observations of the almost daily eclipses by Jupiter of its four principal moons: the difference in two different local times of a given eclipse

would give a difference in longitude. In the summer of 1679 Picard
went from Paris to Belle Isle and Ushant, islands in the Atlantic off
Brittany, and then to Brest, to do what Toinard, a keen wildfowler,
called "sniping" at the moons of Jupiter. With simultaneous sniping at
the observatory in Paris (the "duck pond" Toinard called it), it was then
possible to determine the longitudes of France's western extremities in
relation to Paris. Their observations that summer showed that France
did not extend as far as had been believed.[14]

Toinard urged on Locke the importance of having observers at
other places too and asked him to get people in England involved.
Locke interested Boyle (and, via him, Hooke) in the project, and
Rømer solicited the help of Flamsteed. As a result, observations were
made the following year at the new Royal Observatory at Greenwich
when Picard was at Bordeaux and Bayonne. Locke promised to see
whether he could do something himself at Oxford, but he does not
appear to have done so.[15]

By mid-August Locke had not, despite the urgency, yet been able to get
to Somerset to see to his affairs there, and visits to Oxford and to
Thomas in Salisbury must have been on his mind too. As he told
Toinard, "I had not thought I would be in London more than twenty
days after my arrival, yet here I still am nearly five [*sic*] months later".
Apart from anything else, his two horses had been doing no more
than "exercise their teeth"! "I wish", he said, that the Cartesians (who
believed that animals were mere machines) would invent a horse that
"one could mount when one wished, without wasting hay and oats
when idle".[16]

However, with Shaftesbury shortly to leave for Dorset, Locke spent
the third Sunday in the month preparing to leave for the West Country
the next day. Unfortunately, his own business had to suffer even longer,
for late that night he was summoned by Sir John and Lady Banks to
attend to Caleb who was sick, and the next day he rode to Olantigh in
Kent instead, where the Bankses were staying. His journal records the
detailed course of Caleb's feverish sickness which stayed with him at
least until the end of September; it also records that he too was ill, for
upwards of a week: "When I waked this night I found myself something
ill in my stomach.... In the morning...I began to fall into a sweat
which without increasing the clothes I ordinarily had upon my bed or
taking anything but a little warm small beer once or twice continued
with great violence and a grievous pain in my head." Besides being

concerned with Caleb's and his own illness, Locke prescribed for the gardener who had been suffering from a fever, as well as for others in the area, so it is hardly surprising that the Bankses' host, Henry Thornhill, should have written to Locke after his return to London thanking him "for all the kindnesses and charity he showed at the infirmary of Olantigh". Retailing the local gossip, Thornhill dryly reported on a recent marriage. Being made one flesh, he said, "is a kind of Hoc est Corpus trick",* as was proved by the groom, "who laying his hand on his wife's found no difference it caused in him more than when it was on his".[17]

When Locke got back to London at the beginning of October all chance of going to the West Country, or even to Oxford, was fast disappearing. Having dissolved Parliament in July, some weeks before it was due to re-assemble, the King decided in mid-October not to meet the new one until well into the following January; moreover, because of further threats that Shaftesbury was making to James's position, he dismissed him from his post as Lord President of the Privy Council. "Things since my return are still in such confusion", Locke told Toinard the day before this dismissal.[18]

DECEMBER 1679–APRIL 1680: "A CONDITION AS MIGHT MAKE YOUR FRIENDS APPREHENSIVE"[19]

Shortly before Christmas Locke went to Oxford, where he stayed until February. He had various pieces of business to attend to, most immediately to see to his college finances: the carefully documented account he received showed he was due nearly £200 from the Butler and the Treasurer, and from rent from the sub-letting of his rooms. (His medical attention to Pricket, a college servant who was suffering from a fever, and on which he made extensive notes, was probably gratis.)[20]

There was also some business of Toinard's he had undertaken. He had brought back to England some wooden die stamps which would print ligatured Latin letters, and in response to Toinard's continued requests that he interest printers and publishers in them, Locke showed them to the Bishop of Oxford, John Fell, who for some years had been in charge of a university press. Unfortunately, Fell was not particularly taken with them, and his reaction only reinforced Locke's belief that "if they are new the most worthwhile things only impress those who have a specific use for them".[21]

Besides spending time in Oxford with James Tyrrell and George Walls (perhaps reminiscing about their time together in France), Locke was occupied in writing out his "Observations upon the Growth and Culture of Vines and Olives", which brought together all the information he had gathered and recorded on these topics during his years in France. Having dedicated it to him, Locke sent a copy to Shaftesbury who, one of his associates said, "received it with great joy;... he perused it greedily, and I see him at it very intent last night again".[22]

Locke was thinking of Shaftesbury's grandson too, and bought him a bow and arrows. For himself he bought a Bachelor of Medicine gown – not having been in Oxford since being awarded the degree in February 1675. Bourne took this as implying that he was thinking of taking up long-term residence in Christ Church again, but perhaps straightforward pride in dressing according to his status whenever he was in college is sufficient explanation. When he left Oxford in early February the new gown, along with a manuscript, "Intellectu", a manifestation of another of his long-term interests, was put into the care of Walls.[23] His ultimate destination was Somerset, but he went first to Salisbury. He and David Thomas had not seen each other since the autumn of 1671 and must have had much to talk about in the week Locke was there: medical matters figured, of course, and Locke took down recipes for a variety of complaints (cankers, hydrophobia, quinsies, and suppressed menstruation).[24]

Leaving Thomas, Locke at last made directly for Somerset. The previous November his uncle Peter, then into his seventies, had written anxiously about his coming to attend to his business. The old man's worry was partly rooted in feeling "at the brink of the grave", and that "it would trouble me to die before I see you and even our accounts". But also Locke's accounts had become disordered during the years of his absence. "Some of your rents I cannot gather because I know not what it is some will not pay supposing I believe you are dead." The owners of the coal works on some of Locke's land would similarly not pay their rent except to Locke himself; the legal situation with respect to some other tenancies needed some attention; and there were, said Peter Locke, many other things to go over.[25]

Since that letter, Peter Locke's son-in-law William Stratton had taken over as Locke's legal agent, and, during the next two months, besides discussing matters with him, Locke travelled around the district, collecting rents and his share of money from the coal works, entering into new lettings, and settling some of his and his uncle's debts. Peter Locke had not exaggerated the seriousness of the situation, for seven years' back-rent was collected from some tenants.[26]

On a visit to Bristol, Locke was rather severely kicked in the ribs by a horse, an unfortunate incident which necessitated being bled twice, and the services of a bone setter. While there he picked up a letter from Shaftesbury, thanking him for a locally made Cheddar cheese he had sent. "We long to see you here", Shaftesbury wrote from London, "and hope you have almost ended your travels. Somersetshire, no doubt, will perfect your breeding; after France and Oxford, you could not go to a more proper place."[27]

But Locke was not yet ready for Thanet House when he left Sutton Court in the first week of April. For one thing he had some business of Shaftesbury's to attend to at Shilton, eight miles from Oxford. A couple of months earlier Samuel Birch, a dissenting Presbyterian who had been ejected from Oxford city, had died, leaving his daughter Elizabeth to cope with the school they then ran. Concerned for her, an ex-governess of his grandson, Shaftesbury wondered about her plans. Did she wish to keep on with the boarding of the pupils, taking on a master for their teaching, or did she want to give the whole thing up? Her decision was to restart, and in a matter of months Shaftesbury's grandson, now nine, whom Shaftesbury had taken into his care, was attending her school in Clapham near London, shortly to be joined, under Locke's watching eye, by David Thomas's son William.[28]

From Shilton Locke went on to Oxford, where he stayed for a week. His journal for these days records giving Jacob Bobert at the Botanical Gardens a list of some dozens of seeds which Magnol in Montpellier was hoping for. Another entry, an account of making leavened bread which Locke had recently received from Charleton, exhibits one of his incidental though unfleeting interests. Locke did not understand some of the local measures in the account ("une truquette d'eau", "une piche d'eau", "une hemine de farine"), and made inquiries of Toinard concerning them. Toinard sent Locke a further recipe, for bread made the French way; he thought that Syl, even though Swiss, should be able to get good results with it. For his part Locke thought that bread would never taste so good as when eaten with Toinard, seasoned with his wit. Two years later Locke would record yet a third recipe for bread.[29]

When he left Oxford for London in mid-April he was not, it appears, in the best of health; indeed Fell thought his condition was rather worrying.[30]

APRIL–NOVEMBER 1680: "FORTUNE CONTINUES TO CROSS ALL MY PLANS"[31]

Since the dissolution of Parliament the previous July the King kept postponing the meeting of a new one, and this was now not due until November – thus depriving the whig opposition of any institutional way of pursuing their aims and increasing their fears of Charles's use of prerogative. Locke, and others of Shaftesbury's household, were among almost sixteen thousand protestors who put their names to a petition presented to the King in mid-January, requesting that he summon Parliament, since "there has been and still is, a most damnable and hellish plot".[32]

In May, Charles was ill for a short while, and so gave an urgency to the question of the royal succession. Lord Grey, one of those who was present at the discussions which took place at Thanet House, later said (though in the unreliable circumstances of a "confession") that it was decided that in the event of the King's death there should be an armed rebellion to forestall James, and a meeting of Parliament to settle the succession. No doubt Locke was aware of, even if he was not a party to, these discussions, and it was perhaps on some business of Shaftesbury's that at the end of May and into June he spent four or five days in Hertfordshire, at least some of the time at the Earl of Salisbury's, one of Shaftesbury's associates in the Lords.[33]

For a time in June the weather was very cold. This cannot have helped Locke's health which had been so poor on his return from Oxford in April, and his cough grew worse. A brief escape from the London air was offered by a short overnight trip he made at the end of the month to Esher, thirteen miles out of London, to see Sir Thomas Lynch, recently returned from Paris where Locke had last seen him the previous year, and via whom Toinard had sent copies of a yearly astronomical almanac and a medical journal he had wanted. Besides picking up these things, he was provided by Lady Lynch with a recipe by which Lord Brounker had been cured "of pissing blood and stinking pus and ... kept off the gout".[34]

Early in July, Locke was in Oxford on a brief visit. He had "a little interest" there, he told Toinard, and, so far as we can tell, this was to get access to a trunk, record its contents, and send it to Tyrrell for safekeeping. Legal documents, largely to do with his Somerset affairs, were the trunk's main contents, but a manuscript entitled "Intellectu" was amongst them.[35] Locke clearly placed considerable trust in Tyrrell and was a frequent visitor to his house at Oakley, a few miles northeast of Oxford. He did not, however, confide in him to the extent he did in Thomas and other friends; having known him over twenty years he was presumably aware of aspects of his character which would later annoy him greatly.

Later in July, probably accompanying Shaftesbury, he left London for Wimborne St Giles. After a week there he went to Salisbury to stay, on his way back to London, with Thomas. He was there for just two days, during which, besides acquiring yet more medical recipes and discussing some of Thomas's cases, he wrote down some reflections on how God's omnipotence is not a perfection unless regulated by his wisdom and goodness.[36]

For a month or so there had been the possibility that Locke would travel to France towards the end of August. Part of the initial idea had been to accompany Lady Northumberland, whose husband was still the ambassador in Paris; but his going did not wholly depend on this for it was still something of a possibility even after she decided not to go. Cranston suggested that Locke's intended journey may have had some connection with Shaftesbury's political planning.[37] Whether or not there was any such hidden purpose in it, probably the initiating reason for the journey was to accompany a young man, the son of a Major Knatchbull, to Saumur where, under the eye of Mrs Anna Grigg, he was to attend the Protestant academy there.

Of course the chance of seeing Toinard was in Locke's mind too. "The hope I had of seeing you", he told him, "was the greatest reason for the journey I was planning, but fortune continues to cross all my plans as it has always done since my return to England." Presumably "fortune" took Shaftesbury's shape, for it does seem likely that it was his work with him that had made it difficult for Locke to get to Oxford or to Somerset, but there is no reason to think that the abandonment of the journey to France came about by anything other than a change of mind on Knatchbull's part.[38]

Shortly after getting back to London from Dorset, Locke went to Stringer's in Essex. He was there for over two weeks; perhaps he went on behalf of Shaftesbury (who was still in the country), but we do not really know whether left to himself he would have "disposed of himself" differently had he been free to do so.[39]

On his return from Stringer's he wrote to Toinard, apologising for not having yet studied the sheets of the "Harmony" which he had sent earlier in the month. He had been completely taken up with various short journeys, he explained; and indeed, two days later, on 1 September, he was off again, and again for reasons unknown, this time to Aylesford in Kent where Sir John Banks was now living in his recently completed house. He returned to London on 6 September.[40]

A few days later Shaftesbury returned too, in response to the King's decision a couple of weeks earlier to meet Parliament on 21 October. Locke must have been involved in some way, however minor, with the ensuing discussions which took place in Thanet House as to how Parliament should deal with the question of the succession and with the Duke of York, both directly by way of impeachment or more generally by a further attempt to get an exclusion bill through. But he still had time for his own interests, being shown by Boyle the results of some recent chemical experiments, and visiting various watch and clock-makers on an errand Toinard had wanted him to carry out — to locate a very efficient device he had heard of for cutting toothed clock-cogs (a task in which Locke eventually sought Hooke's help).[41]

Early in October, Locke told Toinard that he was soon going to Oxford unless something were to prevent him. Whether or not it was Shaftesbury's business that might have stood in his way, nothing did, and shortly afterwards he set out on the two-day journey. While there a letter from Thomas asked him to come to Salisbury if his business in Oxford was not such as to detain him long; there were various things he was experimenting with which he wanted to discuss, especially a fever cure which did not use expensive Peruvian bark. Thomas wondered whether Locke was in Oxford with a view to improving his medical qualifications, "to do exercise and proceed Doctor". This must have been something the two had discussed, and something that was a live possibility. But though Locke's journal for the month he was in Oxford contains much in the way of medical notes and recipes, there is no real indication that he was there working towards an M.D. He visited the Botanical Gardens where he handed over seeds of about twenty plants

which he had been sent from Montpellier, and, partly having in mind
the Royal physic garden in Paris, picked up some others to send
to Toinard. He spent a couple of nights at Oakley, where he
administered to Tyrrell's sick wife, and Tyrrell visited him in Oxford
(a visit from which he "got a great cold" through "sitting in your hot little
stove, and then going out into the cold raw air"). He also bought "a steel
ring", for £1 6s. What must have provoked this was what Toinard had
told him in a recent letter and which he had copied down into his
journal, about a cure for "the migraine". "Make a ring of good steel, all
in one piece without joints, and wear it on the little finger of the right
hand. This ring can be made with a piece of steel which you pierce with
a hole the size of a finger." Locke wanted the ring, not for himself,
but for a friend, and quizzed Toinard as to what exactly he meant by
"migraine".[42]

Toinard's migraine cure was just one of the amazingly various topics
that had continued to crop up in his correspondence with Locke
(a correspondence in which Locke, perhaps feeling his French slipping
away, began to write in Latin). Amongst the others were a superior
spinning machine; a method for breathing under water (which Locke
thought ran foul of his still-held view that the purpose of respiration
was to provide fuel to the heart's vital flame); the effects of a vacuum on
humans; a narcotic prepared from thorn-apples; a method of cooking
in a closed vessel without the use of fresh water, in which Boyle too was
interested; coloured glass; air-guns; a double-hulled ship or catamaran
of a kind being experimented upon by Sir William Petty; drinking sea
water; medical recipes; the possible commercialisation in England
of the glass stoppers Toinard had devised and of an idea he had for
making ships perfectly watertight; a device for regulating clock
pendula; a specially designed bed at Thanet House for gout sufferers
(Shaftesbury was one); a theory of Toinard's about the variation of the
magnetic compass; and the dissection of an elephant, which led Locke
to joke that if this revealed that this huge animal's pineal gland was
proportionably large, the Cartesians would have to say it had a large
soul: "but if it is true that elephants can write I wouldn't want them to
be given paper and ink lest they leave to posterity in their memoirs that
we are nothing but machines and that only they have understanding".[43]
Things other than information and ideas passed between them too:
travel books, medical journals, fishing rods, seed potatoes, and trees
which Locke wanted for Shaftesbury's house in Dorset.

NOVEMBER 1680—MARCH 1681: "1641 IS COME AGAIN"

The new session of Parliament began in November while Locke was in Oxford. It again first debated the Popish plot, and threats to Parliamentary government posed by the King's constant recourse to prorogation and dissolution; and when Locke went back to London on 9 November the Commons was debating an exclusion bill. This got through all its readings, but was rejected by the Lords who favoured the King's proposal of limitations. Despite this, Shaftesbury and his colleagues believed that Charles, in return for a Parliamentary vote of money, might be brought to sacrifice James, but early in January (having been encouraged to think that Louis would resume his financial help) he reiterated his opposition to exclusion, and then, on 10 January, announced a ten-day prorogation.[44]

Three days later, Locke set out for Oxford. After an overnight stop in Beaconsfield ("supper and breakfast 9d") he arrived in Oxford in time to buy billets for the fire, and candles. The following Tuesday, before going to Tyrrell's at Oakley, he took some more seeds to the Botanical Gardens, in exchange for which Bobert gave him some recommendations of botanical authors.[45]

"I heartily wish you refreshing by Oxford air", Stratton's wife said, when her husband wrote to Locke at the time about his business affairs, but at Tyrrell's Locke had become confined to his bed, ill with a severe cough, "almost constantly in a breathing sweat". Though he spent most of the two weeks or so he was at Oakley in bed, he was still able to produce, often by dictation to Tyrrell ("my operator when I kept my bed"), a good part of a long point-by-point series of critical notes on a published sermon "The mischief of separation", preached the previous May by Edward Stillingfleet, Dean of St. Paul's, and a more recent defence of that sermon, *The Unreasonableness of Separation* (December 1680).[46]

Stillingfleet was concerned at the danger he saw in the separation of dissenting nonconformists from the Church of England. Not only could such divisions within Protestantism be made use of by the common Catholic enemy, but also, he felt, wearied by these internal disputes people might even long for the unity of a papal tyranny. His aim, he said, was not to stir up persecution of dissenters, but to encourage union with the established Church which he saw as "that great bulwark against Popery".[47]

Underlying all that Stillingfleet said was a certain view shared by other bishops about the status and authority of the Anglican Church and its relation to the state. Stillingfleet's belief was that it was divinely instituted and had a legitimate claim to the truth. Dissent from it was therefore a manifestation of original sin, a wilful recalcitrance to see the truth. It was, moreover, one function of the civil government to act in complicity with it, upholding it and persuading people to it by imposing penalties for dissent.

Locke shared Stillingfleet's worry that there is "mischief" in a lack of unity "at a time when popery so threatens and so nearly surrounds us". But particularly "at a time when [Catholics] are making their approaches towards us and ready openly to attack us", he was doubtful of the wisdom of explicitly focusing on that disunity rather than "letting the controversy sleep". His comments make plain the thought that though he himself is "of the Church of England", what is required is unity in true religion, in Protestantism as such, rather than a unity with the established Church. Unity, he thought, does not require conformity with the Church of England; it is a matter of Christians being "in peace and charity" rather than agreeing in "all the circumstances of outward worship".[48] So long as there is peace between them, separate churches do not destroy unity.

Locke's view embodied an anti-clericalism which had increasingly become and would remain a feature of his thought. What caused dissent from the national Church, he thought, was the insistence on and imposition of certain ways of worship, by ambitious clerics jealously guarding their own ways: peace between "the kneelers and not kneelers at the sacrament . . . between the bowers and not bowers at the altar", is best achieved and preserved by there being no compulsion about it.[49]

Locke clearly was what in a later year he claimed to be, an "evangelical" rather than a "papist" Christian: the latter have a pretence of infallibility and seek to impose on the consciences of others; the former, only seeking truth, want it to be established by reason, and are forgiving of human weakness and fallibility.[50]

Consequently he now argued for the desirability of the "comprehension" within Anglicanism of as many dissenters as possible by relaxing the requirements for a uniformity of worship: "had those ceremonies which are confessed to be but things indifferent been lessened, and the borders of the Church enlarged, the Church of England must needs have had more partisans and less contentions". The success of this enlargement, however, depends on the accommodation being mutual: "both sides [need] to remit something, and to meet in an amicable yielding to each other". In fact, with respect to comprehension there was little difference between Locke and Stillingfleet who, Locke said, was the first of the Anglican clergy he had known of "that would ever hearken to the least abatement of... the precise rigour of their forms".[51]

As for toleration, however, while Stillingfleet's view was that it encouraged dissent and a religious querulousness, Locke's was that it was more likely to put an end to disputes and divisions than was the imposition of uniformity; the religious intolerance of the previous twenty years had not, he pointed out, "cured our separation".[52] Freely belonging to different churches does not make for contention; being denied that freedom does. Forced uniformity is what produces disunity. Peaceful union among Protestants is to be achieved by gentleness and charity rather than the imposition of uniformity. Locke was, moreover, still of the view he had expressed earlier in the "Essay concerning Toleration", that punishing dissenters was likely to make them politically dangerous, more likely to unite with each other than with the national Church.

It was, of course, the *political* danger from Catholicism that was a large part of Stillingfleet's and Locke's concerns, and this was one kind of "dissent" which, in Locke's view, should be punished. Catholicism involves "extravagant and senseless opinions" ("the protestant religion and transubstantiation cannot subsist together"); but this of itself is no reason why Catholics should not be treated as other dissenters, if anything it means they might be given "an allowance of greater pity". But Catholics should still not be tolerated, because (as Locke noted in the "Essay concerning Toleration") being of that religion goes along with "being subjects to a prince that has declared emnity and war to us". In effect the Catholics in the country, few though they may be, are "either enemies in our bowels or spies among us, whilst their general commanders whom they blindly obey declare war, and an unalterable design to destroy us". Protestants, said Locke, "ought now by all ways to be stirred up against them as people that have declared themselves ready by blood, violence, and destruction to ruin our religion and government".[53]

In various ways, Locke's notes on Stillingfleet continued the doctrines of the earlier "Essay concerning Toleration": speculative opinions "concerning things of another life" and "my praying to God in this or that fashion" have no effect on my neighbours' "well-being, or preservation in this world"; "I must choose my own way to salvation", and not, "without further examination", adopt clerically advocated precepts and practices, even when these are of the established national Church. Locke continued to believe, in firm disagreement with Stillingfleet, that the established Church was in no privileged position with respect to ceremonials and doctrines and had no particular duty, over and above any duty other churches had, to bring people into it. All churches will say "we only are in the right".[54]

Rather than having, as Stillingfleet thought, a duty to take part in the "unity of an outward conformity", we have one, Locke thought, "to take care of the salvation of [our] own soul". It is with this business in mind that we should be free to join one church rather than another, according as we find it more "edifying", according as we find its ways of worship better able to "inform the understanding and subdue the will". St Paul's injunction that things should be done "decently and in order" was no more important, Locke pointed out against Stillingfleet, than that they be done "unto edifying". There can be no sin in a person's separating from the established Church if in the judgement of his conscience he finds the ways of another church better able to give him an understanding of Christ's teachings, and to help and encourage him to virtue. Observing the rules of the gospel is more important than merely observing ceremonies; "thinking to please God with outward ceremonies and bodily performances which he neither requires or expects" is "superstition".[55]

While Locke was still confined at Tyrrell's, the need arose for him to be back at Oxford. On the day Locke had ridden to Oakley the King had dissolved Parliament, shortly before it had been due to meet again. He had announced too that he would meet with a new one on 21 March, but this time in Oxford (where, given the University's loyalty, he felt he would be safer than in London from civil protests and demonstrations should he decide again on dissolution).[56] Shaftesbury commissioned Locke to arrange accommodation for him and his party in Oxford.

Locke did what he could from his sick-bed in Oakley, but early in February Stringer told him that Shaftesbury had sent someone from London to deal directly with things; Locke was not to trouble himself further, certainly not to try to go Oxford. But this freedom to "proceed in the recovery of your health" and not do "anything that may be

unsafe or disadvantagous to your condition" came too late, for, even as
Stringer wrote, Locke had been back in Oxford for two days. Despite
having been in bed for just two of the four weeks he thought he
needed, he had got up and out of his room for a day, "to fit myself the
best I could to bear the cold open air", and had then "galloped most of
the way" to Oxford. He was most concerned not to have been
immediately at Shaftesbury's service, "exceedingly ashamed that
a suspicion how I should be able to bear the air should give your
Lordship so much trouble".[57]

After three days back in Oxford he reported that it was impossible to
arrange for a college to take the whole party, but that he had the option
on the house of Dr Wallis, the Savilian professor of geometry, for
Shaftesbury's immediate household and perhaps one or two of his close
friends and associates. He sent Shaftesbury a lengthy and detailed
description (including measurements he took himself) of what was
available. Wallis was prepared to dismantle his study, but Locke,
"knowing how troublesome a thing it [is] to remove books", did not
pursue this. Locke's conversations with Wallis extended beyond this
immediate business of settling Shaftesbury's lodgings, for besides these
domestic issues they discussed questions of chronology, the lengths of
the various years, epochs, and golden numbers.[58]

Locke was also involved in political preparations for the new
Parliament, being asked by Shaftesbury to get some of his supporters to
stand down in Oxfordshire elections, so as not to compete among
themselves. It was, moreover, expected that he would not remain
behind the scenes when Parliament eventually met. He was to be
properly dressed for the occasion, and Stringer arranged, at a cost to
Locke of £3, for "some of the hair prunella [a kind of cloth] to be
bought for you to put you in a fit decorum for entertaining of the
courtiers", and Mrs Stringer and Lady Shaftesbury set to work to
fashion it into a gown.[59]

When he opened Parliament on 21 March the King again expressed
himself utterly willing to consider any suggestions for limiting the
power of a Catholic successor, and keeping the administration
in Protestant hands. But the Commons, besides debating the Popish
plot and the King's treatment of Parliament, again resolved that
nothing less than exclusion would do. Faced with the usual opposition
and with the expectation of being able to survive with French subsidies,
Charles dissolved what would prove to have been his last Parliament.
In a powerful "Declaration" he justified this on the grounds that his

opponents were unreasonable in being unwilling to compromise. In its attacks on him and James, Parliament was acting as it had with his father and the main threat to the country was from it: "Who cannot but remember that religion, liberty and property were all lost when the monarchy was shaken off, and could never be revived till that restored."[60]

No doubt glad to escape "the worry and confusion" of the recent weeks, Locke left Oxford two days after the dissolution. He went first to Wycombe, twenty miles southeast (where Shaftesbury had stayed on his way to Oxford), presumably to prepare for Shaftesbury's return journey, before returning north the next day to Oakley, where he stayed a few days before going back to Oxford.[61]

APRIL 1681—APRIL 1683: "NOT A WORD EVER DROPS FROM HIS MOUTH"[62]

It was not until towards the end of May that Locke returned to London. Quite possibly he had spent some more time on his "Defence of nonconformity"; certainly he made some notes on the need for miracles and inspiration to be answerable to reason. He was, however, busy in other ways too. He made two short visits to Oakley where Tyrrell's wife was ill, and towards the end of April spent two days with Thomas in Salisbury. If this visit with Thomas (during which he noted down cures for nose bleeding, gonorrhoea, and earache) had been on the way to Somerset he changed his mind, for instead he rode north to Gloucester where he saw "Lysis", Nathaniel Hodges, who since his appointment by Shaftesbury in 1673 was a prebendary of Gloucester Cathedral. For some reason his week's stay there involved a journey to Worcester and back, twenty miles further north.[63] Nine of the fifteen days of this period were spent on horseback, at an average of twenty-three miles a day.

When Locke left Oxford for London it was perhaps because he was hoping soon to see Toinard. But, as on previous occasions, Toinard's projected journey to England did not materialise, and Locke had to content himself with catching up on his correspondence with him, and drinking to his health when he had supper one June evening with their mutual friend Brisbane. That same month he made an overnight visit to Sir Thomas Lynch's, thirteen miles away in Esher. Lynch was shortly to go out to Jamaica as governor and they discussed the possibility of Locke's going out there too. Right up to the point of his sailing in December, Lynch persisted in trying to get Locke to go, but he eventually conceded that he was "very reasonable in preferring the tranquillity and conversation of Oxford to the dangers and uncertainties of the winds and seas".[64]

During this early summer period Locke spent some time studying various works of Hooker, particularly on law, and made some lengthy notes on his perennial topic of knowledge, distinguishing between knowledge proper (based on ideas) and "opinion" (based on experience). He thought that so long as we had suitable ideas of God, and ourselves as his creatures, we would be capable of a "demonstrative certainty" about morality. He also met various medical friends from whom he took down recipes; in particular he spent time with Boyle, from whom he learnt a method of preserving and embalming insects. Charleton, who was intending shortly to return to England from Montpellier with his collection of insect and animal specimens and other natural curiosities to be forwarded into Locke's care, had recently asked him whether he knew a good way of doing this.[65]

Towards the end of June, Tyrrell wrote asking Locke what his plans were for the summer. "But I do not blame you", he said, "for not letting Fortune know too long beforehand what your intentions are, for fear the Jade should put one of those dog tricks upon you that she has done so often."[66] Unfortunately, after the pleasantness of the past few weeks, another "dog trick" was about to be played.

Following his blow to whig opposition by his sudden dissolution of the Oxford Parliament, the King began increasingly to exert his power. At the beginning of July Shaftesbury was arrested, accused of getting witnesses to testify falsely concerning the Popish plot; and Thanet House, presumably including Locke's rooms, was searched for incriminating papers.* Having appeared before the King and council Shaftesbury was sent to the Tower, charged with high treason. Together with Stringer, and others of Shaftesbury's immediate circle, Locke set to work on investigating the case against him, and arranging for his defence.[67]

Locke became involved at the same time with the case against one of Shaftesbury's supporters, Stephen College, who had been arrested a few days before Shaftesbury, accused of conspiring to capture the King to force him to make concessions. An attempt on 8 July to indict College at the Old Bailey failed, and it was thought than an indictment for treason might succeed at Oxford, since his activities there during the Parliament earlier in the year were the basis of the charge against him. The next day Locke left for Oxford, no doubt to keep a close eye on the proceedings there. The Oxford Grand Jury successfully indicted College on 15 July (with a trial to begin the next month), and Locke set off back to London the next day, travelling via Oakley where he spent two days with Tyrrell.[68]

Locke returned to Oxford on 1 August. Presumably he went after discussions with the imprisoned Shaftesbury, to be on hand for College's trial which was to begin on 17 August. Indeed he had been reluctant to go, but, as he said later, he was "unexpectedly obliged". To what extent he was involved in preparations for the trial is not clear, but he was observed to be spending time with the main defence barrister, Robert West. Prideaux, the college librarian, later reported to John Ellis, an Under-secretary of State, that Locke had "treated [West] at his chambers and caressed [him] at so great a rate when College was tried here at Oxford". The evidence of Locke's food bill for the day of College's trial is that he treated West to a dinner which included a shoulder of mutton and six chickens.[69]

College's trial,* at which he was convicted of various traitorous acts and words, went on into the early hours of 18 August. No doubt this explains why that morning Locke made his weather observations at the unusually early hour of four o'clock, and then returned to London. He would have wanted to do this anyway to bring the news of College's conviction and to discuss with Shaftesbury's circle its possible bearing on Shaftesbury's case; but he had a further reason in that during the previous two days he had received an urgent letter from Stringer asking him "to hasten to town" because Shaftesbury was seriously ill: "My Lord's ague being returned...he is reduced to an extreme weakness and we all fear in exceeding danger.... We all hope better success from you than he is like to have from the other doctors."[70]

Before being tried by his peers Shaftesbury had to be indicted by a grand jury of commoners, and towards the end of August the government, aware of the support he had in London, looked into the question of whether the judges had the power of reforming a jury already constituted by the sheriff (so removing people who were sympathetic to Shaftesbury). Locke too sought legal opinion on this, besides investigating the legal complexities himself. He also saw to the payment of various legal fees, and, in company with Lady Shaftesbury, delivered an offer, which the King refused, that Shaftesbury would remove from London, even exile himself in Carolina, in exchange for release and a pardon.[71]

Yet Locke still found time for reading and note-taking on his many and various interests (particularly medical, but also geographical and, on one occasion, the question of our ability to acquire "perfect knowledge"). He also, at last, was able to investigate a towing engine which operated on the Thames below Blackwall, and about which Toinard had been persistently asking him for a year; he was keen to know whether such a machine might be suited for towing boats up the St Lawrence river from Quebec to Montreal. Hooke had been going to publish an account of it but had not yet done so, and, towards the end of September, Locke went to survey it. The device consisted, he found, of a pair of oar-powered boats on which was mounted a horse-powered windlass (the gearing of which he noted in detail); in stages, by means of temporary anchorings, "six horses will tow a vessel of 500 tons half a league per hour against the tide".[72]

Shaftesbury was still in the Tower in October, awaiting the proceedings of the Grand Jury, when a pamphlet in his defence, *No Protestant Plot*, was published. Robert Ferguson, one of Shaftesbury's associates, later admitted to being its author, but at the time some suspected that Shaftesbury himself had written it, and others, in Oxford, thought Locke was responsible (and had left the country for France). Eventually, towards the end of November, the jury refused to indict Shaftesbury on a charge of making various treasonable remarks against the King, and of saying, just before the opening of the Oxford Parliament, that he and his associates were ready and prepared to use force to get the King to accept an exclusion bill. He was released on bail.[73]

At the very end of the year (1681) Locke was introduced to Damaris Cudworth, a young woman in her early twenties, twenty-eight years his junior, the daughter of Ralph Cudworth, of Christ's College at Cambridge and one of the so-called "Cambridge Platonist" philosophers. She was visiting London at the time, staying in Salisbury Court, near Fleet Street, at the house of Lady King. Locke was very taken with her and, at the start of what would be a significant friendship, ventured to write to her. He received an encouraging reply: "Be it under what pretence you please that you have sent me a letter, you ought not to fear that it should be ill taken.... You might...without any apprehension have writ to me all that you pleased." There were references in her letter to the poetry of Vincent Voiture, and to characters out of the novels of Madame de Scudéry – references which no doubt indicated the tenor of their earlier conversations, conversations which, she said, she found "so agreeable an entertainment". Signing herself "Philoclea", the name of a character in Sidney's *Arcadia*, but also one which punningly indicates "friend of Locke", she hoped that it "will be acceptable to you that I reckon you in the number of those of my friends for whom I have a more particular consideration". A highly intelligent and literate woman, she seems, certainly at the time, to have been prone to moods, a "fantasticalness and inequality of humour", in which she felt at odds with herself and the world. She also suffered from some "indisposition" for which Richard Lower treated her.[74]

Locke met Damaris Cudworth probably through Edward Clarke, a West Country barrister, who also stayed in Salisbury Court when he was in London on business. Clarke had recently been appointed a trustee of part of Shaftesbury's estates and became well known at Thanet House, though he and Locke had perhaps first met during Locke's visit to Somerset in early 1680. About eight years Locke's junior, Clarke was married to Mary Jepp, a niece of John Strachey, and had recently inherited the estate of Chipley Park, near Taunton in Somerset. He and Locke became close and lasting friends. Locke often corresponded directly with Mrs Clarke, taking the opportunity to practise his gallantry: "Madam, wit and good nature meeting in a fair young lady as they do in you make the best resemblance of an angel that we know", he wrote later this year. She joked in reply that she had to read the address of the letter ten times before she could be sure that it was not intended for Damaris Cudworth, her "pretty overhead neighbour".[75]

Early in the new year Locke took the coach to Oxford. It was not long before he resumed his observations of the weather, and not long either before he wrote to "Philoclea". She had, he appears to have told her, impressed him as having "something more in her than is common to the rest of her sex". Perhaps part of what he had in mind was her recent suggestion for rather more serious reading than the romances they had talked of when they first met: *Selected Discourses*, a book first published about twenty years earlier by John Smith, another "Cambridge Platonist".[76]

Locke bought the book a couple of days after his arrival in Oxford. He was particularly interested in the first of Smith's discourses, "The true way or method of attaining to divine knowledge". At first he was not sure that he understood it properly, and asked "Philoclea" to explain it to him. Rather than giving, as it promised, an account of four kinds of knowledge, one of them "above reason", it seemed, he thought, to be describing something rather different, different degrees of virtue and love of God. "A love and practice of virtue may ... give a man a greater knowledge of god ... yet I cannot allow that it is a different sort of knowledge or any knowledge at all above his reason." Her reaction – that "what you comprehend not I am not very likely to make you" – was based on some shy dislike of being put on the spot and having to answer questions, as was being expected of her on social occasions at Lady King's: "I have of late so mortal an aversion for it ... that I almost wish sometimes that I were dumb, and am in a fright every time that anybody begins to speak to me." When Locke "put her upon this again", she teased "were you not afraid that in revenge I should have asked your advice about making me a new petticoat?"[77]

In April, in the course of what by now was a very regular correspondence, she asked Locke again about Smith's *Discourses*. His reply was based on some notes he had made earlier. The question had arisen between them of whether Smith's fourth and highest kind of knowledge (a kind possessed by someone who by rising "up above his own logical or self-rational life ... endeavours the nearest union with the Divine Essence") really was no more than a kind of spurious personal vision or imagination, what Locke called "enthusiasm". She had suggested that there was "something between" the two extremes of reason and vision, wondering whether it was not possible, while "constantly adhering" to reason's dictates, "to be acted by a higher principle" and to attain "a degree of perfection ... to which the powers of mere unassisted reason will never conduct a man". Locke had replied in effect denying her "something between": reason can be assisted "by education, discourse, contemplation or otherwise", but this does not result in knowledge "above reason"; on the other hand, though some things concerning God and religion may "seem as clear and operate as strongly as true knowledge", if they have no "foundation of reason" they amount to enthusiasm. Spelling this out, he explained that by "enthusiasm" he meant "a strong and firm persuasion of any proposition relating to religion for which a man has either no or not sufficient proofs from reason but receives them as truths wrought in the mind extraordinarily by god himself and influences coming immediately from him". This, he suggested, "can be no evidence or ground of assurance at all nor can by any means be taken for knowledge". In reply "Philoclea" agreed with him about enthusiasm, "to which I hope I am as much an enemy as you", but said that when she read Smith's book she had not taken his fourth kind of knowledge to amount to it. Indeed, without in any way wanting to put reason aside for something more illuminating, she was obviously inclined to place more value than Locke on "purity of life as the only true way of attaining to divine knowledge".[78]

While Locke was in Oxford all charges against Shaftesbury were dropped. He was still under suspicion by the government, though, and, in loyalist Oxford, Locke was under it too. In mid-March, Prideaux informed Ellis that Locke "lives a very cunning unintelligible life here, being two days in town and three out, and no one know where he goes, or when he goes, or when he returns". "Certainly there is some whig intrigue amanaging", he thought, "but here not a word of politics comes from him, nothing of news or anything else concerning our present affairs, as if he were not at all concerned in them. If anyone asks him 'What news?' when he returns from a progress, his answer is 'We know nothing'." He wrote again five days later:

Where J.L. goes I cannot by any means learn, all his voyages being so cunningly contrived; sometimes he will go to some acquaintances of his near the town, and then he will let anybody know where he is; but other times, when I am assured he goes elsewhere, no one knows where he goes, and therefore the other is made use of only for a blind. He has in his last sally been absent at least ten days, where I cannot learn. Last night he returned; and sometimes he himself goes out and leaves his man behind, who shall then to be often seen in the quadrangle to make people believe his master is at home, for he will let no one come to his chamber, and therefore it is not certain when he is there or when he is absent. I fancy there are projects afoot.[79]

Locke's journal for the period certainly does record some coming and going, but (for what it is worth) it does not support Prideaux's account of his movements which, it appears, were *only* to "acquaintances near the town" (though according to Damaris Cudworth he was "almost expected" by friends in London on 7 March): he was at Tyrrell's at Oakley from 17 to 20 February, from 2 to 5 March, and (having spent the previous night at nearby Abingdon) for two weeks from 7 to 22 March. His return to Oxford on 22 March was three days after Prideaux had reported him as having been "absent at least ten days". His weather register squares with the journal and indicates no other absences from Oxford.[80]

If Prideaux continued to keep his eye on Locke he would have seen him again leaving Oxford one day at the end of April; having made his weather observations at 5 a.m. he was going to Burford, twelve miles away, from where he returned the next day. As far as we know, however, he went there to order a saddle, "as good as ever I did make", the saddler reported a couple of weeks later. It may be, though, that his next absence, a month later, when he was away overnight in Reading (about halfway between Oxford and London), was more significant, for he perhaps met Stringer there. On his return he immediately went to Oakley, again just for an overnight stay; and then, after one day back in Oxford, he took the coach to London. He evidently intended to be away from Oxford for some time for he arranged for his horse Sorrel (together with "saddle pistols* and holsters") to be taken from its usual livery stables in Oxford to Tyrrell's.[81]

Whether or not Locke's frequent absences from Oxford in the spring had, as Prideaux had suspected, anything to do with some "whig plot", Locke must, on his return to Thanet House, have discussed the political situation with Shaftesbury. It was clear by now that Charles was determined to do without Parliament and would not call another one. The idea of either assassination or some kind of armed rebellion must at the very least have crossed Shaftesbury's mind and been discussed amongst his associates as some kind of possibility; according to some later (and not straightforwardly reliable) evidence, provided in confessions after Shaftesbury's death by his erstwhile supporters, this was indeed the case. Forde Grey testified that Shaftesbury had talked of (though not planned for) rising against Charles and James at various times (in May 1680 at the time of the King's short illness; in November 1680 after the defeat of the exclusion bill; and at the time of the Oxford Parliament in 1681).[82]

According to Grey's confession, as also to the later confession of Robert Ferguson, ideas of this sort were alive and discussed over the summer. Supposedly Shaftesbury was involved in discussions with the Earl of Argyll about the possibility of the latter's starting a rebellion in Scotland, and with various associates about the possibility of simultaneous uprisings in London, the West Country, and Cheshire. Whether or not Monmouth's visit to Cheshire in September was, as Grey said, for further consultations about this, his popular reception in Chester was so enthusiastic that he was arrested for causing a riot.[83]

Whatever their exact details, Locke must have known of at least the general drift of these discussions and possible plans, but there is no evidence that he took any particular part in them, and in any case he of course left no record of what he thought of them. It must, however, have been in their connection that he went (at least as a go-between, or perhaps as an aide if he went with Shaftesbury) on 18 September (in fact two days after the issue of the warrant for Monmouth's arrest) to Cassiobury in Hertfordshire, the home of Shaftesbury's colleague the Earl of Essex, where he stayed for two nights.[84]

But even if it was partly absorbed by Shaftesbury's affairs, Locke's time over the summer was certainly not wholly taken up by them. He was unable to see Damaris Cudworth, for she had gone back to Cambridge about a week before he arrived from Oxford in May, but their friendship continued to develop by letter. He had time for old friends too, such as Herbert, whom he had regularly seen since his return from France, and Thomas, and Boyle, from whom he took down medical recipes. He was also able to go to two book auctions, buying upwards of thirty books at each, for a grand total of about £13.[85]

In August, moreover, he went with the Clarkes (as he had planned for some months) to take the waters at Tunbridge in Kent. He spent two weeks there: a rather untypical entry in his journal records paying one shilling towards some musical entertainment; more typical are the observations of a comet (the one that became known as Halley's) and the note that tea leaves acted on the waters at Tunbridge as galls did, turning them purple.[86]

On 23 September Locke returned to Oxford, presumably knowing something of what plans Shaftesbury must have then been making. Time was running out for Shaftesbury for, after months of political machinations, the government was succeeding in its attempts to replace the London sheriffs on whose support Shaftesbury had relied for their choice of grand jurors. In these circumstances, any charges that might have been brought against him were unlikely to be dismissed, and towards the end of September, the day after two new tory sheriffs were sworn in, he went into hiding. There is evidence, again mainly from later confessions, that during the next few weeks Shaftesbury was involved in further discussions and meetings concerning either some insurrection or an assassination of Charles and James. Towards the end of November, along with associates such as Ferguson, he left the country and was in lodgings in Rotterdam by 28 November.[87]

In Oxford, Locke and his movements (as far as we know, to Tyrrell's at Oakley, from 30 September to 11 October, from 20 to 27 October, and then again from 28 October to 8 November) seem not to have excited much concern. Towards the end of October, Prideaux informed Ellis that "John Locke lives very quietly with us, and not a word ever drops from his mouth that discovers anything of his heart within". Now that "his master" Shaftesbury had fled "we shall have him all together", Prideaux supposed. "He seems to be a man of very good converse, and that we have of him with content; as for what else he is he keeps it to himself, and therefore troubles not us with it nor we with him."[88]

In early December, Locke set out on horseback for London, presumably having heard of Shaftesbury's safe arrival in Holland. Some weeks later he took a boat up river to Clapham, where Shaftesbury's grandson, now nearly twelve, was at school. Shortly after his arrival he was taken ill, and was confined to his bed in the lodgings he had taken, when, on 26 January, he heard that Shaftesbury had died five days earlier.[89] There is no record of his feelings.

Shaftesbury had wanted to be buried at Wimborne St Giles and, on Locke's suggestion, his body was brought back to Poole in Dorset. On the day of the funeral, towards the end of February, Locke made a very brief note in his journal (along with some notes on Cicero's *De Natura Deorum* and on van Helmont's *Traité des fièvres*), which recorded the end of a lengthy era in his life: "E. Shaftesbury buried".[90]

The house was to be taken over by Shaftesbury's son, and Locke helped Shaftesbury's widow with business related to this and to Shaftesbury's death itself – as, for example, by a visit he made to Poole, and by sorting through Shaftesbury's papers. He found the weeks he was at St Giles too long, complaining to Damaris Cudworth not only that being in the country was dull but also that it was making him so too. But he made the best of it, spending time reading and making notes on a variety of travel and medical literature, and also making abstracts from some of Shaftesbury's manuscripts. He copied out some rather homely recipes and wrinkles (for various equine ills; for soldering broken glass; for curing the cramp by wearing a thistle apple), but was most interested in a lengthy and systematic list of "Inquiries concerning the use and cultures of the kitchen garden and winter greenery". He was also able to meet Clarke, who was passing through Salisbury from Chipley on his way to London. He stayed some days there with Thomas, with whom of course he discussed medical matters.[91]

Eventually Lady Shaftesbury was ready to leave, and in early April, Locke set out with her on the two-day journey back to London. Her intended move from Thanet House involved the dispersal of various goods and furnishings, some of which Locke bought: he recorded paying Stringer for "twenty-three plates weighing 26 pounds at 9d per pound, 19s 6d; for three blankets, 9s; for a quilt, £1; for three carpets, 18s".[92]

TWO TREATISES OF GOVERNMENT

After returning from France in 1679 Locke was able, as we have seen, to combine his involvement in Shaftesbury's affairs with his own intellectual interests: medicine, the human understanding, and religious toleration. There was, however, much else going on which we have not yet reviewed, for during these years he also composed two lengthy works about the nature of government. The political climate during these years explains both the content of the works and the lack of contemporary evidence, not only about their being produced, but also about their very existence. If, for example, these manuscripts had been discovered when Shaftesbury's house was searched and their content digested, Locke would have been at serious risk. It is not surprising that there are no open references to them in Locke's surviving correspondence and other papers. They are, however, usually thought to have been disguised as a work he and friends referred to as *De Morbo Gallico*.* Syphilis was what was conventionally known as "the French disease", but absolute government, against which Locke was writing, might, at the time of Louis XIV, also have been described in this way.

Though it is likely that at least one of these works was begun without much thought of the other, they come together in that one rejects a view according to which political power ultimately derives from the sovereignty of Adam, while the other argues positively that it derives from the consent of the governed; and when Locke came to publish them some years later it was as two parts of one volume, *Two Treatises of Government*. While it is clear that they were largely composed during the four or so years following Locke's return from France, there is disagreement as to precisely when he wrote them. The composition of the first, in which *The False Principles and Foundation of Sir Robert Filmer, and his Followers are Detected and Overthrown*, has been put at various periods* between early 1680 and late 1681. The second, *An Essay concerning the True Original, Extent, and End of Civil-Government*, has usually (though not always) been thought to have been begun after the first, and has been put at various periods and times between 1681 and 1683. The *Treatises* are works of political theory; unlike the *Letter from a Person of Quality*, say, they are not detailed commentaries on recent events. Nevertheless the general thrusts of their arguments, and sometimes their detail, respond to the nature of King Charles's reign.

The first is a point-by-point, polemical rebuttal of a book, *Patriarcha: or the Natural Power of Kings*, by Robert Filmer, published in 1680 as a contribution to the then-current arguments concerning the powers of the King, and was used as a support for the court's belief in Charles's divine right to rule with arbitrary power. Tyrrell was writing against this book at the same time as Locke, but they seem not to have discussed it together, and Locke kept his work on it secret from him.

Through all of what Locke called "the windings and obscurities... of his wonderful system", Filmer addressed the question, "What is the basis for the authority of a government and for the obedience of subjects to that government?"; are rights and liberties "derived from the law of natural liberty", for example, or "from the grace and bounty of princes?" Filmer rejected the first of these alternatives, and attacked what he called "the common opinion", that mankind is free "to choose what form of government it please, and that the power which any one man has over others was at the first... bestowed according to the discretion of the multitude". To Filmer's mind this not only contradicted Scripture, from which he typically sought support for his views, but was dangerous in encouraging the idea that "the people or multitude have power to punish or deprive the prince if he transgresses the laws of the kingdom".[93]

Filmer's view was that regal authority is divinely instituted, and has its foundation in the natural authority which Adam had over his children. As such, it is absolute: a subject's rights and liberties are derived from the ruler's "grace and bounty"; there is no limit to royal prerogative and parliaments have no power but merely to advise the King and their meetings are dependent on his favour. According to Locke's summary of Filmer's position: "Men are not born free, and therefore could never have the liberty to choose either governors, or forms of government. Princes have their power absolute, and by divine right.... Adam was an absolute monarch, and so are all princes ever since."[94]

Locke directly opposed this: men are born free of all political authority; they are at liberty to choose their governors who, as a consequence, are not absolute and arbitrary but answerable to those who have chosen them. But in his first treatise he did not argue for these ideas; instead he raised objections to Filmer's view.

The precise details of Filmer's thought prove to be unclear when what he said is looked at closely, as Locke did. Filmer did not always, for example, ground political authority on Adam as the first father. He sometimes also appealed to the fact that (according to Genesis) Adam was given dominion over all living things. But, Locke pointed out, even if paternal power and unlimited ownership went together in Adam, they were different things, and their going together was not inevitable. According to Filmer, on Adam's death, his "next heir", his eldest son, inherits his power. But even if one allowed (as Locke did not) that a first-born has some natural right over its siblings and that property naturally descends to the eldest son, paternal power does not; for paternal power is not inherited, it comes only from being a father.

The main thrust of Filmer's view, however, was that the absolute and unlimited regal power which he claimed was first possessed by Adam, was possessed by him as the first parent, being grounded in the divine command to "Honour thy father" (as Locke wryly noted, Filmer "contents himself with half" of the fifth commandment). Objecting to this, Locke pointed out that Filmer was wrong in the first place about what paternal authority is like. Filmer spoke as though a father has "an absolute,... unlimited... power over the lives, liberties, and estates of his children".[95] But the duty which children owe their fathers is different from what they owe a ruler.

Furthermore, how exactly is regal authority supposed to be derived from paternal authority? Are we to suppose as many absolute rulers as there are fathers, or are we to suppose a father to have absolute jurisdiction not only over his children, but also over his children's children? This last would mean that grandchildren would not, despite the commandment, have to honour their father, and this would mean that the right the commandment gives to parents cannot after all be one of absolute political dominion.

At first sight it is not implausible that Adam possessed regal power because of his paternal power and because God gave him dominion over the earth. But the idea was revealed to have further problems when Locke turned to the passing on of Adam's sovereignty. Again Filmer was not always of one mind, sometimes speaking of its being *granted* to his successors, sometimes of its being *usurped* by them. What he chiefly insisted on, however, was that it is *inherited* by them.

Now so far as dominion over the earth goes, Locke reiterated that Adam in fact had nothing in particular, no specific privileges, for his heir to inherit. All men, not just Adam, have been told by God (by "Reason, which was the voice of God in him") that they have a right to make use of the earth and its creatures for their own self-preservation, so "Adam's sovereignty built on property...comes to nothing".[96]

Adam could, Locke agreed, have had private property, which his children both could and had a right to inherit. Since God has planted in man a desire, not only for self-preservation, but also for reproduction, parents have a duty to preserve their children, and so their children have a right to their parents' property. But since all Adam's children had this right, it is not one which could "convey right of sovereignty to any one of his posterity over the rest".[97]

Moreover, though children have a right to inherit their father's property, they have no right to inherit any sovereignty or political power he might have. Property is for the use and preservation of its owner, and children have a right to parental property for their preservation. But the power of government is quite different, being for the preservation, not of the governor, but of all the governed: "The sword is not given the magistrate for his own good alone."[98]

How, then, is sovereign power to be passed on? That depends, said Locke, on what was envisaged when it was first acquired. If power was originally bestowed by God, then the right of succession depends on what God had in mind when he first granted it. If, on the other hand, "the agreement and consent of men first gave a sceptre into anyone's hand...that also must direct its descent and conveyance".[99]

Of course, Filmer's view was that sovereign power was originally bestowed on Adam by God, but Locke found on close examination that there is no clear account of how Filmer, though he talked generally of its passing to Adam's heir, envisaged the right of succession to that power. On Adam's death, Filmer said, sovereign power is to pass to the "eldest" parents. But are these those who are of the greatest age, or those who have had children the longest? Filmer also, and differently, said power is to pass to Adam's "eldest son"; but what if he had had no son, and does a grandson by a daughter have a right before a nephew by a brother?[100]

Locke did not deny that these questions could be settled by civil law; rather, he denied Filmer's view that they had been settled by God. God would not have placed sovereignty in Adam yet have left it unclear how it was to be passed down, and, consequently, unclear who possessed it now.

In the second of the two treatises, *Concerning the True Original, Extent, and End of Civil Government,* Locke presented his own view: government is based on the consent of the governed; rulers are answerable to the people, who may, if their trust is abused, use force against them. His "Essay concerning Toleration" of 1667, in rejecting the idea of rule by divine right, had already gone beyond the earlier "Tracts on Government", which were neutral between that and rule by consent; but Locke had certainly not allowed, as he did now, that active resistance to the government could ever be legitimate.

Locke rejected outright Filmer's starting point that the natural state of mankind is one of complete subjection to a divinely instituted absolute monarch. He began with a different picture of our place on earth, our relation to our fellows, and to God. Our natural state is one of "liberty...free from any superior power on earth, and not...under the will...of man but [with]...only the law of nature for [our] rule". Though we are not equal in terms of talents and physical abilities, there is a natural equality of power or authority, a natural freedom from subjection to the will or authority of others. Locke described such a state, in which people are living together "without a common superior on earth, with authority to judge between them", as "the state of nature".[101]

The "state of nature" is a "state of liberty", but it is not a "state of licence", for even though people in it are not bound by the will of another, they are subject to the divinely ordained "law of nature". As Locke had said years earlier in his "Essays on the Law of Nature", this law is discoverable by reason, by which we can come to see that we are all the "workmanship of one omnipotent and infinitely wise maker", all his servants "sent into the world by his order, and about his business", all "furnished with like faculties, sharing all in one community of nature". It follows that we cannot suppose "any... subordination among us that may authorise us to destroy one another, as if we were made for one another's uses, as the inferior ranks of creatures are for ours".[102] We are, therefore, bound by the law of nature to preserve ourselves and also, so far as we can, to preserve others.

We do, though, have a right to harm others in fair and reasonable punishment if they transgress the law of nature. Someone who breaks that law "declares himself to live by another than that of reason ... which is that measure God has set to the actions of men, for their mutual security" and so commits "a trespass against the whole species". Thus, since all men have the right to preserve mankind in general, "every man has a right to punish the offender, and be executioner of the law of nature".[103]

Locke did not think of people as being "alone" in the state of nature. God has so constituted human beings that "necessity, convenience, and inclination ... drive [them] into society". There are, though, different kinds of society: for example, society between man and wife, between parents and children, master and servant, and, finally, political society. The last of these was Locke's main concern, but his detailed discussions of the others (their "different ends, ties, and bounds") are of great interest in themselves; for example, according to his account of parental society, a disciplined upbringing in which a child owes obligations to its parents does not deny the child's "natural liberty", but rather has it as its guiding light.[104] They also underline the superficiality and misguidedness of Filmer's attempt to ground political power on parental power, even if, as Locke agreed, Adam, the first father, might in fact have also been the first sovereign.

While people might be in various societal groupings in the state of nature, they leave that state when they form a specifically political or civil society. In entering into political society, people give up the right or power they have in the state of nature to protect themselves and to punish offences against the law of nature; they put that power into the hands of the society itself, the chief end of which, said Locke, is "the preservation of property" ("property" meaning "life, liberty and estate"). People put themselves "out of the state of nature into that of a commonwealth, by setting up a judge on earth, with authority to determine all controversies, and redress all injuries"; where there is no such power to appeal to, "there they are still in the state of nature". In that state we are judge in our own case and must exact punishments ourselves; whereas a civil society has "political power", which Locke described as the "right of making laws with penalties ... employing the force of the community, in the execution of such laws".[105] We give up the right to protect ourselves and others against breaches of the law of nature because we calculate that a civil society will afford us better, more stable and systematic, protection. It will make clear what the law is, it will provide judges to determine breaches of the law, and it will have the force to punish those breaches.

The move from the state of nature into political society can only be one of free choice: "being all free, equal, and independent, no one can be put out of this estate, and subjected to the political power of another, without his own consent". In making that choice, people do lose the freedom they had to take the law of nature into their own hands, but they do not lose the basic freedom with which they were born: "the liberty of man, in society, is to be under no legislative power but that established by consent...and not to be subject to the...arbitrary will of another".[106]

On the face of it, the black slaves who formed part of the trade of the Royal African Company were people who had been robbed of their natural rights and "subject to the arbitrary will of another" quite without their consent. Is there an inconsistency between Locke's having investments in that company and the political theory he was developing here? The *Second Treatise* does allow the taking of slaves as "captives...in a just war", such as a defensive war waged by innocents against an unjust agressor; for such captives have, by putting themselves into a state of war, forfeited their lives. But Locke can hardly have thought that slave raids were just wars; and he explicitly denied that such aggressors forfeited the lives of their children as well as their own, and so could not even begin to justify hereditary slavery. Though there is no consensus on this whole question, there certainly seems to be "a glaring contradiction between his theories and Afro-American slavery". But even though Locke left nothing to show that he addressed this contradiction, it does not necessarily follow that he "averted his eyes" from it; perhaps the selling of his African investments fifteen years before composing the *Second Treatise* indicates a change of mind on the legitimacy of slavery.[107]

Locke intended his account of the origin of civil society not only to explain what constitutes legitimate government, but also to reflect the historical facts. He rejected the objection that we cannot find cases of "a company of men independent and equal one amongst another, that met together, and in this way began and set up a government". Not only is there *some* historical evidence of such cases, but also it is not surprising that there is not more. Civil societies naturally tend not to have records of their beginnings: "with commonwealths as with particular persons, they are commonly ignorant of their own births and infancies".[108]

But though Locke thus thought that his ideas about man's natural state are answerable to historical facts, they clearly are not just purely empirical. In discussing this objection he said at one point that "*reason* [is] plain on our side, that men are naturally free"; and we could use this claim as a basis for interpeting the idea of an original "state of nature" in which men have natural liberty, as a piece of fiction which brings out how we are to understand the status of people in abstraction from a political state, and so also, by contrast, in relation to one.[109]

The idea that the right to govern is grounded in the consent of the people, and not in some right which God gave Adam, had an obvious general relevance to the situation of those who believed that Charles II was a threat to their liberties and religion. What Locke went on to say about the structure of government sometimes had a particular relevance too.

The "supreme power" of a civil society, he said, is its "legislative" power, the power it has to make laws to allow men "the enjoyment of their properties in peace and safety"; then, echoing his earlier tracts on government and his essay concerning toleration, he said that legitimate legislative power is limited by the good of the society: any specific law must accord with the law of nature, in particular that "fundamental law of nature" which requires the preservation of mankind.[110] Though these theoretical remarks were not restricted to any particular form of government, Locke considered at one point what was in fact his own situation, where the legislature consisted of an assembly of hereditary nobility (the House of Lords), an assembly of representatives elected by "the people" (the House of Commons), together with a hereditary person (the King).

Now the political power of a civil society consists, he explained, not only of the supreme "legislative power" but also of an "executive power".[111] It is best, he thought, that (as in the particular case just described) these two functions be separate and in different hands: for, besides the fact that the legislative need not be in permanent assembly while its laws need a "perpetual execution", this would prevent the legislative making and executing laws to its own advantage.

Locke's own King possessed this executive power and it allowed him to call together, or dissolve, the legislative assemblies. Because of the "uncertainty and variableness of human affairs" there need, Locke thought, be no fixed rule about when the legislature should assemble, and the executive should call it together when need be. This power did not mean that the executive was more powerful than the legislative; Locke saw it as being entirely a matter of trust, and in describing theoretically possible abuses of that trust he must have had in mind actual abuses by Charles: "When the Prince hinders the legislative from assembling in its due time, or from acting freely, pursuant to those ends, for which it was constituted", and when he "deliver[s]...the people into the subjection of a foreign power", he "takes away the legislative and puts an end to the government". He must have had in mind Charles's continued and determined attempts, financed by the French King, to rule by prerogative power, and (by repeated prorogations and failures to summon it) without Parliament. He must also have had in mind, and endorsed, the possibility that Charles could be removed by force. In hindering the meeting of the legislature, the executive puts itself into a state of war with the people, he said, and they have a right to remove it. "Having erected a legislative with...the power of making laws, either at certain set times, or when there is need of it; when they are hindered by any force from what is so necessary to the society...the people have a right to remove it [the executive] by force."[112]

In these remarks about failure to call the legislature, Locke allowed that the executive government should have a certain degree of prerogative discretion (a considerable degree if it is good and wise). But prerogative power, he argued, is not an arbitrary power which the executive has of right; it is no encroachment on it for the legislature to place limits on it. It is, moreover, held "with this trust, that it shall be made use of for the good of the nation, as the exigencies of the times, and variety of occasions shall require".[113] In the end the people are justified in using force against an executive monarch who attempts, as did Charles II, to rule without recourse to a separate legislature.

When the executive acts contrary to the trust placed in it, contrary to the preservation of the liberties and properties of the people, it is *it* who is guilty of rebellion; it is it who has put itself into a state of war with the people. It is, moreover, clearly up to them to decide whether the prince has acted contrary to the trust placed in him; "for who shall be judge whether his trustee...acts well, and according to the trust reposed in him, but he who deputes him, and must, by having deputed him, have still a power to discard him, when he fails in his trust".[114]

Though this "doctrine of a power in the people" obviously gave some justification to rebellion, Locke denied that it was an *encouragement* to it. People, he thought, are in fact slow to act, and they are "not so easily got out of their old forms, as some are apt to suggest"; moreover, "revolutions happen not upon every little mismanagement in public affairs". People will rebel only after "a long train of abuses, prevarications, and artifices". In what in effect was a summing-up of the course of Charles's reign, Locke said,

> if all the world shall observe pretences of one kind, and actions of another; arts used to elude the law, and the trust of prerogative ... employed contrary to the end for which it was given: if the people shall find the ministers and subordinate magistrates chosen suitable to such ends, and favoured, or laid by, proportionably as they promote or oppose them: if they see several experiments made of arbitrary power, and that religion underhand favoured (though publicly proclaimed against) which is readiest to introduce it; and the operators in it supported ... if a long train of actions show the councils all tending that way, how can a man ... hinder himself from being persuaded in his own mind which way things are going; or from casting about how to save himself?[115]

APRIL–SEPTEMBER 1683: "THE TIMES GROWING NOW TROUBLESOME"[116]

Not long before Shaftesbury's funeral Robert Ferguson returned from Holland, and (according to his later confessions) had engaged in plans to assassinate the King and the Duke of York, at Rye House on the road to London, on their return from the races at Newmarket in March. The plot failed because, if for no other reason, the royal party left earlier than expected; and plotting continued, it was confessed, into April and May. It was probably in some connection with these ongoing conspiratorial discussions that, on 24 April, Locke hired a horse and rode the sixteen miles from London to the Earl of Essex's at Cassiobury where he stayed overnight; but exactly what the connection was is unclear. One suggestion is that Locke, again acting as a go-between, had been sent to bring Essex back to London for an imminent meeting of the conspirators. But it is not clear why Locke should particularly have been needed for this.[117] It seems more likely that, at a place some safe distance from London, he wanted to ascertain what was going on. Exactly what he learnt we do not know.

At the end of May he removed from Thanet House to stay with a friend, Dr Charles Goodall, at the College of Physicians in Warwick

Lane, but there is neither reason nor need to think that he was going into hiding, as a result of some warning.[118] More simply, Locke's residence at Thanet House had been under Shaftesbury's patronage, and even if his son had been inclined to continue the favour, Locke is unlikely to have wanted it.

He did not stay long at Goodall's, and left London in mid-June. Some days earlier a man named Josiah Keeling had provided the government with information about the Rye House plot; but, contrary to what has been suggested, Locke's departure was not done "hastily" and as a result of this, for if he knew before he left London that the government had such information, he knew it before the conspirators themselves did. Of course he might, in general terms, have seen advantages in distancing himself from events, but he had had his mind for some time on a remove to Oxford, and had been preparing for it. In Salisbury in March he had arranged with Thomas to direct to him in Oxford "a little square deal box nailed and corded", and also a bed (presumably from St Giles). Then, more recently, in early June, he had arranged for the carriage of ten boxes of goods and some furniture from Goodall's to Oxford. He seems at the time to have seen his life as relatively safe and stable, for he was not merely taking care of his stock of worldly goods, but troubling to add to them, not only by the various things he had acquired from St Giles and Thanet House, but also by a cane chair and table he bought on the day he left London for Oxford.[119]

This was on 14 June when, having booked two days earlier, he took the coach to Aylesbury, where he and Syl hired horses for the further eight miles to Tyrrell's at Oakley. The next day he rode on to Oxford, to his rooms in Christ Church. Before settling down to such routine matters as his weather observations, which he resumed a week later, he had his business interests in Somerset to see to.[120]

For some time, his agent Stratton had had some expectation of seeing him in Somerset, but had suggested a meeting in Cirencester (between Oxford and Bristol) as an alternative possibility. It was presumably for just such a rendezvous that Locke spent the night of 18–19 June there. On 23 June he again went to Tyrrell's, and returned two days later.[121]

But if Locke's intention in removing to Oxford had been simply to refigure his life after fifteen or so years as a member of Shaftesbury's household, his actions did begin to be influenced by political events.

The discovery of the Rye House plot gave the King even more opportunity to move against his enemies, and coincident with Locke's first week back in Oxford, warrants were issued for the arrest of various of the conspirators whom Keeling had named, one of whom, Robert West, gave himself up and, by 26 June, was said to have confessed both about the March plot and about earlier plans, plans in which Shaftesbury had been involved. Locke and West were well known to each other, for, apart from any other contact they may or may not have had, they had had dealings the previous year when West* was a defence lawyer in the trial of Stephen College. The discovery in general of plots and plans against the King and his brother, and West's detention and confession in particular, quite evidently caused Locke some concern. "As soon as the plot was discovered", Locke, according to Prideaux, "cunningly stole away from us, and in half a year's time no one knew where he was":

As soon as he [West] was secured, he [Locke] thought it time to shift for himself for fear West should tell all he knew. When West was first taken he was very solicitous to know of us at the table who this West was, at which one made an unlucky reply, that it was the very same person whom he treated at his chambers... when College was tried here at Oxford, which put the gentleman into a profound silence; and the next thing we heard of him was that he was fled for the same.[122]

As it happens, West did not implicate Locke in any plotting, perhaps there was nothing to tell. But Locke could still have been concerned that in a speedily heating political climate, in which the King continued to gain support as a result of the horror many felt at the thought of royal assassination, and in which various enemies of the King were being arrested (Lord Russell, Algernon Sidney, and the Earl of Essex), he, as an associate of Shaftesbury, might be arrested for questioning, or that someone else might mention his name, or even falsely testify against him; he did, after all, know several of those who had been arrested.[123] He certainly began to act as though out of a feeling of vulnerability, and it was likely during his "profound silence" at the loyalist Christ Church dinner table (probably on 25 or 26 June) that Locke decided as the "next thing", not so much to flee, as Prideaux put it, but to set about hiding or even destroying his papers, and to be discreet in his movements.

He began one or two days later by taking papers to Tyrrell's at Oakley on 27 June. At first that visit was noted in his journal, but he evidently thought again, and attempted to delete the note; and for the next couple of months he made no explicit record of his movements. He was, though, back in Oxford by 29 June, when he saw Robert Pawling, someone else with whom he deposited some of his papers. Pawling, a mercer, who had been mayor in Oxford from 1679 to 1680, was known as an anti-Royalist, a "notorious conventicler", and as someone disaffected with the government.[124] Though Locke took these precautions about the manuscripts and other papers in his rooms, he seems as yet to have had no particular worry about the safety of the books and other goods there. This would come a couple of months later when he was rather precipitately about to leave England.

The next day, 30 June, he made a last entry in the weather record which he had optimistically restarted just ten days earlier, but he was still in Oxford on 4 July, when he paid his college servant Mrs Gristy what he owed her to date. He then, as Prideaux said, "cunningly stole away from us" and went to London, where, at any rate by 10 July, he was again at the Goodalls'.[125]

Unless it was his very activities that excited interest, Locke's caution about his papers was not misplaced. On 13 July the Secretary of State, Sir Leoline Jenkins, was officially informed that it had been noticed in Oxford

that from Mr Locke's chamber in Christ Church, that was a great confidant, if not secretary, to the late Earl of Shaftesbury, in a clandestine way several hand baskets of papers are carried to Mr James Tyrrell's house at Oakley.... Mr Tyrrell and Mr Pawling...are reported to be disaffected. It is thought convenient to make a search...at Oakley,...and if you at the same time direct a search...at Mr Pawling's and that the Bishop of Oxford and the Vice-Chancellor then search Mr Locke's chamber,* it may conduce to his Majesty's service.[126]

Just days after Locke left Oxford, the University, shocked by the revelations of the Rye House plot, set about drawing up a list of "damnable doctrines" which encouraged such plottings, and on 21 July issued a decree officially anathematising them. Some of the twenty-seven propositions were there to be found in the manuscript of Locke's two treatises: political authority originates in the people; there is a compact between prince and subjects; tyrants forfeit the right to govern; and there is a right of resistance against them. He would have been an uneasy witness had he been there in Oxford to see the various "pernicious books" identified as containing these doctrines being taken from the Bodleian Library and publicly burnt.[127]

Perhaps he was still in London when, shortly afterwards, the *London Gazette* published the decree. He had certainly been there when (on 13 July) the Earl of Essex committed suicide or was murdered in the Tower, and during Lord Russell's trial (13–14 July) and sentence of death. But by 24 July he was in Salisbury with Thomas, discussing chemistry apart from anything else. He was on his way to Somerset, where he was by 1 August, seeing to some business affairs with Stratton until at any rate 10 August. Between 15 and 26 August he was again at Salisbury, probably having gone there via the Clarkes at Chipley.[128]

Some of Locke's financial and business dealings during these weeks could indicate he had in mind that it might eventually be prudent to leave England. In London, perhaps with a view to liquidating some of his assets, he sold a silver tankard to Goodall; then, more significantly, in the West Country he gave power of attorney to William Stratton and to Edward Clarke in respect of various of his interests in Somerset, sold his £100 Shaftesbury annuity to Thomas for £500, and bought another from Clarke for £800.[129]

It does seem, then, that Locke raised with Clarke the possibility of his eventually leaving England, but there was no apparent urgency. On 24 August Locke wrote him a relaxed letter, hoping to see him in London before his now pregnant wife was due to give birth. (It is not clear when the birth was expected, but at any rate certainly before late November.) Only two days later, however, his assessment of his situation had quite evidently and dramatically changed, and he now clearly intended to flee to Holland as soon as he could, for on 26 August he again wrote to Clarke, but this time making many arrangements (with regard to both Oxford and London, concerning valuables, money, manuscripts, business matters, and clothing) in connection with leaving the country; in particular, he had "upon consideration . . . thought it best to make a will . . . by which you may be legally entitled to whatsoever I leave". He asked Clarke to keep him informed of the progress of trials against the plotters. In another letter he sent a numerical cipher, for which "there may possibly be some occasion", to encrypt ten names, including Shaftesbury's widow, Thomas, Clarke, Pawling, Tyrrell, and Stratton.[130]

It is clear that his intention now was to go with some haste to Holland, and that, if he meant to go via London (or Oxford), he would be there only briefly (not long enough even to collect "wearing linen, flannel shirts, waistcoats, stockings", which he wanted sent on, certainly not long enough for a social visit to the Clarkes). Exactly when and from where Locke left England we do not know; we do know that, having left Syl behind to deal with various matters and to join him later, he was in Rotterdam just over a week later.[131]

But it is far from clear what had produced the rather abrupt change in his plans. On 23 August he was at Wimborne St Giles, a dozen or so miles southwest of Salisbury, where the steward paid him his annuity from Lady Shaftesbury; on 24 August, when he wrote to Clarke about meeting him in London, he was at Purton, a small village some forty miles north of Salisbury and so not far from Oxford; on 25 August, when his journal records his receiving £50 from Thomas, he was back in Salisbury; and he was still in Salisbury when he again wrote to Clarke on 26 August.[132] It seems clear that Locke had learnt, either by letter or by word of mouth, something deeply disturbing, either at Purton on 24 August (but after writing his letter to Clarke) or at Salisbury on 25 or 26 August.

At Purton he may, for example, have learnt from Robert Pawling that on 24 August a fellow of Lincoln College, James Parkinson, had been released from detention, on Pawling's own security, pending his appearance at the local assizes in early September on charges, arising out of the recent decree, of "holding, maintaining and defending some unwarrantable and seditious principles and accused of several things...inconsistent with and destructive of our present government". Parkinson had, for example, "asserted frequently and defended several of the propositions publicly condemned in Convocation at Oxford, as for instance... 'All civil authority is derived originally from the people',... 'the sovereignty of England is in the king, lords and commons',... 'birth-right and proximity of blood gives no title to rule and government; and it is lawful to preclude the next heir from his right and succession to the crown',... 'there lies no obligation upon Christians to passive obedience when the prince commands anything contrary to the laws of our country'."[133] Though Locke had always carefully refrained from the overt provocativeness which Parkinson had shown, all of these propositions were asserted in his recent and still existent manuscript on the nature of government. (The first and the last of them were also asserted in manuscripts of Algernon Sidney which were used against him in his trial, which did not take place until November, but which, as Locke would have learnt, led to his execution.)

For all we *know*, however, it may not have been until he returned from Purton to Salisbury that Locke came by information or advice that determined him to flee to Holland, and we do not know what that information was or how he came by it.

Though it throws no particular light on the details of the matter, the account Damaris Cudworth gave some years later, of Locke's state of mind at this time, is of interest:

The times growing now troublesome to those of my Lord Shaftsbury's principles as to public matters, and more especially dangerous for such as had been intimate with him, Mr Locke, with reason apprehended himself not to be very safe in England; for though he knew there was no just matter of accusation against him, yet it was not unlikely, as things then were, but that he might have come to be questioned; and should he on any pretence, have been put under confinement, though for no very long time, yet such was the state of his health that his life must have been thereby much endangered. On this account therefore he thought it most advisable for him to withdraw. And going first into the west of England to some friends he had there, he soon after retired out of England.[134]

Holland and the United Dutch Provinces in general were the refuge of various radical whig plotters, and the question would arise, and Locke would be forced to answer it, whether it was because of, or despite that fact, that he chose to go there.

6

Holland and the United Provinces (1683–1688)*

SEPTEMBER 1683–OCTOBER 1684: "MUCH IN MY CHAMBER ALONE"[1]

Locke landed in Holland on 7/17 September at Rotterdam, a town which struck him by its "cleanliness...and convenience for shipping to come almost into every street". He left the same day, and was in Amsterdam two days later. He initially took lodgings with a Mr Wilm, but after five weeks he moved to the house of a man called Reinburg, moving again the following July to Jacob van der Velde's, a bookseller whom he had met soon after his arrival and who was well known to English refugees.[2]

As a stop-gap he had intended to draw on some money Shaftesbury had left in Amsterdam, but before long various arrangements were being made for his friends to transfer money to him. His journal recorded some of what was happening to his belongings in England: a box of manuscripts, quilt and blankets, and Turkey carpets were taken from London to Tyrrell's house near Oxford, and other things were removed from Goodall's.[3]

In November, Locke wrote to Clarke concerning something he referred to as "Tractatus de morbo Gallico": if Clarke had access to more than one copy of it, he would like one sent over, "for I have heard it commended and shall apply myself close to the study of physic by the fireside this winter". He may have been referring to a genuine medical book, *Morbus Gallicus. Omnia quae extant de eo* (Venice, 1566); but since part of one copy was, he said, in the keeping of Rabsy Smithsby (a woman he had known for some years and whose sister Anne had been a domestic at Exeter House), it is more likely that this was a coded reference* to manuscripts of his *Two Treatises*. His uncertainty about how many copies there now were would reflect the fact that the previous August he had told Clarke to burn whatever of his papers he saw fit.[4]

Nevertheless, medicine certainly was one thing which occupied Locke over his first winter in Holland, when he renewed his acquaintance with the physician Peter Guenellon, whom he had met in Paris in 1678. Guenellon introduced him to another physician, his father-in-law, Egbert Veen, and it was perhaps also through Guenellon that he met Dr Caspar Sibelius; with all of these Locke spent time discussing medical matters. Medical notes figure prominently in his journal for his first months in exile, and by the spring he was a member of a semi-formal medical group or "college", along with seven others whose names he listed: Philip van Limborch, Matthew Sladus, Egbert Veen, Abraham Quina, Peter Guenellon, Peter Bernagie, and Abraham Cyprianus. No doubt it was with some of them that a few days after making this list Locke, at Guenellon's, made observations on the development of a chicken embryo.[5]

Locke was more than once entertained (with "tea and the like") at Sibelius's house. He was impressed there by a trumpet device Sibelius used to aid his lungs ("the bellows . . . that nature has given") to blow on the peat fire, and he learnt there from a Mr Bremen, who (to Locke's great interest) had lived for some years in the East, a way of mixing egg yolks, sugar candy, macaroons, and rose water into tea. Bremen also showed the company some drawings of a Papuan native "with a tail which was as long as a deer's"; Bremen did not know, Locke recorded, "whether all the people of that place had such tails, but he had been assured by several credible Hollanders . . . that several of them had".[6]

In January of the new year Guenellon performed the dissection of a lioness which had died in the exceptionally cold weather. Among the observers was Philip van Limborch, a professor of theology at the Remonstrants' seminary in Amsterdam, to whom Locke introduced himself. According to Limborch, "we afterwards had many conversations about religion, in which he acknowledged that he had long attributed to the Remonstrants doctrines very different from those which they held, and now that he understood what they really were, he was surprised to find how closely they agreed with many of his own".[7] What Locke discovered he had in common with Limborch, with whom he formed a lasting friendship, was a belief in the importance for

Christianity of tolerance and a virtuous life, and of studying the New Testament as a guide to faith.

Locke was also "much in my chamber alone" over the winter, sitting by the fire, reading, or writing home to friends such as Clarke and Tyrrell. His reading and note-taking was varied: besides medical books there were books on travel, the French philosopher Malebranche's *Recherche de la Vérité*, and Cicero's *De Officiis*. Yet what kept him "busy there for the most part" was not the "study of physic", which he had said he was going to devote himself to, but rather, so he told Clarke some months later, another of his abiding interests, the study of the human understanding. By contrast with his papers on civil government, he had brought his *De Intellectu* over to Holland with him, expressly having it in mind that away from the company of friends and with time on his hands, he would have something to occupy himself during his "solitary hours". "I was now willing in this retreat", he said, "to turn into a less confused and coherent discourse, and add what was wanting to make my designs intelligible to such of my friends who had desired it of me, and to whom I had promised a sight of it, when it was a little out of the rubbish."[8]

Of course the papers were not in the state they had been when Locke had begun them in 1671; they had been with him in France, and from time to time he had worked on material which became incorporated in them. As he told Clarke, the understanding was "a subject which I had for a good while backwards thought on by catches and set down without method several thoughts upon as they had at distinct times and on several occasions come in my way".[9]

Over the next two or three years, Locke's thoughts would emerge sufficiently "out of the rubbish" for him to think about publishing them – they became *An Essay concerning Human Understanding*, the work for which he would become lastingly famous. But he would never, he told Clarke, have had "the patience to have revised and new formed my old scattered notions" (an exercise which took up "more time and pains with less pleasure and profit than the pursuit of new ones"), had not "so much time...been upon my hands...in the absence of my friends and almost all company" during this winter in Amsterdam.[10]

A copy of *De Intellectu* had been left with Tyrrell, who had been one of those with whom the topic had first been discussed; and, perhaps inspired by Locke's telling him in January that he had been hard at work on it, Tyrrell reviewed it too. He carefully read the papers over a second time, "and like them better than at the first, which I take to be one main sign when I am not fed with empty notions"; he "made bold since it is your foul copy to note...where I doubt anything; or where I think I can illustrate anything you have said by a fitter example".[11]

Clarke and Tyrrell would have been amongst the friends who wanted Locke to continue work and to "make my design more intelligible". Thomas Herbert, now Earl of Pembroke, to whom Locke would eventually dedicate the *Essay*, would undoubtedly have been another. The following December, Locke offered to send him a part of what he had been doing unless it was too much "to suppose you continue the same willingness to see my odd notions when in some tolerable order as you were pleased to express formerly". One of the ways he had begun to put his ideas in order was by dividing them into "books", and it was probably a copy of the second of these which he was offering to Pembroke.[12]

Despite its having been "the hardest winter in the memory of man", in which the ice on the canals was well over two feet thick, Locke's health had been rather good; the Dutch use of peat as a fuel, with its less pernicious smoke, was no doubt a major factor. "I thank God I have not been so well these many years in winter. If you please to come hither you shall not hear me cough once in a whole day together", he told Mrs Clarke in February; then, in March, congratulating her on being delivered of a daughter, he said he had had a deliverance too, "of a scurvy cough, which I think had I been on your side the water this fierce long cold weather would have delivered me over to the worms. But I thank God I have had more mastery of it this very contrary season here than in England I used to have in the most favourable."[13]

In the spring Locke was in renewed contact with his old friend Toinard. One topic they revisited was a method Locke had devised for indexing notes. Some years earlier they had discussed the problems faced by someone who wants to record miscellaneous short notes and comments on his reading or conversations with others. How best are such notes to be arranged? How best are they to be indexed as to be recovered, re-read, or referred to? In about 1660, some years into his university career, Locke had devised and had begun to use what seemed to be a good system. This indexed an entry, made in a notebook, under some "head" ("some important and essential word to the matter in hand"), by entering its page number into a pre-prepared skeleton index against the first letter and first vowel of the "head".

Toinard was most impressed and said that some description of it should be published. Locke had thought it too slight for that but, stimulated by the renewal of Toinard's urging, he spent some time in the summer drawing up an account of it. Toinard's enthusiasm was certainly genuine for he prepared and circulated among friends blank pro forma indexes and pages laid out in the way Locke had devised. "I have", he said, "made by it an infinity of friends whom I have told I got it from you."[14]

Having begun to be persuaded about publishing it, Locke gave much thought as to the best way to present it. It was not long enough to make a single volume on its own, and would be best included in one of the new learned periodicals which were then appearing; but because of its apparent complexity someone needed to be on the spot to make things clear to the printers. Locke wanted Toinard to translate what he had worked out and then to see to its publication in France. Unfortunately, Toinard did not feel up to the translation into French, and though Locke feared he had lost the facility he used to have with Latin, he sent a Latin version two weeks later.[15]

By August he had not been out of Amsterdam, save for a few days in May when he went to nearby Haarlem and Heemstede. The purpose of that journey is not known, but among the things that caught his eye were some official standard lengths made from iron ("the Haarlem's foot is the universal 1.843") and the local method of bleaching linen. (Having started to describe this method in his journal he seems to have lost interest, suddenly concluding "the process is too long and of too little consequence to be writ all particularly".)[16]

In mid-August, however, he set out on a circular tour of the United Provinces of the Dutch Republic, which lasted nearly three months. By wagon and boat he went north to the capital of Freisland, Leeuwarden, noting on the way details of the dress of the natives, of the style of their houses and roads, of the method and cost of sea defences, and of their land taxes. Near Leeuwarden, which he reached in less than a week, was a religious settlement, founded by Jean Labadie at Wieuwerd. His visit there was on behalf of Damaris Cudworth, who, apparently believing he would not want to hear from her, had at first not written for some time. When (and perhaps as a result of Locke's asking Mrs Clarke about her) she had eventually written she had been in a "discontented humour", finding the world she was in to be "base, false, foolish", where "people sell their honesty for imaginary profit, and their happiness for the senseless reputation of being wise". She thought that if Locke could tell her something about the Labadists, it would much reconcile her to the world to know it somewhere contained "a better sort of people than those where I am". She wanted to know "what their manner of living is; and whether it be that, or any peculiar principle, or opinion, in their religion which unites them together"; she asked "whether they be learned, or unlearned; and whether in their lives and conversation one amongst another they do really differ from the rest of the world, and do appear to have more true honesty amongst them".[17]

Locke had already sent her some volumes by Labadie, but without "the encouragement to come into Holland" for which she had hoped, she had to make do at second hand with the long account he wrote of what he found during the day he was at Wieuwerd. Despite a letter of introduction it was not easy to gather information "about their manner and rule of living and discipline", and he thought this "not altogether so suitable to the pattern of Christianity". But, suspecting there was "a little of Tartuffe" in them, he did not see this reticence as stemming from shyness. It was rather that "they seemed to expect that a man should come there disposed to desire and court admittance into their society, without inquiring particularly into their ways; and if . . . they see the signs of grace in him, they will proceed to give him further instruction". As it happens, Locke's diagnosis of the Labadists as hypocritical chimed with what "Philoclea" had meanwhile learnt about them — that so far "from being better than others, . . . they are indeed so much worse as under a show and appearance of religion there are not really greater libertines in the world".[18]

East of Leeuwarden was Groningen, the capital of the province of the same name, "a big town very regularly fortified with 17 bastions the distance of each 470 steps".[19] In the couple of days Locke was there he again made notes on local taxes, besides recording that the university library was open two days a week and that the catalogue of their books ran to 171 small folio pages.

Leaving Leeuwarden on the last day of August, Locke went south to Deventer in Gelderland, where he stayed for nearly two weeks. He made something of a study of the two Protestant nunneries, but the main attraction was Caspar Sibelius, who had moved from Amsterdam and set up a new medical practice. Locke filled many journal pages with medical notes, based partly on Sibelius's own experience, but mainly on that of Sibelius's erstwhile mentor, Dr Johann Webfer (to whom Sibelius, aided by Locke, composed a letter seeking more information about a variety of topics – fevers, epilepsy, cauterization, and poisons).[20]

From Deventer, Locke travelled via Nijmegen and Gorinchem, by wagon and boat, to Utrecht. There is little on record to show what he did during the three weeks he was there (besides making notes on some medical and travel reading). He asked his friends in Amsterdam to send letters care of a painter, van Gulick, but he lodged first at "the Jerusalem" and then in the house of a Mr Grimont.[21]

When he left Utrecht for Amsterdam, he obviously intended to return, for he had as yet not paid* the Grimonts for his lodgings. But rather than going back to Utrecht as soon as he had tidied things up in Amsterdam, he went instead, after five days, to Leiden, where he stayed for just over a month. An immediate reason for going there seems to have been a book auction, where he added at least thirty-five to the good number of books he had already bought in Amsterdam in March and April.[22]

Besides its book auctions Leiden also had the attraction of a medical school, and Locke spent time with its teachers and students. Paul Herman, a professor of botany, gave him much first-hand information about Ceylon, its people, its plants, spices, and fruits. They discussed colic, the endemic disease there, and Locke was led to think about its causes and possible cures; it was in this connection that he recorded an "odd story" about a man who was cured by changing the order in which he put on his stockings in the morning. Another professor, Lucas Shacht, introduced him to a museum devoted to various anatomical specimens, animal, human, and insect, prepared by Swammerdam, the Dutch microscopist who had recently died; Locke remarked particularly on some foetal skeletons, various specimens of rectal and colonic muscles and valves, and noted that the material of the female clitoris was indistinguishable from that of the male penis, "perfectly made porous and spongious".[23]

Locke also spent time in intervals in the book auction making a draft of some "Directions" for the upbringing, or "breeding", of the Clarkes' eldest child, Edward, now aged about three. These were based on things he had already said in letters he had been sending Clarke since July, and which he had intermittently worked on before and during his "ramble" in the Provinces. Calling it "my first chapter on the subject", he sent a copy of it to Clarke at the end of November. The "Directions" focused on the boy not simply as a child, but as a gentleman's son, someone who would need to see to an estate and play some part in public affairs. But he said that many of them were obviously applicable to a gentleman's daughters too (about whom he sometimes wrote specifically to Mrs Clarke).[24]

Fifty-two, unmarried, and childless, Locke was well aware that he was offering Clarke an "old bachelor's advice", and that child-rearing was "a business with which my course of life has made me little acquainted". But it was advice which the Clarkes had sought, and Locke was in a position to have some views on the matter. It is quite clear that he was a keen and reflective observer of the young. Someone once remarked that "you love to converse with children and see the natural productions of the mind, unassisted by art and unpossessed by others' notions".[25] Years earlier he had been given charge of Shaftesbury's grandson, and his experience as a tutor at Oxford and with Caleb Banks in France had given him material for reflection about the education of boys in the second decade of life.

Of course none of that equated with actually being a father; at one point, having advised that a child should not physically be "cockered" or treated too tenderly, he anticipated that Mrs Clarke would conclude he was "a little too hard" and would find it "apparent he has no children of his own".[26] There must be room for argument as to whether parental feelings are necessary for sound educational advice; but necessary or not – and, Locke said, they can easily turn into harmful indulgence – they surely cannot be sufficient. In any case it is clear from the toys he bought for his friends' children and the interest he showed in them that Locke was quite capable of affection of a paternal kind.

Despite all of this, Locke was aware that his instructions, as written down, had never been put into practice ("I am too sensible of my want of experience in this affair"), and that, with their underlay of theory, they might not always be easy to follow: "the speculations which please a contemplative man in his study are not so easy to be put in use out of it". He was keen to learn from Clarke how what he had said was working.[27]

Locke was in no doubt about the importance of early upbringing: "nine parts of ten, or perhaps ninety-nine of one hundred, are what they are, good or evil, useful or not, by their education". Moreover, a central feature of a child's development is the acquisition of habits: "The little and almost insensible impressions, on our tender infancies, have very important and lasting influences.... You cannot imagine of what force custom is." So education, whether physical, moral, or intellectual, is, he continually stressed, largely a matter of inculcating and reinforcing good habit and carefully avoiding bad. What a child gets from his upbringing are "habits woven into the very principles of his nature" which will "sway and influence his life". Habits are acquired, not by the learning of rules, but from the example of parents and servants, and by the association of certain behaviours with praise or disapprobation (certainly not with physical punishment). The habits to be encouraged are, first and foremost, those of virtue ("to make him valued and beloved by others, acceptable or tolerable to himself"); wisdom ("in the popular acceptation . . . a man's managing his business ably, and with foresight in this world"); good breeding ("not to think meanly of ourselves, and . . . of others"); and, last and most definitely least (perhaps surprisingly from the "mouth of a bookish man"), learning.[28]

Locke's instructions began with health (something which "you may rather expect, from that study I have been thought more peculiarly to have applied myself to"). The aim here was that children should not be spoiled by "cockering and tenderness", and should learn to endure discomfort and unfamiliar circumstances. They should be treated like farmers' sons, hardened to all weathers. A child should "have his feet washed every night in cold water, and to have his shoes so made that they may leak. . . . Consider how mischievous and mortal a thing taking wet in the feet proves often to those who have been bred nicely. . . . A fever or consumption follows from just an accident." Some years later, when these instructions came to be published, their apparent harshness provoked comment. But when Locke wrote them he perhaps remembered that years earlier he had treated his young fourteen-year-old cousin Peter Locke for a violent dry cough, which (so his case notes recorded) arose from a cold he had caught "through not sufficiently protecting his feet from the damp of the roads". He further thought this hardiness would prevent corns, "to some men . . . a very valuable consideration", and he included himself here for a few years earlier he had told Toinard about his protracted seach for a remedy for corns which "sometimes make me very lame".[29]

Diet should be "very plain and simple", with a minimum of meat and plenty of bread, eaten at irregular times, "for, when custom has fixed his eating to certain stated periods, his stomach will expect victuals at the usual hour, and grow peevish if he passes it". Sleep, "the great cordial of nature", is the only thing children are to be indulged in, "nothing contributing more to . . . growth and health"; though after the age of seven they should be gradually reduced to eight hours, "which is generally rest enough for healthy grown people". Beds should be hard and made up in different ways: "He that is used to hard lodging at home, will not miss his sleep . . . in his travels abroad, for want of his soft bed."[30]

The strength of the body, then, lies "chiefly in being able to endure hardships", and the same applies to the mind: "the great principle and foundation of all virtue and worth is . . . that a man is able to deny himself his own desires, cross his own inclinations, and purely follow what reason directs as best". The habit of being "obedient to discipline, and pliant to reason" should be planted early on, when the mind is "most tender, most easy to be bowed". Locke recognised that this instruction that an infant's desires should be "subject to the rules and restraints of reason" might conflict with the natural affection parents have for their children, but he insisted that "reason watch . . . that natural affection very warily [and not] let it run into fondness". Parents do their children no favours if they cherish their faults and "indulge their little irregularities". They are merely planting the weeds of bad habits: "he that is not used to submit his will to the reason of others, when he is young, will scarce hearken or submit to his own reason, when he is of an age to make use of it".[31]

So the first thing children should be encouraged in is the "principle of all virtue and excellency". This "lies in a power of denying ourselves the satisfaction of our own desires, where reason does not authorise them". They should be taught to realise "they were not to have any thing because it pleased them, but because it was thought fit for them". "Their being little and wanting something is not a good reason for them to have it", and they should certainly not be allowed to think they can get it by crying.[32]

A child's curiosity is to be encouraged as much as possible, for "one great reason why many children abandon themselves wholly to silly sports . . . is, because they have found their curiosity baulked and their enquiries neglected". Their questions should be answered forthrightly: "let nobody trifle with him and deceive him with false reasons or wrong accounts of things; it will but teach him the trick to dissemble and make excuses".[33]

On the more specific matter of learning to read, Locke suggested, as a start, pasting the letters of the alphabet on the sides of a number of dice or of a single polyhedron, and awarding prizes (apples, raisins, or almonds) for the throwing of certain letters.[34]

NOVEMBER–DECEMBER 1684: "SUSPECTED TO BE ILL-AFFECTED"[35]

Locke left Leiden for Amsterdam on 8/18 November. He did not mean to stay long in Amsterdam, being merely "in...passage" on the way to Utrecht, where he intended to stay at any rate for the duration of the winter. But at that very moment ill-fortune was crossing his plans and, in Tyrrell's phrase, "put[ting] one of those dog tricks" upon him.[36]

Two days earlier, a letter had gone from Whitehall informing the Dean of Christ Church that the King wished Locke to be deprived of his Studentship. He had been informed that "one Mr Locke, who belonged to the late Earl of Shaftesbury, and has upon several occasions behaved himself very factiously and undutifully to the Government, is a student of Christ Church"; consequently his wish was that Locke be "removed from being a student, and that, in order thereunto, your lordship would let me know the method of doing it".[37]

According to Damaris Cudworth's account of the matter some years later, John Fell, the Dean, "had ever expressed much esteem for Mr Locke and...had lived with him on terms of friendship; so that it is not to be doubted but that he received this harsh command with trouble". He spoke with Tyrrell about it, "and was so well satisfied of Mr Locke's innocence that instead of obeying the order he had received he summoned him to return home by the first of January following...to answer for himself". Locke himself expressed the somewhat different view that Fell had wanted him to return "to answer for himself", not because he thought him innocent, but simply because, innocent or guilty, he should be given a hearing. Some years later he said that Fell, "finding it against the rules of common justice as well as the ordinary methods of the college, to turn out anyone without hearing...especially one who had lived inoffensively in the college for many years, did...summon [me]...to answer anything that should be alleged".[38]

If we go by what Fell replied to the King's representative, the second of these accounts was nearer the truth but was still some distance from it. Fell did suggest that Locke should be given a chance to speak, but he did not say (as Damaris Cudworth had it) that he thought Locke was obviously innocent, whereas an appeal to "common justice" (as in Locke's report) can perhaps be seen in what he did say. Yet (contrary to both reports) what Fell suggested, rather against Locke,

was that Locke's having "lived inoffensively" in the college was a
carefully constructed façade. In replying to the court Fell said that since
Locke, having been "much trusted by the late Earl of Shaftesbury", was
"suspected to be ill-affected to the government", he had for some
years "had an eye upon him". However,

> so close has his guard been on himself, that after several strict inquiries I may
> confidently affirm there is not any one in the college...who has heard him
> speak a word either against or so much as concerning the government; and
> although very frequently, both in public and private, discourses have been
> purposely introduced, to the disparagement of his master, the Earl of
> Shaftesbury, his party and designs, he could never be provoked to take any
> notice or discover in word or look the least concern; so that I believe there is
> not in the world such a master of taciturnity and passion.

Fell continued by explaining that Locke "has here a physician's place,
which frees him from the exercise of the college, and the obligations
which others have to residence in it, and he is now abroad upon want of
health", but said that he had

> summoned him to return home, which is done with this prospect, that if
> he comes not back, he will be liable to expulsion for contumacy; if he does,
> he will be answerable...for what he shall be found to have done amiss; it
> being probable that, though he may have been made thus cautious here,
> where he knew himself to be suspected, he has laid himself more open
> in London, where a general liberty of speaking was used, and where the
> execrable designs against his majesty and his government were managed and
> pursued.

Fell promised that "if this method seem not effectual or speedy
enough, and his majesty...shall please to command his immediate
remove...it shall accordingly be executed".[39]

It is possible, however, that Fell's real attitude to Locke is not to
be found in this reply and that he was acting "through a principle
of fear". At a social gathering (at the Stillingfleets' as it happens)
a few month's after Locke's expulsion, Damaris Cudworth heard
a friend of Fell's say that Fell "had often said that nothing had
ever happened to him which had troubled him more than what he
had been obliged to do against Mr. Locke; for whom he had ever
had a sincere respect: and whom he believed to be a man of as
irreproachable manners, and inoffensive conversation as was in the
world".[40]

It was not till 20/30 November at the earliest that Locke first heard
anything of this and learnt of Fell's summons, by what means we do

not know. As is apparent, Fell had no great expectation that Locke would obey it, and his feeling was shared by others in the college. Prideaux reported that "it is supposed he will rather choose forfeit his place by still absenteeing than venture his neck by coming any more within the reach of the King's justice".[41] But they were quite wrong. Locke determined to return to England to answer what was alleged against him.

Pembroke "was much surprised", he told Locke, "when I heard the reason of your coming so soon", but he took comfort when he considered how "many men of good reputation, by being accused, have had an advantage publicly to prove themselves honest men". Knowing Locke as he did, he said he gave no "credit to others' words". He promised his support and assured Locke that "nothing shall hinder me from hazarding all I am worth, when it may be advantageous to such a friend".[42]

We do not know exactly what charges Fell had summoned Locke to answer. The court's letter to Fell had said no more than that Locke had behaved "very factiously and undutifully towards the government"; and, as is plain from his reply, Fell took it that this behaviour was supposed to have been before Locke left for Holland. But, whatever the charges were, apparently Locke was confident that he could answer them satisfactorily.

He was not, however, to have the chance, for by the time he read his summons from Fell, things had moved on. In a letter dated 12/22 November, at least a week before Locke had learnt anything at all of the matter, Fell had been told that the King now wanted, not some proposal as to how things should be managed, but Locke's immediate expulsion. "Whereas we have received information of the factious and disloyal behaviour of Locke ... we have thought fit hereby to signify our will and pleasure to you, that you forthwith remove him from his student's place, and deprive him of all the rights and advantages thereunto belonging." Some people in Oxford thought the expulsion was not before time: "I was very glad to hear that Locke is turned out of Christ Church", one wrote to another, "but methinks it had become the Bishop [Fell] to have done it of his own accord long before, and not to have let the King's bread to nourish and comfort his Majesty's enemies, and the retainers of such great and apparent villains as the late earl of Shaftesbury was."[43]

In moving from simply wanting a proposal for Locke's removal to wanting that removal "forthwith", the King was acting on some

fresh information sent from Holland, information which changed
the charges against Locke. A letter (dated 11/21 November) had
been sent from The Hague by Thomas Chudleigh (envoy to the States-
General) to Charles Middleton, Secretary of State:

Herewith I send your Lordship a most impudent and horrid libel that
the malice of Hell itself could possibly invent. It has for title 'An impartial
inquiry into the administration of affairs in England with some reflections
on the King's Declaration of July 27, 1683'. It has been with great difficulty
that I have procured it from Amsterdam where I doubt not but it was printed,
and by the style and language of it I dare swear it to be the twin brother of
that other libel which I sent you lately that undertakes to prove the Earl of
Essex's being murdered, but what their common father be I may possibly give a
guess, but it will be impossible to prove it; I should be loath to wrong any man,
but since the Lord Shaftesbury is gone I can think none more likely for such a
work than one with whom he may have left his spirit and his malice behind, and
that is his secretary Locke, who has been some time in this country, dividing
himself between Leyden and Amsterdam, whither he pretends to be come for
the benefit of the air.

Locke's faculty place at Christ Church, Chudleigh continued,

was never intended for the maintenance and support of such as seek
to overthrow the government, and to bring the King's sacred person
into contempt and even into horror with all men as if he were the worst
of tyrants and the worst of men, for so His Majesty is more barbarously
pointed out in this libel; and whether he be the author of it or not I do
not see for what reason Mr Locke should be so much indulged as to
keep his place in Christ Church whilst he lives amongst the worst of our
traitors here.

The college should be contacted "and directed to summon him home,
and in case of his refusal to bestow his place on some other that better
deserves it". The letter continued with some information about the
company Locke had been keeping:

It is said that Mr Ferguson* and the Goodenoughs are gone to keep company
with Sir William Waller in Luneborg but I hear with more certainty that
Nelthrop, who has passed for some time at Amsterdam by the name of
Gardner, is now either gone or just upon going thither in company with
Waller's wife and his own.... This Nelthrop was one of Locke's companions,
and another of them is said to be newly dead and buried at Leiden, which is the
Lord Louden Campbell.[44]

The accusations against Locke having been increased by Chudleigh's
letter, the King decided on immediate expulsion. Writing not long

after, Wood recorded that Locke was expelled from Christ Church "for Whiggism":

The reason because he kept company and was great with Robert Ferguson and . . . Lord Grey of Wark at The Hague, which was complained of by Thomas Chudleigh, resident of The Hague, to . . . Charles Middleton, secretary of state to the King in England, who giving notice thereof to Bishop John Fell and wondering why he was suffered to keep his place, was therefore expelled. . . . This Locke is supposed to be the author of 'The Hue and Cry after the Earl of Essex his blood'.[45]

It was on 28 November/8 December, while preparing to return to England in answer to Fell's summons, that Locke received a letter (in fact by the same post as Pembroke's letter of support) informing him of his expulsion on the basis of these additional accusations, of being the author of defamatory pamphlets and of having associated with undesirables not now just in England, but in Holland too. Just who it was from we do not know (Fell?), but, in obvious and great distress, Locke immediately set about writing a lengthy and self-justificatory letter to Pembroke, a letter which has been seen by some as "disingenuous if not untruthful", but which nevertheless gives some interesting insight into Locke's picture of himself and the course of his life.[46]

Locke appealed to Pembroke whether he had ever known him to keep bad company or to speak against the King.[47] Had he "ever observed the least appearance of anything in me of the kind I am charged with; but quite the contrary"? Fell too would surely acknowledge that Locke had never exhibited "the least mark of undutiful against the government either of the church, state, or college itself" and that there was no "appearance of turbulency, faction, or sedition in my nature". It is clear, though, from Fell's letter to the court that he was not prepared to testify as straightforwardly as this on Locke's behalf. The very fact (witnessed to by Prideaux also) that it seems to have been a kind of game in the college to try to provoke Locke into speaking against the government shows what was generally suspected; the fact that he never did so speak, but simply said nothing, clearly seemed to be rooted, not in his having nothing to say, but in his keeping his mouth firmly shut. Prideaux had spoken of Locke's reacting with "profound silence" to the attempts to provoke, and to Fell (at least in his formal report), Locke came over as a supreme "master of taciturnity".

Locke suggested to Pembroke that these accusations had been made against him just because "chance, and not my own seeking" happened to bring him into Shaftesbury's sphere of influence – something which, with an unpleasing lack of loyalty, he portrayed as not having been a completely good thing. His behaviour at Shaftesbury's, he said, had been no less blameless than it had been at Christ Church; "if it had been, it would have belied my mind and temper". He had kept out of his patron's political affairs, never doing anything "undutifully against his Majesty or the government". "I know nothing in my life scandalous, or am conscious of anything that ought to give any offence; I have never been of any suspected clubs or cabals, I have made little acquaintance, and kept little company in an house where so much came, and for that little my choice was of bookish not busy men." This choice, moreover, was "the natural product of my unmeddling temper, which always sought quiet". It is simply unfair, complained Locke, that "any imputation that lies upon him [Shaftesbury] should draw suspicions upon me".

Locke's claim that he kept himself apart from the many visitors to Thanet House would be contradicted by Shaftesbury's grandson (aged ten in 1681), according to whom Shaftesbury "entrusted [Locke] with his secretest negotiations".[48] But in a mood of abject self-pity he went on to regret the way things had developed with Shaftesbury:

Either through attention, or good luck, I happened to do him some acceptable service in that great, and strange disease, when he was opened, so that he was afterwards pleased to own, that he owed his life to my care; and possibly the memory of that, might make him treat me ever after (as I confess he did) with great civility and kindness. Yet some of my friends, when they considered, how small an advancement of my fortune I had made in so long an attendance have thought that I had no great reason to brag of the effects of that kindness.

He was not, Locke told Pembroke, meaning "to complain of my dead master"; that would be "no way decent in me", he said. Yet "in this extremity, I cannot but complain of it as an hard case, that having reaped so little advantage from my service to him whilst living I should suffer so much on that account now he is dead". In words which are surely not lacking in disingenuity, Locke suggested that had he spent the past years exactly as he had but "in any but my Lord Shaftesbury's house, I might now search my health, and enjoy my pittance, and privacy anywhere, quietly without being suspected of libels, or any other miscarriages". The accident of "falling into a great man's family" had "(I know not by what witchcraft) confounded the quiet, I always sought; and the more I endeavour to get into some quiet retreat, the more still I find myself in a storm".

Locke then turned to "the company I am said to keep at Coffee houses", an idea he claimed was ridiculous. "Coffee houses it is well known I loved and frequented little in England, less here... having no great delight either in the conversation or the liquor." Is it likely, he asked, that he would come to Holland and get to know and "keep company" with people "whom everyone that would be safe shuns, and who were never any of my associates in England, when they were under much better circumstances"?

So as for "those who are particularly named for my companions", he simply denied the reports: "I assure your Lordship with the truth I would speak my last breath, I never saw out of England nor in a long time before I left it." Since we do not know exactly who had been named to him, we do not know exactly what he was denying here, but it is easy enough to make some suggestions. According to Wood, Chudleigh had complained that Locke kept company with Robert Ferguson and Forde Grey; Chudleigh's letter as quoted above mentioned Nelthrop and Lord Campbell as his companions; and Prideaux had recently reported that the last thing he had heard of Locke was that "he had consorted himself with Dare of Taunton, and they two had taken lodgings together in Amsterdam". If the last of these, Thomas Dare (a known subversive, who had been close to Shaftesbury in Amsterdam, and who worked with Monmouth in organising rebellion), had been mentioned, then Locke can be convicted out of his own mouth of lying: according to Locke's own journals, Dare had been acting for him as a banker from shortly after his arrival in Amsterdam, and only two days after writing his letter to Pembroke Locke left various things with Dare, including a copy of his *De Intellectu*.[49] As regards Campbell, Ferguson, Grey, and Nelthrop, Locke himself has left no actual evidence that he knew them at this time or later; in later months, however, he would be further reported by English agents as being in the company of some of them.

The suspicion of writing various "scandalous and seditious libels" Locke again blamed on his association with Shaftesbury, for "I have often wondered in the way that I lived, and the make I knew myself of, how it could come to pass, that I was made the author of so many pamphlets, unless it was because I of all my Lord's family happened to have been most bred amongst books".

Quite possibly the "many pamphlets"* Locke had in mind included "A Letter from a Person of Quality" of 1675 and "No Protestant Plot" of 1681; though the second of these was by Ferguson, the first, according to Shaftesbury's grandson, was amongst the writings for which Shaftesbury "made use of [Locke's] assistant pen in matters that nearly concerned the State, and were fit to be made public to raise that spirit in the nation which was necessary against the prevailing Popish party". But, as he said, suspicion had followed him to Holland, and (as we see from Chudleigh's and Prideaux's letters) he was suspected of writing a pamphlet entitled "Hue and Cry after the Earl of Essex his blood" and "An impartial inquiry into the administration of affairs in England". Exactly what these were is not clear: the first reference may be to "An Enquiry into ... the Barbarous Murther of the late Earl of Essex", which was again by Ferguson in fact; but according to the State Papers there were a "great number of libels relating to the death of the Earl of Essex" coming over from Amsterdam. Locke pointed out that differences of "matter and style" in the pamphlets which were attributed to him made it unlikely they were by the same person; but in any case he vehemently denied being responsible for them. Apart from the verses he had published, he "solemnly protested in the presence of God" that he was not the author, "not only of any libel but not of any pamphlet or treatise whatsover in print good bad or indifferent". His friends, who knew full well of "the apprehension and backwardness I have ever had to be in print even in matters very remote from anything of libellous or seditious", would support him here.[50]

Apart from the question of the "Letter from a Person of Quality", there is no reason to suppose Locke had engaged in the writing of occasional pamphlets; yet, unknown to his accusers, at that very moment there were in England manuscripts of his which contained propositions which at best would have led him, like Parkinson, to be expelled from Oxford, or at worst, like Sidney, to the execution block. Perhaps Locke was hinting at these and at what should be done with them when he told Clarke that he was so far from writing any libels that "I take care not to read anything that looks that way ... and if a letter from a friend should have in it but the title or mention of any libel, I should think it a sufficient reason to burn it immediately ... and I desire no other usage for my letters to themselves". The thought that Clarke was meant to read between these lines, lines which Locke was afraid other and hostile eyes might see, is further encouraged by the fact that even if he had not read it, there is amongst his surviving papers a libellous manuscript arguing that Essex had not killed himself but had been murdered.[51]

On Locke's account, it was certainly not to engage with political refugees and subversives that he came to Holland; indeed their presence there was a disadvantage, and he had been at pains to avoid them, he said, "industriously avoiding company, to that degree, that it was reproached to me here, that I was a man by myself". In a similarly self-justificatory letter he wrote to Clarke a month later, he suggested that his isolating himself had been misinterpeted by some malicious person in his lodgings ("I fancy I could guess pretty near the very person"), who had suspected that, alone in his room, he was engaged in the composition of libels.[52] In fact, during these many "solitary hours I spent alone", he had, he told both Pembroke and Clarke, been devoting himself to his work on the understanding:

My time was most spent alone, at home by my fireside, where I confess I wrote a good deal, I think I may say, more than ever I did in so much time in my life, but no libels, unless perhaps it may be a libel against all mankind to give some account of the weakness and shortness of human understanding, for upon that my old theme de Intellectu humano... has my head been beating, and my pen scribbling.

Though Locke's letter to Pembroke did not make the surely false claim that it was on account of his health that he left England, it needed no discussion that it was in fact better for his lungs to be out of England. Nevertheless it had been asked, he said, why he had come to Holland, rather than France, "for change of air"? It has since been suggested that France, which had begun quite serious persecution of its native Protestants, would have been odious to him, but he did not mention this. Rather, he had already tried France, he said, and though it had done his cough some good it had not cured it; he had thought, therefore, to give Holland a try, and in fact, "beyond my expectation", had found it "effectual, and I have reason to hope in time a perfect cure". Besides, he said, wine, the common French drink, was noticeably hurtful to his health, water ("since my last sickness") gave him colic, "and there is but little beer* in France, none in the southern parts".[53]

Locke did not mention the possibility, which Pembroke had hinted at, of getting a pardon from the King; as he explained to Clarke, "though the consideration of his Majesty's great clemency and of my own innocence give me reason to hope a restoration", he thought the time was not yet right ("great men are not pleased to have innocence pleaded in the first heat of their suspicions, however raised by misinformation") and that Pembroke should not be troubled in the matter.[54]

Whether he had joined in or not, Locke must have at the very least known of the kind of discussion that had gone on at Thanet House; in Holland he undoubtedly at least knew political subversives; and something of his political views can be seen in his two treatises on government. But was there more to it than this? Whether or not there was, his letters to Pembroke and Clarke express a deep timidity, and the anxiety of a man who, despite his best efforts, finds himself in the line of fire. Someone who knew him during his worrying years in Holland would describe him as "of a peaceable temper, and rather fearful than courageous".[55]

DECEMBER 1684–SEPTEMBER 1685: "TO BE SEIZED AND BANISHED"[56]

Even had it not become impossible, a return to England would now have been pointless, and Locke resumed his intention to remove to Utrecht. He had already asked two of his Amsterdam friends, van Limborch and Sladus, for letters of introduction to Joannes Graevius, a professor of politics and history at the University of Utrecht, and, through him, to other learned people. What Sladus had to say is interesting as an account of how Locke, already fifty-two, appeared to his contemporaries: "a scholar and a medical practioner of distinction, who also turns his hand to poetry from time to time".[57]

Why, when he had begun to acquire a circle of friends in Amsterdam, did Locke want to leave for Utrecht? Bourne suggested that he reckoned Utrecht would give him "more leisure and better opportunities for quiet thought and work with his pen", and also that, being inland, it had a "milder climate and healthier position as compared with Amsterdam, then much less protected by artificial barriers from inclement weather than now". But, most important for Bourne (who generally wished to detach Locke from any suggestion of subversive political involvement), was that in Amsterdam Locke "appears to have...found himself forced into the society of other English refugees, with whose political designs he had little or no sympathy".[58]

Unless he was being curiously naïve, avoidance of political involvement can hardly have been Locke's reason for going to Utrecht, however; it could seem, indeed, that involvement must have been just what he was seeking. Even before mid-December, when Locke returned there, and to his lodgings with the Grimonts, his plan to do so was known to his enemies, and had aroused even more suspicion. Chudleigh, in the letter which precipitated Locke's "immediate expulsion", had informed his masters that Locke "speaks now of going to reside at Utrecht, where is the greatest nest at present of the King's ill subjects". But, whatever the truth about Locke's involvements, it is no surprise that it was noted in Utrecht that he always left the room when English affairs were spoken of.[59] It is quite clear from what Fell had said about his behaviour at Oxford, and from his own letter to Pembroke, that, whether or not what Locke really wanted was not to be involved, he was certainly keenly and carefully concerned to avoid any appearance of being so.

He was not successful in this, however. So far as his own records go, his activities seem innocent enough. He continued his work on his "notions de intellectu humano", and by the end of April these had grown to "such a bulk" that, he said, it would take some time to get a fair copy of them for Pembroke, who (apparently to Locke's relief) had expressed a desire to see something of them. In February he was in Amsterdam for two weeks (rather longer than expected), and was there again in April for a few days; but all he has left us to know is that on the first of these visits he saw Limborch and left some root vegetable seeds for Clarke with Thomas Dare. But at the same time he was, justly or unjustly, under observation by English government agents. "I was informed at Utrecht", Bevil Skelton, the English envoy at The Hague, reported back to England, that "Sir Patience Ward,* Papillon, Starkey and Locke do constantly reside there, and that Ferguson is often with them".[60]

When that report was made, there was increased activity amongst the English political refugees in Holland. King Charles had died in February, and, as had become inevitable, had been succeeded by James. In response to fears that the country was now even more than ever at risk of Popery and arbitrary government, serious plans were being evolved for an invasion of England by supporters of the Duke of Monmouth. In the first part of April rebels seemed to be congregating in Rotterdam, and rumours of invasion got back to England.[61] Skelton's report continued: "I was also told at Utrecht that all these rogues intend very suddenly for England", and in fact within a few days the Earl of Argyll left Amsterdam with three ships, loaded with men and arms, with the aim of making a rising in Scotland. This was to be followed by one in England by Monmouth, who sailed at the end of May and landed on 11/21 June at Lyme on the English Channel coast.

Both invasions failed, and by the middle of July Argyll and Monmouth had been captured and executed. Grey, Goodenough, and Ferguson, who had been with Monmouth, all got back to Holland. According to Le Clerc, Locke "had not such high thoughts [of Monmouth], as to expect any thing from his undertaking", and the isolated notation, "vanitas vanitatum" (vanity of vanities), in Locke's journal at the beginning of June presumably was some comment on his enterprise.[62]

Locke's visits to Amsterdam (in February and April) postdated Charles's death and the beginnings of serious plotting for invasion. At the very least he must have known what was going on. It would certainly have been ironic if he had not, for the English agents in Amsterdam thought he was involved. "John Locke, previously the secretary to Lord Shaftesbury" was on a list of people seen on board one of Argyll's ships, and unless this was a case of mistaken identity the sighting would have been between 15 and 20 April when Locke was in Amsterdam, Argyll's port of departure. It is not clear whether the report claimed that Locke was still on board when the ships left for Scotland; if it did it was mistaken, though it was not mistaken about others it mentioned, for example, Sir John Cochran and William Blackader, who did sail with Argyll.[63]

Though Locke certainly did not go with Argyll, he has been supposed to have provided financial support for these invasions, either personally or as a treasurer of the money of others. The most obvious evidence for this is in confessions made by two captured insurrectionists. Nathaniel Wade, in his account of the development of the conspiracies, included "Mr Locke" as someone who had financed both Argyll (to the tune of £1000 of the £9000 cost of the invasion) and Monmouth (£400 towards a cost of over £5500). Similarly, Grey informed that Argyll had received "near a £1000 from Mr Locke", and that Monmouth too had got money from "Mr Locke". Bourne's reaction to Grey's confession ("now known to abound in fabrications, and to be untrustworthy in every part") was that what he said about Locke was "preposterous", and others have argued that Grey and Wade* were not referring to Locke at all, but to a different man, one Nicholas Locke.[64]

But whether Locke was involved or not in any way in these insurrectionary ventures, he must have known something of the planning for them. With whatever degree of closeness, he was at least acquainted with some of the people involved (Dare, Grey, and van der Velde); places he had visited since his arrival in Holland (Amsterdam, Utrecht, Leiden, and Rotterdam) were places where the plotters lived and met (Argyll at Utrecht, Monmouth at Amsterdam). Even if it is wrong to think, as Ashcraft does, that he was in those places to meet and plan with them (wrong, for example, that his movements in April and May between Amsterdam and Utrecht related to such meetings), at least he must have come across them there.[65]

At any rate, it has to be recognised, for what it is worth, that Locke was supposed by the English authorities to be involved. Getting wind of Monmouth's intentions, James took measures against the English fugitives sheltering in the Dutch Republic, and on 1/11 May, Skelton was sent a list of eighty or so people he wanted the States-General, the Dutch governing body, to expel from Holland, if they were there and could be found. Locke was not on that list, but Skelton had permission to make additions as he saw fit. See fit he did, and on the list* which he presented to the States-General he put "Mr John Locke who was secretary to the Earl of Shaftesbury", as someone else who was to be "seized and banished".[66]

Locke left Utrecht on 23 May. But just as his presence there had been reported back to England, so too was his departure. It was thought that, travelling under the name of "Johnson", he was "returning to Lubeck where he will take yet another name", but in fact he went to Amsterdam. Perhaps he left simply because the winter, which he had wanted to spend inland, was now over — though this is unlikely, as he now entered a period of living in hiding and under false names. If Ashcraft's interpretation of it is correct, his move was connected with the imminent departure of Monmouth's army. But even if Locke merely knew of and was in no way connected with the invasion plans, his name had appeared on an official list of undesirables, and simple prudence might have indicated a move to Amsterdam, for it was seen as something of a relatively safe haven for English refugees. It had been described by Skelton to his masters back in England as a place that would "not so readily execute these orders" from the States-General, but would "rather shelter those traitors". According to Le Clerc, the move back to Amsterdam had been suggested by his friends there for this very reason. Guenellon, Veen, and Limborch "saw his danger [in Utrecht], and that it was time to do him a kindness", and in fact

when they "consulted one of the chief magistrates of the town
[Amsterdam], to know if he might be safe there", they were told "he
could not protect him, if the King of England sent for him, but that
he would not deliver him, and would not fail to give notice of it to
Mr Veen".[67]

Locke's preference was to stay with Guenellon, "but he excused
himself, because it was not the custom of their city to give lodgings
to strangers, though otherwise he had a great esteem for him [Locke]
and was very well pleased with his visits"; but Guenellon "generously
engaged his father-in-law Mr Veen to entertain him in his house".
Some years later Limborch reported that he put these arrangements
into effect. On Veen's instructions he offered Locke Veen's house
"as a place of concealment, in which he could stay without anyone's
knowledge". "I took him there", Limborch recalled, and "often visited
him in his solitude, and conversed with him for many hours at a time."
Locke arranged for his letter to be sent to Limborch "so that his
honourable hiding-place might not be discovered". Furthermore, said
Limborch, "he entrusted to me his will and other valuables, and gave
me in writing the names of his nearest relatives, in order that I might
communicate with them if anything happened to him". Limborch's
account is something of a sketch, for Locke first stayed where he had
stayed before, with van der Velde, the bookseller, and friend and
supporter of English fugitives. He probably made the secretive move
from there to Veen's in mid-July. Whether he knew it or not, the move
was fortunate: not only had it been known for some time that he was in
Amsterdam, along with "divers others" who had fled Utrecht, but also a
further "List of wanted dangerous and disaffected" persons was about
to be issued, one which identified him as someone "regarded as
dangerous", to be kept under observation, and said to be living "(in
great privacy) at Mr van der Velde's".[68]

The caution and secrecy of Locke's life, which extended even
to keeping his exact whereabouts hidden from Syl, who lodged
elsewhere, is manifest in two letters he wrote to Limborch. According
to the first, perhaps written shortly after his arrival back in Amsterdam,
"I am most eager to see you. . . . If you care to call on me this messenger
will show you my lodgings. . . . But if you think it more convenient that
I should call on you, I will be at your house this evening after
nine o'clock; meanwhile please say nothing about me." In the second,
written on the day of his removal to Veen's, he said, "I shall be with
you after nine, and after that I shall betake myself to the lodging

which has so kindly been arranged for me, and which I should not wish to be known either to my servant or to any of my fellow countrymen."[69]

In June, Damaris Cudworth ceased to be "Mademoiselle C", as she put it, and became "Lady Masham". One topic of the regular correspondence she and Locke had been having had in fact been her "puzzling difficulty about matrimony" (to marry or not to marry?). This seems to have been compounded with more general feelings of being at odds with things: she had a general "quarrel with the world" (which led her to talk, variously, of becoming a stoic, a Labadist, or a nun), but she accepted that this perhaps resulted from "want of a servant [a suitor]", and complained that Cambridge, where she had largely spent her life, was a dull place which had offered no "occasion for a heart". If, at the beginning of the year, she was only "half armed against matrimony", it was because Locke himself had given her "reasons and arguments" for it.[70]

At that point, marriage to Sir Francis Masham was perhaps not yet in question, but it soon became so — not that she had been swept off her feet. In announcing her impending marriage, two weeks before the event, she spoke of it as a merely political event, and in terms of what she was losing: "after a long and glorious reign" she was going to "resign her authority, and submit herself henceforward to the more humble quality, and condition, of a subject". She was quick to assure Locke that things need not change between them. She was altered only in name, and he would "always find her as much your friend as she ever was, or as you can desire that she should be".[71]

At thirty-nine, Francis Masham was thirteen years Damaris's senior. A widower for four years, he had been left with a number of children, for at least three of whom (aged sixteen, ten, and five) his new wife soon had responsibility. Though she had found Cambridge a dull place filled with scholarly pedants, the conversation even there was more diverting than what she had exchanged it for, "the repeated entertainments of the price of corn, and the best management of a dairy". She found the depths of rural Essex and the Masham manor house of Oates, near the village of High Laver, "the wretchedest neighbourhood in the whole world", "a solitary wilderness". The new life of "family cares" to which she had committed herself, a life which required her to be "busy to acquire the necessary reputation of a good country housewife" was not to her liking. She continually complained to Locke that matrimony and its domestic duties made her dull. "Household affairs are the opium of the soul", she said, and made her lethargic and robbed her of "poetry". "Business and the impertinent concerns of a mistress of a family will never have any place in my heart", she had concluded after eighteen months of marriage. "The gentleman you know of", as she referred to her husband in writing to Locke, seems to have had no place in her heart either, or indeed in her mind: "the business of this world almost wholly employs him when he is at home, so that I have very little of his company".[72]

It is not clear from the letters Damaris Cudworth wrote to Locke in the year or so before her marriage whether she was looking for, or how she would have responded to, a proposal from him; nor is it clear how much any such thing was ever in his mind. What is clear is that the possibility of romance seems to have been in the air almost from the outset. If a pair of poems, "On Damon's loving of Clora", they wrote and exchanged probably early in 1693 reflect the course of one chapter of their relationship, then for a while Locke "laughed at love,... disease of fools, fond lunacy", and wanted no more than friendship – only to find that that friendship "warmed [him] with desire and lodged in [him] a secret fire" which she then disdained: "The friendship once I gave retain but think from me no more to gain to whom thy passion comes too late." Locke's female friends Mary Clarke, Jane Stringer, and Anna Grigg all archly hinted at romance between him and Damaris, and she herself unembarrassedly told Locke of a social occasion when someone playfully introduced the idea that "you [Locke] love me exceedingly".[73]

It is also clear that after a very brief period in which they both seem to have felt that her marriage required their relationship to move from one of "friendship" to one of "respect" and "esteem", her feelings for him became openly enlivened, and she pined for his stimulating companionship. Along with her domestic duties, she soon grew tired of letters which congratulated her on her marriage: rather than being wished joy, she told Locke, she would prefer "that you will endeavour to give me some by saying something that is more new to me". Less than half a year after her marriage she told him in terms she would not have used before, "I cannot help telling you that there is scarce anything I would not give to see you here in my closet where I am now writing to you".[74] There is no evidence that any of this was unwelcome to Locke, and, given the modus vivendi they would come to in future years, one could easily think he welcomed her marriage as making it possible for them to have what perhaps he was easier with, close intellectual companionship without the responsibilities and expectations of a marriage.

SEPTEMBER 1685: "WHAT GOD HAS THOUGHT FIT"[75]

A life in which he did not want any Englishman, or even his trusted servant, to know where he was staying, "going out only in the nights to prevent being discovered", must have been unpleasant in the extreme. Veen must have been more keenly aware of this than were his other friends; at any rate he took steps to find him some alternative. According to Limborch, though Locke had "all the services that friendship and good nature could render" at Veen's house, "the confinement was painful to him, the access of only two or three friends being allowed to him. Solitude wearied him, and he wished to breathe a freer air." However, Limborch said, "a certain gentleman" persuaded Veen that Locke "would find a safe and comfortable asylum at Cleve":

I and Dr Guenellon objected to his going, for I knew this gentleman to be fond of making great promises which often came to nothing; but through Veen he persuaded Mr Locke to leave us, his friends, and go...that he might enjoy more liberty. Veen and Guenellon and I conducted him to the boat which goes from here to Utrecht, and hardly could we bear to part from him.[76]

It was probably on 11 or 12 September when Locke was taken to the boat for Utrecht, and 15 September when he arrived at Cleves, after an uncomfortable journey. A couple of weeks earlier he had told Clarke that he was "packing to go I know not whither"; he perhaps suppressed the destination of Cleves, about eighty miles away, simply out of a cautious secrecy, but he may anyway have had some idea about travelling on from there to Germany. In Cleves, having been welcomed by a friend of Limborch, a Mr van der Key, Locke took up lodgings, under the name "Lamy", with Mayer, the secretary of the Elector of Brandenburg.[77]

During the six or so weeks he was in Cleves, Locke continued reading a manuscript of Limborch's *Theologia Christiana* which he had begun in Amsterdam. He found little in it to criticise, but did have some objections to another book he read, *Sentimens de quelque théologiens* by one of Limborch's colleagues at the Remonstrants' seminary, Jean Le Clerc. He agreed with Le Clerc that many things said

by the Apostles could have been said without divine inspiration, but felt
that the way Le Clerc presented this point invited the conclusion that
there was nothing of divine authority in the Scriptures.[78]

Locke was working on something of his own too – his investigations
into the understanding. Quite possibly the manuscript he had with him
was what survives today as "draft C",* headed "An Essay concerning
human understanding" and carrying the date "1685".[79]

Though Locke continued to work on his ideas, the correlation
between this draft (which consists of only the first two of the four
"books" into which he had divided his work) and what he would
eventually publish is close enough for a general appreciation of its
contents to be got by referring to that later form.

The first chapter of book one is an "Introduction" to the whole
Essay, and in it Locke explained his overall purpose. His conception
of this had remained essentially the same since he began his
investigations in 1671. It was to "inquire into the original, certainty,
and extent of human knowledge; together, with the grounds and
degrees of belief, opinion, and assent"; thus he aimed to "consider the
discerning faculties of a man, as they are employed about the objects,
which they have to do with", to give an "account of the ways, whereby
our understandings come to attain those notions of things we have, and
can set down any measures of the certainty of our knowledge, or the
grounds of those persuasions, which are to be found amongst men".
These "persuasions", he commented, are "so various, different,
and wholly contradictory; and yet asserted somewhere or other with
such assurance and confidence... [we] may perhaps have reason
to suspect, that either there is no such thing as truth at all; or
that mankind has no sufficient means to attain a certain knowledge
of it".[80]

According to the note on "The Understanding" which Locke wrote
in Montpellier in 1677, such extreme scepticism would be quite
mistaken, and Locke now made use of the main ideas in that note.
There is, he thought, such a thing as truth and it is not completely
beyond our reach, but there are also pretty obvious limits to our
understandings and to the knowledge we can acquire by them ("the
comprehension of our understandings, comes exceeding short of the
vast extent of things"). But the shape of the map of our knowledge is
not something for which there is no explanation. It is, Locke intended
to show, a function of the nature of our understandings, a nature which
is God-given, so in the end our knowledge is shaped by what a

benevolent God wanted us to know. God has given us faculties which are sufficient for our needs, and these are of two kinds. He has seen to it that we are able to learn to cope with the practicalities of our earthly mortal life, and also that we are able to discover our moral duties to each other and to God, obedience to whom is relevant to our deserts after death. God "has given [people] ... whatsoever is necessary for the conveniences of life, and information of virtue. ... However short soever their knowledge may come of an universal, or perfect comprehension of whatsoever is, it yet secures their great concernments." We have, then, "reason to be well satisfied with what God has thought fit for" us.[81]

A survey of the understanding, its powers and limits, will stop our inquiring into things which are none of our God-given business; it will be of use "to prevail with the busy mind of man to be more cautious in meddling with things exceeding its comprehension. ... We should not then perhaps be so forward ... to raise questions, and perplex ourselves and others with disputes about things, to which our understandings are not suited." Not everything lies in "broad sunshine", but the "candle [our reason], that is set up in us, shines bright enough for all our purposes. The discoveries we can make with this, ought to satisfy us." We are guilty of a kind of meddling pride, and run the risk of discontented pessimism and scepticism, if we seek knowledge beyond our God-given natural limits. "Our business here is not to know all things, but those which concern our conduct. If we can find out those measures, whereby a rational creature put in the state, which man is in, in this world, may, and ought to govern his opinions and actions depending thereon, we need not be troubled that some other things escape our knowledge."[82]

Locke was of the view, then, that there are limits to what is illuminated by the "candle" of our understandings. And in aiming to show just where these are, he hoped to show that they are natural boundaries, which stem from our natural constitutions and the kind of creature we are. He hoped to show how solely by the use of natural faculties "we may acquire all the knowledge we have", gradually and as a process of learning through our lives.[83] But he did not set about this until book two. Instead he devoted the rest of book one to arguing against an alternative view about our knowledge and beliefs according to which they are not all gradually and progressively derived, in an entirely explicable way, by the use of the faculties God has given us, but that some of them are innate at birth.

According to this view, "God has imprinted on the minds of men the foundations of knowledge and the rules of living". Of course if Locke were able to establish his own account of the matter, this doctrine of innateness would thereby be rendered otiose, for "it would be impertinent to suppose, the ideas of colours innate in a creature, to whom God has given sight...and no less unreasonable would it be to attribute several truths, to innate characters...when we may observe in ourselves faculties, fit to attain as easy and certain knowledge of them". But because his own view was a "little out of the common road", he thought he should look directly at this common view and "set down the reasons that made me doubt of" it.[84]

The "foundations of knowledge" of the doctrine of innatism are very general principles of reasoning – for example, "nothing can both be and not be", or the "whole is bigger than the part". The "rules of living" are basic moral principles – for example, "one should do as one would be done unto", or "it is the duty of parents to preserve their children". A prime reason why such principles have been supposed to be innate is that they "are universally agreed upon by all mankind", and Locke's basic strategy was to argue against this. Of the first kind he said that they are "so far from having an universal assent, that there are a great part of mankind, to whom they are not so much as known"; it is surely evident that "all children and idiots, have not the least apprehension or thought of them". It is "near a contradiction", he suggested, "to say, that there are truths imprinted on the soul, which it perceives or understands not".[85]

Locke argued that the supposedly innate moral principles have no "universal assent" either:

He that will carefully peruse the history of mankind, and look abroad into the tribes of men...will be able to satisfy himself, that there is scarce that principle of morality to be named, or rule of virtue...which is not, somewhere or other, slighted and condemned by ... whole societies of men, governed by practical principles, and rules of living quite opposite to others.

And here he brought into play the wide reading he had done over the years in the literature of exploration and travel: "Are there not places, where at a certain age, they kill, or expose their parents without any remorse at all?...There are places where they eat their own children."[86]

A further reason for rejecting innate moral principles is that there are no self-evident rules of morality, none for which a reason may not be asked. Promise-keeping "is certainly a great and undeniable rule in morality",

but yet, if a Christian, who has the view of happiness and misery in another life, be asked why a man must keep his word, he will give this as a reason: because God, who has the power of eternal life and death, requires it of us. But if an Hobbist be asked why; he will answer, because the public requires it, and the Leviathan will punish you, if you do not.[87]

In rejecting the idea of innate God-given "rules of living", Locke was not denying that there is a God, not denying that there is a God-given objective morality. Different societies have different moralities, and people who agree in their principles may give different reasons for them, but Locke did not think this showed there are no moral truths or that we cannot come to know them. The relativism he found among practices, beliefs, and justifications was no indication for him of moral subjectivity. It was still his view, as it had been in the 1660s, that there are "laws of nature", discoverable by a proper use of our reason. He still believed in a "true ground of morality; which can only be the will and law of a God, who ... has power enough to punish the proudest offender". For Locke, differences in people's moralities show only that moral principles have not been inscribed innately on our minds by God; they do not show that there are none. Yet those who believed in divinely inscribed moral principles found it hard to see how, in rejecting innatism, Locke was not rejecting a God-given morality. But it must be clear that he was not: "I would not be here mistaken, as if, because I deny an innate law, I thought there were none but positive [i.e. civil] laws." There is, he said, "a great deal of difference between an innate law, and a law of nature; between something imprinted on our minds in their very original, and something that we may attain to the knowledge of, by our natural faculties". The rejection of an "innate" morality did not involve the rejection of any objective morality attainable by other means.[88]

In the final chapter of book one Locke provided some other considerations against innatism. He appealed to a distinction, one implicit from the very start of his investigations, between propositions, which form the content of what we believe and know, and what he now called "the materials of our knowledge", ideas or notions which are "the parts, out of which those propositions are made". So, for example, the principle "the whole is bigger than a part" is made up from the ideas of "whole" and "part"; the proposition "God is to be worshipped" has amongst its parts the ideas of "God" and of "worship". The point made on the basis of this distinction was a simple one: no proposition can be innate unless the ideas which make it up are innate: "it is hard to conceive how there should be innate moral principles, without an innate idea of a deity: without a notion of a law-maker, it is impossible to have a notion of a law, and an obligation to observe it". He then argued that there are no innate ideas. He pointed out, again appealing to his reading of books of travel and exploration, that not everyone has the idea of God, so our idea of Him cannot be innate. Recent travellers had encountered "whole nations, at the bay of Soldania, in Brazil, in Boranday, and the Caribee islands, etc. amongst whom there was to be found no notion of a God".[89]

Apart from its first, introductory, chapter, book one is essentially negative, it argues *against* the doctrine of innateness rather than positively *for* an account of the origin of our knowledge; by contrast, book two develops the first part of Locke's own account. The distinction between propositions, the "content" of our knowledge, and ideas, the "materials" that make them up, is a hinge on which the course of that whole account turns. First there needs to be an "inquiry into the original of those ideas...which a man observes, and is conscious to himself he has in his mind; and the ways whereby the understanding comes to be furnished with them", and this enquiry is the task of book two. Only then can there be the investigation of what knowledge, beliefs, and opinion we have "by those ideas".[90]

Over the years since Locke first began thinking about this subject he had not changed his mind about the origin of "the materials of reason and knowledge", but he now explained things at somewhat greater length and with rather more style and panache. If indeed there are no innate ideas, then the mind must have acquired its ideas by degrees and by some process. So if we suppose that the mind is at first like "white paper, void of all characters, without any ideas", we can then ask "how comes it to be furnished? Whence comes it by that vast store, which the busy and boundless mind of man has painted on it?" Locke's answer, in a word, was "experience". In experience "all our knowledge is founded; and from that it ultimately derives itself. Our observation employed either about external sensible objects; or about the internal operations of our minds, perceived and reflected on by our selves, is that, which supplies our understandings with all the materials of thinking." At birth, or not long before, a child's mind is as blank paper, on which experience then writes: "He that attentively considers the state of a child, at his first coming into the world, will have little reason to think him stored with plenty of ideas, that are to be the matter of his future knowledge. It is by degrees he comes to be furnished with them."[91]

In the rest of book two there are chapters discussing general properties and kinds of ideas: ideas may be clear (or obscure), distinct (or confused), adequate (or inadequate), real (or fantastical). More stress is laid on and use made of the distinction between simple and complex ideas, and there is greater discussion than before of the various operations of the mind: "retention" or "memory", "perception", "discerning", and "thinking". Furthermore, following his early drafts but more extensively, there is discussion of particular ideas, such as "space", "duration", "number", "infinity", "substance", "power", and "cause and effect". As before, while these discussions fit into Locke's general scheme in that they are attempts to show, by consideration of difficult cases, how various ideas, which we undoubtedly have, could have arisen from experience, they also have something of the character of digressions which Locke had entered into for their own sake. They add to the impression that what is now a great landmark of philosophy was often, during its composition, simply something of a pastime, a cherished diversion with which its author entertained and consoled himself during exile, and which, had circumstances been different, he would never have been sufficiently single-minded to complete.

SEPTEMBER 1685–SEPTEMBER 1686: "THAT FAITH WHICH WORKS, NOT BY FORCE, BUT BY LOVE"[92]

About the time he went to Cleves, Locke had a letter from Pembroke who, having recently distinguished himself against Monmouth at the decisive battle of Sedgemoor, was in favour with the King. Pembroke had been speaking to James on Locke's behalf, and he urged him to return to England:

I have omitted no opportunity of contradicting all false reports.... I have so satisfied the King, that he has assured me he will never believe any ill reports of you. He bid me write to you to come over; I told him, I would then bring you to kiss his hand, and he was fully satisfied I should. Pray, for my sake, let me see you before this summer is over.

There was some possibility of Pembroke's coming over to Holland on government service, and towards the end of September Locke anxiously though vainly awaited his arrival.[93]

Yet, even if, thanks to Pembroke, Locke's safety would now have been ultimately assured, he was still under observation. He had not been in Cleves for many weeks before his exact whereabouts, even under the guise of "Lamy", were again a matter of report. According to a dispatch, various dissidents had gone from Utrecht to Cleves where they made contact with "Dr John Locke who belonged to the late Earl of Shaftesbury in your list, and now lodges at one Mr Meer's house in Cleves . . . [and] who was with them every day."[94]

Perhaps it was because of something said at one of these meetings that Locke was back in Amsterdam by the end of October (possibly having spent some time in Utrecht at the Grimonts); or perhaps he returned because he knew he was under observation in Cleves, imperfect though this was, for into November he was still being reported as being at Meer's house in Cleves. Limborch put his return down to the fact that the "braggartly promises" of "a safe and comfortable asylum" in Cleves "were as vain as we anticipated". At first he again hid at Veen's and, "that there might be the less chance of his being discovered, passed by the name of Dr Van der Linden".* Outside of Limborch there is no other record of Locke's using this alias; could it have been Limborch's version of "Mr John Lynne", a name Locke had sometimes used at least since early in the previous year?[95]

During the whole of November and a good part of December, Locke was engaged in a Latin composition, *Epistola de Tolerantia*. Since considering the question of toleration at length in his "Essay" in 1667, he had continued to be interested in the subject as in his extensive notes on Stillingfleet, and had recently been thinking about it. It was something he and Limborch must have been discussing; Limborch's manuscript, which Locke had read in Cleves, was partly concerned with it, and it is possible that even before going there Locke had given him something he had already written towards the *Epistola*.[96]

What Locke wrote must have been given impetus by his uncomfortable awareness that his own country was, since the accession of James, even more in danger of an intolerant Catholicization, and that recent events in France showed what that could involve. Though the Edict of Nantes of 1598 had granted French Protestants a degree of toleration, Locke himself had been witness during his years in France over a decade earlier that they were not free from persecution, and in recent years Louis XIV had begun increasingly to subject them to physical cruelties and persecution: excluding them from various professions, closing their institutions, and forcing "conversions" by torture. The danger of their situation dramatically changed when in October of this year the edict was explicitly revoked.

The *Epistola* moved even further than the "Essay concerning Toleration" from the early "Tracts on Government", in the direction of stressing that religion is essentially of no civil concern. The "Tracts" had rejected Bagshaw's distinction between religious and non-religious indifferences, and had urged that there were no limits on what some-one, given the opportunity, might not claim to be against his con-science and to be a matter of religion. Moreover, while the "Tracts" had seen the need for firm impositions on potentially querulous people, and the "Essay" had been very much more balanced in its assessment of that need, the *Epistola* saw the problem as lying in a need to rein in religious persecution by the civil authorities. It solved this via a clear distinction, which Locke had laid down very clearly over twenty years earlier in a manuscript piece endorsed "Excommunication", between the different purposes of state and church.[97]

Underlying all that Locke said in the "Letter" was the belief he held all his life, that "every man has an immortal soul, capable of eternal happiness or misery; whose happiness depending upon his believing and doing those things . . . prescribed by God". It follows from this, he said, that "our utmost care, application, and diligence, ought to be exercised in the search and performance of [these things]; because there is nothing in this world that is of any consideration in comparison with eternity".[98]

Locke had been asked (presumably by Limborch), he said, for his "thoughts about the mutual toleration of Christians in their different professions of religion", and his first, rather passionate, paragraphs expressed a conviction that Christianity as such requires toleration; toleration, he said, is "the chief characteristical mark of the true church". He was, therefore, scathing about states which persecute religious dissidents "with a pretence of care of the public weal, and observation of the laws", or of national churches which persecute them "under pretence of religion". "True religion", he was in no doubt, has nothing to do with "erecting an external pomp, nor to the obtaining of ecclesiastical dominion, nor to the exercising of compulsive force; but to the regulating of men's lives according to the rules of virtue and piety". It is clear, he thought, that "if the Gospel and the apostles may be credited, no man can be a Christian without charity, and without that faith which works, not by force, but by love".[99]

The need for toleration between different churches received more emphasis here than in Locke's earlier writings, though of course it had been one theme in his "Defence of nonconformity". His initial concern had been the question of toleration by the state, and, against the background of this claim that Christianity as such is a religion of toleration, Locke returned to that question, introducing it by setting down the "just bound" that separates "the business of civil government from that of religion".[100]

A state, or commonwealth, he said, is constituted "only for the procuring, preserving, and advancing the civil interests" of those in it, interests such as "life, liberty, health...money, land, houses". The "whole jurisdiction" of government "reaches only to these civil concernments", and, consequently, "it neither can nor ought in any manner to be extended to the salvation of souls". Three considerations underlay this claim that the state has no proper concern with "the care of souls". First, God has given a governor no authority "as to compel any one to his religion"; nor have his subjects left it to him to "prescribe...what faith or worship [they] shall embrace"; nor would they do so since no profession of faith or outward worship is acceptable to God unless it is accompanied with inner conviction. "I may be cured of some disease by remedies that I have not faith in; but I cannot be saved by a religion that I distrust, and by a worship that I abhor."[101]

Second, a ruler is anyway unable to bring about conviction in his subjects' minds – a point which had been made in passing in the "Essay concerning Toleration" and the "Defence of nonconformity", but which Locke now underlined. His power consists in outward force and earthly penalties and these are not able to bring about "inward persuasion": "Such is the nature of the understanding, that it cannot be compelled to the belief of anything." It is impossible simply to believe what we are told to believe. Punishment, or its threat, is not able to influence belief: "it is only light and evidence that can work a change in men's opinions; and that light can in no manner proceed from corporal sufferings, or any other outward penalties".[102]

Third, even if it were possible for the state to impose religious belief, in many cases that imposition would not save souls. While there is, Locke believed, "but one truth, one way to heaven", there nevertheless is a "variety and contradiction of opinions in religion, wherein the princes of the world are...divided"; so state interference in religious matters means that our eternal happiness or misery would depend on where we were born. The government is not better placed to "discover [the] way that leads to heaven more...than every man's private search and study discovers it unto himself".[103]

Such was Locke's case for religious toleration by the state. It means, as indeed Locke thought in his earlier "Essay", that the "magistrate ought not to forbid the preaching or professing of any speculative opinion in any church, because they have no manner of relation to the civil rights of subjects"; thus "if a Roman Catholic believes that to be really the body of Christ, which another man calls bread, he does no injury thereby to his neighbour". But though the state's sole proper concern is the civil interests of its subjects, it might properly enact laws which had consequences for some sects or churches. Even in their sacred rites, chuches should not be permitted things which are prejudical to the state and its members, nor should the magistrate tolerate "opinions contrary to human society, or to those moral rules which are necessary to the preservation of civil society". Though Locke thought open or explicit examples of this were rare, there were cases where doctrines "in effect opposite to the civil right of the community" are "covered over with a specious show of deceitful words". No sect or church would deny the obligation to keep promises, or hold that a government might be overthrown if it is not of the right religion, but these things are in effect said by those that teach "that faith is not to be kept with heretics", and that "kings excommunicated forfeit their crowns and kingdoms". Equally, a state should not tolerate a church where membership involves allegiance to another earthly power, for then it would be allowing "a foreign jurisdiction in [its] own country". What Locke had in mind in these cases was Roman Catholicism; but this was not the only group to whom religious toleration was to be denied, for, on the grounds of a similar untrustworthiness, atheists were another: "those are not at all to be tolerated who deny the being of God. Promises, covenants, and oaths, which are the bonds of human society, can have no hold upon an atheist. The taking away of God...dissolves all."[104]

Locke resisted the suggestion that there are yet other groups which should be denied toleration. There certainly had been religious groups and sects which had been "nurseries of factions and seditions", but his thought was that they were not seditious naturally but only as a result of persecution. "If men enter into seditious conspiracies, it is

not religion inspires them to it . . . but their suffering and oppressions."
If it were once established that "nobody ought to be compelled in
matters of religion . . . all ground of complaints and tumults upon
account of conscience" would be taken away, and "there would remain
nothing in these assemblies that were not more peaceable, and less apt
to produce disturbance of state, than in any other meetings".[105]

In the *Epistola* Locke was concerned not only with religious
toleration by the state, but also with mutual toleration of different
sects, churches, and their members. What he said here turned on an
account of the nature of a church: a society of people who have
voluntarily come together for "the public worshipping of God, in such
manner as they judge acceptable to him, and effectual to the salvation
of their souls". Any society needs its rules, and, in Locke's view,
a church's authority to make and apply them resides in members.
He thus explicitly denied the necessity for "a bishop or presbyter with
ruling authority derived from the very apostles, and continued down
unto the present times by an uninterrupted succession". Though not
ruling out that people might opt for an episcopalian or a presbyterian
church, his point was only that there is no explicit edict by which Christ
required that churches have governments of these kinds; he promised,
indeed, to be present "wheresover two or three are gathered together
in his name".[106]

A church is not bound to tolerate anyone who "continues
obstinately to offend against" its laws. But since its aim is, in the end,
"the acquisition of eternal life", it should not (even if it had some
power by virtue of being nationally established) impose any penalties
relating to worldly interests. Here, rather more explicitly than he had a
handful of years earlier in his notes on Stillingfleet, Locke spelt out that
the principle that the state has no proper concern with religion, is
matched by the correlate (which denies what he called "the great and
fundamental Popish doctrine") that the Church should not use secular
power for its ends. Beyond "exhortation, admonitions, and advice",
the only punishment a church can properly inflict is excommunication.
In general, the nature of a church means that "nobody . . . neither
single persons nor churches [nor "bishops, priests, presbyters,
ministers"] . . . nor even commonwealths, have any just title to invade
the civil rights and wordly goods of each other, upon pretence of
religion".[107]

In short, "the care of each man's soul . . . is left entirely to every
man's self". To understand Locke properly here, we should see that

he is *not* allowing that someone might enter into a supposedly private and solitary communion with God. In fact he left very little record of his own churchgoing;* but there is no reason to think he was not assiduous in following (probably as a non-dissenting Anglican) his own injunction here that "God ought to be publicly worshipped". Particularly those who enjoy religious liberty "are to enter into some religious society . . . not only for mutual edification, but to own to the world that they worship God . . . [so that] they may draw others unto the love of the true religion". He is *not* saying either that there are many, equally good ways to eternal happiness: he more than once expressed the view that there is but one, "one only narrow way that leads to heaven". But it is not for the state, or some church having behind it the power of the state, to prescribe what it is. "Those things that every man ought sincerely to inquire into himself, and by meditation, study, search, and his own endeavours, attain the knowledge of, cannot be looked upon as the peculiar possession of any sort of men." "The principal consideration", as he called it, for this view was that even though there is only one narrow way to heaven, it is a necessary (though not a sufficient) condition of my being on it that I am "thoroughly persuaded in my own mind": "I cannot be saved by a religion that I distrust, and by a worship that I abhor", such worship is offensive and not acceptable to God.[108]

Without going into detail, Locke made the point more than once that there are certain articles of faith and actions which are necessary for salvation. He thought that these are given expressly in the Scriptures, which "are acknowledged by all Christians to be of divine inspiration"; no church or sect can be following the "road to heaven" unless it embodies this "substantial and truly fundamental part" of religion. Yet though there is only one road, a road defined by these "fundamentals", there are "several paths" in it, which involve beliefs and actions about which there might be sincere disagreement whether they are "consequences deduced from Scripture", or even whether they are agreeable to Scripture. It is differences about these that produce different sects. Locke mentioned here just the kind of thing which his tracts on government had argued should be subject to decision and imposition by the magistrate: whether ministers should wear a white surplice, or be crowned with a mitre; he mentioned, too, the different ways of worship of the Lutherans and the Catholics, and doctrines such as that of the Trinity. Particularly since what distinguishes these sects and denominations are things not necessary for salvation, there should be peace and friendship between them without any claims of superiority.[109]

At the end of the year Locke moved from Veen's to lodge with Guenellon — according to Jean Le Clerc, to whom Limborch introduced Locke that winter. At the time Le Clerc was starting a new periodical, *Bibliothèque universelle de la Republique de Lettres*, which provided an admirable opportunity for Locke to publish his "Method of Commonplacing". He had supposed that Toinard would have sought to have it printed in the Paris journal *Journal des Savants*, but it was now over a year since he had sent him the latest version he had prepared, and nothing further had been said about it. So he published in the *Bibliothèque* later that year under the title "Méthode nouvelle de dresser des Recueils, communiqué par l'Auteur" ("Method of indexing a commonplace book"). Other than the handful of verses he had published at various times, this "bagatelle" (as he described it) was Locke's first publication, at the age of fifty-four. From time to time he made further contributions to the *Bibliothèque*, such as short reviews of English publications.[110]

During the winter Locke sent Clarke a further instalment of the "Directions" for the upbringing of his son. Supposing that by now the boy could read "pretty well", he again recommended Aesop's Fables, "which being stories apt to delight and entertain a child, may yet afford useful reflections to a grown man". He certainly did not recommend the Bible. "The promiscuous reading of it, though by chapters as they lie in order, is so far from any advantage to children, either for the pleasure of reading, or principling their religion, that perhaps a worse could not be found." Most of it, he said, is beyond a child's capacity to understand, though carefully chosen parts would give them the principles of religion.[111]

Latin should be learnt, but not by rules of grammar as in schools; this was something Locke had "long had thoughts about". It should be learnt as English was learnt; "for if you will consider it, Latin is no more unknown to a child, when he comes into the world, than English: and yet he learns English without master, rule, or grammar". Locke recommended that someone be employed to speak Latin with the boy who could learn other things at the same time, such as some geometry, geography, astronomy, and history. The significance of those subjects is that they "fall under the senses". It is with such things that knowledge should begin, and not be founded in "the abstract notions of logic and metaphysics", which (as "I could assure you on my own experience", Locke said) strike young people as dealing with nothing but "hard words and empty sounds". Locke similarly recommended the reading of Boyle's experiments and observations as "fittest for a gentleman", as opposed to speculative systems in natural philosophy (though if there were any desire for them Locke recommended Descartes's principles, not as perfectly true, but as perhaps the most intelligible).[112]

Such recommendations were clearly based on Locke's critical reflections on his own education. We may remember that Descartes showed him as a student that there was some alternative to the sterilities of scholasticism; and there were further things which he did not want Clarke's son to suffer. The formal rules of rhetoric and logic, he said, are of little use in learning to speak "handsomely" or to reason well: "right reasoning is founded on something else than the predicaments and predicables and does not consist in talking in mode and figure". He was equally against the composition of themes and verses in Latin which had formed so much of his Westminster education. Verse writing in English was ruled out too: "I know not what reason a father can have to desire to have his son a poet"; consider what "company and places he is like to spend his time in" if he became "a successful rhymer". Learning music was almost as undesirable: it "wastes so much of ones time" to acquire any skill, and, like poetry, "engages [one] in such odd company".[113]

Two things which Locke did favour for Clarke's son were drawing, and the keeping of accounts. The first would be useful "especially if he travel", enabling him to "express in a few lines ... what a whole sheet of paper in writing would not be able to ... make intelligible"; and from the sketches to be found in Locke's letters and papers of various pieces of apparatus and mechanisms this clearly was an ability he found useful himself. As for the keeping of accounts, Locke did not have in mind setting down "every pint of wine, or play that costs him money", in the kind of meticulous detail which is often to be found in the accounts* kept by him and for him by his servants; nor did he have in mind that the father would want to keep a check on the son (no doubt part of the point behind the detail Locke required from his servants). He was thinking, rather, that the recording of "general ... expenses" will "keep a man within compass" of his finances.[114]

In May, when the States-General issued another list of people wanted by the English as accomplices in Monmouth's failed invasion, Locke (perhaps thanks to some friend, such as Pembroke) was not amongst them. A few weeks later, however, he met up with some visitors who *had* been under arrest at the time of that affair: Sir Walter Yonge, an old supporter of Shaftesbury, with whom he had been acquainted for at least two or three years; and John Freke, a lawyer who had worked for Robert Ferguson and had been implicated in the Rye House plot, and whom Locke may have known from Shaftesbury's time. With Yonge ("the little baronet") were his married sister Isabella Duke, his "fat brother"-in-law Richard Duke, and his widowed sister-in-law Elizabeth Yonge. The Yonges and the Dukes were near-neighbours of Edward Clarke; they referred to their three country houses, which lay on a straight line (respectively at Escot, Otterton, and Chipley), as "the Row". Yonge was keen to have Locke's help and advice in buying books in Holland, eventually for a library in a new house he was building. The party was completed by Locke's friend "Adrian" Thomas (known to them all as "Dr Taffy").[115]

Within days of meeting him Locke had a quarrel with Duke, over some "course of railery" which had begun between them. The teasing and banter of raillery was something for which Locke acquired a reputation amongst his friends: two of them would remark upon it in obituaries. He was, one said, "No foe to railery, provided it were delicate and perfectly innocent", while according to another "he practised it better than anyone":

railery in him was so far from expressing the least disrespect, that when he began to speak to you with that air, you might almost be assured he was going to say what it should be for your credit to have said; or at least to make you a handsome compliment. And to jest at anyone's misfortune, or imperfection, was a thing abhorent from his nature.

Besides practising it, Locke had also thought about it and "often spoke against [it], as being of dangerous consequence, if not well managed", and it would seem that on this occasion he, or Duke, slipped up in some way (or perhaps Locke simply did not like being subjected to it himself). Locke started it, and Duke, as he admitted later, continued it in "too gross and dull a manner". He thought that "the heavy constitution of a fat man might have excused" this, but Locke took offence, for Duke later accused him of "calling names, or giving ill language". The episode must have underlined for Locke what he had written in his educational "Directions", that "the nice management of so nice and ticklish a business" as raillery or banter is hard to maintain and "a little slip may spoil all".[116]

But things were not irrevocably spoilt. Duke soon forgot "both the quarrel and the occasion of it", and after some days in Rotterdam the party went to nearby Delft. There they met the microscopist van Leeuwenhoek and made some minute observations of the blood, a tooth, and canine spermatozoa, with one of his instruments (not "the best" which "he does [not] show . . . to any one"). Then, towards the end of June, and after some time in Utrecht, Locke and Thomas returned to Amsterdam while the others travelled south to Spa, to drink the waters, and to carry out a task Locke had set them, of testing the mineral content of the waters with galls.[117]

The Dukes had some thought of spending the winter in Utrecht and Locke promised to spend it there with them, but in the event, in mid-September, he was with them at The Briel when they embarked for England. Clarke, so Isabella Duke reported later, seems to have expected that Locke would have returned with them, "yet he advises you nothing", she said, "but leaves you to be determined by your own reason".[118]

SEPTEMBER–DECEMBER 1686: "CHANGING ONE'S ABODE IS INCONVENIENT"[119]

About a week later Locke was in Utrecht again. "Many things have drawn me to this city", he told Limborch "whether they will keep me here I do not know. If I had my way I would soon return to Amsterdam to you and our friend Guenellon and Veen and the "college"; but this body needs a roof, bed, and lodging, nor are these things easy to find in that city. . . . I hope all the same to visit you all shortly."[120]

John Freke had not returned to England with the others, and Locke had him as company for a week in November. When he left he took with him a copy of the recently issued *Bibliothèque Universelle* which contained the account of his method of commonplacing, to give to Benjamin Furly, an English Quaker in Rotterdam, to whom Freke had introduced him when they were there earlier in the year. Furly had been in Rotterdam for twenty to thirty years, where his trade as a merchant left him time to study, and to associate with intellectuals and some of the English radicals. Locke became good friends with him and his family.[121]

In late November or early December, Locke left Utrecht and went to Rotterdam. Limborch had come by the idea that the Utrecht authorities had in fact expelled him as an undesirable, an idea which

Locke was anxious to dispel: "as to what you have heard about expulsion, I neither understand the matter so nor should I wish a word to be said about it. . . . I should be most unwilling for such a description of the matter to get abroad." Exactly what "the matter" was, or how Locke understood it, is not clear; but Freke, after his stay with Locke, had reported from Rotterdam that a "design" they had discussed against a certain person in Utrecht was being "talked of everywhere but none can tell what it is". Freke's letter left the person's name a blank, though of course it was known to Locke, and is likely to have been Locke himself. Freke added that the "Lord M. business at your town" had upset this "design", "spoiled it and either broken or altered their measures". The "business" referred to an (unsuccessful) attempt by an informer in Utrecht to denounce Charles Mordaunt to the English authorities.[122] But even if the "design" was not against Locke, Utrecht may again have felt uncomfortably warm.

Opinions differ whether Locke's choice of Rotterdam was determined by its proximity to The Hague, where revolution against James II "was being plotted for most eagerly". But in any case he did not find it satisfactory there for some reason, and within a week or so he wrote to Limborch in Amsterdam asking him to "consider the question of a lodging there, and discuss the matter with our two friends the Doctors, your neighbours [Veen and Guenellon]". This inquiry was not something he made lightly, for moving around in this way was not attractive to him. Tyrrell, who had had an account of Locke's way of life from Thomas, remarked that "I envy it not". Even though Locke appears to have been remarkably buoyant about it, he felt it forced upon him by events outside of his control: "Changing one's abode in this fashion is, I confess, somewhat inconvenient on account of the business with one's luggage. I want my books, for which it is not easy to find a place; if I fail to do so elsewhere please forgive me if I send them to you." Imposing on his friends, he said, was the one thing that really troubled him, "the rest does not move me". "These things are fortune's sports with us, or rather the ordinary accidents of human life."[123]

In all Locke's moving around, fortune did not sport with him to the extent of depriving him of sufficient time and peace of mind to continue work "de Intellectu". Having got its first two books into a decent state by the autumn of the previous year, he had been in a position this summer to send Clarke a fair copy of the third book (following the first two earlier in the year). Now, at the end of December, he sent him the fourth and last book. "Read it...as a friend's act", he asked, but "judge of it as a stranger's, and let me have your opinion of it".[124]

His own opinion was that more needed to be done on the presentation, which showed the effects of his having worked on his ideas intermittently and in various places for well over a decade. "I see now more than ever", he told Clarke, "that I have reason to call them [my thoughts] scattered, since never having looked them over all together till since this last part was done, I find the ill effects of writing in patches and at distant times...there are so many repetitions in it, and so many things still misplaced." He was, though, satisfied with the ideas themselves: despite the repetiousness, "you will find very little in the argument itself, that I think...needs altering".[125]

Book three of the *Essay*, "Of Words", expanded massively on what Locke had said on this topic in his early drafts. At first he had thought he could move straight on from the first two books about ideas as such, to ideas as the "instruments, or materials, of our knowledge", and how the understanding uses them in coming to knowledge itself.[126] But he had come to see that he needed first to consider language, because of the close connection between ideas and words, the "marks" or "signs" of ideas, and because knowledge is often expressed in words.

Some of the material (on indefinability of the names of simple ideas, abuse of words, and imperfection of language) was taken over from the early drafts. A crucially important advance, which now enabled Locke to explain just why our knowledge has its limits, was a distinction between real and nominal essence, the mere rudiments of which had been there in draft B.

Locke observed that most words are general, names for kinds of thing (man) rather than for particular things (Alexander); one reason for this being that knowledge, "though founded in particular things, enlarges itself by general views". Now words become general, he said, by being made to stand for general ideas, and a general idea such as *man* is formed by our "abstracting" from ideas of particular things (Alexander, Peter, Paul) "the circumstances of time, or place, or any other ideas, that may determine them to this or that particular existence".[127]

It is by this abstracting that general natures, or the essences of sorts of thing, are produced; they are nothing other than abstract ideas. "General and universal, belong not to the real existence of things;

but are the inventions and creatures of the understanding." In claiming this, Locke was disagreeing with a strand of thought within Aristotelian scholasticism according to which particular things belong to this or that species or kind on account of being "made according to", or their "partaking in", certain essences, which were thought of as "forms or moulds, wherein all natural things, that exist, are cast, and do equally partake".[128] In order to mark this disagreement Locke spoke of our abstract ideas, which are what he supposed "general natures" are, as *nominal essences*, as opposed to the *real essences* supposed by the scholastics.

In Locke's first thoughts about the understanding there had been a rather unstressed distinction between ideas of "substantial beings", and other ideas. By this time the distinction had become developed and formalised, and, making considerable use of the notions of real and nominal essence, he discussed at length two kinds of complex idea, "substances" and "modes".

The nominal essence of a substantial kind, such as gold, or horse, is an abstract idea made by the mind. In making such ideas we put together ideas of qualities we have observed together in nature. "Nobody joins the voice of a sheep, with the shape of a horse; nor the colour of lead, with the weight and fixedness of gold." Nevertheless, as Locke had observed in his early drafts, there is considerable variation in precisely which ideas are put together. Some people "content themselves with some few obvious, and outward appearances of things", and so "yellow shining colour, makes *gold* to children", whereas others "add weight, malleableness, and fusibility".[129]

It is, Locke said, an imperfection in our words that, because different people put together different qualities, they often stand for different ideas; and with some feeling he regretted the consequence that people often argue at cross-purposes and engage in merely verbal disputes. Since these imperfections are to an extent avoidable, he was even more heated about those who "abuse ... words", who, sometimes wilfully, use words without any clear idea, or with varying ideas in mind, or with new and unexplained meanings. Revisiting one of the themes in "Anatomie" and *De Arte Medica*, he contrasted the pointless "disputing and wrangling", the "learned gibberish", which arises from these abuses by "learned disputants" or "all-knowing" academics, with the "improvements of useful arts" effected by "the illiterate and contemned mechanic (a name of disgrace)".[130]

Now the scholastics appealed to their "forms" or "real essences" not only to explain what it was for a particular thing to be of a general kind (an account to which Locke opposed his doctrine of nominal essence ideas formed by taking note of regularly conjoined qualities), but also to explain why various qualities were "united" and naturally conjoined in the first place, and how things came to have the properties they did.

In his first thoughts on the understanding, as also in *De Arte Medica* and "Anatomie", Locke believed we could know nothing about the inner workings of nature, and was neutral as between a mechanical explanation of nature and one rooted in the forms and essences of scholasticism. Now, however, he was plainly inclined towards understanding the natural world mechanically, as though it were a clock with "springs and wheels, and other contrivances within". For, distinct from what the scholastics say, there is, he said, another "and more rational opinion" of real essences which holds "all natural things to have a real, but unknown constitution of their insensible parts, from which flow those sensible qualities, which serve us to distinguish them one from another" in accordance with our abstract ideas.[131]

Locke did not commit himself absolutely wholeheartedly to this corpuscularian, mechanical theory of the world, saying at one point that it is merely the best account to be had. But one difference between the two "opinions" of real essences seems to be that, as he would later say, "the modern corpuscularians talk, in most things, more intelligibly than the peripatetics": the mechanical, corpuscularian understanding is at least comprehensible, whereas supporters of the scholastic view really "know not what" their essences are, their "substantial forms [are] wholly unintelligible, and whereof we have scarce so much as any obscure, or confused conception in general".[132]

So, though Locke certainly did talk of the "real essence" of substances, he insisted, first, that they are not what we classify things by; and, second, as what might be supposed to underlie regularly conjoined qualities, they are best thought of as "a constitution of insensible parts", on which all those qualities depend.[133]

Again, however, we do not know that nature really does work mechanically, leave alone know any of the detail: human experience and knowledge, he thought, was, inevitably, literally superficial; we are like someone who sees the motion of the hands of a clock and hears it strike, but knows nothing of its internal mechanism. Because of this,

he explained, there is a divergence between substances' real and
nominal essences. If, on the other hand, the detail of their real essences
was known, if someone's idea of gold was of a specific arrangement
of corpuscles of a certain shape and size, rather than of a certain
collection of observable properties, then real and nominal essence
would coincide.

In the case of modes, however, they do coincide. Modal ideas are not
modelled on likenesses of natural things as ideas of substances are, but
are made "very arbitrarily, made without patterns, or reference to any
real existence". Ideas such as those of murder and parricide are made
according to our own purposes and conveniences. So it comes about
that the nominal essence of a mode is also its real essence. Since these
abstract ideas are "the workmanship of the mind, and not referred to
the real existence of things, there is no supposition of anything more
signified by that name, but barely that complex idea, the mind itself
has formed". In this case it is this idea "on which all the properties of
the species depend and from which alone they all flow: and so in these
the real and nominal essence is the same".[134]

The divergence of real and nominal essence with substances and
their coincidence with modes is, Locke said, of some "concernment...to the certain knowledge of general truths". This becomes
clear in book four which Locke began with a definition of knowledge as
"the perception of the connexion and agreement or disagreement and
repugnacy of our ideas". This applies easily to "general" or "universal"
propositions, for some propositions of this kind are true because their
constituent ideas are connected and related in such a way as to make
them true: the general, universal truth that every number is even or
odd results from a connection between the idea of "number" and those
of "evenness" and "oddness". By "perceiving" these relations we come
to have knowledge. As Locke said, "in some of our ideas there are
certain relations, habitudes, and connections...visibly included in the
nature of the ideas themselves". Knowing that the three angles of a
triangle add up to two right angles is a matter of "perceiving that
equality to two right ones, does necessarily agree to, and is inseparable
from the three angles of a triangle".[135]

Of course many universal propositions are true because they are
merely "verbal" and merely affirm one idea of itself (e.g. parsimony is
frugality) or predicate part of a complex idea of the term for the whole
(e.g. gold is a metal, where being metal is part of the idea of gold). But
it was not this sort of idea-containment or idea-identity that Locke

was thinking of when he talked about there being "relations, habitudes, and connections" amongst ideas. For there are, he said, *two* sorts of proposition which we can "know with perfect certainty": the first are "trifling" propositions which, because they have to do with the containment or identity of ideas, have but a "verbal certainty"; but we can *also* be certain in propositions "which affirm something of another, which is a necessary consequence of its precise complex idea, but not contained in it", for example the proposition that an external angle of a triangle is greater than either of the internal opposites. That relation between the angles, he said, is not part of the complex idea of a triangle, so this proposition is both certainly true and "conveys with it instructive real knowledge".[136]

Locke made a sharp distinction between knowledge, and belief or opinion. Where either intellectual incapacity or lack of any actual connection means that we cannot perceive a connection between various ideas, then, "though we may fancy, guess, or believe, yet we always come short of knowledge".[137] But to what extent and in what cases can we have "instructive real knowledge", and to what extent, and when, are we restricted to belief? When he first considered this his view had been that we can have no instructive knowledge of general propositions about substantial beings specifically: such propositions, he held, are either certain but merely verbal, or, if they are instructive, are uncertain and merely believed. This was still his view, but he had much more to say about it.

What Locke now said about the extent of knowledge, about the limits of our understandings, was structured by the distinction between different kinds of complex idea, modes and substances, and made use of the distinction between nominal and real essence. He now explained *why* general instructive propositions about substances are uncertain and cannot be known to be true. Given that our idea of gold is of a yellow fusible stuff and malleability is not a part of it, then there is no connection between those ideas, and we merely believe on the basis of our observation and experience that gold is malleable. It is, he said, because that idea of gold is not of its real essence, its corpuscular constitution, that we can see no connection between the various ideas. Any connection which malleableness has with the other qualities of gold is only "by the intervention of the real constitution of its insensible parts", but since we do not know this constitution "it is impossible we should perceive that connection". Conversely, if we knew "the figure, size, connection, and motion of the minute

constituent parts of any two bodies, we should know without trial
several of their operations one upon another". Why gold and silver do
not dissolve in the same acids "would be then, perhaps, no more
difficult to know, than it is to a smith to understand, why the turning
of one key will open a lock, and not the turning of another".
Substances "afford matter of very little general knowledge" because we
lack ideas of their real essences.[138]

By contrast, however, since modal real and nominal essence
coincide, there is here the possibility of instructive general knowledge.
Geometry was a favourite example. A "figure including a space
between three lines", he said, "is the real, as well as nominal essence of
a triangle". It is "not only the abstract idea to which the general name is
annexed, but the very essentia or being, of the thing itself, that
foundation from which all its properties flow, and to which they are all
inseparably annexed". And it is because of this that geometry has been
developed as a body of demonstrative knowledge, a systematic and a
priori science. The difference between the cases of substances and
modes was marked: if our idea of gold were of its real essence, rather
than of its observable properties, "then the properties we discover in
that body, would depend on that complex idea, and be deducible from
it, and their necessary connection with it be known; as all the properties
of a triangle depend on, and as far as they are discoverable, are
deducible from the complex idea of three lines, including a space".[139]

Geometry was not the only case where a knowledge of real essences
might give rise to a demonstrative science. Recurring to an idea he had
had five years earlier, Locke was "bold to think" that morality too was
capable of demonstration "since the precise real essence of the things
moral words stand for, may be perfectly known".[140]

In explaining how our knowledge is limited by our ignorance of real
essences, Locke provided a theoretical underpinning for the methodology of careful observation which, under the influence of Sydenham,
he had advocated in his writing on anatomy and medicine as being the
way forward in investigations of the natural world. "In our search after
the knowledge of substances ... the want of ideas of their real essences,
sends us from our own thoughts, ... to the things themselves", and
"experience must teach me, what reason cannot". "This way of
attaining, and improving our knowledge in substances only by
experience and history, which is all that the weaknesses of our faculties
in this state of mediocrity, we are in in this world, makes me suspect,
that natural philosophy is not capable of being made a science."

The purpose of such investigations is, of course, a practical one: from such "experiments and historical observations...we may draw advantages of ease and health". It does not matter that natural philosophy cannot be demonstrated with certainty with reference to hidden causes, and it would be unseemly to want it otherwise: "Men have reason to be well satisfied with what God has thought fit for them since he has given them...whatsoever is necessary for the conveniences of life, and information of virtue."[141]

The purpose of the *Essay* was to inquire into, not only the extent and certainty of knowledge, but also "the grounds and degrees of belief, opinion, and assent". The second draft in 1671 had already included some account of judgement, probability, and degrees of assent, but an important and related addition to the final work was a chapter on "Faith and Reason, and their distinct provinces", which itself reworked and developed some notes* which Locke had made in the summer of 1676. Faith is defined as assent, not on the basis of reason, but "upon the credit of the proposer, as coming immediately from God", a way of "discovering truths to men" which is called "revelation". (Locke mostly had in mind "traditional revelation", by which he meant revealed Scriptural truths.) Truths which are discoverable by reason, "by the natural use of our faculties", have no need of revelation; indeed, divine revelation of some geometrical truth already discovered by reason would not make us any more certain of it, for before accepting something on the basis of some supposed revelation we need to judge, on the basis of reason, whether it really is of divine origin, and we cannot be as certain of this as we already are of a truth known by reason. "To believe, that such or such a proposition, to be found in such or such a book, is of divine inspiration" is not simply a matter of faith with which reason has nothing to do. "Whatever God has revealed, is certainly true; no doubt can be made of it...but whether it be a divine revelation, or no, reason must judge." Given that a revelation is answerable to reason for its authenticity, it follows that a genuine revelation will never be contrary to reason: "there can be no evidence, that any traditional revelation is of divine original,... so clear, and so certain, as those of the principles of reason: and therefore, nothing that is contrary to, and inconsistent with the clear and self-evident dictates of reason, has a right to be urged, or assented to as a matter of faith". The province of revelation, "the proper matter of faith", consists, then, in things which are "above reason" in the sense that, though they are not contrary to reason, they lie "beyond the discovery of our natural faculties"; for example, that the "bodies of men shall rise, and live again".[142]

Locke did not discuss in this chapter just how the judgement of something's being a genuine revelation is to be made, on what basis we are to give "credit to the proposer of it, as coming immediately from God"; but from something he would write later we might suppose he had in mind that "credit" is got, as in the case of Jesus, by the doing of miracles.* Had he made this explicit no doubt he would also have repeated what his journal noted in 1681, that "reason must be the judge of what is a miracle and what not".[143]

The dispatch to Clarke of this last part of a work which had occupied Locke on and off for so long, naturally led to reminiscence and reflection. "Some friends upon an accidental discourse started me upon this enquiry", he recalled, and despite "some pains in thinking, it has rewarded me by the light I imagine I have received from it, as well as by the pleasure of discovering certain truths, which to me at least were new". He set on examining the human understanding in a quasi-natural philosophical way, "not by others' opinions, but by what I could from my own observations collect myself". And so, he said, he "purposely avoided the reading of all books that treated any way of the subject, that so I might have nothing to bias me any way, but might leave my thought free to entertain only what the matter itself suggested to my meditations". His aim had been "only truth so far as my shortsightedness could reach it, and where I have misstated it in part or in the whole I shall be glad to be set right". Locke's claim to have "avoided the reading of books", to be interested only in the truth as he seemed directly to find it, is repeated in the *Essay* itself.[144] It is one he is fond of making. But the fact that that finished work deletes the references of the earlier drafts to Descartes is some indication that the claim involves an element of disingenuous self-construction.

DECEMBER 1686–MARCH 1688: "BUSY AS A HEN WITH ONE CHICK"[145]

Following the inquiry he had made of Limborch, Locke was back in Amsterdam by the end of 1686, staying at Guenellon's. With Sladus and Graevius, who was visiting from Utrecht, he discussed the question of his safety, a matter which continued to occupy him, and concern about which led him to ask Clarke to have the half of the politically dangerous *De Morbo Gallico* manuscript which was with Rabsy Smithsby in London removed elsewhere. But it was probably because suitable long-term lodgings were not to be had in Amsterdam, that in early February 1687 he reluctantly took the canal boat back to Rotterdam, "very sad at being torn away" from his Amsterdam friends. "Warm me to life again with your letters", he wrote back to Limborch, "lest I grow utterly torpid."[146]

One thing Locke soon missed was a weekly discussion group which he had got Limborch and Le Clerc to set up with some others; nearly twenty years later Le Clerc still had "by me the rules, which he [Locke] would have had us observe written in Latin in his own hand". Shortly after his arrival in Rotterdam, Locke told Limborch that he now heard "little about politics... and so far still less about learning". But things must have got better when, not much more than a month later, he went to live with Furly, for given their common interests there must have been no lack of lively conversation.[147]

The Furly household was lively in other ways too. Fond as Locke was to become of Furly's young children, their crying filled the house with "unpleasant and unbecoming noise". This stimulated him to send Clarke an addition to his "former discourse concerning education" in which he discussed two sorts of crying which he had observed, "stubborn and domineering" and "querulous and whining". But Locke's and Clarke's concern for the young Edward, who by now (though Locke was curiously unclear about this) would have been about six, was focused on getting him a tutor. They were both anxious to keep the child away from the servants; not only would he acquire bad habits from them, but also, Clarke had observed, "he grows more and more fond of such people as divert him from... learning". But it was also important, Locke stressed, that any tutor Clarke engaged should agree with his educational doctrines and aims. By March, a Frenchman, M. Foukett, had taken up the post at Chipley, and Locke sent Clarke a summary of the general principles that should be followed. A child must learn "mastery over his inclinations" and "how to resist the importunity of present pleasure, or pain, for the sake of what reason tells him is fit to be done", though his mind must not "be curbed, and humbled too much" (if the tutor knows how to steer the course between the two he has "got the true secret of education"). He stressed again that corporal punishment was to be avoided: it would not teach the boy to resist his desires, but would simply encourage him to govern his actions, not by reason, but by the search for pleasure and the avoidance of pain; similarly he should not be rewarded "by things that are pleasant to him" (this simply authorises his love of pleasure). Shame and applause are the "spur or bridle", the pleasure or displeasure of the parents and the tutor are the way.[148]

Though, Locke said, he counted learning "the least matter", he also advised Clarke on what work the tutor and his charge should do together: once the child has learnt to understand the tutor in French they can turn to anatomy, botany, and astronomy; in a later letter he added geography and chronology, for without these, history, "the great mistress of prudence and civil knowledge", is not easily learnt and would otherwise just be a jumble of facts.[149]

It was perhaps through Furly that Locke soon met Francis Mercure van Helmont, the son of J.B. van Helmont whose medical work Locke had studied at Oxford. Some of his philosophical interests and ideas were rather mystical and speculative, such as his theory of metempsychosis according to which we have a thousand years to live, spread over twelve lives. He also had interests in chemistry and alchemy, and practised as a physician. It was perhaps these more practical interests which formed the basis of his friendship with Locke, who took down from him notes on a machine for polishing precious stones, on a preparation for the care of boots, and on making a ring made from a nail drawn through the hind hoof of a gelding (the purpose of the ring is not recorded).[150]

Towards the end of the year Locke had had a letter from Graevius, from whom he had not heard since their discussion in Amsterdam in January, about Locke's safety. Graevius recounted how two years earlier the information that the English authorities wanted Locke and others to be arrested had been taken to Utrecht by a Dutch official, Everard Dijkveld. At some point in the summer just gone, Graevius and some friends had been able to sound Dijkveld out as to whether Locke was still in any danger. Graevius, presumably reporting what Locke must at some point have told him, put it to Dijkveld that "any suspicion of offence that the king might have had had long been removed and cleared away through your [Locke's] friends, and that you [Locke] were fully assured of this on reliable grounds". Dijkveld, who had recently returned as an ambassador from England, had "no doubt" that things were as Graevius had said. Nevertheless he had suggested they should wait for the return of the English envoy to the United Provinces. "If he on his return", the suggestion was, "did not renew those complaints or make any new move there could be no further risk and you might take up your abode where you wished." In reply Locke pressed Graevius as to whether Dijkveld had mentioned the King himself at all. "If you know this or can fish it out of him when occasion offers, I earnestly beg you to let me know it as soon as possible; I have good reason for pressing you rather urgently on this point."[151]

Dijkveld's confidence about "how matters stood" with regard to Locke related to his assessment of affairs in England following a radical shift in James's domestic policy. In April, James, in a Declaration of Indulgence, had dispensed with the penal laws against Protestant and Catholic dissenters, and with the Test Act of 1673 which required public office holders to be communing members of the Church of England. Some of Locke's friends, perhaps concentrating on what this promised for toleration of Protestant dissenters, rather than for the filling of offices with Catholics, and perhaps ignoring the fact that James had used his prerogative power to suspend Parliamentary statutes, had welcomed these apparent relaxations and thought they put Locke's position in a changed light. In May, Tyrrell had urged Locke to return, at least for the summer to "see the face of things here"; you would, he said, "find a strange alteration in men's humours: and need not doubt a favourable reception"; similarly, Yonge had hoped Locke would have come over in the spring, "I do not yet see any reason you could have had to repent it." Later in the year they had felt no differently about it: in October, Yonge's sister spoke of the "peace, the liberty, the tranquillity, sweet England affords us...it is the merriest time in England that ever I remember", and in December, Tyrrell would again say that "as things stand here you need not doubt of a good reception", adding that Locke could "be restored to your place [at Christ Church] again if you think it worthwhile to confine yourself any more to a collegiate life".[152]

There are, however, other things in this exchange of letters between Locke and Graevius that it would have been good to know more about. Just when did Graevius learn (presumably from Locke) that James's suspicion of offence against Locke had "long been removed", and when did Locke learn? (Presumably one thing Locke was going on was what had been said at Pembroke's meeting with the King in August 1685, and which Pembroke reported* to Locke.) What was Locke's "good reason" for pressing Graevius at this particular time to find out what James's attitude towards him was? It is tempting to think he had recently heard that "Will. Penn has moved the King for pardon for you, which was as readily granted" – something which in August Tyrrell had hinted to Locke that Penn could do: "W.P. is a great favourite at court; and can upon recommendation do you any kindness he pleases." But it seems he did not learn of this until some days after his letter to Graevius. As we will see, Locke was most concerned about this whole question of a royal pardon.[153]

Towards the end of 1687 Locke also heard from Pembroke, who expressed his qualified approval of a plan Locke had asked him about earlier. In the summer he had sent Pembroke an abridgement of his *Essay* seeking permission for it to be published with a dedication to him. Pembroke approved of the publication and "would not alter anything in it", but he declined the dedication, on the grounds that the piece was an abbreviation of something larger: "a chain is not to be commended for its strength by taking it asunder", he said. He was, however, keen to see the whole *Essay*, which he thought should be printed too.[154]

To satisfy Pembroke as soon as possible, Locke asked Clarke to send him the copy he had received in instalments over the previous year, taking care to hide the fact that Pembroke was getting it at second hand: "be sure carefully to tear out all that is writ particularly to you at the beginning or ending of any of those little books it is bound up in. For it would be a little ungraceful that a copy which I send him should carry the marks of being intended for anybody else." Early in the new year Clarke was able to report that he had delivered the manuscripts to Pembroke who "received them with all imaginable kindness . . . and was very solicitous for your return into England this spring".[155]

In mid-December, Locke went to Amsterdam in order to supervise the printing of the French translation of the *Essay* abridgement which Le Clerc had produced. After three weeks he delightedly reported back to Furly that he was "as busy as a hen with one chick"; ten days later, however, some of the delight had worn off. He was having to wait on "the leisure of drunken workmen, who have so great a reverence for the holydays, that they could not till today quit the cabarets, the places of their devotion, and betake themselves to their profane callings". Eventually, nearly three weeks after that, the last sheet was about to be printed.[156]

Le Clerc published the abridgement in his *Bibliothèque Universelle* under the title "Extrait d'un Livre Anglois qui n'est pas encore publié, intitulé Essai Philosophique concernant l'Entendement.... Communiqué par Monsieur Locke". He presented it as "the outline of an English work which the author has been good enough to publish, to oblige one of his particular friends, and to give him an outline of his opinions". "The author is not very anxious to publish his treatise", Le Clerc explained, "and though he thinks he would be wanting in respect to the public if he offered them what satisfied himself without first knowing whether they agreed with it or thought it useful, yet he is not so shy as not to hope that he will be justified in publishing his whole treatise by the reception accorded to his abridgement." Some readers understood from this that the name "Locke" was a fiction, and believed that the "Extrait" was a trial balloon by Le Clerc himself, "fathered...upon an Englishman, to know what the world thought of it".[157]

Some sets of the sheets that came off the press were treated separately, for private circulation to Locke's friends under the title "Abrégé d'un ouvrage intitulé Essai philosophique touchant l'entendement", and (unlike the "Extrait") with a dedication to Pembroke. Locke was keen to get his "chick" (his "little Frenchman", as Damaris Masham called it) across the sea to friends in England, and fretted that it was not easy to find people to send copies by. He was, of course, particularly anxious that Pembroke should have one as soon as ever possible.[158]

Particularly from his friends and polite acquaintances the general reaction to the *Abrégé* was extremely favourable. "Choose some other person to descry the errors you would have me find there, since in my opinion there are none", the wife of John Guise, one of the English dissidents in Utrecht, told Locke; and he himself remarked proudly to Clarke that "my little treatise has drawn on me some compliments, and I doubt not but that I shall receive others upon the same occasion". But where reactions were more considered there were some substantive worries and serious disagreements: for example, about the conception of the soul as a passive *tabula rasa*, void of innate ideas, or about the proof of the existence of God. Lady Masham, to whom Locke of course had sent a copy, had something to say about both these things – as he had hoped, she was not "practising all the rules of the neighbourhood" and letting her kitchen and dairy take up all her time. She wondered, mistakenly, whether though he rejected innate ideas Locke would nevertheless have accepted the Cambridge Platonist view that we have an innate disposition to certain ideas, "an active sagacity in the soul whereby something being hinted to her she runs out into a more clear and large conception". Though she preferred the proof of the existence of God given by her father's colleague Henry More, she thought that Locke's argument from a first cause was "sufficient".[159]

The abridgement of the *Essay* was not all that Locke got the printers in Amsterdam to do; they also produced some copy sheets he had designed for teaching children to write. At the top of the page to be copied would be, in engraved handwriting,* "the alphabet in common letters". Then there would be "twenty-four proper names, each begin-ning with a great letter, and the whole name written in a little bigger hand than the alphabet whereby we shall also have the twenty-four great letters, which it is not necessary children should write before they can write the little letters well, and begin to write join hand". The sample letters were initially done for Furly's son Benjamin, but Locke had also had in mind Clarke's son and soon sent them for approval to Clarke.[160]

The upbringing of Clarke's son seems never to have been far from Locke's mind, and while he was in Amsterdam he wrote again adding to his earlier thoughts. Clarke would doubtless think, he said, that what he now had to say was the product of an overheated brain, but, the fact was, he thought the boy should learn a trade – painting, gardening, woodworking were his first suggestions; but then he warmed to the cutting and polishing of precious stones, even suggesting that Clarke's son should, when the time came, be apprenticed abroad, where he might also earn a living at it for a while. Since it was a given that "gentlemen" did not work with their hands, certainly not to earn a living, Clarke might well at first have thought that this was, as Locke put it, "visionary" extravagence. But the point (in accordance with what he written some years earlier to Grenville) was that the manual skill would eventually be exercised recreatively as an occupation which had the required refreshing contrast with a gentleman's usual business.[161]

Time was far better spent on this, Locke thought, than on "any of the idle sports in fashion". He recounted how, though not averse to the occasional game of cards (the financial outcome of some of which is recorded in his journal), he was for one period of his life "frequently called" upon to play, and was "more tired with it than ever I was with any the most serious employment". Perhaps he had in mind his time with Shaftesbury when, it seems, he had sat by whenever the cards were "called for". Shaftesbury's grandson, in illustration of Locke's "mixture of pleasantry and a becoming boldness of speech", recorded one such occasion when Locke declined to engage at cards with Shaftesbury and his friends:

Mr Locke sat by as a spectator for some time; at last, taking out his table-book, began to write something very busily, till being observed by one of the lords, and asked what he was meditating. My lord (said he), I am improving myself the best I can in your company, for having impatiently waited this honour of being present at such a meeting of the wisest men and greatest wits of this age, I thought I could not do better than to write your conversation, and here I have it in substance, all that has passed for an hour or two. There was no need of Mr Locke's reciting much of the dialogue. The great men felt the ridicule and took pleasure in improving it. They quitted their play and fell into a conversation becoming them, and so passed the remainder of the day.[162]

MARCH 1688–JANUARY 1689: "AN EXPECTED INVASION"[163]

Having completed his business with the Amsterdam printers, and perhaps not wanting to overstay his welcome with Guenellon with whom he had been staying, Locke returned to Rotterdam in early March. At the end of the month he was again joined by David Thomas.[164]

Thomas brought some things for Locke's wardrobe, collected together with the help of Clarke and Rabsy Smithsby. When asking for these Locke had told Clarke that he was "past fashion and finery and am now only for things of use", but this does not seem to have been exactly true, for the details he was exactingly particular about pertained not just to use. He wanted a cloak "of the best boiled chamlet that is to be got, that will endure wetting and of a dark colour, not apt to stain.... The lining I would have of a very good shalon, unless there be anything lighter and as strong"; "a good beaver hat made the diameter of the inside of the crown at the band, which I have here below marked by the two black lines.... I desire the hat may be made as high as the fashion will bear"; "a peruke very deep, the caul of a middle colour between black and flaxen, and a little longer than a parson's". The kind of interest in his clothes shown here seems unrecognised in Damaris Masham's simple record that "his dress was neat, without either affectation or singularity".[165]

During the month they were together, Locke discussed with Thomas the publication of his *Essay*. He asked him to make inquiries in London about publishers' terms. "For good books of which they may venture to print 1000 or 1120 they give sometime 20s sometime 30s the sheet for the copy if written fit for the press", Thomas later reported, saying also that he had discussed the *Essay* with Pembroke ("he longs to discourse you about your book having more to ask and to receive answers to than can be well done in one letter and...longs to see you"). Later in the year Pembroke again told Thomas of his support for the *Essay*, and told Clarke that he wanted Locke to "proceed in your design of publishing it, with the first opportunity, as a performance that will not only exceedingly oblige him [Pembroke], but all the considering and learned part of mankind".[166]

One thing in particular in connection with the *Essay* that Locke and Thomas discussed was an unfortunate and unpleasant situation that was developing, one which was deeply angering to Locke. A few weeks earlier he had asked Clarke to get from the Stringers "the picture they have of mine...that I may take order to have a plate graved from it" to use as a frontispiece. The picture* in question was a portrait, for which Locke paid £15 in "dry money" (hard cash), done some years earlier by John Greenhill, Thomas's brother-in-law. Mrs Stringer had earlier told Locke that, quite apart from the "great honour and esteem" she had for him, "I think it the best picture I ever saw", and this no doubt contributed something to the energy with which her husband protested to Clarke that the picture was theirs and would not be given up without a promise of its return.[167]

This protest was in a letter to Clarke which Thomas had brought over for Locke to read. On the face of it, the letter was rather extraordinary. "I am not willing to weaken my title unto it [the picture]", Stringer had written.

I have his [Locke's] word and my wife has his hand to show how he has once disposed of it and we are now too old for childrens' play to have a thing given and then to have it called for again; you know possession in this case is a good confirmation of my title, and, unless he will give me good security on that point, I am resolved...to stand stoutly in defence of it...until I am well assured of its return.

Stringer then accused Clarke (and Locke) of disingenuity: "what you write of engraving a plate from it, I take to be but a colourable excuse, because Doctor Thomas has one that is generally thought better painted and is of a much less size, and consequently may be better secured from danger of hurt in carriage"; besides, said Stringer, engravings are better done from black and white drawing than painting, and Locke is well placed in Holland ("there being better artists") to have something suitable done there. Stringer's vehemence and the accusation of a "colourable excuse" perhaps had behind it his not being entirely in good faith himself and feeling unsure of his ground; but in fact this was not the first time the picture had been a bone of contention between him and Locke.[168]

It had first come into Stringer's hands when, together with other possessions, Locke left it with him when he went to France in 1675. On his return, after Shaftesbury had moved house, Locke "found at Thanet house the things I had left with Mr Stringer at Exeter House... except my picture which he had removed to his house at Bexwells". Some time after, during a visit to Bexwells, Locke mentioned "removing my picture" from there. To his surprise Stringer had said, in all earnestness, that he "should have it no more", and Locke, "not having then any place, where I was settled, to remove it to", decided not to press the matter, "not willing to come to a heat upon this occasion, which so fierce and positive a man as Mr Stringer was but too apt to break out into". But by 1682 the picture was hanging in Thanet House, from where, shortly before Shaftesbury's death, it again came into the Stringers' hands and was moved to their house.[169]

Having read what Stringer said to Clarke, Locke composed a lengthy letter, for Thomas to take back to England. Stiffly polite, Locke quite evidently thought that Stringer was not in good faith. "If you believe yourself when you say I gave you my picture... [why] deny it me on this occasion. Sure I am you will never persuade anybody else, that you think bona fide I gave it you, whilst you dare not trust it again in my hands." No one who knows me, said Locke, would "imagine I deserve to be suspected of a design to cheat a... friend of what I had given him". As for Stringer's further temporising and evasive "skilful discourse", "I hope I may be allowed to be of age enough to know if I would have a print of myself, what kind will best please me".[170]

Despite the relative restraint and surface calmness of Locke's letter, when Stringer received it on Thomas's return, he claimed to have been much heated by it, so much so that he needed time to cool down "before I did dare trust my temper to adventure you a reply".[171] Even so, his reply read like the blustering reaction of a person attempting to take a firm stand on rather soggy ground.

The picture clearly meant much to Locke. He repeatedly told Clarke that he had always intended to have it "in my chamber in Oxford when I came to settle there", and the affair (stoked by Stringer's "overflow of gall and spite") rankled deeply with him. He wrote a long and biting letter in which he untangled with forensic skill what he saw as Stringer's disingenuity and evasiveness. Clarke was sure that Locke was in the right, and he certainly "could not get a sight of that letter of yours", in which (so Stringer claimed) Locke had "convey[ed] the unquestioned right you once had in the picture". To an extent he was able to calm Stringer down, but, as we shall see, it would be some time before the picture could be got out of the Stringers' hands.[172]

Thomas must have witnessed during this discussion what was later said of Locke by others who knew him, that he was "naturally choleric" and that the "passion he was naturally most prone to was anger". Lady Masham said that "his great good sense, and good breeding so far subdued this that it was rarely troublesome"; but since we are also told that if he "retained any resentment" about his outbursts "it was against himself for having given way to so ridiculous a passion", we might wonder whether it was firm self-control rather than a return to genuine good temper that meant his anger "never lasted long".[173] Certainly he could be unforgivingly cold when he thought he had been slighted or ill-used.

Unfortunately there was another infuriating matter which Locke and Thomas had to discuss: the question of the King's pardon about which Thomas (reporting Tyrrell) had told him the previous December. At the time Locke had, he told Clarke, been surprised to learn from Thomas that Penn had got him a pardon. He was at a complete loss. He knew nothing about it.

You will therefore do well to inform yourself as dexterously as you can from Mr P. by a third and skilful hand what there is in it. For your cousin [i.e. Locke] thinks himself concerned to know; though in a business of the nature it will not become him to appear inquisitive.... When you inform me of the truth and particularities of the story you shall have my opinion concerning the case, for as this may be I know not how far this may alter his measures.[174]

Locke had not yet heard from Clarke what William Penn himself had to say about it. Thomas, however, had brought with him a letter from Tyrrell, and this gave more information about the story. Tell Locke, Tyrrell had asked Thomas, "that I found out Will Penn; and spoke to him ... but he told me the pardon was not for JL. but one Mat. Locke* excepted in the proclamation: so I desired him to meddle in no such thing as to JL. unless particularly desired; which he promised". It is not clear from this whether Penn had actually made an approach to the King or not, nor is it clear whether Penn was correcting an assumption he himself had made about who had been pardoned, or merely correcting one that Tyrrell had made. But, whatever the facts about this, the "proclamation" referred to here was one which the King had issued in March two years earlier, which gave a very general pardon, except that a number of persons were mentioned by name, one of whom was a certain "Joshuah Lock, jun". It was this "Locke" who had been pardoned.[175]

Locke was certainly annoyed by Tyrrell's "imprudent meddling" in his concerns, without any consultation or even telling him directly about it. He felt put into a difficult position, "brought into straights", by it. According to Damaris Masham, writing after Locke's death, Penn ("as I am told", she said) both asked for and was successful in procuring a pardon for Locke; but though it was "actually offered" to him he "would not accept of it as not owning that he needed it". Perhaps she was misremembering or was misinformed, but the report, false as it is, does indicate something of the "straights" Locke saw himself as being brought to. Quite apart from the annoyance at Tyrrell's having taken things upon himself and the discomfort of being the subject of discussion and in ways not subject to his control, apart too from the awareness that, as he said to Clarke, "to refuse what is granted is to bid defiance", Locke did not want a "pardon" (particularly not one which it might seem he had himself sought). To be safe was one thing; to be safe on the basis of a "pardon" (which would have involved conceding there was something to be pardoned for) was another. Presumably similar feelings were involved when in May of the previous year Locke seems to have crossly rejected the suggestion that Freke might use his influence with Penn to have Locke restored to his place at Christ Church.[176]

A further thing which concerned Locke was the possibility of affronting Penn, something that weighed on him heavily when eventually he asked Clarke that either he or Thomas would see to it that Tyrrell would speak to Penn again and "redress as much as is possible, what his meddling has done". He wanted Tyrrell not only to "unsay" to Penn what he had said to him in the first place about a pardon, but also to "own to him that it was without the order or privity of the person concerned [i.e. Locke]; and so take off the suspicion of slighting or affront, which it cannot but be prejudicial ... to lie under with a man of that interest". Finally, Locke may have been further concerned that a pardon granted through some intermediary other than Pembroke might be offensive to his noble friend; after all, when Tyrrell first told Thomas about Penn's approach to the King, Thomas had roundly retorted that if Locke "either wanted or desired" a pardon he would pursue the matter via Pembroke.*[177]

Something happened in the spring which "straightened" Locke even further, for when he wrote to Clarke in mid-May there were "fresh reasons" why Tyrrell should "unsay" what he had first said, reasons, Locke said, having to do with the fact that "what you thought was quite laid by, is now again on foot". Whatever these "fresh reasons" were, they seem to have been material in some way to Locke's relationship with Pembroke, for he seemed to allude to them the next month when, having learnt that Tyrrell had been talking of the matter with Pembroke, he urged Clarke that if Pembroke mentioned this to him he must say that Tyrrell "meddles in business wherein he has neither commission nor knowledge":

This I think is best to be said to him, for I think not seasonable to discourse to him at large that whole affair, nor to show him how my name has been brought in question without any desire or so much as knowledge of mine.... But at present I think there be reasons why it should not be mentioned to him.[178]

Though Locke and Tyrrell had been in direct written contact during this period, this matter was barely, if at all, mentioned between them. Although Tyrrell had not told Locke of his approach to Penn, he was nevertheless piqued that Locke gave no sign of being aware of it. "I am not worthy to be concerned in any business for him", he complained to Thomas, "which is all one to me; I have enough of my own to do." For his part Locke was utterly incensed and disgusted by Tyrrell's whole behaviour: "He loves to be a man of business. At any rate it would choke him, if his tongue might not go, whether with rhyme or reason it matters not. The very mention of holding his peace is like a cork that makes perfect bottle beer of it, and yet it must sputter."[179] He either would not stoop or could not trust himself to discuss the matter with Tyrrell himself.

During the month in which Locke had Thomas's company they spent time not only in Rotterdam (meeting Furly and van Helmont) but also in Leiden and Amsterdam. When "Adrian went away" he took with him to England letters and copies of the Abrégé to be delivered to friends. He forgot to leave behind the sash from his morning gown, which Locke was in need of, but he did leave a recipe for cinnamon and vanilla chocolate (a recipe which he troubled to refine in a letter on his immediate return).[180]

Three months later, after months of prompting, Locke was visited by the person to whom he had not long before proclaimed "I love you more than any man in the world". Edward Clarke had come together with his wife and five-year-old daughter Betty, and from Rotterdam they visited Amsterdam and Antwerp. As their neighbour Isabella Duke had envisaged, Locke's "complaisance to the ladies, would carry [him] from town to town, rambling with them". She had thought that Locke might return to England with the Clarkes, but they left without him, and he was again alone when he returned to Rotterdam in mid-September.[181]

It is not absolutely clear why, despite this and earlier expectations and hopes, Locke remained in Holland. His health was, his friends all accepted, an important consideration, particularly with regard to London winters. As Tyrrell pointed out, however, he could always have spent just the summers in England.[182] Perhaps, despite the fact that in the past couple of years his friends had felt that politically he was safe, he had assessed things differently. If so, his mind would soon be changed.

In the second week of June, King James's wife had caused consternation by giving birth to a son (though many believed that the baby was not really hers and had been smuggled into her bed in a warming-pan). The realisation that a line of Catholic succession to the throne was virtually assured now combined with what had been an increasing concern about James's continuing unlawful policy of infiltrating Catholics into public office, about his claims (implied in his Declarations of Indulgence) of a prerogative right to act without a Parliament, and about his setting up of an Ecclesiastical Commission which disciplined Anglican clergy who attacked Catholicism. At the end of the month, Prince William of Orange was invited by a number of senior statesmen, who assured him of a majority of English support, to come from Holland to England with an army to intervene in the country's affairs and save it from "Popery and Slavery". William and various of the political refugees in Holland began detailed planning, and in the next few months there were increasing rumours and reports in England that an invasion was being prepared.

Towards the end of October, Isabella Duke told Locke about these "rumours of wars, and the daily alarms of an expected invasion"; indeed, she said, "it is full three weeks since that we were told the Dutch were on our coast". She complained that he had given her no early "hints of this storm", which she might then have avoided by coming over to Holland and wintering there, but, as it was, "now we must take our fate; for we did not believe common reports, because we had so good a friend on the place that gave us no intimations of any such thing".[183]

Two days after she wrote, William's fleet, which had been held up by adverse winds, set sail and arrived at Brixham, on the English Channel coast, on 26 October/5 November. With little resistance the Protestant army advanced towards London, where on 18/28 December, a week after James had fled, William arrived. Then, on 24 December, the day after James finally left the country for France, "the Lords spiritual and temporal met at Westminster", Charles Goodall reported to Locke, "and passed the following order: We...do desire your Highness [William] to take upon you the administration of public affairs...and the disposal of the public revenue for the preservation of our religion, our rights, liberties, and properties and of the peace of the nation." Excitedly, Goodall spoke of the "wonderful success which God Almighty has given to the Prince of Orange...to deliver our miserable and distressed kingdoms from popery and slavery, which mercy we in England esteem no less than the Israelites' deliverance from Egypt by the hand of Moses". Offering Locke lodgings with him and his wife, Goodall hoped "that this news will encourage you to return to London".[184]

The Lords' request to William to take on the government of the country was not an offer to him of the crown, nor would the assembly, the Convention, which William then called for 22 January, be at first a true Parliament, for that could only be called by the monarch. There was much for the Convention to discuss. At least publicly, William's intention in invading had simply been to put pressure on the King, to protect the Protestant religion and to ensure that James would not continue to rule without recourse to a Parliament.[185] But whatever he had intended, the constitutional situation was quite unclear, and people took different views. Was the throne vacant or not? Was James still king, even though he had fled the country? If so, William, or someone else, should be appointed as regent, to act in his absence, permanent though that might be. Or had James stepped down from the throne, thereby passing it on to the next in line of hereditary succession (if not his infant son, then his daughter Mary, William's wife)? Or had James been deposed from a throne whose legitimate occupation was dependent on the consent of the people? – in which case William should be offered the crown. William was certainly not prepared to act either as a regent, or as Mary's consort; Mary was not prepared to take the throne alone, but only jointly, with her husband as king.

In any of these cases, however, Locke was, as Graevius commented, now "free from the troubles and dangers you have contended with", and he must have been excited by these developments; but whether he now thought of returning to England must have depended to an extent on how genuine or weighty were the reasons he had given Pembroke as to why he came to Holland in the first place, for these still stood. At any rate, it appears that he did not want to return before the spring, for he hoped to see Graevius in Utrecht when the winter was over. But he did not have his way. His sense of duty (and perhaps an eye to the prospect of some future patronage) intervened. He was asked by Lord Charles Mordaunt, who had gone with William's forces to England, to come with his wife, a member of Princess Mary's court party, when the time was right. Even though it meant leaving his friends, Locke could not say no: it was his duty, "a request not to be refused to the position of him who made it and to the claims of friendship, far less to the deserts of a most illustrious lady". There were advantages, too, in getting back to England: "the expectations of my friends", "my private concerns now so long neglected"; it will, moreover, be "a light-hearted company" (with the attractive and flirtatious Carey Mordaunt), and the royal convoy of "so many ships of war" will offer safety "now that the sea is everywhere infested by pirates".[186]

He still planned on being able to visit his friends in Amsterdam, to say goodbye in person. But on 22 January/1 February, the day the Convention opened, Princess Mary was requested to come to England immediately, and two days' later Lady Mordaunt, giving him three days' notice, told Locke to ready himself. Accordingly he packed up to twenty boxes (mostly with books, but including one "with old linen and wollen in it", and another "with [an] iron furnace in it"), made various financial arrangements by way of transferring his money back to England, and, no doubt in honour of Lady Mordaunt, bought a lace cravat. Syl was put in charge of the baggage and made his own way back to England, arriving after various delays in early May, some time after Locke.[187]

Shortly afterwards, Locke heard details of the first day's proceedings of the Convention. He was dismayed. It had received a letter in which William had said he had done his best to secure "public peace and safety", and it was now up to the Convention more radically to "lay the foundations of a firm security for your religion, laws, and your liberties".

Locke thought there was "weight and wisdom" in this, and his concern was that the Convention seemed not to have heeded William's urging to avoid "too great delay in your considerations"; Irish Protestants were under attack in Ireland, William had reminded them, and England's help was required by the Dutch (who, in the shape of William, had just helped England) in the war which Louis XIV had declared against them the previous November. Instead, and even before it turned to settling constitutional matters, it had (Locke complained, when he heard about it), as though it were "a formal Parliament, and not something of another nature, and had not business to do of greater moment and consequence", spent the rest of the day setting up committees, in particular one which would look into individual complaints relating to the recent elections for the Convention. "Men here", he wrote to Clarke, "very much wonder" to hear of such irrelevant trivialities.

Ironically, unknown to Locke, one of the fourteen petitions whose receipt took up some part of that day was from his friend David Thomas "complaining of an undue election and return of citizens for [Salisbury]". Locke deeply regretted that the members of the Convention, to judge by the proceedings of their first day, were not too concerned about attending to questions regarding the constitution, the "great frame of government" which, if their grievances of the previous years were justifiable ones, had been "invaded" and put "out of order". Moreover, even apart from matters of such lasting moment, how, he wondered, could the members sleep while the Irish and European situations required attention. The nation needed to "put itself in a posture of defence and support of the common [Protestant] interest of Europe". "The spring comes on apace", he fretted, "and if we be, France will not be idle."[188]

Adverse westerly winds delayed the departure of Mary and her court for some days, days during which the Convention had turned to constitutional matters. Saturday 2/12 February saw Locke travelling from Rotterdam to The Hague, to see Lady Mordaunt, before continuing on to Amsterdam to see Limborch. In envisaging this he was trusting "not so much to the wind as to the Princess's religious scruples, for I hardly thought she would be willing to start on a journey on Sunday, even though an east wind might invite it". But that day he had already been twice "drenched by a pretty violent downpour", and Lady Mordaunt "absolutely forbade" him the overnight journey to Amsterdam "as too dangerous to my health"; and he stayed at

The Hague for three days (where the court party was "waiting for nothing but a suitable sailing wind, and as soon as that comes we must rush to the ships"). Three days later, he returned to Rotterdam to "dawdle there", frustratedly waiting for a favourable wind: "nothing is a greater annoyance", he wrote to Limborch, "than to be saddled with inactivity until one is sick of it, and yet not to have time for what one wishes to do most of all. How I wish I could be granted an hour or two with you all." Eventually the wind shifted (though not before, as his journal records, Locke bought another cravat), and on Sunday 10/20 February, Furly accompanied him down to The Briel where he embarked on the *Isabella*. The ship sailed at about three in the afternoon, bound for Harwich; the pleasant and pervasive idea that Princess Mary was on that same ship is mistaken.[189]

Locke was now aged fifty-seven and the future may well have seemed a little empty, if not bleak. His association with Shaftesbury had been a partial cause of his not pursuing a career as a physician, and it had led to his losing the one home he had had independently of Shaftesbury's patronage (and even that was now over). It had "confounded the quiet I always sought", and in the end had led him, so he had complained to Pembroke, into "a storm", in the course of which he had lost his Student's place at Christ Church, with its guarantee of rooms for himself and his books, and of maintenance (about £25 per annum), and "which I always so valued, as the highest convenience for a retired single life, that the keeping of it (which was always my great care) was what most satisfied me in the not getting other things". Homeless and without any kind of regular position, he was wholly dependent on the income from his Somerset rents, and the annuity he bought from Clarke before going to Holland, in total approaching £200 per annum. His public face was simply as "he who was Shaftesbury's secretary", or even, demeaningly, as he who "belonged to" Shaftesbury. Though he had spent much time in writing, he had nothing to which his name was put, except for his early verses and the abridgement of the *Essay*, and even that was suspected by some really to be the work of Le Clerc. The publication of the whole was of course something which he must have been looking forward to, and he seems to have had the intention of "resuming the study of natural things", perhaps in connection with practising as a doctor.[190] On the credit side he had influential friends in Pembroke and, more recently, Mordaunt, and partly under their patronage, a new man of fame and fortune (though of increasingly ill-health) was about to emerge.

7

London (February 1689–December 1690)

FEBRUARY–DECEMBER 1689: ANNUS MIRABILIS

Safely across "the great ditch" of the North Sea, Locke wrote to Guenellon "as soon as I landed [in Harwich] to tell him about our voyage and how well timed it was, for I felt that the first thing to be done on returning to my fatherland was to give evidence of a mindful heart to those who had provided me with a fatherland on foreign soil"; the next day (12/22 February), two days after leaving Holland, he arrived in London, "that sink of sin and sea coal" as Yonge had called it. Having seen Lady Mordaunt reunited with her husband in Whitehall, he went to the College of Physicians in Warwick Lane, where Charles Goodall had invited him to lodge with him and his wife. On his first full day back, the Convention made a Declaration of the Rights of Parliaments and subjects in relation to the monarch; and William and Mary were offered and agreed jointly to accept the English throne. In Holland, Limborch's son "shed tears of joy" as soon as he heard of this; it meant that Locke would never again have to masquerade in exile under assumed names: he prayed that "Mr Locke may ever be closely united to Mr van der Linden, and that no tempest in the state may sunder the one from the other".[1]

Though pleased that constitutional matters were at last being addressed, Locke's concern that the international situation was being ignored continued. Four days before Parliament, as the Convention had become, got round to debating what revenue would be available to the King and Queen, Locke had complained to Mordaunt about the "dilatory methods and slow proceedings...when there is not a moment of time lost without endangering the Protestant and English interest thoughout Europe, and which have already put things too far back".[2]

Parliament quickly resolved to "stand by and assist the King with their lives and fortunes, in supporting his alliances abroad, in reducing of Ireland, and in defence of the Protestant religion, and the laws of the kingdom" – surely much to the delight of Limborch, who had said how important it was that England should join with Holland in order to restrain the French.[3] Nevertheless it was not until 7 May that William felt able to declare war on France.

Besides being concerned about affairs of state, Locke began to be drawn into them. Within two weeks William (acting on the suggestion of his recently appointed privy councillor Mordaunt) offered him some position of importance. Exactly what this was is not clear. According to Lady Masham he was given a choice, between "going as Envoy either to the Emperor [Leopold I, in Vienna], or the now King of Prussia [Frederick III, Elector of Brandenburg, who became King of Prussia in 1701], or to a third place which I remember not". Locke's swift reply to Mordaunt, who had informed him of the matter, referred to just one post – perhaps the mission to Brandenburg, for, without naming it, he recognised it as "one of the busiest and most important in all Europe".[4]

Whatever the post was, Locke declined it. Though recognising duty, he pleaded ill-health: "the most touching displeasure I have ever received from that weak and broken constitution of my health which has so long threatened my life, [is] that it now affords me not a body suitable to my mind in so desirable an occasion of serving his Majesty".[5]

A quarter of a century earlier, when he had declined the offer of a similar but far less important position with the ambassador to Spain, Locke had wondered whether he had let slip "the minute that they say everyone has once in his life to make himself". The chance of "making himself" was in his mind again now, for there was sincere regret in his recognition that William's offer had enough honour in it "to satisfy an ambition greater than mine, and a step to the making of my fortune which I could not have expected". But, he explained to Mordaunt, it would not be fair to the King to accept the post. Even were he able eventually to acquire the diplomatic "skill and dexterity to deal with not only the reasons of able, but the more dangerous artifices of cunning men, that in such stations must be expected and mastered", his body still might let him down: what could such acquired capacity and fitness "do with a body that has not health and strength enough to comply with them? What shall a man do in the necessity of application and variety of attendance on business to be followed there, who sometimes, after a little motion, has not breath to speak?" But besides having this reason "to apprehend the cold air of the country" in question, Locke (perhaps not quite so seriously?) also mentioned "another thing in it as inconsistent with my constitution, and that is their warm drinking". "It is no small matter in such stations", he said, "to be acceptable to the people one has to do with, in being able to accommodate oneself to their fashions; and I imagine whatever I may do there myself, the knowing what others are doing is at least one half of my business"; since there is "no such rack in the world to draw out men's thoughts as a well managed bottle", the King would do better "to send a man of equal parts, that could drink his share, than the soberest man in the kingdom".[6]

Beyond presenting a compelling case to Mordaunt (and to William, who besides suffering from an asthmatic chest himself, also disliked social drinking), why he would not be doing right by the King, Locke in fact also felt that the post abroad was not what he wanted for himself. Apart from anything else he just did not have the heart for it. He told Limborch that, though he could have travelled via Holland and seen him and other friends, he had used his health "as an excuse for avoiding an office which is honourable enough, and which I should undoubtedly seek if I were in the prime of life and in the enjoyment of my full powers; as it is, my only concern now is for peace and quiet for myself and my country".[7]

But, in declining to serve abroad, Locke was not meaning to close the door on acting in any public capacity in the post-revolution country. He urged Mordaunt to look on his refusal "not as the discourse of a modest and lazy man but of one who has truly considered himself, and, above all things, wishes well to the designs which his Majesty has so gloriously begun for the redeeming England, and with it all Europe". "I... shall never be sparing of my mite where it may contribute", and may be more useful to the King at home: "If there be anything where I may flatter myself I have attained any degree of capacity to serve his Majesty, it is in some little knowledge I perhaps may have in the constitutions of my country, the temper of my countrymen, and the divisions and interest amongst them."

Locke's first weeks back in London were busy ones, and the coal smoke, from which he had been free for over five years, was immediately troublesome. Since returning, he told Limborch in March, his time had been quite taken up. Besides the exchange of visits with friends and the collecting together of his scattered possessions, there had been, if not the taking on of some public business at the expense of his private leisure, then at any rate the effort to avoid doing so; and worst of all, there was the injury to his health from the pernicious London smoke.[8]

By April, when he again wrote to Limborch, his lungs were less troublesome, his breathing freer, and his cough less severe; though whether this relief was due to the warmer spring air or to growing re-accustomed to the pernicious air he was not sure. But he was no less busy. Even though he had not taken on any civil service, "public affairs and the private concerns of friends somehow keep me so busy that I am entirely torn away from books". He had no time even to view "a big auction sale of quite good books" which was being held. He could only hope that his "old and longed-for leisure will soon be restored to me, so that I may return to the commonwealth of learning".[9]

When he first wrote to Limborch on his arrival back in England, Locke spoke of the national situation as regards one of their common concerns, religious toleration. Parliament, he explained, was then discussing it under two aspects: comprehension ("the enlargement of the boundaries of the Church by removing some ceremonies, so that people may be induced to conform") and indulgence ("toleration of those who are either unwilling or unable to unite with the Church of England even on the proposed conditions"). He was not sure yet exactly how these things might be applied in practice, but he did know that the Anglican clergy did not favour them. Limborch was not surprised; like Locke, he was pessimistic that "those enjoying power and authority in the Church" would accept much in the way of comprehension and would "hedge about too narrowly". He was more hopeful about indulgence, however: this "might offer a way of providing for the security of all, if those whom their conscience . . . does not permit to join themselves to the Great Church were allowed to meet together by themselves without fear of punishment". Although the speed with which things moved was too slow for Locke's liking (perhaps something which lay behind his confessing to Clarke at the time that "I grow more and more sick of this world"), a toleration bill was eventually passed and received the royal assent in late May; but the proposals for comprehension were laid aside. The result, he told Limborch, was "not, perhaps, to the extent which you, and such as you, sincere, candid, and unambitious Christians would desire". Nevertheless, perhaps "those foundations of peace and liberty have been laid, on which the Church of Christ should be established". With the exception of Catholics, no one was "absolutely forbidden the exercise of their own form of worship or subjected to penalties, if they are but willing to take the oath of allegiance and renounce transubstantiation and certain dogmas of the Roman Church".[10]

Locke's own recent work on toleration, the *Epistola de Tolerantia*, was published in Holland towards the end of April. Limborch sent him some copies, but copies from the Dutch booksellers took some months to reach the English shops. The *Epistola*, Limborch commented, had much to teach England: "it demonstrates so irrefutably, on grounds never hitherto so set forth, that all religious persecution is contrary both to the spirit of religion and to the law of nature".[11]

Though Limborch knew that the anonymously published *Epistola* was Locke's, he reported that many people were curious as to its author. Keeping up the pretence of ignorance, lest others read his letter, Limborch said that "the subject-matter and the manner of its treatment lead some people to infer that it is a product of the Remonstrant workshop"; but there was no one "to whom we could attribute so learned and elegantly written a production". In a sense it is not strictly true that the author "remains hidden" for, according to the title page, the *Epistola* was written to "clarissimum virum T.A.R.P.T.O.L.A." and by "P.A.P.O.I.L.A.". These letters, as Limborch explained after Locke's death, meant "Theologiae apud Remonstrantes Professorem, Tyrannidis Osorem, Libertatis Amantem"* (Professor of Theology among the Remonstrants, Hater of Tyranny, Lover of Liberty) and "Pacis Amante, Persecutionis Osore, Joanni Lockio, Anglo" (A Friend of Peace, Hater of Persecution, John Locke, Englishman).[12]

Locke did not lodge with the Goodalls for long and removed in March to Dorset Court in Channel (now Cannon) Row, Westminster. His new rooms (at a rate of £5 per quarter, and apparently some which Clarke was vacating) were in the house of Rabsy Smithsby*, the woman with whom he had left a partial copy of his *De Morbo Gallico* before he left for Holland, and who had been storing other of his belongings.[13]

After the years away in Holland the rents and agreements for Locke's Somerset properties required review. It was perhaps mainly for this purpose that William Stratton was in London in April; but Stratton also wanted Locke to use his influence to get him a surveyor's place ("or any other creditable office of profit") in the Custom House in Bristol. That influence, presumably in the first place with Mordaunt, was used to get Clarke appointed as the Queen's auditor. The business was "not much", he told Clarke, and the "salary is but £100 per annum", but Locke thought the post would get his friend an entrance into the court and give him a "countenance in the country".[14]

In May, Locke himself acquired a place, as a Commissioner of Appeals for Excise. If Damaris Masham's report is correct, Locke actively sought this position (from Mordaunt in whose gift, as one of the Treasury Lords, it partially was): he had never been paid for his work nearly twenty years earlier with the Council for Trade and Plantations, and reckoned that the annual payment of £200 in relation to the work involved was fair recompense. Locke was so highly esteemed, she said, by those "who were in credit, and power, after the revolution", that he could easily have obtained a more profitable employment. However, aware that the government was short of money, and so not wanting to ask "so much as for a debt due to him for his service . . . in Charles II's reign which he could have had for asking", he "requested no more than to be one of the Commissioners of Appeals a place honourable enough for any gentleman, though of no greater value than £200 per annum: and suitable to Mr Locke on account that it required but little attendance". Locke was more than once asked to sell the post, as would then not have been unusual; he declined and continued to receive the salary until the day of his death, some time after he had ceased to attend meetings with his fellow Commissioners.[15]

Locke himself led Limborch to believe that the position would not be too onerous or time-consuming. But the post would prove to be no sinecure and would involve him in some trouble, and it was not long before he must have thought that its salary was not sufficient recompense for what he was owed. The following February he petitioned the King for payment of the salary which was "still in arrears from Midsummer 1673 to the dissolution of the said council". The petition was referred to the Treasury for advice.[16]

Not long after his appointment to the Appeals Commission, Locke made another attempt to have past wrongs righted, and petitioned the King, in his capacity as Visitor to Christ Church, to be restored to his Studentship. Having outlined the immediate circumstances of the removal – King Charles's order to the Dean that he lose his place,

the summons to appear in Oxford, the further royal order for immediate removal – Locke asked that William "would out of your great
justice and goodness be graciously pleased to direct the...College to
restore your Petitioner to his student's place, together with all things
belonging unto it which he formerly enjoyed". He was clearly not
asking for any kind of "pardon" for the things of which he had been
accused, but rather for the restitution of rights of which he had been
unjustly deprived. Though rooms in college were amongst the "things
belonging unto" the Studentship, Locke envisaged using them only
from time to time, and there is no reason to think he had any desire to
live in Oxford permanently. For one thing, a draft of his petition
included a request for "liberty to be absent" from Oxford on the
grounds of "employment in his majesty's service" (as Commissioner of
Appeals). For another, at least according to what he must have told
Damaris Masham, he wanted restitution only "as an acknowledgement
that he had been wronged".[17]

Locke's honour was satisfied for, as Wood recorded towards the end
of the year, "the news here is that John Locke of Christ Church has
a mandate to be put into his student's place wherein he was ejected".
But in the end (by March 1690) he declined the place, having found that
accepting it would have meant dispossessing another Student.[18]

Towards the end of May, urged by his friends he said, Locke came to
an agreement with the bookseller Thomas Bassett to print and publish
An Essay concerning Human Understanding. The agreement provided
that "printing shall be begun immediately"; the manuscript was not to
be delivered as a whole but in blocks sufficient to produce two sheets at
a time. The book, it was estimated, would run to fifty-eight sheets (for
each of which Locke would receive ten shillings). He was to receive
twenty-five free copies and was entitled to buy, within the year after
publication, up to twenty-five more at a halfpenny a sheet.[19]

In June, Locke heard a voice from the past in the form of a rather
pathetic letter ("I am fully assured your interest and goodness may
befriend me") from his former love Elinor Parry. The man she had
married a year after going to Ireland twenty years earlier had died,
and she was now in Wales, a Protestant refugee from Ireland, and
a widowed mother of four. Badly in need for the further education of
her two eldest children, she solicited Locke's help and advice, to
retrieve some money she was owed, and with a charity for distressed
Protestants. Even if Locke's letters to her had survived, it may still have
been hard to discern just what his feelings were; hers to him show only

that, perhaps with a certain reserve, he did what he thought he should. Over the next year, and out of what she repeatedly described as "friendship", "kind concern", and "goodness", he lent her smallish amounts of money ("till she should be in condition to repay it", he noted in his account book), gave advice and help in pursuing her debtors, wrote to people on her behalf, acted her part with the charitable fund, and gave some help and guidance to one of her sons at Cambridge.[20]

Early in July, Locke was in the studio of the painter Herman Verelst to have a portrait done at the request of the Clarkes. Particularly with the production of the *Essay* so much on his mind, it must have seemed an extraordinary coincidence to him that there, in the studio, was the portrait the Clarkes had earlier unsuccessfully tried to get from the Stringers, for an engraving to be made to front the *Essay*. As Locke matter-of-factly put it to the Stringers, the picture "came very opportunely for the desire I had to have a print of it before a book of mine to which I thought to prefix it being now in the press"; so, he said, "when I saw the painter where it was had no more to do with it I sent for it to my lodging to have a plate graved after it".[21]

In fact the portrait was there in Verelst's studio because Mary Clarke herself had taken it there for Locke to find; though exactly when Locke was told this is not clear. Even though she had told the Stringers no more than that she wanted it in town, she had been able to get them to have it delivered to her.[22]

However much or little Locke knew when he removed the portrait from Verelst's studio, doing so was, by his own punctilious lights, surely wrong; perhaps the strong belief that the painting really was his was uppermost in his mind. Again, there was less than his usual punctiliousness in the letter Mrs Clarke got him to write to Mrs Stringer to explain that the picture she had borrowed was out of her hands. Given the "familiarity" amongst them all, the Clarkes, the Stringers, and himself, he had felt free simply to remove the picture "without offense to anybody".[23]

But Jane Stringer was, she said, "heartily glad" about it: she and her husband had guessed why Mary Clarke had wanted to borrow the picture, and would only have been more delighted if Locke himself had asked. "I hope you cannot doubt but your picture is at your own dispose both for time and place." Particularly given their earlier history, this letter, and another she wrote five days later, are remarkable for their apparent friendliness: "I hope you believe me truly sensible of the great debt I owe you for your abundant great favours to me and mine and though some things unaccountable has passed amongst us I doubt not but you that are strong can forgive the infirmities of weak brethren." Locke seems, however, to have remained "coldly disposed" (as Mrs Stringer put it) towards them, perhaps because, as Clarke told him, though the Stringers were willing the picture "should remain in your hands till the plate be finished", Thomas Stringer still "maintain[ed] his pretended property therein". It is not clear whether the portrait eventually made its way back to the Stringers, nor whether an engraving was ever made from it; but in any case the first edition of the *Essay* lacked a frontispiece.[24]

By early summer, Dutch, French, and English translations of Locke's Latin *Epistola* were underway. In his will Locke said that the English translation was done "without my privity". He cannot have meant it was done without his knowledge, for he told Limborch in June that he understood an Englishman was working on it. Presumably he meant that it was done without his endorsement, endorsement which would have involved revealing his authorship to the translator; his vague reference to "some Englishman" is similarly accounted for by wanting to respect the translator's anonymity, rather than by his not knowing who he was. In fact he was a certain William Popple, who had been a merchant in France for a good number of years and had returned to England only the previous year, when he had published two books in support of freedom of conscience. There is no reason to think Locke did not follow the course of the translation; indeed, given that copies of the *Epistola* were not available in the English bookshops even in September, when Locke reported that the translation was completed, it is likely that Popple got to know of the *Epistola* through Locke himself. The translation was published in November under the title *A Letter concerning Toleration*.[25]

Popple was probably a founder member of a discussion group which Locke started this year. Referred to as a "Dry Club", it was not so informal, matter-of-fact, and "dry" as not to have a set of rules. When Furly learnt about the club he thought the rules were good, except that it was too much to expect that everyone, whether or not they felt they had anything to say, should speak to every question, even to those that had not been announced beforehand. He thought this would "terrify a modest man from offering himself to your society. I think a month or six weeks time, till a man has learned a little confidence might be allowed a novice."[26]

By the end of August, Locke had another work ready for the printers: the *Two Treatises of Government*, which had largely been composed before he went to Holland. After his return to England, Locke found that a considerable part of the *First Treatise* had been lost.* Though he had "neither the time nor the inclination to repeat my pains", he had done more work on it, not merely to prepare it for the press, but also to take some note of the changed political situation.[27]

In the Preface, Locke hoped that the work would be "sufficient to establish the throne of our great restorer, our present king William; to make good his title in the consent of the people; which being the only one of all lawful governments, he has more fully and clearly than any prince in Christendom". These words used to be taken to imply that the *Two Treatises* was written after the event to justify the "Glorious Revolution" against James II, which brought William to the throne. As explained earlier, however (see p. 182), they were conceived and largely written in the context of "a revolution to be brought about", a revolution which in fact never happened, a revolution against Charles II.[28]

This is not to deny, however, that Locke's purpose in *publishing* them was to provide an ideological justification of the later and actual revolution against James. One interpretation of the events of that revolution was that James had abdicated the throne which had, by the usual succession, passed to his daughter Mary (together with her husband). A more radical interpretation was that James had been unseated by William, but this interpretation was shared by two rather different groups. Some held that William was a usurper and James still the rightful King; others thought that James's unseating was right and just. Locke's theory of government in the *Treatises*, according to which legitimate government derives from the consent of the people, clearly provided support for the last view (just as it would have done for rebellion against Charles). Having broken trust with his people, James's removal from the throne was (according to the argument of the *Treatises*) a lawful act. As Locke said, the *Treatises* "make good [William's] title, in the consent of the people, which ... [is] the only one of all lawful governments".

Besides providing a Preface which brought the *Treatises* "up to date" as it were, Locke made some additions and changes to the text, alluding to the events and nature of James's reign: his ruling without Parliament and his prerogative suspension of Parliamentary statutes.

Thus, some of his more forceful remarks against the "absolute arbitrary power" of a ruler who has "put himself into a state of war with the people by dissolving the government", about "a manifest perverting of justice, and a barefaced wresting of the laws to protect . . . some men, or party of men", were, it has been suggested, added with James in mind. Another passage refers to a king who does not think he is "bound to govern by established standing laws . . . and not by extemporary decrees". One passage in particular speaks of a ruler's acting contrary to trust when he tries to get the election of those "who have promised beforehand what to vote, and what to enact"; this is too circumstantial to have been written had not James at one point set out to do just this, by preparing to call a Parliament primed to accept his Declaration of Indulgence and Test Act suspension.[29]

Finally, the support which the *Treatises* gave to William's actions against James is exhibited in what reads as a commentary on the events of the revolution itself: James's leaving the country, the request to William to take over the administration, the eventual offer of the throne, and the transformation of the Convention into a Parliament. A government may be dissolved, Locke wrote, "when he who has the supreme executive power, neglects and abandons that charge": this means that even the "laws already made can no longer be put in execution", and so "the people are at liberty to provide for themselves, by erecting a new legislative, differing from the other, by the change of persons, or form, or both, as they shall find it most for their safety and good".[30]

On 3 December, Locke announced (triumphantly), "Today, as I hope, the last sheet of my treatise on the Human Understanding has been printed". His hopes were not dashed for later in the day his bookbinder, Graves, picked up the complete set of sheets for twelve of his free copies.[31]

The book (carrying the date "1690") was on sale within a week or so, and so some thoughts, which began in private conversation twenty years earlier, were now out in public, openly acknowledged by their author: "the die is cast, and I am now embarked on the open sea", Locke remarked to Limborch. Nearly fifty copies, bound in gilt or in leather, were presented to friends and colleagues, Pembroke and the Queen being amongst those who received the most expensive Turkey-leather-bound copies.[32]

In his "Epistle to the Reader", Locke described the *Essay* as having been "the diversion of some of my idle hours". If it gave "half so much pleasure in reading, as I had in writing it, thou wilt as little think thy money, as I do my pains, ill bestowed". But he was still uncomfortably aware that, having been written "by catches, and many long intervals of interruption", it was long, cumbersome, and possibly repetitious: "when I first put pen to paper, I thought all I should have to say on this matter, would have been contained in one sheet of paper; but the further I went, the larger prospect I had: new discoveries led me still on, and so it grew insensibly to the bulk it now appears in". "Possibly it might be reduced to a narrower compass than it is", but, "to confess the truth", he said, "I am now too lazy, or too busy to make it shorter".

With particular reference to the third book, in which he criticised various aspects of scholasticism, Locke portrayed what he had done as "removing some of the rubbish that lies in the way to knowledge". Describing this "rubbish" at greater length, he then took up a theme which he had played over the past twenty years, ever since his *De Arte Medica*, contrasting the "vague and insignificant forms of speech, and abuse of language [which] have so long passed for mysteries of science [and been] mistaken for deep learning and height of specu-lation" with "true knowledge". Fortunately, he said, "the common-wealth of learning" is not without those who have avoided these "covers of ignorance" and "whose mighty designs, in advancing the sciences, will leave lasting monuments to the admiration of posterity"; not that he was one of those, he said (perhaps regretfully recognising that his own empirical interests had never been fully satisfied), "every-one must not hope to be a Boyle or a Sydenham". His own contri-bution was simply as an under-labourer, "clearing ground a little" for the "master-builders", such as "the great Huygens and the incompara-ble Mr Newton".

With a play at modesty that covered the pride Locke must have felt about what he had now produced after so many years' work, he further stressed that the *Essay* had not been intended for the public but that he had been "brought to let it abroad" by his friends. One of these was Pembroke of course, the *Essay*'s dedicatee:

This treatise, which is grown up under your Lordship's eye, and has ventured into the world by your order, does now, by a natural kind of right, come to your Lordship for that protection, which you several years since promised it.... Things in print must stand and fall by their own worth, or the reader's fancy...[but your] approbation of the design of this treatise, will at least preserve it from being condemned without reading.[33]

Since his arrival back in England, Locke had been a regular attender at an intellectual salon which Pembroke ran. Indeed, so Lady Masham recorded, "of all the contentments" which Locke had at this time "there was none greater than that of spending one day every week with my Lord Pembroke in a conversation undisturbed by such as could not bear a part in the best entertainment of rational minds, free discourse concerning useful truths". One "useful truth", though a minor one, which Locke learnt from Pembroke and troubled to record in his journal, was that if trees are watered with a weak solution of saltpetre, "the fruit will be much better tasted". But Pembroke had a taste for more speculative matters too, and expounded what Locke described as a "noble and vast system" in which he derived all sciences mathematically from first principles.[34]

At Pembroke's, Locke made the acquaintance of Isaac Newton, who less than two years earlier had published his own "noble and vast system", the *Principia Mathematica Naturalis Philosophiae*, the *Principles of Natural Philosophy*, on which Locke had spent some time in Holland studying for a review, for Le Clerc's *Bibliothèque*. According to John Desaguliers, who said he was told ("several times") by his colleague Newton himself, "the celebrated Locke...was incapable of understanding the *Principia* from his want of geometical knowledge [and] inquired of Huyghens if all the mathematical propositions in that work were true. When he was assured that he might depend upon their certainty, he took them for granted, and carefully examined the reasonings and corollaries deduced from them." One result of this "careful examination" was Locke's asking Newton about the elliptical movement of the planets, for early the next year Newton provided Locke with a lengthy demonstration of this.[35]

In discussion at Pembroke's, Locke also acquired from Newton what he enticingly described as "some dim and seeming conception how matter might at first be made, and begin to exist by the power of the eternal first being". When Locke came to refer to this in the second edition of the *Essay* he made no mention of Newton, and said no more than that to understand it we need to "emancipate ourselves from vulgar notions, and raise our thoughts, as far as they would reach, to a closer contemplation of things". As was commented later, in saying this Locke merely "arouses our curiosity but is unwilling to satisfy it".[36]

The "whole mystery" remained until some years after Locke's death when it was "unveiled" by Newton, to whom the point happened to have been mentioned: "Smiling, he [said] firstly that it was he himself who had devised this way of explaining the creation of matter, the thought of it having come to him one day when he happened to touch on this question" with Locke and Pembroke. Newton had suggested to them that "one could in some fashion form an idea of the creation of matter by supposing that God could through his power prevent everything from entering a certain portion of pure space, space being by its nature penetrable, eternal, necessary, infinite; for thereafter that portion of pure space would possess impenetrability, which is one of the essential qualities of matter".[37]

Towards the end of the year Locke, a little wearily, told Graevius of the "difficulties and perplexities", both "public and private", that he had been involved in since his return, and spoke of the "trouble my six or seven years absence [*sic*], together with the new aspect of affairs in England...have caused me". He similarly described himself to Limborch as "continually harassed by matters of business that arise daily". But, difficult as the year might have been for him, he had, at the end of it, considerable cause for congratulation and celebration. Though still partially under the cloak of anonymity he was, after years of study and private discussion, now, for the first time, "embarked on the open sea" with the publication of the *Epistola*, the *Two Treatises*, and, above these, his *Essay concerning Human Understanding*; he was, too, in demand for public office. Finally, so far, through the early months of the winter, his health had been holding. Perhaps realisation of all of this was affecting him in mid-December when he wrote, with an untypical degree of excitement, to Mary Clarke, at home in Chipley, "Madam, I am at the tavern with your husband and other blades of his gang as debauched as he".[38]

JANUARY–SEPTEMBER 1690: DISPUTES AND DISAGREEMENTS

Reactions soon began to appear to Locke's three newly published works. Just before the new year, in response to an offer of a complimentary copy, Tyrrell reported that the *Essay* "came down to Oxford last week and many copies are sold of it, and I hear it is well approved of by those who have began the reading of it". (It must have been particularly pleasing to Locke when he later received a request for a copy from the library at Christ Church.)[39]

Locke's relationship with Tyrrell had been badly damaged by the episode concerning a royal pardon. Now they were in the same country and reunited, it was soon revealed to be "a decaying friendship", as Tyrrell described it. Over the previous months Locke had not (according to Tyrrell) repaid his visits in London and had not kept him informed of his movements. Apart from the kindness of the offer of the *Essay*, he found Locke's letter "cold, and short", and embarked on a long and hurt complaint about Locke's treatment of him in recent years:

I thank God I am not conscious to myself, of falling out with, or leaving my friends upon small quarrels, or groundless suspicions, or think myself set loose from the bonds of friendship, and gratitude, if a person to whom I am obliged for many kindnesses . . . lets me see by his constant coldness and reservedness, that he has put me from the first rate of friends into the second or third of his ordinary acquaintance.[40]

Feelings of hurt and animosity were perhaps present in January when Tyrrell sent Locke a report that opinions in London about the *Essay* were more mixed than they had initially been in Oxford. "Mr Locke's new book", it said, "admits of no indifferent censure, for it is either extremely commended, or much decried, but has ten enemies for one friend; metaphysics being too serious a subject for this age."[41]

By February he had received the copy Locke had promised him and had "begun to read [it] over with great satisfaction: and to refresh those old notions which I had from your manuscript copy concerning that matter". But he again suggested there was room for doubt about how well the book was going down in London. One objection to it, Tyrrell suggested, was its denial of innate ideas: "I find the divines much scandalized that so sweet and easy a part of their sermons: as that of the law written in the heart is rendered false and useless".[42]

Stung by the idea that its enemies outnumbered its friends by a factor of ten, Locke retorted that from *his* observation in London the *Essay* "takes so much among the inquisitive and ingenious". He wanted to know who the informant to the contrary had been, but all Tyrrell would say was that he was "a disciple of Will's* Coffee House and you know how capable those sorts of sparks are of judging of such things".[43]

Tyrrell had further cold water for the *Essay* in March. With what looks like mock-innocence and some *Schadenfreude*, he wrote "and now for want of somewhat to fill up this paper I will let you know what the good nature of some people of this place have invented to disparage your book": he had been told by a friend "that he had had it from one who pretends to be a great judge of books that you had taken all that was good in it from divers modern French authors". Tyrrell had replied that to his knowledge "you utterly refused to read any books upon that subject, that you might not take any other mens notions", and that "if you have fallen upon the notions of others, it was by a necessary train of thought". "If you have any better defence than this to make pray let me know it and I will make it for you." In a now lost letter Locke did put up some defence, which Tyrrell acknowledged "all to be true" and promised to produce it "as oft as there is occasion".[44]

In the spring, the screen of anonymity behind which Locke had hidden his authorship of the *Two Treatises* and the *Letter concerning Toleration* led to acrimonious exchanges. The first of these was with Tyrrell who, perhaps in a mischievous attempt to draw Locke out, had said the previous December that there was some thought abroad that he, Tyrrell, was the author of the *Two Treatises*, and he asked Locke, perhaps disingenuously, to ask the publisher who it really was. Locke simply ignored the request of course, but by March others thought he was the author, and Tyrrell asked what he should say "to those that make you here the author of three new treatises: the first a Treatise of Government...the second of Toleration (a pamphlet) and the third...of human reason in religion: which they will needs have to be yours". Tyrrell came to the conclusion that the third book was certainly not Locke's* (the whole style and manner is "not your usual way of writing"), but he wanted to discuss the others with him. Locke's initial and tart reply was that since people at Oxford "would not have [him] to be the author of a book that [he] owned [i.e. the *Essay*, because plagiarised from the French], [he] did not think it worth while to give them any satisfaction in those that [he] did not own at all". Locke also offered to convince Tyrrell about the mistakes in all of this when next they met.[45]

At some time between then and August Locke and Tyrrell had this further discussion, but it led to a further rift between them: Locke jealous of his anonymity, and Tyrrell inquisitive and meddlingly gossipy, as was his style. What happened first, when Tyrrell called on Locke in his lodgings, was that, as he said, "I fell purposely in talk of [the Two Treatises] and, said that whoever had writ it, whether yourself or another I thought him very much in the right in most things". Tyrrell had then, he said, pointedly given Locke the chance of denying his authorship, "which since I found you did not, but rather...turned...to another subject I must confess I did then (as I do still) entertain some suspicions of your being the author of it, as I must do till you are pleased positively to aver the contrary".[46]

What happened next was that Tyrrell "uttered this suspicion" to "a very good friend" of Locke's who must then have passed it back to Locke. In a now lost letter Locke complained to Tyrrell who was led to justify himself at some length. He had discussed the matter with "Mr P" (Popple?) only because he was a good friend of Locke's; he had told him that he was not confident about it and even "gave him some reasons why he might gather that the book was not yours". "So that I hope when you consider better of it, you will find that you have no reason to take my uttering my private opinion ill.... Whether you own or disown it you shall never find that I publish the suspicion to your prejudice or ever speak so much again of it."[47]

A second unpleasant exchange concerning Locke's anonymity began in April. This one related to the *Epistola de Tolerantia* and was with Limborch who, having known all along that this was Locke's, gave the secret away to Guenellon. Locke had never had other than a warm and unalloyed friendship with Limborch and it must have hurt him more deeply than his disagreement with Tyrrell, with whom his relations never recovered their earlier cordiality. Guenellon had heard from someone whose brother was in England that Locke was the author of the *Epistola*; and Guenellon, together with Veen, had asked Limborch whether this were true. Under pressure from such a close friend, Limborch, so he confessed to Locke, felt unable to deny it; after all, he reasoned, Guenellon might later learn the truth elsewhere and be angry with him for evading or lying. Limborch was uncomfortably aware that now that three people knew it the secret could easily spread, but he suggested it might be a good thing if in fact it did get out: Locke's name would attract readers and give authority to the work.[48]

Locke was shocked that Limborch should break a confidence and did not accept he had really been presented with a real dilemma and had been forced into divulging the secret. But, the question of personal trust aside, what deeply concerned and angered him was that he believed Guenellon's informant was involved in a ruse to elicit information:

Some here who have a not too friendly curiosity about me [have been] able to fish out of you what I had hoped was deposited in safe keeping. When certain irresponsible reports...were being spread in this country I was not troubled about them, as they were likely to die down soon of their accord.... But now that you have disclosed the writer's name they have got hold of it for certain.

Limborch stoutly protested that Guenellon had not been put up to it and had since told his informant that Locke denied being the author and that the reports were false. Guenellon himself wrote to Locke; his informant, he insisted, was not involved in any ruse, and added, perhaps rather naïvely, that he was now "so dissuaded that I am assured that he would judge that it is false" that the book was by Locke.[49]

During April a concern Locke had had about ongoing debates, both in Parliament and outside, as to the nature and legitimacy of the occupancy of the throne by William and Mary, led him, apparently encouraged by Clarke, recently elected to the Commons, to compose a document on the matter, perhaps with a view to publishing it as a pamphlet. The *Treatises* left no doubt about its author's view that rebellion against the government could be justified, and that the basis of its legitimacy lay in the consent of the people. Locke's "Call to the nation for unity" explicitly applied that view to the revolution against James, seeking unified support and endorsement on its basis for the justice of William's actions and his present position. He wanted this not only to stop acrimonious and unsettling debate, but also to secure William's position and unite the nation in the face of threats of "popish rage and revenge" from France and the ousted James. "We have a war upon our hands of no small weight. We have a potent and vigilant enemy at our doors [who will]...blow up any doubts or distrusts among us into disorder and confusion." If ever James returns, he said, "under what pretences soever, Jesuits must govern and France be our master".[50]

Locke's call was for all to "join in a sincere loyalty to his present Majesty and a support of his government". What he required was that people, in "a solemn and public renunciation", completely and explicitly disown the doctrine of divine right by which some regarded William as simply a regent acting in place of an absent king; they must reject the idea that William was owed simply the de facto allegiance that any successful usurping conqueror would acquire. What they must do, and do it explicitly, is acknowledge "King William to be our King by right". It was, Locke said, "the miscarriages of the former reigns [that] gave a rise and right to King William's coming and ushered him into the throne", but this former misrule justified William only if, in consenting to his rule, the people explicitly condemned that previous misrule; unless there really were misrule "our complaints were mutiny...and we ought to return as fast as we can to our old obedience".[51]

Locke had been unwell for a couple of weeks in late February or early March, but had apparently recovered before the end of March. In April, however, he suffered a relapse, and seems to have reported being "dangerously ill": the problem was the chronic one associated with his lungs. The Mordaunts invited him to stay at their house in Fulham a few miles out of London, and at the end of April he took a boat up the river to Chelsea, and then a coach to Parson's Green. As Lady Masham later recalled concerning this period,

his old enemy the town air did indeed sometimes make war upon his lungs: but the kindness of the [Mordaunts]...(who both of them always expressed much esteem and friendship for Mr Locke) afforded him...accommodation on these occasions at a house of their's near the town advantaged with a delightful garden (which was what Mr Locke always took much pleasure in).

Locke's relationship with the Mordaunts clearly benefitted him by the patronage Mordaunt bestowed on him. There seems also, however, to have been some real rapport between them, despite the fact that on the face of it they were peculiarly ill-matched. Mordaunt, about thirty-six years Locke's junior, was described by a contemporary as "a man of much heat, many notions, and full of discourse: but he had not true judgement, and less virtue: his thoughts were crude and indigested: and his secrets were soon known. He was both vain, passionate, and inconstant." Queen Mary, noting his impestuosity, said simply that he was "mad"; as for his wife, "who governs him", she is "madder". Over twenty-five years younger than Locke, she seems from their first meeting in Holland to have been taken by him at least to the extent of wanting openly to flirt. "The impresions receaved from Mr Locke... [are not] so slight: as to bee worne out in a months styme: no thay will grow and thrife haveing taken deepe route in a soile that is nott sandy though in a wman hart." Perhaps it was this lively flirtatiousness (which may have been part of a game she played with her husband) that attracted Locke to her, certainly not, as with Damaris Masham, her intellect; her letters are remarkable for their illiteracy.[52]

At the Mordaunts', Locke wrote to Goodall about his cough and shortness of breath. Goodall felt that Locke was "so much master of our profession" that there was little he could say which Locke did not already know. Besides remarking that "country air, diet, and attending symptoms are of greatest use", he also mentioned some pills commended by a Dr Morton, the author of a book on phthisis, whom Goodall said he would arrange for Locke to meet over dinner.[53]

Locke also received advice he had sought some weeks earlier from a new acquaintance, a Dr William Cole, specifically about the fact that his cough was associated with the expectoration of what he took to be purulent pus. Like Goodall, Cole protested that surely Locke had no need of his help, "for I have been informed that your own studies in physic have been such, as to make you as great a judge in it as any man"; but, so far as a remedy was concerned, Cole said the matter was not simple since a phthisis, specifically "phthisis pulmonaris (the case under consideration)", varied so much both seasonally and from person to person. He tentatively suggested, however, moderate phlebotomy, forced vomiting, the use of opiates at bedtime if his cough was worse at night, and, so far as diet was concerned, either non-muscular flesh such as calves' feet or snails, or a whole milk diet, perhaps sometimes varied with gruel or milk-porridge.[54]

Cole's letter was lengthy, perhaps wanting to impress, for at the time he was seeking Locke's advice and help about moving from Worcester and setting up practice in London. He made an even lengthier reply to Locke's own long report about the progress of his symptoms and to the news that there had been a great alleviation in them. He was now inclined to think that like "most of thinking men (physicians not excepted)" Locke was perhaps exaggerating *his own* symptoms and condition: "magnifying them, or not so distinctly perceiving them through their immediate and great concern . . . as the eye does an object brought too near it". Cole felt that, given Locke's symptoms had improved somewhat, it was possible that what he was suffering from was not phthisis or tuberculosis, as he thought: "I hope what you take for a purulent discharge [as in consumption] may be only a pituita [as in bronchitic catarrh] better ripened than ordinary."[55]

Despite his physical condition, Locke was able to work at Parson's Green on a reply to a recently published criticism of his *Letter concerning Toleration*. No doubt fuelling the speculation and rumours concerning its authorship there had been two recent attacks. To one of these, *The "Letter for Toleration" deciphered*, written by one Thomas Long, Locke gave no public answer. But he gave considerable attention to the other, *The Argument of the "Letter concerning Toleration" briefly considered and answered*, a brief pamphlet published anonymously by an Anglican clergyman, Jonas Proast.

Proast doubted that true religion could gain by the toleration which Locke's *Letter* advocated: "I am sure the fruits of a toleration not quite so large as our author's (some of which still remain with us,) give no encouragement to hope for any such advantage." But rather than argue against toleration as such, he restricted himself to arguing against Locke's argument for it. Locke's claim that the "whole jurisdiction of the magistrate reaches only to...civil concernments;...and neither can nor ought in any manner to be extended to the salvation of souls" had had three supports, and though he disagreed with them all, Proast's focus was on the second: that since beliefs are not under the control of the will, the state can hardly enforce on its subjects those beliefs which are required for salvation. He accepted entirely that religious belief is to be produced "by reason and argument, not by outward force and compulsion", but he denied that this meant that force is "utterly useless for the promoting true religion and the salvation of souls". Force, Proast argued, might nevertheless be used "*indirectly* and *at a distance*"; it might, that is, be used to get people to "consider those reasons and arguments which are proper and sufficient to convince them, but which, without being forced, they would not consider". It is evident, Proast thought, that people do not in general consider these reasons and arguments, and that they take their religion from their upbringing and from fashion. So there is a need to get them to consider them, and the force of penalties is the way to do it. Proast had in mind that the force should be "duly proportioned" to its aim of getting people to "weigh matters of religion carefully and impartially", and here he certainly agreed with Locke that "to prosecute men with fire and sword, or to deprive them of their estates" would not be right, and might even be counter-productive. But beyond describing it as "moderate", and as what would be "ordinarily sufficient to prevail with men of common discretion, and not desperately perverse", he did not specify what degree of force and penalty was appropriate. As to who should apply this force, Proast, in clear denial of Locke's view about the separation of state and Church, thought that primarily this should be the "civil sovereign". Civil interests, he agreed, certainly are *a* concern of the state, but they are not the *only* concern, for the state might, in the way Proast explained, usefully promote men's "*spiritual* and *eternal* interests" too. Indeed, Proast thought, and again in opposition to Locke, a duty to do this has been imposed on the magistrate by God.[56]

Furly's sarcastic reaction to Proast's pamphlet was that it must have been printed at the author's own expense, "the paper being so good, and the stuff so singular"; the author himself was either "a ninny, or he writes booty". But Locke must have thought it needed a reply, and by the end of May,* while he was still with the Mordaunts, he had composed *A Second Letter concerning Toleration*.[57] Perhaps because he was suspected of being the author of the first *Letter*, Locke wrote this second one under the pretence of being a newcomer to the debate, "Philanthropus", lover of mankind.

The *Second Letter* was longer than the first, but it consisted entirely of a detailed, repetitious, *ad hominem* attack on Proast's shortish and succinct pamphlet. Locke did not deny the core of Proast's point that though people's beliefs and convictions are not under the control of their will, they can nevertheless choose to consider arguments and reasons which might change those beliefs and convictions. He did not deny that people might be brought to do this by means which in themselves are inappropriate to influence their understandings directly. Instead, he painstakingly picked at and probed all possible surrounding aspects of Proast's suggestion that the state might adopt this indirect procedure in the case of religious belief. Among many other things, he claimed that the suggestion was needless since, despite what they might claim, persecuting states are not in fact interested in the religious *convictions* of their subjects, but only in their outer compliance and conformity. "When any dissenter conforms...is he ever examined to see whether he does it upon reason, and conviction, and such grounds as would become a Christian concerned for religion?" He also pointed out that because so few rulers are "of the true religion; it is likely your indirect way of using of force would do...as much harm as good.... And your way of applying force will as much promote popery in France, as protestantism in England." He objected that Proast had left unclear exactly to whom this force should be applied; many dissenters may already have considered the reasons and arguments for their beliefs, and many conformists may not have done. He found it hard to believe that Proast would advocate applying force to members of the national Church; yet if force were not to be applied to them, punishment would turn out, after all, for not being of the magistrate's religion, "the very thing you deny he has authority to do". He observed that there is no scriptural warrant for force to be used in this way, and that Proast had not defined what he meant by "moderate" force. He questioned Proast's view that "if the *spiritual* and *eternal* interests of men may any way be procured or advanced by political government, the procuring and advancing those interests must in all reason be reckoned among the ends of civil societies, and so, consequently, fall within the compass of the magistrate's jurisdiction".[58]

Though Proast's words sometimes suggested otherwise, the supposed point of the "moderate" force which he advocated was not simply that people should consider and take their religious beliefs and convictions seriously; nor was it (though Locke suspected otherwise) that they should come to accept the doctrines of the national religion. It was that they should come to the true religion. But, as Locke pointed out, there is no agreement about which this is, and so, "without a judge of truth", people would be punished "for you know not what": it is as if "you should whip a scholar to make him find out the square root of a number you do not know". Inevitably it will be the magistrate that decides: "men will never, in his opinion, 'act according to reason and sound judgement', which is the thing...you say men should be brought to by the magistrate...till they embrace his religion".[59]

Locke's *Second Letter* was well received by his friends. Furly thought it an "ingenious reply" in which Proast was "as ingeniously corrected" and "I wish he may be the better for it"; while Le Clerc thought it "a very careful and sound piece of work".[60]

Though punctuated with a number of trips to London, the stay with the Mordaunts lasted into early June. Parson's Green, with its "good air" and some "warm weather", had, Locke thought, done him much good, and it was not long before he went to the country again. This time, on what was perhaps his first visit there, it was to Oates, the Mashams' house at High Laver in Essex, where he stayed for the last two weeks in June. When he returned to London it was not to the Smithsbys', but to new lodgings, also in Dorset Court. These (for which he paid around a pound a month) were in the house of his old acquaintance Robert Pawling, who had recently moved from Oxford. Despite the move Locke continued, until the end of his life, to rely on Rabsy Smithsby for various items of domestic business.[61]

At the end of June, Tyrrell saw fit to needle Locke again. "I have began again to read over your excellent Essay, with great satisfaction", he began; "and discoursing with some thinking men at Oxford... I found them dissatisfied with what you have said concerning the law of nature (or reason), whereby we distinguish moral good from evil." The dissatisfaction turned on the fact that though (in his denial of innate principles) Locke had later asserted that "there is a law, knowable by the light of nature, i.e. without the help of positive revelation", he seemed in a later chapter, so Tyrrell suggested, to detach morality from the law of nature and to reduce it "to the praise or dispraise that men give to certain actions in several... societies", a reduction which makes morality purely relative.[62]

Basically, there were two criticisms here: that Locke first asserted and then denied the existence of a law of nature; and that as well as denying it he gave a very unsatisfactory basis to morality. Locke found these objections hasty, ill-considered, and ill-natured. We do not have his initial reply to them, but it appears from Tyrrell's rather sulky response that Locke had taken it that Tyrrell was in fact putting his own objections under the disingenuous pretence of passing on those of others. "I am sorry", Tyrrell said, if "anything I said... should make you believe the conclusions which some had drawn... should proceed from myself, for I did intend no more than to give you an account not of my own but other mens censures: and therefore desired your meaning... that I may know how to answer them." Sourly Tyrrell concluded "if you do not like that I should tell you what objections the world make against what you write I shall for the future be more reserved".[63]

Locke must have pointed out in his initial reply that though he did "make the law, whereby men judge of virtue and vice, to be nothing else, but the consent of private men", he also, in a slightly earlier passage, said in reference to "divine law" that "God has given a rule" for our actions.[64] Tyrrell responded that he had indeed pointed this passage out to his friends, but that they took it to refer not to a "law of nature" discoverable by reason, but to a law revealed in the Scriptures.

Of course the acknowledgement that Locke had spoken of laws other than "the law of reputation and fashion" rather defuses the accusation that he reduced morality to that law. But Locke did not stress that, and was more concerned with the accusation that he denied a law of nature discoverable by reason. The fact is, he said, it did not matter for his purpose whether by "divine law" he had meant something discoverable by reason or had meant Scripturally revealed law. What he had been wanting to do was to explain that men form the ideas of "virtue" and "vice" by referring their actions to some law, and all he was doing was listing various kinds of law to which people might make that referral.[65]

Tyrrell had earlier said that if by "Divine law" Locke had meant some law discoverable by reason, he could have explicitly said this and removed the unclarity by adding the words "which others call the law of nature": indeed, "so I should have advised you to have worded it, if I had had the honour of having it communicated to me before it had been made public, for in those notes you left in my hands there is nothing said" of this. Locke's rather testy response was that his friends "might have considered better what I writ. I imagine, what I was there to make out I have done very plainly." But though in the heat of this discussion Locke was not prepared to concede much to Tyrrell, he did come to think again. In the second edition of the *Essay* he would explain that by the divine law he meant what "God has set to the actions of men, *whether promulgated to them by the light of nature or the voice of revelation*": this law, he would say, is "the *only* true touchstone of moral rectitude".[66]

JULY–DECEMBER 1690: QUESTIONS OF ECONOMICS

After a couple of weeks in his new lodgings at Pawling's, Locke again went to Oates. He was intending to spend some time in August at Bath with Cary Mordaunt, but by the beginning of September he was still at Oates, kept there by "constant rain", together with "the entreaties" of the Mashams, "joined to my cough, which with the ill weather began a little to return". It was not until mid-September that he was able to get back to town, where he decided to stay put, perhaps encouraged by Mordaunt, Pembroke, and other friends who had complained of his long absence. Unfortunately, as he had to confess to Lady Masham, after two weeks in London his cough had "a little increased".[67]

Following the entry of England into war against France there had been an increase in the legal interest rate, and then a renewed demand to reduce it from 6 to 4 per cent. Stimulated by this, Locke again turned his mind to this question, taking up the work which he had done in 1668, reorganising and adding to it, sometimes with information about the situation in Holland which he had got from Furly and from his own observations there in the 1680s.[68] He was still against any imposed reduction, and aimed to show that it would not have the consequences some people supposed. His specific conclusions were set against the background of some theoretical considerations about money and interest rates in general.

An official interest rate is needed, Locke thought, to settle legal disagreements in cases where no rate had been agreed, and as the rate at which the government repays loans. He was, however, completely set against any attempt to manipulate the economy by means of enforcing a legal rate for private loans. His thought was that alongside any rate which the government might try to enforce by law there will be a market rate – a rate at which people are prepared to lend and borrow money: "It is the want of money drives men to that trouble and charge of borrowing; and proportionably to this want, so will everyone have it, whatever price it cost him." Now if the legally enforced rate were set lower than the market rate, the law would be broken by bankers and others skilled in "the arts of lending", to the detriment of the ordinary borrower: they would take money on deposit from private indviduals at the legal rate, and lend it out at the higher market rate.[69]

Moreover, even if the law were kept, a lower legal rate would have questionable consequences. It would involve a loss to those, such as widows and orphans, "who have their estates in money" rather than in land; while on the other hand it would mean increased profits for middlemen such as merchants who could borrow more cheaply to buy goods to sell on for undiminished profits. There was, Locke thought, no good reason why money should be redistributed in this way, taken away from "a great and innocent part of the people", and at no advantage to the country as a whole.[70]

Moreover, an adhered-to legal reduction would not, Locke argued, have the consequences promised for it by its proponents, such as an increase in productive trade due to a lower cost of new investments. The passion with which Locke argued here shows how dangerous he thought this promise was: it consists of "gilded words" with nothing substantial in them; it sets "men's mouths a watering" for money at a decreased rate, but it does not actually produce the money. A lower interest rate, Locke thought, would simply reduce the money available for borrowing. Even with the legal rate as it was, there were, he suggested, more borrowers than lenders, and with a reduced rate ordinary people would be reluctant to lend to private tradesmen, "the reward not being judged proportionable to the risk".[71]

Higher prices were supposed to be a further consequence of a lower legal interest rate; the argument being, as Locke reported it, that since money would be worth less, the value of the goods with which it exchanged would be correspondingly more: "As much as you take off from the value of money, so much you add to the price of other things which are exchanged for it; the raising the price of anything being no more but the addition to its value in respect of money, or, which is all one, lessening the value of money."[72] According to Locke the conclusion of the argument was false, and prices would in fact fall due to the decrease in investment in trade. But in any case the argument was based on a confusion about the notion of "the value of money".

Locke suggested that money has a "double value". In one respect it is like land, whose value is that it can be rented out; money can, that is, be lent for interest. This parallel between the two goes further in that tenanted land produces crops which sell for more than the rent, while borrowed money is invested in a business which produces goods which sell for more than the interest. So usurers, Locke suggested, are no different from landlords; indeed, he argued, they take a smaller proportion of their clients' profits than do landlords.

The second part of the "double value" derives from a similarity between money and commodities. Besides themselves being "necessaries, or conveniences of life", commodities can be exchanged for other commodities, and money can be exchanged for them too.[73] Money differs, of course, from the commodities which it buys, being neither a necessity nor a convenience; moreover, unlike them it is taken to have a fixed worth and to be the measure by which we reckon their value.

Thus Locke argued that a reduction in the "value of money", in the sense of a reduction in the interest rate, is not the same as a reduction of its exchange value in the inflationary sense that it will now exchange for fewer goods. The idea that cheaper money will produce higher prices is just confused.

In his discussion of the exchange value of money, Locke saw money simply as a commodity (albeit of a special kind) along with the commodities which it buys, and on this basis he developed a general theory of exchange value or price. He began with the intuitive thought that prices will be low when there are many sellers and few buyers. He then developed an account of price in terms of the notions of "quantity" and "vent": to estimate the value of anything, we must consider "its quantity in proportion to its vent, for this alone regulates the price".[74] The "quantity" of any exchangeable commodity (whether silver coins or wheat) is simply the amount which is available; its "vent", a function of demand, is the amount sold over a given period; and its value is the ratio of quantity to vent. So, the greater the quantity for a given vent (or a lower vent for a given quantity), the lower the value. Consequently one commodity (say wheat) is more valuable than another (say cloth), and will exchange for a greater amount of it when it has the greater quantity/vent ratio of the two.

Money is a special commodity. It neither decays nor is consumed, and is used as a store of value: when they have more than sufficient necessities and conveniences, people are always willing to exchange their excess for money in particular. As a consequence, money has a pretty constant vent: "because the desire of money is constantly almost everywhere the same, its vent varies very little".[75] Moreover since its quantity, too, alters but slowly over the months and years, its value remains constant, and is used as a fixed measure. So, commodities have a "price": the exchange values which wheat has in relation to cloth and to coal can be compared via the intermediary of the exchange values that the three commodities have in relation to money. We think of money as having a fixed value and of the prices of other goods having a rise and fall in relation to it. Since, as a matter of fact, both the quantity and vent of the staple commodity of wheat vary little over the years, its value could be used as a fixed measure; but because of its bulkiness and propensity to rot, it is not suitable as a store of value.

Money is a special commodity in another way too. Besides having an exchange value, a commodity typically has an "intrinsic, natural worth...[which] consists in its fitness to supply the necessities, or serve the conveniencies of life". Obviously the two kinds of value have a connection, but it is not straightforward: an absolute necessity with a large intrinsic value such as air, has, because of its large and freely available quantity, neither vent nor price; on the other hand, people will pay any amount "for whatsoever is absolutely necessary, rather than go without it", and here "scarcity...alone makes the price". Though not thinking of their decorative use or use as plate, Locke spoke of silver and gold as having an intrinsic value too, but in their case it is of an "imaginary" kind:

mankind, having consented to put an imaginary value upon gold and silver, by reason of their durableness, scarcity, and not being very liable to be counterfeited, have made them by general consent, the common pledges, whereby men are assured, in exchange for them, to receive equally valuable things, to those they parted with for any quantity of these metals.... Having, as money no other value, but as pledges to procure what one wants or desires, and they procuring what we want or desire only by their quantity, it is evident that the intrinsic value of silver and gold, used in commerce is nothing but their quantity.[76]

As has been noted, because of its interest value (as opposed to its exchange value) money may be compared with land, and, Locke said, one would expect that the value of land would depend on the interest rate. It was indeed thought that a further consequence of an enforced lower interest rate would be an increase in the value of land in exchange for money. One interpretation of the capital value of land (as an exchange commodity) was that it was equivalent to the yearly rent over a certain number of years; hence, it might be supposed, given that an interest rate reduction from 6 to 4 per cent would mean an increase from nearly seventeen to twenty-five years in the time it would take to get a one hundred per cent return on loaned money, so (given that rents or the interest value of the land remained constant) the capital value of land should be reckoned to have increased from around seventeen to twenty-five times the yearly rent.

Though Locke thought that ideally the return in rents on capital in the form of land should roughly equate to the return in interest on a sum of money, he also thought that the exchange value of land neither was nor should be determined by the interest rate. It was, rather, determined, as was the price of any other commodity, by the goodness of the land and by the number of buyers and sellers.

The fall which the country had seen in the rental value of land (which was making landowners poorer) was, Locke argued, not due, as was thought, to high interest rates (which were only making bankers richer). The two things were just not connected, he thought, and it was a mistake for landowners to press for lower rates with rents in mind. The fall in rents was really due to a poor balance of international trade: "If the landed gentleman will have, and by his example make it fashionable to have, more claret, spice, silk, and other foreign consumable wares, than our exportation of commodities does exchange for, money must unavoidably follow to balance the account, and pay the debt."[77]

Another question of contemporary concern which Locke addressed in the last quarter of the year was the country's coinage.[78] Coins were not, as now, merely official fiduciary tokens; rather, they took their value from the amount of metal in them, so that with the stamp of the Royal Mint on them they were authenticated amounts of valuable metal (primarily silver, but gold to a secondary extent) of a certain degree of fineness. Some silver coins (shillings, or the five-shilling piece, the crown) had a denominated face value in terms of "the money of account" (pounds, shillings, pence). Gold coins, such as guineas, had no denominated value.

In the course of circulation over the years many coins had become devalued, sometimes by as much as half their official weight, by "clipping", the illegal cutting-off of strips of silver from the edges (a practice which the introduction of some milled coins in 1663 made more difficult). Clipped coins usually passed at their denominated face value (though foreign trade was compromised because foreigners would not accept them), but it began more and more to be recognised that something needed to be done. According to Lady Masham, Locke saw this before others: "what loss our nation suffered by the slowness with which men were made sensible, what must be the remedy to our disease, in the debasing and clipping of our coin might, had [Locke] been hearkened to, have had much earlier cure". Soon after his return from Holland, she said, "(when nobody else seemed sensible of this matter) he was very much troubled concerning it":

And when at my lodgings in London (the company there finding him often afflicted about a matter which nobody else took any notice of) have railled him upon this uneasiness as being a visionary trouble, he has more than once replied [that] we might laugh at it, but it would not be long before we should want money to send our servants to market with for bread and meat which was so true five or six years after [around 1695], that there was not a family in England which did not find this a difficulty.[79]

One commonly suggested solution to this problem was a recoinage in which the new coins would be "raised" (as it was described) by their nominal denomination being put at a value above that of the metal they contained. A bill to "raise" or "enhance" the coin had been considered by the Commons the previous May (but had lapsed), and in the autumn there was another bill (which eventually failed) to raise the rating of the crown from 5s to 5s 3d.[80]

In Locke's view, the idea of "raising the coin" had not been thought through ("I wish those that use the phrase of raising our money had some clear notion annexed to it"), and he was against a reminting at a devalued rate. What the idea amounts to, he said, is calling something "a crown now, which before, by the law, was but part of a crown". His basic thought was that what is paid in rent or for goods is essentially a certain quantity of silver (though a quantity which, by virtue of having been officially coined, has been guaranteed as being of a certain weight and degree of fineness). "If anyone thinks a shilling, or a crown in

name, has its value from the denomination, and not from the quantity
of silver in it, let it be tried; and hereafter let a penny be called
a shilling, or a shilling be called a crown. I believe nobody would be
content to receive his debts or rents in such money." It is, Locke was
adamant, "the quantity of pure silver...makes the real value of
money".[81] As a consequence of a devalued recoinage, landlords would
be robbed of a percentage of their rents and all creditors of a
percentage of what they are owed; similarly, a recoined crown would
simply not buy as much as an old one did.

Those who proposed an "enhanced" (devalued) recoinage
suggested that it would increase the domestic value of the bullion of
old full-weight coins, and make them less attractive to melt down and
export as bullion.[82] Locke argued, however, that bullion is exported
only because of the balance of trade.

There were, then, in Locke's view, a number of disadvantages and
no advantages to a devalued recoinage. "It will neither bring us in more
money, bullion or trade; nor keep that we have here, nor hinder our
weighty money...from being melted [so] to what purpose should the
kingdom be at the charge of coining all our money anew?"[83] Though
he could conceive of a time when things had become so serious that
clipped coins would not exchange with standard weight ones, he seems
to have thought that this could be avoided by keeping up the legal
pressure against coin clipping.

In October there was talk of Locke's going to Holland. "I hope London
will agree with your lungs", Thomas wrote to him early that month,
"though I fear it but perhaps Holland may". Perhaps his plan was to go
for the winter and for the sake of his health; and perhaps it was with
this, or a possibly longer stay, in mind that, between January and April,
he had been depositing a total of £700 with Guenellon in Amsterdam.
But, whatever his plans had been initially, they began to involve the
possibility that, whether privately or in some official capacity, he would
make the journey with Pembroke, who was going to The Hague in
connection with a planned visit there by William.[84]

Thus, in the middle of the month, he wrote to Clarke from Oates, to
where he had just gone, that he would come back to town as soon as he
was "sent for". "And therefore pray let me not fail to hear from you,
if...there be any preparations made or orders given concerning the
King's journey. But I would willingly finish what I came for before

I return if I may; but that still shall give way to any commands from my Lord [Pembroke]."[85]

Whether it was because he had been "sent for" or because he had finished what business he had at Oates, he took the coach back to London at the end of October. What that business had been is unclear, but considerations of health had played a part too in his visit to Oates, for shortly afterwards Thomas expressed himself "glad you are so well as to return to London. I hope your lungs will bear it."[86]

The journey to Holland with Pembroke remained a live possibility for some weeks. Towards the end of November, Furly was looking forward to some "winterchat" with "your sweet self", and Locke's "old quarters were ready", along with an eiderdown Mrs Furly had specially prepared. But at the end of November, Locke wrote that Pembroke's yacht had left, with him not on it. Not wanting Locke to be without it, Mrs Furly sent the eiderdown to England.[87]

Pembroke's departure left Locke in what was by now a "wet and foggy winter". A few days earlier Thomas, though marvelling that Locke's lungs seemed to be "perform[ing] their office better than I expected", had suggested that for their sake, and if "you can be so far from London a retreat at my house at Savernake [in Wiltshire] is at your service". But Locke made other plans, and in mid-December he took the Bishop's Stortford coach back to Essex.[88]

8

Oates (January 1691–December 1695)

Isaac Newton was a Christmas visitor at Oates too. He and Locke, together with Lady Masham, discussed what he called his "mystical fancies" about which he was writing, his interpretation of parts of the biblical books of Daniel and Revelations (for example, that "the Son of man" (Dan. 7) is the same as "the Word of God upon the White Horse in Heaven" (Apoc. 19)).[2]

Newton had left when Locke rode back to London in early January. Though he was able to get various small jobs done, such as settling some of Lady Masham's business with a jeweller, it proved to have been a very bad idea to have gone. In little more than a week he was planning to return to Oates, "I bear the winter pretty well here", he wrote to Furly early the next month, "but, going to London at Christmas I wanted breath presently, and was almost dead in a fortnight."[3]

Some years later Lady Masham recalled that when Locke returned to England from Holland she and her husband were in London, where their stay there for a number of months "gave the opportunity of improving our acquaintance and in little more than a year and a half after this (having by visiting us here at Oates experimented the suitableness of this air for him) he made this place his home; the necessity of his health constraining him to leave London except for some months in the summer". His company, she said, was "very desirable to us, and he had all the assurances we could give him of being always welcome here". "To make him easier in living with us", Lady Masham went on, "it was necessary he should do so upon his own terms; which

Sir Francis at last, consenting to, Mr Locke then believed himself at home with us; and resolved (if it pleased God) here to end his days."[4]

Exactly when Locke "resolved" to make Oates his home is not clear. Lady Masham said that he did so "in little more than a year and a half" after coming back to England (which would bring us to August or September 1690), but she also said that he "made trial of the air of this place" during "some considerably long visits... during the years 89, 90, and part of 91". More or less consistently with this second statement, we might suppose that when he went to London in early January, Locke saw himself as simply returning to his lodgings at Pawling's after a Christmas visit, but that, finding it so painful there, he then concluded he must make Oates his permanent home. Martha Lockhart, a relation of Sir Francis Masham and one of Queen Mary's ladies-in-waiting, seems to have thought of his January journey back to Oates as marking the beginning of a new life: "I could not forbear to send this", she wrote the day before Locke left, to wish "all the good success you expect from change of air, and that it may so far make so perfect a cure upon you... that you may at least sometimes be able to oblige your friends in the town, as well as those in the country".[5]

On the other hand (and consistent with the suggestion that his decision to make Oates his home was made in the late summer or early autumn of 1690), he spoke a week or so after leaving Oates in mid-September as though it was already a given that Oates was now permanently available to him as a "retreat and security". That this was indeed so is perhaps indicated by the fact that when Locke paid money to Sir Francis the following May for "board... for me and my man", on the terms they had agreed of twenty shillings a week, the payment of twenty pounds* ran back to 19 December, six days after he arrived at Christmas, his first period at Oates since the previous September.[6]

But whenever this new chapter in Locke's life really began he soon told his friends in Holland about it. "I eagerly await the publication of the book [on the History of the Inquisition]", he wrote to Limborch in March, "as also does Dr Cudworth's daughter,* whose name I mentioned to you some time ago as that of a remarkably gifted woman and one of my familiar friends. She [and her husband]... have taken me into their house as a guest and have provided a most opportune refuge for my present state of health."[7]

The household of which Locke became a part was quite an extensive one. Its head, Sir Francis Masham, who, as the local MP, was often away in London, was about fourteen years Locke's junior. By a first marriage he had a number of sons, and a daughter, Esther (known to Locke, who became very fond of her, as "Landabridis" or "Dib"). By his marriage to Damaris he had a son, born in 1686, Francis ("Totty" or "little Frank"), of whom also Locke became very fond. Lady Masham's widowed mother was a further member of the household, which was completed by ten servants (and Syl).[8]

Until it was destroyed by fire in the nineteenth century, Oates was a small moated manor house in the Essex parish of High Laver. Locke sometimes travelled between there and London on horseback, but more usually he went by the public coach. This left Bishop's Stortford (six miles from Oates, thirty-one from London) on Mondays and Fridays, returning on Tuesdays and Saturdays; travelling south through Harlow and then through Epping Forest it would arrive in the City at the Pewter Pot in Leadenhall Street. Because of the shorter distances (three miles from Oates, twenty-five miles from London) Locke usually got the coach at its stop at the King's Arms in Harlow. Travel between Harlow and Oates was on horseback, or in Sir Francis's carriage. For the two to three miles between the Pewter Pot and the lodgings which he retained at Pawling's in Westminster, Locke usually took a hackney coach.[9]

He was a paying guest at Oates, but sometimes his board money (though always paid) was left for as long as sixty-six weeks, and he quite evidently was a warmly welcome member of the family inner circle. In a variety of ways he contributed much to the household (sometimes, one might occasionally think, as something of a dogsbody, doing things which the Mashams might otherwise have had a servant do). His letters and notebooks are filled with details of various imported luxuries he had delivered to Oates (presumably not just for himself) by Lenham, the local carrier: Seville and Portuguese oranges by the hundredweight; Jamaican cacao nuts or beans by the quarter hundredweight; stockfish by the barrel; and French wines by the dozen bottles. He sometimes had young Frank Masham in his care at Pawling's, buying his shoes, arranging for his dancing lessons (an activity he thought highly of, as giving children "manly thoughts and carriage"); and he frequently did various pieces of business in London for Lady Masham, buying items of clothing, going to jewellers, and having her watch mended.[10]

His friendship with Lady Masham clearly was close and warm, in some ways perhaps more so than hers with her husband. Cranston suggested that Sir Francis was something of an affable bore and that "it looks as though he and Locke found it easy enough to accept the other, without being bothered by, or even perhaps much noticing the other's presence". Locke and Lady Masham shared activities such as gardening that in other marriages husband and wife might have shared. "Working in a garden" was something "he very well understood", she said, and he often ordered seeds and trees for her. Most importantly, of course, they had intellectual interests in common. As a writer herself she took a close interest in his work, and she was a party in discussions with friends who visited him. Writing to Limborch about his work on the Inquisition, Locke said that Lady Masham and he were eagerly looking foward to it; when the book was eventually published he told Limborch that he had it with him at Oates so that "by your kindness Mrs Cudworth* and I may this winter enjoy the evenings, which could only be enhanced by the presence of the author".[11]

In the months following the hasty January return from London, Locke gradually settled into his new home. His personal quarters were two first-floor rooms, a study, with windows facing east and south, and a sleeping room, in which he had his own furniture, some of which (carpet, eight Dutch-bottomed chairs, and bed curtains) spilled over into other rooms. At the end of April he received the eiderdown which had been promised the previous autumn at the Furlys, shipped over in a bag marked "JL".[12]

Until the time of his expulsion, Locke had thought of his permanent home as being at Christ Church, and it must have been with considerable feeling that he now set about retrieving and transferring to Oates the belongings, particularly the books and manuscripts, he had left there when he went to Holland. They were of course no longer in Oxford itself, having been removed from there to Tyrrell's. The process of repossession was not without its difficulties and disappointments. Some things, such as a gilt spoon, cutlery, and plates, were missing (perhaps stolen from the Christ Church rooms before his expulsion, or removed for safekeeping by his bedmaker, who could not be traced). Locke's carefully compiled catalogue of his books was missing too, and Tyrrell had to make a new one. With Tyrrell periodically away from home there were delays in the packing of goods (in particular because a "little hair trunk" in which he wanted to pack some of Locke's manuscripts had been lent to his daughter in Wales). Finally, one very large consignment ("six great boxes, two smaller ones, with one trunk, a great bundle, and a cane chair"), which were to be carted back to Oxford to be taken down the Thames to London, were held up, first by the unavailability of a cart and a barge, and then by broken lock gates.

But gradually, over the year, bundles, boxes, trunks, cases, and chests of various goods, meticulously listed, catalogued, and inventoried, eventually made their way to Pawling's in London and thence, via the carrier, to Oates: amongst them, many books, a telescope, velvet riding cap, linen, a locked leather writing box ("I hope your knife, spoon, and fork may yet be there", Tyrrell wrote), a travelling scriptor, a bottle of elixir, a comb case, a little black ribbon, an iron hook, five cramp rings, a cane chair ("I have given the bargeman a great charge of it", said Tyrrell), a table, and a quilt. There were further things yet to come: more books and manuscripts, carpets, cushions, a terrestrial globe, a barometer, one of Locke's own-design manuscript cabinets, and glass bottles of seeds.[13]

He must have been particularly keen to have his books out of storage and back with him. His unsettled life had made him uncomfortably aware of how burdensome these cherished things could be. "Now that it is gone I know not what to do with my books, having nowhere to place them", he had complained miserably when he lost his Studentship. But at last, for the first time since 1667 when Christ Church ceased to be his only residence, he was in what promised to be a permanent and undivided home, and could have all his books housed together and readily available; and he and Syl, making use of the printed catalogue of the Bodleian Library, set to work listing and cataloguing them, systematically placing them on new walnut shelves. By this time he had about two thousand titles, a number which would nearly double before his death.[14]

Though Locke could not have lived without books, seeing them as the "instruments of truth and knowledge", he nevertheless had come to the conclusion that they were "pestilent things" which infected those that traded in them – printers, binders, and sellers. These, he thought, have "so odd a turn and corruption of mind, that they have a way of dealing peculiar to themselves, and not conformed to . . . that general fairness that cements mankind". Perhaps, he fantasied, it was that the books themselves, with their "noble ends", could not bear being meddled with by those with commercial purposes, and so revenged themselves on book-traders, who "prostitut[ed] them to mean and misbecoming designs".[15]

It appears that Locke's general intention was to resume the study of natural philosophy. Even though he passed on some of his medical books to Thomas's son, he was clearly still interested in medicine, at least to the extent of recording in his journal throughout the year a number of medical recipes, and of giving medical advice, but it seems that his present focus was not as narrow as this. The books he had first wanted to retrieve from Tyrrell were volumes of Boyle's works, and he told Tyrrell of his plan "of again resuming the study of natural things".[16]

As Martha Lockhart had hoped, Locke was not in permanent exile at Oates. He was in London for nearly a dozen days at the beginning of April, for three weeks a month later, and then again for nearly two weeks in July. During one of these stays he visited the watchmaker Thomas Tompion from whom, besides a 5s brass clock-weight, he bought an £11 watch. The watch was bought on trial, for Locke's receipt allowed him a full return if he were not satisfied, and on each day for a month he duly made comparisons of it with some other timepiece at Oates ("watch too fast" he decided).[17]

At the end of July there was confirmation of a visit to Bath which Locke had been planning with the Mordaunts. Understanding their departure to be within two or three days, Locke left immediately for London. In the event he did not set out with the Mordaunts in their coach on the ninety-mile journey to their country seat at Dauntsey until over a week into August. They were at Bath, about twenty miles further on, a few days later; and Locke was able to report "not only continuance but increase of...health, by drinking the Bath waters".[18]

Isabella Duke wrote to him there hoping soon to be able to ride over from Otterton to see him at Chipley, where for some time the Clarkes had been wanting him to visit. He was with the Clarkes in late August, and then went to Bristol, where Stratton was now living. He no longer wanted to look after Locke's business affairs in the country and wanted to settle his account with him (in fact he continued dealing with Locke's affairs for some time).[19]

Locke got back to his London lodgings in the second week of September, leaving after a few days for a week at Oates. He was in London for some days into October, during which time he visited Parson's Green (staying to dine with Carey Mordaunt while her husband went to dine in town). He met Boyle on at least one occasion, taking from him the details of a liquid concoction which was "very useful for ulcers", and lending him a travel book. They seem also to have discussed an experiment Locke had in mind, because a short while later Locke wrote to him from Oates, asking for a quantity of some chemical he needed: "I have water, and I have vessels, I only want soap to be at work. Whatsoever you shall give this bearer for me will be safely brought me." The bearer was Syl, sent down from Oates with papers relating to Boyle's *General History of the Air* which Locke had been working on.[20]

He also spent time with Edward Clarke, in town with his again pregnant wife. In March of the previous year Clarke had been elected as Member of Parliament for Taunton, a fact which gave Locke, by his welcome suggestions and advice, some means to influence national affairs. On this occasion they discussed the problems of the interest rate and the deteriorating currency, and agreed that Locke should publish what he had written the previous autumn. On his return to Oates he put his papers into some order and a couple of weeks later was able to tell Clarke "they only want transcribing". A bill to reduce the interest rate to 5 per cent was introduced in Parliament in mid-November and soon passed a first reading. As a consequence, Locke's (anonymous) *Some Considerations of the Consequences of the Lowering of Interest and Raising the Value of Money* were hurried through the press and appeared at the end of the month. Clarke gave copies to Francis Masham and four or five other members, a piece of lobbying which, he said, was "so advantageously" done that it was already doubtful whether the bill would have a second reading: everyone who had read Locke's piece was "clearly of opinion the arguments therein are abundantly sufficient to destroy that bill, and all future attempt of the like kind". Clarke had heard "the whole treatise generally much approved of and commended"; people were keen to know the author, "and I must tell you", he said, "there have been many that have shrewdly guessed at him". But Clarke also reported that there were some who, while they approved of the book's ingenuity, would not forgive the author for some of his views, if only they knew who it was. Locke replied that he was sure this was so and asked Clarke to tell Lord Ashley (Shaftesbury's grandson, now aged twenty, and himself an MP) to be cautious about this.[21]

Clarke proved to have been unduly optimistic about the effect of *Some Considerations*, for the bill went through second and third readings in the Commons in January. He wrote to Locke, on the day of that third reading, that while many of "the greatest and best men in our House were obliged to that treatise for all the arguments they used", they did not prevail: "it is not reason, but a supposed benefit to the borrower that has passed the bill, and I believe it is that will carry it through the House of Lords likewise". But a month later, when Parliament was adjourned, the bill had not yet passed the Lords, and it was lost shortly afterwards when Parliament was prorogued.[22]

After his return to Oates in October, Locke spent time not only on preparing *Some Considerations*, but also on the manuscript of Boyle's *History of the Air*. The papers were in a rather chaotic state, and much effort of an editorial kind was needed to rearrange and correct them. Locke was forthright in his comments ("I should not make a right use of the freedom you expect from me, should I not without reserve offer my thoughts to you"). "I have", he said, "read them all over very carefully, numbered them according to the titles they belong to, and laid them in that order, the best I could, according to the state they are in. I have besides corrected many of the mistakes of your amanuenses." Even so they were not ready for publication: "there are some faults in the writing, which, without consulting you, I dare not correct; and in other places defects and omissions, which I could not supply". He was not sure what urgency Boyle felt about publication, but told him he would be glad to come to town to discuss things. Despite the cautions Locke had about the presentation of Boyle's material, he clearly thought it worthwhile: "Besides the many strange and pleasant remarks . . . and uncommon experiments you have made yourself about the air, your design opens a large and useful field, and I must confess gives me a larger view than I had before of this subject, which yet I have a long time thought deserved much to be considered."[23] This was not just idle praise for Locke had his own interest in the matter. Indeed, he included with Boyle's papers "a copy of my register of the air", the record of the daily weather observations he had made in Oxford between 1666 and 1683.

Locke saw Boyle again when he was in London for nearly three weeks in November, and no doubt it was as a result of a conversation with him that he wrote to Stratton asking him to collect from the Mendip mines "some of the earth that lieth with the lead ore". For some time Boyle had experimented on mercury combined with a certain kind of "red earth" in an attempt to transmute it into gold. Until two years earlier such experimental work on "multiplying" gold had been illegal, and it had been largely through the efforts of Boyle himself that the statute banning it was repealed.[24]

When Locke left town towards the end of November it was earlier than he had intended; but he was "driven" out by Clarke, concerned for his health. He and Syl were not alone in the coach, for two of the four seats they had booked were occupied by Clarke's son Edward and his tutor, Mr Passebon. Locke and Clarke had been concerned for some time about what progress the ten-year-old was making under the care of Passebon, and had decided that Locke should observe them together for a while.[25]

On reflection Locke realised that he had been "very ill" when he left London, but he already felt better after only one day back at Oates. Well enough, indeed, to embark on a project he had had in mind for some time and which would take more than another ten years to reach fruition, an illustrated interlinear English translation of the Latin from the classical book *Aesop's Fables*. In themselves, he thought the stories not only "apt to delight and entertain a child" but also to "afford useful reflections to a grown man"; presenting them as he planned would enable a child to perfect its reading of English and to learn Latin at the same time. Within a couple of days he was able to send Clarke the first sheet of the book, asking him to pass it on for printing "as soon as you can" to Awnsham Churchill, a bookseller and publisher (with his brother John) with whom Locke often dealt.[26]

Having forced him out of town, Clarke must have been surprised to see Locke back there just a week later. One likely reason for his return was to get Boyle's *History of the Air* to the publisher, since it was now in a fit state to be printed, and Boyle himself was increasingly unwell. But even before he could deliver the book he realised he had again been foolish to leave Oates, and he retreated back there after six days. Again, however, he soon recovered at least his spirits, and wrote to Clarke the next day, "I fancy myself a little better already, though I feel my lungs yet cruelly oppressed".[27]

At the same time he asked Clarke to arrange for his son and tutor to leave Oates as soon as convenient. Locke and Passebon had agreed that he was getting nowhere with the boy — apart from anything else the two quarrelled — and that he should give the job up. Locke proposed that before the child be got another tutor he should have him at Oates for "some time by himself to try his temper and see whether he has that aversion to his book Monsieur complains of, or whether it were only to him and his method. And whether it be sauntering and listlessness, or intention upon play...that makes him less intent...than we would have him in his studies." Clarke, however, soon had another tutor in mind, and Locke's main concern was that he should follow Locke's principles. "This I think you would do well to discourse beforehand with the person you have under consideration, to see whether he be not superstitiously wedded to the methods he himself was educated in, for from such a man I should not expect much."[28] In fact there is increasing evidence that there were features in Clarke's son's personality which Locke's "method" could not reach. Though Locke would perhaps never fully recognise this, he must nevertheless have been saddened that young Edward's upbringing was not going as smoothly as he might have hoped.

On the last day of the year Locke heard from Pawling that Boyle had died that very day. The news must have saddened him greatly; not only had he seen much of Boyle in the past year, but their friendship went back to Locke's early Oxford days. He was, moreover, carrying on some of Boyle's interests, for his work on the *History of the Air* had stimulated him into again making regular weather observations, often twice and once five times daily. These observations, which he had recommenced in early December, continued into his penultimate year. They were made typically as early as seven in the morning, and frequently as late as midnight, and with a few exceptions Locke missed them only when he was away from Oates (when once, for a period of a month, he got a local rector to do them for him). Over the years his weather station was variously positioned, in his "chamber", "closet", "the large room", the "large chamber", and the "great chamber". Besides general observations of wind, cloud cover, and precipitation, the record consists mainly of readings of his hygroscope, thermometer, and barometer; but the emotional temperature rises twice a year (usually in April and September) when very large, capital letters record the happy arrival and depressing departure of the migrating "SWALLOWS".*[29]

JANUARY–DECEMBER 1692: "YOU WON'T BE WELL IF YOU STAY IN TOWN"[30]

Early in February, Mrs Clarke brought her son to Oates again. His father had not yet got a new tutor, and now agreed that Locke should have sole charge of him for a while. Locke was soon satisfied that Edward "wants not parts", and that his lack of progress was entirely due to "want of application, which as far as I can guess is owing something to a saunteringnesss that is in his temper [and] . . . a good deal to an unsteadiness of mind which is quickly tired with a bookish attention, which he takes no great pleasure in". The boy stayed into April under Locke's care, medical as well as educational, for he suffered for some time from a cough, for which Locke had him bled. Despite Mrs Clarke's "aversion to a tutor", Locke was sure it would be best to have one: "if master has somebody that will constantly drive him, but so as to apply right to his temper by mixing reason and liberty . . . he may be brought to do something, and the principle (which we want) of industry and love of reputation be put into him".[31]

Jonas Proast had not been silenced by Locke's reply in June 1690, and the following April had published (again anonymously) *A Third Letter concerning Toleration*. Locke had been too busy to reply immediately and seems eventually to have decided not to do so at all, since "business" continued to occupy "much of the time my health would allow". But later "some of my friends", he said, "sufficiently satisfied of the weakness of [Proast's] arguments . . . persuaded me [a reply] might be of use to truth". So in March, having had Churchill send him a copy, he re-read Proast's *Third Letter* and began a reply. He was working on this when, towards the end of the month, he was wearying of winter life in rural Essex: "The world goes here as it used to do", he wrote to Mary Clarke, "only that nobody rejoices to find ill, rainy, stormy weather that confines them within doors, when they expected fair sunshine to tempt them abroad into the fields. . . . We have no other diversion here but telling of tales by the fireside; for it is both wet and cold." Perhaps it was due to the lack of any outside activity, such as walking, which he liked when his lungs would allow, that he had recently put on weight, and Carey Mordaunt, who did not "love the loss of shape", urged him to come to Parson's Green to "recover your's here". His coming would do her good too. "Leave your learned lady", she commanded him; "one of those afternoons you have been so liberal of to my lady Masham would dissipate the mist [I am living under] and show me things in their due proportion: pretend no more the bleating of sheep is music to your ears."[32]

Things improved towards the end of April, and Locke was tempted by a spell of fine weather to go to London, where he stayed for eight days. Then, little more than a week into May, he went to Cambridge. Newton had been thinking of inviting him to visit, "now the churlish weather is almost over", and Locke certainly had aimed to see him there, but he had been particularly "drawn thither by business that was very necessary to be dispatched", so he told Clarke. Doubtless this was to fulfil an earlier request from Furly (who at the time was interested in the historical foundation for the sacrament of Communion) to check a certain manuscript version (unique to Cambridge) of Luke's Gospel, for the occurrence of the words "Do this in remembrance of me".[33]

Locke must have spent some of his time with Newton discussing work that the latter had done on the extent to which there were well-attested miracles later than the time of Christ and the Apostles, for the *Third Letter* to Proast on which Locke had begun work a couple of months earlier shows considerable interest in the historicity of miracles. They probably also discussed Boyle's ideas about transmutation, for, besides sharing something of these with Locke, Boyle had also revealed them to Newton. Boyle had never given Locke the samples of "red earth" he had promised, and it was fortunate that Pawling happened to meet a servant of Boyle's who promised to get the earth (though "he fears amongst so many sorts as they have he shall not know the right"), and it seems that Locke soon got some.[*34]

To different extents, Locke and Newton both had notes on various parts of Boyle's process, and Locke told Newton that he "had a mind to prosecute" it; indeed it seemed to Newton that Locke was "persuaded" about the possibility of transmutation into gold. Newton himself had "no opinion of it" and was not inclined to experiment with it. Though he was "satisfied...that mercury, by this recipe, may be brought to change its colours and properties", he did not think "that gold may be multiplied thereby". He eventually said "there is one argument against it which I could never find an answer to" — though he did not say what it was. Yet, despite his skepticism, Newton wanted some of Boyle's earth himself, and was, he told Locke, prepared to "assist you all I can". Locke sent him some of what Pawling had got for him; he also, to replace what Newton had "lost...out of my pocket", sent him copies of the notes he had taken down from Boyle.[35]

Locke stayed only three days in Cambridge, "less time than I could well have spent there, and was very much importuned to", but Lady Masham had wanted him not to go at all because her mother was unwell, and might have needed his advice and assistance.[36]

At Bishop's Stortford, on his way back to Oates, Locke picked up a letter from Clarke who was hoping to consult with him about the health of the Mordaunts' son, who had been ill for some time. Rather surprisingly, Locke was reluctant to involve himself: "my notions in physic are so different from the method which now obtains, that I am like to do little good, and not being of the College [Royal College of Physicians] can make no other figure there but of an unskilful empiric". A few days later Clarke urged Locke to come up to London nevertheless, and this request Locke was not so inclined to refuse. "Any desire of yours, or any of my friends there to bring me to town are not very forwardly resisted by me at any time, and therefore I think I shall come." He was, however, in an indecisive "distracted" mood, apparently having reservations about town yet (after only two weeks) dissatisfactions with the country: "whip me if I can think what I shall do in a crowd, or a smoke. I find my head as little suited to one as my lungs to the other. And I am so morose . . . or moped by a country retirement, that all the world appears a bedlam to me, and a madness to meddle with it."[37]

In the event it was to be another month before he got himself to London, in mid-June. There was some suggestion of accompaning Carey Mordaunt and her aunt to Rotterdam, and it may have been with this in mind that, before leaving Oates, he settled accounts with Sir Francis Masham for his board and noted in shorthand in his journal that his will was with Lady Masham.[38]

Five days later Locke put some finishing touches to his *Third Letter for Toleration to the Author of the Third Letter concerning Toleration*. The next month he sent chapter eight to Newton, hoping he would have the leisure "to read, correct, censure, and send it back" before the week was out; and in late November Churchill sent him a printed copy.[39]

Proast's *Third Letter* had matched Locke's *Second*, not only in length, but also in its *ad hominen* nature, its careful quotations, its painstaking line-by-line dismantling of each argument – and also, it must be said, in its bad-tempered rudeness. Perhaps Proast had been provoked by Locke's marked unwillingness to be charitable and by his reaction to Proast as a fool not to be suffered gladly; certainly Proast sometimes seems bewildered at being subjected to Locke's intense fire.

One of Locke's pervading thoughts throughout this dispute was that Christianity has "a beauty, force, or reasonableness", and so can "shift for itself" and "prevail by its own truth and light": "a religion that is of God wants not the assistance of human authority". He spoke of the mildness and gentleness of the Gospel, "which is apter to use prayers and entreaties, than force, to gain a hearing".[40] Proast's contrasting thought was that Christianity is constantly in danger, requiring some special protection against the weaknesses of the flesh.

Locke's reply was far more systematic than his *Second Letter*. "I have endeavoured to bring the scattered parts of your scheme into some method", he said, "to give a fuller and more distinct view of them." Accordingly, he rehearsed all the points of disagreement. Can "propagating the true religion for the salvation of men's souls" be a concern of the state? From where would the magistrate get the authority to involve himself in such matters? Why should the magistrate be the judge of the correctness of religion? – everyone "must be judge for himself".[41] If failure to consider religious matters deserves punishment (even though the Scriptures say nothing about the need for force in religion), then members of the magistrate's church should be liable too. Exactly what degree of punishment does Proast have in mind?

Noting Proast's insistence that force should be used to bring people only to "the true religion", not to the magistrate's religion, Locke argued, more explicitly than before, that in practice this distinction cannot be made: if the magistrate "be obliged to use force to bring men to the true religion, it will necessarily follow, that every magistrate, who believes his religion to be true, is obliged to use force to bring men to his". A dutiful magistrate can do no more than act on his sincere and considered beliefs, and so since most rulers are of false religions "force will be employed for the promoting of those".[42]

Though much of the *Third Letter* simply repeated Locke's earlier reply to Proast, there are ways in which it moved on. Besides showing an increased interest in the interpretation of specific scriptural passages, he was much concerned with the historical evidence for miracles; the question whether there were miracles later than those of the Apostles is something which he raised at this time with Limborch, and with Le Clerc, and which he had discussed with Newton.[43]

A further development was a sustained concern with the question of religious fundamentals and with what the "true religion" might be. Locke argued that it would be wrong simply to identify Anglicanism as "the true religion", as he believed Proast did, for this would be to suppose that everything "required of one in that communion, is necessary for salvation". Locke's thought was that "the true religion", of which, he said, there is but one, is one "whose doctrine and worship are necessary to salvation". He granted to Proast that this "doctrine and worship" *is* "taught and professed in the Church of England", but argued that this did not mean that its religion is the only true one. For there may be further things required by that church which are *not necessary* for salvation, things which another church "does not receive" even though it also teaches and professes "all that is necessary to salvation". (Locke cited the Athanasian creed and the doctrine of original sin as Anglican teachings which can hardly be necessary for salvation, since many people, such as "ploughmen and milkmaids at church", do not understand them.) So, even if the magistrate, guided by an "infallible certainty", knew that his national church upheld the fundamental doctrines of the Christian religion, he would still have no right to require conformity to it if it also upheld and imposed things which were not necessary.[44]

Christians, who accept the Scriptures as "the word of God and rule of faith", are, Locke said, in possession of "a revelation that contains in it all things necessary to salvation". But not everything they contain is necessary for salvation. It is true that Christ suffered under Pontius Pilate, but believing this is not necessary for salvation (even though it, rather than the equal truth that he was born in Bethlehem, is part of the Apostles' creed). There are many scriptural truths of which someone may be ignorant "without any danger to his salvation".[45]

Scripture also reveals baptism to be necessary: "Christ commanded...to baptize in the name of the Father, the Son, and the Holy Ghost." But this was all he commanded. The use of the cross in baptism (which many dissenters found objectionable) was not part of this command. Such a practice is not ruled out of course; St Paul commanded us to do things "decently", and anyone who sincerely believes that decency requires crossing should be allowed to do it. But it is not *necessary* for salvation and should not be required.[46]

While putting the finishing touches to the *Third Letter* during the summer in London, Locke also busied himself with various matters for his friends. Besides dispatching Syl down the river to Leadenhall Street, to the Bishop's Stortford carrier, with some things ("a parasol, a split bonigrace, six pairs of gloves") that Rabsy Smithsby had bought on his behalf for Lady Masham, he himself went across the river to Lambeth Palace to call on the Archbishop of Canterbury, John Tillotson, on behalf of Limborch who wanted to dedicate his forthcoming history of the Inquisition to him.[47]

On a visit to the Churchills' shop he picked up a recently published book, *Dioptrica Nova. A Treatise of Dioptrics*, which had been sent him there by its author William Molyneux, a Dublin savant with interests in astronomy and optics. In its dedicatory letter to the Royal Society (of which he was a fellow), Molyneux, in speaking of logic, wrote that

to none do we owe for greater advancement in this part of philosophy, than to the incomparable Mr Locke, who, in his *Essay concerning Human Understanding*, has rectified more received mistakes, and delivered more profound truths, established on experience and observation, for the direction of man's mind in the prosecution of knowledge, (which I think may be properly termed Logic) than are to be met with in all the volumes of the ancients.

Locke has, Molyneux wrote, "clearly overthrown all those metaphysical whimsies...whereby they feigned a knowledge where they had none, by making a noise with sounds, without clear and distinct significations". Clearly flattered, Locke wrote to thank Molyneux for his "extraordinary compliment". It had made "great advances of friendship to me" he said – an encouragement which Molyneux received "with all joy imaginable". He had had the "highest esteem" for Locke since he read the *Essay* ("I have not in my life read any book with more satisfaction"), and had been "ambitious of making a friendship with you".[48] So began a warm and open relationship in which Molyneux would prove to be a friend not only to Locke, but also to the *Essay*.

Molyneux had been so taken with the *Essay* that two summers ago he had made inquiries in London as to Locke's other writings: "I was recommended, by some, to *Two Discourses concerning Government*, and a little *Treatise concerning Toleration*. There is neither of them carries your name; and I will not venture to ask you, whether they are yours or not." Locke ignored this discrete invitation to acknowledge his authorship (he coyly said later he thought that saying nothing was "the best way of answering"), but it did not affront him, and he reaffirmed his acceptance of Molyneux's advances of friendship:

You must, therefore, expect to have me live with you hereafter, with all the liberty and assurance of a settled friendship. For meeting with but few men in the world, whose acquaintance I find much reason to covet, I make more than ordinary haste into the familiarity of a rational enquirer after, and lover of truth, whenever I can light on any such.[49]

Locke then made a request which turned out to be of great consequence, and asked for Molyneux's "advice and assistance" about a second edition of the *Essay*. "You have, I perceive, read it over so carefully, more than once, that I know nobody I can more reasonably consult, about the mistakes and defects of it." There were three things in particular about which he wanted an opinion. The "Epistle to the Reader" had acknowledged that he had been "too long upon some points", and that there were "repetitions that by my way of writing had got in". Though he had let these things pass ("but not without advice so to do"), he now wondered whether it would be better to cut out "a great part of that, which cannot but appear superfluous to an intelligent...reader". If Molyneux agreed, perhaps he would, Locke asked, indicate which passages are "fittest to be left out". He wondered also whether there were any mistakes: "deal freely with me...for

I flatter myself that I am so sincere a lover of truth... I count any parcel of this gold not the less to be valued... because I wrought it not out of the mine myself". Finally, Locke wondered whether there were gaps in what he had said, things missing which "belong to my subject" or which need further explanation.[50]

As it happens, Molyneux had already mentioned one thing about which he wished more had been said. He hoped that Locke "would think of obliging the world with A Treatise of Morals, drawn up according to the hints you frequently give... of their being demonstrable, according to the mathematical method.... There is nothing I should more ardently wish for than to see it." In reply, Locke sounded slightly regretting of these hints, but he promised to think about the matter further:

> though by the view I had of moral ideas, whilst I was considering that subject, I thought I saw that morality might be demonstratively made out; yet whether I am able so to make it out, is another question. Everyone could not have demonstrated what Mr Newton's book has shown to be demonstrable; but to show my readiness to obey your commands, I shall not decline the first leisure I can get, to employ some thoughts that way.[51]

Following Boyle's death the executors had appointed Locke and Drs Edmund Dickinson and Daniel Coxe to inspect Boyle's chemical papers. The three met one Saturday in mid-July (when "they took out one box of chemical processes, and spent some hours... but went not through above half of it"), and then again the following Tuesday. Lacking "the key or keys of the chemical terms, without which they could order nothing", it was not easy dealing with these papers which Boyle had written for his own use. But Locke was able to transcribe two that he knew would be of interest to Newton.[52]

During the summer the Treasury at last got round to considering the petition Locke had made two years earlier for payment of salary for the Council of Trade and Plantations. As secretary and treasurer Locke had received some money for incidental running expenses, and the Treasury asked him to give an account of that first, a request which had in fact been first made back in March 1685.[53]

Unfortunately, in working this account out Locke again ran into a disagreeable situation with Stringer. He discovered that he was being charged with £250 more than, so far as he had known, he had ever received. On further investigation he discovered in the Exchequer a signed receipt for this very amount, dated 6 December 1676, paid to

Thomas Stringer as his assignee. Having asked Stringer for his "assistance further to clear up this account", he received a long and testy reply, of a kind which was at least consistent with a guilty conscience. Stringer said that he was in no position to help. Locke should remember, Stringer suggested, that when he had returned from France, Stringer had "delivered with your accounts all the papers... related unto you, or any business I had transacted in your behalf into your hands. And not expecting to be ever examined about it I did not make such memorandums thereof to help a bad memory, as sixteen years after does most necessarily require." Stringer certainly did remember that, having been made Locke's agent, he had on his behalf, as ex-secretary, signed a document which paid £250, not to Locke but to another member of the Council; but this, he said, would be traceable in the papers he had already given him. Locke, who was doubtful that any such papers had ever been passed to him, searched in vain, and asked Stringer to look among his papers: "I fear that if they cannot be produced... somebody or other will be liable to repay this money again." Rightly or wrongly, Stringer, portraying himself as a plain sincere man under attack from someone skilled in the use of innuendo and cunning argument, angrily took this as a veiled threat: "what I wrote before, and intended for a satisfaction to you, is by a fit of the spleen and a new way of arguing strained to be a charge upon myself".[54] How matters were resolved between Locke and Stringer is not known, but Locke continued to work on the account.

In mid-August Locke set out for Oates. As the coach was passing through Epping Forest there was an encounter with a group of highwaymen. Young Francis in particular must have been glad to see him back unscathed, for the previous month he had most charmingly written, "Dear Mr Locke, I long till you come down. I should be very glad to see you for I love you mightily. I desire you to come and teach me some Longitude. I am afraid you won't be well if you stay in town."[55]

Locke spent just over three weeks in the country before again going to London, a "very fair" day, he recorded before setting out. A few days later, when he happened to be at Whitehall, there was an earthquake. Naturally he recorded the details: it "was observed by my watch to be about five minutes past two in the afternoon [and] by the Queen's pendulum which the shake of the Earth made stand still just at two of the clock and by Mr Tompion's less than a minute before two which agrees well enough with my watch. For adding to the pendulum the equation of the 8th September which is six minutes the time of day will fall about five minutes past two pm." Locke heard that (though "not at all" in Dublin) the earthquake had also been felt in Bristol, Rotterdam, and Cologne, and speculated that "if there could be found people, that in the whole extent of it, did by well-adjusted clocks exactly observe the time, one might see whether it were all one shock, or proceeded gradually from one place to another".[56] Perhaps not exactly one of the possibilities Locke had in mind, an earthquake proceeds by rippling out from an epicentre.

In mid-October Locke returned to Oates, the past six weeks in London having been at some cost to his health. Being at the mercy of ill-health was clearly something which depressed him: "it be one of the inconveniencies I suffer from my ill lungs that they usually drive me out of town when most of my friends and those whom I would wish to be near are in it".[57]

His leaving town on this occasion precipitated an unpleasant personal episode, and one which, like the earlier ones with Stringer and because of Locke's forensic tenacity, developed into baroque complexity. This time it was with John Norris, a man who, a couple of years earlier, had published some criticisms of the *Essay*, *Cursory Reflections upon a book called An Essay concerning Human Understanding*. Norris had dedicated two other of his books to Damaris Masham, and it was perhaps as a favour to her (for she certainly seems to have taken interest if not pleasure in it) that earlier this year Locke had used his influence with Pembroke to give Norris one of his clerical livings, the rectory of Bemerton near Salisbury.[58]

On 15 October (after a visit to Lady Masham at Oates) Norris arrived in London, having in his possession a (now lost) letter from her for Locke. The letter was delivered to Locke's lodgings, not by Norris himself but by an employee of his publishers, on Thursday 20 October, two days after Locke had gone back to Oates. It had been opened before it arrived at Pawling's ("cracked" as his maid noted), and Pawling firmly believed that Norris had been "peeping" into it: "god deliver me from such proud clergymen. They are not fit for human society, unsavoury salt, etc." He also thought Norris had purposely delayed delivery until after Locke had left. "His design was to look into it and therefore would not send it till Mr Locke was gone, and now he thinks I or some of my family may bear the odium of it, but he is entangled and can't wipe off the reproach from himself." Martha Lockhart thought Pawling was being too severe and that Norris's motives for the intrusion (which she did not doubt) would not have been completely disreputable: "I believe what he did, was out of a very good design, that he might take an occasion to advise you both* as to some matters that he expected to find in it."[59]

At Locke's request, Pawling made detailed inquiries from Norris's publisher; "here is exactly what you aimed at and desired to know", he reported back: "Mr Norris went out of town on Friday October 21; he delivered the letter to Mr Manship [the publisher] the Thursday being the day before; that same day Mr Manship brought the letter and left it with the maid; which exactly agrees with our account, for Mary received it on Thursday October 20." Unfortunately we do not have the angry letter Locke wrote to Norris, but Norris's reply accused him of going off at half-cock: "I am sorry to see a person of your real sense and seeming civility make such haste to express a resentment upon so doubtful an occasion. I am less concerned upon my own account, because I apprehend myself to be in very little, if any fault." Perhaps without mentioning that the letter was open when it got to Pawling's, and without reporting what Pawling had been told by Manship, Locke must have asked Norris why he had not delivered it earlier and why he had committed the effrontery of leaving it with a third party to deliver. Norris replied that, having arrived in London on Friday 15 October, he had not had the letter sent the next day because he had intended to call round with it himself the following Monday; but other business intervened, he said, and "being to go out of town the Wednesday following" (i.e. 19 October), and therefore busy preparing for his journey, he left the letter with Manship on the Tuesday (i.e. 18 October), who promised that he personally would deliver it the next day. "What could I do more or better?", he asked Locke; "there was no care, nor respect wanting on my part." "I am so little sensible of anything I have done justly to deserve your [displeasure]", Norris concluded, "that I must think you less a philosopher, less a gentleman, and less a Christian than I have hitherto taken you for, if upon this account you continue to have any resentment."[60]

Given the conflict between Norris's saying that he was "being about to go out of town" on Wednesday the 19th, and Pawling's information that he left on Friday the 21st, Locke did not believe Norris: "the gentleman went not out of town Wednesday as he pretends", he said to Clarke. His reply to Norris was therefore surely merely a pretence at amelioration, one which perhaps even hid a desire to have Norris perjure himself. "To show you how forward I am to acquiesce in what

gives you ground to ask 'what could you do more or better?' which is all
built upon your going out of town Wednesday", Locke said, he would
accept Norris's explicit word on it "that you went out of town that
Wednesday you speak of so willing am I not to lose your good word or
opinion you shall not find any reason to 'think me less a philosopher
less a gent or less a christian than you have hitherto taken me for' if
a due acknowledgement to you may preserve me that reputation with
you".[61]

Unfortunately this reply was mislaid, leading Norris to complain that
Locke had rudely failed to tell him whether or not he was satisfied.
Locke had to send him a copy, and it was not until the end of the
following February that Norris replied. Somewhat starchily, he said
"I am glad to find in you any tendency towards a reconciliation, but
wonder you should be so straight in the terms of it as to put it all upon
my going out of town precisely on that Wednesday". Moreover, he
retorted, "my plea was not built (as you will have it) upon my actual
going that very day, but upon my 'being' to go". On the Tuesday, he
said, when he gave the letter to Manship, he *was* going to leave town the
next day, but, as it turned out, he did not go until the Friday (on the
Tuesday evening he learnt that his wife had arranged to stay till then).
"If this will satisfy you, well and good, but if not, I have no more to
say."[62] It seems unlikely that Locke was satisfied given that, apart from
anything else, he thought Norris had opened the letter.

Perhaps provoked by this disagreement and by the recent
appearance of a second edition of *Cursory Reflections*, Locke turned
his thoughts to what Norris had said against the *Essay*, and wrote
upwards of a thousand words in "Answer to Mr Norris". Like Furly,
who had read the *Cursory Reflections* in its first edition of 1690, Locke
found nothing in what Norris had said about his account of the origin
of ideas, and dwelt on Norris's uncharitable and unconstructive
approach: with "the privilege of a cursory reflector" he does not take
things in their context but "takes notice of or passes by what he
pleases"; he is not "willing to understand what the author intends";
he is not prepared to read an author's words "in the most favourable
and most consistent meaning".[63]

In November, Popple thought that Locke might, in his absence from
it, be interested in the progress of the discussion club they had formed
three years earlier. It had four new members, he told him, and outlined
the last of the subjects they had discussed: given that "God has given
some general and uniform rule, or at least one same way of knowing

his will", what is that rule? Having "dispatched" that question they were, next time, to consider "of what weight or authority that general rule is in comparison with any other particular pretended or real rule". Given "how unequal our shoulders are to such burdens", Popple hoped that Locke would be "so charitable as to let us have your assistance".[64]

Some weeks later Popple wrote again about the club, Locke's "off spring". It "requires a little of your care. Nay I am inclined to say it deserves it. It is a hopeful child, and now grows apace: and, what is more, it is pretty towardly. So that it is a great pity you should let it grow out of your knowledge, and leave it destitute of your further instructions"; a few weeks later he told him of yet more new members.[65]

After a month back at Oates (even though it was one of rain, fog, hard frost, and snow) Locke felt well enough for London. But yet again it proved to have been a mistake to have gone. After just one day he could hardly breathe. "The malady continually increased upon me, till I was quickly driven away from town, though to the inconvenience of neglecting all my affairs there." He was able to carry out his initial purpose in going – to deliver Limborch's now published history of the Inquisition to the its dedicatee, the Archbishop of Canterbury. But he had to leave unfinished his review of the sheets of Boyle's *History of the Air*, which was at last going through the press. Delay to Boyle's book was becoming an annual event for it had, of course, been about to go to the printers exactly twelve months earlier, when again Locke's health had forced him out of London.[66]

The *History* came out in December. "I think the very design of it will please you", he told Molyneux when he sent him a copy.

It is cast into a method that anyone who pleases may add to it...as his reading or observation shall furnish him with matter of fact. If such men as you are, curious and knowing, would join to what Mr Boyle had collected and prepared...we might hope, in some time, to have a considerable history of the air, than which I scarce know any part of natural philosophy would yield more variety and use.

(He himself contributed to it not only his weather "register" but also a letter on the barometer he had sent Boyle in 1666 at the time of his abortive attempt to record the air pressure in the Mendip mines.)[67]

Locke had lasted little more than a week in London, but he recovered just as quickly; after only a couple of days back at Oates, though his cough was still troublesome his "lungs move easier than they did". There was more improvement during December and, as Tyrrell remarked, this confirms that "experiment that you have so often tried at your own cost, that this town is no safe place for you in winter".[68]

Towards the end of December there was some answer from Molyneux about the *Essay*. He was rather oleaginous about the worry that it was too long and perhaps required some editing: "the same judicious hand, that first formed it, is best able to reform it.... I never quarrelled with a book for being too prolix, especially where the prolixity is pleasant, and tends to the illustration of the matter in hand, as I am sure yours always does." But he did make three or four positive, though brief, suggestions, one of which was that more needed to be said "about man's liberty and necessity" (as at E: 2.21.7–47). "This thread", said Molyneux, "seems so wonderfully fine spun in your book, that, at last, the great question of liberty and necessity seems to vanish. And herein you seem to make all sins to proceed from our under-standings... and not at all from the depravity of our wills." Molyneux was not alone in having some dissatisfaction about Locke's treatment of human liberty, for one of his acquaintances, William King, the Bishop of Derry, had some too.[69]

Locke was not surprised that Molyneux found what he had said about liberty "a little too fine spun". It was not a subject he had really expected to go into when he first thought about the question of the power of the will, and it was only at the insistence of "some of my friends" that he kept it in.[70]

At any rate in its first stage it does rather seem that "the great question" of whether humans have free will and can be held responsible for their actions was made to vanish. For Locke began by arguing that the question whether the will is free is not a proper one: "it is as insignificant to ask, whether man's will be free, as to ask, whether ... his virtue [is] square"; the will, he argued against some then-current thinking, is not a faculty with its own powers, not a "distinct agent". We can, however, ask whether "a man is free", and Locke's answer here was that sometimes we are and sometimes we are not. Freedom consists in being able to act "according as we shall choose or will". So someone has freedom not to jump over a cliff because he has it in his power not to jump; at least, he has such freedom and his not jumping would be voluntary, so long as paralysis or some external physical restraint would not have prevented him from jumping anyway. But it was not because he thought Locke had reduced the "great question" of freedom and moral responsibility to the question of whether or not we are subject to some kind of physical compulsion or constraint, that Molyneux was led to speak of its having been made to vanish; this was not the end of Locke's story. For Locke allowed that our will or choice or preference (for example, not to jump over the cliff) "is determined by something without itself". It is, though (and he was adamant about this), not determined by a prior act of will, for this would simply unfold into an infinite regress: we would be willing to will to . . . will not to jump. But he neglected a possibility which William King raised, namely that there is *no* determining antecedent to the original act of will which "proceeds merely from the active power of the soul, without anything from without determining it" – in other words, that we simply will not to jump. Locke's view was that our choice, our preference, our act of will, is determined by our thinking that not jumping is a greater good than jumping, good being what affords pleasure rather than pain, and hence what conduces to our happiness. "Good, then, the greater good, is that alone which determines the will." Though a "libertarian" of King's kind might disagree with him, for Locke it was not an imperfection in us to be determined in this way. It would, he said, be an even greater imperfection if we were indifferent as between the consequences of not jumping or jumping. (King's view about that was that something is said to be good because we have chosen it, rather than that we choose or prefer it because it is good.)[71]

Though he raised no objection to most of what Locke had said, it was at this last point that Molyneux thought the "great question" of liberty and necessity had vanished. Locke, Molyneux said, was making "all sins to proceed from our understandings", as though we do the wrong thing simply because we have misjudged. Yet surely, he thought, there are occasions when our wrongdoing stems "from the depravity of our wills"; there are times when, despite knowing full well what it would be right to do, we nevertheless fail to do it, due to some weakness or depravity of will.[72]

JANUARY–DECEMBER 1693: "IT WERE BETTER IF YOU WERE DEAD"[73]

Clarke was at Oates in early January. He had been helping with the account of Council of Trade expenses that Locke was required to prepare for the Treasury and brought with him a draft to work on. He also brought a recent anonymously published pamphlet,

For Encouraging the Coining of Silver Money in England. This had been written to support a bill introduced the previous month which proposed to stop the exportation of silver and to attract it in for coinage by increasing the Mint price by something over 3 per cent to the current market price; the proposal would have entailed a corresponding reduction in the silver content of new coins, and so a devaluation. For tactical reasons Locke had not been inclined to write against the bill, but decided to do so against the pamphlet, perhaps because its last paragraph made some criticism of his *Some Considerations.* Towards the end of January he set to work writing a short piece. He completed it in four days, and immediately sent it to Clarke telling him to make of it "what use ... in what manner you think fit"; in fact the bill was already coming to nothing, and the piece remained unpublished for some time.[74]

The author of the pamphlet was probably Thomas Neale who, as Master of the Mint, Locke sarcastically pointed out, would gain personally by any recoinage. Locke considered each of its points, arguing, for example, that bullion left the country rather than being attracted to the Mint for coinage because of adverse overseas trade balances. He also denied that uncoined silver was worth more than coined. This claim of Neale's was specifically aimed against Locke's *Considerations,* one of whose foundations was that silver was the measure of value, so that whether as bullion or stamped as coin, one ounce of silver must be worth any other ounce of silver; coin, that is, has its value from the quantity of silver in it and not "from the stamp and denomination". Locke recognised that merchants who needed bullion for their overseas payments would pay more for silver than would the Mint, but he held that they (unlike the Mint) would make this payment only in lightweight, clipped coin.[75]

Though he had forebodings about its stifling smoke, Locke was expecting soon to be in London. Shortly after he arrived in early February he was "bidden" to visit the Archbishop of Canterbury to pick up a letter and a book of sermons for Limborch. Tillotson, so Locke was able to report to Limborch, was full of praise for him and his book about the history of the Inquisition. He was also busy with the small stuff of life: he got copies of the just published *Third Letter for Toleration*; picked up some books from Furly; collected from Mrs Smithsby some more gloves for Lady Masham and for himself, together with three flannel shirts and two holland caps; and paid for a cloth hat and for the "scouring" of his beaver hat.[76]

But a main purpose of his visit must have been to swear to, and then to submit for audit, the account that he and Clarke had prepared for the Treasury. Aside from the unpaid salary, Locke was personally out of pocket by £64 os 6d in incidental expenses (some of which were incurred in getting the account passed), and he had, no doubt to his annoyance, to petition the Treasury again for this further money. This was paid him the next year; but he was not, or not immediately, paid the arrears of his salary for in September 1695 he would, yet again, petition the Treasury, for £750 in respect of eighteen months' salary.[77]

Locke had not planned to stay long in London and went back to Oates after eleven days (even so the visit was at some cost to his breathing). He narrowly missed Thomas Bassett, the publisher of the *Essay* who called at his lodgings. It was time for a second edition, for the first had nearly sold out, and Bassett needed some alterations and additions that Locke had showed him earlier. With Molyneux's considerable help Locke had worked on these since the previous autumn, his new friend having sent him lists of typographical errors and suggestions, very often of an editorial nature. He also suggested to him what he called "a jocose problem". This, which has become known as "Molyneux's problem", asked whether a man blind from birth, but able to distinguish a sphere from a cube by touch, could distinguish them by sight if he were made to see. In fact Molyneux had already sent this problem some years earlier to the *Bibliothèque Universelle*, just after it had published the *Abrégé* of the *Essay*. It had been ignored then, but this time Locke took it up, in the new edition (with the result that it attracted much attention in the next century).[78]

One thing he had been thinking of adding, "though not fully resolved" about it (so he told Molyneux in March), was a new chapter on "Malebranche's hypothesis of seeing all things in God". This chapter would have been based on some work Locke had been doing on Norris and on Malebranche. In continuation of the short piece he had written the previous year about Norris, Locke had turned his attention to Malebranche, whom Norris acknowledged as the source for his views about the origin of ideas. The result of this was a manuscript,* endorsed "JL. Of Seeing all things in God 1693", which discussed various aspects of Malebranche's *Recherche de la Vérité*. He continued this not long afterwards with "some other loose thoughts which I set down as they came in my way in a hasty perusal of some of Mr Norris's writings, to be better digested when I shall have leisure to make an end of this argument".[79]

Locke was inclined to think that ideas are produced in our minds by motions in our sensory organs caused by the objects we perceive. He also thought this solved a problem (which Malebranche had found with a somewhat similar causal theory) as to how we can see things at a distance, things which are not in direct contact with our eyes. Why not suppose, he said, "that from remote objects material causes may reach our senses, and therein produce several motions that may be the causes of ideas in us". But he acknowledged that we have no understanding of exactly how *bodily* motions produce *mental* ideas. "Impressions made on the retina by rays of light... and motions from thence continued to the brain", all of that may easily be conceived, he thought; and, he was persuaded, these motions really do produce ideas in our minds. But exactly how they do he could not say: the manner of production is "to me incomprehensible"; "I can resolve [it] only into the good pleasure of God, whose ways are past finding out".[80]

On consideration, however, he saw that Malebranche's theory contained an exactly parallel difficulty. According to Malebranche, we do not perceive material things directly since, being extended, they cannot be united to the soul; rather we perceive them indirectly, we "see them in God", with whom our souls are united: God "shows" or "discovers" ideas of material things to us when we are "in the presence of" those things. But this tells us no more than does the causal view that ideas "are by the appointment of God produced in the mind by certain motions of our bodies, to which our minds are united". That suggested explanation may be incomplete, but it is no worse than what Malebranche confidently asserted. The hypothesis to which Locke was inclined, that "God has made our souls so, and so united them to our bodies, that, upon certain motions made in our bodies by external objects, the soul should have such or such perceptions or ideas, though in a way inconceiveable to us", seems, he thought, "as true and as instructive" as what Malebranche held. Malebranche's assertion that we see our ideas "in God" is no improvement on saying that they are produced in our minds by bodily motions by a law established by God. In both cases I have ideas, and in both cases God is the primary cause of my having them.[81]

According to the view to which Locke inclined, material bodies are real or efficient causes at the beginning of a chain of motion which eventually leads, via our sense organs, to ideas in the mind; according to Malebranche they are merely what he called "secondary" or "occasional" causes, they are what "occasion" God to "exhibit" ideas to us: "God shows us the ideas in himself, on occasion of the presence of those bodies to our senses." Locke asked why, on this theory of occasionalism, there was any need for our sensory organs to be so complex: if perception "depended on nothing but the presence of the object affording an occasional cause to God Almighty to exhibit to the mind the ideas of [that object] all that nice and curious structure of those organs is wholly in vain".[82]

The answer, of course, is that that structure is no less necessary for perception in a system of occasional causes than it is in one of real causes. Without its structure an eye would just not play the same part in the causal system, irrespective of that system being one of efficient or of secondary causes. And though Locke did not explicitly recognise this, it seems to be implicit in his questioning of the belief which Norris took over from Malebranche, that the reason why material bodies and motions in them are only secondary causes or occasions for God to act is that they are passive and have no power. Evidently, he pointed out, they have the power to act on God! Occasionalism involves, Locke argued, accepting that God has given "motion in the optic nerve a power to operate on himself" but yet "cannot give it a power to operate on the mind of man". As Locke in the end came to see, the acceptability or otherwise of Malebranche's theory depends solely on rather general considerations: does God need to be the only thing with power in order to be all powerful? Surely God himself lacks power if he can give none to the things he creates: "this is to set very narrow bounds to the power of God, and, by pretending to extend it, takes it away".[83]

Towards the end, Locke's remarks on Norris became increasingly sketchy and he concluded that "the finishing of these hasty thoughts must be deferred to another season".[84] But he never did "have leisure to make an end of this argument" with Norris. He would never include a chapter on Malebranche's "Opinion of seeing all things in God" in any edition of the *Essay*, and would leave it to his executor to decide whether these papers were worth posthumous publication.

Besides a second edition of the *Essay* there was another work which, at the instance of "some of my acquaintances", Locke was thinking about, if not already working on: putting together and arranging for publication all the directions on education that he had sent Clarke over the years from 1684. He had finished this in early March, and by the end of the month it had gone to the printers. Even at that late stage he

was undecided whether he would put his name to it, and in the event
he did not, though a further edition two years later acknowledged the
book as his. *Some Thoughts concerning Education* was published in July,
and Clarke, to whom Locke had naturally dedicated it, soon received
a copy. "The printing of the book", Clarke said, "is certainly a great
service to the public and a particular obligation on all...parents of
children." Molyneux (who had been looking forward to it for use with
his four-year-old child) was sent a copy too. As might have been
expected, he was full of praise, but had some question about Locke's
saying that "a child should never be suffered to have what he craves, or
so much as speaks for, much less if he cries for it". He realised that what
Locke had ruled out was the satisfaction of arbitrary "wants of fancy",
not reasonable "wants of nature", but said he knew of others who had
"stumbled" at the passage. Perhaps it was because of Locke's general
doctrine that desires should be trained and educated by reason that
Tyrrell thought Locke was right not to have put his name to the book,
for "you must expect to find all fond mothers...enemies to your
method".[85]

In late March, Mordaunt was hoping that Locke would be coming
to town, and, offering his coach for the purpose, suggested he come
from Oates direct to Parson's Green ("there is a little philosophical
apartment quite finished in the garden that expects you"); but just
the day before (one of thick fog) Locke had taken the public coach, and
he was already in London. As usual, his health "paid so dear
for...being in town", and he returned to Oates within a month. One
of Sir Francis Masham's relations suggested he should have gone to visit
her instead, just southwest of London. She wished that "instead of
taking a longer journey you would have tried Battersea where you
should have found a hearty welcome though worse company. It is now
very sweet with woodbines and bean blossoms the natural perfumes of
the season." But spring was evident at Oates too: the swallows had
arrived while he had been away, and the garden was ready for the
things he had bought in London: a dozen tuberose roots, some
Spanish broom seed, together with various tools such as a hatchet and
a grafting saw.[86]

In early May, Syl collected Popple and Lord Ashley from the coach at
Harlow, for a visit which had been on the cards for about two months.
With Locke and Lady Masham they spent some of the time during the
four days they were there in philosophical discussion. One of their
conversations concerned whether the imagination, in some unknown

way, is able to communicate thoughts; but the general theme of their discussions was the possibility of plain teaching in religion as opposed to the obfuscations of the clergy.[87]

The following week Locke went to town again. He had, he told Limborch, been "called" there, and said that "the compulsion of affairs, or at least something like affairs, keeps me so busy that time to send you a greeting is scarcely allowed me". It is not clear what "affairs" had called and now occupied him – perhaps he was seeing his *Thoughts concerning Education* through the press – but they did leave time for some shopping (books, some silver gilt sweetmeat spoons, knives, and forks, a hat and some worsted stockings, and a shagreen table book for Mrs Guenellon) and time to look out some of Boyle's manuscripts for possible publication.[88]

Through showers of rain, he went back to Oates nearly two weeks later, but he did not stay long, and after only eight days he was up at six to record the weather (having last done so only six hours previously) and, in the "dim sunshine", to catch the London coach. One of his tasks during the next week was to arrange for approaching two tons of belongings (more than twenty boxes of books and other items such as chairs and a table) to go from London to Oates.[89]

By this time, in response to Molyneux's earlier criticisms, Locke had worked out some radical changes to the chapter on "Power" for the second edition of the *Essay*. He had "got into a new view of things", one which, "if I mistake not, will satisfy you". He gave Molyneux "a short scheme" of the changes by listing the headings of some new sections, but, as Molyneux replied, "I dare not venture, upon those short hints you give me, to pass my opinion". The most obvious and basic feature of Locke's "new view" of what determines the will was that he now denied that it is determined by a *belief*, or understanding about what is good, and argued that it is determined by a *feeling*. Like many other people, he said, "I took it for granted" that "good, the greater good, ... apprehended and acknowledged to be so" determines the will; whereas, he now had come to see, our apprehension and belief about the good does not determine the will "until our desire, raised proportionably to it, makes us uneasy in the want of it":

Let a man be never so well persuaded of the advantages of virtue, that it is as necessary to man who has any great aims in this world, or hopes in the next as food to life: yet till he 'hungers and thirsts after righteousness'; till he feels an uneasiness in the want of it, his will will not be determined to any action in pursuit of this confessed greater good.

Locke used this idea, that what moves and determines the will is
a feeling of uneasiness, a desire for some absent good, to take account
of Molyneux's earlier objection that he had made immoral actions
depend on failures of the understanding, and to find a place for
weakness or depravity of will. He gave the example of a drunkard who
knows full well that he is endangering his health, but who nevertheless
continues to join his drinking companions. He "sees, and acknowledges" what is best, and "in the intervals of his drinking hours, will take
resolutions". But when "the uneasiness to miss his accustomed delight
returns, the greater acknowledged good loses its hold, and the present
uneasiness determines the will" to drinking.[90]

Locke certainly gave a reasonable description here of a weak-willed
person, but it is not clear that *even as a description* it is one which his
"new view" can allow. If that view were simply that beliefs are one thing
and desires quite another (i.e. that beliefs in no way determine the
will, and that what moves it are desires), there would be no question
but that we could act against our beliefs. But though Locke now
thought that feelings and not beliefs are what move the will, he did not
hold that there was no connection between beliefs and feelings, or
between beliefs and the will. It was not that beliefs played no part in his
"new view" and were quite disconnected from the will, for even the
drunkard's *belief* in the acknowledged good was said to "lose its hold"
on the will. Similarly, Locke talked of our desire being "moved by" our
beliefs. With the interposition of desire between belief and the will it
cannot be, as previously, that belief *directly* "determines" the will, but if,
as Locke said, it still is what "ultimately determines", then it was not
clear why Molyneux, with his objection about weakness of will, should
find this "new view" any better than the old.[91]

There is a further complication (or, perhaps, a contradiction, as
one of Locke's correspondents, one John Jackman, suspected) in the
question of the exact relation, on Locke's new view, between belief and
the will. Despite earlier protestations to the contrary, Locke said that
"there is a case wherein a man is at liberty in respect of willing". He
said that someone can "suspend the act of his choice from being
determined for or against the thing proposed, till he has examined
whether it really be of a nature in itself and consequences to make
him happy or no". This case, which involved our ability to suspend the
determination of our will by our desires in order to examine things
more carefully, was not a stray or exceptionable one. Locke said that
it involves "the hinge upon which turns the liberty of intellectual

beings", and stressed that it is our duty as rational beings to exercise this ability.[92]

After working on the chapter on "Power", Locke continued to busy himself with revisions to the *Essay*, and by the end of August it was "now very near ready". He had, in particular, got round to taking up Molyneux's earlier suggestion that more was needed about the so-called "principium individuationis", the principle by which different things of the same kind have their self-identity, for all Locke had, so far and in passing, said, was that personal identity could not require an unchanging body. The result was a whole new chapter, "Of identity and diversity".[93]

The idea of identity, Locke said, is formed by "considering anything as existing at any determined time and place [and] compar[ing] it with itself at another time". But it is crucial, he said, to see that in making such comparisons identity is relative to the kind of thing we are considering: while the identity of a mass of certain atoms would not survive a change of its parts, "a colt grown up to a horse, sometimes fat, sometimes lean, is all the while the same horse". Given that, Locke's main focus in the chapter was the identity of *persons*, and what he said was essentially a development of a short journal note he had made over ten years earlier.[94]

His strategy in the new chapter was to build on an initial account of the identity of living animals, by way of a distinction between the same *man* and the same *person*. As just noted, the identity of an animal does not depend on its having a body made up of the same particles of matter. What it does depend on derives from the definition of an animal, which is "a living organized body": the same animal, therefore, "is the same continued life commmunicated to different particles of matter, as they happen successively to be united to that organised living body". The same goes, Locke suggested, for the identity of a man, a man being "an animal of a certain form". It too consists "in nothing but a participation of the same continued life, by constantly fleeting particles of matter, in succession vitally united to the same organized body". It is a noteworthy characteristic of these accounts that the identity of an animal or a man does not depend on the identity of some substance such as its body. The body of a man when young is a different object from that when he is old, but it is the same man: the man is the "continued life" carried, as it were, by ever changing matter.[95]

The identity of a *person* also derives from the relevant definition, and it consists in something analogous to a "continued life", namely a continued self-consciousness. A person "is a thinking intelligent being, that has reason and reflection, and can consider itself as itself, the same thinking thing in different times and places". "As far as any intelligent being can repeat the idea of any past action with the same consciousness it had of it at first, and with the same consciousness it has of any present action; so far it is the same personal self."[96]

Locke was keen to stress that the identity of a person (like that of a man or animal) is not, or does not depend on, that of a continuing substance. "Personal identity consists, not in the identity of substance, but...in the identity of consciousness." It is perfectly possible that the "continued consciousness" which is a person, is "carried" by a succession of different substances, whether material or immaterial. He added, however (though he gave no reason for saying it), that the probability is that "this consciousness is annexed to, and the affection of one individual immaterial substance".[97]

One strand in Locke's discussion related to moral responsibility: in personal identity is "founded all the right and justice of reward and punishment". "Person", he said, is a "forensic term appropriating actions and their merit; and so belongs only to intelligent agents capable of a law, and of happiness and misery". In support of this he pointed out that a man who has recovered his sanity is not punished for what he did when mad, for he was "not himself". But why, then, he asked against himself, are people held responsible for what they do when drunk, or when sleepwalking, even if they were not later conscious of what they had done? It is, he said, because we cannot be sure that they really cannot remember what they did earlier. On the Judgement Day, however, the "secrets of all hearts shall be laid open" and we may be sure that God will not make people answer for what they genuinely know nothing of.[98]

Molyneux's reaction to Locke's new chapter was typical: "everything you write therein is delivered with such convincing reason, that I fully assent to all". Three months later, however, "one thought suggested itself to me, which on my first reading did not occur". He thought Locke had mischaracterised, or at least not fully specified, the reason why the drunkard is punished. He had made nothing of the fact that drunkenness, unlike sleepwalking, is both a deliberate and an unlawful act, so that, even if the drunkard really did not remember what he had done, he should still be punished for it. In reply, Locke acknowledged that "drunkenness being a crime, one crime cannot be alledged in excuse for another", but suggested that this was not really relevant to his point (and, on the face of it, actually went against it, if it showed that a man *could* be punished for something that it was agreed he was no longer conscious of). Molyneux's point that any "criminal action infects the consequences of it" (as in an example he gave of a poacher shooting someone accidentally) had nothing to with consciousness.[99]

Locke's account of personal identity as constituted by a continuity of consciousness has formed the basis for most discussions of the topic ever since. It has been harder pressed than it was by Molyneux, and has been revealed to have vaguenesses and weaknesses (which sympathetic readers have tried to deal with in various ways). Surely it is possible for me to be apparently conscious of, to seem to remember, something I did in fact not do, or, conversely (as possibly in the case of the drunkard), to have forgotten something I did do. But this distinction between real and apparent memories seems to involve a distinction between an action's being mine and my being conscious of it being mine, and this is ruled out if, as Locke held, a continuing person *is constituted by* his memories. Furthermore, a paradox arises if we suppose (along with George Berkeley and Thomas Reid in the eighteenth century) a person who can remember what he did in middle age, but who since middle age has forgotten what he did as a boy. It would follow on Locke's account that the elderly person is not the same as the boy, even though he is same as the middle-aged person, who in his turn *is* the same as the boy.

In September, Locke had a strikingly sad and apologetic letter from Newton ("your most humble and unfortunate servant"). The background to it is not clear, but some time earlier Newton had been told that Locke was "sickly and would not live", and had answered, so he now said, "it were better if you were dead". This "uncharitabless", for which Newton now begged pardon, arose from a curious mixture of "hard thoughts" which he had entertained about Locke. Besides thinking (and putting it about) that Locke had "struck at the root of morality" in denying innate ideas in the *Essay*, he had believed that Locke not only had dealt badly with him in connection with some official employment, but also had "endeavoured to embroil me with women". Besides having "hard thoughts" about Locke, Newton had been equally paranoid about Samuel Pepys, supposing him to have accused Newton of using his name to gain some advancement. In fact Newton had, he told Pepys, been in a highly disturbed state for the past year. Recently indeed, as he told Locke, he "had not slept an hour a night for a fortnight together, and for five nights together not a wink". Locke's draft reply to this sad letter is gentle and forgiving in the extreme:

I have been, ever since I first knew you, so entirely and sincerely your friend, and thought you so much mine, that I could not have believed what you tell me of yourself, had I had it from anybody else. And though I cannot but be mightily troubled that you should have had so many wrong and unjust thoughts of me...I receive your acknowledgement of the contrary as the kindest thing you could have done me, since it gives me hopes that I have not lost a friend I so much valued.... I wish for nothing more than the opportunities to convince you that I truly love and esteem you.... To confirm this to you more fully I should be glad to meet you anywhere.[100]

Locke saw no need to defend himself: "after what your letter expresses, I shall not need to say anything to justify myself to you". It is, of course, quite conceivable that he should have taken part in some discussion vis-à-vis Newton* and some official post (he had done so two years earlier and did again later), but it is hard to imagine him even thinking, leave alone "endeavouring", to "embroil him with women". The remark about innate ideas, however, gave him some concern: "my book is going to the press for a second edition and...I should take it as a favour, if you would point out to me the places that gave occasion to that censure".[101]

Over the summer and into the autumn Locke's health had been good, so much so that it seems not to have suffered any set-back during the six weeks he spent in London in November and December. Congratulating him on the strength of his lungs, Thomas hoped his time there had to do with "other than public affairs which cannot deserve it". How much public affairs, such as the Commission for Appeals, did take up Locke's time we do not know (though he certainly met with at least one of his fellow Commissioners, who informed him that their salaries were being wrongly taxed); we do know, though, that, closer to his heart, he made arrangements for the production of the second edition of the *Essay*. Besides leaving Popple with the final text for delivery to the printer, he had Syl pick up and make a final payment for an engraving he had commissioned the previous June for use as a frontispiece; this time there had been no problem about getting the original for the engraver to work from — a drawing of Locke which Syl himself had done.[102]

JANUARY–DECEMBER 1694: "DISCOURSE ON MATTERS OF
IMPORTANCE"[103]

Francis van Helmont, whom he had met in Rotterdam in 1686, was
with him when Locke returned to Oates just a few days before
Christmas. Helmont had already visited Oates (lodging at the Crown
in Harlow), having been in England for some months. This time he
stayed until mid-April, when he returned to London on his way home
to Rotterdam. Locke was busy with the second editions of both the
Treatises and the *Essay*, but the many iron and earthen crucibles, and
other equipment such as tiles, pulleys, and tongues that Locke had
sent from London in January and February, were possibly for experiments he and van Helmont were conducting. The gallon of rapeseed
oil that he also had delivered was perhaps for some plan for lighting
Oates, for he had recently made inquiries about the lamps which were
being introduced in the London streets, and had found that this was
what they burned.[104]

Towards the end of April, a few days after saying goodbye to van
Helmont, and during an unseasonal spell of beautiful cloudless
weather, Locke went to London. A couple of days later the royal
assent was given to a Parliamentary bill which gave birth to a national
bank whose aim was to capitalise on future government revenues, by
issuing promissory notes. Locke was against this institution of the Bank
of England, partly because of the political danger in affording the
monarch a means of getting money independently of Parliament, and
partly because of the possibility that the Bank might get a monopoly
over the money supply. But, presented with the Bank as a fact, Locke
was not averse to becoming a subscriber, making an investment of
£500.[105]

In May, the second edition of the *Essay* was on sale. In what
Samuel Pepys thought was "a useful sample [= precedent] for future
reprinters", also available were loose printed sheets of all the
alterations and additions, to be inserted into copies of the first edition.
This would, Locke commented to Molyneux (and presumably having in
mind that the sheets were free), make copies of the first edition "useful
to any young man". Locke was soon sending copies to friends.
Unfortunately, David Thomas was not now on his list, for the previous
month this "long and steady" friend for nearly thirty years had died
after an illness of some months.[106]

During eight days at the beginning of July Locke was on a "ramble", which took in visits to Overwinchenden in Buckinghamshire (the estate of Thomas Wharton, Comptroller of the Household), Staunton Harold in Leicestershire (the seat of Lord Ferrers), Bretby in Derbyshire (the Earl of Chesterfield), and Boughton in Northamptonshire (Lord Montagu).[107] A highlight of these travels was the gathering and eating of early ripening peaches, oranges, and grapes.

A couple of days after his "ramble" in the Midlands, Locke was back at Oates. As ever, eight-year-old Francis would have been pleased to see him for just the previous month he had written, "I desire that you should know I love you very much, and I long to see you that we may talk Latin together, and that you may see how much I am ready to please you in everything". Had she not been away, "little Frank's" half-sister, Esther, would have been pleased to see him too, for, as she wrote to him, "I have yet found nothing so pleasant as being in the garden digging with my John". In fact there would have been no gardening anyway for, as Locke wrote to her from Oates towards the end of August, "Pray, when you return, bring a little summer with you if you intend to do anything in the garden with your John. For we have had nothing but winter weather since you went, and I write this by the fireside, whither the blustering wind and rain like December has driven me."[108]

Just before eight that morning Locke had recorded "a solemn hard rain" and "a hard and whistling wind" from the southeast, of a force which, according to his system, was between a fresh gale and a storm; while just after five that afternoon, though the rain had stopped, the wind was still strong. Such weather (which the swallows left behind a fortnight later) can hardly have helped Locke's cough, which had not yet recovered from his last period in London. As he told Clarke about the same time, "my long stay in town the last time made so lasting an impression on my lungs that I have scarce yet got it off... I shall not be very forward to come thither yet a while". Clarke had recently returned to London and Locke hoped to have from him an occasional "little account how the world wags". He was obviously getting a bit bored, for in mid-September he wrote to Hans Sloane thanking him for sending "news from the commonwealth of letters into a place where I seldom meet with anything beyond the observation of a scabby sheep or a lame horse". A few days later a break was offered him by Mordaunt, who suggested that either they meet one day, at some place between Oates and Parson's Green, "from whence we may both get home at night", or, if Locke had any need to go to London, "I will send my coach for you". But Locke had already booked a seat on the public coach and that very day he went "to Mr Pawlings", intending to "stay but a little while".[109]

"Mr Pawlings" now meant, not Dorset Court, but Little Lincoln's Inn Fields, where Pawling had moved that summer, nearer to his work with the Treasury, to which he had recently been appointed. "The chamber we design for you", he wrote to his lodger, "has the same furniture the other had and I think will be altogether as convenient." When Locke returned to Oates nearly three weeks later he was carrying with him six pairs of white gloves and two neckerchiefs for Lady Masham. He was looking forward to seeing Esther, who had recently returned after her summer away, and perhaps she was with him when he resumed his weather observations not long after seven that evening.[110]

He got down to work that same day too, writing a short piece about uneasiness and its determining of the will for Le Clerc, to whom he had sent a copy of the printed sheets of additions and alterations to the *Essay*. He must have been glad to get out of town: he told Clarke less than a week later, "I thank God the country air begins a little to relieve me from those impressions [which] were made on my lungs by your London smoke, which ... I perceive I must not make too bold with at this time of the year".[111]

At the end of November, Freke and Clarke told him that Sir John Somers, the Lord Keeper, had "enquired with great concern for you and asked when you would be in town because he has great occasion to discourse with you on matters of importance". He had asked them to beg Locke to come as soon as possible. "There are many things of weight wherein he desires your opinion and advice", Freke said, one of which was a project for raising an immediate £5 million for the government from investors who would be repaid over ten years by a tax on land. The project was to be discussed in the present session of Parliament and Freke and Clarke too were keen to have Locke's opinion: "besides the service you will do us you will likewise contribute much to the public service".[112]

This letter is the first we have which refers to the trio of friends, Locke, Freke, and Clarke (a Member of Parliament for Taunton and a Commissioner of the Excise), as "the College", perhaps when specifically concerning themselves with national and political matters. Over the next years Locke would receive and reply to many such

"College" letters, in which Freke came to be referred to as "the Bachelor", Clarke as the "Grave Squire", and Locke as "the Castle", in reference to Oates, with its moat.

As requested, Locke went up to London a few days later. There is no record of what he said about the financial project to Somers (or to Freke and Clarke), but it seems never to have been formally proposed and debated. He did not expect to stay long: "my lungs labour and my health will not permit", he wrote to Limborch in an interval "between town affairs and the panting of my labouring lungs".[113]

In the event he stayed a fortnight. Syl booked seats in the return coach not only for themselves but also for young Edward Clarke. About three weeks later, when he sent him back to his father, Locke reported his observations on his development: he was impressed by the boy's Latin ("in a little time now he will be master of that tongue"), but a little concerned that he would not benefit from his dancing lessons unless his "postures, carriage and motions" were "looked after and minded" even "when he is out of the dancing master's hands".[114]

JANUARY 1695: "WHEREIN THE CHRISTIAN FAITH CONSISTS"[115]

During the winter Locke began, so he told Limborch, "seriously considering in what consists Christian faith". What prompted him, he later said, was that "the controversy that made so much noise and heat amongst some of the dissenters, coming one day accidentally into my mind, drew me, by degrees into a stricter and more thorough inquiry into the question about justification". This controversy, which seems not to have attracted his interest when it began in 1690, concerned the relation of repentance and obedience to God's gift of saving faith, and it led Locke to wonder exactly what the content of that faith is. Whatever the saving tenets of Christianity were, it seemed to him they were to be discovered in the New Testament, "separate from any opinions and orthodoxies of sects and systems". This belief that there were certain essentials to the faith that was required for membership of Christ's Church on earth and for eternal salvation in heaven, was a prominent feature of the second reply Locke had made three years earlier to Proast in defence of his *Letter concerning Toleration*. However, he had not, in that reply, developed the idea, but had simply continually stressed that a distinction was to be made between the essentials of the one true Church and the inessentials of doctrine and ceremonies of worship added by various sects and denominations.

He was now interested in exactly what those essentials are.[116] The upshot, not many months later, was the anonymous publication of *The Reasonableness of Christianity, as delivered in the Scriptures.*

After "a careful and diligent reading" of the New Testament, he told Limborch, its teaching became "clearer than the noonday, and I am fully convinced that a sincere reader of the Gospel cannot be in doubt what the Christian faith is". His reading was followed keenly by Damaris Masham, who "every day, from the beginning to the end of my search, saw the progress of it, and knew, at my first setting out, that I was ignorant whither it would lead me; and therefore every day asked me, what more the scripture had taught me". Not only was Locke determined to ignore what various sects and systematic theologians taught about the fundamentals of Christianity, but also he restricted himself to the teaching of Jesus and the Apostles as reported in the Evangelists and in the Acts of the Apostles. Other parts of the New Testament, such as Paul's Epistles, were, he reasoned, written for those who were already Christians, and so might contain more than the absolute basics of Christianity. Two thoughts guided Locke's reading: the Scriptures were designed "for the instruction of the illiterate bulk of mankind" and so should be "understood in the plain direct meanings of the words...without such learned, artificial, and forced senses of them, as are sought out and put upon them, in most of the systems of divinity"; second, that verses should not be taken out of context in order to support preconceptions, rather "we must look into the drift of the discourse, observe the coherence and connexion of the parts, and see how it is consistent with itself and other parts of scripture".[117]

Repeated careful reading revealed that there was just one fundamental tenet that marked one out as a Christian believer. "The great proposition" that was argued about at the time of the Apostles was whether Jesus was the Messiah, the son of God, or not; and it was assent to that proposition, Locke saw, which distinguished believers from unbelievers. There were, however, some "concomitant articles" to this belief that Jesus was the Messiah and "constituted the lord and judge of all men, to be their king and ruler": namely, that there is "one invisible, eternal, omnipotent God, maker of heaven and earth" (whose son Jesus was), and that Jesus was resurrected and so not "under the power of death". To hold the one fundamental, together with its "concomitants", was, Locke concluded, what it was to be a Christian, even though the Scriptures contain further truths which, though not "a necessary part of the law of faith, (without an actual assent to which [God] will not allow anyone to be a believer)", must be believed by an obedient Christian who can understand what they are.[118]

So far as its essential fundamentals go, Christianity is an eminently reasonable religion "suited to vulgar capacities": the "bulk of mankind" can easily understand and believe that Jesus is the Messiah. But this is not all that is necessary for salvation. That belief, if it is to justify and save, must go along with repentance and obedience: there must "be not only a sorrow for sins past, but...a turning from them into a new and contrary life.[119]

But what is salvation and why is anything required of human beings to gain it? "It is obvious", thought Locke, "to anyone, who reads the New Testament, that the doctrine of redemption...is founded upon the supposition of Adam's fall." So to understand "what we are restored to by Jesus Christ, we must consider what the Scriptures show we lost by Adam". They do *not* show, he thought, that Adam's posterity is doomed to eternal punishment; it would not be consistent with divine justice that millions who had never heard of Adam and had not authorised him "to transact" for them or be their "representative" should be punished for *his* sin. But they do not show either that there is no place for the idea of redemption and that Jesus is "nothing but the restorer and preacher of pure natural religion". What they *do* show is that once Adam had been banished from paradise as a punishment for his sin, and so lost immortality, all his descendants lost it too: not because they inherited Adam's sin and were punished for it, but simply because they suffered the unfortunate consequences of being born outside of paradise, namely, the mortality and eventual death which results from being "out of the reach of the tree of life".[120]

Christ, however, can restore to us what we have lost. If we believe in him as the Messiah and repent of our sins (for we are all sinners in fact) and are obedient so far as we are able, he can (if he so wishes, for we have no rights in the matter) count us on the Judgement Day as though we were blameless and resurrect us to immortality; the wicked, however, are condemned to punishment for a time and then to a final death. Locke said nothing in the *Reasonableness* about our state in heaven, but his view in the *Essay* was that we would be like the angels who have an enhanced intuition and there would be "thousands of things, which now, either wholly escape our apprehensions, or which, our short-sighted reason having got some faint glimpse of, we, in the dark, grope after".[121]

As early as the "First Tract on Government" in 1660, Locke held that moral precepts were expressions of God's will and that we know his commands to us either as a law of nature by means of our reason and natural faculties, or through the revelations of the Scriptures. This view was retained throughout his life. The "Essays on the Law of Nature" had gone some way to showing both how the content of natural law, and various of its presuppositions such as the existence of God and our having an obligation to obey the divine will, might be known on the basis of our natural faculties. But they did not show, what he himself said was necessary, that there is an afterlife* in which we might receive divine reward and punishment. Locke had recognised the importance of, and the need for, some such demonstrations in the drafts of the *Essay* in 1671, but he had deferred them to a "fit place". Apparently the *Two Treatises* were no such "fit place", and simply took for granted that there was a law of nature; nor were the opening books of the *Essay* (more or less in their final form by 1685), which just reiterated that "God has given a rule whereby men should govern themselves". The right place, he seems to have in decided in 1687, would be in a concluding chapter of the *Essay*, "Of ethic in general". In a draft of this proposed chapter which remained unfinished, Locke noted a common failure to recognise genuine moral precepts for what they are, "the commands of the great god of Heaven and Earth" who would "retribute to men after this life"; and he said that in order "to establish morality . . . [on] such foundations as may carry an obligation with them we must first prove a law which always supposes a law maker, one that has a superiority and right to ordain and also a power to reward and punish according to the tenor of the law established by him". Remarking that he had already proved the existence of "this sovereign law maker" (i.e. at E: 4.10.-, also E: 1.4.9), but not mentioning that he had also shown we are to "honour, fear, and obey" God because we see our dependence on him (E: 4.13.3), it followed that "the next thing to show is that there are certain rules, certain dictates which it is his will all men should conform their actions to, and that this will of his is sufficiently promulgated and made known to all mankind".[122] At this point, however, the draft simply came to a halt.

Despite failing to go into the matter, the *Essay* was optimistic that God's laws could be known by the natural means of our reason, even to the point of raising difficulties about the other source of such knowledge, revelation. Referring to the multiplicity of interpretations of the Bible, Locke said that "when clothed in words" God's will is "liable to doubt and uncertainty"; by contrast, however, "the precepts of natural religion are plain, and very intelligible to all mankind": in his goodness God has "spread before all the world, such legible characters of his works and providence, and given all mankind so sufficient a light of reason that they...could not (whenever they set themselves to search) either doubt of the being of a God, or the obedience due to him". His talk about evolving a demonstrative morality on the basis of our knowledge of the real essences of moral ideas added to what was said in the "Essays on the Law of Nature" about coming to a knowledge of moral precepts and the law of nature by the use of our reason. It developed an idea he had made notes on ten years earlier:

The idea of a supreme being, infinite in power, goodness and wisdom, whose workmanship we are, and on whom we depend; and the idea of ourselves, as understanding, rational beings...would, I suppose, if duly considered, and pursued, afford such foundations of our duty and rules of action, as might place morality amongst the sciences capable of demonstration: wherein...the measures of right and wrong might be made out, to anyone that will apply himself with the same indifferency and attention to the one, as he does to the other of these sciences.[123]

Locke was less optimistic about the systematic discovery of moral precepts on the basis of our natural faculties when he told Molyneux in 1692 that a rationally demonstrated complete body of moral principles would be an achievement comparable with that of Newton's *Principia*. This in itself said nothing either way about revelation as a source of knowledge of divine law, but three years later, by the time he came to write the *Reasonableness*, he was correspondingly more optimistic about it. He now obviously thought it was not too difficult by careful reading of the Bible to find at least the essentials of God's will. A year later still, in answer to Molyneux's further pressing about the idea of a complete ethics derived solely by our natural faculties, he would say not only that we did not *need* one since "the Gospel contains so perfect a body of ethics, that reason may be excused from that inquiry", but also that reason "may find man's duty clearer and easier in revelation than in herself".[124]

He was not saying here, however, that revelation is *necessary* and that our natural faculties are *insufficient*. This was not what he said in the *Reasonableness* either. In considering those people "to whom the promise of the Messiah never came, and so were never in a capacity to believe or reject that revelation", he explained, as he had all along, that all mankind has the natural revelation, by means of the light of reason, of what laws we are under and how we should atone the good and merciful God when we have transgressed. "He that made use of this candle of the Lord, so far as to find what was his duty, could not miss to find also the way to reconciliation and forgiveness, when he had failed of his duty." He later offered Cicero's *De Officiis* as "a good specimen" of "how far human reason advanced in the discovery of morality".[125]

Locke's position seems to have been that though "natural revelation" was in principle sufficient to show us our moral duties, people had not always used their reason effectively. Sometimes they had "put out or neglected this light" and so had seen neither their duty nor the way to reconciliation with their creator if they neglected it. He outlined a historical story which explained why, as a matter of fact, the law of nature in its full extent had never been discovered by natural reason. Overly concerned with their sensual natures, or under the influence of priests of false religions who "excluded reason from having anything to do in religion", people had failed to recognise the existence of God, even though "the works of nature, in every part of them sufficiently evidence a deity".[126] Again under the influence of the priests of false religions, people had failed to look into and to acquire a knowledge of their duties according to God's laws.

Added to this was the kind of thing Locke had said to Molyneux about a demonstrable morality: "It is too hard a task for unassisted reason to establish morality in all its parts, upon its true foundation, with a clear and convincing light.... Some parts of that truth lie too deep for our natural powers easily to reach ... without some light from above to direct them." Even if someone had produced for us "ethics in a science like mathematics, in every part demonstrable", we would still need to be assured that these were indeed rules of morality which we had an obligation to obey.[127]

For these largely historical reasons, there was a need for a complete morality to be revealed to the world by the authoritative teachings of Jesus. Surely "one coming from heaven in the power of God ... giving plain and direct rules of morality" is more likely to enlighten us than is "reasoning ... from general notions and principles of human reason". Anyone who is persuaded "that Jesus Christ was sent by God to be a king, and a saviour ... needs no more, but to read the inspired books, to be instructed: all the duties of morality lie there clear, and plain, and easy to be understood".[128]

Jesus did more than present the world with a complete body of ethics. He also gave a clear assurance of an afterlife and rewards for virtue – something which from the start, as in the "Essays on the Law of Nature", Locke had said was a presupposition of the law of nature, but which he had not shown was knowable by natural reason. For a number of years he must have thought, or at least hoped, that on the basis of our faculties we could at least see some probability in this. In a note made during his years in France he wrote that it is "at least probable" that there is "another life wherein we shall give an account for our past actions in this". He did not explain why it was "probable"; and such detail was again absent when in the notes he wrote in 1681 against Stillingfleet he made the stronger claim that the "light of nature" shows us not only that there is a God to whom we are obliged, but also that "our eternal happiness and misery" depends on him. Again without explanation, he wrote in his journal the next year of the "strong probability amounting almost to certainty" that God will "put the souls of men into a state of life or perception" after our bodily death.[129]

If Locke had thought our immortality could be demonstrated by reason, he would not have been alone, for in 1682 he had ruminated on the common Cartesian argument which took as a premise that an immaterial thing, such as our soul, is naturally indestructible. But he thought this did not show that after bodily death our souls would be conscious and susceptible to happiness or misery. Moreover, at any rate by the time of the *Essay*, he did not think it could be taken for granted that the soul *is* immaterial anyway. This, however, was of no consequence for the question of immortality, for "all the great ends of morality and religion are well enough secured, without philosophical proofs of the soul's immateriality": whether we are material or immaterial, God who created us as sentient intelligent beings "can and will restore us to the like state of sensibility in another world, and make us capable there to receive the retribution he has designed to men, according to their doings in this life". Locke still did not say why he believed that God "will" restore us, but presumably he was not thinking of revelation – as he was when Stillingfleet later questioned him about it, and when he came to write the *Reasonableness*: "Before our saviour's time, the doctrine of a future state, though it were not wholly hid yet it was not clearly known to the world"; Jesus revealed to us the possibility of "a perfect complete life, of an eternal duration".[130]

The idea of divine rewards and punishments associated with God's laws was present in Locke's thought from the start: "law is to no purpose without punishment", he said, in the "Essays on the Law of Nature", and, more elaborately, in the *Essay* years later, that "the true ground of morality . . . is only the will and law of a God who . . . has in his hands rewards and punishments, and power enough to call to account". But his view about what role those rewards and punishments play seems to have undergone some change. In his "Essays" he said that what puts us under an obligation to follow God's will is "not fear of punishment", but rather a "rational apprehension of what is right". He also said, however, that people "who refuse to be led by reason" may be led to obey and be constrained by the fear of punishment; and the thought that what motivates us to action are considerations of pleasure and pain is something which became more prominent in his mind.[131]

In the proposed *Essay*'s chapter "Of ethic in general", Locke expressed this thought in no uncertain terms. People act with moral rectitude and conform their actions to God's law only because of the rewards and punishments which God has annexed to the performance of various actions. At first he went so far as to say that there could be "no reason to direct my action" were it not for these consequences, and that a hungry man would be a fool not to raid his neighbour's barn "if no evil would follow from his taking what was not his". But he then crossed this passage through, leaving a softer claim that consideration of the consequences is the "motive or restraint" to our actions. As he said in the *Essay*, God's "enforcement of good and evil" is there to "determine" our will.[132]

Of course all of this presupposed some authenticity and authority for the Scriptures, and in the *Reasonableness* Locke simply assumed that the Bible was divinely inspired and a source of genuine revelation. The Scriptures, as he said in his notes on Study, are "an eternal foundation of truth as immediately coming from the fountain of it". The *Reasonableness* was not the place to discuss, as he had earlier in the *Essay*, the role of reason in evaluating the genuineness of some supposed divine revelation, but what came out much more clearly here than in the *Essay* was the theme that Christ's divine authority was established by the miracles he performed. Jesus "was sent by God: his miracles show it; and the authority of God in his precepts cannot be questioned. Here morality has a sure standard, that revelation vouches, and reason cannot gainsay."[133]

Locke spoke of miracles as being "the confirmation of some truth [which] requires it", and something of what he meant by this was perhaps explained in some notes he made in 1681. Though God might perform miracles "for the confirmation of truths", we should not think he would do them to enforce doctrines "not conformable to reason, or that we can receive such for truths for the miracles sake". Even with the doctrines of the Bible "which have the greatest proof of revelation from God and the attestation of miracles to confirm their being so the miracles were to be judged by the doctrine and not the doctrine by the miracles".[134] In the light of this and of what the *Essay* said about the role of reason in judging the authenticity of revelation, Locke plainly meant that miracles "confirm" in that they give us an external reason to believe something which is "above reason" and which we would otherwise have no reason to believe. Locke appeared not to recognise any circularity in supposing that scriptural messages are confirmed by miracles when those same Scriptures are what attest to the occurrence of miracles in the first place.

JANUARY–AUGUST 1695: "NOT ONE WORD OF SOCINIANISM"[135]

While he was studying the Gospels, Locke was also involved with more worldly matters. He and the "College" were concerned with the renewal of the Licensing Act which regulated the printing of books. This Act had last been renewed in 1693, despite the common objection (which at the time Locke urged Clarke to get his Parliamentary colleagues to consider) that it gave the "company of ignorant and lazy Stationers" a monopoly. They were, for example, able to claim copyright on classical texts, even to the extent of controlling the import of better and cheaper editions: "it is a great oppression upon scholars, and what right can anyone pretend to have to the writings of one who lived a thousand years ago".[136]

The Act was now up for renewal again, and a committee had recommended its continuation. Locke composed some detailed comments on it. These repeated his earlier objection about the Stationers' monopoly, particularly of classical authors and books over fifty years old, but they also objected to the prohibition on "heretical, seditious, schismatical or offensive books...contrary to Christian Faith, or...the Church of England". Locke thought this too vague, and too subject to the transient fancies of the Church and state authorities. In any case, he objected in principle to any such censorship: why should someone "not have liberty to print whatever he would speak; and to be answerable for the one, just as he is for the other.... Gagging a man, for fear he should talk heresy or sedition, has no other ground than such as will make fetters necessary, for fear a man should use violence if his hands were free, and must at last end in the imprisonment of all who you will suspect may be guilty of treason or misdemeanour."[137]

In February the recommendation that the Act be continued was rejected by the Commons, and another committee, of which Clarke was a member, was appointed to draw up a bill for a new Act. In March, some days after Clarke, on behalf of the committee, presented this bill for a first reading in the Commons, Locke wrote some comments on it, for which the College was "extremely obliged" and which they intended to "make a right use of... if the bill goes on which we much doubt". The new bill avoided Locke's worries about the Stationers' monopoly, but Freke and Clarke still had objections to it, even though they did not share Locke's concern that continuing censorship of things "heretical" and contrary to the Christian religion "as it is established by law" was too vague; a precise meaning for these words was, they said, laid down by statute. Freke was right that the new bill would not pass, and in April the Lords tried for a renewal of the old Act. Clarke's committee drew up a list of reasons against it (including those Locke had set down in January) and the attempt failed.[138]

At the end of January a suggestion was made which must have pleased Locke greatly. Almost from the outset, Oxford tutors had been recommending the *Essay* to their pupils, at least one of whom was "extremely pleased" with Locke (except, perhaps, with his tendency to repetition):

There is a great deal of very good sense in him; and I believe a great part of it is his own: besides, his language is sound, proper, and pure; and his instances so familiar, that anyone may understand him. If he says the thing over and over, I think we are obliged to him; for he has nothing but what will bear reading twice at least.

Now one tutor, John Wynne of Jesus College, had come to the conclusion that "the greatest service that could be done for the judicious and thinking part of the world, next to the composing of it, would be to bring [the *Essay*]... into common and general use". Wynne suggested that Locke should produce an abridgement which contracted "some of the larger explications (some of which are but incidental to the general design of the work)"; it would be "of excellent use" for young students. Wynne knew of the *Abrégé* that Locke had done for Le Clerc, but, besides being in French, this was not sufficiently available. He himself, Wynne said, "would willingly contribute any assistance . . . to ease you of the trouble".[139]

Locke asked Freke and Clarke to make inquiries about Wynne, and in replying to Wynne told him of his surprise at having "so great a commendation of my book from a place where I thought it little taken notice of". When he published the book ("which was writ for the diversion of my idle hours") Locke had supposed, he said, that "those who had leisure to throw away in speculations a little out of the road . . . might perhaps look into it"; he certainly had not thought it "the serious business of studious men who know how to employ their time". He agreed that "most of the larger explications may be looked on as incidental . . . [and] those repetitions which . . . I let it go with may be omitted". But he had no health or leisure to do the work himself, and in any case it was long since that he had read any systematic academic texts of the sort he understood Wynne wanted for his students. Locke did not, though, give Wynne complete and wholehearted encouragement to go ahead; he still needed to know something about him, and nearly two months after his initial request, Freke eventually had something to report. Meanwhile, however, Wynne had forged ahead: "since you thought fit to decline", he told Locke, and did "judge me in some measure qualified for it, I did immediately set about it and have almost finished it". He had not reformed or restructured the book but had simply "contracted it into a narrower compass", partly by leaving out the whole of book one on "Innate Ideas". Three weeks later he had finished it, and Locke thought well enough of it to put Wynne into contact with Churchill. Even so, he did not want to be too closely identified with it: having told Freke and Clarke "it was not for me to oppose it or go about to hinder him", he asked Wynne to delete from his proposed prefatory epistle a suggestion that Locke had been responsible for the publication. Since a third edition of the *Essay* itself was on the way, Wynne left the timing of the publication of his abridgement to Churchill. In the event, the third edition of the *Essay* was published by the end of the year, and was soon followed by *An Abridgement of Mr Locke's Essay concerning Human Understanding*.[140]

The failure of the coinage bill in 1692 had been followed by other attempts to deal with the deteriorating currency, but these too had been unsuccessful. Meanwhile the problem had got worse, and by the beginning of 1695 domestic trade had begun to be seriously affected. Even for domestic purposes, clipped coins could no longer be exchanged for full-weight ones without payment of a premium; and full-weight ones themselves, because of a rise in the price of silver, were in short supply. The effect on Locke's business must have been typical: in the first part of the year Stratton complained about difficulty in collecting Locke's rents, "money is so bad and country people being so ignorant that I know not how to receive money for they are offended with me if I will not take one third or half bad"; and Locke asked Clarke whether he could refuse clipped money. "I take it not to be the lawful coin of England, and I know not why I should receive half the value I lent instead of the whole."[141]

In January the Commons set up a committee under Francis Scobell to consider the situation. Clarke and Masham were on it and worked to dissuade their colleagues from devaluation, with the help of the short piece on the coinage which Locke had written two years earlier, and which he now published anonymously under the title *Short Observations on a paper, entitled, "For encouraging the coining silver money in England, and after for keeping it here"*. At first Freke feared that Locke's pamphlet would do little good: "you have set that matter in its due light...but those that make most ado about it will not be brought to understand your treatise and are still puzzling themselves about methods that will rather increase than cure the evil". But in early March, shortly before the committee reported, he was more hopeful. He thought Locke's paper "has and will do a great deal of good...and we endeavour as much as we can to make it looked into and considered by the members of the House of Commons who now have this matter under consideration".[142]

The committee recommended a recoinage (at an estimated cost of £1 million) with a devaluation around 10 per cent (in line with a further increased market price of silver). One resolution, made at Clarke's insistence, was that new crowns and half-crowns should be of the old weight and fineness (though with an increased rating). Clarke thought that when the Commons came to debate the matter "that resolution would destroy all the rest", and indeed, as the College hoped, the Scobell devaluationist proposals were eventually rejected. Things were left much the same, except for an increase in penalties against clipping.[143]

Since January the winter had been hard, with snow and frost, and had held Locke "so close...prisoner within doors", that a day in early March was only the second in three months he had been out of the house ("and that only a mile in a coach"). His "inability...to breathe London air in cold weather" completely ruled out any hope of going to town for some time of course. Though the swallows arrived in early April, "spring was so slow in bringing us back warm suns and pleasant days", Locke wrote to Graevius. A visit to London required careful planning: "my breath is yet short", he told Clarke in May, "and I know not how long stay it will permit me in town, and therefore having business that will call me to town, but not presently, I must husband my time there as well as I can". In any case, he said, "we have still winter weather bating a little warmth". A week later his business was not "yet ripe" for the visit, and nor was the weather: "I write this by the fire's side, and know not yet how I shall be able to bear London air." But then the weather turned warm, and at the very end of the month Locke took the coach to London.[144]

It is not clear what business it was that needed to ripen. Part may have been to do with the Commission of Appeals, part with his recent appointment as a Commissioner for Greenwich Hospital. For five or so years there had been a project (in which Pawling was much interested and involved) for the care of sick and disabled seamen, but only relatively recently had it really begun to develop.[145]

But perhaps what Locke really had in mind was completing and preparing for publication his work on the essentials of the Christian faith, for when he eventually went up to London he took with him a finished manuscript, which the publishers contracted to print. Locke had cautioned Limborch when he told him about the project that "these things are whispered in your ear". But he was not averse to the thoughts themselves, as opposed to the identity of their author, being made public. He wrote later that when he saw

what a plain, simple, reasonable thing Christianity was, suited to all conditions and capacities; and in the morality of it now, with divine authority, established into a legible law, so far surpassing all that philosophy and human reason had attained to, or could possibly make effectual to all degrees of mankind, I was flattered to think it might be of some use in the world.

In particular, he thought what he had worked out might be of use against "deists" whose arguments against Christianity were really against Christianity misunderstood as something which went beyond reason, and who held either that "there was no need of revelation at all", or that "the revelation of our Saviour required the belief of such articles for salvation, which the settled notions, and their way of reasoning in some, and want of understanding in others make impossible to them".[146]

Highwaymen were again at work in Epping Forest when Locke returned to Oates, but this time the public coach was not troubled by them. After a week back at home he wrote to Graevius that "shut away in the country by the weakness of my lung I am as it were an exile from London; if I ever make an excursion to it I return speedily, like a dog at the Nile". Despondent and worried as he was about his health (he told Molyneux at the time that it did not "promise me any long stay in this world"), he had held out in London for three weeks, and would very shortly be there again for another six.[147]

During the summer Locke acquired, after many years of effort, what became known at Oates as his "brewhouse". According to Esther Masham, "Mr Locke drank nothing but water. What he calls his brewhouse was a stone in form of a great mortar of so spongy a stone that water being put in use to run through in a very short time and strained the water from any dirt that might be in it". Locke had been drinking water in preference to wine for at least twenty years, and his consequent interest in methods of filtering it (as through sand, at Venice) had been particularly caught by Toinard's telling him of certain porous stones (presumably of volcanic origin) from the sea to the north of Gran Canaria which, suitably fashioned for straining water, could sometimes be obtained in Cadiz. Locke had pestered Toinard to find out more about these stones, and to track one down. On two occasions over the years Toinard had been almost ready to send one (about fifteen inches in diameter and eleven in depth, mounted in a wood and iron frame), but it was only now that at long last Locke had one.[148]

In his later years and among his friends, Locke acquired a reputation for "leaving off wine and malt liquors"* in favour of water, and he seems to have been something of a proselytising advocate for this as a healthy regime. Lady Masham said he thought that ordinarily drinking nothing but water "was the means of lengthening out his life to such an age". He so thoroughly converted Pawling to water and the use of a filtering stone (his "tavern") that Pawling would not have servants who drank malt, and claimed there would never be "a thorough reformation in England till [water] becomes the chief drink; it will cure men of drunkenness and many other vices". Some years later a visitor to Oates would tell Locke that he had won him over to water-drinking, "and I hope in a little time to reach perfection. Like a young convert, I'm very zealous to propagate the doctrine."[149]

Esther Masham's testimony that Locke drank "nothing but water" is presumably not to be understood just like that; in fact there was a time when he thought that unadulterated water as opposed to beer gave him colic. Though he did not like the taste of coffee, he certainly acquired an interest in tea in Holland, and chocolate, made from a paste of roasted, ground-up cacao nuts or beans mixed with water, was obviously something he had a liking for at Oates.[150]

William Stratton, who had been looking after Locke's Somerset affairs, died in August. Locke had not seen him since 1691, on what proved to have been his last visit to Somerset, and now that he was dead not only had he lost a long-standing friend, but also he faced the situation he had feared for some years: that he now knew no one in the area who could manage his affairs. "Death has taken away all my old friends and acquaintances thereabouts, and my long absence out of the country has scarce left me so much as the names of anybody . . . to whom I could now apply myself", he said to a local man, Cornelius Lyde, when he successfully solicited him to take over Stratton's responsibilities.[151]

Locke's *The Reasonableness of Christianity* appeared in August, and he soon began to get reactions to it. He noted that though some spoke of it "with great commendation", most people "censured it, as a very bad book"; indeed, as he would later say, it caused a "buzz, . . . flutter, and noise", and "the reports which were raised, would have persuaded the world, that it subverted all morality, and was designed against the Christian Religion". At least parts of the world were persuaded of this and two years later the book, along with some others on religion, was reported by the Grand Jury of Middlesex as denying the Trinity and contributing to Socinianism and atheism – "a matter of dangerous consequence", Molyneux said, "to make our civil courts judges of religious doctrines".[152]

It was soon widely believed that Locke was the anonymous author, and by November Furly in Rotterdam had been assured that "it was sufficiently known to be yours". Molyneux was too discreet to "presume to inquire" whether such beliefs were true, but he reported, more favourably, that a bishop had told him that "if my friend Mr Locke wrote it, it was the best book he ever laboured at; but, says he, if I should be known to think so, I should have my lawns torn from my shoulders".[153]

Others did not have Molyneux's discretion, and in September, just weeks after publication, Locke received a letter adressed to him by name. Its anonymous writer, who had taken "the trouble, as well as charge to buy and seriously to peruse" it, did not accuse Locke of being "against the Christian Religion", but in seeking guidance on the meaning of the doctrines of the Trinity and the Incarnation he obviously felt that something should have been said about these contentious issues.[154] The letter was decent, simple, and sincere, completely unlike the printed attack made on Locke that same month in *Some Thoughts concerning the Several Causes and Occasions of Atheism*, by John Edwards, an Anglican clergyman.

Appearing just five weeks after the *Reasonableness*, Edwards's book had been largely written before he had read Locke's, and his attack occurred as an afterthought, "for his bookseller's sake" Locke suggested. The "Brief reflections on Socinianism and ... *The Reasonableness of Christianity*" appeared towards the end of the book in connection with the eleventh of the causes which Edwards found for atheism, namely the way theological disputes were used by ill-disposed people to reject the teachings of the Scriptures and the existence of God. For example, the dispute about the Trinity unsettles minds and makes people "waver about the truth and certainty of the main articles of our religion", and also the writings of many on the unitarian side of the dispute have in themselves "an atheistic tang", a "tendency" towards atheism. Edwards found this tendency not only in incidental remarks made by such writers (whom he describes as "Socinians"), but also in "their own avowed principle, which is that they are to admit of nothing [in Christianity] but what is exactly adjusted to nature's and reason's light, nothing but what is entirely clear and evident". At the bottom of all, he said, is that "the trinity and such like doctrines are above their reason, and natural ideas, and therefore they are not matter of their faith". Similarly, when their principle is applied to the nature of God it is found to be "not commensurate to our conceptions ... not adjusted to our ideas" and so God himself must be disowned. "Consequently one would be apt to gather that a Socinian, so far as he is led by this principle, is an atheist, or ... one that favours the cause of atheism."[155]

The name "Socinian" derives from the sixteenth-century Italian theologians Laelio and Fausto Sozzini. There was no clear and settled group of doctrines which constituted so-called "Socinianism" (often just something of a term of abuse), but the doctrines Edwards attributed to it give a good indication of it. The "leading card", as Edwards put it, was the rejection of the Trinity, but it was also Socinian to deny the divinity of Jesus and to deny that he died in satisfaction of our sins.[156] It was Socinian to deny original sin, the immateriality of the human soul and even of God (and his omniscience and omnipresence), and to say that our resurrection does not involve the resurrection of the same body. It was Socinian to reject the priesthood as a special calling or mission.

The whole tendency of Socinianism was towards "Deism", towards the rejection of the Bible as a source of divine revelation, and, according to Edwards, "it will appear at last that Atheism lurks under the refined name of Deism". This move towards "natural" and away from "revealed" religion involves, Edwards explained, the submission of doctrines to reason, and their consequent rejection, because they are "mysterious" and opaque to the understanding. "What is above our reason to apprehend, is", it is held, "also above our belief".[157]

Towards the end of his book, Edwards turned to yet another doctrine which, because of its implications (particularly of unitarianism), he vilified as "Socinian". He found this "more particularly fully and distinctly" in the *Reasonableness of Christianity* where, he said, it is given "over and over again ... that nothing is required to be believed by any Christian man but this, that Jesus is the Messiah ... there is no other article of faith necessary to salvation; this is a full and perfect creed".[158]

Edwards rather fancifully proposed that behind this lay the hope that "when the faith is thus brought down to one single article it will soon be reduced to none: the unit will dwindle into a cypher". But even without the possibility of that ultimate reduction (about which Locke later joked that the idea of "but one article ... has no more tendency to atheism, than their doctrine of one God"), Edwards was certain that some essentials were being ignored. This reduction of the Christian faith to just one belief means, Edwards said, that the author "forgot, or rather wilfully omitted a plain and obvious passage in Matthew 28.19 which speaks of 'the Father, the Son, and the Holy Ghost'". Yet a belief in the Trinity is also "necessary, absolutely necessary, to make one a member of the Christian Church". It was this implied rejection of the Trinity that he found particularly objectionable, making it the object of his frequent rhetoric: "this gentleman is resolved to be a Unitarian, for one article of faith, as well as one person in the Godhead". But other important doctrines are being rejected too if there is but one article of faith, and it is because of this, Edwards said, that the *Reasonableness* neglected the Epistles – "because they are fraught with other fundamental doctrines" such as original sin, satisfaction by Christ's crucifixion, the importance of the priesthood, and the resurrection of human bodies. A further motive behind Locke's simplifying reduction of the Christian faith to one article, according to Edwards, was the Socinian belief that "there must be nothing in Christianity that is not plain, and exactly level to all men's mother-wit and common apprehension", and that "religion should have no difficulties and mysteries in it". All of this, said Edwards, shows that the author "is all over Socinianised". Whatever objections anyone might have to Socinianism should be levelled against the *Reasonableness* too.[159]

In his criticisms of the anonymous *Reasonableness*, Edwards typically referred simply to "the author", but there is no doubt he believed this to be Locke. With the pretence of suggesting otherwise, he said it was hard to believe that "a person of ingenuity and good sense" would disguise his Socinian aims, and that this made him doubt "the ingenious gentleman" who is supposed by some to be the author really is. "I question whether we have the right author because I have so good an opinion of the gentleman who writ of Human Understanding and Education."[160]

Locke was very quick to react, and by the beginning of November his shortish reply, *A Vindication of the Reasonableness of Christianty, etc. from Mr Edwards' Reflections* was in the press. In it he said that he would leave Socinians to speak for themselves as to whether they are really atheists or favour atheism; for himself, he later claimed, he had "never yet read" any Socinian writers ("So we must", Edwards would reply, "number him among the Ignoramus-Socinians").[161] His "vindication" lay instead in examining and rejecting Edwards's "proof" that he was a "Socinian".

A central strand of Edwards's argument was that Locke's contention that there was just one essential article of faith was a disguised way of rejecting a number of other beliefs, which Socinians found objectionable, besides being in itself a manifestation of the Socinian aim to make religion into something non-mysterious. In answer, Locke said that he had not set out with the *insistence* that there be just one basic belief (as a kind of symbol of unitarianism, as Edwards had suggested), nor with the requirement that religion be something non-mysterious and "plain and easy". It simply turned out that there was just one, and, thanks to "the goodness and condescension of the Almighty", one which "the labouring and illiterate man may comprehend".[162]

Locke also reminded Edwards (perhaps not as forcibly as he might have done) that in claiming that the belief that Jesus is the Messiah is the Christian fundamental, he was speaking "not of all the doctrines of Christianity, nor all that is published to the world in it: but of those truths only, which are absolutely required to be believed to make any one a Christian".[163] He was not saying that all else is to be rejected.

Since Locke had made no point of specifying any of the non-essential, but nevertheless true, Christian doctrines which can be found in the Scriptures, he exposed himself to a number of other strands in Edwards's accusation of Socinianism. Edwards had pointed out that, in speaking of the advantages of Christ's coming, Locke had not cited (as a Socinian would not have done) his purchasing our salvation by his death. Locke was able to point to a passage where he had said that Christ restored mankind to life, but his main defence was that he had been writing mainly for people who were "not yet thoroughly, or firmly Christians"; so he had mentioned only those advantages on which everyone was agreed, and not any which were not urged by Christ and the Apostles "as necessary to be believed". He repeated, what he had said in the *Reasonableness*, that he had not made use of the Epistles because they were written for those who were Christians already, so that fundamental articles were "promiscuously, and without distinction, mixed with other truths"; it was not, as Edwards had claimed, because the Epistles contained doctrines that he wanted to deny.[164]

Locke similarly insisted that his neglect of other doctrines which Edwards thought important was not wilful; it was rather that Christ and the Apostles had not proposed them "as necessary to be believed, to make men Christ's disciples". In fact, he pointed out, there were "omissions" which Edwards had not mentioned: Edwards had picked only on those which would enable him to accuse Locke of Socinianism. "Socinianism then is not the fault of the book, whatever else it be.... There is not one word of Socinianism in it."[165]

AUGUST–DECEMBER 1695: "OF GREAT USE TO YOUR COUNTRY"[166]

Locke was taken up with currency matters again in the second half of the year. An increased shortage of standard-weight silver money had led to a dramatic increase in the price of gold guineas (from under twenty-three shillings to around thirty), one result being that foreigners were bringing in their gold and taking away English silver. The Lords Justices (the council in charge of the country while King William was abroad), hoping to stabilize matters and to draw a line under the decline of silver as currency, had concluded that a recoinage was now necessary.

They had considered various reports before reaching this decision, and in early August William Trumbell, Secretary of State, had asked Locke to comment on one of these, "Concerning the Price of Guineas". Apologising for "having troubled you so often about the lamentable condition of our money", Trumbell again wanted Locke's views: "I have so great a desire to understand this matter fully, and to contribute my part towards some cure of this great evil, that I depend upon your goodness... to instruct me." Locke replied with a short paper, "Guineas". A nominal thirty shillings worth of clipped coins now contained less silver than twenty shillings worth of full-weight coins, and it was not reasonable, he said, that the Exchequer should (as had been proposed as a solution) simply refuse to accept guineas at the current price. He now thought clipping had gone too far and that it was pointless to hope it could be prevented, and suggested that the real solution was to address the cause of the problems, and make it illegal for clipped money to exchange at its face value, so making it worth only its actual weight in silver. Quite simply, the government should stop shoring up the deteriorated parts of the currency.[167]

But the Lords Justices were set on recoinage and asked the Treasury Secretary, William Lowndes, to work out the practicalities. Lowndes showed Locke, in London since the beginning of September, a preliminary draft of his "Report containing an Essay for the Amendment of the Silver Coins" and, as Locke said, "made me the compliment to ask me my opinion of it". We do not know what Locke said to Lowndes, and in any case it was not very extensive. "Though we had some short discourse on the subject", Locke later reported, "the multiplicity of his business, whilst I stayed in town, and my health, which soon after forced me out of it, allowed us not an occasion to debate any one point thoroughly."[168]

One point Locke might have commented on was the nature of the recoinage Lowndes advocated. Though he had not yet considered recoinage, a non-devaluing one would have been the next step on from Locke's preferred option of reducing clipped coins from their nominal value to their value by weight. But a devaluing recoinage, which was what Lowndes, along the lines of the Scobell committee, argued for, was something Locke had always been set against.[169]

Lowndes was not the only one who wanted Locke's view of a draft of his report. But even if Locke was able to favour John Somers, another Treasury Commissioner, with the half-hour discussion for which he asked, we do not know what he said; however, a third private request for a preliminary assessment of Lowndes, this time again from Trumbell, resulted in another paper, "Money".[170]

By the time he wrote this, Locke had come to accept the necessity for a recoinage, but was adamant that it should maintain the standard. He was against the proposal that clipped coinage should continue to circulate at face value until it was brought in for reminting, to be compensated for from a fund built up from taxation. This would simply invite more clipping, and at the taxpayers' expense. Given that legislation against clipping did not work, the only remedy was to make clipping unprofitable; and what would do this was what he had told Trumbell in August – to make clipped money pass by weight, and be eventually brought into the Mint (without compensation) for recoining to the standard.

Shortly after Somers had asked Locke to see him, and shortly before Locke left London, the Lowndes report was formally received by the Lords Justices. They were undecided about its recommendations and, "desirous to know the opinions of some other persons versed in those matters", determined to seek advice from various people who, starting with Locke, included Newton, Wren, and Wallis.[171]

Locke must have received the request for advice either shortly before or shortly after leaving London at the end of September. A few days earlier he had been intending to go back to Oates that week, but something happened one morning which made him leave immediately. Perhaps it was a sudden and violent asthmatic attack; at any rate he told Trumbell that his lungs were in a very poor state, and he later reported that he was "forced out of town by my health". On the other hand he also said that, apart from his health, there was some "pressing occasion" for his needing to be at Oates.[172] It may well have been that Lady Masham's mother had fallen ill.

A week into October, Somers asked Freke to get Locke to hurry with the paper for the Lords Justices. But Locke was detained at Oates longer than he had hoped, and it was a further two weeks before he went up to London with some "Propositions" which he submitted two days later. In these few pages he again argued for retaining the standard of the coinage: "Men in their bargains contract not for denominations or sounds; but for the intrinsic value, which is the quantity of silver by public authority ascertained to be in pieces of such denominations." Raising their value adds no value to silver coins, "one may as well hope to lengthen a foot by dividing it into fifteen inches instead of twelve". Devaluation of the coinage is simply clipping by public authority. Again Locke insisted that clipping must be made unprofitable by making money go by weight; in the end this would bring lightweight money in for recoining.[173]

On delivering his "Propositions", Locke was asked to address some further, direct questions on specific points in the Lowndes report; he submitted his "Answer to my Lord Keeper's Queries" a week later. Unlike Lowndes, he did not think, he explained, that coins should be devalued commensurately with the rise in the price of silver bullion; that rise simply reflected payments being made in clipped coinage which no longer exchanged freely with unclipped. The price of bullion would fall if there were only full-weight money to buy it with. "Raising the coinage" would not bring any more bullion to be minted and stop its export, for that was due entirely to our balance of payments.

Locke's ideas (along with those of Wren) were discussed at a meeting of the Council in late October. Apart from his objections to compensation for lightweight coin, they were accepted and (no doubt at least partly because the King, newly returned to the country, had already declared for retaining the monetary standard) it was decided that there should be some recoinage but no devaluation.[174]

Just a few days after that, Locke, perhaps seeing that things were going his way, asked Somers to use his influence to get him appointed as Comptroller of the Mint (a position, worth £300 per annum, which fell vacant a year later). Somers told him, what he probably already knew, that Newton had already been recommended "as proper for that place", but Locke was "still very desirous that his name might be mentioned".[175]

Lowndes's report (which had been submitted in September) was published in mid-November. Anxious about the influence its proposals for devaluation might have in Parliament, Somers and the College were

keen that it should have some public refutation. Somers tried to get
Locke to provide this, pointing out that the request at the end of the
report for comment from people who had thought about the matter
was "in some sort directed to you". Locke agreed to write something,
but he was unable to do anything immediately. A sudden departure was
precipitated by being "sent for into the country by an express", which
told him that Lady Masham's mother had died the previous day.[176]

In his haste to get to Oates he was also unable to complete what he
had hoped for a friend of Molyneux, one Ezekiel Burridge, whom
Molyneux had mentioned some months earlier as an excellent
possibility as a Latin translator for the *Essay*. Having met him, Locke
thought that Molyneux had "got a better than I could have expected",
and that Burridge "is the man you speak him to be". Burridge was in
London with a Latin translation of another work which he hoped, with
Locke's help, to get published. Locke had wanted to have "settled that
matter, before I left London", but could only get as far as arranging for
Awnsham Churchill to call on Burridge. When Burridge started on the
translation the following March, Locke was "past all hopes to have any
leisure at all" to review and correct what Molyneux sent him of it.
Burridge had other things to do too and did not get on as quickly as
Molyneux would have liked, but two years after he had started it was
almost finished. It was eventually published in 1701.[177]

Locke expected to be at Oates with the grieving Lady Masham and her
mother's affairs for about three weeks, and Freke and Clarke were
impatient about his being away at such a crucial time. They chided him
for it, complaining that "your being in town would be of great use to
your country many ways. Your influence is needed to make the business
of the coin . . . to be considered rightly." The "Country gentlemen" of
the recently re-elected Commons, they said, "can hardly be made to
understand this business". They were also impatient about the reply
to Lowndes which Locke had promised: "you might in your absence
be further serviceable . . . by sending us your thoughts on Mr Lowndes's
book to be made public as I have daily expected you would".[178]

Though quite happy that manuscript copies of what Freke and
Clarke had of his on the subject (his "Propositions" and "Answer")
could be given to anyone "who would be serviceable in the debate",
Locke was in fact not keen on any further publication. He had once
been told, he said, that "arguments that were in print were quite lost
when made use of in the house [of Commons] and signified nothing".
As for writing anything further for private circulation, as he had

promised, he retorted that his time at Oates was not being ill-spent: he had been at work "writing what you desire", but "whatever may be expected from me, I cannot dispatch faster than my health and leisure will permit".[179]

So far as his health was concerned, Locke was "grievously tormented" with a cough and toothache, and they required "some allowance of time to be made to them"; as for leisure, there had been very little of that. He had been occupied during the first week back with business concerning a trust that had been set up following the death of Lady Masham's mother. Despite all of this, he stressed, "I have not been wholly idle"; and in fact he was well on the way to a composition based on three of the papers he had written earlier in the year together with some new material in further refutation of Lowndes.[180]

In early December, Freke reported on recent proceedings in Parliament: a Commons committee had voted for recoinage, and the Lords had voted to ask the King to demonetarise clipped coins. He was even more impatient to have Locke's reply to Lowndes: "the sooner it appears the greater will be its...usefulness". Locke sent him some papers three days later, but again expressed reluctance to have them published (because, it has been suggested, he had just heard that the Commons were already about to investigate compensation for clipped money). Freke, however, was determined that they should be published, and showed them to Somers (whom Locke had intended as a dedicatee). Somers wanted them printed as quickly as possible, and they appeared, entitled *Further Considerations concerning the Value of Money*, before the end of the month.[181]

By this time Parliament had agreed that clipped coins should cease to be legal tender, and had formulated a programme extending over some months for their gradual demonetarisation and recall to the Mint for recoinage according to the old standard. Clipped crowns and half-crowns were the first to go, and at the beginning of January Pawling reported to Locke that "his Majesty's coffers fill apace with half crowns, they gallop to town from all quarters". With a gap of some weeks, clipped shillings were similarly to be phased out.[182]

As Locke had feared, the decision that demonetarisation was to take place over a period, with compensation to be paid for lightweight coins, gave scope for the cunning to engage in further clipping, while the simple, confused by the whole affair, were taken advantage of. Locke would soon tell Clarke of a local carpenter who had been paid a debt with a mass of half-crowns and shillings no one else would accept.

Pawling, as a Treasury official, offered to help him get them to the Treasury:

If your poor carpenter brings up his coin I will assist him; and if he pleases to buy up as many small half crowns for twelve pence a piece ... I can help him off with them; or if he could lawfully do it, if he could with his chisel chip off six pennyworth of silver more from most of those he intends to bring up I can, by virtue of an order from our Board to the Receiver, make him take them at two shillings and six pence.[183]

Advice on the currency was only one of the "many ways" in which the College thought Locke would be "of great use" were he in town. There was also the matter of his position as Commissioner of Appeals:

you would also serve your country by taking care to execute your office and hear the appeals ... for if they are not heard there will be complaints and possibly to Parliament and then though you have a good excuse for yourself an occasion may be taken to break the commission wholly ... and then the Revenue of Excise will be ruined and come to nothing which at this time I think is not a desirable thing.

A few days later Freke underlined this reprimand by saying that the other Commissioners "know not what to do without you".[184]

Locke was annoyed about this: his journeys to London that year had been at least partly with Appeals business in mind, and he had "with my utmost endeavours ... laboured to get a quorum". He pointed out to Freke and Clarke that he had asked them to find out whether or not his fellow Commissioners were now in a position to meet. Unless they were, he would be forced to make yet another journey to town only to "wait there to the danger of my health" until his colleagues were ready. "I cannot hear appeals myself", he acidly observed. Ironically, his colleagues were just then in a position to meet, for the day before Freke and Clarke had complained to him, their Register had written to Locke's London lodgings, telling him that three of them had agreed to meet the next day (30 November). Not surprisingly, Locke was not at that meeting, nor at the next one, arranged for a week later.[185]

9

"A Gentleman's Duty" (December 1695–March 1700)

DECEMBER 1695–NOVEMBER 1696: "YOUR COUNTRY CALLS FOR YOUR HELP"[1]

Locke became involved in yet more state business towards the end of the year, business which would come to take up very much of his time: in mid-December he was appointed by the King as a Commissioner for Trade. Since 1675, when Shaftesbury's Council of Trade (of which Locke had been secretary) was abolished, the whole question of trade and colonial business had been in the hands of a committee of Privy Councillors. But reform had become necessary: due to a lack of interest by its members, the committee had become rather haphazard; besides which, colonial administration was beginning to fail.[2] A proposal that the whole business of trade should be remitted to a Board chosen by Parliament forced the King, jealous of his prerogative, into appointing a new Council himself. Even so, he temporised, and Parliament decided to make its own appointments.

Mordaunt, from inside the Privy Council, told Locke in some disgust about the fiasco: "I cannot but write to you to give some ease to my ill-humour, for, though accustomed to see such follies committed, I cannot be insensible ... when the public and a friend is concerned." He explained that some days earlier the King had been pressured to form a Council of Trade, "where some great men were to assist, but where others, with salaries of one thousand pounds a year, were to be fixed as the constant labourers. Mr Locke being to be of the number, made me have the better opinion of the thing"; but that when everything had been worked out, with "the patent ready for the seal", the

King would not sign. With the King delaying, Parliament "fell upon it, and are going to form such a commission, to be nominated by themselves". Mordaunt was at a loss to know what the outcome would be, "but for the little I am able, I shall endeavour Mr Locke may be the choice of the House, as well as the King's: if it takes that course."[3]

William Trumbell recognised the different pressures that Locke must have felt in connection with this appointment: he hoped, above all, that it would not be prejudicial to his health "in giving sometimes your attendance: if that point be secure I am sure the public will have the advantage.... I beg of you to sacrifice a little of your philosophical inclinations to the great necessities we labour under in this matter of trade; and now the voice of your country calls for your help do not refuse it."[4]

Freke and Clarke gave Locke a detailed account of the duties and responsibilities of the new Council: it was to investigate the state of trade and of manufacturing in the country, how they might be improved and protected, and what to do with the unemployed poor. It was also to look into the state of the overseas plantations, what naval stores they might provide, and how well they were being governed and administered.[5]

Locke hardly hesitated in accepting a part in these responsibilities, and he took the coach to London at the request of Somers (who had suggested Locke's appointment to the King). By now, however, his help was being called for on more than one front, and he went not only in response to Somers, but also urged by the College to advocate and explain his views on the currency, and to take part in hearing some Excise appeals. Predictably, and contrary to Trumbell's hope, there was immediately some prejudice to his health, and eleven days later, on the last day of the year, he was "forced...out of town in haste" by a serious cold.[6]

The conflict between health and "the voice of the country" became sharper when, by the "express order of the Lords of the Treasury", Locke was required to be in London on 7, 9, and 10 January in his capacity as a Commissioner of Appeals: "they lay great stress on the cause, and your being present at the decision of it, and therefore expect you should not be absent". This time his health (or lack of it) prevailed, for he was "more than ordinary indisposed" ("very ill ... not without some apprehensions of my life" he later told Molyneux), and three days before he was due in town he wrote to Clarke (from his bed, and rather alarmingly) that he would "always readily obey the orders of the Treasury to the utmost of my power", but he was certain that if "the very ill estate of my health" were made known, "wherein I at present suffer more from my lungs than ever I have done since their first disorder", he would surely be excused. Finding his "usual helps" not working, Locke had recourse to "my last refuge of keeping my bed". This gave him some relief, and towards the middle of the month there had been "a stop to the increase and violence of my cough". Even so, it was not quite gone, "as it was before I last came up to town", he told Clarke, and he was still "very short" of breath. Fortunately he was not forced to decline another summons to appear on Appeals business, for Pawling acted in the matter for him. He had been at the Treasury, he told Locke, "just after the order came and I there acquainted the Clerk that signed it that you was ill and I hoped they might dispense with your absence".[7]

Popple wrote to Locke that same day, appealing not to his sense of duty, but to what Trumbell had called his "philosophical inclinations". Having in mind that sooner or later a Council for Trade would get set up and Locke would be called to serve, he told him that in the meantime "you can always render yourself no less useful to the public even in your most private retirement". Without actually attributing the *Reasonableness of Christianity* to him, Popple suggested that "however reasonable a book it be", he doubted it would have much effect on people who "deny all immaterial beings", people who "laugh not only at revealed but even natural religion". Such people had gone to this extreme of atheism and irreligion in an attempt to escape the other extreme of "the mischiefs of superstition", and of religion mixed in with obscurantist clerical verbiage. What was needed was a book which would show religion "in a pure light", and, Popple thought, Locke was just the person for it.[8]

This need was something they and Lady Masham had discussed during Popple's spring visit to Oates nearly two years earlier,* and the idea was hardly something that Locke would have found fault with. Nevertheless he had "too just grounds to decline", and Popple set about writing something himself. Two months later he sent Locke what he had "lately scribbled", asking that he and Lady Masham would give their comments on it. Of course they agreed to do so, but there is no record of what they thought.[9]

In February, with the process of collecting in the silver currency for recoinage underway, attention again turned to the question of the high value of gold.* Parliament set the value of a guinea at a maximum of twenty-eight shillings, a value which by mid-April was set at twenty-two. There was some resistance to this in the Treasury, where it was hoped that a high guinea might lead, contrary to government policy, to a "raising" or devaluation of the silver currency; Clarke, by contrast, was in favour of it, thinking it would cause clipped money to be valued by weight. Locke was not fully in agreement with Clarke on this: he too wanted clipped money to pass for no more than its weight, but thought it was pointless to try to fix the value of the guinea by law, it would find its own level: "you may as well regulate the price of wheat as gold". What could be legislated for was for clipped silver money still in circulation to be valued by weight, and that would regulate the price of gold, because what had raised it was the currency of "light and base" silver money.[10]

Though his concerns about the evils of continued clipping were as intense as ever, Locke was rather regretting his involvement in "the business of our money" when he complained to Molyneux in April that because "I had played the fool to print about it, there was scarce a post wherein somebody or other did not give me fresh trouble about it".[11]

The instability of the currency continued to occupy Locke on a more personal level too. In February he instructed his new agent Lyde to accept from his Somerset tenants any coins that would be accepted in Bristol. Then, having forgotten to mention guineas, he added in early March that he would accept them for twenty-six shillings, even though he thought that, when people began to use the heavy milled silver coins they had been hoarding, they would fall to twenty-one or twenty-two. The beginning of May was the date fixed for the demonetarisation of any remaining lightweight silver coins, and Locke was anxious that Lyde should see to it that any of these he had received would reach him by then, so that he could get them off to the Treasury.[12]

It is perhaps not surprising that Locke declined Popple's suggestion of writing a book which would show religion "in a pure light", since he had other plans for writing. Twice in the following months he mentioned to Molyneux that there were "some thoughts my mind is sometimes upon", if only he could get some "quiet and leisure, and a competency of health" to perfect them. Whatever it was he had in mind was denied him, at least for some time: "business" and the "service of my country", things which are "not those I now relish, or that do, with most pleasure, employ my thoughts", had already been taking up more time than his health really allowed.[13]

Popple could not have been alone in the opinion he had expressed of Locke at the beginning of the year, that "if public service call you, I know you will take the best measures you can to comply". Nevertheless, Locke learnt in April of complaints that he was failing in his duties with the Appeals Commission. Clearly annoyed, he reminded Freke and Clarke, who had alerted him to this, of the three occasions the previous year when he had been in town (2–28 September, 21 October–18 November, and 20–31 December) trying to get a quorum, and pointed out that "I could do no more than I did unless I could have heard and judged by myself". Since then, he said, he had punctiliously replied to every summons he had received (even though he had excused himself from them on the grounds of health).[14]

The complaints were doubly annoying since "the ill impressions" his lungs received when he was last in town were "not so wholly worn off...that I should be forward to return into that mischievous air till settled warm weather has made it a little safer for me. I am hoarse still almost every evening.... I should be very sorry any urgent business should force me thither sooner." Unfortunately, however, business began to appear before better weather, and in the second half of May pressure began to build up for him to be in town for a matter which, he had previously confessed to Molyneux, "I...shall not be sorry, if I escape". The King had again passed a warrant for a bill appointing Commissioners of Trade, and this time it had received the Great Seal. A stirring letter from Trumbell alerted Locke to the fact that the new Commissioners should now meet: "I am now to call upon you in behalf of the public, whose service requires your help, and consequently your attendance." The Council of Trade "must go on with effect, or the greatest inconveniences and mischief will follow. I hope your health will permit you to come and make some stay here; and what reluctancy soever you may have to appear ... I know your love to your country, and your great zeal for our common interests, will overcome it." Pressure was increased by another letter, from Sir William Honeywood, an Appeals commissioner: they were shortly to meet, "and believing it will be not only necessary but also very advantageous to us to have your assistance we entreat you to be there".[15]

Locke was not quite ready for these summonses. The day before the first was issued, he had told Clarke that it was "with us perfect winter weather and I write this by the fireside" (at both ends of the day he recorded "misling rain" and a "hard and whistling wind" from the northeast). Not knowing how long he might have to spend in town, he wanted to be as well prepared as possible, and needed at least a week's warmer weather "to get off the remainder of my cough before I venture into that enemy air".[16]

Nevertheless he replied to Honeywood immediately that "neither health nor weather" would keep him away longer than need be. He would, he said, be there in town as soon as was practicably possible; unfortunately this would not be soon enough, for the next coach was on the day of the Appeals meeting and in any case it was already filled. He went in the next after that, four days later; whether or not he was there for any of it, the Appeals business did not last long, and he was soon back at Oates.[17]

A week later he set out again for London, with over two weeks in hand before his first meeting with the other newly appointed Commissioners for "promoting the trade of this kingdom and for inspecting and improving his plantations in America and else-where". With Popple nominated and admitted as secretary (possibly due to Locke's influence), the Commissioners resolved to meet "upon Monday next at four a clock in the afternoon and from thence forwards continue to meet regularly every Monday at the same hour; and every Wednesday and Friday at ten a clock in the morning".[18] In fact they sometimes met more often even than this, and the Board of Trade joined ill-health as a prominent feature of Locke's life.

He had missed only two of the fifteen meetings that had been held so far when he wrote in early August to Molyneux, who had congratulated him on his appointment. "If you would give me leave to whisper truth without vanity", he said, it was something by which he would get nothing:

My age and health demand a retreat from bustle and business, and the pursuit of some enquiries, I have in my thoughts, makes it more desirable than any of those rewards, which public employments tempt people with. I think the little I have enough, and do not desire to live higher, or die richer than I am. And therefore you have reason rather to pity the folly, than congratulate the fortune, that engages me in the whirlpool.[19]

Pierre Coste would record that it was said of Locke "that he was in a manner the soul of that illustrious body. The most experienced merchants were surprised that a man, who had spent his life in the study of physic, of polite literature, or of philosophy, should have more extensive and certain views than themselves, in a business which they had wholly applied themselves to from their youth."[20]

Despite the "whirlpool" of Trade business, Locke was able to spend some time with a friend, Alexander Cunningham, "an extraordinary man of parts and learning", discussing a short paper the German philosopher Gottfried Leibniz had written, "Quelques remarques sur le livre de Mons. Lock intitulé Essay of Understanding". It had been passed to Cunningham by one Thomas Burnet who, earlier in the year, had got it from Leibniz himself. Leibniz (already impressed by Locke's *Thoughts concerning Education*) had found "many things to my liking" in the *Essay*, and hoped his remarks on it would be seen and responded to by Locke.[21]

Leibniz disagreed with Locke on a number of points: he thought that ideas are innate and "come from within our own soul", that "the soul is never without some perception", and that there is no vacuum. But he also agreed on others (for example, that "a mass of matter, whose parts are without perception, cannot make a thinking whole"), and he was continually generous in his praise ("he gives us important thoughts of his own invention; his penetration and fairness appear everywhere. He is not only an assayer, but he is also a transmuter by the increase of good metal he gives").[22]

Many of the works on which Leibniz's reputation as a great philosopher now rest were unpublished at the time and he was best known as a mathematician. Even so, as Locke told Molyneux, "Mr Leibniz's great name had raised in me an expectation"; it was, however, one to which "the sight of his paper did not answer", for when he and Cunningham read the piece over "paragraph by paragraph" together, there were some passages Cunningham could not understand and others where Locke thought Leibniz's opinion "would not hold". The suspicion was that Leibniz, with a poor grasp of English, had sometimes misunderstood Locke. In any case, Leibniz's own views, merely hinted at and left sketchy, must have been rather baffling to Locke: his seemingly extraordinary claim about innate ideas that "we not only have a reminiscence of all our past thoughts, but also a presentiment of all our future thoughts" would not have been to Locke's rather down-to-earth taste. Locke's negative reactions to Leibniz's paper were shared by Molyneux and Le Clerc; the latter, despite a thousand good things he had heard "of this mathematician", thought that "he does not understand you, and I doubt that he understands himself very well".[23]

Leibniz was disappointed that Burnet could not tell him much of what had passed between Locke and Cunningham. Burnet was able to report that Locke "much esteemed" Leibniz and had taken his paper "as the greatest compliment", but he had to say that Cunningham had not been "so free" in passing on Locke's opinion of its contents. Though conscious that Locke might be busy with his work for the government, he got Burnet to prompt him to let him know that "your great and just admirer... desireth even to be instructed from you", and early the next year Burnet sent Locke another copy of the paper.[24]

At least as mediated by Burnet, there was no lack of cordiality between Locke and Leibniz, and they sent each other copies of their publications (in Locke's case the collection of his *Several Papers relating to Money, Interest and Trade*). But Locke was not to be drawn into philosophical discussion and, after he had said that lack of time prevented him giving Leibniz's paper the attention it deserved, Leibniz decided not to press him further, telling Burnet that, after all, his "metaphysics is a little more Platonic" than Locke's, and so not to the general taste. Burnet later told him some of the truth, that Locke could not fully understand the "Remarks", and Leibniz was anxious to know where the difficulties were. But it was not until after Locke's death, when his letters to Molyneux were published, that Leibniz learnt that Locke's reaction had basically been one of scorn.[25]

Considerations of time aside, Locke's reluctance to enter a discussion must have had something to do with his low view of Leibniz's philosophical acumen, a view which was confirmed when he read a published article which Leibniz had sent him, and concluded that "even great parts will not master any subject without great thinking, and even the largest minds have but narrow swallows". The "sort of fiddling" that Leibniz had produced, Locke said, "makes me hardly avoid thinking that he is not that very great man as has been talked of him".[26]

Locke took a break ("convenient for my health and necessary for some business I had") from Board meetings towards the end of July when he absented himself from two and went to Oates for some days. The business related to an action that Damaris's brother John was taking against the trustees of the trust set up by their mother, an action which points to an excess of self-satisfaction in Locke's later boast that "I do not use to set my hand and seal till I have advised with those who are better skilled in those matters than I, by which means I have all my life avoided suits and controversies".[27]

During the next month, at Molyneux's request, Locke found the time to sit to a portrait painter, Michael Dahl. Molyneux was impatient to have the picture (not least because someone had told him "I something resembled you in countenance; could he but assure me of being like you in mind too"). It was finished by September, when Locke (who complained that it "made me look grave") told Molyneux, "the honour you do me in giving me thus a place in your house I look on as the effect of having a place already in your esteem and affection, and that made me more easily submit to what I thought looked too much like vanity in me". "Painting", he explained, "was designed to represent the gods, or the great men that stood next to them" – to which Molyneux replied that in fact that was why "I desired your picture"![28]

Trade matters continued to make great demands on Locke's time (he certainly was not free to go to Somerset to see to his affairs, as he had hoped). Besides the meetings themselves – and he conscientiously attended them all until mid-November (fourteen in August, twenty in September, sixteen in October) – there were inquiries to make, and letters to write and to answer, on a wide variety of topics such as ship wrecking in Norfolk, arbitration of merchants' disputes, and the manufacture of linen. At the beginning of September he wrote to young Esther Masham that though "my head . . . belongs now to a man of trade, and is thwacked with sea-coal and fuller's earth, lampblack and hob nails and a thousand such considerable things, yet there is room empty and clear kept on purpose for the lady, and, if you did but see how you sit mistress there and command all the ambergris and pearls, all the fine silks and muslins which are in my storehouse, you would not complain".[29]

In mid-November, Locke left off his public duties and returned home. Earlier in the year, despite feeling well, he had been a little unconfident: "the flattery of my summer vigour ought not to make me count beyond the next winter", he had told Molyneux; and more recently that anxiety must have seemed to have been justified. Latterly in London, besides his chronic cough and shortage of breath, there had been acute cramps which "tormented . . . constantly every night". Fortunately, a day or so after getting back to the country he was able to tell Clarke that these had gone, perhaps because of "the goodness of the air which helping relieve me of those crude humours which this way rack me in town". As for his other ailments, "my cough continues to shake me cruelly, though I find my lungs move better than they did in town, and I am not so much oppressed with short breathing as I was there".[30]

Syl had not come back with Locke to Oates, for the previous month he had, after eighteen years' service as servant, valet, and anamuensis, left to take up employment (at twenty times the salary) as a clerk, under Popple as secretary to the Commissioners of Trade. No doubt Locke often came across him in Whitehall, but they remained more in touch than that, for Syl often shopped for various small items which he had delivered to Oates, where he was an occasional visitor. When they came to finalise the meticulous daily domestic accounts that Syl had kept, Locke was owed a sum approaching Syl's yearly wage; however, as the account book records, he generously decided to "remit and forgive the said debt of £3. 13. 11". Some years earlier, when Syl had left Locke's service for a brief period, Locke had thought it would take a miracle to find someone else so "trusty, sober, diligent, well conditioned, read and write well, and some other good qualities, in fine excellent". So Timothy Kiplin, who replaced him at 15s a quarter, 5s less than Syl, had a lot to live up to. From the very start "Tim" was not going so be as useful as his predecessor: for one thing he could not copy French.[31]

NOVEMBER 1696—FEBRUARY 1697: "A CLIPPED CHRISTIANITY"[32]

Locke was not long back at Oates before he read a very recently published book, *A Discourse in Vindication of the Doctrine of the Trinity* by Edward Stillingfleet, now the Bishop of Worcester. In defence of the doctrine of the Trinity against objections "from reason", Stillingfleet spent time criticising Locke's *Essay* account of knowledge. Molyneux felt it not worth Locke's while to make a specific point of replying: it is "not of that moment; but perhaps you may find some accidental occasion of taking notice thereof, either in the next edition of your Essay, or some other discourse you may publish".[33] Locke judged differently, and immediately set about writing *A Letter to the Bishop of Worcester.*

On the face of it, Molyneux was right, for much of what Stillingfleet said was unclear and based on misunderstandings. Moreover, the reason for replying which Locke gave Limborch was, again on the face of it, hardly strong enough to outweigh his dislike of public controversy; namely, that "I ought to give my reasons why I adhere to my opinion when I cannot discover it to be contrary to truth".[34]

But what lay behind this, as is plain from his *Letter*, was the concern that Stillingfleet, a bishop in a position of authority in the established Church, had publicly connected the *Essay* with heretical Socinian attacks on church doctrine. Yet not only did the *Essay* give no support, certainly not explicitly, to anti-Trinitarianism, Locke wanted (whatever his private views on the matter) to rebut, and as soon as possible, any suggestion of being associated with what were officially proscribed heresies.

It is not clear whether he thought Stillingfleet's associating him with religious heterodoxy was in any way malicious and part of some concerted move against the *Essay*, but he did think something of that sort was in the air. A short time later, when the *Letter* was being printed, he told Molyneux that William Sherlock had recently delivered a sermon against his rejection of innate ideas, charging it with "little less than atheism", and then commented on a general change of attitude to the *Essay* which he thought he had discerned. Three years earlier, and commenting on how fast the *Essay* was selling, he had rather brashly said that "however heterodox it may be" it had not "as yet found an assailant". Now, with rather more concern, he said that though "my book crept into the world about six or seven years ago, without any opposition, and has since passed amongst some for useful, and, the least favourable, for innocent", it seems that "it is agreed by some men" that this should change.

Something, I know not what, is at last spied out in it, that is like to be troublesome, and therefore it must be an ill book, and be treated accordingly. It is not that I know anything in particular, but some things that have happened at the same time together, seem to me to suggest this: what it will produce, time will show.[35]

Stillingfleet's last chapter defended the Trinity against the objection that it is "a mystery, and therefore above reason, and we cannot in reason be obliged to believe any such thing". In his *Letter*, Locke continually expressed himself at a loss why his account of knowledge should be connected with this objection and those who made it: "I have the good luck", he remarked dryly, "to be joined with others for what I do not say...which, how it came about, your lordship can best resolve."[36] Both overall and in detail the train of Stillingfleet's thought is far from easy to discern (not because of any depth, but because of confusion and sloppiness). As a result Locke could not outline what Stillingfleet had said, but was forced into lengthy quotation and line-by-line polemical comment.

Stillingfleet approached the objection "from reason" by investigating "what we understand by reason". But rather than being positive about this, he chose simply to attack an account he attributed to those who made the objection. In some recent unitarian pamphlets he had found little beyond some reference to "clear and distinct perceptions", but he had found more in a recent book by John Toland, *Christianity not Mysterious*, which argued that the revelations of the Scriptures were acceptable only if they were not "above reason".[37]

Toland had been known to Locke since 1693 when he was introduced to him via letters from Le Clerc, Limborch, and Furly. It is possible that Locke had seen some part of Toland's book (which was objected to by the Middlesex Grand Jury at the same time as the *Reasonableness of Christianity*) while it was still in manuscript. Toland had not mentioned Locke by name, but the reference to an "excellent modern philosopher" was clear, for there were many echoes of the *Essay* in his book, including an account of reason as the perception of agreements and disagreements between ideas derived from experience.[38]

On the basis of his reading of Toland, Stillingfleet erected as a target an account according to which certainty and knowledge depend on our perception of agreements and disagreements between ideas which not merely are derived from experience but also are clear and distinct. He then embarked on a rather *ad hominem* critique of Locke, aiming to show how very unsatisfactory this account is, and so to undermine the idea that we should not believe anything "above reason", anything which was a "mystery" in not being "clear and distinct" to our understanding. By reference to Locke's proofs of the existence of God, and of material and thinking substances, Stillingfleet argued that Locke's own practice did not always square with this theory, and that therefore Locke had hardly provided "any reasonable foundation for rejecting a doctrine proposed to us as of divine revelation, because we cannot comprehend the manner of it".[39] He argued also, by reference to Locke's accounts of substance in general, and of what it is for two people to be the *same* (both persons) yet *different* (two in number), that when Locke's practice did follow his theory it put him firmly on the side of those who rejected the "three persons in one substance" of the Trinity.

Locke was determined to rescue the *Essay* from any connection with unitarianism, and with Toland's rejection of things above reason. He continually questioned why he had been publicly brought into the matter in the first place. The *Essay* had been written, he said, "without any thought" of the Trinitarian controversy, yet Stillingfleet gave the impression to anyone who had not read the *Essay* that it was deeply concerned with it. Since in over twenty-eight pages of text all Stillingfleet's references were to the *Essay*, "the world will be apt to think that I am the person who argues against the Trinity, and denies mysteries, against whom your lordship directs those pages ... [yet] I do not see how what I say does at all concern the controversy your lordship is engaged in".[40] As for the account of knowledge which Stillingfleet had attributed to him, Locke pointed out over and over that though he held knowledge to be the perception of agreements between ideas, it was no requirement of his that those ideas be "clear and distinct", and their not being so was not a reason for rejecting them. He did not think, he repeatedly said, that ideas needed to be clear and distinct in all respects for us to discern agreements between them. Moreover, he said, what Stillingfleet himself said about reason, knowledge, and certainty (in so far as he had said anything) differed only in terminology from Locke's talk of perception of agreements between ideas.

As for having given an unsatisfactory account of substance, Locke replied that his did not differ from Stillingfleet's. Where he said we cannot conceive how qualities "should subsist alone", and so "suppose them ... supported by some common subject ... we denote by the name substance", Stillingfleet held that because it is a "repugnance to our conceptions, that modes or accidents should subsist by themselves", we "conceive a substratum, or substance". Permit me then, Locke said, "to boast to the world" that what he had said about our general idea of substance "has the honour to be confirmed by your lordship's authority. And that [what I say about it] has no objection in it against the Trinity; for then your lordship will not, I know, be of that opinion." Finally, if Stillingfleet found that what Locke could say, on the basis of ideas derived from sensation and reflection, about the *sameness in nature* yet *difference in number* of two people was unsatisfactory, Locke found what Stillingfleet had said of no help either, and "learned nothing out of your elaborate discourse". If Locke could be accused of anti-Trinitarianism because he did not give a clear account of "the distinction between nature and person", then Stillingfleet could too.[41]

In ending, Locke summed up his bafflement about the bishop's dealings with him: "I can scarce find upon what ground this controversy with me stands, or whence it rose, or whither it tends.... Give me leave to wish, that your lordship had shown what connexion anything I have said...has with any objections, that are made by others against the doctrine of the Trinity or against mysteries." He stressed that it was no requirement of his that everything be "clear and distinct" and transparent to reason. He was able to accept "mysteries above reason": "The holy scripture is to me...the constant guide of my assent; and I shall always hearken to it, as containing infallible truth.... And I wish I could say, there were no mysteries in it.... But where I want the evidence of things, there yet is ground enough for me to believe, because God has said it." I shall, he said, withdraw anything I have said "as soon as I am shown that it is contrary to any revelation in the holy scripture. But I must confess to your lordship, that I do not perceive any such contrariety in anything in my Essay of Human Understanding."[42]

Lengthy as it was, Locke had completed the *Letter* by the end of the first week in January. He sent it to Freke to look over before passing it to Churchill for publication. Apart from making a few verbal alterations, Freke had no criticism except for "the too frequent repetitions...which I observe in it after the example of your Essay". By mid-March it was published.[43]

Though no longer exposed to the London air, Locke was not well in the weeks after his return to Oates in November. At the beginning of December there was mention of some "recovery", and an expectation of being in London again "some time hence", but then, at the turn of the year, he was kept within doors "under the confinement of my ill lungs". His weather observations being from indoors, he was still able to make these. It was very much on his mind that "business of several kinds would make it necessary to me to go to London as soon as possible". By then he had missed over two dozen Board of Trade meetings and cannot have been pleased to be reminded of this. "Some of my brethren", he wrote to Somers,

I understand, think my stay in the country long, and desire me to return to bear my part, and to help to dispatch the multitude of business.... I cannot but say they are in the right; and I cannot but think, at the same time, that I also am in the right to stay in the country, where all my care is little enough to preserve those small remains of health.

Perhaps his displeasure led him to continue by offering his resignation:

there remains, therefore, nothing else to be done but that I should cease to fill up any longer a place that requires a more constant attendance than my strength will allow; and to that purpose, I prevail with your Lordship to move his Majesty, that he would be pleased to ease me of the employment he has been so graciously pleased to honour me with.[44]

Somers was "very sorry for your ill health" of course; he hoped Locke would "have so much regard to yourself, your friends, and your country, as not to think of returning to business till you are recovered". But he would not hear of relaying a resignation to the King, certainly not until he had seen Locke. Locke's reply was firm, perhaps a little impatient: "If my ill lungs would permit me...to come to town and wait there the opportunity of discoursing your Lordship, I should not have reason as I have to desire to quit this employment." He suggested that "the great indulgence your Lordship expresses to my infirm constitution, makes me hope it will extend itself further and...do [no] less than make your Lordship bethink yourself of a man to substitute in the place of a shadow".[45]

Nevertheless, just over a week later, on a close, windless day, Locke travelled up to London "with an intention to make some stay there", and two days later was again at a Board meeting (having now missed the last fifty-nine). Pressure of business forced the Commissioners to meet in the evening as well as the afternoon on that Saturday, and likewise on the following Monday; they met again on the Tuesday and on the Wednesday, and the agreement for yet another meeting the next day seems to have been too much for Locke, and he absented himself, both then and the next day. Perhaps he attended an Appeals meeting on that Friday, but, "after a week's uneasy and gasping stay", was forced "precipitately" to return to Oates the next day. "My illness", he later said, "grew so fast upon me that in less than a week my life was in danger and I was forced to get out of town."[46]

Despite feeling himself to be "an infirm old man", Locke had managed much during these few days in London. Besides the multiple Board meetings, he attended to some of his own interests and business. He made a point of seeking out Hans Sloane, now secretary of the Royal Society, to whom he had promised an account of the extraordinarily long nails of a man he had once seen in Paris. He had brought with him from Oates, not his written account of the case (which he could not immediately find amongst his papers), but rather some clippings of the "monstrous nails" themselves, "pieces of horny substance", which he must have carefully preserved over the past twenty years. Sloane took them to a Society meeting (which decided they should placed in their museum, "too great an honour to those odd nails", Locke thought) and had Locke's account of them published in their *Philosophical Transactions*.[47]

Astonishingly he also had called on Churchill with yet another manuscript, *A Second Vindication of the Reasonableness of Christianity*, which was published the next month. It is unclear when he had been able to write this lengthy reply to further attacks by John Edwards. If, as has been suggested, he wrote it in the present year, it must have taken him just a few weeks; on the other hand the closing months of the previous year had already seen the composition of the *Letter* to Stillingfleet. Initially Locke had intended no reply to Edwards's *Socinianism Unmasked* when it had been published early in the previous year, thinking that "every considerate reader" would see it deserved "nothing but contempt". But more recently there had been another book, *The Socinian Creed*, in which Edwards had taunted that Locke "would have answered him if he could". So in the end he had set about doing so, "that the interest of Christianity may not suffer by my silence".[48]

Edwards's criticisms replayed, at length, his theme in *The Causes of Atheism*, that, if not actually an atheist, the author of *The Reasonableness of Christianity* and its *Vindication* was a Socinian. The recourse to anonymity, a device typical of Socinians, indicated this: "he would not set a Christian name before that book wherein he so grossly abuses Christianity". In *Socinianism Unmasked*, Edwards challenged the "vindicator", as he dubbed their author, to make himself known, but he was in no doubt that "Locke" was the name in question. In *The Socinian Creed* he was sly about this. It is the common "belief and vogue of his very friends and favourers" that *The Reasonableness of Christianity* is Locke's; and since "they call it by his name, I hope it is no offence in me to say so". There was sly unpleasantness too in Edwards's tepid praise of the *Essay* and *Thoughts concerning Education*: "I am apt to think well of the gentleman himself. . . . He had got some credit by his former attempts concerning *Human Understanding* and *Education*; and now . . . he is further tempted to show his parts. . . . I pity him for his unhappy choice of his notion, and his more unhappy and successless defending it." Later, having purported to praise Locke's "acute and ingenious" writings on money, he said "but...I can't approve of his introducing a clipped Christianity, and thrusting upon us a false coin, a counterfeit stamp in religion".[49]

Edwards furthered his general accusation of Socinianism by remarking that those who had applauded the *Reasonableness* were all avowed Socinians and anti-Trinitarians. He noted also (as Locke had in the *Vindication*) the "flutter and buzz" which the *Reasonableness* had raised even when still in the press, and he claimed to find something rather sinister in this: "There were certain factors and emissaries who extravagently extolled it, and it was observed this applause came from the Racovian quarter."* In fact, Edwards suggested, the very publication of the book was part of a concerted plot, into which Locke had been drawn: "Socinianism was to be erected at this time,...all hands are to be employed, i.e. all that they can get. Among others they thought and made choice of a gentleman, who they knew would be extraordinarily useful to them; and he it is probable was as forward to be made use of by them." The plan, Edwards suggested, was to deny (as Locke did) all knowledge of Socinianism and then to advance it surreptitiously: "if there be but one point necessary to be believed, then the doctrines concerning the Trinity, concerning the Incarnation and Divinity of Christ, concerning his satisfaction, etc. are rendered unnecessary as to the making us Christians".[50]

Amongst those whom Edwards picked out as involved with Locke was Samuel Bold, the rector of Steeple in Dorset. In a sermon, *A Short Discourse of the True Knowledge of Christ Jesus*, published towards the end of the previous year along with a lengthier tract, *Some Passages in the Reasonableness of Christianity, etc. and its Vindication...with some Animadversions on... "Socinianism Unmasked"*, Bold had defended Locke against the attacks so far made on him by Edwards. In his sermon he had happened to uphold what Locke had argued for, that there is just one article of faith required to make a Christian, and numerous others in the Scriptures which it is incumbent on a Christian to believe. Some time later he was led by Edwards's *Causes of Atheism* to re-read *The Reasonableness of Christianity*, and "came to be furnished with a truer, and more just notion of the main design of that treatise than I had, upon my looking over it cursory presently after it was published". So, realising that the views of the the *Reasonableness* were close to his own, and that Edwards had not understood them, Bold had been moved to defend them. Praising the *Reasonableness* for its likely tendency to "overthrow and ruin faction in religion", he rated it as "one of the best books that has been published for at least these sixteen hundred years". ("I'm of opinion...it is one of the worst", Edwards later chimed in.)[51]

Bold's criticisms of Edwards were remarkably clear and illuminating; they were also very fair and gentle. It is no wonder that Locke warmed to him, and came to his defence in the *Second Vindication*, whose preface contained an open letter to Bold. He had been surprised, Locke wrote, to find Bold defending him at a time when there was such an outcry against the *Reasonableness*, and, having found that Bold talked very good sense ("you seem to me to comprehend what I have laid together"), he thanked him, and commiserated with him for having had to put up with "the bespatterings of Mr Edwards's dunghill".[52]

In particular, Edwards had accused Bold too of being involved in a supposed Socinian plot: Bold's sermon was simply the production of a "journeyman" who had been commissioned to defend Locke. So far as the *Animadversions* were concerned he had been "made a tool of", for Edwards did not believe that Bold had written it ("Mr Bold would [not] offer such a crude and shallow thing to the public"), and he thought there were distinct differences in style between the initial sermon and the consequent *Animadversions*. Moreover, the "very objections and cavils" which were used in the *Animadversions* were identical with what Edwards had heard that Locke was now proposing. In short, said Edwards, Bold had been asked to put his name to the *Animadversions*, "that it might be said...that a man with a name, and with open face...warranted the...*Reasonableness of Christianity*; that it might be said that a clergyman...vouched these strange notions". In fact, however, "though they appear under the name of S.B. yet they might more truly have had J.L....prefixed to them".[53]

It is not clear where Edwards had heard of what, supposedly, Locke was thinking, and what exactly he had heard, but, realising that there were parallels between Bold's *Animadversions* and what he himself was about to say, Locke felt bound to defend Bold against this accusation:

I ought to acknowledge to Mr Bold, and own to the world, that...his notions do so perfectly agree with mine, that I shall not be afraid, by thoughts and expressions very like his, in this my second vindication, to give Mr Edwards...a handle to tell the world, that either I borrowed this my Vindication from Mr Bold, or wrote his Animadversions for him. The former of these I shall count no discredit, if Mr Edwards thinks fit to charge me with it; and the latter, Mr Bold's character is answer enough to.[54]

Though there may have been "perfect agreement" between the overall views of Bold's *Animadversions* and Locke's *Second Vindication*, agreement in tone with the gentle Bold was quite another matter. Locke said more than once that he had not written for the sake of controversy, but for the sake of truth and things of "everlasting concernment" (a claim borne out from time to time by impressively passionate passages in support of toleration). But he was quite incapable of Bold's pleasant moderation and avoidance of detailed polemic, and he reacted strongly when Edwards was malicious and rudely personal. Locke had been said to be an "egregious...a notorious dissembler", who "nibbles at wit according to his mean talent"; he replied that Edwards was unhelpfully unconstructive (where "arguments are not at hand...railing...is much easier than reasoning") and unfair (Edwards's "business is not to convince me of any mistakes,...but barely to misrepresent me").[55]

Locke's approach was to answer every small point in detail; he found it his "business...to show the world that he [Edwards] is captious and scurrilous...whose disputes are only calumnies directed against the author, without examining the truth and falsehood of what I had published". In doing this he was, as Edwards had observed, not above biting sarcasm and personal invective himself; he concluded a meticulous unpicking of one of Edwards's confidently misguided arguments with the remark:

and there ends the rattling for this time; not to be outdone by any piece of clockwork in the town. When he is once set agoing, he runs on...always in the same strain of noisy, empty declamation, (wherein everything is supposed, and nothing proved) till his own weight has brought him to the ground: and then, being wound up with some new topic, takes another run.[56]

In *Socinianism Unmasked* and *The Socinian Creed*, Edwards, unmoved by Locke's *Vindication*, repeated his earlier criticisms, and because Locke tried to answer him at every point, the *Second Vindication* is at least twelve times the length of the first, from which Locke often quoted. But, tedious though it sometimes is, the repetitive nature of the dispute does mean that some earlier brief points received fuller discussion. Edwards's accusation that Locke took "'the Son of God' to be no more than the 'Messiah'" and so denied Christ's divinity, was first made rather in passing in his *Causes of Atheism*. It was put with much more force in *Socinianism Unmasked* and Locke answered it at great length. Locke, Edwards said, follows Socinus and others in not taking the phrase "son of God" to mean "was God" (i.e. "was begotten from eternity of the substance of the Father by an ineffable generation"), and in equating it simply with "messiah", which is no more than the name of his office. In reply Locke sidestepped the question whether he denied Christ's divinity, and restricted himself to making the debating point that "son of God" could legitimately be used interchangeably with "messiah", as some non-Socinians had done.[57]

Moreover there are some ways in which this phase of Locke's controversy with Edwards moved on. In having to repeat that nothing turned for him on whether what was required to make a Christian was a single uniform belief, Locke reminded Edwards that in both the *Reasonableness* and the *Vindication*, he had also spoken of various associated beliefs. There was nothing evasive about this. Locke's interest was in seeking for *whatever it was* that was required in the way of belief to make a Christian. It was of no concern to him whether that requirement neatly reduced to one, and he was quite prepared, with no sense of discomfort, to speak not only of the "fundamental article" that Jesus is the Messiah, but also of various "concomitant articles" which picked out "characteristical marks" of Jesus being the Messiah and which were "convertible with" it, such as "his resurrection, his ascension, his rule and dominion". Similarly, when Edwards claimed that the faith Locke spoke of, that Jesus is the Messiah, was for him a mere belief which even devils could share, he reminded him that the *Reasonableness* made plain that "the faith which makes a Christian" is a matter of people "entering themselves in the kingdom of God; owning and professing themselves the subjects of Jesus, whom they believe to be the Messiah".[58]

To an extent, then, there was room for some agreement, at least in principle, between Locke and Edwards when the latter claimed that there are things we need to believe, on pain of not knowing what we are believing, when we believe Jesus to be the Messiah — otherwise we shall think that "Jesus is the Messiah" is intended "for a charm or spell, and that the very syllables will suffice to make one a true believer". As Edwards said, "it is impossible anyone should firmly embrace . . . the doctrine of the Messiah" unless he also knows who Jesus is, and what he requires from us.[59] But some of the things that Edwards listed as "essential articles" (original sin, atonement, Jesus's divinity, and the doctrine of the Trinity) went far beyond anything Locke could accept as fundamental requirements of Christian belief.

In what at first appears to be a curiously crabwise move, Locke asked why Edwards's list of "fundamental articles" of Christian belief was not even longer, given that what qualified a belief for inclusion was its being something with divine authority which can be found in the Scriptures. A desire like Edwards's to produce a collection of fundamentals on this basis inevitably and tragically leads, Locke argued, to "creed making" and to a narrowing of Christianity, to systems, sects, and disagreements between them. Not knowing "where to stop, when they have once begun", people simply stop with those fundamentals and texts which suit their particular systems. Between *his* fundamental that Jesus is the Messiah and the whole of the New Testament there is, Locke said, no half-way: "I will be bold to say, that... either only the article of his being the Messiah their King... is the only necessary article... or else, that all the truths contained in the New Testament are necessary articles to be believed to make a man a Christian: and that between these two, it is impossible anywhere to take a stand."[60]

What, then, is special about the belief that Jesus is the Messiah? It is of course far from being all that Christians need concern themselves with. Locke had been insistent from the start that the Scriptures contain other divine truths, which must be believed by obedient Christians who, perhaps after reading and study, are able to understand what they are. But if Locke agreed that "a great many of the truths revealed in the gospels... a man may be ignorant of; nay disbelieve, without danger to his salvation", and also elevated the belief that Jesus is the Messiah above others as necessary to be believed, why is Locke not a "creed maker" and "system builder" himself?[61]

Much of Edwards's disagreement with Locke and Bold arose from a failure to see the answer to this. Quite simply, that belief is distinguished from other truths contained in the New Testament in being what is *"required to make* a Christian"; others are beliefs *"required of* a Christian". In the *Second Vindication*, Locke castigated Edwards for failing to grasp this distinction; it is, though, one which certainly was not clear from the *Reasonableness* or the first *Vindication*.

In fact the need to clarify this crucial distinction and how to do so were perhaps things that Bold showed to Locke; possibly realising his debt, Locke praised Bold for having "excellently explained the difference between that faith which constitutes a man a Christian, and that faith whereby one that is a Christian believes the doctrines taught by our Saviour, and the ground of that difference". As Bold explained it, the grounds for belief in the two cases are quite different: we believe that Jesus is the Messiah (which "is Christianity itself") because of "the evidence and proof [e.g. miracles] that is given that he was". Our further beliefs are grounded on our having accepted the first. It is the "formal consideration" for the others: a person must have been a Christian before he believed other articles – why else would he believe them? Paralleling this, Locke's own subsequent explanation was that "a man must be a subject, before he is bound to obey": the difference between accepting Christ as the Messiah and believing other things in the Scriptures is like (is indeed one instance of it) the difference between, on the one hand, accepting someone as our King, and then, on the other hand, discovering and accepting his laws.[62]

Locke's point, then, was that there is a difference in kind between the belief that Jesus is the Messiah and a belief in other Gospel truths. Moreover, so far as the latter go, it is impossible to mark out amongst them any which are more fundamental or more important than others; they are all, together, simply the whole of God's revelation to us, and all of them, when we discern what they are, must be believed unless we renounce our allegiance to Christ. "Particular acts of an explicit assent" to what we find in the Scriptures depend on what each of us understands; but underlying them there must be what Locke called a general "obedience of assent", an assent "implicitly to all that is delivered" in the Scriptures. Because a Christian is obliged to believe all that he finds revealed in the Scriptures according to his understanding, it follows, said Locke, that each of us in effect does have a "distinct catalogue of fundamentals". Such a catalogue would not, after the manner of Edwards and other system builders and creed makers, be a "set bundle of fundamentals, culled out of the Scripture...according as best suits anyone's fancy, system, or interest"; rather it would be "all those propositions, which he, according to the best of his understanding really apprehends to be contained...in the Scripture" (together with, implicitly, "all the rest, which he is ready to believe, as soon as it shall please God...to enlighten him").

The idea that the Scriptures contain some "set bundle of fundamentals" is, in Locke's view, what had led to the setting up of sects, to "schisms, separations, contentions, animosities, quarrels, blood and butchery, and all that train of mischiefs which have so long harassed and defamed Christianity...and which must still continue as long as any...shall take upon him to be the dispenser and dictator to others of fundamentals". By contrast, for Locke, "nobody can tell what is fundamental to another.... This catalogue of fundamentals everyone alone can make for himself...according as God has...opened each man's understanding, that he may understand the Scriptures." There is, then, on Locke's account of the matter, no scope for the setting up of sects and creeds (beyond Christianity itself, the belief in Jesus as Messiah). "Everyone is orthodox to himself" and there is no reason why I should seek to impose my orthodoxy, my set of fundamentals, on others. Toleration between Christians has an objective basis in the fact that, beyond the belief that makes one a Christian, there is no objective set of Christian fundamentals. Anyone who pays serious attention to the Scriptures and is ready to believe and obey what, according to his own individual understanding, he finds there, "is a true and faithful subject of Christ's kingdom; and cannot be thought to fail in anything necessary to salvation".[63]

To what extent were Edwards's accusations of Socinianism accurate? Locke's claim that he "had never yet read" any Socinian writers was just not true. But it was surely not a disingenuous attempt to hide who his fellow-travellers were. Why, anyway, should reading books entail agreement with them? Rather, it expressed the desire of an independent mind not to be tarred with an indiscriminatingly broad brush. After all, his whole aim with the *Reasonableness* had been to read the Scriptures as they stood, "separate from any opinions and orthodoxies of sects and systems".[64]

At the same time some of his views (whether in the *Reasonableness* or as expressed later), for example about original sin or about bodily resurrection (see pp. 338, 405 and 414), do place him in company which would at least have included Socinians.[65] It is certainly not clear, however, that Edwards (and, later, Stillingfleet) was right to accuse him of playing the "leading card" of Socinianism, the rejection of the Trinity.

He was certainly right to notice that texts which might be supposed to favour the Trinity had been ignored by Locke, or given an interpretion which withdrew that favour. He saw this as a rejection of the doctrine, but Locke could have been simply avoiding the debate as irrelevant to his purposes, and attempting to leave his central argument acceptable to both sides. Perhaps Locke was speaking the simple truth when he said that it was not to the point of the *Reasonableness* to discuss or even mention the Trinity, for it was not a doctrine which Jesus or the Apostles "preached, and required assent to, to make men believers", nor one mentioned in the Apostles' creed. To deny, as indeed many Trinitarians did, that belief in the Trinity was essential to make one a Christian, was not of itself to deny that further study might not lead one to it. It would in any case not be suprising if Locke took the opportunity to avoid the question. The truth, and even the meaning, of this doctrine had been a matter of so much contentious debate in the past half-dozen years that "for preserving of unity in the Church, and the purity of the Christian faith, concerning the trinity", the King (early in 1696) had seen the need to ban discussion of the doctrine and to require the Church to subject opponents of it to civil prosecution.[66]

Locke may in fact have been quite undecided about the Trinity. The evidence of his reading, notes, and jottings shows that, increasingly from the late 1670s and markedly at the time of writing the *Reasonableness*, he was interested in the matter. It also shows that his early positive view that, although the Scriptures had not made the idea of the Trinity comprehensible to us, we should accept it as something which God wanted us "to know and believe", did not survive. But it does not show whether he came to reject the doctrine, or felt that the biblical evidence for it was not so clear as he had earlier thought. His considered view may have been what he expressed to an anonymous correspondent who had written to him in the midst of the Trinitarian controversy in 1693, that in so far as he could understand it, revelation had not made the matter clear, and, considering his own limitations, he was easily persuaded that "there might be unfathomable depths in the incomprehensible nature of that infinite first being".[67]

FEBRUARY 1697–JANUARY 1698: "TOLD I MUST PREPARE MYSELF FOR A STORM"[68]

Having arrived back at Oates towards the end of February, Locke set about catching up on his correspondence. To Molyneux he apologised for not having replied to a letter from the previous September. Nearly every day he had meant to, but something had always intervened. "You would have pitied me to see how much of my time was forced from me this winter...by crowds of letters, which were therefore indispensably to be answered, because they were from people whom either I knew not, or cared not for, or was not willing to make bold with." Limborch was another friend to whom Locke owed a letter. He had been "put last" along with Molyneux, precisely "because you are my friends beyond ceremony and formality".[69]

There were further letters from people he "knew not". One, long and anonymous, asked him to write something in support of the General Naturalisation Bill then going through Parliament, a bill which would have encouraged immigration: "since the strength of a Kingdom is not only money, but people...by your successful pen encourage the multiplication of the latter, as you have preserved the former". The writer went on to answer objections to immigration ("schism in a greater multitude"; immigrants "will outtrade, under-work, underlive and eat the bread...out of [our] mouths") and to rehearse the arguments in favour ("by the many strangers coming here [we have] gotten the perfect manufactory knowledge and insights into the arts and trade of Holland, Spain, and France"). Whether or not Locke did write anything in support of the bill, he was in favour of its aims: four years earlier he had written a short piece according to which "naturalisation is the shortest and easiest way of increasing your people...[who] are the strength of any country or government. It is the number of people that makes the riches of any country."[70]

While Locke had been writing the *Second Vindication*, Bold had been writing his own answer to Edwards, *A Reply to Mr Edwards's Brief Reflections* (something he would not have done, he later said, had he known that the *Second Vindication* was in progress). It was by a very pleasant coincidence that towards the end of March, when Churchill sent Bold printed copies of his *Reply*, he also sent one of Locke's *Second Vindication*. Clearly delighted to find that its author had "stooped so low" as to vindicate him against Edwards, and had thereby acknowledged that they had a common cause, Bold wrote to Locke via Churchill. "Your very rational, exact, and full answer to Mr Edwards...confirms me", he said, "in my persuasion of your pious design and most judicious procedure in your most excellent treatise", *The Reasonableness of Christianity*. Edwards had acted "very injuriously, and with detestable disingenuity": "How deplorable is our case, when those who are peculiarly engaged to study the Christian religion, do make it their business, rather to give the world proofs of the raging furious spirit of a party, than of the meek and charitable spirit of that holy and good religion they are obliged to instruct people in." In words more fitting of himself, he complimented Locke on the calmness of his reply to Edwards, "so becoming a sincere disciple and follower of your meek and patient Lord".[71]

When Churchill sent Locke his copy of his *Second Vindication* he also sent one of his *Letter to the Bishop of Worcester*. The *Letter*, which had not been anonymous, received much praise. "Every judicious reader must own you to be much warier, and more exact, and distinct...than your adversary", Robert South told him; Freke and Clarke had heard an eminent churchman say that "there was not a word amiss in it". Bold was full of praise for it too, "excellently well done...a most delicate, neat, and clear answer". Yet Bold's letter also showed that Stillingfleet had his supporters. Some weeks earlier, he told Churchill, some clergymen asked him what he thought of Locke, "now that great man the Bishop of Worcester had shown the weakness and the dangerous-ness of his chief principles in that book I so admired, his Essay on Human Understanding". His answer had been to wonder why "so great a man should write so little to the purpose". For, Bold had said, "the Bishop does not quote right, he misrepresents Mr Locke's sense, and his own arguments are not concluding". Apparently "this occasioned a little heat", but, Bold told Churchill, "I fetched down both books, and made out what I said so clear in several instances they could not reply a word. But at last concluded, the mistake must be in me, for they could not believe a man of such prodigious learning and reason should be out."[72]

Besides attending to correspondence, Locke began to think of what additions he might want to make to a fourth edition of the *Essay*, and in early April he was at work on the subject of a possible new chapter, "Of the Conduct of the Understanding". "I know not how far it will lead me", he told Molyneux. "I have written several pages on it, but the matter, the farther I go, opens the more upon me...[it] will, I conclude, make the largest chapter of my Essay." But he never fully completed the envisaged chapter, and it was one of a number of "imperfect draughts...intended to be revised and farther looked into", which he eventually left to his executor to deal with "as you think fit".[73]

Our understanding, said Locke, guides us in all we do. Care should therefore be taken "to conduct it right". The *Essay* as it already stood gave an account of the workings, as it were, of the understanding; this proposed chapter explained how it might be ill-used or used to best effect. Locke later spoke as though it dealt exclusively with the ill-health of the understanding, its "miscarriages" and "diseases", various "faults" in its use. Often it did, for example in sections on how our "present circumstances and interest" can prejudice our beliefs; on how we often "hunt after arguments" to support "opinions that best comport with [our] power, profit, or credit"; or often skip in a desultory way from one subject to another.

But besides offering "remedies" for these diseases, Locke also gave advice (some of which would have been in place in his *Thoughts concerning Education*) on how a healthy well-being of the understanding is to be developed and maintained. We must strive to be "indifferent" to the truth, in the sense of not being "in love with any opinion, or wish[ing] it to be true" until we know that it is; we must be open to the examination of our opinions; we must not only read and receive information, but also reflect on, digest, and make notes on what we read; we must cultivate the habit of "reasoning closely and in train", a habit we can learn by some study of mathematics and then "transfer to other parts of knowledge". While we must avoid "a little smattering in everything...filling our heads with superficial notions", it is good that we nevertheless pay attention to subjects beyond our day-to-day concerns: this is not for the "sake of talk and vanity", but because doing so will "accustom our minds to all sorts of ideas, and the proper ways of examining their habitudes and relations". Besides giving the mind a suppleness, it will give it a kind of freedom: "let a man be given up to the contemplation of one sort of knowledge, and that will be everything.... A metaphysician will bring ploughing and gardening immediately to abstract notions.... An alchemist shall reduce divinity to the maxims of his laboratory; explain morality by sal, sulphur and mercury."[74]

Locke had thought his *Letter* to Stillingfleet might have passed for "a submissive complaint of what I did not well understand rather than a dispute", but the bishop was not for peace, and Locke soon found himself embroiled further in unpleasing public argument. Just a couple of months after the appearance of the *Letter*, Stillingfleet published an *Answer*, a copy of which reached Locke at Oates in early May. "It does not satisfy me at all" was Bold's sharp comment, while Molyneux was "mightily surprised" to see Stillingfleet had replied at all: "I thought he would have let that matter fall."[75]

Almost immediately Locke set about a second reply, dating his *Reply to the Bishop of Worcester's Answer to his Letter* a couple of months later, 29 June. He told Molyneux after writing it, "I am not delighted at all in controversy, and think I could spend my time to greater advantage to myself.... I had much rather be at leisure to make some additions to [my book of Education] and my Essay of Human Understanding, than be employed to defend myself against the groundless and, as others think, trifling quarrel of the bishop." But it is not difficult to see why Locke again saw the need to reply in defence of his own name and that of his cherished *Essay*. Stillingfleet had a senior position in the Church and, as Bold's experience had shown, was of some reputation: so much so that an acquaintance, Elizabeth Berkeley (later married to a bishop), admonished Locke for his concern with himself, and for being too critical of "small faults in the exactness" of Stillingfleet's writing. Stillingfleet's "reputation for learning is so justly established and of so public benefit", she said, "that all needless reflections ought to be avoided since it is of less ill consequence to have it thought you mistook my Lord than that my Lord mistook the truth.... [You should have] more willingly used your art to clear what was I own too obscure in my Lord's book than to make that obscurity more observable."[76]

Moreover, quite apart from feeling the need to defend himself against someone who otherwise might automatically be supposed to be right, he still suspected that there was some concerted plan to convict him of irreligion. He told Limborch a few months later that after years of silence

faults, which were not apparent at first, have begun to be discerned. And, oddly, it is claimed that matters of religious controversy can be found in this book in which I had had the plan of treating questions of pure philosophical speculation only.... Since a debate has arisen between the bishop of Worcester, who has attacked me on far-fetched pretext, and myself, the cassocked tribe of theologians has been wonderfully excited against my book, and that dissertation that had hitherto been commended now teems throughout with errors or at least contains the latent foundations of errors or scepticism, which must now at last be laid bare by the pious diligence of learned men.

He told Molyneux that "what I told you formerly of a storm coming against my book, proves no fiction.... Mr Sergeant, a popish priest has bestowed a thick octavo upon my Essay, and Mr Norris, as I hear, is writing hard against it." At the end of the year (by which time another critic of the *Essay*, Thomas Burnet, had emerged) Bold too made a similar observation to Churchill. He did not know exactly what it was that had made "a cluster of writers appear as it were just at the same time (and so many years after the publication of the Essay)"; but he was sure "there is something at the bottom, which they do not yet speak out".[77]

Stillingfleet had seen Locke's *Letter* as consisting partly of a defence against criticisms that Stillingfleet had made against things he claimed to find in the *Essay*, and partly of a complaint. In answer to Locke's complaint, that the *Discourse* had unfairly and unjustifiably connected the *Essay* with the rejection of the Trinity as being "above reason, and therefore not to be believed", Stillingfleet simply repeated what he had already said: that in searching for what the anti-Trinitarians meant by "reason", he had been led via Toland's *Christianity not Mysterious* to Locke's *Essay*. Locke, in his second letter of *Reply*, quite rightly saw this as no advance: it was simply "a short narrative" of what Stillingfleet had said before. It did not justify his being aligned with unitarians, and being saddled with the doctrine that certainty requires clear and distinct ideas. Having had no satisfaction from him, Locke now made his own diagnosis of Stillingfleet's loosely connected train of thought: Toland was coupled with the unitarians because both he and they supposed that certainty required clear and distinct ideas; and Locke was coupled with Toland because they both talked about reason being a matter of perceiving connections between ideas, and because what Toland said about the origin of ideas echoed what Locke had said. "Who can deny", said Locke, that "so ranged in a row, your lordship may place yourself so, that we may seem but one object, and so one shot be aimed at us altogether? Though, if your lordship would be at pains to change your station a little ... we should visibly appear to be very far asunder."[78]

Stillingfleet had been so little moved by Locke's initial complaint that he now tried in his *Answer* to connect him even more firmly with Toland. Implying that Locke himself was somehow at fault for it, Stillingfleet said that it was quite clear that Toland's approach to religion was based on what Locke had said in the *Essay* about knowledge and certainty, and that Locke should take responsibility for this:

there is too much reason to believe, he thought them ["your expressions and his method of proceeding"] the same, and we have no reason to be sorry that, he has given you this occasion for the explaining your meaning.... And if your answer does not come fully up in all things to what I could wish, yet I am glad to find that in general you own the mysteries of the Christian faith...I cannot believe you intended to give any advantage to the enemies of the Christian faith; but whether there has not been too just occasion for

them to apply them [your principles] in that manner is a thing very fit for you
to consider.[79]

In his *Reply* to this, Locke retorted that nothing more by way of
explanation of his meanings was required from him than what he had
already said, namely "that I lay not all foundation of certainty in clear
and distinct ideas; and so there was no reason to join me with those
that do".[80] He took Stillingfleet's patronisingly lofty remarks to
reveal a belief that he really was one of those who rejected
any doctrine of which we had no clear and distinct understanding
and so which was "above reason", and also a determination to
find fault with the *Essay* because he disapproved of its author. With
some justification, Locke clearly felt that he was being wilfully
dragged into a controversy in which he was quite innocent and had
no part.

In fact, as Locke clearly saw, Stillingfleet in his *Answer* had changed
his ground. He was claiming his target not to have been the basing of
certainty on clear and distinct ideas specifically (which Locke did not
do), but rather the basing of it on the perception of agreements
between ideas in general (which Locke did do). His target now was
simply "the way of certainty by ideas": this, said Stillingfleet, has
been "made use of by ill men to promote scepticism and infidelity,
and to overthrow the mysteries of our faith". Locke could make little of
this as a charge against him. "If it be a reason to lay by anything
as bad, because it is, or may be used to an ill purpose, I know not
what will be innocent enough to be kept"; and if his account of
certainty and knowledge in itself (rather than the use some people
had seen fit to make of it) did endanger the doctrine of the Trinity, why
did not Stillingfleet defend that doctrine by giving another account?[81]

Locke argued further that what he had said about certainty, whether
correct or incorrect, could not be of dangerous consequence to
religion, for it was of no consequence to it at all. Knowledge and faith
are two different things. Whatever is said about certainty not "in the
least concerns the assurance of faith". "Faith stands by itself, and upon
grounds of its own; nor can be removed from them, and placed on
those of knowledge." He went no further into this distinction between
knowledge, with its grounding in reason, and faith, grounded in the
revelations of the Scriptures, but the details of what he had in mind
should have been familiar to Stillingfleet from the *Essay*'s chapter* on
the matter.[82]

Another point at which Stillingfleet's *Answer* reinforced his earlier criticisms concerned the "grounds of identity and distinction", or, in other words, what was involved in two *different* people being of the *same* nature, both persons. He had claimed in his *Vindication* that it was impossible on the basis of experience to have clear and distinct ideas about "the distinction between nature and person", ideas without which "we must talk unintelligibly" about the Trinity. Locke had said in his *Letter* that this might make him "a mistaken philosopher", but it did not put him on one side rather than the other with respect to the Trinity. But now, in his *Answer*, Stillingfleet said directly that if what Locke had said about these ideas was true, it was not possible to defend the Trinity. What he had in mind is what Locke had said in the *Essay* about how general terms, such as "man", have their meaning by standing for abstract complex ideas: these, said Stillingfleet, "are only notions of the mind" and nothing in reality, with the result that the doctrine of the Trinity is left foundationless, "one nature and three persons can be no more". For there to be three different persons co-existing in one divine nature it is necessary, Stillingfleet held, that the universal natures of various kinds of thing lie in the things themselves and are not just complex ideas in our minds. "It is certain", in Stillingfleet's view, "that God created not only individuals but the several kinds, with the differences, which they have from each other; it is certain, that these difference do not lie in mere names or ideas."[83]

What seemed certain to Locke, however, was that Stillingfleet's "way of speaking of the same common nature, being in several individuals" is just mistaken: "there is no such thing as one and the same common nature in several individuals; for all that...is in them is particular".[84] Locke had claimed in his *Letter* that he simply could not understand what Stillingfleet's *Vindication* had said about this, and his *Reply* expanded on this, mainly by reporting a conversation he had with friends about it. What Stillingfleet had said was often confused and hasty, but rather than making a serious attempt to engage with it, Locke and his friends seem to have been set on sport, and amused themselves picking it to pieces.

In an appendix to his second reply Locke addressed a short pamphlet, *Remarks upon an Essay concerning Human Understanding*, published earlier in the year by a clergyman, Thomas Burnet. Under the cover of anonymity, Burnet had said that he could not see how "the principles of that ingenious essay...will give us a sure foundation for morality, revealed religion and a future life". He could not see how the distinctions between good and evil, virtue and vice could be discerned by the senses (in accordance with Locke's "general principle of picking up all our knowledge from our five senses"), nor how morality could, as Locke claimed, be as capable of demonstration as mathematics. Further in connection with that demonstration of morality, he was unsure what Locke's mind was about the "reason or ground" of divine law. Was it "the arbitrary will of God, the good of men, or the instrinsic nature of the things themselves": "You seem to resolve all into the will and power of the law-maker. But has the will of a law-maker no rule to go by?"[85]

As to revealed religion, Burnet did not see how Locke could prove that divine revelation was actually true. "You have", Burnet said, "proved very well an eternal, all-powerful and all-knowing being", but how do we know from these attributes that the supreme being is good, just, holy, and veracious? He could not see either that Locke could prove the immortality of the soul. According to Locke, God could, for all we know, endow a system of matter with the power to think; but if the soul were not distinct from the body, then when that "is corrupted and dissolved, 'tis manifest she must be dissolved also".[86]

Locke thought these remarks did not deserve an answer. If their claim to be looking for elucidation were genuine, their author would have approached him directly rather than publishing his remarks; moreover, the author's anonymity prevented Locke from knowing "how to suit my answer to him". He was worried, however, that the *Remarks* might be part of the concerted move against the *Essay*: "Before anything came out against my *Essay* the last year, I was told, that I must prepare myself for a storm that was coming against it; it being resolved by some men, that it was necessary that book of mine should . . . be run down." Nevertheless his reply was brief in the extreme. He had, he said, not claimed actually to have produced a demonstrative morality, and as for Burnet's concern about the ground of divine law, this was simply out of order, and a sign of infidelity. "Whoever sincerely acknowledges any law to be the law of God, cannot fail to acknowledge also, that it has all that reason and ground that a just and wise law can or ought to have; and will easily persuade himself to forbear raising such questions and scruples about it." The insinuation that Locke held that "the distinction of virtue and vice was to be picked up by our eyes, our ears, or our nostrils" showed either ignorance or malice, and "deserves no other answer but pity". The accusation that he had failed to show the veracity of an infinitely powerful and wise being received similar short shrift: "anyone who appears among Christians, may be well ashamed of his name, when he raised such a doubt...unless falsehood be in such reputation with this gentleman, that he concludes lying to be no mark of weakness and folly". As to immortality, "I will tell him a principle of mine that will clear it to him; and that is, the revelation of life and immortality of Jesus Christ, through the gospel".[87]

Later in the year, in reply to Locke's answer, Burnet published *Second Remarks*. Though this too was anonymous, he accused Locke of the same failing: "as to the crime of concealing my name...I think of all men I know Mr Locke had the least reason to make that criminal: he who has written too many books without putting his name to them.... Put your name to all the books and pamphlets you have writ and I will put my name to this." We cannot be sure just what Burnet had in mind; perhaps the pamphlets which Locke had been wrongly accused of writing from Holland, perhaps the *Letters concerning Toleration*, perhaps the *Two Treatises*, perhaps the *Reasonableness of Christianity*. Burnet was obviously taken aback by what he saw as Locke's "domineering answer" to him, "writ in such an angry style, and with such undeserved and ill-grounded reflections". Whatever Locke had heard about "a storm...coming...and a design hatching to run down your book", Burnet had heard of no such thing and protested, quite rightly, that every line of his remarks had been "calm and peaceable". The same was true of every line of his second set of remarks, which expand on all of the questions raised by his first set: immortality, the basis of morality and its relation to God's will, and the trustworthiness of revelation.

Unlike Stillingfleet's rather too detailed and partisan way of dealing with Locke, Burnet's questioning showed much more acumen in getting to essentials, and in pressing Locke for elucidation and clarification. The question of the "reason and ground" of God's laws is a sensible one, on which Locke had had something to say in his "Essays on the Law of Nature", holding there that they were not arbitrary but that there is a "harmony" between them and our rational nature. It is quite clear that Edwards was not raising any doubt about God's veracity, but was objectively asking how Locke's principles supported it. Reasonably enough, Locke thought that it followed from goodness, but the *Essay* had simply assumed that God is good and when it did say that this and other attributes can "easily be deduced" from God's being eternal, omnipotent, and omniscient, it did not show how. According to the *Reasonableness of Christianity* too, God's goodness is discoverable (somehow) by reason, but is something which is best shown in his "peculiar care of mankind" as expressed "in his promises to them" in the Scriptures. The question of what authenticates the Scriptures* is something which, we have seen, Locke was prepared to consider, but he clearly was not prepared to do so with Burnet. He did not address himself further to him, whom he seemed to have seen as a contemptible disbeliever, but there is no doubt that later students of Locke's thought would have benefited more from his seriously doing so than from his polemical replies to Stillingfleet.[88]

In June, Locke felt able to "venture to town with less danger", and went to London taking with him his almost finished *Reply* to Stillingfleet. Shortly afterwards, after an absence of seventy-one meetings, he resumed attendance at the Board of Trade, and at the Commission for Appeals, whose meetings he had recently promised to "constantly attend".[89]

One concern that summer was to find a tutor for Francis Masham, now aged eleven. Having had one person he interviewed decline the post, Locke turned to another Frenchman, Pierre Coste, a young man in his late twenties, who had been wanting such a position for some time. Locke had already had dealings with Coste, in connection with a French translation of *Some Thoughts concerning Education*, since when Coste had also translated *The Reasonableness of Christianity* and had embarked upon the *Essay*. By the end of the year he had taken up residence at Oates. "His skill in mathematics and natural history... is not much", Locke reported to Molyneux, "but he is an ingenious man, and we like him very well for our purpose" – a purpose which, given his work as a translator, must have been partly personal to Locke.[90]

During August there were Trade meetings nearly every day; though one Sunday in the middle of the month Locke was able to have a day out to Walthamstow, with Hans Sloane and a friend. The Board considered schemes relating to trade with Ireland, specifically in wool and linen. Since its climate was particularly suitable, it would benefit Ireland if the cultivation of flax and hemp and its manufacture into linen, and sail-cloth and cordage for the navy, were encouraged there; and this, as Molyneux saw when Locke had discussed the matter with him the previous year, would also be of benefit to England by protecting its all-important woollen industry. "England, most certainly, will never let us thrive by the woollen trade", he remarked to Locke, "this is their darling mistress, and they are jealous of any rival. But I see not that we interfere with them, in the least, by the linen trade. So that that is yet left open to us to grow rich by." Of the three schemes the Commissioners produced, Locke's in particular was "pitched upon" and, over two meetings, considered "paragraph by paragraph".[91]

Locke's initial premise was that woollen manufacture in Ireland was "wholly incompatible with the fundamental trade of England, on which the prosperity of this nation so much depends", and his first recommendations were of ways to suppress it, by taxation and the prohibition of exports. For what are clearly pragmatic rather than moral reasons, the paper went on to recognise that since it is usually ineffective "to drive men from the trade they are employed in by bare prohibition, without offering them at the same time some other trade...we humbly propose that the linen manufacture be... so encouraged in Ireland as may make it the general trade of that country as effectually as the woollen manufacture is and must be of England". Locke's paper then turned to a good number of suggestions and recommendations for this encouragement, ranging from the simple prohibition of linen imports into Ireland to a highly structured nationalisation of the industry: the setting-up of "spinning schools" which children of poor parents should be obliged to attend to learn the trade; the provision of public bleacheries and workhouses; and the standardisation of "the breadth, length, and other qualities [including nomenclature] of the several sorts of linen cloth", of "the length of reels whereupon to wind the linen yarn (which length it is supposed may most conveniently be such as to contain two yards in circumference"); and annual spinning competitions for the best and most thread spun in an hour, and for the best piece of sail-cloth. The spinning schools were to use a very efficient "double wheel" which had been invented by an old friend of Locke's, Thomas Firmin, and which had been demonstrated at the Board the previous August.[92]

The scheme, much as Locke had initially submitted it, was adopted by the Board and sent on to the Lords Justices at the beginning of September.* Though it was appropriate that Locke should have shaped his official report in terms of national self-interest and considerations of political prudence, some remarks to Molyneux reveal more personal feelings on the matter:

I think it a shame, that whilst Ireland is so capable to produce flax and hemp, and able to nourish the poor at so cheap a rate ... that so much money should go ... to enrich foreigners, for those materials, and the manufactures made out of them, when ... people in Ireland, by the advantage of their soil, situation, and plenty, might have every penny of it, if that business were but once put in the right way.... I mightily have it upon my heart to get the linen manufacture established in a flourishing way in your country.[93]

In early September, a couple of days after his report had been approved and signed by his colleagues, Locke was able to squeeze in a quick visit home, leaving immediately after one meeting and getting back just in time for the next one, four days later. Young Esther would have been glad to see him; she had recently complained of his being away for so long (even wishing for the return of his "old and great enemy" winter, because that would keep him at Oates). Though he had told her that it was not "my inclination" that kept him in town, and assured her that "to live is to be where and with whom one likes", his friend Mordaunt seems to have picked up a slightly different idea: "I hope in four or five days ... to see you in London; for I take it for granted, the Essex lady [Lady Masham] is not to attract, while the sun has so much influence."[94]

Later that month the Board set itself to work producing more schemes, this time "to consider of some proper methods for setting on work and employing the poor of this kingdom, and making them useful to the public, and thereby easing others of that burden". Locke began his report (one of those which were considered in detail over a number of meetings) by supposing that pauperism did not stem from "scarcity of provisions nor from want of employment for the poor": "upon a very moderate computation", he said, "it may be concluded that above one half of those who received relief from the parishes are able to get their livelihood". Rather, he suggested, the increase in numbers of the poor was caused by lack of discipline and "corruption of manners". Laws made for the relief of the poor had been improperly applied: "they are turned only to the maintenance of people in idleness, without at all examining into the lives, abilities, or industry of those who seek relief".[95]

Locke's report has been described as an "appalling document", but it was not completely so. He made a clear division between those who, for unspecified reasons (perhaps because they were old and infirm, perhaps because there simply was no work to be found), *cannot* support themselves, and those who can but who don't "maintain themselves by their own labour". The "begging drones" and "idle vagabonds" whose "suppression" Locke discussed are quite explictly those "who live unnecessarily upon other people's labour", they are people "sound of limb and mind", they are those who adopt the "pretence" that they cannot find work. Amongst Locke's proposals for such people were impressing them into the navy, reforming them by putting them to work in "houses of correction" until they were prepared to find work for themselves, and offering others the chance of employing them at low rates of pay. He proposed a system of "working schools" for the children of families too large for their parents to support, where they would learn some handicraft useful to the country, such as "spinning or knitting or some other part of the woollen manufacture".[96]

It is certainly true that the punishment he advocated for anyone caught begging with a forged permit is harsh — he "shall lose his ears for the forgery" for the first offence, and for the second "shall be transported to the plantations, as in case of felony". But Locke's thought throughout was the entirely reasonable one that those who can work should work, and should be facilitated to do so; those who cannot should be supported. Damaris Masham was clear about this. While Locke, she said, was naturally compassionate to the needy, "his charity was always directed to encourage working, laborious, industrious people, and not to relieve idle beggers.... People who had been industrious, but were through age or infirmity passed labour, he was very bountiful to; and used to blame that sparingness with which such were ordinarily relieved... they had (he said) a right to live comfortably." He regularly gave twenty shillings in bread at Christmas to the poor of Pensford ("especially to those that are old and cannot work", or those with too many children to maintain, "though still preferring the honest and industrious to... the lazy and vicious"). And his will set aside ten pounds yearly for the "industrious poor" in his native parishes, especially for "the binding out apprentices... to honest art, vocation, or trade".[97]

In September, Bold received from Churchill a copy of Locke's *Reply* to Stillingfleet. This time, however, it had been sent as a present from the author (in silent acknowledgement of Bold's support of the author of the *Reasonableness*). This, Bold told Locke, was a greater honour than if any bishop "had conferred the best preferment in his diocese on me". Though Stillingfleet "was never so gently treated", Bold said, no one was ever "so effectually answered, and vanquished". Locke's reply to Bold has not survived, but within a year they were meeting each other. Locke also presented Robert South with a copy of the *Reply* – "in which", South said, "with great strength you follow your own blow and with equal dexterity ward off, or rather repel, his; so that for my own part I cannot see how he will be able to encounter you for the future".[98]

Towards the end of the month Locke read yet another attack on him by John Edwards, *A Brief Vindication of the Fundamental Articles of the Christian Faith, as also of the Clergy, Universities, and Public Schools, from Mr Locke's Reflections on them in his Book of Education*, published a couple of months earlier. As the title indicates, Edwards had moved from pretending to suspect (in *Causes of Atheism*) that Locke could not have been the author of the *Reasonableness*, through suggesting (in *Socinian Creed*) that he might be, to saying positively (because in the *Vindication* Locke did not deny it) that he was. Locke must have been completely shocked by Edwards's renewed attack. With its unpleasant rancour and gratuitous personal invective, its aggressive and vicious rudeness, Edwards surpassed even himself ("so much unmannerly passion and Billingsgate language", "such a poor wretch, he deserves no notice", Molyneux remarked). There was no real argument, simply a series of personal attacks, and pompous claims to be setting Locke right. Edwards spoke of Locke as "this adversary, whose obstinate hypocrisy and dissimulation call for no other than the severest chastisements and corrections": "When I saw our Holy Religion endangered by his sacreligious attempts...and his rude encroachments on the professed schools of learning I found it was a public cause." Christianity, Edwards thought, was not all that needed his "vindication": the clergy, universities, and public schools needed defence against the misunderstanding, misrepresentation, and exaggeration of what the "sniveling and pitiful" Locke, a "lewd declaimer...of invectives", an "ill bred and wandering pedagogue", had said about them in his *Education*.[99]

Edwards was particularly obnoxious concerning what Locke had said in the *Education*, about teaching children "to evacuate dextrously": Locke "very feelingly and concernedly discourses" of the guts, Edwards said, "as if they were that part of the body which he most minds". It is true that, having said costiveness* was "an indisposition I had a particular reason to inquire into", Locke had devoted six sections to "making court to Madam Cloacina"; but Edwards's remark that a child will succeed in a daily stool "only when the party [Locke] is present, it being promoted by his vespasian looks" is sheer embroidery.[100]

Edwards's *Brief Vindication* had been printed bearing the commendation of the Vice-Chancellor of Cambridge University, the Regius Professor of Divinity, and other Cambridge notables, including John Covel, Master of Christ Church. Locke thought this so disgraceful that he wrote to Covel expressing his disapproval with bitter sarcasm. In fact, Covel had not actually read the book before it was published, and was now covered in shame − "you may really count me a fool and a coxcomb". He explained how Edwards, an old student acquaintance whom he met by chance in the street, had (without saying much about it) told him that he had a new book ready for the press, and had led him to believe that the Regius Professor and the Vice-Chancellor had agreed to give their names to it.[101]

Locke also took the matter up with the Archbishop of Canterbury, Thomas Tenison, and the Vice-Chancellor of Cambridge, Henry James. Tenison explained that when James saw the book before it was printed he had ordered the deletion of various passages, and was later assured by Edwards that "he had smoothed many things". One "smoothing" was the omission of a certain word ("too horrid to name"), another was of a passage according to which "Mr Locke was governor of the seraglio at Oates". There is no good reason to suppose that the Masham *ménage* was *à trois*, but, for all his rudeness, Edwards did seem to have had a good insight into the domestic structure of Locke's past and present life, for his book still described him as an "itinerant", a "travelling tutor" who "fixes nowhere, has no habitation", who "creep[s] into houses, and insinuat[es] into families". Locke was not satisfied with things as Tenison explained them: "The book is gone and goes abroad into the world with those Reverend licencers names to the imprimateur.... It is alleged that they and others are displeased with [Edwards] for it, but the world sees not any mark of the least displeasure."[102]

In mid-October, still in London, Locke complained to Esther that in a recent letter she had "made such show" of being plump: if her feelings for him were as she claimed she should "pine away a little". As for himself, "thin as I am when I part from you,

I always return thinner. But what I am abated in bulk, I always return increased in affection." Pleasant as this sentiment was, there were more tangible reasons why Locke should wear away. "All the day from my rising", he later told Molyneux, "was commonly spent in [business], and when I came home at night, my shortness of breath, and panting for want of it, made me ordinarily so uneasy, that I had no heart to do anything; so that the usual diversion of my vacant hours forsook me, and reading itself was a burden to me." At the time of his writing to Esther there had been seventy-six Board meetings since he went up to London in June, and he had attended all but one. There had been Appeal meetings, and the almost daily Board meetings continued through November. He was too busy to review the accounts that Lyde sent him from Somerset, and, pressed for time, he had to write to Limborch in French rather than the usual Latin ("lack of practice ... prevents my writing it easily"). Eventually, at the end of November, he missed two Board meetings and returned to Oates.[103]

As he told Clarke whom he had seen the day he left, Locke regretted having left it so long before getting out of town, "foolishly letting the shortness of breath grow so far upon me". But only days after his return to Oates he was much better; so long as he sat still he could breathe "pretty easy", and at night was free of "that panting for breath which so often tormented me in town and made my life there not worth the keeping". Yet he had only to cough or move and he was short of breath, "and the very dressing or undressing me is a labour that I am fain to rest after".[104]

December was spent convivially by the fireside. Afternoons passed "agreeably and jocundly" in the parlour with three or four of the family (which by now perhaps included Pierre Coste) — his letters sometimes ended with greetings from "my lady and all our fireside". He caught up on his corrrespondence with Molyneux, at last went over the Somerset accounts sent him by Lyde, and was kept up to date by Clarke with proceedings in Parliament. By mid-January he had not yet been out of the house, and it is quite possible that he first went out on 21 January, when he left on a journey which brought him, he said, to "the jaws of death".[105]

JANUARY–JULY 1698: "AT THE JAWS OF DEATH"[106]

On Friday 21 January, in response to a summons from Somers, Locke went to London and, two days later, had an audience with

King William. Lady Masham had been told that "the King had a desire to talk with him about his own health; as believing that there was much similitude in their cases". She did not believe this. After all "the King it was thought had too great regard for Mr Locke's health to expose it by such a journey without some important reason for so doing"; and she was right, for the purpose of the meeting was to offer Locke an appointment. Just what this was is not clear: secretary to the ambassador in Paris has been one suggestion; the rather more important position of Secretary of State has been another. Whatever it was, Locke "begged his Majesty to think of some fitter person, and more able to serve him in that important post". He explained to Somers some days later that

> my temper, always shy of a crowd of strangers, has made my acquaintances few, and my conversation too narrow and particular, to get the skill of dealing with men in their various humours, and drawing out their secrets. Whether this was a fault or no to a man that designed no bustle in the world, I know not. I am sure it will let your Lordship see that I am too much a novice in the world for the employment proposed.

"Want of experience" was not the only thing he pointed out to the King; "my own weak state of health" was another, and his point was very shortly to be illustrated quite dramatically. Having seen the King, Locke was supposed to see Somers, but, unfortunately missing him that Sunday evening, he determined to call again early the next morning. The night before had already been bad, but this next one was worse. He could not breathe lying down and had

> to sit up in my bed, where I continued a good part of the night, with hopes that my shortness of breath would abate, and my lungs grow so good-natured as to let me lie down to get a little sleep, whereof I had great need; but my breath constantly failing me as often as I laid my head upon my pillow, at three I got up, and sat by the fire till morning.

There was nothing for it, he told Somers, "but to get out of town immediately; for after the two precedent nights without any rest, I concluded the agonies I laboured under so long in the second of those, would hardly fail to be my death the third, if I stayed". So, early on the Monday ("one of the bitterest days I have known", and one on which the Thames began to freeze over), he returned home. Lady Masham said that he was "so much altered as was almost unimaginable in so little a time".[107]

He was not so altered, however, as to be unable to continue his weather records, which he recommenced at eleven that same evening. By his report, though, he had got into a very bad state: "I can lie down again, indeed, in my bed and take my rest; but, bating that, I find the impression of these two days in London so heavy upon me still... which extends further than the painfulness of breathing, and makes me listless to everything, so that methinks the writing of this letter has been a great performance."[108]

Retreat from "the jaws of death" was not swift. At the end of February he gloomily told Clarke that

as for a speedy recovery which you wish me, the little progress I make in the recovering of my breath... gives me no expectation of it. And for a perfect recovery, as you also wish me, my lungs are too much decayed and my life too far spent to permit the hopes of it. The cruel sharp weather... still upon us here is not at all favourable to either.... My time is all divided between my bed and the chimney-corner, for not being able to walk for want of breath upon the least stirring, I am a prisoner not only to the house, but almost to my chair.[109]

A couple of weeks later, however, he was able to get outside the house and "crawl to a seat we have in the terrace walk, where I can at my ease lazily enjoy the sun and breathe the fresh air". But he had insufficient breath to walk much further, "I... have been without the moat but twice since I came hither". He must have been cheered by the reappearance of the swallows, two of them, at the end of the month.[110]

The *Reply* to Stillingfleet the previous year had been incomplete in addressing only those objections which concerned the *Essay*'s being supportive of irreligion; it promised to return later to objections to his views taken in themselves. It is not clear when Locke had had it in mind to do this, and perhaps he had not yet started when, early in January, he had been faced with *The Bishop of Worcester's Answer to Mr Locke's Second Letter; wherein his notion of ideas is prov'd to be inconsistent with itself, and with the articles of the Christian Faith*, and told Molyneux that Stillingfleet "will receive an answer at large in due time". That was shortly before his terrible days in London, but he must since then have been hard at work by the fireside and on his seat in the terrace walk, for by early April he had "an answer ready for the press",* *Mr Locke's Reply to the Right Reverend the Lord Bishop of Worcester's Answer to his Second Letter*.[111]

Stillingfleet had been "not a little surprised" at the length of Locke's second letter to him: "I see how dangerous it is to give occasion to a person of such a fruitful invention to write; for letters become books, and small books will soon rise to great volumes." He must have been stunned by this further reply, for it was nearly four times longer. Locke himself saw that it was "too long": "the plenty of matter of all sorts, which the gentleman affords me, is the cause..., though I have passed by many things worthy of remark".[112]

What really forced him to write at such length was the abysmally poor quality of what Stillingfleet again faced him with. He needed to untangle the mess produced by frequent misquotation, non sequitur after non sequitur, and a sloppy way with pronouns — "Your Lordship's privileged particles", Locke called them, for Stillingfleet seemed to have exempted them from having any precise reference. But, leaving aside that Stillingfleet was still giving the misleading impression that the *Essay* contained heresy, what led him to bother at all was the continuation of the direct challenge to him and his views. That challenge was now far from what it had been initially — that Locke's *views* were to be scrutinised because they had been taken over by Toland. Locke himself had become a direct object of attack, and he complained about the way Stillingfleet had built up fresh accusations against him. No doubt still worried that there had seemed to be some movement against it, he complained that Stillingfleet had "rummaged again" in the *Essay* "to find new and more important faults...and now at last, at the third effort, 'my notions of ideas are found inconsistent with the articles of the Christian faith'...[and] capable to bear a deeper accusation".[113]

Stillingfleet chided Locke for spending so long on "personal matters", and for persisting with his complaint about being wrongly associated with the unitarians. From the height of his bishop's throne, he loftily told Locke that their controversy might have been shortened had he simply declared that he "owned the doctine of the trinity, as it has been received in the Christian church" (as though, Locke pointed out, he was "charged now with evasions for not clearing myself from an accusation which you never brought against me"). This, Stillingfleet said, "would have removed the suspicions of the doubtful.... But when you so carefully avoid doing this...[you] do but leave the matter more suspicious."[114]

Stillingfleet went on to address Locke's complaint that he should never have been associated with Toland, since he (Locke) did not base certainty on clear and distinct ideas. In his sidestepping of the issue Stillingfleet was at his most aggravating. So much the worse, he told Locke, if you did *not* base certainty on clear and distinct ideas, your account of it would be better if you did. "It is a very wonderful thing...for you to pretend to *certainty* by *ideas*, and not allow those *ideas* to be *clear and distinct....* I could not imagine that you could place certainty in the agreement and disagreement of ideas, and yet not suppose those ideas to be clear and distinct."[115]

Locke rather nicely exposed the disingenuity of this, pointing out that Stillingfleet was here supposing, after all, that certainty *can* be attained by the perception of agreements between clear and distinct ideas – how else can that be a *better* account? In doing so, Locke said, "you grant the proposition, which you declare you chiefly oppose; and so all this great dispute with me is at an end".[116]

Stillingfleet's thoughts were not just narrowly focused on whether Locke required ideas to be clear and distinct. He had it in his head that what Locke was claiming to provide was not so much an analysis of what knowledge and certainty is, but rather a way or method of reaching it. So, he took the *Essay* doctrine that there are limits to our knowledge to be a confession that Locke's "way of certainty" was a mistaken failure: "it is still to me a strange thing, that you should talk so much of a new method of certainty by ideas; and yet allow, as you do, such a want of ideas, such a want of connection between our ideas, and the things themselves". In his first letter Locke had already rejected this picture of what he was up to, but he still had to complain in his third that Stillingfleet thought the *Essay*'s offer had been "to put you in a way of certainty different from what had formerly been the way of certainty, that men by it might attain to certainty in things which they could not before my book was writ".[117]

Misunderstanding what Locke's "way of certainty by ideas" amounted to, Stillingfleet spent many pages of his second letter trying to contrast it disadvantageously with his own "way of certainty by reason". Based on straightforward misquotation and misunderstanding, much of what it said went nowhere and forced Locke to spend time simply setting things straight. One thing that perhaps underlay Stillingfleet's confused criticisms was antipathy to the empiricism of Locke's "way of ideas", according to which the ultimate source of all "ideas" was *experience*, and not some innate content or structure of *reason*. This prevented him acknowledging two things that Locke kept urging: first, that his "ideas" (as objects of the mind in thinking) differed only in name from what Stillingfleet called "notions"; second, that though "reason" for Stillingfleet tended to mean "principles of reason", the self-evidence or proof of these still needed a grounding, and this could only be in "reason" as Locke meant it — our ability to perceive the connections and agreements of the ideas in those principles.

As the very title of Stillingfleet's second letter showed, his target was no longer, specifically, an account of certainty based on clear and distinct ideas, nor even, more generally, one based simply on ideas, but, more generally still, what he called Locke's "way" or "notion of ideas" — which, in his slapdash way, amounted, simply, to any and every doctrine in the *Essay* which gave any appearance to him of being inconsistent with some article of orthodox faith!

For instance, Locke's account of personal identity, which "makes not the same body necessary to the making the same person", cannot, said Stillingfleet, be squared with scriptural teaching about resurrection, which he understood to involve the resurrection of the body as well as the soul: "the same material substance must be reunited [with the soul]; or else it cannot be called a resurrection, but a renovation; i.e. it may be a new life, but not a raising the body from the dead". Locke replied that, except for the resurrection of Christ's body, Scripture spoke only of raising "the dead",* not of raising "bodies from the dead". Of course, a resurrected person would have a body, but there was nothing to say that this would be the *same* body he had in life. Besides which, Locke said, even if his account of personal identity did not require it, it did not rule out that people shall be raised "with the same bodies they had before" if God so pleased.[118]

According to Stillingfleet, Locke's "way of ideas" also involved a rejection of the Incarnation (the "union of the divine and human nature in one person") and of the Trinity ("three persons in the unity of the divine nature"). His claim depended, as it had when he discussed the Trinity in his first reply, on his understanding of what was involved for Locke in two *different people* being of the *same nature*, both human. Given Locke's account of the meaning of words in terms of abstract ideas which are "no more than notions of the mind", Christ's sharing in human nature could, Stillingfleet argued, amount to no more and no less than what it would be for a human to share in it, namely, his answering to a certain abstract idea by virtue of having certain qualities. Yet Christ, the son of God, also partook of the divine, and if his sharing in human nature, on Locke's account, "were in him no otherwise than in other men, then the mystery of the incarnation is quite gone, and Christ is to be considered but like other men".[119]

The basic disagreement between Locke and Stillingfleet concerned whether "a general or common nature could be in particulars, i.e. individuals". For Stillingfleet, a general word, like "man", stood for a "common nature or essence" which, though present and the same in all individuals of that kind, has yet a particular and different subsistence in each of them: in three men, Peter, James, and John, there is a "common nature with a particular subsistence belonging to each of them...and so then here we have an identity of nature, and a distinction of persons in the same nature". Locke, on the other hand, claimed just not to understand how there can be a "distinct, common, or general nature,...a real being", that really exists, not in the understanding, but in different individuals in different places.[120] For him there could be nothing general in a particular thing, everything that exists is particular, and the common nature of two different individual men is just their conformity to an abstract idea in the understanding.

Finally, Locke turned from Stillingfleet's second letter and returned to points in the first which, because they were simply "so many philosophical questions", he had not yet answered. For example, how, on Locke's account, can we be certain that there is any such thing as substance? In answer to Stillingfleet's original complaint about what the *Essay* had said about substance in general, Locke had replied that his view and Stillingfleet's in fact amounted to the same thing. Stillingfleet, however, had not been satisfied. For one thing, he thought Locke's talk of "supposing" qualities to be supported by a common subject far too weak: "that is not what I looked for, but something in the way of certainty by reason". For another, and with some justification, he could not see how, purely on the basis of experience, we could arrive at the idea that sensible qualities needed a support: surely qualities themselves are "things or beings; or else there could be no effect of them", and "how came we to know that these accidents were such feeble things" as to require a support? Indeed, how do we come by the very idea of a "support", and the associated distinction between things which have a self-subsistence and things which do not? The idea of self-subsistence and support, Stillingfleet's view seemed to be, is an a priori idea, "it arises from nothing suggested by the ideas of sensation or reflection, but it comes only from the mind itself". Locke, Stillingfleet objected, had simply not explained *why* "we cannot conceive how...sensible qualities should subsist alone".[121]

Locke saw no force in such questions. The idea of "support", he said, was sufficiently well explained by reference to the foundations of a building, be it "laid upon a rock of diamond, or supported by fairies". He appeared to feel no discomfort that this was just metaphor, and that Stillingfleet, with some justification, was wanting some account of what required its application.[122]

The immateriality of the soul was something else which Locke had still to address. Stillingfleet had focused in his book on what he took to be an inconsistency in the *Essay*: Locke had said both that we do not have clear and distinct ideas of the essences of body and of mind, and that we can nevertheless be certain that there are both spiritual and bodily substances. So far as body was concerned, this certainty was based on our experience of the co-existence of sensible qualities which "we presume to belong to one thing"; it was the same with respect to mind or spirit, Locke had said: we notice in ourselves the "operations of...thinking, reasoning, fearing, which we concluding not to subsist of themselves, nor apprehending how they can belong to body...we are apt to think these the actions of some other substance, which we call spirit". Stillingfleet argued that on Locke's principles this was not satisfactory as a proof of "a spiritual substance in us", for Locke also held that since all we know of body and mind are their operations and nothing of their essences, we "possibly shall never be able to know, whether any mere material being thinks, or no".[123]

In the first of his three *Letters*, Locke's response had been to insist that being a "spiritual substance" or "spirit" does not necessarily involve being an "immaterial substance". A "spiritual substance" involves no more than having the power of thinking, whether or not it is also a body or material substance. We do, then, know of the existence of thinking or spiritual substances, even though we do not know that what thinks in us is immaterial. Locke admitted that this claim that "spirituality" did not necessarily involve immateriality and rule out materiality might seem surprising, and one could wonder whether it was simply a device to avoid Stillingfleet's accusation that it was inconsistent to allow that matter might think. Certainly there was some force in Stillingfleet's reply in his first letter that, prior to this claim, Locke did seem to have set up some kind of opposition between body and mind: according to the *Essay*, besides complex ideas of material substances we all have an idea of "immaterial spirit", derived from the "operations of our own minds".[124]

Stillingfleet was in no doubt that the ideas of spirit and of matter are in opposition, and that it confounds the two to suggest that matter might think. In his third letter, however, Locke insisted that while thought and reason are certainly not part of the essence of matter (so if matter thinks it does not necessarily do so), they are not inconsistent with it either; God could make matter think. There is much in the purely material world, he added, that does not follow from the essence of matter, such as gravitational attraction and the reproductive power of animals and plants. Certainly "we cannot conceive how matter can think", but "to argue from thence, that God therefore cannot give to matter a faculty of thinking, is to say that God's omnipotency is limited to a narrow compass, because man's understanding is". Yet even though it is not impossible that we are material thinking beings, there is no possibility that God is. In reply to Locke's suggestion in his first letter, that there is an incompatibility between being an eternal thinking being and being material, Stillingfleet had said that the same must go for *any* thinking being, so that if God must be immaterial we must be too. In his third letter Locke made his argument more explicit: since thought is not essential to matter, any matter which does think must have been produced by some thinking thing to which thought *is* essential, i.e. by an immaterial spirit.[125]

Locke also replied to Stillingfleet's early claim that the suggestion that matter might think is a threat to religion and morality (something which Locke had explicitly all along denied). Stillingfleet's worry had been that if we cannot prove the soul's immateriality we cannot prove its immortality, and, lacking such proof, are less likely to accept our immortality on the basis of revelation. In short, Locke had "lessened the credibility" of this article of faith. Answering this, Locke pointed out that Stillingfleet was here accepting precisely what he had begun by arguing against – Toland's principle of rejecting mysteries of faith which are above reason. He was maintaining that "divine revelation abates of its credibility" in proportion as human reason fails to support it, and that "the veracity of God is not a firm and sure foundation of faith to rely on, without the concurrent testimony of reason". The confused and shifting nature of his attacks had brought Stillingfleet to a position diametrically opposed to his starting point, and one which Locke, unlike Toland, firmly rejected. "If this be your lordship's way to promote religion or defend its articles", Locke taunted, "I know not what argument the greatest enemies of it could use." This is to "resolve all revelation perfectly and purely into natural reason, to bound its credibility by that, and leave no room for faith in other things, than what can be accounted for by natural reason without revelation". As he had made plain in his first letter, "the holy scripture is...the constant guide of my assent...as containing infallible truth.... Where I want the evidence of things, there yet is ground enough for me to believe, because God has said it."[126]

Answering Stillingfleet was not all that occupied Locke in the late winter and early spring. The previous September Johannes Hudde, the burgomaster of Amsterdam, had asked Limborch whether Locke could help in his search for some irrefutable proof that "an eternal being, whether existing by itself or in every respect perfect, is only one" (i.e. that there is only one being of the kind). At first both Limborch and Locke felt that proof was hardly needed: no one who accepted God's existence could doubt his uniqueness. Yet Locke agreed that proof was possible, and was "inclined to think that the unity of God could be as clearly demonstrated as his existence"; he did not, however, want to go into the matter lest it cause some dispute ("I love peace", he told Limborch).[127]

Hudde, too, was reluctant to show his hand. Like you, Limborch told Locke, "he fears the unjust judgements of theologians who are wont to give a black mark to everything that is not drawn from their own school". Nevertheless, Hudde pressed for Locke's arguments. Limborch reported that "he has composed a demonstration for himself, but said that it is too subtle; and as he values your judgement highly he very keenly desires to see your arguments".[128]

In February, Locke sent the proofs, which he had been thinking about at least since the previous October. Given that the "true notion" of God is of "an infinite eternal incorporeal being perfectly perfect", it is very easy, he said, to show his unity. One of the perfections of a perfectly perfect being will be omnipotence. But there cannot be two omnipotent beings: for either they will the same thing or they do not; if they do, then the will of one must be determined by that of the other, and if they do not, then one will must triumph over the will of the other, so that the other is not omnipotent. In a similar way, two beings cannot both be omniscient or omnipresent. Further, as a second proof, given that no things of the same kind can be in the same place, there cannot be more than one thing with the perfection of omnipresence.[129]

Limborch thought that Locke's first proof wanted nothing, and had irrefutably proved God's uniqueness. But caution was needed, he said, about showing the second to Hudde who, being a Cartesian devotee, would not approve of it as it stood. For according to the Cartesians, God is not in space and so not omnipresent in any literal sense. Locke agreed that the second proof should not be passed on, and thanked Limborch for saving him from "Cartesian disputations and subtleties".[130]

During the course of this discussion (which continued into June) Locke was able, in early April, to report that Limborch's son Francis, a young man in his early twenties, had been at Oates. Unfortunately Locke's health had not permitted him to meet him in London ("at a time of all others when I might seasonably have assisted a new-comer and one inexperienced in things here") when he arrived there the previous month. Lady Masham welcomed the young man, as much as did Locke, for their fathers had been friends. He eventually established himself in England as a merchant and was quite a frequent vistor to Oates, which over the years he supplied with various goods, such as Dutch cabbage seeds, stockfish, and, in particular, cacao nuts from Curaçao; he would, however, be unable to provide the Russian fur-lined boots Locke was seeking just before he died.[131]

Despite the activity and the company, however, Locke was in a despondent mood. At the beginning of April, having told Molyneux of some work which he hoped to be able to finish, he said "my ill health gives me little heart or opportunity for it" – an odd comment given that he had recently set down so many words in reply to Stillingfleet. He was despairing of ever seeing Molyneux, who had been planning to come to England in the spring, to take the waters at Bath, and glumly said that there were many things he wanted to talk to him about "before I die". In the middle of the month he spoke of his "listlessness from indisposition", and at the end of the month his mood was still low. From the beginning of the year, he told Furly, he had been

in the chimney corner...by the fireside, for we have here yet no warmth from the sun...and it was but yesterday morning that it snowed very hard for near two hours together. This great indisposition of my health...keeps me here out...of London and the bustle of affairs. I am little furnished with news and want it less. I have lived long enough to see that a man's endeavours are ill laid out upon anything but himself, and his expectations very uncertain when placed upon what others pretend or promise to do. I say not this with any regard to my private concerns, which I own give me no cause for complaint, since my desires are confined in a narrow compass.

His mood then, and throughout the month, cannot have been helped by being "almost quite alone here now". Damaris, Frank, and Esther Masham had been in London for some weeks. Coste had gone with them too, though he was just about to return, bringing with him a letter from Locke's dear Esther, to which he immediately replied, subscribing himself "I am, of all the shepherds of the forest, gentle bergère, your most humble and most faithfull servant, Celadon the Solitary".*132

One thing Locke wanted to discuss with Molyneux was something his friend had raised, as to whether the English Parliament could, "without our consent and representatives", reasonably pass laws which were applicable to Ireland, which had its own Parliament. Molyneux had said that this was a question for "the author of the Two Treatises of Government", clearly meaning Locke. Coyly rather than coldly, Locke avoided the attribution of the Treatises to him, and said they must discuss the matter, cautioning him that if he did this with anyone else "mention not me" (presumably lest it reinforce any connection they might have been inclined to make between him and the Treatises). But before they could talk about it, Molyneux had published a small book, *The Case of Ireland's being Bound by Acts of Parliament in England stated*. The book was inquired into by the English Parliament, and in late June was deemed to be "of dangerous consequence to the Crown and People of England" since it denied the dependence of Ireland on the crown. It had named Locke as the reputed author of the second treatise, and just after the inquiry got underway Locke thanked Clarke (who had been one of its instigators) "for the care you promise me to take that I receive no inconvenience by the indiscretion of a man which mightily surprised me".133

In June, John Covel went over to Oates from Cambridge. He and Locke discussed a variety of topics ranging from the relationship between various calendars (Greek, Jewish, and Chinese) to points of biblical interpretation. But they also discussed the sensitive matter of the imprimateur to Edwards's *Brief Vindication*. Covel satisfied Locke about his role in the affair; and they agreed that he would concoct a letter which Locke might publish, in an attempt to do both of them some justice.134

JULY–DECEMBER 1698: "NOTHING EVER ESCAPES YOU"[135]

The very cold winter was slow to end. The first Sunday in July was only the third day of the year Locke was able "to pass without a fire"; it was in fact "the comfortablest day I have had these six months", and he was able to sit outside in the fresh warm air. Unfortunately the "winterly weather" returned the very next day, but despite this he determined to go to London at the end of the week. He was there for two or three days before he resumed attendance at Board meetings, but from then until towards the end of October, when he left London, he went to all but three of seventy-four meetings.[136]

One of these three was in late August, when he went back to Oates for a few days. He was (surely to his great delight) accompanied by Molyneux, who had at last made his long-promised and long-awaited visit from Dublin. He had crossed the Irish Sea some weeks earlier, and had visited Bath before going to London for his first ever meeting with Locke. They were together for five weeks, during which Molyneux sat to Sir Godfrey Kneller for a portrait. Locke paid Kneller the £16 for the picture, though it seems it was not intended to hang at Oates, but was for Molyneux's brother. Once back in Dublin, in late September, Molyneux wrote, "I cannot recollect, through the whole course of my life, such signal instances of real friendship, as when I had the happiness of your company.... It is with the greatest satisfaction imaginable, that I recollect what then passed between us, and I reckon it the happiest scene of my whole life." Molyneux promised to make a further visit the following year, but just over two weeks later his kidney ruptured and he was dead. He bequeathed to Locke "my excellent friend...author of the Essay concerning Human Understanding, the sum of five pounds, to buy him a ring, in memory of the value and esteem I had for him".[137]

During his weeks with Molyneux, Locke had another first face-to-face meeting, presumably as moving as the one with Molyneux, this time with Samuel Bold. They discussed several subjects, ranging from the passage in Deuteronomy about the Israelites being permitted to eat animals marked out for sacrifice, through Locke's exchange with Limborch about the uniqueness of God, to the question of additions to a future edition of the *Essay*. After their meeting Bold sent Locke some pages he had written in reaction to a recent book (Robert Jenkins's *Reasonableness and Certainty of the Christian Religion*) which had taken exception to Locke's suggestion in the *Essay* that "possibly we shall never be able to know, whether any mere material being thinks or no" (E: 4.3.6). Locke found Bold's reasonings "strong and just", but encouragement from Locke released a stream of self-doubt (doubt which, in the light of the simple and elegant clarity of his reply to Edwards, was quite misplaced): "I wish I could write with some accurateness, and that I knew how to give my expressions such a turn, as might present my thoughts with something of life." In a later letter he further complained of often failing to keep hold of and develop his ideas.[138]

Locke told him "you mistake yourself and your abilities", and the advice he gave, derived from Francis Bacon, was what he had often given young Ashley Cooper: "never to go without pen and ink, or something to write with; and to be sure not to neglect to write down all thoughts of moment that come into the mind" ("I must own I have omitted it often, and have often repented it", Locke said); and, second, to develop one's ideas by getting things down on paper as soon as possible, returning to these initial drafts when time permitted.

You cannot imagine the difference there is in studying with and without a pen in your hand. Your ideas, if the connections of them that you have traced be set down, so that without the pains of recollecting them in your memory you can take an easy view of them again, will lead you further than you can expect. Try, and tell me if it is not so.[139]

Towards the end of October, Locke reported to Limborch that "winter now becoming more severe and hurtful to my lungs, will shortly drive me from the city and my increasing cough and difficulty in breathing urge departure". A few days later he returned to Oates for the winter. A short while earlier the possibility had opened up that (perhaps in the company of the Mashams?) he would winter in Paris and return to England via Holland, but by the time he left London this no longer seemed likely.[140]

Some weeks later the manservant whom Locke had taken on when Syl left him, also left. "My man Kiplin and I are parted", Locke wrote to a friend, "I want a good servant if you can help me to one". Early into the new year he had found one, James Dorington, at an initial wage of £1 per quarter. (Dorington was with Locke for just under three years, when William Shaw took his place.)[141]

Locke's *Reply* (his second "letter") to Stillingfleet was published in November. He was told of some who thought that Stillingfleet "has the advantage", but Freke reported that "Oxford generally gives judgement in your favour against the bishop and say he deserves the treatment he has received from you though it be pretty severe". He did not know what was said at Cambridge, "but the soberest and ablest London divines concur with the Oxonians". Robert South seems to have approved of the detail of Locke's reply: "I cannot sufficiently commend the closeness of your thoughts and reasoning, and your admirable sagacity and exactness in searching into and sifting everything that your adversary says; so that nothing ever escapes you; which must needs render such a loose writer as Stillingfleet, a very unequal match." Covel was less enthusiastic: venturing to report that some people thought Locke's polemic too detailed, he admitted only that he did not see what else Locke could have done against Stillingfleet's vagueness and innuendo.[142]

A welcome visitor to Oates on Christmas Day was a young man in his late twenties, Peter King, the grandson of Locke's uncle Peter. This was not King's first visit to Oates, but it was the first since he had been called to the Bar, earlier that summer. Locke called him his "nearest kinsman", and at some point decided to make him his heir, even though some years earlier he had felt "very little obligation to him" and more to Peter Stratton who, as another grandson of Uncle Peter, was equally closely related. King, however, as a man "of parts", was more what Locke might have liked to have had as a son. When only twenty-two he had published a book on the early Church, and had intended to become a clergyman; but having some caution about the established Church he turned away from this, no doubt with Locke's approval, to study law instead. King was already beginning to do things which would have been done by a dutiful (and trusted) son: from dispatching books, through giving legal advice, to making substantial investments (sometimes in his own name) of money saved from Locke's Board of Trade salary. Before long King was making regular visits to the West Country on the assize circuit and was able to keep a close eye on Locke's Somerset property. His career would blossom, with a knighthood in 1708 and appointment as Lord Chancellor in 1725.[143]

During King's Christmas stay, besides discussing less homely matters, they discussed the problem King was having in keeping his feet warm: the secret sine qua non, Locke advised him, was that the legs be kept warm. It was perhaps during this conversation that Locke asked King to buy him some knitted gloves; but when he received the half-fingered gloves King sent, Locke thought his advice had been taken too far, "for I am as apt to feel cold in the tops of my fingers as you in the tops of your toes. But in revenge if ever you desire me to buy socks for you I shall be sure to take care that they shall not cover your toes."[144]

In his *Thoughts concerning Education*, Locke advised that after a growing boy had learnt terrestrial geography and could recognise the northern stellar constellations, it was time to learn something about the solar system and "to understand the motion and theory of the planets". Following his own advice, Locke composed for twelve-year-old Frank Masham an outline of "The Elements of Natural Philosophy". In this brief account, which he went over with Frank, Locke prefaced a description of the solar system with an account of Newton's laws of motion, and went on to a brief outline of the earth, first as a planet, and then its geology, its meteorology, and its minerology. He followed this with an account of the nature of plants and animals, and of the five senses. In a final chapter, "Of the understanding of man", he summarised the *Essay* in about five hundred words.[145]

His concluding words were a forthright statement of the corpuscularian theory of the inner workings of the natural world: "By the figure, bulk, texture, and motion, of ... small and insensible corpuscles, all the phenomena of bodies may be explained." These words showed none of the caution of earlier years about whether the natural world was to be understood mechanically in terms of properties of matter and the laws of motion, but even if Locke now agreed completely with Boyle about this, he perhaps did not think such an account was sufficient by itself. Five years earlier, at any rate, in the *Thoughts concerning Education* he had suggested that none of the "great phenomena" of nature, such as gravity, can be explained by "any natural operation of matter, or any other law of motion"; gravity* is explicable only by reference to the "positive will of a superior being".[146]

JANUARY 1699–MARCH 1700: "A TOO LONG STAY IN TOWN"[147]

Despite some improvement in health since leaving London in October, mid-January of the new year saw Locke little disposed to read or write. At any rate this was the reason he gave Daniel Whitby for not making a detailed answer to comments that Whitby sent, directed against what he said about the resurrection of the dead in his latest reply to Stillingfleet. But, besides the fact that Whitby had misunderstood his position, it must also have been that Locke was not much interested in the specifics of the matter. Whitby took him to have *denied* Stillingfleet's view that "the dead shall be raised with the same bodies"; as Locke pointed out, though, he merely denied that Stillingfleet had *proved* his view. Though he was certain we would be resurrected and with suitable bodies, he told Whitby that it was quite indifferent whether these bodies are or are not the same.[148]

Leibniz too had been following Locke's dispute with Stillingfleet; despite his low opinion of Leibniz as a philosopher, Locke had sent his first *Letter*, and wanted to know (so Burnet reported) what he thought. Leibniz was disturbed to find that a real clarification of anything serious was hindered by *ad hominem* carpings about misunderstandings which took up most of the dispute, but he was certainly interested in the substantial issues and wrote at some length about them. His thoughts were relayed to Locke via Burnet, as was his desire to learn Locke's reaction to them. Yet, having encouraged Leibniz, Locke was not prepared to reciprocate, telling Burnet that he had neither the time nor the health to do so. A few years later Lady Masham entered into a philosophical correspondence with Leibniz, starting it by sending him a copy of her father's *Intellectual System*. We can only guess what Locke felt about this, but Leibniz's enthusiasm was at least partly due to his belief that Locke had some sort of presence in the letters that reached Hanover from Oates.[149]

Clarke's son Edward was now aged about nineteen, an age at which Locke might have hoped that the fruits of his method of education would be about ripe. Unfortunately he was even now still giving cause for concern when he visited Locke in April. He was suffering from a lethargic depression, to which he seems to have been prone. At first Locke felt the root cause must be physical (perhaps stemming from a childhood illness) and thought Clarke should consult a physician. A mental cause would "have its foundation in some affliction, some weighty cross or other", which, Locke thought, was quite lacking here; but Clarke then suggested as an immediate cause "some desponding thoughts" which he had discovered his son had of himself. Locke was sure that these feelings of worthlessness must themselves have a physical cause (why should "this one of all your children" have such thoughts "when all the rest have vigorous and active minds?"), but suggested that for a while Clarke and his wife should simply try to give "ease and comfort" to his mind, to "apply all the quickening" they can to it.[150]

As May approached, and throughout that month, Locke was again hoping that "the weather and my lungs" would allow him to go to London. It was wintry at the end of April, but through May the weather got warmer, he was at last able to leave the fireside, and on the last day of the month he went to London. Popple (who over the winter had kept him in touch about Board business) had recently been keen for him to attend in order to ensure a quorum, but it was a few days before he resumed attendance (having missed the last 122 meetings). From then on, during the six months from June to November, he attended every one of ninety-eight meetings.[151]

As usual this took up much of his attention, and in a letter which took him a week to write, being "broken into by frequent interruptions", he complained to Limborch at not having the time to read a book he had sent him. Perhaps one of the "interruptions" was a visitor he had recently received at ten in the morning on a day he happened to have free from official business; but it is hard to believe that the twelve hours he spent with him were unavoidable.[152]

Over the summer Locke's health bore up. In mid-August he commented to Ashley that "time never mends an ill pair of lungs in one of my age, though this warm summer has enabled me to bare the inconvenience of them with some tolerable ease". But as winter approached and November wore on, his cough began to develop. Just after missing two Board meetings, he was forced to leave town at the end of the month. One of the last things he did before leaving was to see to the distribution to his friends of copies of a new, fourth, edition (dated 1700) of the *Essay*. This had been projected (with "many additions") at any rate since the beginning of the year when the third had become out of print, and Locke had worked on it during the spring at Oates. Among the additions were two new chapters (on "Association of Ideas" and on "Enthusiasm"), additions which were also available separately, as those for the second edition had been.[153]

The first of these new chapters examined the way in which ideas which have no natural or logical connection can become firmly associated in our minds and produce utterly unreasonable beliefs or habits. One of Locke's examples concerned a young man who learnt to dance in a room which contained a trunk: "the idea of this remarkable piece of household stuff...so mixed itself with the turns and steps of all his dances" that he could not dance anywhere unless a "trunk had its due position in the room". Another example made an anti-Catholic sideswipe: if the idea of infallibility becomes joined in our minds to that of a certain person, then we will "swallow for a certain truth, by an implicit faith whenever that imagined infallible person dictates and demands assent without inquiry", such as that, in a literal view of the Eucharist, one body can be in two places at once.[154]

It is surprising that Locke had waited until now before including a chapter on "Enthusiasm", for, in discussing it with Damaris Cudworth, he had made notes on the topic as long ago as 1681. Like the chapter on "Association of Ideas", this too treated of "assent without inquiry", but in the context of another form of Christianity, that of the Quakers (who are not mentioned by name). As a young man Locke had had a low opinion of this religious movement, finding Quakers "mad folk", whose discourteous practice of keeping on their hats was dangerous for their already hot heads. He believed their religion was irrational ("we are all Quakers" he gloomily said towards the end of the interregnum, when he found that the world seemed to have abandoned reason); and though in later life some of his good friends, Furly for example, were Quakers, he never abandoned this view. Quakers, he thought, were guilty of "enthusiasm".

For Locke, faith, though quite different from reason, is not entirely independent of it: any supposed revelation must be examined by reason.* Enthusiasm, however, is faith adopted independently of reason, and often on the basis of some immediate, personal inspiration, some "peculiar guidance of heaven", some supposedly divine "call or direction". An "enthusiast", said Locke, is one who "laying by reason would set up revelation without it". But to accept a supposed revelation without using reason to decide its authenticity is to accept "ungrounded fancies" or "the conceits of a warmed or over-weening brain". An enthusiast will insist that reason should have nothing to do with revelation and faith, perhaps claim that we are more open to inspiration if we put reason aside. But, Locke argued, divine inspiration and revelation cannot be their own guarantee. The question must always be pressed, "How do I know that God is the revealer of this to me; that this impression is made upon my mind by his Holy Spirit, and that therefore I ought to obey it?" The strength of a person's persuasions is not sufficient for things to pass as being of divine origin: "if reason must not examine their truth by something extrinsical to the persuasions themselves; inspirations and delusions, truth and falsehood will have the same measure, and will not be possible to be distinguished".[155]

Locke had stayed too long in London. Two days after arriving back home he told King that he saw "by my cough's usage of me since I came here, that I gave it too much hold upon me by my too long stay in town". Yet he very soon re-engaged with his correspondence: to Hans Sloane about a proposal for calendar reform, and about the performances of a strong man in London, "which may be a subject of speculation and inquiry to the philosophical world"; to King about his financial affairs ("I have £1000 lying dead by me. I would desire you to consult... what is the best way of turning money to advantage now"), and wanting to know what was going on in Parliament.[156]

At the beginning of January, Locke had the sad news that his former manservant Syl had died; a death which his bereaved wife (to whom he had been married for at least two years) said "has plunged me into such a multitude of troubles that I don't know what to do for my afflictions are more than I am able to bear". One of her troubles was that since the Board of Trade owed a whole year of Syl's £80 salary, she could not pay her debts, including £20 to Locke. Locke told King that he intended "to be kind to her", although, he cannily added, "I doubt whether that will be in forbearing my debt to the end that other creditors may be paid theirs".[157]

In March, Toinard wrote to Locke, "laughingly", but in some excitement, that the possibility of a *deus ex machina* had presented itself to get him out of some ongoing financial and legal difficulty he was in, and would allow him to come to England. He had read of a new lottery, "The Charitable Adventure for the Benefit of Greenwich Hospital", and wanted Locke to buy him tickets. They were of two prices, 5s (with nearly ten thousand prizes, from £3000 downwards) and 20s (with nearly thirteen thousand prizes, from £10,000 downwards). Toinard wanted three tickets in each, but, due to some malpractice, the "large" lottery was abandoned, and he decided on a further twenty-four more for the "small". Locke hoped that at the driaw the *deus ex machina* would be present "to deliver you from the law suit and restore you to my longing arms"; sadly it was not and Toinard won only 36s.[158]

10

"Laying Down His Place"
(March 1700–October 1704)

MARCH 1700–MARCH 1701: "NOTHING BUT WHAT I OUGHT
AND DO EXPECT"[1]

Despite being busy at Oates, Locke must have been missing his
"College" friends, Clarke and Freke. There were things he wanted to
discuss with them. Towards the end of March the "favourable winter"
had raised hopes of doing this soon. But the wind moved round to the
east and "pinched shrewdly", and, he thought, caused "the spitting of
blood, which happened lately to me, and which I am sure came from
my lungs".[2]

When the swallows arrived in the second week of April, he was
drawn outside to see them for himself: "SWALLOWS now first seen
though they had been looked after by several for many days past. Mr
Winwood Masham saw three this evening and I going outwith to the
place where he had just before seen them we could see but one which
we observed a good while but no more appeared. It was a little before
sunset." But cold, unseasonable weather persisted, and despite a break
of a "warm day or two" which he hoped would continue and "quickly
set me up for the town", Locke's time at the end of the month was still
being spent in "the chimney-corner...by my fireside". A couple of
weeks later, however, he was in London.[3]

He went at least partly in response to a request to make up a quorum
at three forthcoming Appeals meetings, but he must also have had in
mind his responsibility with the Board of Trade, the minutes of whose
meetings Popple always carefully sent him. Wearing a new sword (just
bought for £1 10s) he was at a Trade meeting the day after getting

to London, and for some weeks his attendance was regular and without a break. But he eventually found it too much, and on 27 June, the day after his twenty-eighth meeting in forty-four days, he went to the King, told him that "his health would permit him to stay no longer in town", and sought permission to resign. He was almost sixty-eight, just two years short of the age at which (according to the laws he drew up twenty years earlier) he once thought* people need not accept public office.[4]

The King was reluctant to let him go (telling him "his services in that office would yet be very necessary") and tried to persuade him simply to attend when he could. But the next day the Board minutes recorded that Locke, "finding his health more and more impaired by the air of this city, so that he is not able henceforth to make any continued residence in it...had been yesterday to wait upon the King, and desired his Majesty's leave to lay down his place...and that he therefore came to take leave of the Board, and so withdrew". In fact this was not his last appearance, for he was asked to attend a few days later "in order to confer with the Board about the state of coin in the Plantations", a discussion which involved the question whether a mint should be erected in the American Plantations.[5]

No longer expected at Trade meetings, with Clarke and Freke out of town taking the waters at Tunbridge, he had diminishing reason to stay in London. There were of course other friends and acquaintances to see; Bold, for example, had been in London for some time, and he was anxious to discuss various questions which were concerning him: whether there can be any rational objection to the Gospels, and what cast of mind is conducive to the acceptance of divine truth. But, the fact was, Locke was not well. "I have", he wrote to Clarke, "been very uneasy...since you went, and breathe in pain whilst I write this"; and he returned to Oates in mid-July. He was obviously not going to spend so much time in London now, and his servant James followed in the carrier's wagon with three hundredweight of belongings from his lodgings: a clock, a chair, a wig, and a hat, amongst other things.[6]

Awaiting him at Oates was a horse he had been intending to buy. The horse was prone both to lameness and to distemper, and its owner would neither sell it nor give him it, "but if for his own sake you will take a lease of him you will oblige both him and me". It seems that Locke made good use of it, for towards the end of August he reported enthusiastically to Clarke that "I am on horseback every day": "I know nothing so likely to produce quiet sleep as riding about gently in the air for many hours every day." He urged Clarke to join him.

The Tunbridge waters evidently had not helped Clarke's health, and Locke recommended some pills made from steel and Jesuit's powder for his spleen. But they had to be combined with riding: "Ride with them every day, without which I do not expect they should have any great effect. And your riding must not be for an hour or two, but so much and so long every day as when a man travels a journey." As he had learnt from Sydenham years earlier, the succussive or shaking effect of riding stimulates the bodily organs.[7]

But even if Clarke had made the visit, Locke would not have been able to do any riding with him. Despite the exercise and the summer country air which had been doing him some good, he developed a swelling in his back ("they who have seen it, by its bigness and redness think it a boil. I something doubt of it, because it has no head upon it nor is so extreme painful...though it be tender enough"), and this kept him off horseback for two or three weeks into September.[8]

Locke had wanted, and had been expected, to go up to town again for a while before the winter began. But, as summer came to a close, there had first been the swelling in the back, which meant that he could "bear neither horse nor coach", and then, despite the goodness of the air at Oates, he laboured for breath in the morning and knew that the town air would hardly suit. Finally, in early October, things got worse and he was in considerable pain: the "humour" from the back swelling had "fallen into my leg, where it has caused me very sharp pains.... I spend most of my time in bed, and have ate nothing for some days but water gruel." Towards the end of the month the leg was mending, slowly, but sufficiently to allow him to sit up for an hour or two, after which it became "angry and raw".[9]

John Shute, a young man with a family connection to Lady Masham, was a visitor to Oates around this time. He and Locke discussed a book on God and the divine perfections, by Gerard de Vries, of whom Shute had some direct personal knowledge, having studied at Utrecht where de Vries was a professor of theology. "Before I had the honour to see you", Shute flatteringly told Locke when some months later he sent him a copy of the book, "[I thought him] the best man and the best thinker of this age". Like Locke in the *Essay*, de Vries argued against the idea of God being innate, and, as Shute remarked, Locke would find de Vries often "to entertain the same opinions, which you have advanced with so much strength and so much success". In Shute's eyes, similarities between Locke and de Vries did not stop there: "as truth has formed your notions alike, so virtue has made your tempers and your practice to agree too. For Mr de Vries has a great deal of that cheerfulness, that willingness to oblige, that easiness and compliance, that affability, that candour, that communicativeness which as it makes you, so it renders him too a mighty ornament to learning." One return that Locke made two years later for this flattery was to recommend Shute to Pembroke (who had just become High Admiral). Unfortunately, Pembroke had "very few places in his disposal" and "a great many friends to oblige".[10]

By early November, Locke was no longer confined to "the lazy lying much in bed", and looked on the "malady of a sore leg...as quite over"; but he was resigned to "being under the blockade of my old enemy winter", for as the leg had got better his breathing had got worse:

whether it be the coming of winter alone that causes it, or whether the alteration be owing in part to the vent of the humour ceasing in my leg, or wholly to the cold and foggy weather, I cannot be positive. It is nothing but what I ought and do expect. Every winter is, of course, to bring a greater load upon me, till at last it put an end to my breathing at all.[11]

But Locke soon realised that he had been wrong to think the problem with his leg was over, the other one was now giving him "pain and trouble". The bad legs, combined with chronically poor circulation in his feet, produced another problem, as he told Clarke:

you know that I have but one way to keep my feet warm, that are apt to be without a fire icy cold. But now...the sores that yet remain on my legs, as soon as they feel any warmth from the fire, do so burn and shoot that the pain is intolerable. This obliges me to spend a great part of my time in bed, a way of living I do not much like. Though, when I consider well, I think I ought to be content that I am at all amongst the living.

That last gloomy thought was provoked by recent news of the death of Nathaniel Hodges, a friend of his and David Thomas from early Oxford days: "they two are gone, and who could have thought that I, much the weakest and the most unlikely of the three, should have outlived them".[12]

Peter King came just before the end of the year. Though Locke must have been glad to see him, he had already shown some annoyance that it was not earlier. He had not had a visit from him at the beginning of the month as he had hoped, nor some days before Christmas, and had taken it amiss that "it is now come to 'If I can so order my business I will be at Oates Christmas Eve'". King came with a cousin, the

Reverend Richard King, and stayed some days into January. One topic of their conversation concerned a religious society that Richard King knew of, formed from people "whose spirit is charity and who are Christians without being of a party". He later sent Locke a printed account of it and asked for his opinion and "advice and counsel for the promoting of" the society. Locke was "very glad to see such a spirit raised, for the support and enlargment of religion. Protestants, I think, are as much concerned now, as ever, to be vigorous...for the maintenance of the reformation." In token acknowledgement of the visit, Locke sent him a copy of his "Method of Commonplacing".[13]

Shortly after the Kings' visit Locke's leg and lungs got worse. He hoped that better weather would relieve him, but of course this was not due for some time and during the whole of February, and into April, his leg forced him to spend "most of my time in bed wherein I have no great satisfaction".[14]

In the Parliamentary elections in January Sir Francis Masham was again returned as member for Essex, and Peter King was elected as a new member, for Bere Alston, Devon ("I think it will be much for your advantage in many ways", Locke said). King asked how he should combine a legal career with a Parliamentary one, and was forcefully told that he "should not think of going the circuit", but should attend Parliament. For one thing, this would "give the world a testimony how much you preferred the public to your private interest and how true you were to any trust you undertook". For another, there was some possibility of war with France, and, Locke told King, "I wonder how any one of the house can sleep till he sees England in a better state of defence". Locke also advised him not to be too quick to speak in Parliament, but to "have your eyes open to see the temper and observe the motions of the House, and diligently to remark the skill of management, and carefully watch the first and secret beginnings of things, and their tendencies, and endeavour, if there be danger in them, to crush them in the egg". What "light or apprehensions" you gain in this way, Locke told him, can be passed on "to some honest speaker who may make use of it". In this way "you will more recommend yourself when people shall observe so much modesty joined with your parts and judgement, than if you should seem forward though you spoke well". Locke assured King that he advised him nothing "I would not do myself were I in your place", and only what "I would...my son".[15]

Without a knowledge of English, Limborch had for years not been able to read the *Essay*. But in February he was able to tell Locke that he had at last been studying it, in the French of Coste's translation which had appeared the previous year. He approved of everything in it, but, though he had heard much praise and applause for the book, he had also heard of some Cartesians who objected to the rejection of innate ideas. In fact his grasp of French was hardly perfect and he still hoped for a Latin translation. But when Burridge's appeared just a few months later, Locke told Limborch that, where there was any disagreement, Coste's French should be preferred to Burridge's Latin, "for the author read through the whole of it to me, and corrected it where I discovered that it strayed from my meaning".[16]

In particular, Limborch wanted to understand better what Locke had written about free will. Locke was not surprised that Limborch was "rather at a stand" at what he had written about this. He had, he said, once thought of not including it, because of "the novelty and subtlety of the matter itself", and fearing that readers might not immediately follow it and reject his ideas as "the paradoxes of an innovator or the stumblings of an ill-advised wanderer". But, he said (repeating what he had told Molyneux years earlier), "friends disagreed" and he left it in. He now thought that his initial judgement had been correct; though more people "have entered into discussion with me about this one subject than about all the remaining chapters of the book", he had always been able to answer their questions, he said.[17]

Locke told Limborch that he would be glad to know what he thought when he had looked at the chapter on liberty again: "nothing will be more acceptable to me than to have my mistakes revealed by a friendly hand...; for I hold that not fame or opinion, but truth alone is to be served"; and in March, Limborch wrote that he thought he had understood what Locke was saying, and agreed with him: "You show excellently that Understanding and Will are not two faculties in reality distinct from the soul.... Thence you infer that it is not rightly the will that is said to be free, but the man.... You also define liberty rightly...a power to act or not to act."[18]

But, after a further letter from Locke, Limborch came to see that they disagreed about what Limborch called the "principal question", what moves us to do this or that? What liberty required, in his view, was what he called an "indifferency", which he defined, not as any kind of wavering of judgement, but as an "energy of the spirit, by which when all requisites for acting are present, it can act or not act".

(In effect he was agreeing with what Bishop King had said* some years earlier, that there must be some point at which there is an action of the will which is active and undetermined.) Limborch did not deny that beliefs or judgements have a part to play, for "when a man acts in accordance with right reason he always wills what his understanding judges ought to be done". But someone "can also act against reason and determine his will to the contrary.... If a man does not have liberty herein to determine himself or not to determine himself, and to suspend his action, I cannot see in what liberty consists." Limborch said that he had thought this is what Locke had meant in saying that the soul "has the power of suspending the fulfilment of any of its desires...to consider them successively...and in this consists the liberty of a man".[19]

When Locke replied that in his view there was no place for anything between the judgement of the understanding and an action of willing, Limborch saw that they did differ as to whether we have a power of determining an action contrary to the judgement of the understanding, though he still felt that what Locke had said about suspension of desire really put him on his side.[20]

MARCH 1701–DECEMBER 1702: "THE ORNAMENT OF THIS AGE"[21]

Visits from King, Ashley Cooper, and young Limborch must have kept Locke entertained, yet by the end of May he had "longed for some time to be in London, but the weather continues bad and my legs not right". Two weeks later his legs were as bad as ever "and to come to town to lie abed is not I think worth while". But after a further two weeks he went. This must have been something of a surprise to his landlord Pawling who, just a few days earlier, thought he "would hardly come this summer". But King seems to have wanted to see him somewhat urgently before he left for the assizes in July. They had many things to talk about, but beyond financial affairs it is not clear what these were.[22]

During the "little stay" of just over a week in London, Locke was "in a perpetual hurry". Out for most of the day, between ten and eight, he missed Hans Sloane for whom he had a paper from Furly about a calculating genius, an illiterate youth who "out of his head will reckon any of the most difficult sums you can give him even to the utmost fractions". Shortly afterwards the paper was read at a Royal Society meeting, for which "the company...ordered you their thanks in an extraordinary manner", Sloane reported. Another person whom Locke failed to meet was a certain Charles Hatton, who was out when he called on him (for some unknown reason). Hatton described "the Great and Incomparable Mr Locke" to Churchill as "the Glory of our Nation and the Ornament of this Age". Locke's return to Oates was of course dictated by the effect the week in London had had on his lungs. Nevertheless, he was hoping (fruitlessly) to return within two or three weeks for a longer stay.[23]

Though the "ornament of the age", Locke was not allowed to be merely decorative. He was solicited for medical advice, and despite the public availability of his *Thoughts concerning Education*, for educational and vocational advice too. People wished to be introduced to him, if only to pay their respects, such as a group of nonconformist minsters, who "highly value[d] the lights [he had] given the world". He was bombarded with letters concerning the *Essay*. Jean Barbeyrac, a jurisconsult in Berlin, who had already communicated some stylistic comments to Coste about his translation of the *Essay*, wrote a lengthy, but insubstantial, and merely flattering letter, in which he reminded Locke of a difficulty he had raised with Coste regarding "simple ideas". In due course Locke sent him some comments on this (which Coste incorporated into his translation), and some remarks on work that Barbeyrac was doing on Aristophanes. Locke was also drawn into correspondence with a certain Henry Layton, who, in various books and pamphlets, argued for the materiality (and also the mortality) of the soul. Layton had sent one of his books to Locke "as a very good judge upon this argument and as one who has suffered some measure of persecution, for but saying that thing was possible".[24]

Locke sometimes ignored the letters he received, though it is not always clear why. An anonymous letter suggested that his proof of the existence of God (E: 4.10.-) had assumed and not proved that we had a beginning, whereas it was not self-evidently false that we had existed from eternity, "formed of pre-existent substances, and produced according to the natural course of things". The writer was clear, polite, and sensible, and could fairly claim to have written only as an honest inquirer: "it was neither the vanity of writing to a man of your reputation, nor a humour to cavil and find fault, which made me trouble you; but a sincere desire of finding out the truth". Yet Locke did not reply, causing the man to write again three months later. It was obviously harder to ignore the rather more intrusive and completely unsought visit from a certain J. Maer. Having tried without success on several occasions to find Locke at his lodgings, he went all the way

down to Oates with the "purpose to propose something in chemistry to
you, which if you approve I shall beg your assistance in it". Locke must
have been rather impatient with Maer and, judging from the letter
Maer was moved to send after his visit, gave his proposal rather short
shrift: "If the infirmities of age disgust you with life", Maer said, "and
make you think nothing more in it worth your care, or consideration,
I can only complain of nature for decaying you too soon."[25]

Just as in earlier years Locke had benefited from the patronage of
others (Popham, Shaftesbury, Pembroke, and Mordaunt), so now he
was often asked to use the influence he had acquired ("I have some
acquaintance and interest in some...of our great men", he said to
Cornelius Lyde, when he offered him help). Sometimes the requests
were from people he did not know, and came out of the blue: a John
Tatam asked him to help get an Act of Parliament standardising the
way tithes of hay should be laid out; a nephew of Sir Francis Masham
solicited his help, via Pembroke, and on behalf of another person,
for support for an expedition to the East Indies in pursuit of pirates.
But usually the requests for "recommendatory letters" were for the
advancement of friends, acquaintances, and relations. George Walls,
his old companion in France, asked him to use his influence with
Somers to get him ecclesiastical preferment; Martha Lockhart made a
similar request on behalf of a friend who, she promised, would "not
prove a Mr Norris", and also asked for his help via Pembroke, to get
capital from the King in lieu of a pension for her position as a Royal
bedchamber woman; John Patrick, a barometer maker, asked him
to get financial support from Pembroke to support him in his
experiments concerning air pressure; and Edmond Rumney, a distant
relation, knowing "your acquaintance is great among persons of
quality", wanted him to get some preferment for his son-in-law.[26]

Locke still retained some of his earlier interests in natural philosophy, even though other concerns had stopped him fully realising the
plan he had had on his return from Holland of "resuming his study of
natural things". More than three years earlier he had given up serious
work in medicine and "wholly laid by the study of physic", but he
was as committed as ever to his daily observations of the weather;
perhaps these were something of an obsessive habit, but he also urged
the habit on acquaintances in the colonies, suggesting they take "a
constant register of the air", and even providing them with oat-beards
to use in the construction of hygrometers. A systematic register,
he argued, would not only be of some advantage to the plantations

themselves, but also be of use to "the improvement of natural philosophy" in general. One thing he must have had in mind was the idea that there might be a connection between weather and the spread of disease, in which connection Goodall had asked him a few years earlier whether he had made any further observations "about the influence of the air in reference to acute or chronical diseases, as also endemial or epidemical". This topic had been included in a questionnaire which, four years earlier, Locke had collaborated with Goodall in sending out to medical contacts in different countries. But the interest in epidemic illnesses which Locke had acquired from Sydenham over thirty years earlier was alive this summer, for he made at least three sets of inquiries about the course and nature of the fevers which had recently broken out.[27]

One of his informants, Robert Pitt, a physician who advised him on his own ailments, consulted him in turn regarding a disagreement the Royal College of Physicians was having with the Society of Apothecaries, concerning the fees which apothecaries charged the sick for their medicines and the establishing of a College dispensary to provide physicians with medicines directly.[28]

Locke's health again became of prime concern in the autumn, and with his "old adversary" winter approaching. His lungs and cough were bad and made movement painful "unless it be on horseback", and his legs were troubling him again, forcing him to "lie much abed and so waste a good deal of my time". His friends had plied him with remedies for his legs; Martha Lockhart had recommended "milk turned with a piece of alum to a poset and with pieces of fine cloth dipped in it bathed for an hour or more at a time"; and Tyrrell had suggested "young cabbage or colewort leaves" to draw out the humour. He had, however, "found out a way to fence my legs from the heat of the fire, which used to put [them] ... into a rage whenever I approached it". In fact, as Frank Masham wrote to his sister Esther, "Mr Locke's legs do not pain him now that he has got a screen for them, for which I am extremely glad". Another device in which Frank perhaps had some interest, since he would eventually inherit it, was a "silver screen" that Locke used "to preserve the eyes in reading by candlelight".[29]

In November, Locke was still engaged with Limborch in the discussion concerning free will which had begun in the spring. But besides being physically tired, he had wearied of the whole discussion. By contrast with Limborch's serious attempts to sort things out, he had tended throughout to be patronisingly superior and to sidestep the real issues, perhaps seeing that Limborch would not be brought to agree with him. And now, making plain that he was certainly not going to change his mind, he cut things short by sending Limborch some changes* he would make in the *Essay*, and by which he hoped to make his meaning clearer.[30]

Besides his lungs and his leg, Locke was further troubled in December by "a very great cold" which "very much indisposes me for everything, even writing itself". There was some exaggeration in this for he continued to make his weather observations. But just into the new year even they were sometimes abandoned when he was "miserably tormented" with an intense pain in his left ear, which rather disturbed his sleep. He was not short of advice, not only from Tyrrell and Lockhart, but also from two professionals, Alexander Geekie and Robert Pitt. The pain began to slacken in the second half of January, but he was left with an unfortunate deafness, which Geekie, who sometimes attended him in person, tried to diagnose and treat. The deafness persisted, with the return in April of some pain caused by an ulcer which, by dint of Geekie's treatments, began to discharge in July.[31]

In March, Peter King was considering an offer of marriage he had been made. In Locke's view, "the family and other circumstances have no exception...and the person I have heard commended". Unfortunately, Laetitia Hampden (whom King had never met) suffered from some "defect". King should, Locke thought, satisfy himself "whether that be what he can well bear, and will consist with the comfort and satisfaction" he hoped to have in marriage. He should, moreover, satisfy himself before he showed enough interest as to visit the family. Making a visit, Locke advised, "is yet a sort of address" and "for whatever reason a man may have to refuse a woman that is offered him, it must never be known that it was anything in her person". Locke went so far as to suggest ways in which King might pursue discrete inquiries.[32]

Though these revealed that the "defect" was "not to any considerable degree", King felt that he had to see for himself, and a dinner was arranged with the family. But, having seen Laetitia, King could not make a final decision as he had hoped: it seems that there was more than one defect and that, apart from anything else, her hearing was poor, which meant she did not say much. King hoped to see Locke before making up his mind. Whatever was said when he visited Oates just a few days later, the whole matter seems to have gone no further.[33]

Cold weather and his own ear kept Locke indoors until the beginning of May. But then, having put his will into Lady Masham's hands, he went to London. After little more than a week his ill-health forced him out again, and he returned to Oates, leaving behind at Pawling's Francis Masham and Coste who had come to London with him. During those few days he had managed to see Clarke, and to visit relations of the Masham family (who consulted him on matters of health). He had, however, failed to discuss with fellow Appeals Commissioners the question of petitioning for a renewal of the Commission; and he had also failed, he felt, to persuade Clarke to take more care of his own health. For "my sake, for the family's sake, for your country's sake", he wrote to him from back at Oates, do not "neglect your health": "Get on horseback as fast as you can; it is a thing worth the riding for, and I am confident riding will do."[34]

At the beginning of June Locke was anxious to see King again, not just for personal reasons but also on business. King had talked about travelling to Oates and back in one day, but Locke said that he would never agree to his doing "so wild a thing". He arranged with King that, to do their business, and if he had sufficiently recovered from "the harm which my lungs suffered when I was there last", he would travel to London some days later, for a short, one-night stay (which King had to keep quiet). When the time came he was up to the journey, and perhaps even hoped to stay more than one night; but he returned the next day. It had, it turned out, been his last visit to London.[35]

Towards the end of June Elizabeth Berkeley, now married to Gilbert Burnet, the Bishop of Salisbury, told him of a book, *A Defence of Mr Locke's Essay*, that she had recently read which addressed the three sets of *Remarks* that Thomas Burnet had published against the *Essay*. She had been sent the book, which she thought "commendably performed", by the author, Catherine Trotter, whom she had had occasion to meet a few times. Not only had Catherine and her widowed mother fallen on hard times but also, by "misfortune of ill company", they had been converted to Rome. Elizabeth Burnet told Locke that "if by any accident you see her, or think fit to take further notice by writing to her I wish you could be an instrument to free her from those errors". Besides her Catholicism, Trotter had further "great blemishes on her reputation" because, in order to support herself and her mother, she had been forced into writing plays. As a consequence, though Burnet wanted to help her, she was wary of doing so. Locke was inclined towards giving Trotter a present, and Burnet thought that books might be a good idea. Later she suggested money, and he eventually decided on five guineas. King was called upon to deliver them, "with all the softness and civility imaginable". He was not, however, so civil as not to reveal Locke's name, as he had been asked. This meant, however, that Locke was now free to write openly to Trotter: "I cannot in earnest be angry with him [King] for procuring me, without any guilt of mine, an opportunity to own you for my protectress, which is the greatest honour my Essay could have procured me.... You have ... not only vanquished my adversary, but reduced me also absolutely under your power."[36]

When King came to visit in mid-July, various pieces of business had built up for discussion: mortgages for £2000 and £600 which King was arranging on Locke's behalf; legal niceties relating to the renewal of his office as a Commissioner of Appeals (various oaths, for example of allegiance to the Queen, and certification that he received the Anglican sacrament, were required from him); and a book that King had been working on and had recently published, *The History of the Apostles' Creed*.[37]

The visit did not satisfy Locke's desire for King's company for long, and at the beginning of September, not long after King returned from the assizes, Locke said he must press him to visit again,

not in haste as to one with whom you have business but to let me have your company for some time (a thing you have never done yet).... I thank god my health is not much otherwise than it was when I saw you last. But what this winter will do with me I cannot tell. This I am sure I never ought for the future at the end of one to count upon another summer.[38]

Over the summer and into the autumn Locke had been still suffering from his ear abscess, despite Geekie's continued attention. In October, though not now in so much pain, he was still deaf, and Geekie lent him a silver "ear crutch", an ear trumpet (in two pieces "to make it easier for the pocket"). He must have found it of some use for he asked to have one made.[39]

Locke's ills were unfortunately not limited to his deafness, for, as he told Furly in October, he had recently "so great a pain in my arm when I write that I am often fain to give off". Yet though "my frail tenement has decays in it" and "I think my self upon the brink of another world", he was still of good heart: "I am not grown into a sullenness that puts off humanity, no nor mirth either"; but rather than being concerned with "news and politics", he chose rather "to employ my thoughts about some thing that may better myself and perhaps some few other such simple fellows as I am". He probably had in mind here the close study of St Paul's Epistles that he had been engaged upon for more than two years. It had, of course, been one of Edwards's criticisms of the *The Reasonableness of Christianity* that it neglected these and the other epistles, but though Locke had had reason for this (as he explained in the *Vindications*), he never denied that they contained truths which it was the duty of a Christian to uncover. Locke had focused first on Corinthians, and then on Romans, perhaps because the question (which* had come up in his exchanges with Stillingfleet, and in correspondence with Whitby) as to whether the dead were resurrected with the same body, turned on passages in these epistles.[40]

Towards the end of October, Locke became "confined to the chimney corner", but he had Samuel Bold with him. Over the next three weeks they discussed (perhaps in the company of Lady Masham) a range of things: the idea that God is infinite space, the question of the resurrection of the same body, and the smoking of millefolium leaves to ease asthma (as for tobacco, Locke advised Bold not to exceed three pipes a day). They also, on behalf of a neighbour of Bold's, "discoursed upon the method, a young gentleman should take in his reading and study". The neighbour, Bold later reported, was "mightily pleased" with the "Directions for Reading" which Bold took down from Locke's dictation.

Since the general aim of reading should be to improve the understanding and enlarge knowledge, a gentleman should cultivate the habit of "observing and judging of the reasoning and coherence of what he reads, and how it proves what it pretends to teach". A further and more particular aim of reading is to improve the art of speaking well so that a gentleman "may be able to make the best use of what he knows". Speaking well consists, said Locke, in perspicuity and right reasoning, and with these things in mind he recommended, besides classical writers such as Cicero, Terence, Virgil, and Livy, the writings of Tillotson and of Chillingworth. The directions were explicitly for a "gentleman", whose "calling is the service of his country", and so Locke explained that his reading should be directed specifically to what "treat of virtues and vices of civil society, and the arts of government; and will take in also law and history". For "a full knowledge of true morality" Locke recommended "no other book but the New Testament", though Cicero's *Offices* would give a good account of the ethics of the heathen world; for politics, as it concerns the basis of political power, Locke recommended, besides Hooker and Sidney, his own anonymous *Treatises of Government*. Noting towards the end of his extensive list, which continued through history, geography, law, and exploration, that "another use of reading...is for diversion and delight", he recommended, rather vaguely, "poetical writings, especially dramatic, if they be free from profaneness, obscenity, and what corrupts good manners". As for fiction, however, Cervantes' *Don Quixote* (a book he had often shared with his friends) had no equal in "usefulness, pleasantry, and constant decorum".[41]

By mid-November, Locke had not been out of doors since a couple of weeks before Bold arrived, and he doubted (quite correctly now) that his health would ever let him see London again. "A little venture [there] last year had almost dispatched me", he said to King, recalling his short July visit. It would have been some compensation that Awnsham Churchill paid him one of his frequently promised but rare visits, and even more that he managed towards the end of the month to get to the Crown Inn in Epping to see Charles and Carey Mordaunt who, realising he could not get to London, arranged to meet him there.[42]

As Christmas approached, Locke hoped for yet more visits from friends. "I have been little better than out of the world these twelve months", largely shut out of conversation by deafness, he told Clarke. But now that his hearing was restored "it is in your power to make me yet more sensible of that blessing.... It would be folly in me to count on another Christmas: come, then, and let me enjoy you in this." Clarke raised Locke's hopes that he would come; if he did he would have joined the company of King and young Limborch.[43]

During this year Locke completed a short piece which he had begun the year before, on "Miracles". In this he discussed at greater length than he had in the *Reasonableness* "the testimony which divine revelation receives from miracles". One thing which had stimulated him into thinking again about the authentification of revelation by the occurrence of miracles was his disagreement with William Fleetwood's *An Essay on Miracles* (1701), according to which a miracle is "an extraordinary operation performable by God alone". This definition was something which earlier had been Locke's own, but what seems to have led him to change his mind was no longer wanting to accept its obvious consequence that, since we do not "know how far the power of natural causes do extend themselves", it will be very hard to determine what is or is not a miracle. For what Locke was concerned with in this piece was the function of miracles as things which "give credit", and authenticate an apparent revelation.

What is important from this point of view is not so much what Fleetwood laid stress on — simply that some event should be "beyond natural causes" — as that it should be (what Fleetwood thought irrelevant) startling and surprising. As Locke had said in the *Essay*, "supernatural events…may be the fitter to procure belief, by how much the more they are beyond, or contrary to ordinary observation. This is the proper case of miracles, which well attested, do not only find credit themselves; but give it also to other truths, which need such confirmation." In referring here to miracles as "supernatural events", Locke did not deny that miracles are changes in the course of nature, or violations of natural laws. But he now explicitly rejected this criterion that miracles need actually be supernatural and against the laws of nature: "a miracle", he now said, is an observable event "which, being above the comprehension of the spectator, and *in his opinion* contrary to the established course of nature, is taken by him to be divine".[44]

Locke agreed that what was above the comprehension of one person, and so a miracle to him, might not be so for another. But he thought that neither this, nor his suggestion that a miracle need have nothing "extraordinary or supernatural" in it, "invalidated the use of miracles for the attesting of divine revelation". The point of a miracle is that it be a credential that the deliverer of some supposed divine revelation really is sent from God. Miracles, in the sense that Locke now defined them, are such credentials and "infallibly direct us right in the search of divine revelation".[45]

It was not part of Locke's thought that the point of a miracle is to demonstrate the existence of the one true God; rather its point is to authenticate His pronouncements in the eyes of people who already believe in Him. A messenger from God "cannot be refused belief if he vouches his mission by a miracle…. Where the miracle is admitted, the doctrine cannot be rejected."[46]

But on what grounds, Locke now inquired, should we take "any extraordinary operation" to be a *miracle*, i.e. to be something "wrought by God himself for the attestation of a revelation from him", and not something peformed by some "sorcerer" or "inferior power"? His answer was in terms of the nature not only of the miracle but also of the revelation. "The number, variety, and greatness of the miracles" performed by Jesus and the Apostles were "strong marks of an extraordinary divine power": on their basis Jesus's message stands firm "till anyone rising up in opposition...shall do greater miracles". Moreover, any genuinely divine revelation must be consistent with "the high and awful thoughts men ought to have of the Deity", it must reveal something relating "to the Glory of God, and some great concern of men".[47]

JANUARY–DECEMBER I 703: "NEW LIFE"[48]

Early in the year John Hudson, at the Bodleian in Oxford, told Locke that in updating its catalogue the library had found that it had none of his "excellent pieces". Locke arranged with Churchill to have books sent, and he respected Locke's anonymity by not sending any which had been published without his name. Though they were inscribed "ex Dono Authoris", the books were not listed in "the book of benefactors". For that honour Locke would have to give books worth more than forty shillings; and in fact Hudson was interested in considering any books Locke might have to donate, whoever their author. When Locke did become entitled to an entry in the Register of Benefactors he was fussy about there being a suitable space under his name and was most anxious for all the books he had given to be listed.[49]

Hudson showed a special interest in having the anonymously published *Second* and *Third Letter on Toleration*, which he supposed were by Locke, but these were not among the books which were delivered over the next months; they were not even put under their author's name in Locke's own private catalogue. His hopes were eventually satisfied, however, by Locke's will, which referred to Hudson's original request:

> I did, in return to the honour done me therein present...all the books that were published in my name, which...yet were not understood fully to answer the request...it being supposed that there were other treatises...which had been published without my name to them: in compliance therefore...I do hereby give...these following books; that is to say, three letters concerning Toleration...Two Treatises of government,...the Reasonableness of Christianity..., A Vindication of the Reasonableness..., A Second Vindication.... These are all the books whereof I am the author, which have been published without my name to them.[50]

Towards the end of the winter Locke had a visit from Tyrrell. With him was Anthony Collins, a young man of about twenty-seven; this was certainly Collins's first visit to Oates, and may well have been his first meeting with Locke. Though he had not yet published anything, Collins would, within the next ten years or so, make a reputation for himself, particularly with his *Discourse of Free-Thinking* (1713), as a defender of "free thinking" revelation-independent rational deism. In his writings Collins was much influenced by Locke, and his admiration for him must have been an important fertilising factor in the rather close friendship which soon developed.[51]

Shortly after the visit Locke described Collins to King as "in all respects...a very valuable acquaintance": "a generation of such young men to come upon the stage as the old drop off", he said, "would give new life to the age". Yet Collins was to give "new life" not just to the age, but to Locke himself, for it is clear that his flattering attention was important to Locke not least because it came from a much younger man, a man in whom he perhaps saw his former self, a man with the vigour he had now lost. Perhaps it goes too far to say that Locke became besotted with Collins, but he certainly became deeply charmed, and in some way seduced by his vitality; his relationship with him had a passion not evident in that with King. Just weeks after the first visit Locke told him, "you are a charitable good friend, and are resolved to make the decays and dregs of my life the pleasantest part of it. For I know nothing calls me so much back to a pleasant sense of enjoyment, and makes my days so gay and lively, as your good company."[52]

King himself soon spoke of making a visit. "If I can I will slip down to Oates for a day about Whitsunday" is how he put it, and Locke was not pleased that he was not more definite nor would stay longer: "I do not count upon much time in this world, and therefore you will not blame me...for desiring to see and enjoy you as much as I can." In reply, King suggested that Locke might come up to London, rather than he to Oates, but while Locke agreed that there were many reasons why he might want to be there, "I doubt whether ever I shall see it again.... My shortness of breath...sensibly increases upon me." It was not "in a fit of dispiritedness" or in an attempt to persuade that he spoke of not having long to live, but "upon sober and sedate consideration". "I have several things to talk to you of", he told King, "and some of present concernment to yourself, and I know not whether this may not be my last time of seeing you."[53]

When King came he had with him an anxiously awaited letter from Newton. The previous autumn, during a short stay at Oates, Locke had showed him the "essay" he had written on Paul's Epistle to the Corinthians, and told him that he was busy on the Epistle to the

Romans too. Newton promised to send "his observations and
opinion" on a copy Locke sent him. By the end of April, after four
months, Locke had not heard, and was clearly concerned by Newton's
keeping the papers so long without saying anything about them. He
certainly valued Newton's good opinion, telling King that his knowledge of the Scriptures had few equals, and presumably his worry was
that Newton had come to the view that his work was along the wrong
lines. He must have been relieved to have the letter King brought
with him. Newton was rather brief in his explicit praise ("I think
your paraphrase and commentary...is done with very great care
and judgement"), but he offered detailed and thoughtful comments
on Locke's interpretation of the passage (1 Cor. 7.14) about the
unbelieving husband.[54]

King had come with Collins (whose wife had recently died), in
Collins's "chariot". Writing after the visit, Locke spoke to Collins
of "the confirmation of your friendship" he had received from it,
and told him that "if you knew what satisfaction I feel spread over
my mind by it, you would take this acknowledgement as coming
from something beyond civility; my heart goes with it, and that you
may be sure of; and so useless a thing as I am have nothing else to
offer you".[55]

Locke was no doubt extremely frustrated by his inability to get to
London and to attend to his various affairs. Throughout his life he had
been used to seeing to it that, so far as possible, things, in all their
detail, were as he wanted. But, rather than lowering his sights and
moderating his wishes, he was not slow to make use of his new friend's
energy and mobility to carry out various commissions of a highly
specific nature. After this last visit he sent him a book not merely "with
a desire you will get it bound by your binder", but also with a short
lecture on binding which included some very exact instructions – as
though he saw the physically more able Collins simply as an extension
of his (Locke's) will and judgement, and as having none of his own. "In
the parts of good binding, besides folding, beating and sewing", Locke
instructed Collins, "I count strong pasteboards, and as large margins as
the paper will possibly afford; and for lettering, I desire it should be
upon the same leather blacked, and barely the name of the author."
Locke portrayed his making this request "as a mark that I think we are
past ceremony", but (given the fussy detail) it might be wondered how
much, perhaps despite himself, he was making selfish use of the young
man simply to run the errands he could no longer take care of himself.

At first Collins saw things somewhat that way, and bridled at what he felt was condescension in Locke's "sticking not to waste [his, Collins's] time in looking after the binding of [his, Locke's] books". Locke protested that he wanted a genuine friendship with Collins, to "live upon equal terms" with him, but he had to admit that "I am old and useless, and out of the way, [and] all the real services are then like to be on your side".[56]

At first there was every sign that Locke's estimate about who might be of service to whom was true, not only in practical ways, but in emotional ones too, for shortly after that Locke wrote, as though accusing Collins of seduction, "it is but six days since, that I wrote to you; and see here another letter. You are like to be troubled with me. If it be so, why do you make yourself beloved? Why do you make yourself so necessary to me?" He went on, "I thought myself pretty loose from the world, but I feel you begin to fasten me to it again. For you make my life, since I have had your friendship, much more valuable to me than it was before."[57]

Yet eventually these feelings were reciprocated. Along with accepting Locke's practical impositions on him to the extent of suggesting that he should think of Collins as himself carrying out his own errands, so Collins confessed to being unable to prevent himself falling into "the strain of a lover". Though Locke was "not a young lady, a beauty, and a fortune", Collins took "more satisfaction and pleasure" from his friendship.[58]

Unfortunately, despite Collins and King, there were ways in which Locke really was becoming "pretty loose from the world", for just after nine in the morning of 22 May, a week or so after their Whitsun visit, he left off the habit of half a lifetime and registered the weather for the last time, observing, from "the great chamber", the "rain which began about eight". Yet it was not that he was indifferent to worldly things, for he was not beyond cantankerous and fussy complaints to his tailor. As for the clothes not fitting, he was told in reply, "it is for want of being well put on.... Let your servant put the waistcoat and coat together when you put them on and settle it first and I will be your bond slave if it don't please". A couple of years earlier Locke had complained that a coat had been made up with different pieces of material: he did not wear clothes to make himself ridiculous, he said. Pawling gently and joshingly put it to him that the lining did not show, and that "I believe your tailor will not publish it". He then told Locke a rather good story about the bursar of an Oxford College who lent a collier some money, to be repaid when he next delivered the coal:

The collier came no more, but the bursar meeting him by accident, charged him with his base dealing, and...said...I value not the loss of 40s, but I am vexed that I should be laughed at for being so served. The collier replied, master you need not be troubled for that, for if you will tell nobody I will tell nobody.[59]

A couple of weeks after King and Collins had returned to London, Edward Clarke came with his wife. Three years earlier there had been some discussion of marriage between the Clarkes's daughter Betty, then just seventeen, and Peter King. Locke himself (at least by Mrs Clarke's account) had proposed the match much to their delight: to Edward's, since he believed King "would be a rising man", and to his wife's, because though she could forgive King "if he never be Lord Chancellor", she saw that the match "may do pretty well" if the young pair "can agree together to weedle Mr Locke so as to make them his heirs". (Mrs Clarke was right in her estimation of whom Locke might make his heir, wrong that King might not be Lord Chancellor.) But, as Mrs Clarke saw it, Locke was slow to follow through. "I hope Mr Locke's slow motion will prove the more sure at last especially since it was of his own proposing", she told her husband; and, for whatever reason, the proposal came to nothing – until Mrs Clarke now tried to revive it, for the purpose of their visit was for her to raise the matter again.[60]

Mrs Clarke wanted Locke to endorse and support this renewed proposal (which came with the hint that an improved settlement might be forthcoming), even to pretend that it was his own. Conscious of his relations with both parties, Locke was understandably prepared only to be a go-between; he punctiliously told King that he had no view on the matter and that it was entirely up to him. On the way back to London the Clarkes' coach turned over; fortunately they were unharmed, but the plans for their daughter were upset too, for nothing came of them.[61]

Mrs Clarke took back with her a letter to Dr William Cole in which Locke sought advice about what he now had come to describe as his "asthmatical symptoms". As on a previous occasion Cole was puzzled why he should be consulted: "you who understand physic so well, and cannot but have much conversed with the most eminent physicians that have been these thirty years...in relation to your case, must know as effectually what is proper in it as any man". But, having been asked, the "mite" he added was the use of garlic (eaten "raw, in great quantities, to five or six heads, not cloves of it, in a day"), which he had "observed...has in some persons given great relief"; he also reported various more complex remedies he sometimes used for asthma.[62]

In June Locke had further visitors, among them Samuel Bold. One thing Bold wanted to discuss with Locke and Lady Masham during the two or three days he was there was a lengthy and detailed criticism of the *Essay*, Henry Lee's *Anti-Scepticism* (1702) ("those few in Oxford that have read it, complain of the tediousness of it", Tyrrell had said). Afterwards, Bold reported having been "so exceeding pleased with the conversation at Oates".[63]

Before Bold left London for his home in Dorset, Collins gave him a copy of a recent book, *Psychologia; or an Account of the Rational Soul*, in which John Broughton defended the immateriality of the soul, and argued against some of the things Locke had said in his *Third Letter* to Stillingfleet about the possibility that matter could have the power of thought superadded to it. Perhaps Collins's sole reason in giving Bold the book was that it discussed their friend, for he thought very poorly of it: "a discourse upon nothing, or which is all one on something that nobody knows anything of, or if anyone did, would know less from reading his book", he told Locke. Bold thought much the same: "it has not all enlightened me", he reported, hoping Locke would not think "I have spent all my time since I came home in reading such sort of books as this". He nevertheless saw fit to give him a lengthy and careful account of Broughton's argument, and the following year he had the plan of publishing this, with other material. Locke urged Collins (whose help Bold was seeking) "to stop your hand a little". What Bold intended to discuss (the resurrection of the same body and the immateriality of the soul) are, advised Locke, "very touchy subjects at this time; and [Bold] may, for ought I know be crippled by those, who will be sure to be offended at him, right or wrong". At the very least, Locke said, Bold's name should be omitted: "I doubt not of his reasoning right, and making good his points; but what will that boot, if he and his family should be disturbed." Collins promised that the work would not be published "so long as you think the author is in any danger"; and in the event Bold published after Locke's death.[64]

Early in September, Locke put the finishing touches to a project he had begun some twelve years earlier, the production of an interlineary

English and Latin edition, with engraved animal figures, of the ancient collection of *Aesop's Fables*. Though Locke continued to oversee the whole work, he had arranged at some point for William Grigg, the son of his old friend Anna Grigg, to undertake the actual translation. Printing had been going on, sheet by sheet, over the past year or so, and in mid-November Churchill sent Locke two copies of the finished work.[65]

Towards the end of October, after a visit to Oates during which considerable time was spent discussing Locke's financial affairs, King delivered to Newton some more of Locke's work on St Paul's Epistles. He reported that Newton was "very well pleased with your design and performance, and will critically peruse what I delivered him". Locke was pleased that King was "grow[ing] into a familiarity" with Newton; "you will find him a very extraordinary man". King saw Newton again a couple of weeks later, but, because Newton had other company, they could not discuss Locke's papers. By this time Locke had extended his study to include Paul's letters to the Galatians and the Ephesians. Also, as he was intending to publish the paraphrase and notes that he had done for the letters to the Corinthians, he had done some preparatory work on a preface.[66]

]That autumn Locke commissioned, for about £50, a gold tumbler, which he wanted to present to Carey Mordaunt ("it should be well shaped, and be put into a handsome box covered with leather and lined with baize or the like"). King was instructed to deliver it when it was ready in early November, and was soon able to report that the present was received "with great expressions of respect and kindness for you"; in fact, Carey Mordaunt had fondly reminisced about how Locke had accompanied her back from Holland in 1689 and how (in August 1691) he had visited Dauntsey and Bath with her. On hearing of this conversation, Mordaunt, so King reported, "in his jocular way thinks that he has reason to suspect an intimacy between you and his lady, if he were not sure that you follow the rules of true philosophy".[67]

Shortly after this Locke was somewhat more "out of order" than usual, having caught a cold. He got it in "the surest way that I know in the world to get a cold and all the mischiefs that follow it", namely "to have one's room washed and then sit in it. I never knew it fail." Towards the end of the month he was "every day mending" from it, but his weak lungs went "on their course": "They have lasted longer already than the world or I expected...[but] when breath is wanting for the least motion one cannot be far from ones journey's end."[68]

What with this set-back and his desire to get on with his work on St Paul he can hardly have welcomed, though he may have been flattered, being asked by John Shute, a sometimes visitor to Oates, to write a pamphlet in defence of occasional conformity, the dissenters' practice of taking parish communion once a year as a way of formally complying with the 1661 Corporation Act which required that local and national government office-holders be Anglican communicants. Since the death of the tolerationist King William the previous year, a campaign (supported in the Commons, but rejected by moderate bishops in the Lords) had been growing against this, and Shute's concern was with a recent contribution to that campaign, a book by Humphrey Mackworth, *Peace at Home.* Acting as a spokesman, Shute said that Locke should not wonder

that a parcel of people desirous of liberty and threatened with hardships, defenceless and exposed but secure in a pen which had baffled the boldest champion of slavery and exposed the sophistry of a more refined scheme of persecution should fly to you for protection, and beg of you once more to resume your pen and vindicate the liberty of occasional communion.

The clear suggestion that he was the author of the *First Treatise of Government* attack on Filmer and the *Letters concerning Toleration* against Proast cannot have been welcome to Locke, and no doubt he ignored it; but whether or not it influenced him, he did not write the requested pamphlet. Shute himself took on the job, and the next year published *The Rights of Protestant Dissenters.* It was published anonymously, but Collins told Locke who it was by, and this enabled Shute to send Locke a copy. Since he had not been able to persuade Locke to write, Shute said, "the best thing I thought I could do...was to write upon those principles which you sir have so well established. If there's anything that is not wrong in these sheets they are but deductions from the incomparable Letters of Toleration." The relation between the *Letters* and Shute's book did not escape notice, and just as Locke was supposed (correctly) to have written the former, so he was supposed (incorrectly) to have written the latter.[69]

Clarke, Collins, and King came for Christmas. Having booked the whole of the public coach for themselves, the three were brought directly to Oates rather than to Harlow, on Christmas Day. Some weeks earlier Locke had described himself to Betty Clarke as being in a "gentle descent", but on seeing him her father wrote to her rather more cheerfully about him.[70]

Collins had brought with him a number of things from Awnsham Churchill — various books, some almanacs for the new year to give as presents, and a pair of knitted gloves ("if you wash them in hot lather, they will be thicker", Churchill advised). He also brought a manuscript (a chronological account of Jesus's life) on loan from William Lloyd, the successor to Stillingfleet as Bishop of Worcester.[71]

Locke and King discussed the details of a trust that he wanted to set up for young Francis Masham, and how best his intentions were verbally to be captured in his will; one of Locke's concerns was that King, along with lawyers in general, seemed to make no distinction between "and" and "or".[72]

King hinted that he was again thinking of marriage, a matter which they discussed more fully in letters the next month. He had received a proposal regarding the eighteen-year-old daughter, Anne, of a Glamorganshire gentleman, Richard Seys. "An agreeable woman, thriftily and carefully bred", King said. He was expected to put £4000 into the marriage settlement and the same amount might be hoped for from the girl's aunt. King wondered whether "by waiting he may meet with a greater fortune"; on the other hand it was far from certain that he would ever "meet with a woman and other family circumstances that will better please". In any case he did not want to proceed without Locke's approval.[73]

Locke felt that King himself was best able to decide about "the lady and...the family circumstances", but that it did need to be decided whether the aunt should be pressed about the settlement or whether, without any formal agreement, she could be depended on for the money. He was also advised to find out whether the young woman would be content with a lowish standard of living for a time. "If she comes with an expectation of a coach and equipage and show at first", then either she will be disappointed, "which is a dangerous beginning", or else King "may be engaged in too great a way of expense before he sees where he is". King thought that the aunt would "not come under any legal obligation for futurity", but was sure she promised well; as for the girl's expectations, "she has wit and sense, and will, I believe, be very easy in all those things you mention".[74]

JANUARY–AUGUST 1704: "AT THE END OF MY DAY WHEN MY
SUN IS SETTING"[75]

In February, Locke learnt from Collins that the heads of some Oxford colleges had discussed imposing a ban on his books. They both felt that this effectively amounted to "a recommendation... to the world", but, while making considerable jest, Locke wanted (and was repetitively insistent about it) to know every detail: "the day, the names of those present, and the very words of the order or resolution; and... from whence it had its rise". It appeared that an official announcement had been suggested, but that in the end it had been decided that each head of college should "admonish the tutors not to read to their pupils nor to suffer their pupils to read any of those books".

The most detailed account was given to Locke by Tyrrell, who reported that what lay behind the proposed ban was the feeling that the decline in exercises in logic "could not be attributed to anything so much as the new philosophy which was so much read, and in particular, your book". The Warden of Wadham College had argued against the proposal, partly because it would not look good if the University "went about to forbid the reading of all philosophy save that of Aristotle", and partly because "it would make young men more desirous to buy and read those books". The affair stung Locke into thinking twice about continuing with his gift of books to the Bodleian; but Tyrrell urged that he should not "impute the indiscrete zeal of a few men to the whole university, any more than we should lay the failing of the Bishops to the Church". Locke was assured that the people concerned were "all of them... ashamed of the matter", and indeed that "several... who having read your book [the *Essay*] themselves do not only very much approve of it but also encourage their pupils after they have done with their logic".[76]

That same month Locke raised with Hans Sloane the possibility of publishing in the Royal Society's *Philosophical Transactions* parts of his weather register (a possibility he had first mentioned four years earlier). The register from 1666 to 1683 had already appeared in Boyle's *History of the Air*, of which Churchill had been intending a new edition which might have included Locke's register at Oates from the end of 1691. But this was not yet ready and Locke was anxious that the remains of the register might be lost unless it were published in his lifetime. He believed that from his records alone "there is little to be collected", but the thought was that if something similar were kept "in every county in England...many things relating to the air, winds, health, fruitfulness, etc. might by a sagacious man be collected from them, and several rules and observations concerning the extent of winds and rain etc. be in time established to the great advantage of mankind". Locke had already prepared the register for 1692 (which Sloane published), but the rest remained in his original notes.[77]

King intended to come in early March for one of his regular visits before going off to the Western assizes. He was to bring with him a sermon which had recently been preached to the Commons on the topic of God's wrath in a recent great storm (which had uprooted twelve elms on Locke's Somerset property); a manuscript copy of the chronology of the life of Christ which Bishop Lloyd was now giving him; a Bible from Collins; and some chocolate, "for I know not but a little of that may go down and relish well enough", Locke had told him. Locke anxiously awaited the visit: be "sure to be here early on Friday that we may have the more time", he told King. He was in very poor spirits: "this may be the last time I may see you. I speak not this from despondency of mind but from what I feel in my body. If the coming about of the [warmer] wind to the south or west does not relieve me it is probable my journey will be at an end before your circuit." He was, he wrote just two days later to Carey Mordaunt (thanking her for a visit she and her husband had made two months earlier), a "decayed shell" and a "breathless skeleton".[78]

Shortly afterwards Collins told Locke about a book he had just received, the second part of John Norris's *Essay towards the Theory of the Ideal or Intelligible World* (the first part of which was published in 1701). It contained, Collins reported, some criticism of what Locke had said in the *Essay* against the syllogism. As far as Collins could see, Norris's defence of the syllogism amounted to no more than pointing out that all arguments could be reduced to that form; but, as he noted, this hardly shows that we cannot reason except in that form, nor that it is the most useful form. Norris had also criticised what Locke had said to Stillingfleet about God's being able to superadd thought to material substance; but, according to Collins, he had said no more than that thought, because of its "excellence", has to belong to some other substance. In response to a Malebranchian account of perception according to which ideas are not directly caused in our minds by objects, but rather are "exhibited" there by God "upon the occasion of the presence of objects", Collins suggested something he had entertained for some time − that the essence of Locke's *Essay* was its denial of innate ideas. It therefore followed, he argued, that given Norris himself denied innate ideas, then what he said about perception could not really stand in basic opposition to what Locke said. Given that the *Essay* considers ideas only as "objects of the understanding", it does not matter how they become those objects; what is said there, Collins argued, about the experiential origin of our ideas is neutral with respect to the question which concerned Norris, whether the senses are their real or their occasional cause.[79]

Locke agreed that what Norris said about the "excellency" of thought was not clear, and suggested that his basic fallacy was that just because thought did not naturally belong to matter, it did not follow "that it may not be made an affection of or be annexed to" it. As for the insight that nothing can be advanced against the *Essay* "but upon the principle of innate ideas", Locke complimented Collins on having such a mastery of the book, and on not "stick[ing] in the incidents... which... make nothing to the main design of the Essay, that lies in a little compass".[80]

Collins also hinted that he had discovered Locke to be the author of *Epistola de Tolerantia*. He realised, he said, that he could read enough of the title page as to to work out its author and his nationality. (The last three of the title page letters "P.A.P.O.I.L.A." stood for "Ioanni Lockio, Anglo"). Collins would perhaps have raised this again on his next visit, but this was not to be for some time for he was due to go to Oxford to see some friends. Not surprisingly Locke made no reply about the *Epistola*, but, again not surprisingly, he was able, he told Collins, to "find business for you at Oxford, as well as London". A part of this was to deliver a letter to Tyrrell concerning the Oxford ban on the *Essay*. In recent years Locke's relations with Tyrrell seem to have been cordial enough, but he still saw the need to give Collins instructions for dealing with him: "You must not take his conjectures for matters of fact.... You may avoid all dispute with him; if you will but say after him, though you put him upon things that show you question all he says." Collins thought this second piece of advice, for avoiding disagreeable argument, was "an admirable secret that I shall endeavour to use".[81]

On 11 April, Locke had witnessed what proved to be his final will. There were many bequests: amongst others, £10 or so to each of his friends in Holland, Veen, Guenellon, and Furly; £200 each to Edward Clarke and to his daughter Elizabeth. Sir Francis Masham was willed £10 and "the hangings and other furniture belonging to me in the chamber over my study in his house", while his wife was to receive his ruby and his diamond ring and thirty-two books of her choice from his library. Esther and Frank Masham were each to have £10, though the latter also was to benefit from a £3000 trust and to have various pieces of silver, and half of Locke's library, when he reached twenty-one. (Locke was most concerned that none of the trust money "shall at any time be lent to Sir Francis Masham, which I do to prevent inconveniences which I who am acquainted with the family forsee it would unvoidably occasion".) There were half a dozen designated books and a map for "my good friend" Anthony Collins; and Peter King, named as his sole executor, was to have the remaining half of Locke's library together with "all the rest of my goods, chattels, mortgages, and real securities" – these last, according to some accounting he did late the following September, amounted to over £12,000.[82]

Contrary to his pessimistic prediction, Locke was still alive when King completed his circuit towards the end of April, perhaps because the weather had turned "extremely fine and warm", and he had been able to get outside into the fresh air. Yet it had not been "at all balsamic" to his lungs, and he again urged King not to delay in coming to see him "for if I mistake not the reckoning will soon be at an end". One thing Locke discussed during King's visit was an easy chair that he wanted made, to a design he had very carefully considered:

The hollow mentioned to be made in the middle of the seat of my chair I would not have very deep, and so not wholly without stuffing. But the stuffing should not raise the seat so high in the middle as it is about the sides. This moderate depression in the middle of the seat...makes it both easier for sitting, and makes the cushion lie better without slipping off.

There was a "morning gown and lining" in a trunk at Pawling's which was to provide some of the material.[83]

After King had gone there were other visitors. At the beginning of May young Francis Limborch stayed for some days, a visit he repaid by a present to the household of some stockfish. Collins (who had come with King) was with Locke into the middle of the month, and then, the day after he left, Edward Fowler, the Bishop of Gloucester, came for three or four days. Congratulating himself on having found such a friend as Collins "at the last scene of my life", Locke remarked to him on the contrast between his visit and Fowler's: "in this poor decaying state of my health...I find the charms of your company make me not feel the want of strength, or breath, or anything else", but as for the

Bishop, himself unwell, "I find two groaning people make but an uncomfortable concert". "Enjoy your health, and youth, whilst you have it ... remembering that merciless old age is in pursuit of you", he advised Collins, adding that "I reflect often upon it, with a secret joy, that you promised I should, in a short time, see you again".[84]

Before Collins left, Locke discussed having a light carriage made, a thing about whose details he was most clear and insistent, having formed a lively (and rather self-indulgent) picture of the use to which he wanted to put it: "I think sometimes in the evening of a warm day to sit abroad in it, to take the fresco; but would have a canopy over my head, to keep the dew off." Some details were easily settled: the seat should be good and broad and "the two cushions soft plump, and thick enough", the cloth lining would be of "a dust colour", the "harness and all the whole accoutrements [should] be of as good materials and as handsomely made and put together as may be". But, even so, they were not settled without self-concerned and self-congratulatory pontification on Locke's part: as for decorative brasses, "give me leave to tell you, that, in my whole life, I have been constantly against anything that makes a show. . . . I like to have things substantially good of their kind, and useful, and handsomely made, and fitly adapted to their uses."

Other matters took rather longer to agree. When he made some initial inquiries about types of carriage, Collins reported that "the most convenient sort as well as the cheapest are those that fall back though they be not quite so ornamental as those that have fixed tops; . . . [if you want the former would you] have the top only fall back upon two standing corner pillars or so far that you may have as full a prospect behind you?" Locke was concerned to know about the relative ease of management of the two sorts of cover, and how far over the head each came "as to shelter it from the dew, without shutting you up from the free open air". He was concerned that the cover be such that when erected "one may lean and loll against it at one's ease ... for I am grown a very lazy fellow, and have now three easy chairs to lean and loll in, and would not be without that relief in my chaise". Having got more information with regard to leaning and lolling, Collins was understandably most anxious that Locke should decide, but unfortunately they had been at cross-purposes. "What I enquire about", said Locke "is not a stuffed back for the ease of my head in leaning against it, but whether the back and sides will be strained and stiff enough to bear my leaning against it." There had been discussion about whether there would be room for a footman, but they decided that there was no need for this: "besides the advantage of having it less and lighter I think your servant may as well go on foot to open the gates for you in the fields, as ride behind". As an afterthought Locke thought of a "rope and hook to check one of the wheels going down a steep hill".[85]

Locke was now not alone in thinking that he was in a decline. Coste noted that at the beginning of the summer, "a season which in former years had already restored him some degree of strength", Locke's "strength began to fail him more remarkably than ever". But despite this he was still alert to his business and domestic affairs. He was very keen to have from King "such a knowledge of the present posture of my little affairs that I might be able presently upon any occasion without sending for information, to give orders about them"; and he continued to send orders to his tailor.[86]

As the year progressed his health did not improve with the weather. At the beginning of June he found that "this comfortable, and to me usually restorative, season of the year has no effect upon me for the better: on the contrary, my shortness of breath, and uneasiness, every day increases; my stomach, without any visible cause, sensibly decays, so that all appearances concur to warn me that the dissolution of this cottage is not far off". It was time for one of King's regular visits and Locke was most anxious to see him and that it would not be a fleeting visit:

Pray be sure to order your matters so as to spend all the ... week with me: as far as I can impartially guess, it will be the last week I am ever to have with you.... Refuse not, therefore, to help me pass some of the last hours of my life as easily as may be in the conversation of one who is not only the nearest, but the dearest to me, of any man in the world.

Initially Locke had wanted him to bring some cherries, one of his favourites ("if they could be brought without bruising"), but in the end told him, rather wearily, not to trouble: "they will be troublesome to you; and these things, that entertain the senses, have lost with me a great part of their relish ... such desires are usually but the fancy ... [which] seeks in vain for the delight which the indisposition of the body has put an end to". In any case, he thought, his desire for the cherries was probably a substitute for a desire to see King, and "when I have your company, I shall forget those kind of things". Locke wanted King to retrieve from a trunk at Pawling's what he described as "a steel truss" and to have it re-covered by "Mrs Bernard a truss maker ... who uses to do it for me". It is not clear why he was wanting this truss nor how it relates to one "to be made in sole leather" whose design is described in one of his manuscripts.[87]

King's visit clearly did Locke good, for after it he reported that the ageing man (now in fact approaching his seventy-second birthday) had been "fine and cheery". This was just a matter of surface mood of course, and Locke's abiding thought was that, as he told Churchill, "I hasten apace to my journey's end, and can count upon but a very few days in this world". He was not sleeping well, and in early July made inquiries about various of his problems. For one thing, his stomach was sensitive to pressure, and Cole thought the symptoms pointed to a cachexy, some humoral ill disposition, rather than (as he suspected Locke suspected) to a dropsy, an accumulation of fluid, perhaps in a tumour, in the abdomen, and he prescribed some pills accordingly. At the same time Locke consulted Pitt, not only about his stomach, but also about an increased shortness of breath. Like Cole, Pitt did not think the stomach problem was a symptom of dropsy, and he assigned the difficulty in breathing to the fact that because Locke's cough had been less, his lungs had become clogged. Locke had complained about his swollen legs too, and Pitt thought these should improve when his breathing did, and so also his circulation.[88]

Early in July Locke's "calash" was ready, made by the Queen's carriage-maker (at a cost of nearly thirty pounds), and Collins drove down to Oates in it. Locke had not refrained from giving advice about the journey: "I hope since you are to make the first trial... you will not forget to provide a whip proper for the driver." Joking, Collins said he would not forget the whip for he would be reminded of it by a book he was bringing with him – a short pamphlet, *A Second Letter to the Author of the Three Letters for Toleration*, which, after a silence of thirteen years, Jonas Proast had just published.[89]

The dozen oranges that Collins also brought were probably more to Locke's taste than was Proast's pamphlet, as would have been the six pounds of chocolate that King brought with him when he arrived a week later. Locke was now surrounded by friends, for Samuel Bold and John Shute were there too. It is no wonder that Collins remarked that "the conversation at Oates is so extremely agreeable".[90]

King and Shute stayed only three or four days, but it was long enough, and Locke was well enough, for them to see him out in his calash. Collins stayed on a few days longer, and Bold longer still. If they had not already done so, they would have discussed Locke's work on St Paul's Epistles, for some weeks earlier Locke had asked Collins to prepare for his visit by spending "some spare hours" on the letters to the Corinthians, to see whether he found any difficulties with them: "when I have you here, I hope to convince you it will not be lost labour; only...you must read them with something more than an ordinary application".[91]

The previous year Locke had been preparing to publish his notes and paraphrase of Corinthians, but at some point he changed his mind, for less than a month after these discussions with Collins, he received from the printers the proofs of *A Paraphrase and Notes on the Epistle of St Paul to the Galatians*. The work was published posthumously, and, as he had instructed King, was followed by his paraphrase and notes on the two Epistles to the Corinthians, and then by the paraphrases and notes on Romans and on the Ephesians, and *An Essay for the Understanding of St Paul's Epistles*.[92]

As Locke explained in this last, he had undertaken his work on the Epistles for himself. He had thought it his "duty and interest in a matter of so great concernment to me" to set himself "in earnest to the study of the way of salvation, in those holy writings wherein God has revealed it from heaven". After a lifetime much of which had been devoted to what he now referred to as "the wisdom of the world" (the "knowledge, discoveries, and improvements...attainable by human industry, parts, and studies"), he was now concerned with his ultimate destiny and his mind was almost entirely on the "wisdom of God" (the "doctrine of the gospel coming immediately from god by the revelation of his spirit"). As he would shortly write in his last letter to Collins, he had learnt that "this life is a scene of vanity that...affords no solid satisfaction but in the consciousness of doing well and in the hopes of another life".[93]

But Locke had been repeatedly urged to publish his work on St Paul "by some very sober judicious Christians", who included "learned divines of the Church of England", who found that what he had done enabled them to understand the Epistles "much better than they did before". The divines very likely included Bold and Fowler, with whom Locke must have discussed his work, while Collins, King, Newton, and Damaris Masham would have been among the "sober judicious Christians". Presumably their earlier difficulties with the Epistles were the ones Locke had striven to surmount: the facts that the letters leave out many things known to their addressees; that they were written in koine Greek by a Hebrew speaker; and that Paul's thoughts crowded in on him as he wrote, and so did not produce "an easy and obvious perspicuity". The way in which later editors had imposed their own divisions of the letters into chapters and verses made things more obscure, besides offering mistaken encouragement to "snatch out a few words" here and there as "independent aphorisms", so playing into the hands of sects which had their own partisan interpretations of the Scriptures to defend. Locke's own response to all this had been to read through each letter and at one sitting, "over and over, and over again", in order to discern its "general drift and design".[94] The result of the understanding he got by "consulting St Paul himself" in this way, were summaries and paraphrases of Paul's letters, together with often quite lengthy notes explaining points of translation or of detailed interpretation.

Along with the chaise, Collins brought a recently published book, *A Discourse concerning the Happiness of Good Men*, by William Sherlock. The book included a forty-page "Digression concerning connate Ideas, or inbred Knowledge", in which Sherlock re-presented and added to what he said in a sermon* he had preached in 1697 against Locke's rejection of innate ideas. Giving Locke some foretaste of the book, Collins told him that though "the clergy triumph mightily upon Dr Sherlock", he was of a piece with Stillingfleet: full of "insolent or haughty expressions", of "extraordinary arguments and questions", and of misunderstandings about what Locke meant by there being no "innate" ideas. Sherlock took Locke's rejection of innate ideas to be an invitation to atheism: "There is not a more formidable objection against religion, than to teach that mankind is made without any connate, natural expressions, and ideas of a god, and of good and evil.... The general reason why men are so zealous against these ideas being innate is to deliver themselves from the necessity of believing of god or religion."[95]

Initially Sherlock's attack had been of some concern to Locke, for his sermon had struck him as further evidence of a wider clerical attack on the *Essay*; by now, however, he was unworried, and had promised Collins to "make us merry" with Sherlock's book. When they came to do this, Collins pressed Locke to reply to Sherlock's arguments, so energetically, it appears, that he later begged his pardon for being too fervent about it. But he was not alone in thinking that Locke should reply, for Robert South (no admirer of Sherlock anyway) urged him too: the "pert empty fellow" has not only "wrote against your sentiments", but also, in implying that Locke was an atheist, "has also very virulently reflected upon your person". However, though

Locke (rather surprisingly given his frequent and rather high-minded claims to dislike controversy and polemic) told Collins that replying to Sherlock "would afford as much diversion as any hunting you could imagine", he neverthelesss felt he had neither "strength and breath enough to pursue the chase".[96]

Collins had brought the calash not a moment too soon, for Locke's swollen legs were preventing him from riding. By the early autumn he had given up all hope of being able to take it up again, and passed on his riding horse to the Bishop of Gloucester. Unfortunately he too was not in the best of health; and Locke suggested that if he could not make use of the horse it should be sold, with the money going to the poor (or such of them as fitted the criteria Locke seems to have specified). Presumably it was sold for, though an easy horse, riding it brought about blood in the Bishop's urine (a problem which Locke thought was caused by a stone in the neck of the bladder).[97]

AUGUST–OCTOBER 1704: "A HAPPY LIFE, BUT NOTHING BUT VANITY"[98]

The short pamphlet by Proast which Collins had brought was not long in Locke's hands before, in early August, he was at work on a reply, *A Fourth Letter for Toleration*.[99] In hiding behind the name "Philanthropos" in his first reply to Proast, Locke had perhaps meant to distance himself from his original letter; but it had not worked, for Proast addressed himself "to the author of three letters on toleration" and clearly supposed he was faced with only one author. Proast said that the reason for breaking his silence after so many years was that a recent book had claimed he had given up his case. Wanting to "put a stop to a report so injurious (as well as groundless)", he now wanted to make clear that he had been no more persuaded by Locke's last letter, of 1692, than by anything earlier.

One issue had been whether Proast argued simply for the magistrate's right to use force in matters of religion, or for that right only in the case of *the true* religion. His official position was the latter, but one of Locke's points had been that if a magistrate is obliged to use force to bring people to the *true* religion, then he is obliged to use it to bring them to *his* religion, for he believes his to be the true. Proast now simply denied this inference, and claimed that in the case of the true religion it is possible to have "a full assurance", something which is not possible with a false religion. This "full assurance", Proast said, would show the magistrate which religion he is to promote. In answer to another of Locke's points, that it would be wrong to impose things which were not necessary for salvation, Proast argued that imposing a doctrine does not mean it is thought necessary; doctrines are imposed not as things necessary in themselves, but rather "as instances of that obedience to the bishops and pastors whom God has set over his Church", an obedience "which is necessary to salvation". Proast ended loftily: "I can spend my time better than in unravelling cobwebs, and detecting sophistry; and...[am] now more than sufficiently sensible...that cavils and impertinencies are endless, when a man of parts shall not disdain to make use of them."[100]

It is surprising that Locke had sufficient energy and interest to compose, with the aim of publication, a reply to Proast. Proast had done little more than continue to gnaw over old bones of contention, and Locke did nothing better. He had, however, lost nothing of his deftness as a polemicist. "Sir", he began,

a fresh revival of the controversy formerly between you and me is what I suppose nobody did expect from you after twelve years silence. But reputation...has put a resolution into your heart, and arms into your hands to make an example of me, to the shame and confusion of all those who could be so injurious to you, as to think you could quit the opinion you had appeared for in print, and agree with me in the matter of Toleration.... But yet there are sober men who are of opinion that it better becomes a Christian temper that dispute, especially of religion, should be waged purely for the sake of truth and not for our own.[101]

Locke thought that Proast's new idea, that the true religion gives a "full assurance" of its truth, got nowhere. "All your talk of full assurance pointing out to the magistrate the true religion...amounts to no more but his own religion, and can point out no other to him." Locke was not denying, what Proast was anxious to assert, that there may be better, more rational grounds for the true religion than there are for the false. His point was rather that unless Proast himself were to give some account of what these were, it would, again, simply be up to each magistrate himself to judge whether he has "clear and solid proofs" and whether his grounds are such as to give him full assurance. He insisted, furthermore, that it is not necessarily because they have not thought carefully enough that people take the wrong side in religion. He cited the striking and amusing case of the brothers (one a Catholic, the other an Anglican) who each succeeded in converting the other, and they simply exchanged religions with each other.[102]

In August, Collins expressed a wish to have a portrait of Locke and asked whether he could commission Godfrey Kneller to do one. Locke was gushingly delighted: "I have long since surrendered myself to you.... Judge then, whether I am willing my shadow should be in the possession of one with whom my heart is; and to whom all that I am...does belong." If it were possible, he told Collins, for Kneller "to make a speaking picture, it should tell you every day how much I love and esteem you; and how pleased I am to be, so much as in effigy, near a person with whom I should be glad to spend an age to come". He hoped that Collins would accompany Kneller when he came to do the preliminary drawing, and, intending to entertain Kneller well ("both out of respect and to keep him in good humour that he may draw the better"), Locke asked Collins to bring some food: "some partridges, rabbits or what other good things of that kind the poulterers' shops afford, as also lobsters, craw fish, crabs or prawns". Locke sat for Kneller soon after (as did Lady Masham, at Locke's request), and by early September the paintings* were done. Locke asked Kneller to write names and dates on their backs: "this is necessary to be done, or else...the picture loses of its value, it being not known whom it was made to represent".[103]

King made a short visit of a couple of days in early September. Besides bringing Locke up to date with his affairs in Somerset, they must have discussed King's impending marriage to Anne Seys, which Locke had eventually encouraged, and which took place later that month. On the wedding day Locke (who had arranged a presentation of "a toilet furniture" for the bride) could do no more than drink the couple's health at dinner, but a few days later he was able to entertain them at Oates. They brought with them some of the food Locke had ordered:

four dried neats' tongues; twelve partridges that are fresh; four pheasants..., four turkey poults ready larded, if they be not out of season, four fresh auburn rabbits if they are to be got, plovers, or woodcocks, or snipes, or whatever else is good to be got at the poulterer's, except ordinary tame fowl, twelve Chichester male lobsters if they can be got alive – if not, six dead ones that are sweet, two large crabs that are fresh, crawfish and prawns, if they are to be got, a double barrel of the best Colchester oysters.... I desire you also to lay out between twenty and thirty shillings in dried sweet-meats of several kinds, such as some women skilful in those matters shall choose as fit and fashionable (excepting orange and lemon peels candied, of which we are provided). Let them be good of the kind, and do not be sparing in the cost, but rather exceed thirty shillings. These dried sweet meats must each sort be put up in a paper by itself and then all the papers put up in a box together, I mention this because for want of this care some that my Lady lately sent for were quite spoiled.

Just as Lady Masham had been disappointed earlier with her sweetmeats, Locke had been with some of the game Collins had brought for Kneller, for the list to King included "twelve partridges that are fresh... for it is to no purpose to bring down stinking things... as I was lately served". Typically, these instructions were not all. "One thing more let me mind you of", Locke fussily and laboriously concluded, all these things should

be put in a little hamper and packed with care and the hamper put up before the coach if possible, for if it be put behind and there be no servant that rides behind or follows the coach on horseback you will be in danger to have it cut off (as some of our neighbours have been lately served) unless it be extremely fast tied on and somebody in the coach constantly look out after it especially riding through the town.

There were eight at the celebratory dinner and supper ("plain country entertainment" Locke called it), including the bride's father. Perhaps it was on this occasion (certainly it was around this time) that "though he [Locke] perceived he should not live long... he continued as cheerful and pleasant as before... [saying] 'While we are alive let us live' ".[104]

There was some pleasant early autumn weather that month, and Locke was still able to get out of the house. Coste recalled a conversation he had with him while they sat out in the late afternoon sun:

as he was sitting in a garden, taking the air in a bright sun-shine, whose warmth afforded him a great deal of pleasure, which he improved as much as possible, by causing his chair to be drawn more and more towards the sun, as it went down; we happened to speak of Horace, I know not on what occasion, and having repeated to him these verses, where that poet says of himself "that he loved the warmth of the sun, and that, though he was naturally choleric, his anger was easily appeased." Mr Locke replied, that if he durst presume to compare himself with Horace in anything, he thought he was perfectly like him in those two respects.[105]

Unfortunately there had been no room for Collins at the wedding celebrations. Even whilst the Kings were still there, Locke told him that "to complete the satisfaction I have lately had here, there has been nothing wanting but your company". But whatever pleasure Locke had had from the wedding he was, when it came to it, rather down, so much so that, "tired with so little a motion as writing is", King had to help him write the letter. He urged Collins to visit; King would be witness, he said, that "my infirmities prevail so fast on me, that, unless you make haste hither, I may lose the satisfaction of ever seeing again a man, that I value in the first rank of those that I leave behind me".[106]

The day after King left, Locke put more of his affairs in order, setting down some instructions to him concerning various of his writings. He did not want his "Discourse of Seeing all things in God" to be published, "yet I do not absolutely forbid it. If you and others of my judicious friends should find occasion"; his discourse on "Miracles" was to be published if his friends saw fit, as was his "Conduct of the Understanding". He also mentioned some medical papers, headed *Physica*: these contained first thoughts which needed to be "weighed again and again" and were not fit for publication; but even apart from that they were not yet suited to "the present temper of this age"; exactly what he meant is not clear, particularly since the topic of the papers is unknown. He was least diffident about the last work he had done: "Those who have seen what I have done upon St Paul are all very desirous it should be printed", he said, and specified the order in which it was to appear.[107]

Collins arranged to visit the following week, and was met off the coach at Harlow and taken to Oates in Locke's new chaise. He brought with him yet more fine food which Locke wanted for his entertainment:

You and I have other satisfaction together than eating and drinking, and yet there is no fault in expressing ones welcome to a friend in a good dish of meat. Let that be my excuse for desiring you to bring down with you half a dozen partridges, or some other dish for second course. Let it be pheasants or larks or rabbits or what you like best, and a double barrel of the best Colchester oysters.

Collins did not stay long and may already have left when, two days later, Locke wrote to King asking him to come for a quick visit that weekend: "my strength decays so fast that I doubt whether I may last another week".[108] In fact he had a little longer to last than that, but there is no certain record whether he saw King again.*

On Wednesday 25 October he made some additions to his instructions regarding his unpublished manuscripts. He was worried that the transcribing work he was having done on the notes on Paul's Epistle to the Ephesians would not be finished before he died. This time he was right. He had grown noticeably weaker as each day had gone by, and the swellings in his legs increased; and the next day, when Coste went to see him in his bedroom, he "found him on his knees, but unable to rise again without assistance". Then, on Friday, Lady Masham found him, not in his study, but in bed: he said "he could not bear the fatigue of rising, having wearied himself too much with it the day before, and that he did not know whether he should ever rise again". His legs were "very much swollen" now, and staying in bed unfortunately "made the swelling...get up into his body, [and] immediately took away his stomach and his sleep". He ate little or nothing that day and about five in the evening fell into a sweat and became extremely weak. Everyone including himself thought he was "not far from his last moment": he thought "he might perhaps die that night, but that he could not live above three or four days". He drank a few spoonsful of mum, "to the health of the company, wishing all of them happiness when he should be gone". While Damaris Masham, whose friend he had been "above half my lifetime", stayed with him by his bedside when the others were at supper, he counselled her "to look on this world only as a state of preparation for a better": he had "lived long enough", he said, and "thanked God he had enjoyed a happy life"; but after all "he looked upon this life to be nothing but vanity". He welcomed her suggestion ("if it would not give too much trouble") that the whole family make their evening prayers with him, and for him; so after supper they came to his room and between eleven and twelve he seemed a little better. He spoke

of the goodness of God...exalted the love which God showed to man, in justifying him by faith in Jesus Christ.... He exhorted all about him to read the Holy Scripture attentively and to apply themselves sincerely to the practice of all their duties; adding expressively that by this means they would be more happy in this world, and secure to themselves the possession of eternal felicity in the other.

Locke would not allow Lady Masham to sit with him through the night, saying that "perhaps he might sleep, and that if he should find any alteration he would send for her". The next day, Saturday 28 October, even though he had not slept at all, he determined to get out of bed, and, being too weak to walk, asked to be carried into his study. Here he dozed fitfully in an easy chair, until after some time, "thinking himself somewhat better", he asked not only to be dressed but even for a drink of small beer. After that he asked Lady Masham, "who was reading to herself in the Psalms, while they dressed him, to read aloud, which accordingly she did". For a while he was very attentive and in his full senses, "till he was hindered by the nearer approaches of death, upon which he desired her to read no more, and died* a few minutes after...about three in the afternoon" − from, it has been suggested, "congestive heart failure secondary to chronic bronchitis and emphysema". He was seventy-two, though he himself had forgotten how old he was, and his friends "computed that he was about sixty-six".[109]

Shortly afterwards Lady Masham wrote to a friend that

All the faculties of his mind were perfect to the last, but his weakness, of which only he died, made such gradual and visible advances that few people, I think, do so sensibly see death approach them as he did. During all which time no one could observe the least alteration in his humour, always cheerful, civil, conversible, to the last day; thoughtful of all the concerns of his friends, and omitting no fit occasion of giving Christian advice to all about him.[110]

Locke would have fallen foul of one of the laws* he drew up a quarter of a century earlier, according to which "the will and testament of him that dies a batchelor past fifty shall be nul unless he be killed in the wars of country". But of course the terms of his will were followed, and he was "buried in a plain wooden coffin not covered with cloth or any otherwise adorned", for, as he had added, "that cost will better be laid out in covering the poor and therefore...four honest poor labouring men of the neighbourhood...shall each of them have a coat and pair of breeches of cloth, a hat, a pair of shoes and stockings which will be better than the vain waste of a covering and other ornaments on my coffin". The plain wooden coffin was entombed at All Saints' Church, High Laver, on 31 October 1704.[111]

Expository Notes

xxviii laundry lists:	See illustration page xiv.
1 somewhere:	Perhaps he was thinking of the list of various birthdays on the loose leaf, endorsed "Age" by him but written by his father (NA PRO 30/24/47/31).
2 portrait of Locke:	See illustration p. xv.
6 house:	See illustration p. xvi.
19 verses:	In the first half of 1662 he (along with over a hundred others) also contributed to a book of poems compiled for King Charles and Queen Catherine (dB: vol. 1, 191).
31 reading:	About 167 of the 350 or so books he read during that period were medical, and a further 59 related to natural science (in all about 63 per cent). By contrast, theology and religion, and politics and law, come rather lower (respectively 55 books/15 per cent and 7 books/2 per cent) (J. Milton 1994: 35–7). At the end of his life, in his library of over 3500 books, approximately 11 per cent were medicine (402 books), 6.6 per cent natural science (240), nearly 24 per cent

	theology (870), 10.7 per cent politics and law (390), and 7.4 per cent philosophy (269) (Harrison and Laslett: 18).
57 shorthand:	See illustration page xvii.
66 Ambassador:	The new ambassador, Lord Sandwich, left on 2 March (dB: vol. 1, 257).
66 preparations:	For an account of the work, recorded in MS Locke f.25 (for which see Walmsley and Milton), see Dewhurst 1963a: 20.
67 valued at £872:	After taxes the yield in rents was about £72 per annum (Kelly: 101).
72 not clear:	The weather register is blank 27–29 July, and then again 1–14 and 17–28 August, and there is other evidence that he was at Astrop during that last period (Locke 1692d: 657, L206, L207).
75 not writing:	A letter from her had perhaps been lost (L214).
86 medical crisis:	Ashley's problem, as diagnosed later from Locke's own descriptions, had been a suppurating hydatid cyst of the liver (Haley: 204, Osler). Locke made copious notes on the case (NA PRO 30/24/47/2), and discussed it at length (L230, L250).
91 played a part:	J. Milton 1990 reviews most of the evidence for Locke's involvement.
96 sea coals:	soft, bituminous coal brought down by sea to London from Newcastle.
106 start:	See illustration page xviii.
109 Fellow:	Four months later he had been appointed to a committee "for considering of and directing experiments to be made from time to time at their weekly meetings" (Birch: vol. 2, 328, Stewart 1981: 26).

111 Adventurer:	According to Cranston: 115, Locke invested a further £200 the next year; according to Davies: 65, Locke sold his stock in 1675.
113 alterations:	MS Locke b.1, fols. 13−14 records Locke's paying for various bits of joinery, shelves, and so on, "at my Lord Chancellor's".
116 degree:	Prideaux was also wrong that Locke had "wriggled" into a place vacated by Thomas Ireland; that went to William Allestree (Bill: 351).
120 tours:	See map p. xix.
122 decimal measurement:	See pp. 156f.
137 little Tour:	to towns on the Loire, to Rennes, La Rochelle, Bordeaux, and back to Paris via Poitiers (dB: vol. 1, 572).
138 Launay:	See illustration p. xiv.
151 name after me:	Locke (now Edisto) Island on the Edisto River (CSPC: vol. 7, 585 (no. 1284)).
153 Let us pray...:	A motto in the "Mercurius Coelestis" almanac for 1682 in which Locke wrote his journal that year.
159 Hoc est corpus trick:	from the Mass, "Hoc est enim corpus meum" (later hocus-pocus) = for this is my body.
172 papers:	Amongst the papers which were taken away were a version of *De Intellectu* and the "Observations upon the growth and culture of vines" which Locke had presented to Shaftesbury (NA PRO 30/24/6a/349).
173 trial:	College was put to death at the end of the month.

178 pistols:	Bullets and gunpowder figure on Locke's shopping lists as does the discharge and cleaning of pistols (Locke 1680a: 197, 200, 1681a: 27, 50).
181 *De Morbo Gallico*:	See, for example, the journal shorthand entry Locke 1681a: 104 (18 July).
182 various periods:	J. Milton 1995a: 357.
192 West:	See p. 173.
193 chamber:	According to Wood 1891–1900: vol. 3, 117, Locke's rooms never were searched.
197 United Provinces:	See map p. xx.
198 coded reference:	See p. 181.
203 not yet paid:	He eventually paid at the end of the following January, for the four months from 30 September (Locke 1685: 257).
210 Ferguson, etc.:	Robert Ferguson and Richard Goodenough had been involved in the Rye House Plot; Ferguson and Waller had fled to Holland with Shaftesbury.
214 many pamphlets:	See pp. 116–17, 174.
215 beer:	The idea that it was the beer that had drawn him to Holland has been said to be "so singular as to be positively comical" (Cranston: 249). On the other hand, the claim that Locke disliked coffee houses was surely quite genuine. "I do not go once in three months to a coffee house and never to seek company but to find someone with whom I have particular business", he later said, in circumstances which gave no particular reason to dissemble (L2384).
217 Ward, etc.:	Patience Ward and Thomas Papillon were whigs who had had been involved in City politics; Henry Starkey had been one of Shaftesbury's servants.

218 Grey and Wade: Ashcraft argues, however, that Grey and Wade were reporting the truth when they said that "Mr Locke" contributed money to Argyll and Monmouth, and that in saying so they had in mind "Locke, he who was Shaftesbury's secretary" (Ashcraft: 457–62).

219 list: Two or three weeks later Locke was included on a further list from England, but in transmitting this to the States-General, Skelton left him off, as "I had put him into the first list" (BL Add. MS 41812, fol. 100, Skelton to Middleton, 26 May/5 June 1685).

224 draft C: Inscribed "For Edward Clarke of Chipley Esq., James Tyrrell of Oakley Esq., or Dr David Thomas of Salisbury", the manuscript seems not to have left Holland during Locke's life (Aaron: 56–7).

230 der Linden: The linden or lime tree was a whig symbol.

235 churchgoing: We do know, however, that he particularly enjoyed the sermons of the tolerant, non-dogmatic Latitudinarian Benjamin Whichcote (1609–83).

237 accounts: See illustration p. xxi.

247 some notes: See pp. 126f.

248 miracles: See pp. 434f.

251 Pembroke reported: See p. 229.

254 engraved handwriting: See illustration p. xxii.

256 picture: See illustration p. xxiii. This is possibly not the portrait which was in Stringer's possession (dB: vol. 8, 446) but must have

been done about the same time. It is in any case the earliest known portrait of Locke.

258 Mat. Locke: Tyrrell's mention of "Mat Locke" was just a temporary mistake; "Josiah Locke" is the name Penn actually gave him (L1049). It was on the basis of a letter of 20/30 April 1686 from Skelton, which discussed a pardon for "Joshuah Locke ... now at Amsterdam", that Bourne believed that Locke had been pardoned (NA PRO SP 84/220, fol. 14; Bourne: vol. 2, 26). But it is clear from the letter (and from another of Skelton's of the same date (BL Add. MS 41813, fol. 110r) that this "Locke" was someone involved in woollen manufacturing.

260 Pembroke: Shortly after this exchange between Thomas and Tyrrell, Tyrrell told Locke that (as a non-Catholic) Pembroke's influence with James was declining, "and I wish you were here whilst his interest lasts for I fear it will not be long" (L985, also L1016).

270 Libertatis
Amantem: But LeClerc: 13–14 has "Limburgium Amstelodamensem" ("Limborch of Amsterdam") rather than "Libertatis Amantem" (Lover of Liberty).

270 Rabsy Smithsby: See p. 197.
275 part ... had
been lost: As on p. 197, one manuscript of *De Morbo Gallico* was divided into two parts, and stored in different places.

280 Will's:	a leading Covent Garden coffee house for men of letters (dB: vol. 4, 23).
281 not Locke's:	*A Discourse of Humane Reason with relation to Matters of Religion* was in fact likely to have been by Popple (dB: vol. 4, 37).
287 end of May:	The book was internally dated "May 27".
298 seraglio at Oates:	See p. 399.
299 twenty pounds:	These terms, together with one shilling a week for "feeding for horse at grass", still held ten years later (MSS Locke c.1, 331, b.1, fol. 154).
299 Dr Cudworth's daughter:	Limborch had corresponded with Ralph Cudworth (dB: vol. 4, 238).
301 Mrs Cudworth:	i.e. Damaris Cudworth, as Limborch thought of her.
307 SWALLOWS:	See illustration p. xxiv.
309 got some:	Stratton also sent him some of the earth from the Mendips (L1448, L1484).
317 advise you both:	The topic of the possible advice is unknown.
323 manuscript:	Eventually mainly published as Locke 1693c.
332 vis-à-vis Newton:	See p. 357.
339 afterlife:	See p. 57.
349 malt liquors:	ale and beer.
363 earlier:	See pp. 326–7.
363 value of gold:	Two months earlier Locke had sold thirty-seven gold rings on behalf of Lady Masham (Locke 1695a: 296, 298).
377 Racovian:	Rakow, in Poland, was a centre of Socinianism.
390 *Essay*'s chapter:	E: 4.18.-; see pp. 247f.
394 authenticates the Scriptures:	See pp. 343–4.

395 September:	Its later progress was impeded by the need to consider a proposed bill from the Irish Parliament on the question (Bourne: vol. 2, 373; dB: vol. 6, 220, L2324 and others).
398 costiveness:	A psychoanalyst might guess from the perhaps obsessive note-taking and record retention that Locke, as he once told Clarke, was "naturally costive", a problem to whose cure he had devoted quite some thought, coming up in the end with what sounds like a sure recipe for piles: "After my first eating, which was seldom till noon, I constantly went to the stool, whether I had any motion or no, and there stayed so long that most commonly I attained my errand" (L799).
402 ready for the press:	Dated 4 May, the answer was published the following November (L2507).
405 raising "the dead":	Locke was surprised to have found that this was so, and admitted that the *Essay* had said that "the bodies of men shall rise" (E: 4.18.7); but, having now seen that this was wrong, he determined to change it in the next edition. A denial that resurrection is of the *same* body is, according to Edwards, a Socinian belief (SC: 95).
411 Celadon the Solitary:	Esther noted on this letter that the allusion was to the *Romance of Astrea* (a book by Honore d'Urfé), which "I use to read him after suppers" (E. Masham: 43).
415 gravity:	In this same passage Locke suggested that Noah's flood was best explained by supposing "God's altering the centre of gravity in the earth for a time" (see also L1684, 3LS: 461).

418 examined by

reason:	See pp. 247f.
421 once thought:	See p. 150.
426 King had said:	See p. 321.
430 changes:	Presumably he sent Limborch the changes eventually made in the fifth edition at 2.21.48, 56, 71, changes which made clearer how his position differed from Limborch's.
433 which:	See pp. 405f. and 415f. for Stillingfleet and Whitby.
453 said in a sermon:	See p. 371.
456 paintings:	See illustration p. xv.
458 saw King again:	According to Campbell: vol. 4, 563, King saw him during his last three days, "in time to see how a Christian should die".
459 died:	Esther Masham reported a less dignified end, one which, had he known of it, would have delighted Locke's enemy John Edwards, who some years earlier (see pp. 398f.) had been so rude about the sections on costiveness in the *Thoughts concerning Education*, remarking that the guts were that part of the body of most concern to Locke: on the last morning "he resolved to rise, and was carried into his study, and in his chair got a little sleep, was very sensible, and between twelve and one he called for the close-stool, and was no sooner sat upon it but he died, closing his eyes himself" (Esther Masham to Mrs Smith, an ex-servant, 17 November 1704 (BL Add. MS 4311, fol. 143)).
460 laws:	See pp. 150f.

Bibliographical Notes

Unless indicated otherwise, numbers in these notes are page numbers.

INTRODUCTION

1. L163.
2. Coste: 174; trans. Bourne: vol. 2, 560–1.
3. Thacker: 29.
4. Coste: 166–7.
5. D. Masham: 187.
6. D. Masham: 192, Coste: 164–5.
7. Coste: 169, D. Masham: 191; L191, L797, L417, L182, L163.

CHAPTER I

1. Locke 1660: 119.
2. Bourne: vol. 1, 2, D. Masham: 171; genealogical information mainly from dB: vol. 1, endpaper.
3. NA PRO 30/24/47/31; Bourne: vol. 1, 4.
4. Bourne: vol. 1, 12.
5. Cranston: 4; BL Add. MSS 4222, fols. 224–6; 28273.
6. D. Masham: 171–2, L3.
7. L803, TE: §40.
8. BL Add. MS 28273, fols. 138r, 141r–57r, 102r, 139v; 125rv, 130rv; L114; D. Masham: 173.
9. MS Locke c.25, fol. 7.
10. Cranston: 14; L1739.
11. Locke 1660: 119.
12. Cranston: 1, 4, 11, Marshall 1994: 3–4.
13. BL Add. MS 28273, fol. 135v.
14. Cranston: 16; BL MS Add. 28273, fols. 86rv; 28, 105v–109r, 116r–18r.

15. Cranston: 16, Bourne: vol. 1, 9.
16. Cranston: 17, D. Masham: 171.
17. BL Add. MS 4222, fols. 224–6, Cranston: 17, Bourne: vol. 1, 16–17, Leyden: 15.
18. L1471.
19. Cranston: 21, MS Locke f.11, fols. 77r, 83r. For much of this and the following I am indebted to Sargeaunt.
20. MS Locke f.11, fols. 76r, 79r; 75v, 85v, 78v, 69v, 68v; 86vr.
21. South: vol. 1, 431; dB: vol. 1, 153; L. Tanner: 18.
22. Sargeaunt: 118; L177.
23. Cranston: 22, MS Locke f.11, fol. 84r.
24. Sargeaunt: 279–82.
25. Quoted in Cranston: 19, L1471, L929, TE: §§47, 54, Edwards 1697a: 10.
26. TE: §171.
27. MS Locke f.11, fols. 2r, 77v; 75v.
28. Bill: 92, 94, L5.
29. L4, Bill: 92, L3, L4, L6.
30. L3, L4.
31. J. Milton 1994: 30.
32. D. Masham: 173.
33. L7, L8.
34. MS Locke f.11, fol. 4r; L148, dB: vol. 1, 203; Locke f.11, fol. 60v.
35. Bourne: vol. 1, 26, Bill: 106.
36. For information about Locke's Studentship I am much indebted to J. Milton 1994.
37. Bill: chap. 4, Fincham: 199.
38. Bill: 276; Feingold 1997a: 215 (quoted from Ward: vol. 1, 65–7).
39. MS Locke f.11, fols. 60v, 7r; Feingold 1997a: 227, 1997b: 404.
40. D. Masham: 172–3.
41. TE: §98; D. Masham: 173.
42. TE: §188; Le Clerc: 2.
43. D. Masham: 173, dB: vol. 1, 28, L22.
44. L18.
45. Cranston: 32, 34.
46. Quoted in Bourne: vol. 1, 51.
47. MS Locke f.11, fols. 60v, 7r, L17.
48. Cranston 37, L24; Bourne: vol. 1, 52.
49. D. Masham: 172.
50. L27.
51. L29; D. Masham: 172.
52. L30; dB: vol. 1, 42.
53. Feingold 1997b: 429.
54. Bourne: vol. 1, 52, D. Masham: 172.

CHAPTER 2

1. L77.
2. L54.
3. L59; L68, L43; L77, L68.
4. L68, L88, L66, L77, L80, L79; L82.
5. L51, L79, L104, L122, dB: vol. 1, 74, 119; L51; L34, L58, L62, L72, dB: vol. 1, 48, 82, Leyden: 19; L60, MS Locke e.6.
6. L66, dB: vol. 1, 95.
7. dB: vol. 1, 130, L71, L83, L86, L84, L65.
8. L71, L74.
9. dB: vol. 1, 130, L48.
10. L69.
11. L69, L70; D. Masham: 189.
12. L72.
13. L74.
14. L54, L79.
15. L79.
16. L80.
17. L87.
18. L87, L89.
19. D. Masham: 173.
20. D. Masham: 173; J. Milton 1997: 148–50; MS Locke e.4, 5–7, 18–21; 20, 24, 23.
21. L38; MS Locke e.4, 111; 27, 33, 68, 73.
22. J. Milton 1997: 143, MS Locke, f.18.
23. J. Milton 1997: 150–1, 154, MS Locke f.47.
24. Abrams: 32.
25. Leyden: 21; L75.
26. L75.
27. L91.
28. L85, L91.
29. Bill: 138–65.
30. J. Milton 1994: 31; Bill: 131–8.
31. J. Milton 1994: 31.
32. L93, L94.
33. L91.
34. Frank 1997: 507–16, Porter: 99–100.
35. Frank 1980: chap. 3, 64.
36. Frank 1980: 66, 179–80; L97, L101.
37. J. Milton 1994: 37–8, 2001: 226, D. Masham: 173.
38. L91.
39. Worden: 770, Beddard 1997a: 809–11; L91.
40. L80.
41. L59.
42. L59.
43. L81.

44. L82.
45. L95.
46. dB: vol. 1, 151, L101.
47. 1T.
48. L97, L105, L106.
49. Leyden: 38, dB: vol. 1, 155.
50. L106.
51. 1T: 124.
52. 1T: 118.
53. 1T: 126.
54. 1T: 159, 160.
55. 1T: 119, 157, 158.
56. 1T: 124, 122, 126, 125.
57. 1T: 137.
58. 1T: 139, 140.
59. 1T: 167, 146, 167, 145, 128.
60. 1T: 138, 138–9.
61. 1T: 146.
62. 1T: 120.
63. L110, L95.
64. L111.
65. L113; 7 February (MS Locke c.25, fol. 6).
66. D. Masham: 171, L110, L43.
67. MS Locke c.25, fol. 6.
68. MS Locke c.25, fol. 7.
69. L108, L115, L118.
70. 1T: 119, 120.
71. 1T: 117; L797; 1T: 118.
72. L127, L129; Marshall 1994: 9–12.
73. L112.
74. L119.
75. L119.
76. L118, L119; J. Milton 1995b: 114; Bill: 197.
77. MS Locke f.11, fol. 8; J. Milton 1995b: 102, 111, 114; Bill: 343.
78. MS Locke f.11, fols. 10v–13v, L3328; MSS Locke c.41, b.7, Gough.
79. MS Locke f.11, fols. 7v–57; L138 and others; L133.
80. L155 and others; L154, L157.
81. L137 and others.
82. L200.
83. Locke 1661: 317; Biddle: 307.
84. Locke 1661: 317, 321.
85. Locke 1661: 323.
86. Locke 1661: 326–7.
87. J. Milton 1995b: 114; Abrams: 16; 2T: 241, 212, 210.
88. 2T: 211, 212, 211–12.
89. 2T: 214.
90. 2T: 238, 225.

91. ELN: 173.
92. J. Milton 1997: 145–6, Dewhurst 1963a: 11–12; MS Locke f.19, 42–50, 52–7, 60–3; Walmsley and Milton: 97, Wood 1891–1900: vol. 1, 472, 474; L1681, Walmsley and Milton: 95.
93. J. Milton 1994: 31; Bourne: vol. 1, 88, L163.
94. J. Milton 1995b: 114.
95. Leyden: 7–12.
96. ELN: 109.
97. ELN: 199.
98. ELN: 125–7, 137–9.
99. ELN: 141.
100. ELN: 127, 129.
101. ELN: 129–31.
102. ELN: 165.
103. ELN: 123, 151.
104. ELN: 153, 183, 157.
105. ELN: 173.
106. Locke 1664b: 221–3.
107. Leyden: 247–51, TE: §161; Locke 1692a: 140, 1696a: 318, 1678: 172, 1675: 5.
108. Frank 1980: 186 (BL Add. MS 32554, fols. 53v–54r, 100v–101r).
109. Frank 1980: 144; BL Add. MS 32554, fol. 48r.
110. Frank 1980: 144–6.
111. Frank 1980: 183–8, Dewhurst 1963a: 13 (Locke MS f.19, 212–13, 226–7).
112. BL Add. MS 32554, fol. 49r.
113. Frank 1980: 186–7 (MS Locke f.19, 227, 158), 109–12, 117–21.
114. Frank 1980: 187–8 (MS Locke f.19, 227); MS Locke f.25, 33.
115. MS Locke f.27, 64.
116. MS Locke f.27, 64, 61; L176 and others; L183.
117. L176, L178, L181.
118. L184, L180.
119. L177.
120. L180.
121. L180.
122. L180.
123. 1T: 159, L175.
124. L198, L204.
125. L184, L186.
126. L182.
127. L186, L187; L207.
128. L183, L191.
129. L185, L193; L192 and others; L198, L204, L1681.
130. L193, MS Film 79, 12; MS Locke f.12, 6–7 (10–26 April), dB: vol. 1, endpaper, Kelly: 101; MS Locke f.12, 5.
131. Meynell 1995: 187, MS Locke f.12, 7; L197.
132. Stewart 1981: 24.
133. Locke 1692d: 655; Locke 1705a: 1919, Dewhurst 1963a: 18–19.
134. Locke 1666a: 266.

135. Locke 1666a: 266–7.
136. Locke 1666a: 267.
137. Locke 1666a: 264–5.
138. Locke 1666a: 264.
139. Frank 1980: 165–6.

CHAPTER 3

1. L797.
2. L797.
3. Wood 1820: vol. 4, 638–9; dB: vol. 1, 283; Dewhurst 1962a (MS Locke d.9, 68); L797, L208.
4. L203, L204.
5. Haley: 27, 185.
6. dB: vol. 1, 287; D. Masham: 174.
7. D. Masham: 175, L205, Shaftesbury 1705: 329.
8. D. Masham: 175; L205.
9. Locke 1692d: 658, L209, Locke 1692d: 660, D. Masham: 177.
10. NA PRO 30/24/47/8 (3 November).
11. J. Milton 1994: 31, Bill: 134.
12. Dewhurst 1963a: 26; quoted in Bourne: vol. 1, 131 from NA PRO 30/24/47/22.
13. Locke 1692d: 660, D. Masham: 177, L212.
14. L217.
15. L219.
16. L220.
17. L222.
18. L225.
19. Locke 1666b: 207.
20. Locke 1666b: 207, 208.
21. Descartes: 138.
22. Locke 1666b: 208.
23. Locke 1666b: 208, 209; Romanell: 61, 64, Walmsley 2000: 388.
24. L223, L224; MS Locke f.25, 136.
25. MSS Locke f.12, 9, also Film 79, 10; Locke 1692d: 668; L224; MS Locke f.12, 12; MS Film 79, 7 (30 May); D. Masham: 177.
26. D. Masham: 177.
27. Haley: chaps. 1–10.
28. dB: vol. 1, 28, 74, 90, 155; Shaftesbury 1705: 330, Haley: 220.
29. L182.
30. Haley: 215, MS Locke Film 79, 39–40, 42; BL Add. MS 5714, Bourne: vol. 1, 331–3, L228.
31. L857; D. Masham: 189, Coste: 340.
32. D. Masham: 188–9.
33. Tomalin: 435; L240, L241; dB: vol. 1, 334.

34. Haley: 209, Dewhurst 1963a: 35, MS Locke d.11, fol. 79v, Boyle 1772: vol. 6, 648—9.
35. Sydenham: 227, L1593.
36. Marshall 1994: 42.
37. T: 174.
38. T: 175, 178.
39. T: 176.
40. 1T: 145, T: 176, 1T: 128.
41. T: 176—7.
42. 1T: 159; T: 177—8.
43. 1T: 146; T: 176, 177.
44. T: 180—1.
45. T: 182, 177.
46. T: 183, 184.
47. T: 187, 188, 189.
48. T: 191, 189.
49. Shaftesbury 1705: 329.
50. Dewhurst 1963a: 36, Haley: 205.
51. L1593. There is some disagreement whether "Anatomie" is by Locke (Meynell 1994, J. Milton 1996: 119).
52. Locke 1668a: 87, 89, 88.
53. Locke 1668a: 85, 87.
54. Locke 1668a: 86.
55. Locke 1668a: 86.
56. Shaftesbury 1705: 229—30.
57. Kelly: 8, 71.
58. Locke 1668b: 202, 172.
59. Locke 1668b: 171.
60. Locke 1668c.
61. D. Masham: 188.
62. L225, L232; dB: vol. 1, 69.
63. dB: vol. 1, 354, Haley: 230, 239, 241—2, 248; Shaftesbury 1669: §§95, 97.
64. Locke 1823: vol. 10, 150; L279.
65. Shaftesbury 1669: §96, Haley: 245, Locke 1823: vol. 10, 194; Locke 1690a: 57, L1403, L3483.
66. Bourne: vol. 1, 244, Brown: 167, dB: vol. 1, 354, Haley: 253, MS Locke c.30, L254, L270 and others; NA PRO 30/24/48/83.
67. Shaftesbury 1705: 331—2; L235.
68. L236, L237.
69. dB: vol. 1, 324.
70. L238.
71. Locke 1669: 226. There is some disagreement whether Locke is in fact the author (Meynell 1994, J. Milton 1996: 120).
72. Locke 1669: 222, 223.
73. Locke 1669: 223, 224, 224—5.
74. Locke 1669: 223, 225.
75. Locke 1669: 224, 226.

76. Coste: 165, D. Masham: 188.
77. L246, L247, BL Add. MS 5714, fol. 17, L251, L252; L248.
78. L243, NA PRO 30/24/47/10.
79. Shaftesbury to Fell, 8 December 1670 (NA PRO 30/24/47/10).
80. dB: vol. 1, 341; L248, L249.
81. L797, Dewhurst 1959b: 373, 1963a: 47, MS Rawlinson c.406, 4.
82. L797, D. Masham: 174.
83. A: 56.
84. L247, L251.
85. L255, Dewhurst 1954b: 491.
86. Brown: 224, L532, Shaftesbury 1705: 332.
87. Locke 1671a, L255, L258, D. Masham: 178, Tyrrell's note in the margin of his copy of Locke's *Essay concerning Human Understanding* (British Library, c.122); E: Epistle to the reader.
88. A: 56, 57–8 (§§1, 2).
89. A: 56, 57 (§§1, 2).
90. A: 61 (§5).
91. A: 73 (§27).
92. A: 57 (§1).
93. A: 61, 56 (§§6, 2).
94. A: 59, 61 (§§3, 6).
95. A: 60 (§4).
96. A: 63 (§9).
97. A: 56 (§1).
98. A: 66 (§13).
99. A: 73, 76, 74, 83, 82 (§§27, 31, 29, 27).
100. A: 77, 57, 77 (§§31, 1, 31).
101. A: 66, 63 (§§13, 10).
102. A: 77, 66, 67–8 (§§32, 13, 15).
103. A: 64, 65, 66, 64, 67 (§§11, 12, 13).
104. A: 72–3 (§26).
105. A: 77 (§32).
106. A: 83, 78 (§§27, 33).
107. A: 85, 80, 84, 84–5, 86 (§§41, 39, 40, 42).
108. A: 63 (§10).
109. A: 68, 69 (§§15, 17).
110. B: §88.
111. L259.
112. L259, L260.
113. B: §§1, 3.
114. B: §1, Locke 1669: 225.
115. B: §4.
116. B: §§21, 79, 100.
117. B: §§64, 68, 87.
118. B: §§72, 75, 73.
119. Birch: vol. 2, 323–4, 328, 427.
120. Locke 1668a: 86, 1669: 225–6, B: §88.

121. L265.

122. Locke 1692d: 670–1, L262.

123. Cranston: 144, Haley: 297.

124. Haley: 300; quoted by Martyn: 248. The poem was written in a book of Cowley's poems addressed to Greenhill.

125. BL Add. MS 15640, 4, 16, Bourne: vol. 1, 289–93, L270; MS Locke c.1, 76, 81.

126. NA CO 268/1, 11.

127. dB: vol. 1, 366, Locke 1692d: 671; L264, L265, L269.

128. L264.

129. Locke 1676: 402.

130. L265, Haley: 259–60, Bourne: vol. 1, 285 ff.

131. Haley: 304, 311, dB: vol. 1, 372; L267, dB: vol. 1, 260, 373, Bourne: vol. 1, 314, MS Locke c.44, 9, 12.

132. L269, Birch: vol. 3, 59, 61, 64, 69, 112, Stewart 1981: 26, L270.

133. L267, Haley: 307.

134. Haley: 316–17, Ogg 1956: 344–5.

135. Shaftesbury 1705: 333, Haley: 317.

136. Haley: 317–26, Ogg 1956: 350–6, 64–70.

137. Locke 1692d: 672, L276; CSPC: vol. 7 (1669–74), 527 (no. 1151); 531 (no. 1162), MS Locke b.l, fol. 21; CSPC: vol. 7, 633 (no. 1419); L270 and others, see also MS Locke c.1, 16–17, and CSPC: vol. 7, refs. in General Index.

138. Haley: 330–43.

139. Haley: 263–4; Kelly: 11–12.

140. L297; dB: vol. 1, 420–1, Bourne: vol. 1, 333.

141. L295.

142. Dewhurst 1963a: 49, MS Locke b.5, no. 10, Bill: 350–2, Prideaux: 34 (7 February).

143. L302, Haley: 389–90, Locke 1823: vol. 10, 201, Haley: 399.

144. Locke 1823: vol. 10, 152, Haley: 393.

145. Shaftesbury 1705: 330–1.

146. L306, L307, L313.

CHAPTER 4

1. MS Locke c.25, fol. 15, L304; MS Locke c.25, fol. 15, L523; L303.

2. MS Locke c.25, fol. 16.

3. Locke 1675: 1 (14/24 November); Prideaux: 49, L307.

4. L310.

5. Locke 1675: 1.

6. Locke 1677a: 248–50.

7. Locke 1676: 31, 53, 397, 33, 102, 217, 68.

8. Locke 1676: 72.

9. For example, Locke 1676: 34, 44, 47, 54, 55–6, 146–7, 220, 225, 349, 1678: 239.

10. Locke 1676: 52, 365, 1677a: 80–1.

11. L307 and others, MS Locke c.31, fol. 168; MS Locke f.15, 26, 42.
12. Locke 1676: 252, 254, 1677a: 83.
13. dB: vol. 1, 442, L310, Locke 1675: 1, 2, 1678: 270.
14. Locke 1675: 4, 7.
15. D. Masham: 192; Locke 1675: 10, L508, Locke 1676: 37, 257, MS Locke c.31, fols. 173–5.
16. dB: vol. 2, 642; Locke 1675: 9–12.
17. Locke 1675: 25, 1676: 27–34.
18. Locke 1676: 35, L309, L313.
19. Locke 1676: 213–14, 216, 218, 401–2, 406–7; 156–7; 129, 138; 51, 288, 350–3, 434–6, 438–9, 466, 468–9, 483–5, 502, 1677a: 39–40; dB: vol. 1, 451.
20. Locke 1677a: 33–4, 82; L314, L311, L312, L320, Locke 1676: 479.
21. Locke 1676: 455–6, dB: vol. 1, 668.
22. Locke 1676: 299, 303, 305, 309–10, etc.; 317, 394; 289–90, 417–22.
23. Locke 1676: 418–19 (Leyden: 276).
24. Locke 1676: 422–3, 424 (Leyden: 277–8).
25. Locke 1676: 427, 428 (Leyden: 280).
26. Locke 1676: 369–70.
27. Locke 1676: 403, 402, 404, 405 (Leyden: 256–7); Leyden: 255.
28. Quoted by Leyden: 254 from MS Locke c.28, 42; quoted Bourne: vol. 1, 296, from Locke 1828: xxiii.
29. Locke 1677a: 42–3.
30. Locke 1677a: 45, 46.
31. Locke 1677a: 48–9.
32. Locke 1677a: 50–1.
33. L323, L322.
34. L316, L323, L331.
35. Locke 1676: 523, 526, L366, P. Milton 1996.
36. L372, L326.
37. L327.
38. L329.
39. L421, L328.
40. L328.
41. Locke 1677b (from 1677a, 86–140); 1677a: 87, 135, 134, 135.
42. Locke 1677a: 89, 90, 98.
43. Locke 1677a: 124, 122, 114, 125.
44. Locke 1677a: 101, 100, 100–1.
45. Locke 1677a: 137; 1694c.
46. Locke 1677a: 138, L1887.
47. Locke 1677a: 97, 96, 115, 96, 104, 143, 149.
48. L324, L331, L323, L336.
49. L330, L336, L346, L349.
50. L352.
51. Tanner 1929: 306, L341.
52. L373, L376, L381, L384, L387.
53. L383.

54. L386.
55. L335.
56. Cranston: 172.
57. Locke 1677a: 152, 299; 1678: 179, 180.
58. L339, L347, L348, L356, Ward 1740: 276.
59. Locke 1677a: 290, Romanell: 44; Locke 1678: 36, 47, 159.
60. L546; Locke 1677a: 292–3, 1678: 161–2.
61. dB: vol. 1, 579; L397.
62. Locke 1678: 108–9; dB: vol. 1, 580–1; L428.
63. Locke 1677a: 370–1; L359; L360–L364; see Dewhurst 1957; Locke 1678: 189.
64. Locke 1677a: 389; 166–7, 353–68; 1678: 47–8, 60–7; L398, Locke 1678: 27–38, 80–4, 90–101.
65. L372, L374.
66. Locke 1677b: 419, E: 4.12.10, 14.2, 2.10.9.
67. Locke 1678: 172–89.
68. L383; L390, Locke 1678: 191–2, 195.
69. Locke: 1678, 192–3.
70. L390A, Locke 1678: 219, L396.
71. Locke 1678: 227–8.
72. Locke 1678: 253, 191, 236, MS Locke f.28, 16.
73. L397.
74. Locke 1678: 240, 244.
75. Locke 1678: 271, 253, 252, 255.
76. Locke 1678: 257b.
77. Locke 1678: 257b, 260–1.
78. Locke 1678: 262.
79. Locke 1678: 263.
80. L400; Locke 1678: 270–4.
81. Locke 1678: 281.
82. L404, L405, L406.
83. L407.
84. L399, Locke 1678: 287.
85. L417, Tanner 1929: 321–5, L410.
86. Locke 1678: 300–6.
87. Locke 1678: 315, 316, 317, 318; 316–18, L413.
88. L415, L417, Locke 1678: 321 (4 November).
89. L415, L431, L417; Locke 1676: 255, 459–65.
90. L431, Locke 1678: 335, 347.
91. MSS Locke f.28, 24, c.1, 108, L419, dB: vol. 1, 629; MS Locke f.13, 5 (February 1674); MS Locke c.1, 59, L308; D. Masham: 191; MS Locke f.13, 39, L1585, dB: vol. 8, 446.
92. L358, L389.
93. L477, L481, L485, L475, trans. Bourne: vol. 1, 429, L508.
94. Locke 1679: 65, 38–56; 1678: 347, 379, 349, 383; L432.
95. L421, L426.
96. Locke 1679: 13–14, 19–20 (see also 1676: 280, 319).

97. L354; L392, L481 and others; L476 and others.
98. Cranston: 120; L469 (trans. Bourne: vol. 1, 427); L475; L633 and others.
99. L660, L481.
100. L431, L434, Locke 1679: 90–2, L467.
101. L467, Locke 1679: 92–4.

CHAPTER 5

1. L312, L351; Haley: chaps. 21–3; L467.
2. D. Masham: 179, Bourne: vol. 1, 411.
3. Haley: 516–18.
4. Bourne: vol. 1, 414, Haley: 517–28.
5. Haley: 466.
6. L473, L475, Locke 1679: 103; D. Masham: 179.
7. L565; Wood 1891–1900: vol. 2, 431.
8. L473, L475, L483, Locke 1679: 97; L483, L499, Locke 1679: 65, 97, 124–5, 129.
9. dB: vol. 2, 15, 39, L497, Locke 1679: 94–5; Locke 1679: 65; L478, L492, L508.
10. L475, L600, L666.
11. Forbes: 7, dB: vol. 2, 17, 39; L469.
12. L466 and others; L600; L473.
13. L517 and many others; L510 and others; L556 and others; L517 and others, Locke 1679: 33–64.
14. L470 and others; L501; L502.
15. L497, L508; L560 and others; L587.
16. L503, L492.
17. Haley: 544, L503, Locke 1679: 133, dB: vol. 2, 103; Locke 1679: 146–7; L509.
18. Locke 1679: 159; Haley: 537, 548–9, 556; L508.
19. L544.
20. Locke 1679: 187; L523; Locke 1680a: 3, 5–7.
21. L492 and others, Philip and Morgan: 681; L587.
22. Locke 1680b, L528.
23. Locke 1680a: 3; 1679: 189, 1680a: 8–9; Bourne: vol. 1, 436.
24. Locke 1680a: 10–17.
25. Locke 1680a: 19 (12 February); L511.
26. L543, MS Locke c.26, fol. 68; Locke 1680a: 19–50.
27. Locke 1680a: 34, 43, 165, L532.
28. Locke 1680a: 50; Beddard 1997a: 854–5; L528, dB: vol. 1, 418, vol. 2, 154; L561, dB: vol. 1, 418, L572, L612.
29. Locke 1680a: 76; 65–9, L531; L531, Locke 1680a: 50; 168, L538; L545; L556; Locke 1682: 45–6.
30. L544.
31. L565.
32. Knights: 382.

33. Haley: 576; Locke 1680a: 107–11 (31 May–4 June).
34. Locke 1680a: 124–5, L554; Locke 1680a: 125 (30 June–1 July), 1679: 105, L551; Locke 1680a: 127.
35. L554, Locke 1680a: 138 (July 7), L556.
36. Haley: 584, Locke 1680a: 143 (21 July), 145 (July 31), 145–9.
37. L541, L558, L561, L565, Cranston: 197.
38. L565.
39. Locke 1680a: 155, 162 (11–27 August); Haley: 587.
40. L565; Locke 1680a: 167.
41. Haley: 587 (11 September), 587–93; Locke 1680a: 172–4; L569 and others.
42. L580, Locke: 1680a: 184 (7 October); L584; Locke 1680a: 187, L593; Locke 1680a: 185–6 (14–16 October), L590; Locke 1680a: 191, 182–3, L577, L580, L596, L609.
43. L626.
44. Locke 1680a: 191; Haley: 597–602, 615–18, 620–2.
45. Locke 1681a: 4 (14 January), 10, 6–7 (18 January).
46. L614; L620; Locke 1681a: 7 (3 February), 68; L817.
47. Quoted in Locke 1681b: 14.
48. Locke 1681b: 30, 8, 1.
49. Locke 1681b: 60.
50. L2498.
51. Locke 1681b: 9, 10, 31.
52. Locke 1681b: 26.
53. Locke 1681b: 26, 30, 26, 11.
54. Locke 1681b: 76, 5, 86, 43.
55. Locke 1681b: 131, 23, 59.
56. Haley: 620–2, Beddard 1997b: 868–72.
57. L618, L620, Locke 1681a: 68, 9.
58. L620, Locke 1681a: 18–19, 22–3.
59. L625, L624, Locke 1681a: 29.
60. Haley: 632–9; quoted in Haley: 639.
61. L633; Haley 632, 638; Locke 1681a: 29 (30–31 March), 38 (6 April).
62. Prideaux: 134.
63. Locke 1681a: 33–8 (Aaron and Gibb: 114–16); 54, 59, 60 (11–16, 17–19 May), L645; Locke 1681a: 41–2, 44, 45.
64. Locke 1681a: 60 (20 May); L638; L640; Locke 1681a: 66, 67 (June 10, 11); dB: vol. 2, 397, L634 and others; L673.
65. Locke 1681a: 74–83, 113–14 (Aaron and Gibb: 116–18); 83, 87; L636 and others.
66. L645.
67. Haley: 654; Locke 1681a: 91, Haley: 656, Milton and Milton: 187.
68. Locke 1681a: 91 (9–10 July), 104, 105 (16–19 July).
69. Locke 1681a: 108; L656; Locke 1681a: 92–104 (14 August); Prideaux: 139–40; MS Locke b.1, fol. 48 (17 August).
70. Haley: 663; Locke 1692d: 676, 1681a: 113; L653, also Haley: 662.
71. Haley: 664–5, 667, Milton and Milton, Locke 1681a: 138, 146, 147, Prideaux: 115.

72. Locke 1681a: 113; L594 and others; Locke 1681a: 123, MS Locke c.31, fol. 48.

73. Haley: 670; Prideaux: 115, L667; Haley: 675–82.

74. L677; L704 and others; L693. Thanks to Roma Hutchinson for pointing out the significance of "Philoclea".

75. dB: vol. 2, 479, L683, Cranston: 214, L705, L709.

76. Locke 1682: 17 (8–9 February); 1692d: 676 (10 February); L684.

77. Locke 1682: 18; L684, Locke 1682: 33–4; L688.

78. Smith 20; L684; L687, L696, L699.

79. Haley: 691; Prideaux: 129 (14 March), 131 (19 March).

80. L690, Locke 1682: 19, 32, 44, 47, 52; 1692d: 676–7.

81. Locke 1682: 58 (27–28 April), L706; Locke 1682: 61 (25–26 May), L709; Locke 1682: 62 (27–28 May), 63 (30 May); 62, L715.

82. Haley: 710, P. Milton 2000: 651.

83. Haley: 710–11.

84. Locke 1682: 91–2.

85. L709, L714 and others; Locke 1679: 95, 116, 178, 1680a: 115, 1681a: 152, 1682: 90; 75, L723; Locke 1682: 87, 89; 73, 76, 78–9.

86. L709, L724; Locke 1682: 83, 86 (8–22 August); 88, 86.

87. Locke 1682: 94; Haley: chap. 29; P. Milton 2000: 655, Haley: 715, 718–22; 728–9.

88. Locke 1682: 94, 95, 97, 100; Prideaux: 134.

89. Locke 1682: 109 (4 December); 1683: 3 (17 January); L753.

90. L753; Locke 1683: 19.

91. Locke 1683: 24, 44–8; L760; Locke 1683: 44–55; L762, Locke 1683: 56–78 (22–28 March).

92. L766; Locke 1683: 92.

93. T1: 209; Filmer: 4, 2, 3.

94. T1: §5.

95. T1: §§6, 9.

96. T1: §§86, 87.

97. T1: §91.

98. T1: §92.

99. T1: §94.

100. T1: §§108, 123.

101. T2: §§22, 19.

102. T2: §6.

103. T2: §8.

104. T2: §77.

105. T2: §§85, 89, 3.

106. T2: §§95, 22.

107. T2: §85; Farr: 281.

108. T2: §§100, 101.

109. T2: §104 (emphasis added).

110. T2: §§134, 135.

111. T2: §143–4.

112. T2: §§156, 216, 155.

113. T2: §167.
114. T2: §240.
115. T2: §§226, 223, 225, 210.
116. D. Masham: 179.
117. Haley: 717–18, P. Milton 2000: 660; Locke 1683: 93 (24–25 April); 94; Ashcraft: 379–80, P. Milton 2000: 661.
118. Locke 1683: 106 (29 May); Ashcraft: 388, P. Milton 2000: 662–3.
119. Ashcraft: 383, P. Milton 2000: 663; L768, Locke 1683: 81, L769; MS Locke c.25, fol. 35, Locke 1683: 111.
120. Locke 1683: 115, 111; 1692d: 682 (21 June).
121. L767, L755; Locke 1683: 112, 117.
122. P. Milton 2000: 663–4, Haley: 717–18; Prideaux: 139–40 (12 November 1684).
123. P. Milton 2000: 666–7.
124. Locke 1683: 119; Wood 1891–1900: vols. 2–4, *passim*, CSPD: vol. 25 (July–September 1683), 325, 381.
125. Locke 1692d: 683; 1683: 119.
126. CSPD: vol. 25 (July–September 1683), 109–10 (13 July).
127. Beddard 1997b: 892–7.
128. Beddard 1997b: 897; Locke 1683: 120; 121, MSS Locke f.29, 10; c.19, 22; L770; Locke 1683: 122–4, L771.
129. Locke 1683: 119; MSS Locke c.19, 22–3; b.5, nos. 6–8, b.8, no. 11 (dB: vol. 2, 599), nos. 173–4.
130. L770, L773, L771, L772.
131. L771; Locke 1683: 123 (7/17 September), 126.
132. L770, Locke 1683: 124, L771.
133. Wood 1891–1900: vol. 3, 72, 69, 71; Beddard 1997b: 898–900.
134. D. Masham: 179–80.

CHAPTER 6

1. L801.
2. Locke 1683: 123, 125, 142, 155, 1684: 98.
3. L771, Locke 1683: 126–7, 141, 129–30.
4. L773; dB: vol. 2, 601, Withington: 380, BL Add. MS 5714, fol. 8r, MS Locke f.12, 12 (19 September 1667), L771.
5. dB: vol. 2, 738, Le Clerc: 11; Locke 1684: 1, 4, 79, 83.
6. Locke 1683: 161, 162; 1684: 59.
7. Le Clerc: 11; Limborch to Masham (1705) quoted by Bourne: vol. 2, 6.
8. L801, Locke 1684: 8–9, 10–11, 19–26, 32, 33, 34, 56.
9. L801.
10. L801.
11. L775.
12. L797, Locke 1684: 230.
13. Locke 1684: 28, L774, Locke 1683: 163, L777.
14. Meynell 1993: 245; Locke 1686b: 334, 336; L495, L510, L536, L552, L796.

15. L811, L814, L818.
16. Locke 1684: 77–8.
17. Locke 1684: 107–15; L777, L779.
18. L787; Locke 1684: 105, 114–21; L784.
19. Locke 1684: 122.
20. L785.
21. Locke 1684: 176–203, L866.
22. Locke 1684: 203, 204, L797, Locke 1684: 209–11; 36–55, 67–71, L794.
23. Locke 1684: 212–23.
24. L800, L791, L809.
25. L807, L844, L2315.
26. L782.
27. L845, L844.
28. L782, TE: §§1, 14, 42, 135, 140, 141, 147.
29. L782; Withington: 375; TE: §7, L600, also L605.
30. TE: §§13, 15, 21, 22.
31. TE: §§33, 34, 36.
32. TE: §§38, 39.
33. TE: §118; L822, also TE: §120.
34. L807, L822, also TE: §§150–4.
35. NA PRO 30/24/47/22 (8/18 November).
36. Locke 1684: 227, L797, L645.
37. 6/16 November; quoted by King 1884: 149–50 from NA PRO 30/24/47/22.
38. D. Masham: 180, MS Locke c.25, fol. 42.
39. Quoted by Bourne: vol. 1, 484–5 from NA PRO 30/24/47/22 (8/18 November).
40. D. Masham: 181–2.
41. dB: vol. 2, 657, Prideaux: 139 (to Ellis 12/22 November).
42. L795.
43. Quoted by Bourne: vol. 1, 485 from NA PRO 30/24/47/22; BL Ballard MS 12, fol. 5 (quoted by B.: 40).
44. BL MS Add. 41810, ff. 187r–88v.
45. Wood 1891–1900: vol. 3, 117.
46. dB: vol. 2, 661.
47. L797. Ironically this letter is now at Christ Church itself, in the library, which inexplicably ignores even initial inquiries concerning it.
48. Shaftesbury 1705: 330.
49. Prideaux: 139 (to Ellis, 12 November 1684); dB: vol. 2, 623; Locke 1683: 156, 1684: 37, etc; 230 (30 November).
50. Shaftesbury 1705: 330; CSPD: (May 1684–February 1685), 285.
51. L801; Cranston: 250.
52. L801.
53. dB: vol. 2, 665; L797.
54. L795, L801.
55. Le Clerc 13.
56. Add MS 17677 (GG), fols. 262–6.

57. L792, L793, L794.
58. Bourne: vol. 2, 17.
59. Locke 1684: 232 (16 December); 1685: 257; BL MSS Add. 41810, fol. 188v; 41812, fol. 85v.
60. L822, L801; Locke 1685: 258, 261 (1–14 February), L810; Locke 1685: 267, 268 (15–20 April); BL Add. MS 41812, fol. 34r (Skelton to Middleton, 24 April/4 May 1685).
61. Earle: 52, 76.
62. Le Clerc: 13, Locke 1685: 277.
63. BL Add. MS 41817, fol. 5r. Thanks to Jan and Susan van der Werf for a translation from the Dutch; Willcock: 339.
64. BL MS Harleian 6845, fols. 270v, 277r, Grey: 112, 118, Bourne: vol. 2, 20, Cranston: 252, Pringle.
65. Ashcraft: 465.
66. BL Add. MSS 41823, fol. 13r; 41812, fol. 58v (Skelton to Middleton, 8/18 May 1685); 17677(GG), fols. 262–6 (Skelton to the States General, 17 May 1685) (partly reprinted in King 1884: 154–5); Sloane MS 1983B, fol. 38.
67. Locke 1685: 273; BL Add. MSS 41812, fols. 70v, 85v, 41817, fol. 125, Ashcraft: 465–6, BL Add. MS 41812, fol. 100; Le Clerc: 13.
68. Le Clerc: 13; Limborch to Masham, 13 March 1705, quoted by Bourne: vol. 2, 22–3; BL Add. MS 41818, fol. 229v, L825, Locke 1685: 282 (16 July); BL Add. MSS 41817, fols. 125 (10 June), 218v (8/18 July), also 41812, fol. 138r (7/17 July), 41817, fol. 218r–v.
69. L824, L825.
70. L805, L827, L823.
71. L823, L827.
72. dB: vol. 2, 758; L827, L830, L837, L896, L1003.
73. L751, L752; L709, L748, L820, L815.
74. L830, L839, L837.
75. E: 1.1.5.
76. Le Clerc: 13; Limborch to Masham, 6 April 1706 (quoted by Bourne: vol. 2, 24–5).
77. MS Locke f.34, 6, Locke 1685: 289, L829, L831.
78. L834.
79. L834.
80. E: 1.1.2.
81. E: 1.1.5.
82. E: 1.1.4, 5, 6.
83. E: 1.2.1.
84. E: 1.3.14, 1.2.1.
85. E: 1.2.2, 4–5.
86. E: 1.3.10, 9.
87. E: 1.3.5.
88. E: 1.3.6, 13.
89. E: 1.4.1, 8.
90. E: 1.1.3.
91. E: 2.1.2, 6.

92. ET: 6.
93. dB: vol. 2, 728, L828; L833 and others.
94. BL MS Add. 41812, fol. 224 (from Utrecht to Skelton, 2/12 November 1685).
95. MS Locke f.28, 95, 96; BL Add. MS 41812, fol. 218 (8 November); Limborch to Masham (26 March 1706), quoted by Bourne: vol. 2, 25, dB: vol. 2, 760, L1131; dB: vol. 2, 611.
96. Limborch to Masham, 13 March 1705 (Bourne: vol. 2, 34), Le Clerc: 13; J. Milton 1993: 52ff., Locke 1684: 97 (17 July), dB: vol. 2, 744.
97. Locke 1674.
98. ET: 4.
99. ET: 5, 9, 6.
100. ET: 9.
101. ET: 9, 10, 28.
102. ET: 11, 12.
103. ET: 12, 25.
104. ET: 40, 45, 46, 47.
105. ET: 47, 49, 48.
106. ET: 13, 14.
107. ET: 16, 20, Locke 1681b: 103.
108. L1554, L2812; ET: 43–4, 29, 26, 25, 28.
109. ET: 56, 24, 56.
110. Le Clerc: 13, 14; Bourne: vol. 2, 42–3, L814, L818, L790, L926, Cranston: 293.
111. L844.
112. L844.
113. L844.
114. L844; L623, L849, MSS Locke c.31, fol. 98, d.1, 101, Locke 1679: 93–4; MSS Locke f.34, b.1, c.1, c.26, f.11, f.12, f.13.
115. Bourne: vol. 2, 26; Locke 1683: 109, dB: vol. 3, 5, 7, 58, Anselment: 951, L1086, L883, L876; L851 and others; L851.
116. Coste: 165, D. Masham: 189–90; L861, TE: §143.
117. L851; Locke 1686a: 17 (22 June), 18 (11 July); L854, L857, L859, Locke 1686a: 22–3.
118. L860, L867, L872; L873.
119. L879.
120. L865.
121. L874, dB: vol. 3, 39–40.
122. L877, Locke 1686a: 48; L879, L874, dB: vol. 3, 60, de Beer 1974: 37–8; Ellis: vol. 1, 177–8.
123. Bourne: vol. 2, 55, de Beer 1974: 35, 38; L879; L889.
124. L849, L871, L886.
125. L886.
126. E: 2.33.19.
127. E: 3.3.4, 6.
128. E: 3.3.11, 17.
129. E: 3.6.28, 30, 31.

130. E: 3.10.8, 9.
131. E: 3.6.3, 3.17.
132. E: 4.3.16; TE: §193; E: 3.3.17, 6.10.
133. E: 3.6.2.
134. E: 3.5.3, 14.
135. E: 3.5.14; 4.3.29, 1.2.
136. E: 4.8.8.
137. E: 4.1.2.
138. E: 4.6.9; 4.3.25; 4.12.9.
139. E: 3.3.18; 2.31.6.
140. Locke 1681a: 78; E: 3.11.16.
141. E: 4.12.9–10, 1.1.5.
142. E: 1.1.2, 4.18.2, 4, 6, 10, 7.
143. E: 4.18.2; Locke 1681a: 35.
144. L886, E: 1.4.23, 25.
145. L991.
146. Le Clerc: 14; dB: vol. 3, 146, L914, L974, L906; MS Locke f.34, 10 (7–9 February); L905.
147. Le Clerc: 14; L905, L917.
148. L943, L901; L890 and others; L907, L929.
149. L943.
150. L947; dB: vol. 2, 620; MS Locke c.31, fol. 98, Locke 1687a: 3, 1686a: 50.
151. L974, L978; dB: vol. 3, 290.
152. L932, L939, L968, L985.
153. L982, L957.
154. L946, L955, L982.
155. L989, L1000.
156. MS Locke f.34, 14 (16 December); L991, L993, L999.
157. Trans. and quoted in Bourne: vol. 2, 99; Le Clerc: 15.
158. L1003, L1004, L1026, L999.
159. L1025 and others; L1044, L1026; L1024, L1024A, L1053, L1035; L1040.
160. L998, L1004, L1020 and others.
161. L999.
162. Shaftesbury 1705: 330.
163. L1085.
164. L1017, MS Locke f.34, 16 (5–6 March); Locke 1688a: 318 (29 March).
165. L1026, L1020, L1030; D. Masham: 192.
166. L1042, L1077.
167. L1020, L748.
168. L1030, L1028.
169. MS Locke c.25, fols. 16, 17; Locke 1679: 117–18; L1050; L748, Locke 1683: 3, 1684: 88, MS Locke f.29, 26.
170. L1038.
171. L1045.
172. L1047, L1050, L1046, L1060, L1077.
173. Coste: 170, D. Masham: 191.
174. L1026.

175. L1019; NA PRO SP 45/12 (as in Steele no. 3828).
176. L1047, D. Masham: 182, L937.
177. L1047, L1050; dB: vol. 3, 450, L982.
178. L1050, L1057.
179. L1019, L1057.
180. Locke 1688a: 318, 319, MS Locke f.34, 16, L1038, L1042; Locke 1688a: 319 (21 April), L1032, L1049; L1068, Locke 1688a: 319, L1042.
181. L1026, L1070, L989; Locke 1688a: 322–7, L1083; L1085, L1077.
182. L908, L1000, L1019, L1027.
183. L1085.
184. L1096.
185. Baxter: 235–6.
186. L1110, L1107, L1100.
187. L1100, also L1107; dB: vol. 3, 539, L1100, L1101; Locke 1689a: 5; 2–5, L1102; L1127, Locke 1689a: 11, MS Locke f.34, 18–21.
188. House of Commons Jns: vol. 10, 9, 10–11, L1102.
189. L1105, L1107; Locke 1689a: 6, 7, L1114; Goldie: 125, J. Milton 2004: 223, dB: vol. 3, 569.
190. L797, L746; L1378.

CHAPTER 7

1. L1121, L1117, Locke 1689a: 7, L876; L1096, L1121; L1131.
2. House of Commons Jn: vol. 10, 36 (27 February), L1116.
3. House of Commons Jn: vol. 10, 36, L1131.
4. D. Masham: 182–3, L1116, dB: vol. 3, 573.
5. L1116.
6. L187, L1116.
7. Baxter: 248, L1127.
8. L1117, also L1121, L1124; L1120.
9. L1127, also L1125; L1127.
10. L1120; L1122; L1127, L1128, Horwitz: 24–6, 28–9; L1147.
11. L1131, L1134, L1147; L1172, L1178, L1182, L1187; L1131.
12. L1146, also L1158; Limborch to Masham, 24 March 1705, quoted by Montuori: xxi.
13. Locke 1689a: 29 (18 March); 1690a: 44; L1102; L773; MS Locke c.25, fol. 39.
14. L1129, L1128.
15. CTB: vol. 9, 110 (8 May, 1689); D. Masham: 182; L1710, L2461; MS Locke c.2, 70.
16. L1184; MS Locke c.25, fol. 47 (10 February); MS Locke c.25, fol. 47; NA SP 44/236, 186 (CSPD: William and Mary (1689–90), 455 (10 February 1690)).
17. MS Locke c.25, fol. 42v; fol. 41v, D. Masham: 182.
18. Wood 1891–1900: vol. 3, 316 (6 December 1689/3 March 1690), D. Masham: 182.
19. L1172, MS Locke b.1, fol. 109.

20. L1152; L1156, L1176, L1177, L1185 and so on, Locke 1690a: 38, 39, MS Locke c.1, 46.
21. dB: vol. 3, 661, L1165.
22. L1166, L1173.
23. L1165.
24. L1166, also L1173; L1171; L1192; L1167; dB: vol. 8, 444–6.
25. L1158; MS Locke b.5, no. 14; L1147; dB: vol. 3, 623; Montuori: xxxi, xxxv–xxxvi, L1182.
26. Locke 1823: vol. 10, 156–7, 1689e: rule 6, L1562.
27. Cranston: 326; T1: Preface.
28. Laslett 1960: 47.
29. T2: §§171, 205, 20, Laslett 1960: 299, 400, 420; T2: §131, Laslett 1960: 427, 368, 371; T2: §222, Ogg 1955: 186–8.
30. T2: §§219, 220, Laslett 1960: 428–9.
31. L1213, Locke 1689a: 29, MS Locke f.29, 36.
32. L1213, L1225; dB: vol. 8, 449–50.
33. E: Dedication.
34. D. Masham: 183, Locke 1689a: 18, E: Dedication; L1184.
35. Axtell 1965b: 154–7, 1969: 175–6, Brewster: vol. 1, 339, King 1884: 209–16.
36. E2: 4.10.18, Locke 1729 (trans. Bennett and Remnant: 5).
37. Locke 1729 (trans. Bennett and Remnant: 5).
38. L1200, L1213, L1225, L1220.
39. L1225, L1352.
40. L1225.
41. L1239.
42. L1248, dB: vol. 2, 610.
43. L1256.
44. L1266, L1277.
45. L1225, L1266, L1277, L1312.
46. L1312.
47. dB: vol. 4, 116, L1312.
48. L1283.
49. L1285, L1288, L1298.
50. Farr and Roberts: 386, Locke 1690d: 395, 398, 395.
51. Locke 1690d: 395, 396, 397, 396.
52. L1264, L1271; L1301, L1317, L1332; Locke 1690a: 44 (29 April); D. Masham: 183–4; Burnet 1823: vol. 3, 275; quoted by Hattendorf: 14; L1099.
53. L1292.
54. L1290.
55. L1299.
56. P1: 2–3; LT: 10; P1: 3, 5, 12, 14–15, 12–13, 24, 14, 16, 18.
57. L1325.
58. 2LT: 73, 76–7, 126, P1: 18–19.
59. 2LT: 102, 128.
60. L1325, L1330.

61. Locke 1690a: 48, 49, MS Locke f.34, 26, L1301, L1305, L1307; MSS Locke f.29, 63, f.34, 27, Locke 1690a: 51 (17–30 June); Locke 1690a: 51, MS Locke c.1, 221, 223.
62. L1301; E: 1.3.13; E: 2.27.10–12; 2.28.10–12 in later editions.
63. L1309, L1307.
64. E: 2.28.12, 8.
65. L1309.
66. L1307, L1309; E: 2.28.8, my emphasis.
67. MS Locke f.29, 63 (15 July), L1313; Locke 1690a: 56 (17 September), MS Locke f.29, 63, L1314, L1315, L1322.
68. Kelly: 16, 126–9, L1345, L1348, L1350.
69. SCIM: 5, 10.
70. SCIM: 11.
71. Kelly: 71, SCIM: 76, 29.
72. Kelly: 71, SCIM: 30.
73. SCIM: 33.
74. SCIM: 40.
75. SCIM: 40.
76. SCIM: 42, 31, 22.
77. SCIM: 72.
78. Kelly: 129.
79. Kelly: 42, 45; D. Masham: 185–6.
80. Kelly: 17.
81. SCIM: 81, 83, 87, 88.
82. Kelly: 17, Horsefield: 38.
83. SCIM: 103.
84. L1323 and others; Locke 1690a: 34, 35, 37, 40, L1244, and so on; dB: vol. 4, 148.
85. Locke 1690a, 58 (14 October), MS Locke f.29, 63, L1326.
86. Locke 1690a: 59 (27 October), MS Locke f.29, 63, f.34, 29; L1333.
87. L1344, L1345, L1351, L1355.
88. L1342, Locke 1690a: 65 (13 December), MSS Locke f.29, 63, f.34, 31.

CHAPTER 8

1. L2281.
2. L1357.
3. Locke 1691a: 81, MS Locke f.34, fol. 31 (5 January); L1353, Locke 1691a: 82 (17 January); L1356.
4. D. Masham: 170–84.
5. D. Masham: 170, 184; dB: vol. 4, 122, L1353.
6. L1322, Locke 1691a: 90 (Friday, 8 May).
7. L1375.
8. L1758, L2603, Cranston: 344.
9. L2096, L3409, L1433; MS Locke f.34, fols. 6or, 64r, L2825; MS Locke f.34, fols. 6or, 64r.

10. Locke 1699a: 417; 1692a: 147, 1693a: 181, L2368 and others from Bonville, L1839 and others to/from Freke, L3452 and others from Francis Limborch, L2684 and others from Samuel Locke, MS Locke c.2, 27; MS Locke c.1, 232, 265, 230, 338, TE: §67.
11. Cranston: 344, D. Masham: 192; Locke 1692a: 164, L1345 for example, L1429, L1572.
12. Cranston: 343, L3163, Locke 1705a: 1918; MS Locke c.25, fol. 62; L1360, L1371, L1386.
13. L1378, L1477, L1885; MS Locke f.17, see dB: vol. 4, 284; L1430, L1424, L1420; L1403, L1420 and others from Tyrrell, L1528, L1529, Locke 1691a: 98, 1692a: 151–3.
14. L620, L801, L879; Locke 1692a: 172; Harrison and Laslett: 18, 30–2.
15. L3556.
16. L1450, Locke 1691a: 85, 105, 108, 113, L1449, L1476, L1378.
17. Locke 1691a: 84, 88 (30 March–9 April), 90, 95 (8–28 May), 97, 103 (13–25 July); Locke 1691a: 94, 96.
18. L1397, L1403, L1411; Locke 1691a: 103 (31 July), 101 (8 August); L1413, L1414; L1420.
19. L1413, L1406; Locke 1691a: 101 (24 August), 102, L1406; L1406, L1484, L1537.
20. Locke 1691a: 104 (9 September, 12–18 September); L1418; Locke 1691a: 105, 107; L1422; MS Locke f.34, fol. 42r (21 October).
21. L1423; dB: vol. 4, 17, L1586, L1625, L1628; L1423, Locke 1691b, Kelly: 131, L1435, L1436, L1440; L1439, L1440.
22. L1455, dB: vol. 4, 367, 373.
23. L1422.
24. Locke 1691a: 108–11; L1448, Hunter: 113f., Maddison: 176, L1519.
25. Locke 1691a: 111 (21 November), L1431; MS Locke f.34, fol. 42r, L1433, L1435; L1369, L1370, L1376, L1416.
26. L1431; L906, TE: §156, L829, L844, L845; L1431.
27. Locke 1691a: 112 (27 November); Boyle 1692: Advertisement, Locke 1691a: 114 (2 December), L1433.
28. L1435, L1471, L1440, L1442.
29. L1444; dB: vol. 5, 738, L2809, MS Locke d.9.
30. L1510.
31. L1462, L1467; L1471; L1472, Locke 1692a: 130, L1476 and others; L1476.
32. 3T: 141–2, Locke 1692a: 130 (3 March); L1483, D. Masham: 192, L1488.
33. L1497, Locke 1692a: 132, 137 (22–30 April), Locke 1692a: 137 (10 May); L1499; L1501, L1480, L1533.
34. L1465, L1499; L1450; L1466.
35. L1519, L1466, L1513.
36. L1501; Locke 1692a: 139 (13 May).
37. L1501, dB: vol. 4, 453; L1501, L1502.
38. Locke 1692a: 140 (15 June); L1506; Locke 1692a: 140:
39. It is dated "20 June"; L1517, Locke 1692a: 170.
40. 2LT: 63, 64, 76.
41. 3LT: 546, 213, 2LT: 89.

42. 3LT: 143, 163.
43. L1473, L1511.
44. 3LT: 331, 320, 410, 145.
45. 3LT: 153, 327.
46. 3LT: 154.
47. MS Locke f.34, fol. 46r, Locke 1692a: 141, 142, L1507, L1509.
48. Locke 1823: vol. 9, 289; L1515, L1530.
49. L1530, L1857, L1538.
50. L1538.
51. L1530, L1538.
52. John Warr, one of Boyle's executors, to his son (quoted by Maddison: 203), L1517.
53. NA T/27/13, 326 (CTB: vol. 9, 1731 (20 July, 1692)); T/27/9, 18 (CTB: vol. 8 (1685–9), 38 (9 March 1685)).
54. MS Locke c.19, fol. 127, L1542, L1545, L1551, L1563.
55. Locke 1692a: 149 (13 August), L1532, L1510.
56. Locke 1692a: 150 (5 September), 1705a: 1933; Locke 1692a: 153 (8 September), L1538, Locke 1692a: 161, also MS Locke c.42, 290, L1538, also L1534, L1535, L1544, L1562.
57. Locke 1692a: 167 (18 October), L1556, L1565.
58. dB: vol. 4, 443, L1492, L1505.
59. L1548, L1549.
60. L1559, L1564.
61. L1576, L1575.
62. L1595, L1606.
63. L1325, Locke 1692c: fols. 107r, 108r.
64. L1567.
65. L1590, L1608.
66. Locke 1705a: 1933–5, 1692a: 169 (18 November), L1572, L1571; L1571, L1573, L1588.
67. Boyle 1692; L1583; Locke 1692d, L197.
68. Locke 1692a: 171 (26 November), L1571, L1589.
69. L1579, L1544.
70. L1592.
71. E: 2.21.14, 20, 21, 27, 29, 25; L1544; E: 2.21.29; L1544, sect. 31.
72. L1579.
73. L1659.
74. L1548 and others, L1586; L1596, Kelly: 22; L1586, Locke 1695b, L1598, Horsefield: 42.
75. Kelly: 23, Locke 1695b: 129.
76. L1601, L1598; Locke 1693a: 177 (7 February), L1601; Locke 1693a: 178–80.
77. Locke 1693a: 177, L1598, NA AO/1/2303/2, MS Locke b.5, nos. 12–13, c.1, 239; MS Locke c.25, fol. 48; CTB: vol. 17 (1702), 732, 735 (28 June 1694), MS Locke c.25, fol. 49.
78. L1601, Locke 1693a: 180 (18 February); L1610; L1607; L1609, L1620, L1064, E2: 2.9.8.
79. L1620, Locke 1693b, MS Locke d.3, 89.

80. Locke 1693b: §§14, 10.
81. Locke 1693b: §§4, 52, 4.
82. Locke 1693b: §52, 1693c: §3.
83. Locke 1693c: §14.
84. Locke 1693c: §35.
85. L1620, Yolton and Yolton: 47, dB: vol. 4, 627; L1643, L1644, Yolton and Yolton: 48; L1609, L1622, L1652; TE: §106, L1655, TE: §107, L1661, L1665.
86. L1619; Locke 1693a: 181 (24 March); MS Locke d.9, L1625, Locke 1693a: 185 (18 April); L1627, MS Locke d.9, c.1, 239, Locke 1693a: 181–2.
87. L1608, L1626, MS Locke f.34, fol. 50r (6 May, 13 May), L1630.
88. Locke 1693a: 185 (22 May), L1635, Locke 1693a: 185–93, L1634.
89. Locke 1693a: 193 (2 July), MS Locke d.9 (2 July 1693), Locke 1693a: 193 (10 July), 196–7.
90. L1643, L1652, L1655, E2: 2.21.35.
91. E2: 2.21.43, 71.
92. L2105, E2: 2.21.56, 52.
93. L1647, L1655; L1609, E: 2.1.12, E2: 2.27.–, L1655.
94. E2: 2.27.1, 3; Locke 1683: 107.
95. E2: 2.27.8, 6.
96. E2: 2.27.9, 10.
97. E2: 2.27.19, 25.
98. E2: 2.27.18, 26, 20, 22.
99. L1661, L1685, L1693, also L1712, L1744.
100. L1659, Brewster: vol. 2, 142, L1663, L1664.
101. L1405, L1663.
102. L1665, L1679; L1686, L1698, L1704; MS Locke f.34, fol. 53r; dB: vol. 8, 446.
103. L1821.
104. L1650, L1692, L1702, MS Locke f.29, 146 (16 April), L1741; L1690, L1718, L1719; L1696, L1703, L1709, Locke 1694a: 216; L1703; L1696, dB: vol. 4, 791.
105. MS Locke d.9 (12–23 April), Locke 1694a: 222 (23 April); Ogg 1955: 418–21, Kelly: 103, L1844, L1847, L1874, dB: vol. 5, 187.
106. Tanner 1926: vol. 1, 99, L1744; dB: vol. 8, 450, L1695, L1733.
107. Locke 1694a: 237, L1762, L1768, dB: vol. 5, 106.
108. Locke 1694a: 238 (14 July); L1750, L1769, L1773.
109. MS Locke d.9 (20 August, 4 September), Locke 1705a: 1918, L1776, L1785, L1788, Locke 1694a: 241 (19 September), L1790.
110. L1760; Locke 1694a: 246 (9 October); L1795; MS Locke d.9.
111. L1798, also L1767; L1799.
112. L1821.
113. Locke 1694a: 249 (7 December); dB: vol. 5, 200; L1826.
114. Locke 1693a: 251 (22 December), MS Locke f.34, fol. 59r, L1836.
115. L1901.
116. L1901, 2VRC: 186, Higgins-Biddle: xvi–xvii.
117. L1901, 2VRC: 188, RC: 5, 152.
118. RC: 17, 157, 16–17, 20, 156.
119. RC: 157, 105.

120. RC: 4, 5, 7.
121. E: 4.17.14.
122. E: 2.28.8, Leyden: 69, Locke 1687b: 9, 14.
123. E: 3.9.23; Locke 1681a: 78, E: 4.3.18.
124. L1538, L2059.
125. RC: 133, L3328.
126. RC: 133, 135.
127. RC: 139–44, 146.
128. RC: 146–7.
129. Locke 1677a: 50–1, 1681b: 75–6, 1682: 31.
130. Locke 1682: 25–32, E: 4.3.6, 3LS: 474–6, RC: 149–50.
131. ELN: 173, E: 1.3.6, ELN: 185, 183.
132. Locke 1687b: 11–12, E: 2.28.6.
133. Locke 1677b, 95, RC: 143.
134. RC: 85, also E: 4.16.13, Locke 1681a: 37–8.
135. VRC: 167.
136. L1586.
137. L1833, dB: vol. 5, 248; King 1884: 202–3.
138. dB: vol. 5, 248, 785, L1853; dB: vol. 5, 282, 791–6, L1858, L1862; L1860, L1862; dB: vol. 5, 327, L1874.
139. Atterbury: vol. 2, 2; L1843.
140. L1845, L1846; L1868, L1869, L1884, L1872, L1915, L2059.
141. Kelly: 20; L1890, L1908.
142. Locke 1695b, L1853, L1856.
143. L1860, Kelly 21, Horsefield: 47.
144. MS Locke d.9, L1857; L1920, L1903, L1908; L1904, L1911; Locke 1695a: 273 (30 May), MS Locke f.34, fol. 60r.
145. L1972, L2067; CTB: vol. 10, 944–5 (8 March 1695), L1904, dB: vol. 5, 375; L1359 and others, dB: vol. 4, 200.
146. MS Locke b.1, fol. 178 (12 June), L1901, 2VRC: 188.
147. Locke 1695a: 279 (22 June), L1934; L1920, L1921; Locke 1695a: 280, 290 (8 July–20 August).
148. MS Locke c.1, 269 (30 July), Locke 1695a: 299, L2603, E. Masham: 80; Locke 1684: 28–9, 1688a: 320, L884; L910, L916, L919 and others; L1031, L1043 and others.
149. L2880, also L1397, L1411, L1540, L3170, L3172, L3229, D. Masham: 193; L2896, also L2976, L3247, L2945.
150. L797; L840, L1182, L1184, Locke 1684: 35, 59; L2239, L2242, L3616, L3634.
151. L1941, L1944, L2020.
152. Locke 1695c, L2115, VRC: 165; dB: vol. 6, 163, Higgins-Biddle: xlix, L2288.
153. L1961, also L2066, L3174, L2100, L2131.
154. L1939.
155. VRC: 179; CA: 63, 64, 67, 68, 72–3, 74, 75.
156. SC: 215.
157. SC: 134, 132.
158. CA: 104–5.
159. CA: 122, 2VRC: 304, CA: 105–6, 106, 121, 109–10, 115–16, 119, 113.

160. CA: 113–15.
161. VRC: 172; SU: 93.
162. VRC: 175.
163. VRC: 175.
164. VRC: 164, 167.
165. VRC: 166, 167.
166. L1971.
167. Kelly: 24; dB: vol. 5, 415; L1929; Locke 1695e.
168. Kelly: 24; Locke 1695a: 290 (2 September), Locke 1695j: 136.
169. Kelly: 24–5.
170. L1949, Locke 1695f, Kelly: 26.
171. NA SP 44/274, 93; CSPD, vol. 6 (July–December 1695), 71, Kelly: 25.
172. Locke 1695a: 292 (28 September), MS Locke f.29, 147; L1948, L1953, Locke 1695j: 136, 1695h: 381.
173. L1956, Locke 1695h: 375, 380, 1695a: 293 (21 October); Locke 1695g: 375, 380.
174. Kelly: 29 (31 October), 27, 30.
175. Coxe: 400, dB: vol. 4, 288.
176. L1964; L1965, L1966, L1968, Locke 1695a: 295.
177. L1966, L1945; L2038, L2115; L2131, L2407, L2422, L2935.
178. L1971, also L1974.
179. L1972.
180. dB: vol. 5, 466; Locke 1695f, 1695g, 1695h.
181. L1974, L1976; Kelly 31–2; L1976, Locke 1695j, dB: vol. 5, 486.
182. dB: vol. 5, 517, Li: 115–16, L1987, also L1976.
183. L2001, L2003.
184. L1971, L1974.
185. L2067, L1972, L1970, L1975.

CHAPTER 9

1. L1980.
2. Cranston: 400.
3. L1977.
4. L1980.
5. L1981.
6. Locke 1695a: 296 (20 December); L2094; MS Locke f.29, 147, L2067.
7. L1985, also L1989; L1990, L2059, L1988, L1992, L2001; L2003.
8. L2002.
9. L2036, L2041.
10. L2017, dB: vol. 5, 562, L2033; Kelly: 33, L2017, also L2022, L2033; L2018.
11. L2047 and others; L2059.
12. L2015, L2025, also L2039 and others, L2056.
13. L2059, L2115.
14. L2002; L2067, L2074.
15. L2071, L2059; April 30, CSPD: (1696), 154, L2088; L2091, L2092.

16. MS Locke d.9 (18 May 1696); L2090.
17. L2094; L2096, Locke 1696a: 318 (29 May), MS Locke f.29, 147 (2 June).
18. MS Locke d.9 (8 June); f.29, 147 (8 June); NA CO 391/9 (25 June); Laslett 1969: 155; NA CO 391/9 (25 June).
19. L2115.
20. Coste: 168.
21. L2243; G: 185–6, 162, 176, 180.
22. Langley: 15, 16, 18, 19.
23. L2221, L2236; L2243; L2202, Langley: 15; L2221, L2262, L2236.
24. G: 189, L2243; G: 186; L2228; G: 189.
25. G: 197, dB: vol. 6, 62; G: 197, 204, 242, 245, L2565; G: 612.
26. L2243, also L2202; L2254.
27. L2113, MS Locke f.29, 147 (18–27 July); dB: vol. 5, 466–7, L2027 and others; L2230.
28. dB: vol. 5, 699, vol. 8, 447; L2189, L2129, L2131.
29. L2097; L2117, L2122, L2123, L2131, NA CO 391/9, 51ff., 222; L2124.
30. Locke 1696a: 333 (14 November), L2115, L2139.
31. L2244, L2250; MS Locke f.34, fol. 65r; L1050, Locke 1696a: 331 (7 November), 1697a: 342, L2134; L2202.
32. SC: 247.
33. dB: vol. 5, 766; L2189.
34. L2209.
35. L2202, L1804, also L2209.
36. DVT: 230, 1LS: 32.
37. DVT: 231.
38. L1646, L1650, L1653, see also L2605, L1874, Higgins-Biddle: xlix; Toland: 82.
39. DVT: 245.
40. 1LS: 68, 30.
41. E: 2.23.4; DVT: 236; 1LS: 13, 93.
42. 1LS: 94–6.
43. L2179; Locke 1697a: 344 (17 March).
44. L2160, L2202, L2172.
45. L2181, L2179, L2186.
46. MS Locke f.29, 147 (11 February), d.9 (11 February), L2202, NA CO 391/9 (13 February); 391/9 (13–19 February); L2199, L2209, MS Locke f.29, 147 (20 February), L2218.
47. L2209; L2160, also L397, L478, L2219, L2224, L2227, Locke 1697f.
48. Higgins–Biddle: xxvii; 2VRC: 191.
49. SU: A2v, 107, 30; SC: 120, 126–7, 247.
50. SC: 124; SU: Intro.
51. Bold 1697a, 1697b; b: A3, 51–2; SC: 2, 64.
52. 2VRC: 186.
53. SC: 245, 254, 250, 251.
54. 2VRC: 189–90.
55. 2VRC: 236; SU: 98, 108; 2VRC: 262, 204.
56. 2VRC: 204, 266.

57. CA: 112; SU: 89; 2VRC: 362.

58. 2VRC: 341, 349, 284.

59. SU: 33, 9.

60. 2VRC: 230, 231.

61. RC: 156.

62. 2VRC: 415–16; Bold 1697b: 36–7, 1697c: 30; 2VRC: 231.

63. 2VRC: 232, 358, 233, 377, 233.

64. Marshall 1994: 342, 417, Higgins-Biddle: lviii–lx, L1901.

65. Marshall 2000: 161.

66. VR: 166; Marshall 2000: 166–7; quoted by Tyacke 1997b: 616.

67. Marshall 2000: sects. 2, 4, 6; Locke 1661: 323; L1678.

68. LB: 186.

69. L2202, L2209.

70. L2206; Locke 1693e: 487.

71. L2232.

72. Locke 1697a: 344; L2229, L2239, L2233.

73. L2243; L3647.

74. L3647; Locke 1697g: §§1, 14, 15, 11, 7, 18, 19.

75. 3LS: 249; Locke 1697a: 349, L2278, L2288.

76. L2310, L2315.

77. L2340, L2310, L2359.

78. 1SL: 4, 2LS: 102, 108.

79. 1SL: 36–7.

80. 2LS: 117.

81. 1SL: 23, 2LS: 141.

82. 2LS: 146.

83. 2LS: 147, DVT: 252, 1SL: 103, 112.

84. 2LS: 175.

85. 1BR: 24, 23, 25.

86. 1BR: 26, 30.

87. LB: 187, 186, 188, 187, 188.

88. 2BR: 38–55, 3BR: 57, 2BR: 37; ELN 199; LB 187, E: 2.28.8, 4.13.3, 10.6; RC 11, 136.

89. L2218, MS Locke f.29, 147 (18 June); NA CO 391/9, 10; L2218, also L2272.

90. L2284, L2286; L2254, L2269, L1917; L2289, L2376.

91. L2296; L2131; NA CO 391/10, 207, 214–15, 224–5.

92. Locke 1697h: 364, 365, 371; NA CO 391/9, 52.

93. NA CO 391/10, 232, L2376.

94. MS Locke f.29, 147 (2–6 September), NA CO 391/10 (2–6 September); L2301, L2306.

95. Locke 1697i: 377; NA CO 391/10, 276 (23 September); 391/10 (28 September, 19, 26 October, 17, 18, 19, 25 November, 22, 23 December); Locke 1697i: 378, 383.

96. Cranston: 425; Locke 1697i: 378, 379, 381, 380, 386, 385.

97. Locke 1697i: 380, D. Masham: 190–1, L3310, MS Locke b.5, no. 14.

98. L2312, L2486, L2314.

99. L2100, L2240; Edwards 1697a: 77–8, 6, 15.

100. Edwards 1697a: 17, Locke 1693d: §§23–8.
101. L2319, L2322, L2323 also L2347.
102. L2363, L2378, L2281; Edwards 1697a: 53, 74, 68; L2378.
103. L2327, L2376; L2333, L2334; L2332, L2340; MS Locke f.29, 147 (30 November).
104. L2356, L2376.
105. L2376, L3088a; L2372, L2369, L2371, L2376; Locke 1698a: 375, L2412.
106. L2412.
107. Locke 1698a: 375; D. Masham: 184; dB: vol. 6, 306–7, de Beer 1967, L2384, L2424.
108. MS Locke d.9 (24 January), L2384.
109. L2398.
110. L2408, MS Locke d.9 (28 March).
111. L2376, L2414.
112. 2SL: 3, L2414.
113. 3LS: 392, 201.
114. 2SL: 4; 3LS: 202.
115. 2SL: 7–9.
116. 3LS: 221.
117. 2SL: 75; 3LS: 459.
118. 3LS: 331, also 2SL: 44, 3LS: 333–4.
119. 2SL: 45, 52, 57.
120. 3LS: 431, 435, 2SL: 158, 154.
121. 3LS: 442, 1SL: 9, 13, 27, 25.
122. 3LS: 446.
123. E: 2.23.1, 5, DVT: 241, E: 4.3.6.
124. E: 2.23.15.
125. 3LS: 461.
126. 3LS: 474–5, 482; 1LS: 96.
127. L2318, L2340, L2352.
128. L2460, L2352.
129. L2395, also L2340, dB: vol. 6, 783–93.
130. L2410, L2406, L2413.
131. L2413, L2395, L2406, L3486 and others, L3643.
132. L2407, L2414; L2420, L2424, L2426.
133. L2407, L2414, L2422, dB: vol. 6, 377, Ogg: 1955, 9; L2447.
134. L2459, L2477, L2481.
135. L2597.
136. L2468, L2469; MS Locke f.29, 147 (8 July, 25 October), NA CO/31/11.
137. MS Locke f.29, 147 (19 August), L2490, L2471, L2475; L2495, L2589, Locke 1698a: 394; L2490, L2495, L2514.
138. L2486, L2567, L2590, L2493.
139. L1169, L2590.
140. L2498, MS Locke f.29, 147, Locke d.9 (25 October), L2460, L2485, L2519.
141. L2512, Locke 1699a: 405 (11 January), MS Locke c.1, 343, 342.
142. L2518, L2525, L2597, L2549.

143. L2522, L2437, L2455, dB: vol. 6, 425; Bourne: vol. 2, 450–2; L2643, L2448 and others; L2773 and others.
144. L2535.
145. TE: §180, Axtell 1969: 178, Locke 1698b, Locke 1823: vol. 10, 154.
146. TE: §192.
147. L2636.
148. L2526; L2533, L2536, see also L2771, L3188, L3203.
149. G: 197, 242, 257; L2565, L2724A, G: 297–8, 337–9.
150. L2575, L2585.
151. L2576, L2583, L2590, MS Locke f.29, 147; L2503 and others, NA CO 191/11, 191/12.
152. L2615, L2611.
153. L2610, MS Locke f.29, 164 (25 November), L2637; L2640, 2645, L2539, L2566, L2590, L2718.
154. E4: 2.33.16, 17.
155. Locke 1681a: 33–4 (in Aaron and Gibb: 114); L29, L30, also L13, L59, L81; E4: 4.19.5, 6, 3, 7, 10, 14.
156. L2634, L2640, L2643.
157. L2439, L2652, L2663, L2656.
158. Ewen: 175, L2693 and others, L2728 and others; L2734, L2750, Locke 1700a: 463, 467.

CHAPTER 10

1. L2812.
2. L2719, L2695.
3. MS Locke d.9 (10 April), L2711, L2719; MS Locke f.29, 164 (13 May).
4. L2720, MS Locke c.36, c.1, 361, Coste: 168.
5. Coste: 169; NA CO 391/13 (28 June), CSPC: vol. 18 (item 600), 386; NA CO 391/13 (5 July), CSPC: vol. 18 (item 614), 392.
6. L2747, L2687, L2771, L2747; MS Locke f.29, 164 (17 July), L2749.
7. L2745, L2776; L2763 also L2756, L2768; L337, Rawlinson MS c.406, 6–8 (partly quoted in Bourne: vol. 1, 453), Dewhurst 1959b: 372.
8. L2762, L2783, L2768.
9. L2784, L2807, L2768, L2787, L2798, L2800.
10. dB: vol. 7, 352, L2945, L3074.
11. L2808, L2812.
12. L2817.
13. L2819, L2825, L2831, L2843; L2846.
14. L2841, L2859 and others.
15. dB: vol. 7, 222, 226, L2847, L2851, L2874; L2855, L2883.
16. L2857, L2742, L2795, L2979, L3010.
17. L2795, L2857, L2866, L1592.
18. L2866, L2881.
19. L2925, L2881, L2953, E: 2.21.47.
20. L2979, L3010.

21. L2952.
22. L2904, L2923, L2931, L2939; MS Locke f.29, 164 (30 June), L2964; L2948, L2955 and others.
23. L2956, L2986; L2952; MS Locke f.29, 164 (July 8), L2964, L2965, L2975.
24. L2381, L2978; L2926, L2932; L2623; L2487, L3141, L3232, Locke 1700c: 2.15.9, L3590, L3148.
25. L3271, L3323; L3150, L3154.
26. L1960, L2451, L3118, L3000, L2397; L2682, L3089; L2992; L3090.
27. L2310; L2637, L2638; L2055, L1521, Dewhurst 1963a: 301–3; L2984, L2986, L2987, L2991.
28. L3006, L3016 and others, Ogg 1955: 91–3, dB: vol. 7, 424.
29. L3025, L2828, L2975, E. Masham: 153 (7 November 1701), MS Locke b.5, no. 14.
30. L3043.
31. L3058, MS Locke d.9, L3062; L3063, L3071, L3089; L3064 and others, L3063 and others, L3072, L3125, L3165.
32. L3107.
33. L3108, L3111, L3116.
34. L3131, Locke 1702a: 522 (4 May), MS Locke f.29, 164 (4, 13 May); L3144, MS Locke b.1, 252, c.2, 65; L3143, L3144; L3138.
35. L3142, L3147, L3151, MS Locke f.29, 164 (16 June).
36. L3153, L3164, L3207, L3219, L3234.
37. L3159, L3161, L3162, L3163, dB: vol. 7, 643, 648, L3051, L3156.
38. L3186.
39. L3193, L3197, L3206.
40. L3198; Wainwright: 2, 5, dB: vol. 6, 629.
41. L3201, L3243, L3326, Locke 1823: vol. 10, 155, Locke 1702c; L59, L264, L699.
42. L3209, L3218, L3212 and others.
43. L3223, L3233, L3235.
44. Locke 1702b: 265; 1681a: 35 (Aaron and Gibb: 115), E: 4.16.13, Locke 1702b: 256 (my emphasis).
45. Locke 1702b: 257.
46. Locke 1702b: 259.
47. Locke 1702b: 259–62.
48. L3284.
49. L3248, L3261, L3283, L3324, L3283, L3358, L3575, L3607.
50. L3392, Harrison and Laslett: 43, King 1884: 269–70.
51. L3263, L3293.
52. L3284, L3278.
53. L3269, L3272, L3275.
54. L3275, L3233, L3287.
55. L3278, L3276, L3293.
56. L3293, L3301.
57. L3306.
58. L3500.
59. MS Locke d.9, L3309, L3014.

60. L3291, L3292, L3298, Clarke: 97–9.
61. L3300, L3292, L3302.
62. L1299, L3299.
63. L3306, L3195, L3273, L3326.
64. L3311, L3326, L3461, L3465, L3470, L3467.
65. L3315, L1431, L2718, L2781, L3012 and others, L3383.
66. L3348 and others, L3364, L3367, L3369, L3382, Wainwright: 689, 664–7, 672–4.
67. L3364, L3368, L3369, L3373, L3376.
68. L3382, L3388, L3375.
69. L2945, dB: vol. 7, 352, L3394, dB: vol. 8, 134, 311; L3553.
70. L3402, L3405, L3409, L3400, L3430.
71. L3412, L3418.
72. L3414, L3418, L3419.
73. L3415.
74. L3418, L3419.
75. L3361.
76. L3461, L3465, L3467, L3477, L3485, L3511.
77. L3466, L2833, L3489, Locke 1705a, 1919, MS Locke d.8.
78. L3454; L3444, L3481; L3454, L3469, L3471, L3409, L3475.
79. E4: 4.17.4–8, L3490.
80. L3498.
81. L3495, L3500, L3504, L3511, L3506.
82. MS Locke b.5, no. 14, b.1, fols. 283–4, L3647.
83. L3513, L3517, L3522, L3524.
84. L3529, L3528, L3537.
85. L3542, L3539, L3566, L3548, L3544, L3555, L3556 and others.
86. Coste: 172, L3541 and others.
87. L3551, L3541, MS Locke, c.29, fol. 121, Dewhurst 1954a.
88. L3572, L3573, L3580, L3582.
89. MS Locke b.1, fol. 286, L3573A, L3577.
90. L3576, L3581, L3600.
91. L3593, L3592, L3600, L3565.
92. Locke 1705b, L3615, L3647, Locke 1706a, 1706b, 1707a–c.
93. Locke 1707c: 115, 116, Locke 1706a: 175, L3648.
94. Locke 1707c: 109, 104, 103, 110.
95. L3558, L3566, Sherlock: 161–2.
96. L2202, L3570, L3603, dB: vol. 8, 356, L3591, L3608.
97. L3626, L3633, L3642.
98. Le Clerc: 26.
99. dB: vol. 8, 343.
100. P3: 6, 9, 18.
101. 4LT: 549–50.
102. 4LT: 561, 568, 570.
103. L3613, L3624.
104. L3624, L3627, L3631, Le Clerc: 24.
105. L3616, Coste: 170.

106. L3636.
107. L3647, Locke 1693b, 1702b, 1697g.
108. L3638, L3640, L3641.
109. Coste: 172–3, BL Add. MS 4311, fol. 143, Le Clerc: 25–6, G: 365, Dewhurst 1963a: 289.
110. Quoted by Bourne: vol. 2, 556.
111. MS Locke b.5, no. 14, G: 365.

Abbreviations and References

ABBREVIATIONS

1BR: Burnet 1697a; 1LS: Locke 1697b; 1SL: Stillingfleet 1697b; 1T: Locke 1660; 2BR: Burnet 1697b; 2LS: Locke 1697c; 2LT: Locke 1690c; 2SL: Stillingfleet 1698; 2T: Locke 1662; 2VRC: Locke 1697e; 3BR: Burnet 1699; 3LS: Locke 1699b; 3LT: Locke 1692b; 4LT: Locke 1704b; A: Locke 1671a; B: Locke 1671b; CA: Edwards 1695; CSPC: Calendar of State Papers: Colonial Series; CSPD: Calendar of State Papers: Domestic Series; CTB: Calendar of Treasury Books; dB: de Beer 1976–89; DVT: Stillingfleet 1697a; E: Locke 1690b; E2: Locke 1694b; E3: Locke 1695i; E4: Locke 1700b; ELN: Locke 1664a; ET: Locke 1689b/c; G: Gerhardt 1875–90, vol. 3; L: numbered items in de Beer 1976–89; LB: Locke 1697d: LL: numbered entries in Harrison and Laslett 1965; LT: Locke 1689c; P1: Proast 1690; P2: Proast 1691; P3: Proast 1704; RC: Locke 1695c; SC: Edwards 1697b; SCIM: Locke 1691b; SU: Edwards 1696; T: Locke 1667; T1: Locke 1689d ("The First Treatise of Government"); T2: Locke 1689d ("The Second Treatise of Government"); TE: Locke 1693d; VRC: Locke 1695d.

Unless otherwise stated (BL: British Library, London; NA: National Archives, Kew) all quoted manuscripts are in the Bodleian Library, Oxford.

REFERENCES

Aaron, Richard I. 1971. *John Locke*, 3rd edn. Oxford: Clarendon Press.
——and Gibb, Jocelyn, eds. 1936. *An Early Draft of Locke's Essay, Together with Excerpts from his Journals*. Oxford: Clarendon Press.

Abrams, Philip, ed. 1967. *John Locke: Two Tracts on Government.* Cambridge: Cambridge University Press.

Anselment, Raymond A. 2004. Freke, John. In Matthew and Harrison: vol. 20, 950–1.

Ashcraft, Richard. 1986. *Revolutionary Politics and Locke's Two Treatises of Government.* Princeton: Princeton University Press.

Atterbury, Francis. 1783. *The Epistolatory Correspondence of Francis Atterbury,* 2 vols. London.

Axtell, James, L. 1965a. Locke, Newton, and The Elements of Natural Philosophy. *Paedogica Europaea* **1**:235–44.

——1965b. Locke's review of the Principia. *Notes and Records of the Royal Society of London* **2**:152–61.

——1968. *The Educational Writings of John Locke.* Cambridge: Cambridge University Press.

——1969. Locke, Newton and the two cultures. In Yolton 1969:165–82.

B., R.A. 1968. Book reviews and notices. *The Oriel Record,* 40–1.

Baxter, Stephen. 1966. *William III.* London: Longmans.

Beddard, R.A. 1997a. Restoration Oxford and the remaking of the Protestant Establishment. In Tyacke 1997a:803–62.

——1997b. Tory Oxford. In Tyacke 1997a:863–905.

Bennett, Jonathan, and Remnant, Peter. 1978. How matter might at first be made. *New Essays on Rationalism and Empiricism.* Guelph: Canadian Association for Publishing in Philosophy.

Biddle, John C. 1977. John Locke's Essay on Infallibility. *Journal of Church and State* **19**:301–27.

Bill, E.G.W. 1988. *Education at Christ Church Oxford,* 1660–1800. Oxford: Clarendon Press.

Birch, Thomas. 1756–57. *The History of the Royal Society of London,* 4 vols. London.

Bold, Samuel. 1697a. *A Short Discourse of the True Knowledge of Christ Jesus.* London.

——1697b. *Some Passages in the Reasonableness of Christianity, etc. and its Vindication,* etc. London.

——1697c. *A Reply to Mr Edwards's Brief Reflections,* etc. London.

——1698. *Observations on the Animadversions…on a late book, entituled, The Reasonableness of Christianity,* etc. London.

Bonno, Gabriel. 1959. *Lettres inédites de Le Clerc à Locke.* Berkeley and Los Angeles: University of California.

Bourne, H.R. Fox. 1876. *The Life of John Locke,* 2 vols. London.

Boyle, Robert. 1692. *The General History of the Air.* In Boyle 1772: vol. 5, pp. 609–750.

——1772. *The Works of Robert Boyle,* ed. Thomas Birch. 6 vols. London.

Brewster, David. 1855. *Memoirs of the Life, Writings, and Discoveries of Sir Isaac Newton,* 2 vols. Edinburgh.

Brown, Louise Fargo. 1933. *The First Earl of Shaftesbury.* New York: Appleton.

Burnet, Gilbert. 1823. *History of His Own Time,* 6 vols. Oxford.

Burnet, Thomas. 1697a. *Remarks upon an Essay concerning Humane Understanding,* etc. London. As in Watson 1989, pp. 23–32.

——1697b. *Second Remarks upon an Essay concerning Humane Understanding,* etc. London. As in Watson 1989, pp. 37–55.

——1699. *Third Remarks upon an Essay concerning Humane Understanding,* etc. London. As in Watson 1989, pp. 57–93.

Calendar of State Papers, preserved in the Public Record Office, Domestic Series. 1856–. London.

Calendar of State Papers, preserved in the Public Record Office, Colonial Series (America and West Indies). 1860–. London.

Calendar of Treasury Books, preserved in the Public Record Office. 1904–. London.

Campbell, John Lord. 1849. *The Lives of the Lord Chancellors,* vol. 4. London.

Christie, W. D. 1871. *A Life of Anthony Ashley Cooper, First Earl of Shaftesbury.* 2 vols. London.

Clarke, Bridget. 1991. The marriage of John Locke's "wife", Elizabeth Clarke. *The Locke Newsletter* **22**:93–114.

Coste, Pierre. 1705. A letter of Mr Coste... written on the occasion of the death of Mr Locke. *Nouvelles de la République des Lettres,* February 1705, art. 2:154. As in Locke 1823: vol. 10, pp. 163–74.

Cottingham, John, Stoothoff, Robert, and Murdoch, Dugald, trans. 1985. *The Philosophical Writings of Descartes,* vol. 1. Cambridge: Cambridge University Press.

Coxe, W. ed. 1821. *Correspondence of...Duke of Shrewsbury.* London.

Cranston, Maurice. 1957. *John Locke: A Biography.* London: Longmans.

Davies, K. G. 1957. *The Royal African Company.* London: Longmans.

de Beer, E. S. 1967. John Locke: the appointment offered to him in 1698. *Institute of Historical Research (University of London) Bulletin* **40**:213–19.

——1974. Locke: from Utrecht to Rotterdam 1686–7. *The Locke Newsletter* **5**:32–40.

——, ed. 1976–89. *The Correspondence of John Locke,* 8 vols. Oxford: Clarendon Press.

Descartes, René. 1637. *Discourse on the Method.* As in Cottingham et al. 1985.

Desmaizeaux, Pierre, ed. 1720. *A Collection of Several Pieces of Mr John Locke.* London. As in Locke 1823: vols. 3, 10.

Dewhurst, Kenneth. 1954a. Truss designed by Locke. *British Medical Journal* **2**:44.

——1954b. Locke's midwifery notes. *Lancet* **267**:490–1.

——1957. A symposium on trigeminal neuralgia, etc. *Journal of the History of Medicine* **12**:21–36.

——1959a. An Oxford medical student's notebook (1652–1659). *Oxford Medical School Gazette* **11**:141–5.

——1959b. An essay on coughs by Locke and Sydenham. *Bulletin of the History of Medicine* **33**:366–74.

——1960a. Locke's essay on respiration. *Bulletin of the History of Medicine* **34**:257–73.

——1960b. The correspondence between John Locke and Sir Hans Sloane. *Irish Journal of Medical Science* **413**:201–12.

——1962a. Post-mortem examination on case of rickets performed by John Locke. *British Medical Journal* **2**:1466.

——1962b. Some letters of Dr Charles Goodall (1642–1712) to Locke, Sloane, and Sir Thomas Millington. *Journal of the History of Medicine* **17**:487–508.

——1963a. *John Locke (1632–1704), Physician and Philosopher: A Medical Biography*. London: Wellcome Historical Medical Library.

——1963b. Dr William Cole's (1635–1716) letters to Locke. *Centaurus* **8**:147–73.

——1966. *Dr Thomas Sydenham (1624–1689)*. Berkeley: University of California Press.

Earle, Peter. 1977. *Monmouth's Rebels*. London: Weidenfeld & Nicolson.

Edwards, John. 1695. *Some Thoughts concerning the several causes ... of Atheism ... - With some Brief Reflections on Socinianism: and on ... The Reasonableness of Christianity*, etc. London.

——1696. *Socinianism Unmask'd*, etc. London.

——1697a. *A Brief Vindication of the Fundamental Articles of the Christian Faith, as also of the Clergy, Universities and Public Schools, from Mr Locke's Reflections upon them in his Book of Education*, etc. London.

——1697b. *The Socinian Creed*. London.

Ellis, G. A. 1829. *The Ellis Correspondence*, 2 vols. London.

Ewen, C. L'Estrange. 1932. *Lotteries and Sweepstakes*. London: Heath Cranton Ltd.

Farr, James. 1986. "So vile and miserable an estate". *Political Theory* **14**:263–89.

——and Roberts, Clayton. 1985. John Locke on the Glorious Revolution: a rediscovered document. *The Historical Journal* **28**:385–98.

Filmer, Robert 1680. *Patriarcha*. London. As in Sommerville 1991.

Feingold, Mordechai. 1997a. The humanities. In Tyacke 1997a: chap. 5.

——1997b. The mathematical sciences and new philosophies. In Tyacke 1997a: chap. 6.

Fincham, Kenneth. 1997. Oxford and the early Stuart polity. In Tyacke 1997a: chap. 4.

Forbes, Eric G. 1975. Origins and early history (1675–1835). *The Royal Observatory at Greenwich and Herstmonceux 1675–1975*, vol. 1. London: Taylor & Francis.

Forster, T. I. M. 1830 (1847 2nd ed.) *Original Letters of Locke, etc.* London.

Frank, Robert G. Jr. 1980. *Harvey and the Oxford Physiologists*. Berkeley: University of California Press.

——1997. Medicine. In Tyacke 1997a: chap. 8.

Gerhardt, C. I., ed. 1875–90. *G. W. Leibniz: Philosophischen Schriften*, 7 vols. Berlin.

Goldie, Mark, ed. 2002. *John Locke: Selected Correspondence*. Oxford: Oxford University Press.

Gough, J. W. 1962. John Locke's herbarium. *Bodleian Library Record* **7**:42–6.

Grey, Forde. 1754. *The Secret History of the Rye House Plot*. London.

Haley, K. H. D. 1968. *The First Earl of Shaftesbury*. Oxford: Clarendon Press.

Harrison, John and Laslett, Peter. 1965. *The Library of John Locke*. Oxford: Oxford University Press.

Hattendorf, John B. 2004. Charles Mordaunt. In Matthew and Harrison, vol. 39, 13–20.

Higgins-Biddle, J. C., ed. 1999. *John Locke: The Reasonableness of Christianity as Delivered in the Scriptures*. Oxford: Clarendon Press.

Horsefield, J. K. 1960. *British Monetary Experiments, 1650–1710*. London: Bell & Sons.

Horwitz, Henry. 1977. *Parliament, Policy and Politics in the Reign of William III*. Manchester: Manchester University Press.

House of Commons Journals. London, 1803–.

Hunter, Michael. 2000. *Robert Boyle (1627–91)*. Woodbridge: Boydell Press.

Johnston, Charlotte. 1958. Locke's examination of Malebranche and John Norris. *Journal of the History of Ideas* **19**:551–8.

Kelly, Patrick Hyde, ed. 1991. *Locke on Money*, 2 vols. Oxford: Clarendon Press.

King, Sir Peter. 1706. *Posthumous Works of John Locke*. London.

King, Peter, 7th Baron King. 1884. *The Life and Letters of John Locke, with Extracts from his Journals and Common-place Books*. London.

Knights, Mark. 1989. Locke and the Exclusion crisis. *Times Literary Supplement*, no. 4998 (4–13 April):382.

Langley, A. G. trans. and ed. 1949. *New Essays concerning Human Understanding by Gottfried Wilhelm Leibniz, together with ... some shorter pieces*. La Salle, Ill.: Open Court.

Laslett, Peter, ed. 1960. *John Locke: Two Treatises of Government*. Cambridge University Press: Cambridge.

——1969. The great recoinage, and the origins of the Board of Trade. In Yolton 1969, pp. 137–64.

Le Clerc, Jean. 1705. Eloge de feu Mr. Locke. *Bibliothéque Choisie* **6**:342–411. As trans. in *The Life of and Character of Mr John Locke ... done into English by T. F. P. Gent*. London, 1706.

Leyden, W. von. 1954. *John Locke: Essays on the Law of Nature*. Oxford: Clarendon Press.

Li, Ming-Hsun. 1963. *The Great Recoinage of 1696 to 1699*. London: Weidenfeld & Nicolson.

Locke, John. 1660. The First Tract on Government (so called). As in Abrams, pp. 117–81.

——1661. Essay on Infallibility. As in Biddle, pp. 317–27.

——1662. The Second Tract on Government (so called). As in Abrams, pp. 183–241.

——1664a. Essays on the Law of Nature. As in Leyden, pp. 108–215.

——1664b. Can anyone by nature be happy in this life? No. As in Leyden, pp. 220–43.

——1666a. Respirationis usus. As in Dewhurst 1960a, pp. 270–3.

——1666b. Morbus. As in Romanell, pp. 207–9.

——1667. Essay concerning Toleration. As in Bourne, vol. 1, pp. 174–94.

——1668a. Anatomie. As in Dewhurst 1966, pp. 85–93.

——1668b. Some of the Consequences that are like to follow upon the lessening of interest to 4 per cent. As in Kelly, pp. 167–78.

——1668c. Supplement (to 1668b). In Kelly, pp. 178–86.

——1669. *De Arte Medica.* As in Bourne, vol. 1, pp. 222–7.

——1671a. *De Intellectu Humano* (so-called draft A of Locke 1690b). MS Film 77, pp. 56–89, 94–5.

——1671b. An Essay concerning the Understanding, Knowledge, Opinion, and Assent (so-called draft B of Locke 1690b). As in Rand 1931, pp. 15–307.

——1674. Excommunication. As in King 1884, pp. 300–6.

——1675. Journal. MS Locke f.1, pp. 1–25. (Some parts in Dewhurst 1963a, Lough.)

——1676. Journal. MS Locke f.1, pp. 25–527. (Some parts in Aaron and Gibb, Dewhurst 1963a, Leyden, Lough.)

——1677a. Journal. MS Locke f.2. (Some parts in Aaron and Gibb, Dewhurst 1963a, Leyden, Lough.)

——1677b. Of Study. 1677a, pp. 86–140.

——1678. Journal. MS Locke f.3. (Some parts in Aaron and Gibb, Dewhurst 1963a, Lough.)

——1679. Journal. BL Add. MS 15642. (Some parts in Aaron and Gibb, Dewhurst 1963a, Lough.)

——1680a. Journal. MS Locke f.4. (Some parts in Dewhurst 1963a.)

——1680b. *Observations upon the growth and culture of vines and olives; the production of silk; the preservation of fruits.* In Locke 1823, vol. 10, pp. 328–56.

——1681a. Journal. MS Locke f.5. (Some parts in Aaron and Gibb, Dewhurst 1963a.)

——1681b. A defence of nonconformity. MS Locke c.34. As in Stanton: vol. 2 (part in King 1884: pp. 346–58, Bourne: vol. 1, pp. 457–60).

——1682. Journal. MS Locke f.6. (Some parts in Aaron and Gibb, Dewhurst 1963a.)

——1683. Journal. MS Locke f.7. (Some parts in Dewhurst 1963a.)

——1684. Journal. MS Locke f.8, pp. 1–244. (Some parts in Dewhurst 1963a.)

——1685. Journal. MS Locke f.8, pp. 257–309. (Some parts in Dewhurst 1963a.)

——1686a. Journal. MS Locke f.9, pp. 1–81. (Some parts in Dewhurst 1963a.)

——1686b. Méthode nouvelle de dresser des Recueils. *Bibliothèque Universelle* 2: 315–40. As in Locke 1823, vol. 3, pp. 331–49.

——1687a. Journal. MS Locke f.9, pp. 82–311. (Parts in Dewhurst 1963a.)

——1687b. Of ethick in general. As in Nuovo, pp. 9–14.

——1688a. Journal. MS Locke f.9, pp. 317–47. (Parts in Dewhurst 1963a.)

——1688b. Extrait d'un Livre Anglois qui n'est pas encore publié, intitulé Essai Philosophique concernant l'Entendement... Communiqué par Monsieur Locke. *Bibliothèque Universelle* 8:49–142.

——1688c. *Abrégé d'un ouvrage intitulé Essai philosophique touchant l'entendement.* Amsterdam.

——1688d. Review of Newton's *Principia Mathematica. Bibliothèque Universelle* 8:436–50.

——1689a. Journal. MS Locke f.10, pp. 1–32. (Parts in Dewhurst 1963a.)

——1689b. *Epistola Tolerantia.* Gouda. As in Montuori.

——1689c. *Letter concerning Toleration.* London. As in Locke 1823, vol. 6, pp. 3–58.

——1689d. *Two Treatises of Government.* As in Locke 1823, vol. 5, pp. 207–485.

——1689e. Rules of a Society, which met once a week, for their improvement in useful knowledge, and for the promoting of truth and Christian charity. As in Locke 1823, vol. 10, pp. 312–14.

——1690a. Journal. MS Locke f.10, pp. 33–65. (Parts in Dewhurst 1963a.)

——1690b. *An Essay concerning Humane Understanding.* London. As in Woolhouse 1997, occasionally amended in the light of Nidditch, when there are relevant variations between editions.

——1690c. *A Second Letter concerning Toleration,* etc. London. In Locke 1823, vol. 6, pp. 61–137.

——1690d. A call to the nation for unity. As in Farr and Roberts, pp. 395–8.

——1691a. Journal. MS Locke f.10, pp. 81–115. (Parts in Dewhurst 1963a.)

——1691b. *Some considerations of the consequences of the lowering of interest, and raising the value of money.* London. As in Locke 1823, vol. 5, pp. 1–116.

——1692a. Journal. MS Locke f.10, pp. 129–72. (Parts in Dewhurst 1963a.)

——1692b. *A Third Letter for Toleration.* London. In Locke 1823, vol. 6, pp. 141–546.

——1692c. JL to Mr Norris/JL Answer to Mr Norris's Reflections 92. MS Locke c.28, fols. 107–12. (In Johnston 1958 in small part.)

——1692d. Weather Register kept in Oxford (1666–1670, 1681–1683) and London (1670–1681). As in Boyle 1692, pp. 655–84.

——1693a. Journal. MS Locke f.10, pp. 177–209. (Parts in Dewhurst 1963a.)

——1693b. JL Of Seeing all things in God. MS Locke d.3, fols. 1–122. As, largely, in Locke 1823, vol. 9, pp. 211–55 (and largely completed by Johnston 1958).

——1693c. Remarks upon some of Mr. Norris's books, wherein he asserts P. Malebranche's Opinion of our seeing all Things in God. As, largely, in Locke 1823, vol. 10, pp. 247–59 (and completed by Johnston 1958).

——1693d. *Some Thoughts concerning Education.* London. As in Locke 1823, vol. 9, pp. 1–205.

——1693e. For a General Naturalization. As in Kelly, pp. 487–92.

——1694a. Journal. MS Locke f.10, pp. 215–52. (Parts in Dewhurst 1963a.)

——1694b. *An Essay concerning Humane Understanding,* 2nd edn. London. In Nidditch 1975.

——1694c. Adversaria Theologica. In Nuovo, pp. 21–33.

——1695a. Journal. MS Locke f.10, pp. 263–99. (Parts in Dewhurst 1963a.)

——1695b. *Short Observations on a printed paper, intituled, For encouraging the coining silver money,* etc. London. As in Locke 1823, vol. 5, pp. 117–30.

——1695c. *The Reasonableness of Christianity as Delivered in the Scriptures.* London. As in Locke 1823, vol. 7, pp. 1–158.

——1695d. *A Vindication of the Reasonableness of Christianity,* etc. London. As in Locke 1823, vol. 7, pp. 159–80.

——1695e. Guineas. As in Kelly, vol. 2, pp. 363–4.

——1695f. Money: A paper given to Sir William Trumbell which was written at his request September 1695. In Kelly, pp. 365–73.

——1695g. Propositions sent to the Lords Justices (...23 October 1695). As in Kelly, pp. 374–80.

——1695h. Answer to my Lord Keeper's Queries (delivered 30 October 1695). As in Kelly, vol. 2, pp. 381–97.

——1695i. *An Essay concerning Humane Understanding*, 3rd edn. London. In Nidditch 1975.

——1695j. *Further considerations concerning raising the value of money*, etc. As in Locke 1823, vol. 5, p. 131–205.

——1696a. Journal. MS Locke f.10, pp. 309–36. (Parts in Dewhurst 1963a.)

——1696b. *Several Papers relating to Money, Interest and Trade, etc.* London.

——1697a. Journal. MS Locke f.10, pp. 341–69. (Parts in Dewhurst 1963a.)

——1697b. *A Letter to the Right Reverend Edward Lord Bishop of Worcester Concerning some Passages...in a late discourse of his Lordship's in Vindication of the Trinity.* London. As in Locke 1823, vol. 4, pp. 1–96.

——1697c. *Mr. Locke's Reply to the Bishop of Worcester's Answer to his Letter Concerning some Passages...in a Late Discourse of his Lordship's in Vindication of the Trinity.* London. As in Locke 1823, vol. 4, pp. 97–189.

——1697d. An answer to "Remarks upon an Essay concerning Human Understanding". As in Locke 1823, vol. 4, pp. 185–9.

——1697e. *A Second Vindication of the Reasonableness of Christianity*, etc. London. As in Locke 1823, vol. 7, pp. 181–424.

——1697f. An account of one who had horny excrescencies or extraordinary large nails on his fingers and toes. *Philosophical Transactions* **19**:594–6.

——1697g. Of the Conduct of the Understanding. As in Locke 1823, vol. 3, pp. 205–89.

——1697h. Encouragement of Irish linen manufacture. As in Bourne, vol. 2, pp. 363–72.

——1697i. Poor-law scheme. As in Bourne, vol. 2, pp. 377–91.

——1698a. Journal. MS Locke f.10, pp. 373–404. (Parts in Dewhurst 1963a.)

——1698b. Elements of Natural Philosophy. As in Locke 1823, vol. 3, pp. 301–30.

——1699a. Journal. MS Locke f.10, pp. 405–38.

——1699b. *Mr Locke's Reply to the Bishop of Worcester's Answer to his Second Letter*, etc. London. As in Locke 1823, vol. 4, pp. 191–498.

——1700a. Journal. MS Locke f.10, pp. 445–77.

——1700b. *An Essay concerning Humane Understanding*, 4th edn. London. In Nidditch 1975.

——1700c. *Essai Philosophique concernant l'entendement humain...traduit de l'Anglois de Mr. Locke par Pierre Coste*, etc. Amsterdam.

——1701. Journal. MS Locke f.10, pp. 481–507.

——1702a. Journal. MS Locke f.10, pp. 513–35.

——1702b. A discourse of miracles. As in Locke 1823, vol. 9, pp. 256–65.

——1702c. *Some thoughts concerning reading and study for a gentleman.* As in Locke 1823, vol. 3, pp. 291–300.

——1703. Journal. MS Locke f.10, pp. 545–65.

——1704a. Journal. MS Locke f.10, pp. 577–600.

——1704b. *A Fourth Letter for Toleration.* As in Locke 1823, vol. 6, pp. 547–74.

——1705a. A register of the weather for the year 1692, kept at Oates in Essex. *Philosophical Transactions* **24**:1917−37.

——1705b. *A Paraphrase and Notes on the Epistle of St Paul to the Galatians*. London.

——1706a. *A Paraphrase and Notes on the First Epistle of St Paul to the Corinthians*. London.

——1706b. *A Paraphrase and Notes on the Second Epistle of St Paul to the Corinthians*. London.

——1707a. *A Paraphrase and Notes on the Epistle of St Paul to the Romans*. London.

——1707b. *A Paraphrase and Notes on the Epistle of St Paul to the Ephesians*. London.

——1707c. *An Essay for the Understanding of St Paul's Epistles by consulting St Paul himself*. London. As in Wainwright, pp. 102−16.

——1729. Second edition of Locke 1700c.

——1823. *The Works of John Locke. A New Edition, corrected*, 10 vols. London.

——1828. *Discourses: Translated from Nicole's Essays* (ed. Thomas Hancock). London.

Lough, John, ed. 1953. *Locke's Travels in France, 1675−1679*. Cambridge: Cambridge University Press.

Maddison, R. E. W. 1969. *The Life of the Honourable Robert Boyle*. London: Taylor & Francis.

Marshall, John. 1994. *John Locke: Resistance, Religion and Responsibility*. Cambridge: Cambridge University Press.

——2000. Locke, "Socinianism", and Unitarianism. In Stewart 2000, pp. 111−82.

Martyn, Benjamin. 1790. *The Life of Anthony Ashley Cooper, First Earl of Shaftesbury*. London.

Masham, Damaris Cudworth. 1704. Letter to Jean Le Clerc, 12 January 1704. As in Woolhouse 2003.

Masham, Esther. 1722. *Letters from relations and friends to E. Masham, Book 1st*. The Newberry Library, Chicago; Case MS E5.M3827.

Matthew, H. C. G. and Harrison, Brian. 2004. *Oxford Dictionary of National Biography*. Oxford: Oxford University Press.

Meynell, G. G. 1993. John Locke's method of common-placing, as seen in his drafts and his medical notebooks, Bodleian MSS Locke d.9, f.21 and f.23. *The Seventeenth Century* **8**:245−67.

——1994. Locke as the author of "Anatomia" and "De Arte Medica". *The Locke Newsletter* **25**:65−73.

——1995. Locke, Boyle and Peter Stahl. *Notes and Records of the Royal Society of London* **49**:185−92.

Milton, J. R. 1987. Locke's Adversaria. *The Locke Newsletter* **18**:63−74.

——1988. The date and significance of two of Locke's early manuscripts. *The Locke Newsletter* **19**:47−89.

——1990. John Locke and the Fundamental Constitutions of Carolina. *The Locke Newsletter* **21**:111−33.

——1991. John Locke, George Wall and George Walls: a problem of identity. *The Locke Newsletter* **22**:81–91.

——1993. Locke's Essay on Toleration: text and context. *British Journal for the History of Philosophy* **1**:45–63.

——1994. Locke at Oxford. In Rogers 1994, pp. 29–47.

——1995a. Dating Locke's *Second Treatise*. *History of Political Thought* **16**:356–90.

——1995b. Locke's pupils. *The Locke Newsletter* **26**:95–118.

——1996. Locke manuscripts among the Shaftesbury Papers in the Public Record Office. *The Locke Newsletter* **27**:109–30.

——1997. John Locke's medical notebooks. *The Locke Newsletter* **28**:135–56.

——1998. The dating of "Adversaria 1661". *The Locke Newsletter* **29**:105–17.

——2001. Locke, medicine and the Mechanical Philosophy. *British Journal for the History of Philosophy* **9**:221–43.

——2004. John Locke. In Matthew and Harrison, vol. 34, pp. 216–28.

Milton, J. R. and Milton, Philip. 1997. Selecting the Grand Jury: A Tract by John Locke. *The Historical Journal* **40**:185–94.

Milton, Philip. 1996. Denis Grenville and John Locke. *The Locke Newsletter* **27**:75–108.

——2000. Locke and the Rye House Plot. *The Historical Journal* **43**:647–68.

Molyneux, William. 1692. *Dioptrica Nova. A Treatise of Dioptrics*. London.

Montuori, Mario ed. 1963. *John Locke: A Letter concerning Toleration (Latin and English Texts)*. The Hague: Nijhoff.

Newton, Isaac. 1850. *Correspondence of Sir Isaac Newton and Professor Cotes*. London.

Nidditch, Peter H., ed. 1975. *John Locke: An Essay concerning Human Understanding*. Oxford: Oxford University Press.

Nuovo, Victor, ed. 2002. *John Locke: Writings on Religion*. Oxford: Oxford University Press.

Nye, Stephen. 1695. *The Exceptions of Mr. Edwards . . . against the Reasonableness of Christianity . . . examined*, etc. London.

Ogg, David. 1955. *England in the Reign of James II and William III*. Oxford: Clarendon Press.

——1956. *England in the Reign of Charles II*, 2nd edn. Oxford: Clarendon Press.

Ollion, Henry, ed. 1912. *Lettres inédites de John Locke*. La Haye: Nijhoff.

Osler, William. 1900. John Locke as a physician. *Lancet* **2** (20 October): 1115–23.

Philip, I. G. and Morgan, Paul. 1997. Libraries, books, and printing. In Tyacke 1997a, chap. 13.

Porter, Stephen. 1997. University and society. In Tyacke 1997a, chap. 1.

Prideaux, Humphrey. 1875. *Letters of Humphrey Prideaux to John Ellis*, ed. E. M. Thompson. London: Camden Society Publications, New Series 15.

Pringle, Helen. 1992. Who gave money to Monmouth. *The Locke Newsletter* **23**:131–43.

Proast, Jonas. 1690. *The Argument of the Letter concerning Toleration . . . answer'd*, Oxford. As in Schouls.

——1691. *A Third Letter concerning Toleration: in defence of "The Argument of the Letter concerning Toleration...answer'd".* Oxford. As in Schouls.

——1704. *A Second Letter to the Author of the "Three Letters for Toleration", from the author of the argument of the "Letter concerning Toleration...answered".* Oxford. As in Schouls.

Rand, Benjamin, ed. 1900. *The Life of Anthony, Earl of Shaftesbury.* London.

——1927. *The Correspondence of John Locke and Edward Clarke.* Cambridge, Mass.: Harvard University Press.

——1931. *An Essay concerning the Understanding, Knowledge, Opinion, and Assent, by John Locke.* Cambridge, Mass.: Harvard University Press.

Rogers, G.A.J., ed. 1994. *Locke's Philosophy: Content and Context.* Oxford: Oxford University Press.

Romanell, Patrick. 1984. *John Locke and Medicine.* New York: Prometheus Books.

Sargeaunt, John. 1898. *Annals of Westminster School.* London.

Schouls, Peter A. ed. 1984. *The Philosophy of John Locke,* vol. 12. New York and London: Garland Publishing Inc.

Shaftesbury, Anthony Ashley Cooper, 1st Earl of. 1669. *The Fundamental Constitutions of Carolina.* As in Locke 1823, vol. 10, pp. 175–99.

——1675. A Letter from a Person of Quality, to his Friend in the Country. London. As in Locke 1823, vol. 10, pp. 200–46.

Shaftesbury, Anthony Ashley Cooper, 3rd Earl of. 1705. Letter to Jean Le Clerc, 8 February 1705. As in Rand 1900, pp. 328–34.

Sherlock, William. 1704. *A Discourse concerning the Happiness of Good Men.* London.

Smith, John. 1673. *Select Discourses,* 2nd edn. Cambridge.

South, Robert. 1865. *Sermons Preached upon Several Occasions,* 2 vols. London.

Sommerville, Johann P., ed. 1991. *Sir Robert Filmer: Patriarcha and Other Writings.* Cambridge: Cambridge University Press.

Stanton, Timothy, A. 2003. John Locke, Edward Stillingfleet and toleration, 2 vols. Ph.D. thesis, University of Leicester.

Steele, R.R. 1910. *Tudor and Stuart Proclamations, 1485–1714.* Oxford.

Stewart, M.A. 1981. Locke's professional contacts with Robert Boyle. *The Locke Newsletter* **12**:19–44.

——, ed. 2000. *English Philosophy in the Age of Locke.* Oxford: Clarendon Press.

Stillingfleet, Edward. 1697a. *A Discourse in Vindication of the Trinity,* etc. London.

——1697b. *The Bishop of Worcester's Answer to Mr Locke's Letter, concerning some passages...in the late Discourse in Vindication of the Trinity.* London.

——1698. *The Bishop of Worcester's Answer to Mr Locke's Second Letter,* etc. London.

Sydenham, Thomas. 1987. *Thomae Sydenham: Methodus Curandi Febres Propriis Observationibus Superstructura,* ed. G.G. Meynell. Folkestone: Winterdown Books.

Tanner, J. R., ed. 1926. *Correspondence of Samuel Pepys, 1679–1703,* 2 vols. London: Bell & Sons Ltd.

——1929. *Further Correspondence of Samuel Pepys, 1662–1679*. London: Bell & Sons Ltd.

Tanner, Lawrence E. 1951. *Westminster School*. 2nd edn. London: Country Life Ltd.

Thacker, Christopher, ed. 1995. *Voltaire: Selected Writings*. London: Dent.

Toland, John. 1696. *Christianity not Mysterious*. London.

Tomalin, Claire. 2003. *Samuel Pepys: The Unequalled Self*. London: Penguin Books.

Trotter, Catherine. 1751. *Works*, 2 vols. ed. T. Birch. London.

Tyacke, Nicholas, ed. 1997a. *Seventeenth-Century Oxford*. Oxford: Clarendon Press.

Tyacke, Nicholas. 1997b. Religious controversy. In Tyacke 1997a, chap. 10.

Vaugh, Karen Iversen. 1980. *John Locke: Economist and Social Scientist*. London: The Athlone Press.

Wainwright, Arthur, W. ed. 1987. *John Locke: A Paraphrase and Notes on the Epistles of St Paul*. Oxford: Clarendon Press.

Walmsley, Jonathan. 2000. Morbus – Locke's early essay on disease. *Early Science and Medicine* 5:366–93.

—— and Milton, J. R. 1999. Locke's Notebook "Adversaria 4" and his early training in chemistry. *The Locke Newsletter* 30:85–101.

Ward, G. R. M., trans. 1845. *Oxford University Statutes*, vol. 1. London.

Ward, John. 1740. *The Lives of the Professors of Gresham College*. London.

Watson, George, ed. 1989. *Remarks on John Locke by Thomas Burnet, with Locke's Replies*. Doncaster: Brynmill Press.

Willcock, John. 1907. *A Scots Earl in Covenanting Times, being The Life and Times of Archibald 9th Earl of Argyll*. Edinburgh: Andrew Elliot.

Withington, Edward Theodore. 1898. John Locke's "Medical Observations". *Medical Magazine* 7:47–50, 375–87, 573–9.

Wood, Anthony. 1813–20. *Athenae Oxonienses*, 4 vols., ed. P. Bliss. Oxford.

——1891–1900. *The Life and Times of Anthony Wood, Antiquary, of Oxford*, 5 vols., ed. Andrew Clarke. Oxford.

Woolhouse, Roger, ed. 1997. *John Locke: An Essay concerning Human Understanding*. London: Penguin.

——2003. Lady Masham's account of Locke. *Locke Studies* 3:167–93.

Worden, Blair. 1997. Cromwellian Oxford. In Tyacke 1997a, chap. 15.

Wynne, John. 1696. *An Abridgement of Mr Locke's Essay concerning Humane Understanding*. London.

Yolton, John W., ed. 1969. *John Locke: Problems and Perspectives*. Cambridge: Cambridge University Press.

Index